AF778001

Health Psychology in Australia

In today's diverse society, health professionals require a complete understanding of how physiological, social and psychological factors impact physical wellbeing. Health psychology is an increasingly important focus of modern healthcare practice. *Health Psychology in Australia* provides a contemporary, relevant perspective on the unique climate in which health psychology is practised. Drawing on the diverse expertise of the author team, this book gives students the skills to identify and evaluate health risk factors and to intervene in and manage health behaviour.

Each chapter includes learning objectives, case studies with accompanying critical thinking questions and a detailed summary to consolidate learning. The comprehensive glossary and links to online resources help solidify understanding of key concepts and ideas and encourage wider reading. An online instructor's resource manual to enhance teaching practices is available at www.cambridge.edu.au/academic/healthpsychology.

Written with a focus on respectful advocacy of health promotion, *Health Psychology in Australia* provides psychology and allied health students with a comprehensive understanding of the role of the health psychologist as clinician, researcher, educator and client.

Jillian Dorrian is Associate Professor in the School of Psychology, Social Work and Social Policy at the University of South Australia.

Einar Thorsteinsson is Associate Professor in Psychology in the School of Behavioural, Cognitive and Social Sciences at the University of New England.

Mirella Di Benedetto is a lecturer in psychology in the School of Health and Biomedical Sciences at RMIT University.

Katrina Lane-Krebs is a lecturer in the School of Nursing and Midwifery at Central Queensland University.

Melissa Day is a NHMRC Early Career Fellow in the School of Psychology at the University of Queensland.

Amanda Hutchinson is a Senior Lecturer in the School of Psychology, Social Work and Social Policy at the University of South Australia.

Kerry Sherman is Associate Professor in the Centre for Emotional Health, Department of Psychology at Macquarie University.

HEALTH PSYCHOLOGY IN AUSTRALIA

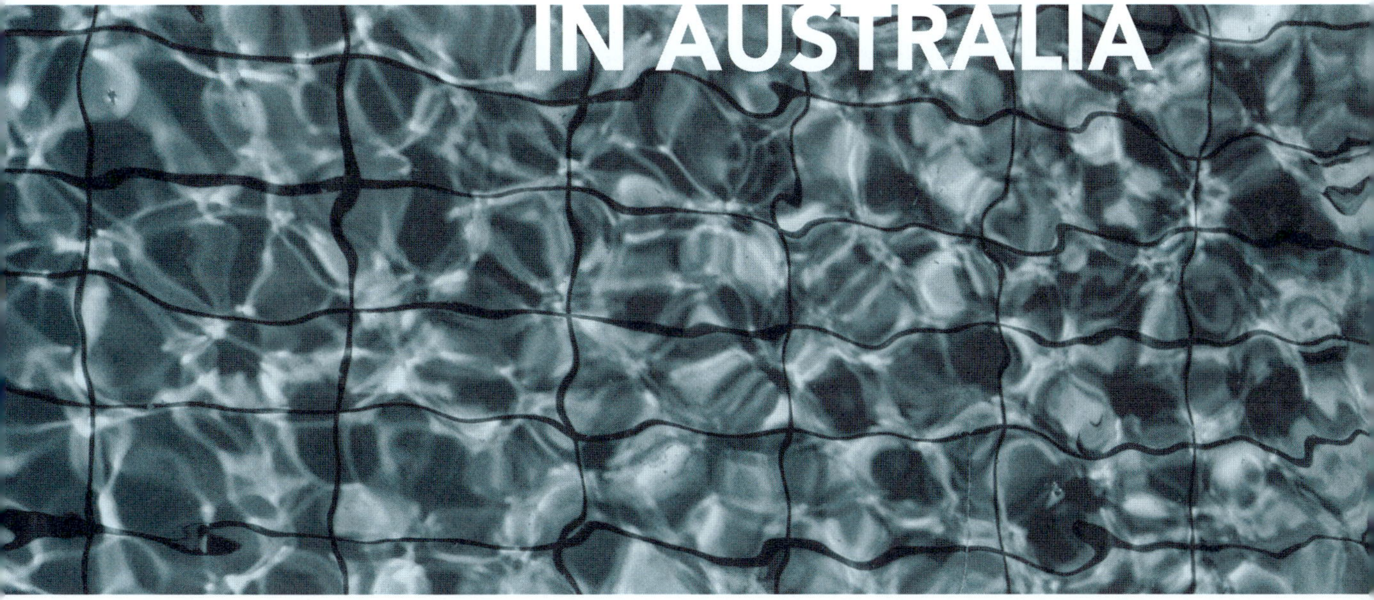

Jillian Dorrian
Einar Thorsteinsson
Mirella Di Benedetto
Katrina Lane-Krebs
Melissa Day
Amanda Hutchinson
Kerry Sherman

CAMBRIDGE
UNIVERSITY PRESS
www.cambridge.org

CAMBRIDGE
UNIVERSITY PRESS

University Printing House, Cambridge CB2 8BS, United Kingdom

One Liberty Plaza, 20th Floor, New York, NY 10006, USA

477 Williamstown Road, Port Melbourne, VIC 3207, Australia

4843/24, 2nd Floor, Ansari Road, Daryaganj, Delhi – 110002, India

79 Anson Road, #06–04/06, Singapore 079906

Cambridge University Press is part of the University of Cambridge.

It furthers the University's mission by disseminating knowledge in the
pursuit of education, learning and research at the highest international levels of excellence.

www.cambridge.org
Information on this title: www.cambridge.org/9781316623954

First published 2017

Cover designed by eggplant communications
Typeset by Newgen Publishing and Data Services
Printed in Singapore by Markono Print Media Pte Ltd, December 2016

A catalogue record for this publication is available from the British Library

*A Cataloguing-in-Publication entry is available from the catalogue
of the National Library of Australia at* www.nla.gov.au

ISBN 978-1-316-62395-4 Paperback

Additional resources for this publication at www.cambridge.edu.au/healthpsychology.

*Please be aware that this publication may contain several variations of Aboriginal and Torres
Strait Islander terms and spellings; no disrespect is intended. Please note that the terms
'Indigenous Australians' and 'Aboriginal and Torres Strait Islander peoples' may be used
interchangeably in this publication.*

Contents

1

Introduction to health psychology

Health

Health psychology is the study of the relationship between behaviour and health including our intentions and norms. However, in order to understand health psychology, we must first understand **health**. This is not as straightforward as it may at first seem. Health is a dynamic concept – if we look back over time we can see clear, marked changes in the way that health has been understood.

Historical perspectives on health and illness

Concepts of health have fluctuated greatly over time. For example, there is evidence that during the Stone Age (10 000–2000 BC), 'evil spirits' were seen as a cause of ill health. Across time, we have seen religious explanations for health, resulting from favour or punishment from God, predominating through Ancient Hebrew (100–300 BC) and early Christian (600 AD) belief systems (Magner, 1992).

In contrast, Greek physician Hippocrates (460–370 BC), credited with the Hippocratic Oath, argued that health depended on balance between bodily fluids or 'humours'. He believed that the mind and body were one, and that external pathogens could lead to humour imbalance, and in turn, ill health (Franco & Williams, 2000; Jackson, 2001). Hippocrates' ideas were later supported by Galen (129–199 AD), who believed that temperament was a product of bodily humours, and that people with different temperaments may be differentially susceptible to illness (Jackson, 2001; Stelmack & Stalikas, 1991). However, this was not an acknowledgement of the psychological impacting on the physical. Rather, temperament and illness were both seen as a reflection of the same underlying physical cause – the change in bodily humours.

Indeed, the mind–body relationship (the role of the psychological and the physical) is a central concept, which is continually revisited throughout definitions of health and illness. French philosopher Descartes (1596–1650) argued that the mind and body were separate. This is the concept underpinning dualism – that the body is visible and material, and is distinct from the mind, which is invisible and insubstantial (Duncan, 2000; Sullivan, 1986). It has been argued, although not by all authors (Duncan, 2000), that this led to conceptions of the body as a machine, and medical professionals became primarily responsible for the workings of the machine. In contrast, issues of the mind were the domain of spiritual experts. We can view this as the foundation for the **biomedical model of illness**, which was also highly influenced by Virchow, the 'father of pathology,' who argued that all disease is the result of abnormal changes to the cells (Magner, 1992). The biomedical model is founded on several tenets (Wade & Halligan, 2004, p. 1398):

- All illness and all symptoms and signs arise from an underlying abnormality within the body (usually in the functioning or structure of specific organs), referred to as a disease;
- All diseases give rise to symptoms, eventually if not initially, and although other factors may influence the consequences of the disease, they are not related to its development or manifestations;
- Health is the absence of disease;
- Mental phenomena, such as emotional disturbance or delusions, are separate from and unrelated to other disturbances of bodily function;
- The patient is a victim of circumstance with little or no responsibility for the presence or cause of the illness; and
- The patient is a passive recipient of treatment, although cooperation with treatment is expected.

The biomedical model has been associated with enormous advances in healthcare. In focusing on the cause of the disease, biomedical science has produced antibiotics, vaccines and countless pharmacotherapies, which have led to substantive reductions in infectious illness (e.g. smallpox) in many societies (Magner, 1992). In Australia, the biomedical model has led to a dramatic shift in the healthcare landscape. In the 18th and 19th centuries, dietary and infectious illnesses such as tuberculosis, diphtheria, measles and influenza represented the primary healthcare burdens. With biomedical reductions in these causes of illness and death, in combination with changes in lifestyle, the majority of the healthcare burden is now driven by chronic illness including cardiovascular disease, diabetes, obesity, cancer and mental health conditions (AIHW, 2011, 2014a, 2014b). Importantly for health psychology, some of the key risk factors for these illnesses are behavioural. In particular, smoking, excessive alcohol consumption, poor diet and physical inactivity are critical and ubiquitous risk factors for chronic illness (AIHW, 2015). In Australia, the contribution of sun exposure to skin cancer risk must also be acknowledged (Chen, Halliday & Damian, 2013). Other behavioural factors, such as sleep loss and disruption of our daily rhythms, are becoming increasingly recognised as risk factors for health (Knutsson, 2003; Rajaratnam & Arendt, 2001). The elevated risk of chronic illness with increasing stress (including stress resulting from job insecurity, burnout, marital/family discord, financial stress and trauma) is also a prominent concern for health psychology (Rozanski et al., 2005; VanItallie, 2002).

These issues are addressed in the following chapters in this book:
Chapter 5: Nutrition, exercise and health
Chapter 6: Sleep, sleep loss, safety and health
Chapter 7: Health risk behaviours: alcohol, drugs and smoking
Chapter 8: Stress and managing stress
Chapter 9: Lifestyle-related chronic illnesses (CVD and T2D) and depression
Chapter 10: Experiencing cancer: an acute and chronic condition

In addition, there are demographic, social, cultural and political risk factors (AIHW, 2015). For example, life expectancy has been estimated at 56 years in male and 63 years in female Indigenous Australians, compared to 76.6 years and 82.1 years for non-Indigenous males and females respectively. These disease-specific discrepancies in mortality rates are higher in Australia than in New Zealand, Canada and the US (Bramley et al., 2004). Such inequalities have been highlighted globally as a matter of social justice.

> There is no necessary biological reason why life expectancy should be 48 years longer in Japan than in Sierra Leone or 20 years shorter in Australian Aboriginal and Torres Strait Islander peoples than in other Australians. Reducing these social inequalities in health, and thus meeting human needs, is an issue of social justice.
>
> (Marmot, 2005, p. 1103)

These issues are addressed in the following chapter in this book:
Chapter 12: Health inequalities

Interestingly, the absence of a concept of biomedical mind–body dichotomy has been discussed as one of the potential barriers to engaging Indigenous Australians in mental health services. Descriptions of Indigenous concepts of health include more holistic beliefs, and can encompass an understanding that 'things aren't well' without specific reference to physical and mental injury. This approach to health goes beyond the biomedical, involving not only interpersonal and cultural factors, but also environmental and historic factors in a multifaceted, interconnected understanding (Westerman, 2004; Ypinazar et al., 2007), with a well-established, widely practised pharmacopoeia (traditional medicine practice) (Best & Fredericks, 2014).

This highlights the importance of **cultural competence** (understanding and consideration of diverse cultural needs; Douglas et al., 2014), **cultural sensitivity** (putting this understanding into practice as a foundation for an effective therapeutic relationship; Fleming & Towey, 2001) and avoiding, at all costs, **ethnocentrism** (the belief that your own culture is somehow superior; Jones & Creedy, 2012). In the Australian context, this includes recognising multiple Indigenous communities with unique cultural practices as well as shared concepts such as the importance of country, elders, ancestors and storytelling (Australian Government, 2015). These ideas extend to the recognition of the many cultural groups in Australia in order to promote cultural safety in healthcare practices, respecting cultural diversity and maintaining cultural integrity at all times (Schnierer, Ellsmore & Schnierer, 2011).

These issues are addressed in the following chapter in this book:
Chapter 13: Cross-cultural psychology

Therefore, it is clear that while genetic and medical risk factors for chronic illness are still important, there is a spectrum of factors that are of central relevance in the current healthcare climate that go beyond biomedical explanations. For these reasons, the biomedical model has been heavily criticised and best practice in healthcare now includes understanding the personal and social context, rather than simply the physical condition (Wade & Halligan, 2004). In other words, we need to acknowledge the psychosocial context – *there has never been a more important time for health psychology!*

The biopsychosocial model

The **biopsychosocial model** builds on the very successful, but increasingly limited, biomedical model by explicitly acknowledging that the biological factors that we know are important (such as genes and physiological dysfunction) interact with psychological factors (such as experience, behaviour patterns, thoughts and emotions) and social factors (such as family, friends, community and societal context) (Figure 1.1). This not only considers how illness is generated, but also how it is experienced and treated.

This is not a new model, but the inclusion of biopsychosocial practices in healthcare – this evolution from the biomedical approach – is still occurring after many decades.

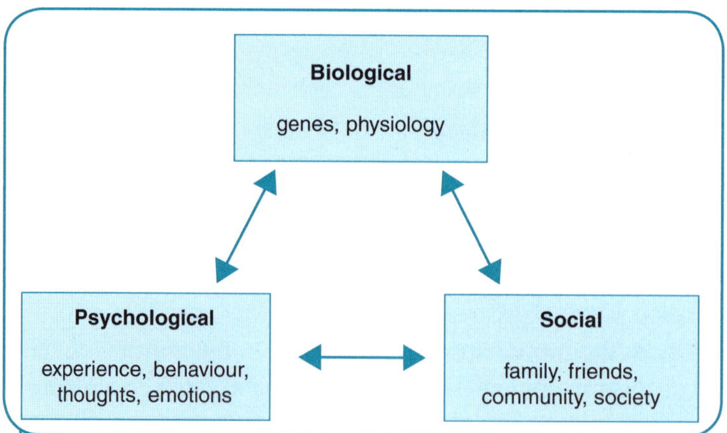

Figure 1.1 The biopsychosocial model of health
Source: adapted from Engel, 1977

In 1977, George Engel published an article in *Science*, one of the leading international journals, arguing for the importance of the biopsychosocial approach. It is recommended reading, especially highlighting the development of biopsychosocial understanding over time (when reading the article, note the gendered language referring to the doctor as 'he'). Engel spoke about the paradox whereby a patient could be provided with a test that shows that they are sick without expressing any feelings of being sick, or a patient could feel sick and seek help from a doctor without any clear underlying physical causes. He also described the interesting example of grief, which can manifest in many debilitating physical symptoms, even without the patient being conscious of the link between their experience, their emotions and these physical consequences. He argues that 'the physician's basic professional knowledge and skills must span the social, psychological and biological, for his decisions and actions on the patient's behalf to involve all three' (Engel, 1977, p. 133). He also noted the importance of referral to relevant allied healthcare professionals, highlighting multidisciplinary healthcare.

Another clear example of biopsychosocial interactions in healthcare is pain. Pain may have a clear biological cause (e.g. broken arm), pain may be experienced in the body in a different location from an injury (e.g. referred pain), or there may be no obvious insult or injury in the body (e.g. phantom limb pain). In all cases, the brain is interpreting signals to produce a pain signal that we experience. Even in the case where pain has an obvious physical cause, we know that the experience of pain can be influenced by psychosocial factors (e.g. focus, **anxiety**, social context and beliefs about the cause and meaning of the pain) (Loeser & Melzak, 1999).

These issues are addressed in the following chapter in this book:
Chapter 11: Pain and its optimal management

What you can see from this discussion is that these models reflect changing understandings of what is meant by 'health'.

Evolving definitions of health

The biomedical approach to health as the absence of disease or illness is inadequate in this context. A definition consistent with the biopsychosocial model that is frequently cited in the current literature comes from the World Health Organisation (WHO, 1946): 'health is a state of complete physical, mental and social wellbeing and not merely the absence of disease or infirmity'.

In this definition, it is clear that health is not simply considered as a binary (healthy/sick), and specifically includes mental and social factors. Consistent with the WHO definition, health has been conceptualised on a continuum (Roscoe, 2009). This acknowledges that at any point in time, a person is in a dynamic state of health that is somewhere along this continuum from death through to optimal wellness (Figure 1.2). Consider the example of the high school student who has no current medical diagnoses, is involved in many

Figure 1.2 Health as a continuum

sports teams, eats a healthy diet, does not drink alcohol and gets plenty of sleep. Would you consider them healthy? Now consider their transition to university life. They still have no medical diagnoses, but now they are socialising much more, have turned 18 and drink alcohol. Their study load leaves them little time for exercise. They often sacrifice sleep for socialising and pull 'all-nighters' to finish assignments. They are often tired, eat chocolate and drink lots of caffeine to compensate (sound familiar?). Would you consider them healthy now? While they have not been diagnosed with an illness, it could be argued that it is likely that their social and behavioural changes might have moved them further from optimal wellness (i.e. they have moved along the continuum in Figure 1.2).

Having models of health that allow us to capture these changes in behaviour and experience gives us a framework for *health promotion* and *preventative healthcare*, and the ability to target interventions before patterns of behaviour over time result in illness.

However, even today, as we feel that we are getting ever closer to a more informed understanding of health, controversies remain. The WHO definition has been criticised for resulting in 'overmedicalisation' as an increasing number of daily lifestyle characteristics are being described as risk factors for illness, and for being impossible to achieve for most people in a global context (i.e. 'a state of complete physical, mental and social wellbeing'). It has also been criticised for undervaluing the ability for an individual to take responsibility for their health-related behaviour and to cope with health-related challenges (Godlee, 2011). In response to these criticisms, a 'global conversation' was initiated, yielding the following definition of health (Godlee, 2011): 'the ability to adapt and self-manage in the face of social, physical, and emotional challenges'.

Arguably, this definition builds even further on the WHO inclusion of psychosocial factors to acknowledge the role of the individual and their behaviour in health. **Health psychologists** are centrally placed to contribute to individual adaptation and self-management, and to understand the combination of social, physical and emotional challenges. *Health psychology is absolutely critical in the current healthcare context.*

What is health psychology?

Health psychology is the study of the effects of behaviour on health and health on behaviour. It examines the pattern of behaviours helping to maintain optimal health and those behaviours leading to illness. One of the main aims of health psychology is to encourage health-promoting behaviours, such as optimal diet and increased activity levels, and to help people quit smoking and reduce alcohol consumption. In helping the individual to achieve better health, health psychology focuses on prevention through education programs and public healthcare policy. The biggest challenges in Australia at the moment are to reduce obesity, increase activity levels (e.g. walking, exercise, sport participation), improve diet, and cut smoking rates and alcohol consumption. Prevention does not reach or work for everyone. Thus, health psychology also focuses on treatment and harm reduction to help 'move' people towards better health (i.e. to move to the right on the health continuum shown in Figure 1.2). In the current healthcare climate, helping people to quit smoking, improve sleep, reduce stress, be 'sun smart' and increase wellbeing are central.

These issues are addressed in the following chapter in this book:
Chapter 2: Understanding health behaviour and evaluating change

Given this broad focus of health psychology and the health status of Australians, there is no shortage of work for healthcare professionals to enable people to improve their physical and mental health. Healthcare workers from different disciplines (e.g. psychology, medicine) tend to approach health differently given their varying perspectives. The biopsychosocial model brings these different perspectives together. In practice, the implementation of the model provides a foundation for multidisciplinary healthcare, allowing healthcare professionals to examine the biological, psychological and social perspectives, and how they overlap. The biological perspective tends to focus on physical 'roots' such as genetic causes of health and behaviour, and dominates in medicine. As described previously, the psychological perspective is not exclusive to psychology and focuses on causal factors such as learning (e.g. reinforcement of behaviour). The social approach is more concerned with society as a whole and the norms it projects via news outlets and magazines in the form of 'role models' such as celebrities and sporting stars. To use smoking as an example, an individual who smokes has not taken up smoking in a social vacuum. It is likely that they were influenced by norms from family, peers, friends and the media. They may also have experienced feelings of being cool, independence, pleasure and being in control of his or her own destiny, thus reinforcing smoking-related behaviours. Biologically, smoking is reinforced through feelings of wellbeing and satisfaction as the nicotine enters the bloodstream.

Many common models in health psychology build on this biopsychosocial understanding of health. For example, the **ecological model** puts individual behaviour in context through interactions with social, environmental and societal factors. The ecological model is just one example of an expansion of the biopsychosocial model and takes into account the dynamic interaction effects that are at play in determining behaviour.

Health psychology is informed by a spectrum of psychological perspectives, including the following.

- Evolutionary: links evolutionary biology and psychology, exploring the processes that have shaped the human mind over time, from natural selection to communal living (Buss, 2015).
- Cognitive: the scientific study of the mind (Braisby & Gellatly, 2012).
- Behaviourist: objective approach to predicting and changing behaviour (Watson, 1913).
- Humanist: client-centred approaches that acknowledge the drive for self-actualisation (Elkins, 2009).

This is critical to informed and evidence-based approaches to understanding the relationships between individual factors, the social context and health more broadly.

Work environment

In Australia, health psychologists need to think and act in a multidisciplinary workplace. The ability to approach different situations from any or all of the different perspectives on the biopsychosocial model is essential for an effective workplace producing optimal outcomes for the clients involved. Health psychologists in Australia are expected to have certain skills in areas of intervention, treatment and research (Australian Psychological Society, 2016b), and are represented by one of the Australian Psychological Society's Colleges (Australian Psychological Society, 2016a).

In hospitals

Health psychologists who work in hospitals should be critical players in multidisciplinary research teams and do so using their skills in bringing together different perspectives and research talents. The skills a health psychologist brings to this team include an understanding of research design (e.g. longitudinal, experimental evaluation of interventions), logistics (e.g. ethics, timeline, funding), statistical analysis and interpretation, report writing for internal purposes, and manuscript writing for submission to peer-reviewed journals, grant and ethics writing and application. Conducting research is rewarding, but so is implementing research findings. A health psychologist will be able to read and disseminate research findings and then implement changes and interventions accordingly through ongoing education. This helps to maintain the focus on best practice given the available evidence, such as for hygiene-related behaviour (Hong et al., 2015). This may include working on improving the hygiene practices of those who enter a hospital (e.g. staff, patients, visitors). There are plenty of such interventions needed in hospitals to target staff and patients; however, for the changes to become permanent and thus effective they need to come not only from research findings but from the staff and patients themselves. Patients need to know the importance of adherence to treatment, from cognitive behavioural treatment through to drug treatment. To understand problems with adherence, a health psychologist needs to know how to conduct surveys and interviews with patients and staff asking not about adherence but lack of adherence and barriers to adherence. Assuming there is a problem will tend to expose the problem in this case.

In private practice

A health psychologist working with clients may incorporate health coaching to enable the client to develop more health-friendly behaviours (Gale, 2007). This will help the client cope with conditions such as diabetes and hypertension. All health psychologists should have the skills and knowledge necessary to enable them to help change clients' behaviours such as quitting smoking, changing diet and adhering to treatment. Another important factor is timing. Health psychologists may not always be able to help their clients change damaging behaviour before it has negative consequences for their health. However, they may be able to do so after the client has been diagnosed with a health condition such as cardiovascular disease or diabetes. A health psychologist may not be able to convince a client to change a diet which is high in sugar and processed food before problems are evident, but can help the client manage their condition following diagnosis. For example, after a client has been in a diabetic coma, health psychologists use their time with clients to alter the behaviours that may have led to the diabetic coma by using interventions to reduce the risk of future diabetic comas. Changes in behaviour need to be driven not just by the health psychologist but by the client as well. The client needs to see the value in change and the method to achieve the desired change, such as to quit smoking or improve diet. The health psychologist also understands the wider context that sustains behaviours such as bad sleep habits and a lack of work–life balance. This context includes the client's norms that may be maintained by culture, family, friends and religion. Changing lifelong habits can require consultation with family and friends. We would like to think that clients can decide to change their diet if they want to, but if they don't have a say in the food that is being sourced or cooked then it may be an illusion to think that the client has many options. There are several models that can be utilised by the health psychologist to help predict behaviour and thus to plan behavioural change.

These issues are addressed in the following chapter in this book:
Chapter 3: Common models in health psychology

The health psychologist can also work with individuals and their support networks (e.g. friends, family) to assist in social cohesion during critical times of adjustment such as diagnosis of a chronic illness, or during treatment regimens that may result in a need for extra support and care (e.g. during chemotherapy). At these points, it is common that those in the support network would benefit from support themselves. Relationships are often put under strain, right at the time when they are particularly necessary. Health psychologists are perfectly positioned to promote health in the whole social network, which ultimately improves outcomes for the individual.

These issues are addressed in the following chapter in this book:
Chapter 10: Experiencing cancer: an acute and chronic condition

Scientific knowledge and research

Psychology research employs various study designs in order to gain scientific knowledge and understanding. Studies relying on correlational designs focus on the relationships between variables. For example, the relationship between adherence, conscientiousness and wellbeing may be examined, revealing that higher conscientiousness is positively correlated with adherence and wellbeing. This study could have a cross-sectional design (participants could answer the survey once) or a longitudinal design (participants could answer the survey more than once and their answers could be linked between Time 1 and Time 2 in the dataset; for an example see Lytle et al., 2013). The time interval between Time 1 and Time 2 depends on the issues being examined and expectations about change. For instance, there is little point in measuring adherence and wellbeing only a week after the Time 1 measurement as a week may not be enough time for any treatment or intervention to have an effect on adherence and wellbeing, thus there is no or little change from Time 1 to Time 2 to examine.

Studies that are quasi-experimental compare two or more pre-existing populations, such as smokers versus non-smokers (e.g. Mendrek et al., 2006). As these are pre-existing populations, there is no baseline (e.g. pre-smoking). Quasi-experimental approaches are often used in human participants to explore health outcomes in two groups with different behavioural exposures (e.g. smoking/non-smoking). Due to ethical issues, animal models are frequently used to experimentally examine questions relating to exposures and health outcomes (e.g. Does second-hand smoke cause cancer?). In these cases, animals (e.g. mice, rats) may be used, and then inferences drawn for humans. Experimental studies use randomisation to allocate participants into different groups so as to examine the effects of exercise on mental health (e.g. Bretland & Thorsteinsson, 2015). Experimental models are also used with human participants. For example, if you wanted to compare the effectiveness of different interventions to assist people to quit smoking (e.g. chewing gum versus spray versus chewing gum and spray) then you would complete your baseline measures and then randomly allocate participants to four (not three) conditions: 1. chewing gum; 2. spray; 3. chewing gum and spray; and 4. control (waiting list). In the end you would have measured your participants at baseline, post-intervention and maybe two follow-ups (perhaps at 3 and 6 months).

When it comes to health psychology, we have to start expanding our study design horizon. We need to do this because the studies we are reading overlap with other health professions (e.g. medicine) and often focus on binary outcomes (e.g. diagnosis versus no diagnosis, heart attack versus no heart attack). Epidemiology, the study of control and progression in health and disease, with its odds and risk ratios, will become familiar to you and you will quickly understand these different indices (e.g. Satman et al., 2002). In many ways, these indices are simpler than the typical indices you are familiar with from your undergraduate psychology statistics lectures. A *t* value from a *t* test has little meaning on its own and a *p* value simply reflects the number of participants your analysis relied on. This is why effect sizes are so important and why ratios like risk, relative risk and odds are effect sizes. These ratios, along with a confidence interval, can then clearly show the danger patients are in (e.g. risk of lung cancer from smoking) and the chances of treatment improving or curing a condition, such as by using a statistic called **number needed to treat (NNT)**.

All this said, if we examine influential (based on the number of citations) papers in the area of health psychology, we do not necessarily see experimental or epidemiology types of studies but rather review or systematic review (e.g. meta-analysis) studies. One such paper is a review by Cohen and Wills (1985) that has over 11 000 citations. This paper examined the association between different types of social support and wellbeing within the main- and direct-effects models. Another type of research that is very influential deals with scale development, such as in a paper by Scheier and Carver (1985) that proposed a measure of dispositional optimism and has now over 5000 citations.

When it comes to enhancing our scientific knowledge, healthcare professionals must not shy away from unfamiliar research designs when they are needed in order to answer the questions at hand.

These issues are addressed in the following chapter in this book:
Chapter 4: Understanding presentation of research in health: research designs, figures and statistics

About this book

Based on published theory and research findings, this book has been developed to provide the reader with a clear understanding of health psychology and what health psychologists have to offer society. Health psychologists work to provide an evidence-based, context-rich understanding of behaviour, and to use this understanding as a basis for intervention to promote behaviour change for positive health outcomes. The aim is to improve the health not only of the individual, but also of societies as a whole, increasing physical and mental wellbeing and reducing the cost to the healthcare system. Health psychologists work with individuals to assist them to look after their health through a nutritious diet, adequate physical activity (e.g. exercise), sufficient sleep and protective sun exposure-related behaviours. It is a question not only of what to do but also of what not to do. Health psychologists also assist people to quit smoking and reduce their alcohol consumption. To do this, they use behaviour modification interventions, education and changes in society-level policies (e.g. increased alcohol taxes). Health psychologists also help people to recognise and cope with daily stress in order to optimise health. When it comes to stress, it is a question of getting the work–play balance right to try to reduce the negative effects stress can have. Taking these factors together (i.e. what to do, what not to do, and balance) we can start reducing the rates of chronic illnesses such as type 2 diabetes, cardiovascular disease and even pain. To further tackle these illnesses, we need to consider and address health inequalities in society and how culture may work both against better health and for it. All of this is conducted on the basis of an understanding and synthesis of research methods and findings from many relevant fields (e.g. epidemiology, public health), and alignment with, and contribution to, the continual debate about how we define health as a dynamic, evolving concept.

With this in mind, this book includes the following chapters.

Chapter 2: Understanding health behaviour and evaluating change. This chapter uses an ecological model perspective to describe methods of societal, environmental, social and individual behaviour change. The final section of the chapter focuses on methods of measuring behaviour and determining whether change is significant and/or meaningful.

Chapter 3: Common models in health psychology. This chapter focuses on the theoretical models that are used in health psychology to help to explain behaviour and to develop strategic, targeted and effective interventions for behaviour change. The empirical support for these models, and also their limitations, are discussed.

Chapter 4: Understanding presentation of research in health: research designs, figures and statistics. This chapter presents common research designs, graphical tools and analytic approaches common to other health disciplines such as epidemiology and public health. In a multidisciplinary context, the health psychologist must understand the scientific languages of these other disciplines in order to connect with all innovations and findings in health research.

Chapter 5: Nutrition, exercise and health. This chapter canvasses the complexity in motivations for food selection and consumption and discusses nutrition, diet and eating disorders. It also discusses the way in which we understand exercise requirements and what is considered adequate to promote health.

Chapter 6: Sleep, sleep loss, safety and health. We are designed to sleep for approximately one-third of our lives, yet sleep is frequently absent from discussions about healthcare. This chapter describes how we understand and measure sleep, what happens when we don't get enough, and the important implications of sleep loss in the healthcare context.

Chapter 7: Health risk behaviours: alcohol, drugs and smoking. Health psychologists must understand the complex and often emotionally laden factors that predispose people to engage in health risk behaviours, and the potential barriers to change. This chapter focuses on alcohol and tobacco addiction as two primary risk factors for chronic illness with the added intricacy of associated social disapproval and stigma.

Chapter 8: Stress and managing stress. This chapter discusses the ubiquitous phenomenon of stress and its role as a risk factor for illness. Coping mechanisms to deal with life's pressures are canvassed, including mindfulness meditation, which is currently receiving much attention as a potentially effective stress intervention.

Chapter 9: Lifestyle-related chronic illnesses (CVD and T2D) and depression. Health behaviours (e.g. diet, exercise), depression and chronic illness are interrelated. This chapter focuses on type 2 diabetes and cardiovascular disease as common examples of chronic illness, and describes lifestyle interventions for prevention and treatment, as well as treatment of comorbid depression.

Chapter 10: Experiencing cancer: an acute and chronic condition. Cancer is a lifestyle disease, which can be conceptualised as having a number of phases, starting with at-risk individuals and moving all the way through to survivorship or end of life. Each phase is associated with specific impacts, not only for the individual but also for their family and friends.

Chapter 11: Pain and its optimal management. Pain is a complex phenomenon that can be a highly adaptive warning sign, but in some cases it becomes chronic, with heavy social and psychological costs. This chapter considers the role of the health psychologist in understanding and treating chronic pain using non-pharmacological interventions.

Chapter 12: Health inequalities. This chapter discusses differences in health profiles as a function of socioeconomic status, employment, family structure, gender, sexual orientation, social connectedness, belief system and geographic location. These factors interact to produce levels of inequality which, as a matter of social justice, we should work to correct.

Chapter 13: Cross-cultural psychology. This chapter focuses on understanding culture and cultural competence in the healthcare context. Cross-cultural appreciation is critical for an effective therapeutic relationship, which can be undone by a conscious or unconscious ethnocentric lens.

Studying health psychology allows you to move from observer to participant in the ever-evolving debate about how we understand health and what we can do to promote health for all. As you read this book, we encourage you to reflect on your own ideas about health and illness, responsibility and advocacy, behaviour change and health promotion, and how you view these issues through your own cultural lens. This study may be part of your journey to becoming a healthcare practitioner, researcher, educator or policymaker, or a combination of several or all of these important roles. Health psychology has never been more critical. What will your contribution be?

Suggested weblinks

Refer to the companion website at www.cambridge.edu.au/academic/healthpsychology for a list of suggested weblinks.

References

AIHW. (2011). National health priority areas. Canberra: Australian Institute of Health and Welfare. Retrieved from: http://www.aihw.gov.au/health-priority-areas/

—— (2014a). *Australia's Health 2014*. Canberra: Australian Institute of Health and Welfare.

—— (2014b). *Cardiovascular Disease, Diabetes and Chronic Kidney Disease. Australian Facts: Prevalence and Incidence*. Canberra: Australian Institute of Health and Welfare.

—— (2015). Risk factors to health. Canberra: Australian Institute of Health and Welfare. Retrieved from: http://www.aihw.gov.au/risk-factors/

Australian Government. (2015). Indigenous arts, culture and heritage. Available online: http://www.australia.gov.au/about-australia/australian-stories/indigenous-arts-culture-and-heritage

Australian Psychological Society. (2016a). APS College of Health Psychologists. Retrieved from: https://groups.psychology.org.au/chp/

—— (2016b). Health psychology. Retrieved from: https://www.psychology.org.au/public/health/

Best, O. & Fredericks, B. (2014). *Yatdjuligin: Aboriginal and Torres Strait Islander Nursing and Midwifery Care*. Melbourne: Cambridge University Press.

Braisby, N. & Gellatly, A. (2012). *Cognitive Psychology*. Oxford: Oxford University Press.

Bramley, D., Hebert, P., Jackson, R.T. & Chassin, M. (2004). Indigenous disparities in disease-specific mortality, a cross-country comparison: New Zealand, Australia, Canada, and the United States. *The New Zealand Medical Journal*, *117*(1207), 1–16.

Bretland, R. J. & Thorsteinsson, E. B. (2015). Reducing workplace burnout: the relative benefits of cardiovascular and resistance exercise. *PeerJ*, *3*, e891. doi: http://dx.doi.org/10.7717/peerj.891

Buss, D. (2015). *Evolutionary Psychology: The New Science of the Mind* (5th edn). London: Psychology Press.

Chen, A. C., Halliday, G. M. & Damian, D. L. (2013). Non-melanoma skin cancer: carcinogenesis and chemoprevention. *Pathology: Journal of the RCPA*, *45*, 331–41.

Cohen, S. & Wills, T. A. (1985). Stress, social support, and the buffering hypothesis. *Psychological Bulletin*, *98*, 310–57. doi: http://dx.doi.org/10.1037/0033-2909.98.2.310

Douglas, M, et al. (2014). Guidelines for implementing culturally competent nursing care. *Journal of Transcultural Nursing*, *25*(2).

Duncan, G. (2000). Mind-body dualism and the biopsychosocial model of pain: what did Descartes really say? *Journal of Medicine and Philosophy*, *25*, 485–513.

Elkins, D. N. (2009). *Humanistic Psychology: A Clinical Manifesto: A Critique of Clinical Psychology and the Need for Progressive Alternatives*. Colorado: University of the Rockies Press.

Engel, G. L. (1977). The need for a new medical model: a challenge for biomedicine. *Science*, *196*, 129–36.

Fleming, M. & Towey, K. (2001). *Delivering Culturally Effective Health Care to Adolescents*. Chicago: American Medical Association.

Franco, D. A. & Williams, C. E. (2000). 'Airs, waters, places' and other Hippocratic writings: inferences for control of foodborne and waterborne disease. *Journal of Environmental Health*, *62*, 9.

Gale, J. (2007). Health psychology meets coaching psychology in the practice of health coaching. *InPsych*, *29*, 12–13.

Godlee, F. (2011). What is health? *British Medical Journal*, *343*, d4817.

Hong, T. S., Bush, E. C., Hauenstein, M. F., Lafontant, A., Li, C., Wanderer, J. P., et al. (2015). A hand hygiene compliance check system: brief communication on a system to improve hand hygiene compliance in hospitals and reduce infection. *Journal of Medical Systems*, *39*, 1–4. doi: http://dx.doi.org/10.1007/s10916-015-0253-z

Jackson, W. A. (2001). A short guide to humoral medicine. *Trends in Pharmacological Sciences*, *22*, 487.

Jones, K. & Creedy, D. (eds) (2012). *Health and Human Behaviour*. Melbourne: Oxford University Press.

Knutsson, A. (2003). Health disorders of shift workers. *Occupational Medicine*, *53*, 103–8.

Loeser, J.D. & Melzack, R. (1999). Pain: an overview. *The Lancet*, *353*(9164), 1607–9.

Lytle, L. A., Murray, D. M., Laska, M. N., Pasch, K. E., Anderson, S. E. & Farbakhsh, K. (2013). Examining the longitudinal relationship between change in sleep and obesity risk in adolescents. *Health Education & Behavior*, *40*, 362–70. doi: http://dx.doi.org/10.1177/1090198112451446

Magner, L. N. (1992). *A History of Medicine*. New York: CRC Press.

Marmot, M. (2005). Social determinants of health inequalities. *The Lancet*, *365*, 1099–104. doi: http://dx.doi.org/10.1016/S0140-6736(05)71146-6

Mendrek, A., Monterosso, J., Simon, S. L., Jarvik, M., Brody, A., Olmstead, R., et al. (2006). Working memory in cigarette smokers: comparison to non-smokers and effects of abstinence. *Addictive Behaviors*, *31*, 833–44. doi: http://dx.doi.org/10.1016/j.addbeh.2005.06.009

Rajaratnam, S. M. W. & Arendt, J. (2001). Health in a 24-h society. *The Lancet*, *358*, 999–1005.

Roscoe, L. J. (2009). Wellness: a review of theory and measurement for counselors. *Journal of Counseling and Development*, *87*, 216.

Rozanski, A., Blumenthal, J. A., Davidson, K. W., Saab, P. G. & Kubzansky, L. (2005). The epidemiology, pathophysiology, and management of psychosocial risk factors in cardiac practice: the emerging field of behavioral cardiology. *Journal of the American College of Cardiology*, *45*, 637–51.

Satman, I., Yilmaz, T., Sengül, A., Salman, S., Salman, F., Uygur, S., et al. (2002). Population-based study of diabetes and risk characteristics in Turkey: results of the Turkish diabetes epidemiology study (TURDEP). *Diabetes Care*, *25*, 1551–6. doi: http://dx.doi.org/10.2337/diacare.25.9.1551

Scheier, M. F. & Carver, C. S. (1985). Optimism, coping, and health: assessment and implications of generalized outcome expectancies. *Health Psychology*, *4*, 219–47. doi: http://dx.doi.org/10.1037/0278-6133.4.3.219

Schnierer, E., Ellsmore, S. & Schnierer, S. (2011). *State of Indigenous cultural heritage 2011*. Report prepared for the Australian Government Department of Sustainability, Environment, Water, Population and Communities on behalf of the State of the Environment 2011 Committee. Canberra: DSEWPaC.

Stelmack, R. M. & Stalikas, A. (1991). Galen and the humour theory of temperament. *Personality and Individual Differences*, *12*, 255–63.

Sullivan, M. (1986). In what sense is contemporary medicine dualistic? *Culture, Medicine and Psychiatry*, *10*, 331–50.

Vanitallie, T. B. (2002). Stress: a risk factor for serious illness. *Metabolism*, *51*, 40–5.

Wade, D. T. & Halligan, P. (2004). Do biomedical models of illness make for good healthcare systems? *British Medical Journal*, *329*, 1398–401.

Watson, J. B. (1913). Psychology as the behaviorist views it. *Psychological Review*, *20*(2), 158.

Westerman, T. (2004). Guest Editorial: Engagement of Indigenous clients in mental health services: What role do cultural differences play? *Australian e-journal for the Advancement of Mental Health*, *3*(3), 88–93.

WHO. (1946). *Preamble to the Constitution of the World Health Organization as Adopted by the International Health Conference*. New York: World Health Organisation.

Ypinazar, V.A., Margolis, S.A., Haswell-Elkins, M. & Tsey, K. (2007). Indigenous Australians' understandings regarding mental health and disorders. *Australian and New Zealand Journal of Psychiatry*, *41*(6), 467–78.

Acknowledgements

I would like to acknowledge Dr Natasha Loi for valuable comments on this manuscript.

2

Understanding health behaviour and evaluating change

Learning outcomes

After reading this chapter, you should be able to:

- explain reasons for behaviour change in health promotion, illness prevention and treatment
- describe approaches to behaviour change at the societal, environmental, social and individual levels
- explain the way in which health psychologists consider behaviour in context, and the importance of understanding the antecedents and consequences of behaviour
- describe single systems designs and their utility for evaluating behaviour change
- design a basic behaviour change intervention and data collection methods, and analyse the data to determine whether a change is meaningful and/or significant.

Introduction

Primary goals of health psychology include preventing illness, promoting good health and assisting with treatment. One way of working towards these goals involves understanding and supporting behaviour change. For example, preventive behaviour change may involve encouraging people to wear sunscreen to avoid skin cancer, promoting good health may involve encouraging people to quit smoking, and assisting with treatment may involve helping someone to change their diet following a diagnosis of heart disease. Behaviour change can be achieved through action at a number of levels through societal change (e.g. policy and mass media), environmental manipulation (e.g. availability of green spaces and fresh produce), social influence (e.g. family and friends) and behaviour modification at the individual level.

At all levels, we need to understand behaviours in context. What are the cues, or triggers, for behaviour? What are the consequences of the behaviour? We also need to be able to evaluate whether our intervention for behaviour change has had a meaningful impact. In order to do this, we must be able to measure the behaviour and then analyse it. In this chapter, the rationale for behaviour change will be discussed, followed by each of the levels of intervention, according to the ecological model (societal, environmental, social, individual). The final section of the chapter will focus on interventions for individual behaviour change and methods for behaviour measurement and analysis to determine whether a change is meaningful and/or significant.

Health behaviour

When we think about health psychology, we often think about the role of psychology in treating or supporting people who are unwell. However, we are not only interested in illness. In fact, health psychologists spend a considerable amount of their time focusing on health behaviours. Health behaviours include, but are not limited to: eating a healthy diet; engaging in physical activity; immunisation; wearing sun-protective clothing and sunscreen; and limiting alcohol consumption.

Why do we focus on health behaviours if people aren't necessarily sick? The first reason is that health behaviour can prevent disease and illness later in life. In Australia, cancer is the leading cause of **burden of disease**, followed by cardiovascular disease. Together they account for over half of the years of life lost due to premature death (AIHW, 2015a). The adoption of a healthy lifestyle significantly reduces the risk for chronic diseases including cancer, cardiovascular disease and type 2 diabetes. In fact, these are sometimes referred to as 'lifestyle diseases' due to the substantial role that health behaviours play. The incidence of chronic diseases around the world could be significantly reduced through the adoption of a healthy lifestyle (AIHW, 2012; Low, Lee & Samy, 2015). Promoting health behaviour in order to reduce risk or prevent disease is called **primary prevention**.

Preventing disease and illness is not the only reason for supporting healthy behaviours. A healthy lifestyle can extend life expectancy by 10 years or more depending on current age (Li, Husing & Kaaks, 2014; Martin-Diener et al., 2014). Perhaps more importantly, a healthy lifestyle is associated with improved quality of life (May et al., 2015; WHO, 1986). This can be defined in terms of physical, emotional and social functioning and therefore impacts all aspects of life.

The final reason for supporting health behaviour is the cost associated with illness and disease. In 2013–2014, total health expenditure in Australia was estimated at $154.6 billion and government health expenditure at $104.8 billion (AIHW 2015b). For the same time period, health costs to the individual were estimated at $6639 per person. The costs associated with poor health are therefore significant both for society and for individuals. It is important to remember that people are often unable to work or need to reduce their work hours due to their illness. Therefore, they may have a reduced income with which to pay for medical expenses.

If healthy behaviour reduces risk for chronic disease, improves quality of life and reduces the financial burden associated with disease and illness, the case is clear for making healthy lifestyle changes. The big question is then, why don't people adopt healthy behaviours? It is often assumed that if people know the benefits of healthy behaviours and the consequences of health risk behaviours, they will make healthy choices. However, knowledge alone rarely results in health behaviour change. The reasons for this are many because health behaviours, like all behaviours, are complex. Some of the common models used to explain health behaviour are presented in Chapter 3. For now, however, we will look at the ecological model in order to understand the broad levels of influence on health behaviour (see Figure 2.1). In this chapter we will examine each of these levels beginning with the broadest level (societal influences) and ending with an in-depth consideration of individual behaviour change.

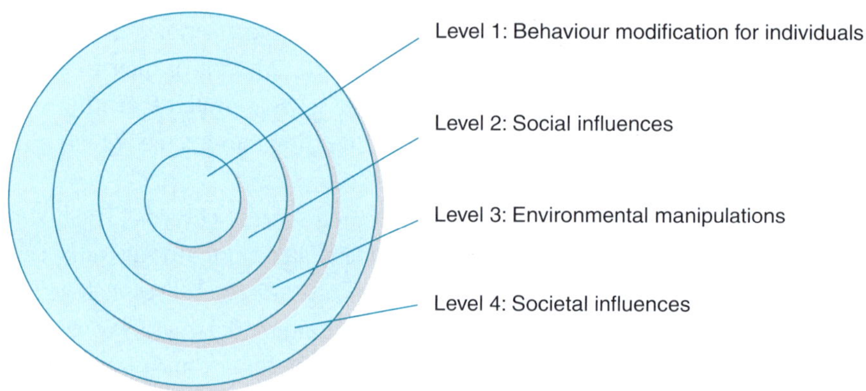

Figure 2.1 Ecological model
Source: adapted from Faith & Epstein, 2007

Mini case study 2.1

Australia has the highest incidence of skin cancer in the world, and skin cancer is the most common cancer type in Australians aged 12 to 24 (AIHW, 2011, 2014b). However, the good news is that skin cancer can be prevented by adopting sun protection behaviours. These include wearing sun-protective clothing (hats, long sleeves and sunglasses), applying sunscreen and seeking shade when UV levels are moderate to extreme. Despite high levels of knowledge about skin cancer prevention in the population, largely due to school-based education programs and mass media campaigns, typically fewer than 50% of Australian adolescents and adults regularly use sun protection during peak times of UV radiation (Hutchinson et al., 2015; Volkov et al., 2013). In fact, adolescents and young adults in particular continue to tan (deliberately sun expose) and believe a tan is desirable (Prichard et al., 2014; Volkov et al., 2013).

Critical thinking question

Identify factors that influence sun protection and sun exposure behaviours at each level of the ecological model as presented in Figure 2.1. Are these likely to vary with age? Gender? Geographic location?

Societal influences

Some influences on health behaviour take place at a societal level. These can occur at the state or national level, but due to the use of social media and increased globalisation, information and trends can easily spread beyond national borders.

Policy

Changes in policy or legislation result in widespread change. Their impact is substantial because the corresponding health behaviours become mandatory. There are many examples of significant changes in policy that impact society and the health of its citizens; compulsory wearing of seatbelts and bans on smoking inside restaurants are now accepted as normal (AIHW, 2014a). Policies are not limited to requiring or prohibiting certain behaviours. Policies may also influence health risk behaviours by creating barriers to engaging in these behaviours, such as increasing taxes on alcohol and tobacco products.

However, not all health behaviours lend themselves to policy changes or the introduction of legislation. Solariums were recently banned in Australia, making the commercial use of tanning beds illegal due to the increased cancer risk associated with 'indoor tanning' (Sinclair et al., 2014). However, imagine the backlash if legislation was introduced making it illegal to go outside during the middle of the day when ultraviolet radiation is at its peak. This type of government involvement in health behaviour would be considered unwelcome by most people. Mass media campaigns present an alternative method for reaching a large proportion of the population with a health message in these cases.

Mass media

Mass media campaigns are used to deliver a message to a large population via television, radio, newspapers or online. In Australia, memorable media campaigns have addressed sun protection, road safety, alcohol consumption and tobacco use. These campaigns have the potential to reach a large number of people either through direct exposure to the campaign or indirectly through exposure to behaviour changes of other members of the social network who have been exposed to the campaign. Another advantage of mass media campaigns is that the message may be heard repeatedly over time and therefore is more likely to be remembered (Wakefield, Loken & Hornik, 2010).

The impact of mass media campaigns on health behaviours has varied. One reason for this may be exposure to inconsistent messages due to competing campaigns, marketing efforts (e.g. by alcohol and tobacco industries) promoting the unhealthy behaviour, and the increased difficulty in achieving widespread exposure due to the variety of media available to consumers (Wakefield et al., 2010). In one case, a tobacco company delivered a campaign designed to decrease smoking in young people. The campaign encouraged children to talk to their parents about tobacco use. Surprisingly, studies revealed that exposure to this campaign actually strengthened intentions to smoke in the future (Farrelly et al., 2002; Wakefield et al., 2006). The reason for this effect may have been that the campaign did not provide a strong reason for not smoking. It has also been suggested that defining smoking as an adult activity may increase its appeal among young people. Tobacco is one area where many mass media campaigns have been successful in reducing smoking intentions and behaviour. However, significant effects of mass media campaigns have been found in a range of areas, including road safety, prevention of cardiovascular disease, nutrition and physical activity (Wakefield et al., 2010).

In order to maximise the chance of success, campaigns should be based on research evidence, tested during development to assess outcomes, achieve widespread exposure (which may require significant funding to support dissemination), and be supported by relevant policies (e.g. restrictions on smoking, provision of nutritional information, financial support for cancer screening) (Wakefield et al., 2010). Providing health-related products in conjunction with mass media campaigns has also been recommended as a way to increase effectiveness. For example, providing nicotine replacement therapy, sunscreen or pedometers alongside campaigns for quitting smoking, sun protection and physical activity (respectively) have also been recommended (Community Preventive Services Task Force, 2014).

Mini case study 2.2

The 'rethink sugary drink' campaign is supported by 12 community and health organisations, including the Cancer Council, Diabetes Australia and the Heart Foundation. The campaign aims to raise awareness about the sugar content of drinks and the health impact of consuming high amounts of sugar. The video states that an adult needs to run 3 km in order to burn off the calories contained in one 600 mL soft drink. The increased risk of weight gain, type 2 diabetes, heart and kidney disease and cancer is also described. The advertisement concludes by suggesting water as an alternative to sweetened drinks. You can view the video and related materials at www.rethinksugarydrink.org.au.

Critical thinking questions

1. Identify a policy that could be implemented to support this campaign.
2. How could this campaign impact people's consumption of sweetened drinks even if they haven't seen the video?

Environmental manipulations

It is important to consider the environment when promoting behaviour change. An intervention designed to promote walking in the local neighbourhood may be less likely to succeed if there are no footpaths in the area or if there is a high crime rate. Similarly, increasing consumption of fruits and vegetables in a remote town will be challenging if there is little fresh produce available and if that which is available is very expensive.

Therefore, changes to the environment may involve removing significant barriers to engaging in health behaviours. These changes may occur at the community level or within workplaces, schools or community groups.

One example of an environmental factor related to health of the community is the creation and maintenance of green spaces or natural environments such as parks and playgrounds. The availability of green space has been associated with increased physical activity, health and wellbeing (Calogiuri & Chroni, 2014; van den Berg et al., 2015). Other environmental changes include the provision of bike lanes to support cycling (physical activity) and increasing the availability of healthy foods to facilitate adoption of a healthy diet. Interventions in the workplace could include establishing a smoke-free workplace, providing free fruit for employees or providing flexible work hours to allow employees to attend the gym at a convenient time. Finally, schools might establish a nutrition program or provide sunscreen and shade in the playground. The success of each of these strategies is likely to vary from setting to setting. A careful consideration of the specific context and potential barriers to health behaviour change is paramount when designing interventions or environmental changes.

Nudging

Health behaviours are often choices. If a health behaviour is not required by law (e.g. wearing seatbelts), or by workplace policy (e.g. not smoking inside), individuals are in a position to choose whether or not to engage in a health behaviour. These choices are influenced by a number of biases. People tend to be overly optimistic about their own performance and about their own personal risk for poor health outcomes. For example, people may predict that their own chance of being diagnosed with cancer is smaller than that of others. This bias may lead them to choose riskier behaviours such as smoking or delaying regular health screenings. The status quo bias also affects our decisions. People tend to continue doing what they are already doing (e.g. sitting in particular seats in the classroom or watching the same TV channel) rather than initiate change.

Optimism and the status quo bias are just two examples of many biases that influence individual choices (Thaler & Sunstein, 2008). These may sound like a problem; however, Thaler and Sunstein indicate that biases can be used to **nudge** people towards healthy choices. For example, placing fruit in a highly visible location in a shop would encourage its purchase without removing an individual's ability to choose alternative snacks. In fact, marketers have used these biases to influence our choices for a long time. The placement of chocolate bars and magazines at eye level next to the checkout in supermarkets is not accidental.

The classic example of a nudge comes from an airport in Amsterdam where the image of a fly was etched into each of the men's urinals. This simple change led men to pay more attention, improve their accuracy and as a result, spillage was reduced by 80%! This example has received so much attention that it has now been implemented around the world (Thaler & Sunstein, 2008).

By designing environments that influence behaviour in a predictable manner, we can nudge people towards better choices without removing their freedom of choice (Thaler & Sunstein, 2008). We know that many people will choose to remain with the default option because of the status quo bias, whether this relates to the notification settings on your phone or the size of the soft drink that comes with a fast-food meal. Therefore, the careful choice of default options can nudge people towards specific choices and can be used to increase the likelihood of health behaviours.

Despite the important contribution of environmental interventions, it is often difficult to evaluate their impact (Lieberman, Golden & Earp, 2013). The majority of health intervention studies focus on individual behaviour change or social networks; these will be discussed in the following sections of this chapter. Further research on the impact of changes to the environment is greatly needed.

Mini case study 2.3

Elizabeth drives for an hour each day to her job in the city. She works in a large office block and works at a computer all day. She is concerned by her lack of physical activity. It is usually dark by the time she gets home and her previous efforts to start walking regularly have been short-lived.

Critical thinking questions

1. What questions could you ask Elizabeth about her workplace or community?
2. You discover that Elizabeth is in a senior position in the company. She also meets regularly with members of the city council. What environmental or policy changes could you explore with Elizabeth for: a. the workplace; and b. the broader community?

Interpersonal influences

Family and friends

Significant others, particularly family and friends, influence health behaviour. This can be explained by **social norms**. Social norms describe behaviour that is perceived as normal or socially acceptable and these norms vary from group to group. Family have been shown to have a significant influence on a number of health behaviours, including dietary choices, physical activity and alcohol consumption (Feunekes et al., 1997; LaBrie et al., 2010; te Velde et al., 2014). Similarly, friends or peers have been shown to influence smoking behaviour, diet, alcohol consumption and physical activity (Go et al., 2012; Holahan et al., 2013; LaBrie et al., 2010; Yun & Silk, 2011).

Given the number of potentially influential friends and family, who are the most influential? The answer, perhaps not surprisingly, is those that are closest. Norms can be defined as proximal or distal. **Proximal norms** reflect those norms of close family and friends while **distal norms** are those associated with broader peer groups or the media (Yun & Silk, 2011). In general, proximal norms influence health behaviour to a greater extent than distal norms (Cox & Bates, 2011; Gilligan et al., 2014; Yun & Silk, 2011). It is important to consider the role of social norms and the influence of peers when promoting behaviour change. If the proposed behaviour is inconsistent with the behaviour of significant others, it will be hard to maintain.

Diffusion of innovations

The **diffusion of innovations** model describes the process by which an idea (or innovation) spreads through a social network. The model was developed in the 1950s and 60s and was first applied to agriculture (Rogers, 2004). Since then, it has been applied to health promotion as well as many other domains. An s-shaped curve of the adoption of an idea or practice over time has been observed, such that initial adoption is slow, followed by a steep increase in uptake before the rate of adoption levels off (see Figure 2.2). This pattern has been found to be similar across diverse areas of research, from planting hybrid corn seed to drug addiction. The rate of adoption does, however, vary from one innovation to another. Innovations that are viewed as advantageous, consistent with values, observable, easily tried and easy to understand or use are likely to be adopted more rapidly and spread quickly (Rogers, 2002). This also applies to health behaviours such as smoking, drug use and online scheduling of medical appointments (Ferrence, 1996, 2001; Haider & Kreps, 2004; Zhang et al., 2015).

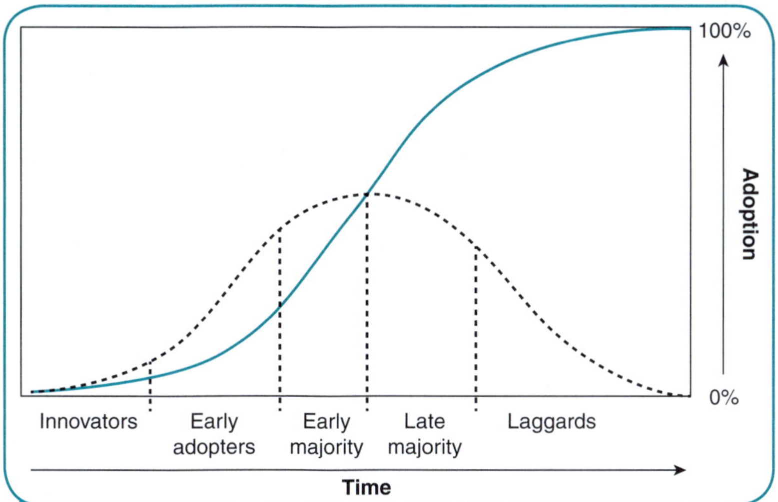

Figure 2.2 Diffusion of innovations model. The blue solid line shows the s-shaped curve of adoption of an idea or practice over time. The spread of the different members of the social system is displayed in the black dotted line.

Interpersonal connections also influence the spread of an idea, behaviour or other type of innovation. Members of the social system can be categorised as innovators, early adopters, early majority, late majority or laggards; innovators are the first to adopt an innovation, followed by early adopters through to laggards, who only adopt the innovation when they are surrounded by others who have already adopted the practice or idea (Rogers, 2002). Early adopters are the focus of many health-related and prevention interventions as they are more integrated in the community than innovators and therefore have the potential to influence others. These influential community members are often called opinion leaders and may include health practitioners or teachers (Rogers, 2002).

Compared to other innovations, the adoption of prevention behaviours tends to be slow. This is probably because the reward for engaging in prevention behaviours occurs in the future (e.g. greater life expectancy), making the behaviour appear less advantageous in the short term. Therefore, it is important to engage opinion leaders, provide peer support and promote communication related to the relevant health behaviour through social networks (Rogers, 2002).

Social networks

Although it is important to consider the behaviour and attitudes of significant others, it is also important to remember that individuals live within a complex social environment, characterised by numerous relationships. This has led to an examination of broader social networks. Social network analysis has been used to examine obesity, relationships, substance abuse and political behaviour, to name just a few applications (Christakis & Fowler, 2009; Valente, 2010). Social network analysis considers how a network influences an individual's behaviour as well as the behaviour of the system as a whole. Ultimately, it views the individual within their social context and examines relationships as well as an individual's behaviour.

Figure 2.3 shows a social network with girls depicted as circles and boys as squares. The lines indicate a relationship between members of the network. Those who are central to the network are likely to be influential and may be opinion leaders. Centrality can

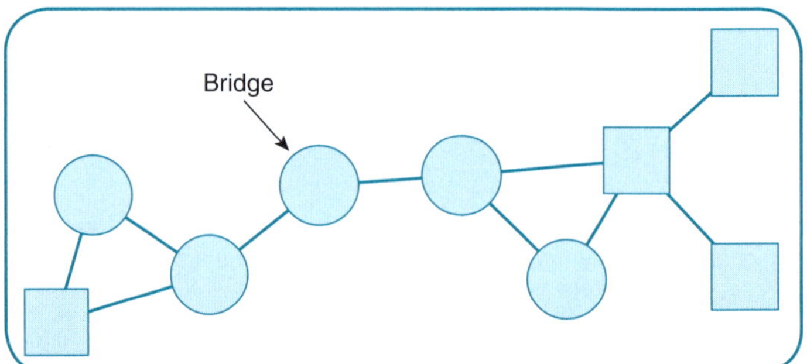

Figure 2.3 Example of a social network. Circles indicate girls, squares indicate boys and lines indicate a relationship between members of the network.

be defined and measured in several ways, including those individuals who are most connected to others and those who are closest to all others in the network. It seems obvious that central members are likely to influence the network. However, those in bridging positions may also be influential as they connect otherwise disconnected groups. These individuals have the potential to spread an idea or behaviour from one group to another. However, they may also represent bottlenecks in the spread of information. Furthermore, their removal is also likely to have a significant impact on network performance (Valente, 2010). So, a person's position in the social network and degree of connectedness may affect how influential their behaviour is on others.

Social networks present an opportunity for interventions to have a broader impact than individual approaches because changes in one person's behaviour may lead to changes throughout the network. Health behaviours may also be more easily maintained if they are consistent with social norms and supported by family and friends.

Mini case study 2.4

Interventions designed to promote health behaviour or prevent disease can have both positive and negative outcomes. When designing interventions, it is important to consider unintended consequences of the intervention. Programs designed to influence behaviour by changing social norms or influencing social networks may also increase stigma towards those whose health or behaviour is inconsistent with the norm. Stigma has been identified as a significant concern for people with diabetes, HIV or mental health problems, for smokers and for people who are obese (De Brun et al., 2014; McCool et al., 2013; Reavley & Jorm, 2012; Scambler, 2009; Schabert et al., 2013; Stuber, Galea & Link, 2008; Young et al., 2010). Although some might argue that stigma can motivate behaviour change, stigma has been shown to result in poorer health outcomes, reduce help seeking and increase health disparities (Puhl & Heuer, 2010; Williamson et al., 2014).

Critical thinking questions

1. What impact might stigma have on individuals who engage in health risk behaviours?
2. How might interventions targeting social networks or social norms address this issue?

Behaviour change for individuals

To design interventions for behaviour change on an individual level, we need to understand the antecedents and the consequences of the behaviour we are interested in changing, frequently referred to as the **target behaviour**. This is often referred to as the ABC approach (antecedents, behaviour, consequences). **Antecedents** come before our target behaviour, and may also be thought of as cues, or stimuli. **Consequences** come after behaviour, and may also be thought of as reinforcing factors. To understand the ABC, we frequently use a behaviour diary in order to record and examine the target behaviour over time (often 1 to 2 weeks). An important underpinning of the behaviour diaries used in health psychology is the understanding that all behaviours occur in a context involving situations, thoughts and feelings. Table 2.1 provides an example excerpt from the type of diary that might be used in this way. You can see from this example that not only are the day, amount and type of food recorded, but importantly, the time, location, people present, activity and mood are also entered for each instance of the behaviour.

Table 2.1 Example excerpt from a behaviour diary, where the target behaviour is diet

	Food or drink		Circumstances				
Day/Date	How much	What kind	Time	Where	Alone or with whom	Activity	Mood
Tues 28/02	2	Weet-Bix	8:00 am	home	alone	getting ready for uni	happy
Tues 28/02	1 cup	Milk (2% reduced fat)	as above				
Tues 28/02	1	Choc chip muesli bar	10:30 am	uni	Claire and Jacqui	break from lectures	tired
Tues 28/02	2 slices	White bread	12:30 pm	uni	Claire	socialising	happy

Planning behaviour change

To understand the way in which we approach individual behaviour change, we need to go all the way back to two definitive theories in psychology: classical and operant conditioning. **Classical conditioning**, of course, was developed by Ivan Pavlov, a Russian physiologist who was studying the digestive systems of dogs. He noticed that when he brought out the food to the dogs, they started salivating in anticipation. This led to the understanding that associations between two related events are learned (e.g. experimenter footsteps, arrival of food), and that this learned association can prompt a physiological response (e.g. salivation) (Pavlov & Anrep, 2003). Learned associations can be important in behaviour change. For example, if we are interested in reducing chocolate consumption, we may look at our behaviour diary and notice that we consume chocolate when we are alone, watching television. In fact, when we think about it, we may realise that just sitting in front of the television makes us crave chocolate. This demonstrates a learnt association between sitting in front of the television and chocolate. So in behaviour diaries we look for antecedents, or cues to behaviours, and then some types of intervention focus on breaking those associations. These are often referred to as **stimulus control interventions**, involving reduction or removal of a stimulus (e.g. television watching) that elicits a conditioned response (e.g. chocolate craving) and prompts undesirable behaviours (e.g. eating chocolate) in order to reduce the frequency of that response, or the introduction or amplification of stimuli that prompt desirable behaviours (Cooper, Heron & Heward, 2007; Faith & Epstein, 2007).

Operant conditioning was developed by Burrhus Frederic Skinner, who was an American behaviourist. He is famous for his work with rats in his operant conditioning boxes, which we now refer to as 'Skinner Boxes'. He demonstrated that the likelihood that a behaviour will recur is dependent on the consequences of that behaviour. Referred to as **reinforcement**, he explained that behaviours with positive consequences are likely to recur, whereas those with negative consequences are not (Skinner, 1963). For example, if we notice in our behaviour diaries that we eat chocolate when we feel sad, and that afterwards our mood improves, then improved mood can be described as reinforcement for the behaviour of eating chocolate. So in behaviour diaries, we look for the consequences of behaviours and then some types of intervention focus on changing those patterns of reinforcement, or creating new ones. These are often referred to as **behaviour modification interventions**, involving behaviour change based on operant conditioning principles, often by setting up (or changing existing) **response contingencies**, which are behaviours that will earn reinforcement.

One way a health psychologist may begin discussion about a target behaviour, often assisted by information collected in behaviour diaries, is through an interview. Some example questions from such an interview are included in Table 2.2. This interview schedule helps to guide a client through the antecedents and consequences of their target behaviour, as well as examining the potential benefits and losses associated with behaviour change. It is critical to acknowledge that every change has potential benefits, but also potential losses. Often, these health behaviours are serving a purpose, which may have negative consequences for health but may be helpful in other ways. For example, people may drink alcohol to relieve symptoms of anxiety (Carrigan & Randall, 2003; Ganz & Sher, 2009) or may eat foods that are high in sugar because they are feeling tired (Persson & Mårtensson, 2006). We need to understand, once we take the alcohol or the sugar away, what might happen. This is critical when we are considering maintenance of behaviour change. If you change a behaviour that was serving a purpose without addressing the need served by the behaviour it may be difficult to maintain change (Faith & Epstein, 2007).

We can use the resulting understanding of the target behaviour in context in order to set behaviour change goals. This is most often done using **goal-setting principles**: working on successive approximation, and setting up goals that are small and attainable to build towards a larger goal. An intervention plan can then be designed to support those goals using stimulus control or behaviour modification interventions.

Table 2.2 Example questions from a behavioural interview for investigating/planning behaviour change

1. How do you feel about your [target behaviour]?
2. In what situations does your [target behaviour] occur?
3. What are you thinking/feeling/doing just before and after the [target behaviour]?
4. What are the factors that maintain your [target behaviour]?
5. Have you attempted to do anything about your [target behaviour]? If yes, how and when?
6. How does your social network influence your [target behaviour]?
7. What are the benefits of you changing your [target behaviour]?
8. What are your future health goals surrounding your [target behaviour]?
9. What ideas do you have about how you could work towards achieving that goal?
10. How committed are you to improving your situation?
11. What do you think will be the losses associated with changing your [target behaviour]?
12. How would you maintain your [target behaviour] change after the intervention?

Measuring behaviour change

Single systems designs

There are very structured techniques that can be used to understand whether an intervention has been successful. These are **single systems designs**, with the behaviour of an individual or group of individuals measured before and after an intervention. A particular target behaviour is chosen and operationally defined, an intervention is planned and implemented, and then change is evaluated. These designs are usually described in phases, where A is the baseline (pre-treatment) phase and B denotes the post-intervention phase. The most basic is the **AB design**, where there is a single baseline phase followed by an intervention phase. This is also the least robust design, since it is open to contaminating effects resulting from changes in people's lives that may happen at the same time as the intervention, and explain any behaviour change (or lack of change) (Bloom, Fischer & Orme, 2006).

In order to reduce confounding, more complex versions of the designs may be used. For example, an ABA design may be implemented, which involves a baseline phase (A), a treatment phase (B) and then a third phase, where the treatment is removed again (A). This can reduce the likelihood that an external factor may be driving any change over time in behaviour that is seen. This can be further extended to become ABAB designs, and so on. However, where the treatment is implemented and then removed, the term **withdrawal design** is frequently used. As you can imagine, ethical issues can arise in withdrawal designs; for example, in cases where a clinician feels that an intervention is very likely to be beneficial, they may not want to suggest withdrawal. For this reason, **multiple baseline designs** may be implemented, where at least three individuals undertake the intervention, but begin the study with their start times staggered, to help to rule out other potential reasons for behaviour change (e.g. change of seasons). An example of a multiple baseline design is the concurrent design, where the second person starts once the first person's baseline has stabilised, then the third person starts when the second person's baseline has stabilised, and so on. Of course, the longer the baseline and intervention periods, the more robust the design (Bloom et al., 2006; Engel & Schutt, 2009; Faith & Epstein, 2007).

Let's consider a situation where we have three clients who are trying to reduce their chocolate consumption. We know from their behaviour diaries that studying is a stimulus for eating chocolate. If we collected baseline data for 1 week during exams, where a lot of chocolate was consumed, and then implemented the treatment at the start of holidays and observed a reduction in consumption, then it would be difficult to tell whether the intervention had resulted in the change, or whether it was simply due to the coincident cessation in studying. If we used a multiple baseline design, which was staggered so that the first participant started their intervention during the first week of holidays, the second participant in the second week and the third participant in the third week, and we found exactly the same results across all participants, then we would be more sure that it was the intervention that was having the effect on behaviour.

Making behaviour measurable

A key to evaluating behaviour change is to operationalise the target behaviour, to make it measurable so that any changes can be quantified. Behaviour can be quantified in terms of the following.

- **Frequency.** How often does the target behaviour occur?
- **Duration.** For how long does the target behaviour occur?
- **Interval.** How long is the period in between observations of the behaviour?
- **Magnitude.** How large/intense are observations of the target behaviour?

For example, if our target behaviour is exercise, and our goal is to increase the amount of exercise that a person does, we could measure frequency (how many times they exercise), duration (how long they exercise, in minutes or hours), interval (how long it is between exercise sessions, in minutes or days) and/or magnitude (the intensity of their exercise, e.g. mild/moderate/high) (Engel & Schutt, 2009). Smoking is an example of a behaviour that may suit an interval approach, especially in cases where it is of interest to examine how long someone can make it without a cigarette, and working on extending that time. We must be clear on the type of measure and the units (e.g. coffee consumption in milligrams, exercise duration in hours, alcohol consumption in number of standard drinks) when defining behavioural goals.

Graphing and interpretation

Once behaviour is measurable, it can then be recorded and plotted on a graph. Plotting the data allows us to identify any patterns. Figure 2.4 displays examples of patterns that may be observed across a week of baseline recording, with a target behaviour of alcohol consumption, operationalised as number of standard drinks. The **linear trend** shows an increase or decrease by the same amount each day, the **stable pattern** shows consistent consumption across days, the *daily changes* show an example where alcohol is only consumed on weekends, the **curvilinear trend** shows an increase or decrease by an increasing amount each day, and the *variable* figure shows changes each day.

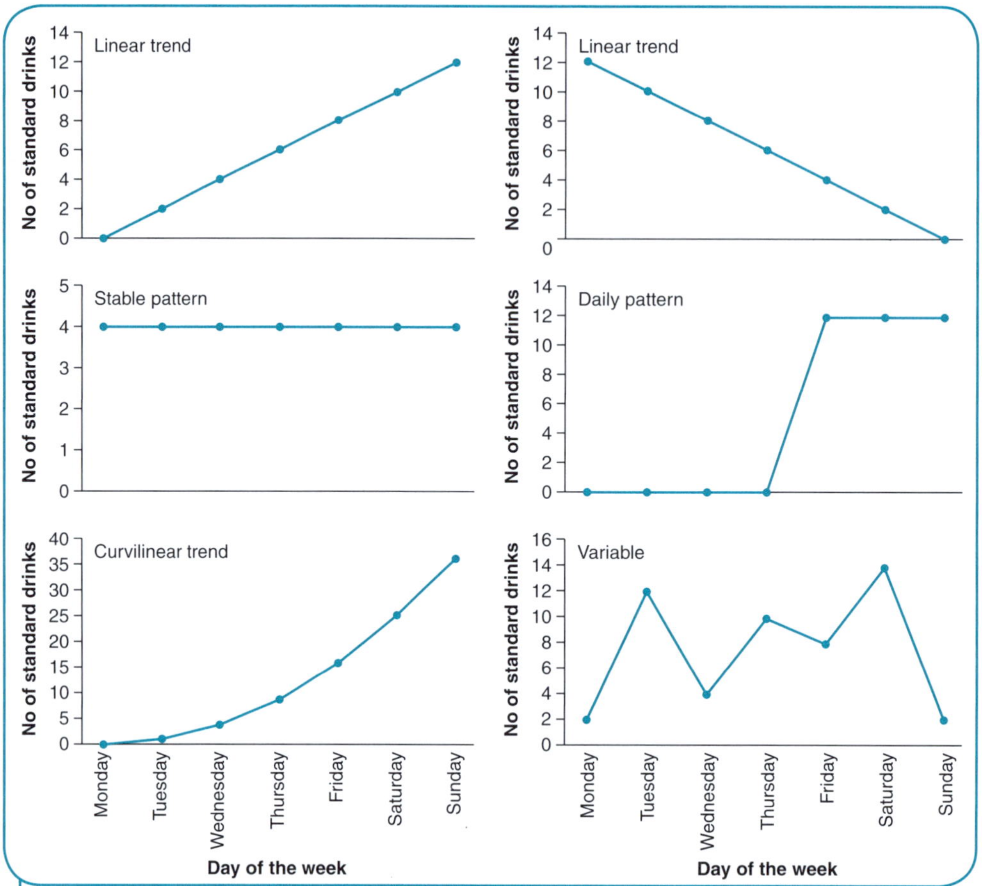

Figure 2.4 Example patterns from a 7-day baseline recording of alcohol consumption (units are standard drinks)

We can plot our behaviour during a baseline period, then compare this to the pattern and the amount of the behaviour following an intervention. Imagine an intervention with a client who has a goal of increasing their daily exercise duration. They record daily exercise in minutes during a 7-day baseline period and then during a 7-day intervention period, which involves a series of rewards for increasing the number of minutes of exercise. Figure 2.5 displays four different potential patterns that could be found, with some graphical tools that can be used to help the reader to see these patterns. On the *x*-axes are days of the week during baseline (left) and intervention (right), and on the *y*-axes are exercise durations in minutes. The top left graph shows an increase in exercise duration in the intervention week. Overlaid on the data points are mean bars (indicating the average minutes of exercise during the baseline and intervention weeks) to clearly show the change in level that has occurred [lines are drawn at the mean during baseline = (20 + 25 + 10 + 20 + 15 + 20 + 10)/7 = 17.14; and the mean post-intervention = (40 + 50 + 30 + 35 + 45 + 40 + 50)/7 = 41.4]. You could also choose to draw lines at the median or the mode to help to describe the central tendency in the data. In the top right graph, the mean

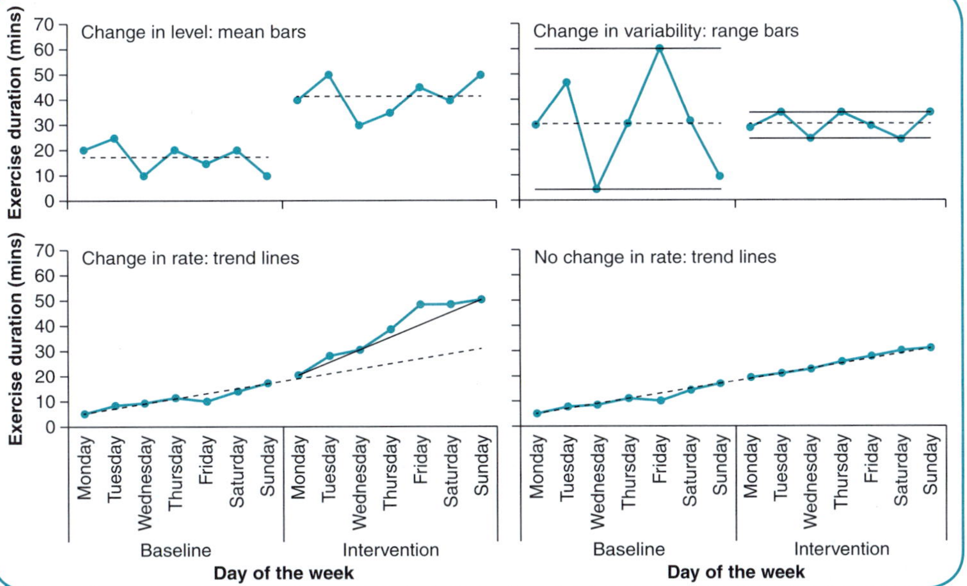

Figure 2.5 Example patterns from a 7-day baseline recording and then a 7-day post-intervention recording of exercise duration (minutes)

bars show no change in level, but there has still been a change of potential interest. The variability has reduced following the intervention. In order to highlight this, range bars have been added (indicating the highest and lowest value observed during the baseline and intervention weeks) (Engel & Schutt, 2009).

Lines can also help to more clearly visualise trends over time. Nugent (2001) proposes a very simple way of drawing trend lines, which involves superimposing a straight line that connects the first and last points in each phase. This has been done in Figure 2.5, lower left graph. In this example, the trend line from the baseline week has been extended through the intervention week. A second trend line on the intervention data clearly shows that the intervention has made the already increasing trend in exercise duration happen more quickly. It should be noted that using this method of drawing trend lines, if the first point happens to be an outlier (if the difference between the first and second points is more than 2.5 times larger than the difference between any other successive points in that phase), then the line should connect with the midpoint of the first and second points. Similar treatment should be given to the final point in the case that it is an outlier (Nugent, 2001). Finally, in the lower right graph in Figure 2.5, you can see an example where there is a consistent trend across baseline and intervention phases. While you might look at this figure very quickly and think that the intervention has increased exercise duration, the data are actually following the same trend that they were already on during the baseline recording. These data suggest that the intervention had no effect. Indeed, one of the problems with these types of studies is that if the data is trending anyway, it can artificially look like the intervention has made a difference (Bloom et al., 2006). What we are looking for is a change in *level*, *variability* or **rate** following intervention. That is why we look at the pre-existing pattern during the baseline phase first, and then consider the post-intervention pattern in that context.

Example case studies

In other chapters of this textbook, case study sections will be relatively short. In this chapter, consideration of case examples is central to illustrating approaches to planning and measuring behaviour change. For this reason, we will devote this section of this chapter to consideration of three case studies, each with a different target behaviour and approach to intervention. As you read these cases, see if you can identify:

- the target behaviour and the goal(s) of the behavioural intervention
- any benefits and losses associated with the planned behaviour change
- the way in which target behaviours were operationalised
- the principles of operant and/or classical conditioning underpinning the proposed intervention
- any measures to account for the losses associated with behaviour change
- the patterns of behaviour during the baseline and intervention
- the graphical tools used to help the reader to notice these patterns
- whether there is evidence for a change in behaviour as a result of the intervention.

We will review these points at the end of each case.

Case 1: Nicola (Brewer, 2016)

Nicola is 43 years old and has identified that she would like to lose weight. To do this, her goal was to reduce snack consumption. She identified snacks as 'indulgences' according to the 12345+ Food and Nutrition Plan (Baghurst et al., 1992; CSIRO, 2005). This allows classification of snacks into 'indulgence' units. For example, one indulgence unit is the equivalent of two sweet biscuits, two cups of soft drink or juice, half a chocolate bar or 75 g (half a cup) of hot chips. To reduce indulgences, Nicola changed the conditions surrounding her eating behaviours. All food consumption was conducted sitting down in the dining room with a plate, knife and fork. She was not allowed to do anything else while eating. This confined eating to circumstances associated with meals, rather than snacking. She also gave herself a single fixed-portion sweet snack reward if she complied with these conditions, in order to reinforce her behaviour as well as reducing her indulgence cravings. Her design was the most basic AB design, with 7 days of baseline recording and 7 days post-intervention. Results of her intervention are displayed in Figure 2.6. During the baseline period, Nicola consumed an average of 2.8 indulgences per day (range = 4 indulgences), compared to an average of 1.4 during the intervention period (range = 3 indulgences). It was cautiously concluded that the intervention had a positive impact on indulgence consumption, keeping in mind the very short time frame of intervention and recording.

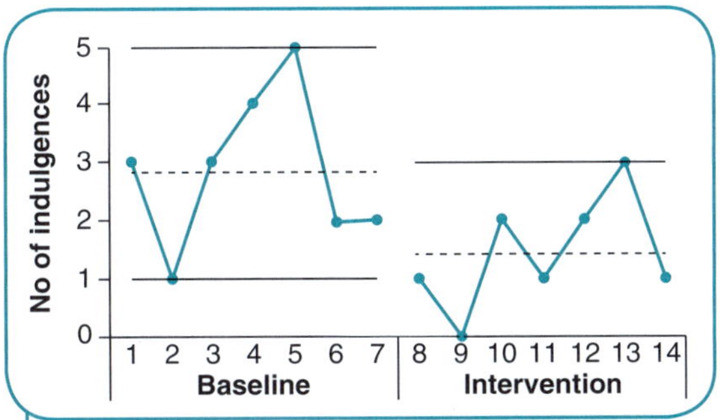

Figure 2.6 Case 1: Nicola. Number of 'indulgences' (*y*-axis) as defined by 12345+ Food and Nutrition Plan (CSIRO, 2005) across 1 week of baseline recording and 1 week of post-intervention recording (*x*-axis). Dotted black lines show mean bars and solid black lines show range bars.
Source: adapted from Brewer, 2016

Case 1 review

Goal(s)	• to reduce snack food consumption
Target behaviour operationalised	• in indulgence units from the 12345+ Food and Nutrition Plan (CSIRO, 2005)
Benefits of change	• long-term change could lead to weight loss
Losses with change	• cravings for sweet snacks
Behaviour change principles	• reducing cues for snacking (opportunities to eat while standing or doing another activity) • only eating under conditions of cues for main meals • portion-limited sweet reward for compliance
Patterns of behaviour during baseline and intervention	• variable pattern during baseline and intervention • mean and variability lower during intervention
Graphical tools used	• mean and range bars
Evidence for behaviour change as a result of the intervention	• evidence for a reduction in indulgence consumption
Design strengths and weaknesses	• most basic single systems (AB) design • very short time frame (7 days per phase)

Critical thinking question

Nicola chose to operationalise her measure of snacking using 'indulgence' units. Why do you think she chose to do it this way? Can you think of an alternative way of operationalising snack food consumption in order to measure it?

Case 2: Lynda (Morphett et al., 2014)

Lynda is 50 years old and was experiencing health problems, including insomnia, stress and headaches. She identified her caffeine intake as consistently high, with a history of seven cups of coffee per day. She felt that her caffeine consumption may be contributing to her health issues. She reported that she used caffeine to help her ameliorate daytime tiredness, and drank cappuccinos as 'little treats'. Lynda recorded her daily caffeine intake in milligrams, using the Australia New Zealand Food Standards Code 2016 to quantify the amount of caffeine in the food and drinks she consumed. She set a series of goals to achieve graduated reduction of caffeine intake over a 10-week period and kept a behaviour diary to record caffeine consumption throughout this time. Week 1 involved baseline recording of typical consumption. In week 2, caffeine was reduced to ≤ 160 mg/day, and in week 3 it was reduced to ≤ 80 mg/day. When this limit was reached, any time another caffeinated beverage was desired, it was substituted with an instant cereal beverage, peppermint or chamomile tea. During weeks 4 to 10, the participant limited her intake to a single green tea per day, containing ≤ 35 mg of caffeine. Lynda used short naps to help with daytime tiredness, and also recorded tiredness, headaches and performance ratings to monitor any consequences (positive and negative) of her changes in caffeine intake. Results of her intervention are displayed in Figure 2.7. During the baseline period, Lynda consumed an average of 353 mg caffeine per day (range = 115 mg). You can see that during the three phases of the intervention, Lynda was able to adhere to her target caffeine limits. Using the intervention, Lynda was able to reduce her caffeine consumption, at least for the period of monitoring.

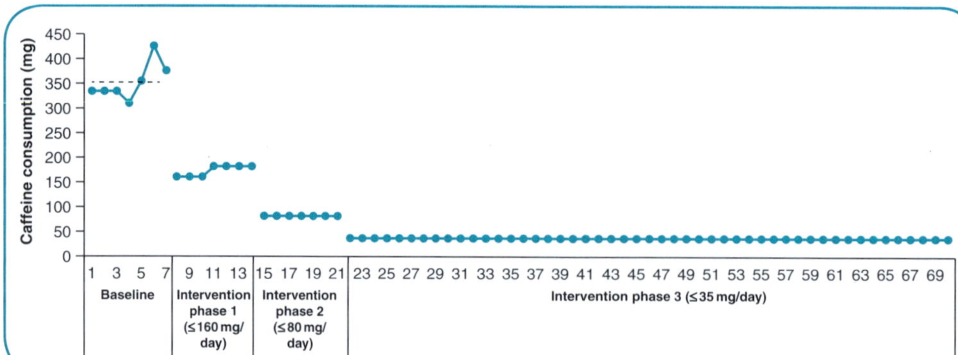

Figure 2.7 Case 2: Lynda. Caffeine consumption in milligrams (*y*-axis) across 1 week of baseline recording, and a graduated intervention period in three phases (*x*-axis): Phase 1 ≤ 160 mg/day; Phase 2 ≤ 80 mg/day; and Phase 3 ≤ 35 mg/day. Dotted black line shows the mean of the baseline period.
Source: adapted from Morphett et al., 2014

Case 2 review

Goal(s)	• to reduce caffeine consumption
Target behaviour operationalised	• in milligrams (mg) of caffeine per day, calculated by recording all the foods she consumed that contained caffeine and using the Australia New Zealand Food Standards Code 2016 to calculate total caffeine
Benefits of change	• reduce insomnia and headaches • longer term health benefits
Losses with change	• daytime sleepiness • loss of treats
Behaviour change principles	• graduated reduction (successive goal setting) • substitution (i.e. herbal tea instead of coffee)
Patterns of behaviour during baseline and intervention	• fairly stable pattern during all phases
Graphical tools used	• mean bar for baseline
Evidence for behaviour change as a result of the intervention	• evidence for a reduction in caffeine consumption
Design strengths and weaknesses	• basic design • longer time frame than Case 1, but still fairly short in terms of demonstrating lasting change

Critical thinking question

When Lynda analysed her data on headaches and sleepiness, she noticed increases in headaches and tiredness during the intervention period, while reducing her caffeine. Why do you think that this may be the case?

Case 3: John (Miller, 1972)

John is 44 years old and went to his doctor following fights with his wife concerning his alcohol consumption. In the last 2 years his drinking had increased. He felt that his behaviour was exacerbated by criticism and disapproval from his wife. John recorded the number of drinks he had each day. To do this, he defined a drink as a single shot of alcohol (~44 mL). John and his wife set a goal of reducing his alcohol intake from 7–8 to 1–3 drinks per day, and recorded a written contract of this agreement. This contract also stipulated that all drinks were to be consumed in the presence of his wife, and that breaking these terms would result in a $20 fine (that his wife would spend on whatever she desired) and withdrawal of attention. His wife also committed to no negative drinking-related comments or gestures, or she would be subject to a $20 fine, paid to John. His design involved 14 days of baseline recording and 30 days during intervention. John also conducted a 6-month follow up for 10 days. Results of his intervention are displayed in Figure 2.8. During the baseline period, John consumed an average of 7.1 drinks per day (range = 4 drinks), compared to an average of 2.8 drinks during the intervention period (range = 8 drinks). Even after 6 months, John consumed an average of 1.3 drinks during follow up (range = 4 drinks). The figure shows a clear downward trend during the intervention phase. It was concluded that the intervention had a positive impact on John's drinking, supported by the follow-up recording.

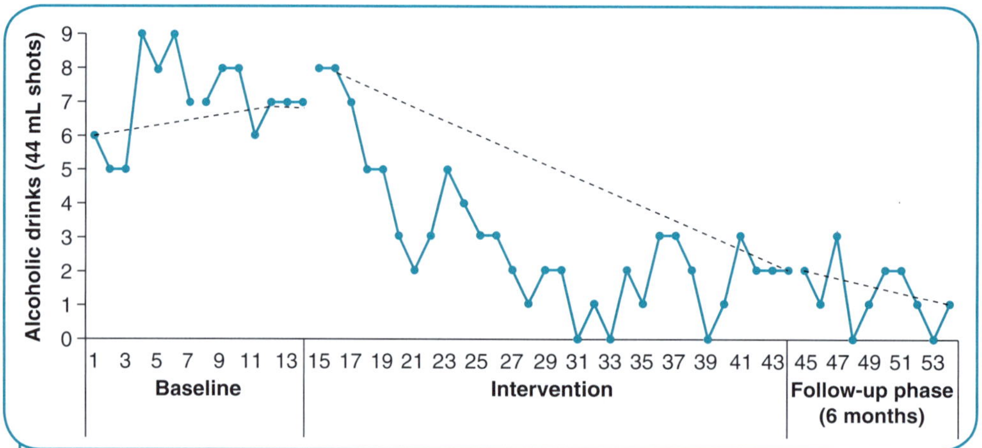

Figure 2.8 Case 3: John. Number of alcohol drinks (44 mL shots) (*y*-axis) across 2 weeks of baseline recording, 30 days of intervention recording and 10 days of follow-up recording after 6 months (*x*-axis). Dotted black lines shows trends during each of the phases.
Source: adapted from Miller, 1972

Case 3 review

Goal(s)	• to reduce alcohol consumption
Target behaviour operationalised	• in number of drinks, defined as approx. 44 mL shots
Benefits of change	• improved relationship with wife • longer term health benefits
Losses with change	• loss of mechanism to cope with feelings regarding relationship conflict
Behaviour change principles	• behavioural contract • undesired behaviour resulted in a fine and withdrawal of attention from his wife
Patterns of behaviour during baseline and intervention	• relatively stable pattern during baseline, downward trend during intervention and baseline
Graphical tools used	• trend lines
Evidence for behaviour change as a result of the intervention	• evidence for a reduction in alcohol consumption
Design strengths and weaknesses	• a 1-month recording period plus a follow up after 6 months to investigate whether behaviour change may have been sustained

Critical thinking question

One loss associated with reducing his alcohol intake was the removal of his mechanism for dealing with feelings about the conflict with his wife. How was this directly addressed in the intervention design?

Evaluating behaviour change

Determining whether a change is meaningful

Once we record behaviour and determine that a change has occurred, we also need to evaluate the change in a clinical context. We could ask the question: is this change likely to make the desired difference in terms of health (or any other) outcomes? One way of doing this is to set threshold scores that meet defined clinical levels. Are there meaningful thresholds for the target behaviour? There are many examples of established guidelines for health behaviours.

For example, our National Health and Medical Research Council (NHMRC) publishes guidelines for alcohol consumption. These recommend no more than four drinks in 24 hours to minimise the risk of injury, and no more than two drinks per day to minimise the risk of lifetime harm (NHMRC, 2009). We can consider this in relation to John's case (Case study 3). During his baseline phase, John consumed between five and nine drinks per day, with an average of 7.1 drinks per day. This level of consumption is above the NHMRC risk indicator levels. During the intervention period, John's level of consumption decreased, and during follow up his average consumption was 1.3 drinks per day, with a maximum of three drinks on a single day. This reduced level of consumption is within NHMRC guidelines. We could therefore argue that John has not only been successful in reducing his alcohol consumption, but importantly, he has made a meaningful reduction that is much less likely to result in risk or health implications.

Other examples of guidelines that can be used include: NHMRC recommended dietary intake (NHMRC, 2013); NHMRC minimum exercise recommendations (NHMRC, 2003); Cancer Council Australia Sunsmart Position Statements and quit smoking guidelines (CCA, 2014); National Sleep Foundation, USA, sleep recommendations for each age group (Hirshkowitz et al., 2015); and the Australian Dental Association recommendations for dental hygiene (ADA, 2016).

However, as we have discussed earlier, when planning behaviour change, we use individual goal-setting principles. That is, goal setting frequently needs to be done in small manageable steps. When the transition from typical behaviour to meet clinical guidelines involves substantial change, the clinical criteria may form a long-term goal, which is divided into a series of shorter term goals for intervention. These shorter-term goals represent successive approximations of the long-term target. We saw a basic example of this in Lynda's case (Case study 2), above. During her baseline phase, Lynda consumed an average of 353 mg of caffeine per day (4 to 5 drinks containing caffeine each day). Rather than aiming to go straight to no caffeine, Lynda reduced her caffeine in three manageable phases. There are several benefits of graduated reduction in Lynda's plan, including reducing potential withdrawal effects associated with lowering caffeine consumption. In other words, while we may not be able to achieve the absolute desired behaviour in a single step, any change towards the desired behaviour is positive and is supported.

Another method for determining whether behaviour change is meaningful is to investigate the impact of that change on ancillary outcomes, such as mood, anxiety, body mass index (BMI) or other health measures. In Lynda's example, she also measured headaches, sleepiness and performance, and had blood tests to measure fasting levels of triglycerides and cholesterol. This allowed her to monitor any positive or negative changes associated with reducing her caffeine consumption. Understanding the broader implications of behaviour change can help to maximise the chances that any positive change can be maintained. If Lynda is sleepier, or has headaches following caffeine reduction, then managing those negative impacts can help with maintenance. Similarly, if Lynda is able to see that the caffeine reduction was associated with improvements in her health, this may motivate her to continue on her reduced caffeine regime. Various ancillary measures can also be recorded in daily diaries, and plotted and examined in similar ways to the behaviour measures we have examined in this chapter.

Determining whether a change is significant

When evaluating interventions in a research context, it is frequently of interest to understand whether a change is statistically significant. It is important to remember that you can have a meaningful change that is not significant, or a significant change that is not meaningful. Can you think of some examples?

When considering significance, many common statistical techniques are not appropriate when you are collecting data on a single individual (or small group) over time. There are a number of techniques that can be useful in this specific situation. We will discuss some examples.

- *Proportion/frequency approach.* This approach can be used when collecting data over time (e.g. daily, weekly, monthly) for an individual or group (Auerbach & Schudrich, 2013; Bloom et al., 2006). First, a 'typical zone' for behaviour is identified, using the middle two-thirds of the data points during the baseline phase. This idea for defining what is 'typical' comes from our understanding of the standard normal curve, where the mean plus or minus one standard deviation is equivalent to two-thirds of the dataset. With 'typical' behaviour defined, significant departures from 'typical' during the intervention phases can be identified. The direction of the change is also considered. For example, if we are trying to reduce alcohol consumption, then consumption that is lower than 'typical' is 'desired' (and consumption that is higher than 'typical' is 'undesired'). We can assess the proportion of 'desired' behaviour during the intervention and determine whether this is significantly higher than during baseline.
- *T-tests against population norms.* This technique is often useful for evaluating ancillary measures with available normed values. It allows individual data from questionnaires to be compared to published values from normative samples using a t-test specifically designed for testing single values against group data (Crawford & Howell, 1998).

For example, if you are interested in whether an intervention to increase exercise over 12 months is associated with a reduction in depression scores for an individual client, you may decide to measure depression using the Beck Depression Inventory (BDI) (Beck, Steer & Carbin, 1988) before and after the intervention. You may then decide to compare BDI scores at Time 1 and then at Time 2 to published norms to determine whether they are significantly different from these typical population values. If you found that after the intervention, scores were no longer significantly higher than normative values, this may provide extra evidence for interpreting the change in this ancillary behaviour as important.

- *Reliable change index.* Consider further our BDI scores before and after our 12-month exercise intervention. You may also want to compare BDI scores at Time 1 to scores at Time 2. One way to do this is to ask: is the change on this measure larger than the expected measurement variation? This can be done relatively simply with published psychometric properties (Jacobson & Truax, 1991). The reliable change index uses test–retest reliability as an estimate of expected measurement variation. Using this technique, you could determine whether the difference in BDI from Time 1 to Time 2 was a significantly larger variation than expected for that measure, again potentially providing extra evidence for interpreting the change as important.

Mini case study 2.5

Mr B is 54 years old and went to his doctor for gum disease, which led to the discovery of liver damage related to excessive alcohol consumption. He had a history of recurrent major depression and two attempts at suicide. He engaged in an intervention to help him abstain from alcohol consumption. Treatment included therapy, acamprosate (a drug to assist in alcohol abstinence) and fluoxetine (a drug to assist with depression) (Spilsbury, 2012). Scores on the Depression, Anxiety and Stress Scales (Lovibond & Lovibond, 1996) were measured before and after treatment. These are shown alongside the clinical cut-off values for each subscale below.

	Cut-off values			Mr B's scores	
	Low	Moderate	High	Pre-treatment	Post-treatment
Depression	10	14	21	21	8
Anxiety	8	10	15	2	0
Stress	15	19	26	20	14

Critical thinking question

Do you think that Mr B experienced a meaningful change in depression from before to after treatment? What is your evidence for this?

Summary

- Lifestyle-related behaviours, including an unhealthy diet, lack of physical activity and alcohol consumption, have been associated with chronic disease risk. Behaviour change promoting a healthy lifestyle can be used to prevent disease and illness, extend life expectancy, improve quality of life and reduce the social and financial burden of disease.
- Behaviour change at the societal level typically involves changes in policy or the dissemination of health-related messages through mass media campaigns. Behaviour change at the environmental level takes the specific environment into account. This may occur in the local community, or at a particular workplace or school. The social level takes the influence of friends, family or broader social norms into account. Behaviour change at this level may utilise social networks or may attempt to change perceived norms. Behaviour change at the individual level requires a comprehensive understanding of the individual, their behaviour and the context in which the behaviour occurs.
- In order to understand a behaviour in context, it is important to understand the antecedents of the behaviour as well as the behaviour's consequences. This is often referred to as the ABC approach (antecedents, behaviour, consequences). The ABCs will identify the potential benefits and losses associated with the proposed behaviour change. Failure to address possible losses may result in a failure to maintain new behaviours.
- Single systems designs are used to assess the success of an intervention. The simplest of these is the AB design, consisting of a baseline phase and followed by an intervention phase. An ABA design (and more complex designs) assess whether change occurs after withdrawal of treatment. The design is made up of a baseline phase, an intervention phase and a phase in which the intervention is removed. Multiple baselines provide another way to determine whether factors external to the intervention are resulting in behaviour change.
- In order to do this, you must identify and operationalise the target behaviour (and any ancillary behaviours that you are interested in monitoring), choose the timing of the baseline and intervention periods, collect the necessary data, plot the data and look for patterns. You can then also consider whether you will use any cut-off values to determine meaning, or tests to determine significance of the change.

Suggested weblinks

Refer to the companion website at www.cambridge.edu.au/academic/healthpsychology for a list of suggested weblinks.

References

ADA. (2016). Australian Dental Association. Retrieved from: http://www.ada.org.au/

AIHW. (2011). *Cancer in Adolescents and Young Adults in Australia. Cancer Series no. 62*. Cat. no. CAN 59. Canberra: Australian Institute of Health and Welfare.

—— (2012). *Risk Factors Contributing to Chronic Disease*. Cat no. PHE 157. Canberra: Australian Institute of Health and Welfare.

—— (2014a). *Australia's Health 2014. Australia's Health Series no. 14*. Cat. no. AUS 178. Canberra: Australian Institute of Health and Welfare.

—— (2014b). *Cancer in Australia: an Overview 2014. Cancer Series no. 90*. Cat no. CAN 88. Canberra: Australian Institute of Health and Welfare.

—— (2015a). *Australian Burden of Disease Study: Fatal Burden of Disease 2010. Australian Burden of Disease Study Series no. 1*. Cat. no. BOD 1. Canberra: Australian Institute of Health and Welfare.

—— (2015b). *Health Expenditure Australia 2013–2014. Health and Welfare Expenditure Series no. 54*. Cat. no. HWE 63. Canberra: Australian Institute of Health and Welfare.

Auerbach, C. & Schudrich, W. Z. (2013). SSD for R: a comprehensive statistical package to analyze single-system data. *Research on Social Work Practice*, 1049731513477213.

Baghurst, K. I., Hertzler, A. A., Record, S. J. & Spurr, C. (1992). The development of a simple dietary assessment and education tool for use by individuals and nutrition educators. *Journal of Nutrition Education*, *24*, 165–72.

Beck, A. T., Steer, R. A. & Carbin, M. G. (1988). Psychometric properties of the Beck Depression Inventory: twenty-five years of evaluation. *Clinical Psychology Review*, *8*, 77–100.

Bloom, M., Fischer, J. & Orme, J. G. (2006). *Evaluating Practice: Guidelines for the Accountable Professional (Vol. 1)*. Boston: Allyn & Bacon.

Brewer, N. (2016). Case study: an integration of external 'situational' and internal 'biological' cues in a behavioural modification intervention to reduce snack-food consumption. The study you can't read between meals without ruining your appetite! *Eat, Sleep, Work*, *1*.

Calogiuri, G. & Chroni, S. (2014). The impact of the natural environment on the promotion of active living: an integrative systematic review. *BMC Public Health*, *14*, 873. doi: http://dx.doi.org/10.1186/1471-2458-14-873

Carrigan, M. H. & Randall, C. L. (2003). Self-medication in social phobia: a review of the alcohol literature. *Addictive Behaviors*, *28*, 269–84.

CCA. (2014). Sunsmart Position Statements. 10 December Sydney: Cancer Council Australia. Retrieved from: http://www.cancer.org.au/preventing-cancer/sun-protection/sunsmart-position-statements.html

Christakis, N. A. & Fowler, J. H. (2009). *Connected: The Surprising Power of our Social Networks and How They Shape our Lives*. New York: Little, Brown and Company.

Community Preventive Services Task Force. (2014). Combination of mass media health campaigns and health-related product distribution is recommended to improve healthy behaviors. *American Journal of Preventative Medicine*, *47*, 372–4. doi: http://dx.doi.org/10.1016/j.amepre.2014.05.032

Cooper, J. O., Heron, T. E. & Heward, W. L. (2007). *Applied Behavior Analysis*. Essex: Pearson.

Cox, J. M. & Bates, S. C. (2011). Referent group proximity, social norms, and context: alcohol use in a low-use environment. *Journal of American College Health*, *59*, 252–9. doi: http://dx.doi.org/10.1080/07448481.2010.502192

Crawford, J. R. & Howell, D. C. (1998). Comparing an individual's test score against norms derived from small samples. *The Clinical Neuropsychologist*, *12*, 482–6.

CSIRO. (2005). *Food and Nutrition Plan: A Simple Guide to Healthy Eating & Weight Control*. Adelaide: CSIRO Adelaide.

De Brun, A., McCarthy, M., McKenzie, K. & McGloin, A. (2014). Weight stigma and narrative resistance evident in online discussions of obesity. *Appetite*, *72*, 73–81. doi: http://dx.doi.org/10.1016/j.appet.2013.09.022

Engel, R. J. & Schutt, R. K. (2009). *The Practice of Research in Social Work*. California: Sage.

Faith, M. S. & Epstein, E. (2007). *Individual Behavior Change*. In: S. Kumanyika & R. C. Brownson (eds), *Handbook of Obesity Prevention: A Resource for Health Professionals* (pp. 377–402). New York: Springer Science & Business Media.

Farrelly, M. C., Healton, C. G., Davis, K. C., Messeri, P., Hersey, J. C. & Haviland, M. L. (2002). Getting to the truth: evaluating national tobacco countermarketing campaigns. *American Journal of Public Health, 92*, 901–7.

Ferrence, R. (1996). Using diffusion theory in health promotion: the case of tobacco. *Canadian Journal of Public Health, 87 Suppl 2*, S24–7.

—— (2001). Diffusion theory and drug use. *Addiction, 96*, 165–73.

Feunekes, G. I. J., Stafleu, A., de Graaf, C. & van Staveren, W. A. (1997). Family resemblance in fat intake in the Netherlands. *European Journal of Clinical Nutrition, 51*, 793–9.

Ganz, D. & Sher, L. (2009). Suicidal behavior in adolescents with comorbid depression and alcohol abuse. *Minerva Pediatrica, 61*, 333–47.

Gilligan, C., Thompson, K., Bourke, J., Kypri, K. & Stockwell, T. (2014). 'Everybody else is doing it' – norm perceptions among parents of adolescents. *Journal of Studies on Alcohol and Drugs, 75*, 908–18.

Go, M. H., Tucker, J. S., Green, H. D., Jr., Pollard, M. & Kennedy, D. (2012). Social distance and homophily in adolescent smoking initiation. *Drug and Alcohol Dependence, 124*, 347–54. doi: http://dx.doi.org/10.1016/j.drugalcdep.2012.02.007

Haider, M. & Kreps, G. L. (2004). Forty years of diffusion of innovations: utility and value in public health. *Journal of Health Communication, 9 Suppl 1*, 3–11. doi: http://dx.doi.org/10.1080/10810730490271430

Hirshkowitz, M., Whiton, K., Albert, S. M., Alessi, C., Bruni, O., DonCarlos, L., ... Kheirandish-Gozal, L. (2015). National Sleep Foundation's sleep time duration recommendations: methodology and results summary. *Sleep Health, 1*, 40–3.

Holahan, C. K., Holahan, C. J., Li, X. & Jung, S. (2013). Social influences on smoking in American workers: the role of the presence of smokers in the workplace and in the home. *American Journal of Health Promotion, 28*, 105–7. doi: http://dx.doi.org/10.4278/ajhp.120604-ARB-283

Hutchinson, A. D., Prichard, I., Ettridge, K. & Wilson, C. (2015). Skin tone dissatisfaction, sun exposure, and sun protection in Australian adolescents. *International Journal of Behavioral Medicine, 22*, 435–2. doi: http://dx.doi.org/10.1007/s12529-014-9441-3

Jacobson, N. S. & Truax, P. (1991). Clinical significance: a statistical approach to defining meaningful change in psychotherapy research. *Journal of Consulting and Clinical Psychology, 59*, 12.

LaBrie, J. W., Hummer, J. F., Neighbors, C. & Larimer, M. E. (2010). Whose opinion matters? The relationship between injunctive norms and alcohol consequences in college students. *Addictive Behaviors, 35*, 343–9. doi: http://dx.doi.org/10.1016/j.addbeh.2009.12.003

Li, K., Husing, A. & Kaaks, R. (2014). Lifestyle risk factors and residual life expectancy at age 40: a German cohort study. *Biomed Central Medicine, 12*, 59. doi: http://dx.doi.org/10.1186/1741-7015-12-59

Lieberman, L., Golden, S. D. & Earp, J. A. (2013). Structural approaches to health promotion: what do we need to know about policy and environmental change? *Health Education & Behaviour, 40*, 520–5. doi: http://dx.doi.org/10.1177/1090198113503342

Lovibond, S. & Lovibond, P. F. (1996). *Manual for the Depression Anxiety Stress Scales*. Sydney: Psychology Foundation of Australia.

Low, W. Y., Lee, Y. K. & Samy, A. L. (2015). Non-communicable diseases in the Asia-Pacific region: prevalence, risk factors and community-based prevention. *International Journal of Occupational Medicine and Environmental Health, 28*, 20–6. doi: http://dx.doi.org/10.2478/s13382-014-0326-0

Martin-Diener, E., Meyer, J., Braun, J., Tarnutzer, S., Faeh, D., Rohrmann, S. & Martin, B. W. (2014). The combined effect on survival of four main behavioural risk factors for non-communicable diseases. *Preventive Medicine, 65*, 148–52. doi: http://dx.doi.org/10.1016/j.ypmed.2014.05.023

May, A. M., Struijk, E. A., Fransen, H. P., Onland-Moret, N. C., de Wit, G. A., Boer, J. M., ... Beulens, J. W. (2015). The impact of a healthy lifestyle on Disability-Adjusted Life Years: a prospective cohort study. *BMC Medicine, 13*, 39. doi: http://dx.doi.org/10.1186/s12916-015-0287-6

McCool, J., Hoek, J., Edwards, R., Thomson, G. & Gifford, H. (2013). Crossing the smoking divide for young adults: expressions of stigma and identity among smokers and nonsmokers. *Nicotine & Tobacco Research, 15*, 552–6. doi: http://dx.doi.org/10.1093/ntr/nts136

Miller, P. M. (1972). The use of behavioral contracting in the treatment of alcoholism: a case report. *Behavior Therapy, 3*, 593–6.

Morphett, L., Heath, G., McIntosh, W. & Dorrian, J. (2014). A case study investigating a behavioural intervention to reduce caffeine consumption. *Journal of Women's Health Care, 3*, 186.

NHMRC. (2003). *Clinical Practice Guidelines for the Management of Overweight and Obesity in Adults.* Canberra: National Health and Medical Research Council.

—— (2009). *Australian Guidelines to Reduce Health Risks from Drinking Alcohol.* Canberra: National Health and Medical Research Council.

—— (2013). *Australian Dietary Guidelines.* Canberra: National Health and Medical Research Council.

Nugent, W. R. (2001). Single case design visual analysis procedures for use in practice evaluation. *Journal of Social Service Research, 27,* 39–75.

Pavlov, I. P. & Anrep, G. V. e. (2003). *Conditioned Reflexes.* New York: Dover Publications.

Persson, M. & Mårtensson, J. (2006). Situations influencing habits in diet and exercise among nurses working night shift. *Journal of Nursing Management, 14,* 414–23.

Prichard, I., Kneebone, A., Hutchinson, A. D. & Wilson, C. (2014). The relationship between skin tone dissatisfaction and tanning behaviour. *Australian Journal of Psychology, 66,* 168–74. doi: http://dx.doi.org/10.1111/ajpy.12039

Puhl, R. M. & Heuer, C. A. (2010). Obesity stigma: important considerations for public health. *American Journal of Public Health, 100,* 1019–28. doi: http://dx.doi.org/10.2105/AJPH.2009.159491

Reavley, N. J. & Jorm, A. F. (2012). Stigmatising attitudes towards people with mental disorders: changes in Australia over 8 years. *Psychiatry Research, 197,* 302–6. doi: http://dx.doi.org/10.1016/j.psychres.2012.01.011

Rogers, E. M. (2002). Diffusion of preventive innovations. *Addictive Behaviors, 27,* 989–93.

—— (2004). A prospective and retrospective look at the diffusion model. *Journal of Health Communication, 9* (Supp. 1), 13–19. doi: http://dx.doi.org/10.1080/10810730490271449

Scambler, G. (2009). Health-related stigma. *Sociology of Health and Illness, 31,* 441–55. doi: http://dx.doi.org/10.1111/j.1467-9566.2009.01161.x

Schabert, J., Browne, J. L., Mosely, K. & Speight, J. (2013). Social stigma in diabetes: a framework to understand a growing problem for an increasing epidemic. *Patient, 6,* 1–10. doi: http://dx.doi.org/10.1007/s40271-012-0001-0

Sinclair, C. A., Makin, J. K., Tang, A., Brozek, I. & Rock, V. (2014). The role of public health advocacy in achieving an outright ban on commercial tanning beds in Australia. *American Journal of Public Health, 104,* e7–9. doi: http://dx.doi.org/10.2105/AJPH.2013.301703

Skinner, B. F. (1963). Operant behavior. *American Psychologist, 18,* 503.

Spilsbury, G. (2012). Solution-focused brief therapy for depression and alcohol dependence: a case study. *Clinical Case Studies.* doi: http://dx.doi.org/10.1177/1534650112450506

Stuber, J., Galea, S. & Link, B. G. (2008). Smoking and the emergence of a stigmatized social status. *Social Science & Medicine, 67,* 420–30. doi: http://dx.doi.org/10.1016/j.socscimed.2008.03.010

te Velde, S. J., Chin, A. M. J., De Bourdeaudhuij, I., Bere, E., Maes, L., Moreno, L., ... Brug, J. (2014). Parents and friends both matter: simultaneous and interactive influences of parents and friends on European schoolchildren's energy balance-related behaviours – the ENERGY cross-sectional study. *International Journal of Behavioral Nutrition and Physical Activity, 11,* 82. doi: http://dx.doi.org/10.1186/1479-5868-11-82

Thaler, R. H. & Sunstein, C. R. (2008). *Nudge: Improving Decisions About Health, Wealth, and Happiness.* New Haven, CT: Yale University Press.

Valente, T. W. (2010). *Social Networks and Health.* New York: Oxford University Press.

van den Berg, M., Wendel-Vos, W., van Poppel, M., Kemper, H., van Mechelen, W. & Maas, J. (2015). Health benefits of green spaces in the living environment: a systematic review of epidemiological studies. *Urban Forestry & Urban Greening, 14,* 806–16.

Volkov, A., Dobbinson, S., Wakefield, M. & Slevin, T. (2013). Seven-year trends in sun protection and sunburn among Australian adolescents and adults. *Australian and New Zealand Journal of Public Health, 37,* 63–9. doi: http://dx.doi.org/10.1111/1753-6405.12012

Wakefield, M., Loken, B. & Hornik, R. (2010). Use of mass media campaigns to change health behaviour. *The Lancet, 376,* 1261–71. doi: http://dx.doi.org/10.1016/S0140-6736(10)60809-4

Wakefield, M., Terry-McElrath, Y., Emery, S., Saffer, H., Chaloupka, F. J., Szczypka, G., ... Johnston, L. D. (2006). Effect of televised, tobacco company-funded smoking prevention advertising on youth smoking-related beliefs, intentions, and behavior. *American Journal of Public Health, 96,* 2154–60. doi: http://dx.doi.org/10.2105/AJPH.2005.083352

WHO. (1986). The Ottawa Charter for health promotion. Geneva: World Health Organisation. Retrieved from: http://www.who.int/healthpromotion/conferences/previous/ottawa/en/index.html

Williamson, L., Thom, B., Stimson, G. V. & Uhl, A. (2014). Stigma as a public health tool: implications for health promotion and citizen involvement. *International Journal of Drug Policy*, *25*, 333–5. doi: http://dx.doi.org/10.1016/j.drugpo.2014.04.008

Young, S. D., Hlavka, Z., Modiba, P., Gray, G., Van Rooyen, H., Richter, L., ... Coates, T. (2010). HIV-related stigma, social norms, and HIV testing in Soweto and Vulindlela, South Africa: National Institutes of Mental Health Project Accept (HPTN 043). *Journal of Acquired Immune Deficiency Syndromes*, *55*, 620–4. doi: http://dx.doi.org/10.1097/QAI.0b013e3181fc6429

Yun, D. & Silk, K. J. (2011). Social norms, self-identity, and attention to social comparison information in the context of exercise and healthy diet behavior. *Health Communication*, *26*, 275–85. doi: http://dx.doi.org/10.1080/10410236.2010.549814

Zhang, X., Yu, P., Yan, J. & Ton, A. M. S. I. (2015). Using diffusion of innovation theory to understand the factors impacting patient acceptance and use of consumer e-health innovations: a case study in a primary care clinic. *BMC Health Services Research*, *15*, 71. doi: http://dx.doi.org/10.1186/s12913-015-0726-2

3

Common models in health psychology

Learning outcomes

After reading this chapter, you should be able to:

- explain the basic aspects of key models in health psychology
- explain the main pros and cons of these models
- discuss the various concepts and issues that are required in order to expand on these common models in health psychology.

Introduction

Three health psychology **models** are examined in this chapter: the health belief model (HBM), the transtheoretical model (TTM) and the theory of planned behaviour (TPB). They are commonly used in health psychology to try to predict behaviour and to try to change behaviour for the better. The desired change in behaviour could be to enable a client to implement regular breast self-examinations, quit smoking, start exercising or increase compliance with healthcare advice.

This chapter examines the evidence for and against these models, how they are applied in research to help understand different underlying factors that can assist in predicting behaviour and how they are applied by healthcare professionals, such as for **interventions**. Their limitations are also examined. You should note that these models are not restricted to the area of health psychology but can be used in fields such as environmental psychology too. Although there are many other models used to explain behaviour these are the key models used in health psychology and your understanding of them will help you master and apply other models.

So what really determines behaviour, and when do interventions to change behaviour work or not? When using and evaluating these models, it is important to consider the role played by factors such as learning, personal control, locus of control, attitudes, intentions, beliefs, emotions, motivations and non-rational processes.

The health belief model (HBM)

The HBM was first developed by psychologists in the 1950s. The model was driven by the United States (US) Public Health Service's need to understand why the public did not **adhere** to its health-related recommendations. The HBM incorporates several measures to produce the predicted behaviour (e.g. breast self-examination) and exists in several versions. Figure 3.1 simply captures the key components of the HBM and does not elaborate on causal directions or interactions.

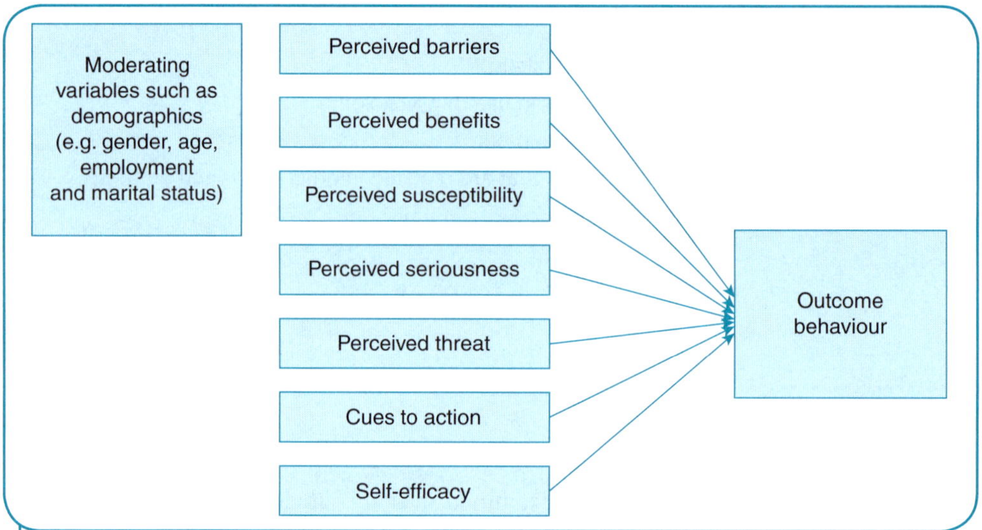

Figure 3.1 The health belief model

Different approaches to the HBM may propose different causal pathways and interactions. Figure 3.1 shows that perceptions are at the core of this model and may interact in different ways depending on the health behaviour being predicted. New health behaviours may be faced with *barriers*. For example, if you want to stop smoking (smoking cessation being the wanted outcome behaviour) then you may have to stop socialising with some of your friends because they will not be supportive of your behavioural change, or at least you think (perception) that they will not support you. *Self-efficacy* will play a role in barriers as you may simply not believe that you can quit smoking. You may also believe that you will not be able to stop socialising with some of your friends. Hopefully, the *benefits* of smoking cessation will outweigh the barriers, but any such benefits may not become apparent unless your health is improving (e.g. feeling fitter, breathing more easily). You may also think about the benefits in terms of increased disposable income if you quit smoking, especially given how expensive it is in Australia. If the benefits are not perceived as exceeding the barriers, then the chances of change are minimal. Smoking has consequences, and *susceptibility* captures your perceptions about any negative health outcome such as lung cancer while *severity* captures the seriousness of contracting lung cancer. However, you may not see yourself as susceptible to lung cancer or you may not see lung cancer as being a serious condition because all the adults in your family smoke and not one of them has died of lung cancer, thus you may not know how dangerous lung cancer is. You may also underestimate the *threat* posed to you by lung cancer. For example, if you are young and you have just started smoking you might mistakenly think that lung cancer only affects older people. Thus reduced susceptibility, severity and threat reduce your chances of ceasing smoking. However, if one of your family members develops lung cancer, then that may act as a *cue to action*, forcing you to re-evaluate your own susceptibility and the threat posed by this disease. As the cancer progresses, you are further forced to re-evaluate the severity of lung cancer. If the family member in question stops smoking, your *self-efficacy* may be increased as a result of seeing someone successfully quit, thus enabling you to take the first steps towards smoking cessation.

The key components of the HBM are then 'framed' by factors such as age, sex and income. These factors may be important predictors of perceived threat. *Age* or how long you have been a smoker may affect the relationship between the perceived threat posed by smoking and the desired health outcome (quit smoking). If you are older, you may not consider smoking a threat to your health if you have not experienced any ill effects and you may have lived longer than most of your uncles and aunts. However, if you are young (e.g. in your 20s) but you have been smoking for several years, then you may perceive a high threat to your health from smoking and you may worry about your smoking cessation self-efficacy. When it comes to factors like earnings, a limited income may limit your options in accessing help to stop smoking, such as travelling from a remote area to see a GP, going to a pharmacist or accessing support groups.

When it comes to education about smoking, the HBM suggests that in order to enable people to quit we need to increase benefits, susceptibility and severity, and reduce barriers. At the same time, information from agencies such as Quitnow suggesting that a smoker can reduce their risks of disease and recover their health after quitting may be counterproductive. Smokers may be inclined to rationalise their smoking by thinking that after they stop it will only take a few years to get back to full health.

Research has shown that the HBM is a useful model, and that it can help predict many different health-related outcomes and a large percentage/proportion of the variance in the outcome measure. This allows healthcare professionals to understand the key factors influencing individuals' health-related decisions. Additionally, it indicates the pathways through which healthcare professionals can influence and help optimise health-related decisions. A study by Noroozi, Jomand and Tahmasebi (2011) in Iran found that a 13-variable HBM (HBM_{13}) explained 62% of the variance in breast self-examination. This means that if healthcare professionals want to predict if a client will perform breast self-examination, they need to measure these 13 variables to get a good idea, not 100%, about the likelihood that clients will perform breast self-examination or not. Knowing that a client is not likely to adhere to recommendations is also beneficial as the healthcare professional can then intervene to try to increase **adherence**. Furthermore, the HBM has been successfully employed to guide recent research into children's oral hygiene practices in the US (Walker & Jackson, 2015) and parental vaccine decision-making in the US (Smith et al., 2011). A study in Australia by O'Connor et al. (2014) examined how the HBM might predict mental health help-seeking behaviour in a student sample. This study found that the students who scored highly on perceived benefits and high on perceived susceptibility scored the highest on intentions to seek help. The study also found that high general health motivation combined with high perceived susceptibility predicted higher scores on intention to seek help. Unexpectedly, the study found that the perceived severity and susceptibility were not found to predict intention to seek help. Overall, the study found that a HBM_{13} predicted 40% of the variance in intention to seek help.

Surveys like these are **cross-sectional studies** (i.e. measure at one time only) and though they are promising, longitudinal studies are needed to examine whether the HBM predicts future outcomes rather than if it is simply associated with a specific outcome. Using a **longitudinal study** design (four months) to examine adherence, Olsen et al. (2008) reported that the HBM explained 21.8% of the variance in adherence to continuous positive airway pressure therapy. They improved the adherence prediction to 31.8% by adding biomedical indices to the HBM. A **meta-analysis** by Carpenter (2010) of 18 studies assessed the HBM's predictive powers over time and concluded that the HBM did not provide strong enough future predictions. The author, however, pointed out that this may partly be due to researchers not using reliable and valid measures to assess the different components of the HBM.

Strengths

Due to its flexibility, the HBM has been found to be a useful model helping to explain various health-related outcomes. However, this flexibility can also be considered to be one of its weaknesses.

Framework for research and health programs

Given that the amount of variance in various outcomes explained by the HBM is relatively high, it suggests that the HBM provides healthcare professionals with a good framework for research and health-related programs. Even some longitudinal studies show strong outcomes for the HBM.

Flexibility

The HBM does not have a set way of measuring the different concepts it contains (e.g. barriers, benefits, threat or outcome behaviour). This flexibility enables researchers and healthcare professionals to tailor the measures they use for a given health-related outcome.

Limitations

Despite the positives of the HBM, it has many limitations. However, these limitations have not really undermined the model but rather limited its application.

Study design

One indirect problem of the HBM is that many of the studies testing the HBM, as well as other models, tend to be cross-sectional when what we need are longitudinal studies that can examine if the HBM predicts future behaviours. Cross-sectional data does not help to clarify causal pathways. Instead of high general health motivation and high perceived susceptibility predicting intention to seek help, for instance, it may well be that students' intentions to seek help predict high perceived susceptibility and high general health motivation. Longitudinal studies can help address these problems around causal pathways but dropout rates and costs can be high.

Irrational behaviour

Behaviour is not always rational or seen to be rational. O'Connor et al. (2014) argued that susceptibility to mental disorders should have predicted the intention to seek help. However, their results did not support this. Following up on these findings, the authors reported susceptibility as a negative predictor of intention to seek help if participants had low motivation and perceived low benefits of seeking help. Thus interactions had to be examined carefully to try to explain the findings.

Variance explained

The amount of variance explained by the HBM in various outcomes is impressive. However, even if the variance is 62% that still leaves 38% unexplained. Unexplained variance suggests that additional variables need to be assessed or that the HBM needs to be improved in some way.

Standardised measures

The HBM lacks standardised measures that can be easily adjusted depending on the outcome in question and this makes it difficult to assess the usefulness of the model (Carpenter, 2010). However, as noted already, this may also be considered a strength in that it enables the researcher to employ different types of measures. These measures could then be selected based on the best measures available at the time and the fit between the measures and the outcome variable in question.

Habitual behaviour

The HBM does not really account for habitual behaviours such as teeth cleaning and flossing. A study by Buglar, White and Robinson (2010) found that the only parts of the HBM model that explained a considerable variance in tooth brushing and flossing were barriers and self-efficacy.

Mini case study 3.1

This mini case study is based on a recent interview with a nurse who is currently finishing a PhD in psychology.

When nurses are engaging with patients, they often resort to parts of the HBM to get the desired outcome behaviour, such as adhering to antibiotic treatment. They do this by referring to the benefits associated with taking the medication and the seriousness of the consequences if it is not used. Nurses also have to assess the potential barriers to treatment adherence and problem-solve their way through these with the patient. Sometimes these barriers may be indicative of the patient's low self-efficacy, suggesting that the nurse will need to give examples of how other patients have solved similar problems in the past to increase the patient's own self-efficacy.

To help a diabetic patient keep to their treatment plan, a nurse may need to teach them about parts of the HBM in order to improve compliance. Thus the nurse will go through the threat and the seriousness posed by lack of adherence. The nurse will then evaluate the barriers to adherence based on other patients' histories. The nurse can then use these examples to explain the benefits (e.g. more energy, able to work, able to engage with family) to the patient as well as to motivate them and increase their self-efficacy by reminding them that they have so far managed this situation as well as similar situations in the past and that they really can change the behaviours that need to change (e.g. diet and activity levels).

Critical thinking questions

1. How would the approach to using the HBM differ between a researcher wanting to study smoking cessation and a healthcare professional wanting to implement a smoking cessation intervention?
2. Examine your own life with regard to health behaviours. Consider a behaviour you would like to quit (e.g. smoking), change (e.g. be more active) or take up (e.g. bushwalking), and consider it in terms of the HBM. Evaluate your own barriers, self-efficacy and other HBM factors with the aim of changing your behaviour for the better.

The transtheoretical model (TTM)

The TTM, or stages of change model, was proposed by Prochaska and DiClemente (1986) and is designed to help in the treatment of addiction. The TTM is rooted in models of psychotherapy and behaviour change and includes Freudian, Skinnerian and Rogerian traditions (Prochaska, Redding & Evers, 2008). The TTM should be able to help researchers and healthcare professionals understand why individuals change their behaviour, especially in relation to substance use. Figure 3.2 shows the five stages of the TTM. The first stage is *precontemplation* whereby the individual does not really know, or does not want to know, about the negative consequences of their behaviour on their health. The individual has no intention to act in the next 6 months. The second stage is *contemplation* whereby the individual is thinking about their behaviour and starting to realise that it needs to change. Thus the individual might be realising, for example, that they smoke too much. This stage is characterised by intention to act in the next 6 months. The third stage is *preparation* whereby the person has started to examine options such as online quit programs including, for example, the Australian Quitnow program (http://www.quitnow.gov.au/). Action is intended in the next 30 days. The fourth stage is *action* whereby the person acts on or has acted in the last few months to address the behaviour, such as when the person has quit smoking. This stage has action taken in the last 6 months. The fifth stage is *maintenance* whereby the person is making sure that they don't start smoking again, thus they may be seeking online support and using nicotine gum to help them abstain. In this stage behaviour change has been maintained for more than 6 months. There are two other important parts to the model: *regression* and *progress*. Regression happens when a person moves 'down' the model; see Figure 3.2. Thus the individual 'falls' from one stage to another. Regression will clearly prolong the duration of the negative behaviour as the individual needs to go through each stage of the model again to get to the 'goal' stage of maintenance. Healthcare professionals need to help their clients move 'up' the model, thus progressing towards their goal 'maintenance'. It is important, therefore, to be able to identify what stage an individual currently is at, as it helps the healthcare professional determine what intervention is needed to move the client up to the next stage.

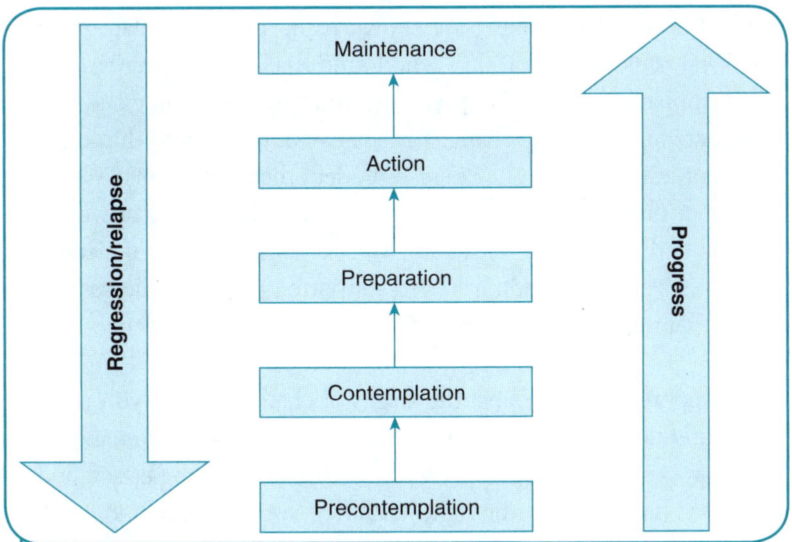

Figure 3.2 The transtheoretical model or stages of change model

The TTM has grown in complexity since its inception. A sixth stage has been proposed (Prochaska et al., 2008), called *termination.* During this stage there is no temptation to take up the behaviour again (e.g. start smoking or drinking). Prochaska et al. (2008) list and define several *processes* of change as part of the TTM (i.e. consciousness raising, dramatic relief, self-re-evaluation, environmental re-evaluation, self-liberation, helping relationships, counterconditioning, reinforcement management, stimulus control and social liberation) and *pros and cons* in decision-making along with *self-efficacy* (confidence and temptation).

When it comes to research and the TTM, a meta-analysis by Marshall and Biddle (2001) concluded that there was support for this model in relation to the target behaviour of physical activity. However, it was noted that its measures need to be standardised. Thus, as with the HBM, the measures used need to be reliable and valid. The results of the meta-analysis showed support for the stages and differences from stage to stage based on outcomes related to processes of change, self-efficacy, and pros and cons of decision-making. The highest variance explained was 19.4% for self-re-evaluation comparing the stage of precontemplation against the stage of contemplation. However, there was no estimation of the variance explained in physical activity by the total TTM as there is a lack of longitudinal studies examining it from the first to the last stage. Researchers might like to use the TTM when *applying* interventions targeting individuals at different stages of change and then *evaluate* their interventions using improved standardised TTM measures of processes, decision-making and self-efficacy.

The TTM is not without its critics. In an editorial in the journal *Addiction*, West (2005) calls for it to be put to rest, stating that the TTM is worse than what we had before it and that it has hindered research attempting to come up with meaningful and useful findings. West suggests that the TTM has only arbitrary stages and it expects rational process from people when rationality is clearly so often lacking. West also points out that many individuals who quit smoking are shown to have had no plan or preparation to support this. West cites Larabie (2005), who found that more than 50% of quit smoking attempts were unplanned. West also points out that the only thing the model shows is that individuals are more likely to change their behaviour if they are thinking about it than not. West calls for a new model of change, a model other than the HBM or the theory of planned behaviour (TPB, discussed in the next section), a model that would incorporate decision-making and motivation. However, West does stop short of clearly formulating such a model. West's condemnation has been supported by others such as Herzog (2005), who points out that the development of the TTM stages has no evidence in peer-reviewed literature.

Given the support for and against the stages of change model, you may wonder if it is justifiable to use it. The answer is 'yes'. You can use the stages of change model until a better model is proposed and supported by research. There are no perfect models in health psychology, so you have to select the right model for your research and interventions.

Strengths

The TTM has its strengths in flexibility and focus on interventions.

Flexibility

The TTM (the same as the HBM) does not have set standardised measures, thus enabling researchers and healthcare professionals to be flexible when applying these models. Flexibility enables you to employ a variety of measures, so that you can tailor-make your research to fit the health behaviour outcome you are trying to understand and measure.

Framework for research and health programs

The relative success of the TTM suggests that it is useful for healthcare professionals when planning and evaluating interventions. Professionals can thus use the stages of change model and its processes to plan and execute different types of interventions with varied outcome targets.

Limitations

In addition to the criticisms detailed earlier, the stages of change model has been criticised for a lack of standardised measures.

Standardised measures

As with the HBM, the measures used to assess different aspects of the stages of change model/TTM have not been standardised using published, reliable and valid measures. As with any other model with such a limitation, this may result in large variations in outcomes from study to study where the same variables are being examined, simply because one study may use better measures to assess the different variables than another study.

Study design

Research into the stages of change model needs to focus on longitudinal studies to support the model's application. Thus future research needs to limit the use of cross-sectional studies.

Critical thinking questions

1. What are the key differences between the HBM and the TTM from research and intervention vantage points?
2. As with the HBM, examine your own life again with regard to health behaviours. However, now use the TTM to examine the behaviour in question. Then contrast the information you obtained from the TTM examination of the behaviour with the information you obtained from the HBM.

The theory of planned behaviour (TPB)

The TPB was developed by Icek Ajzen in the 1980s. It should be noted that the TPB is a modification and update to the theory of reasoned action model. The TPB, like the HBM and the TTM, was developed to predict behaviour, as the final stage of these theories show. There are several components to the TPB (see Figure 3.3): behavioural attitudes and beliefs, subjective norms and beliefs about norms, control beliefs and perceived beliefs about behavioural control, intention, actual behavioural control, and, finally, the behaviour outcome. If you were planning to take up a more active lifestyle (e.g. bushwalking, walking, standing more while working, gardening, or riding your bicycle to work), then the health behaviour you are aiming at is the outcome of the TPB. The part of the model called *behavioural beliefs* captures your expectations about an active lifestyle and what benefits it may have for you. Your *attitudes* towards an active lifestyle are hopefully positive, thus increasing your likelihood of engaging in such a lifestyle. Increasing physical activity in daily life will be made easier if *normative beliefs* support an active lifestyle. That is, whether significant others and society in general is supportive of an active lifestyle. If your friends tend to live inactive lives, then your normative beliefs may hinder an active lifestyle. If you have friends who live inactive lives and consider physical activity a bore, then this will affect your personal or *subjective norm*, reducing your chances of taking up a more active lifestyle. *Control beliefs* capture your self-efficacy in relation to an active lifestyle while your *perceived behavioural control* captures how easy you think it will be to incorporate more activity into your life; again this is tapping into your self-efficacy. *Intention* really captures your goal or purpose in relation to achieving a more active lifestyle, while *actual behavioural control* will clearly moderate your move from

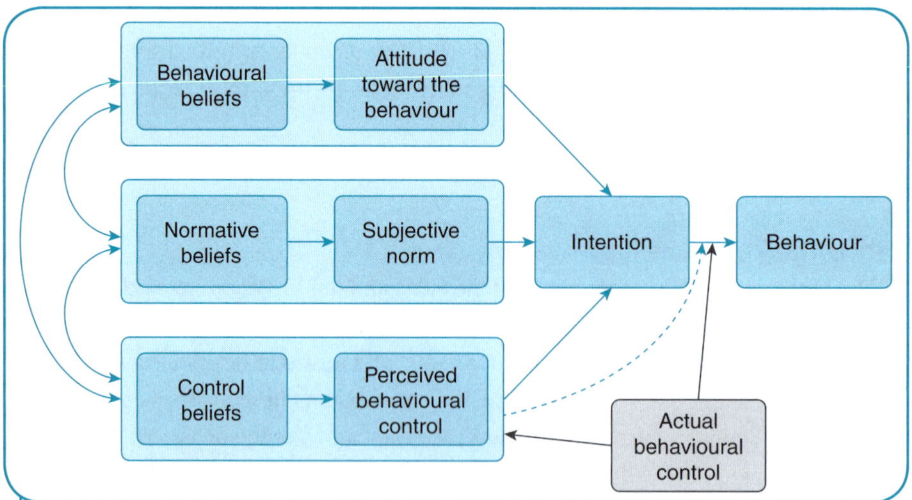

Figure 3.3 Theory of planned behaviour
Source: Icek Aizen, 2006, http://people.umass.edu/aizen/tpb.diag.html

intention to behaviour: if you cannot control how active a life you live then intentions are of limited use in and of themselves.

As with the HBM and the TTM, the TPB has been used extensively to try to predict behaviour, with mixed success. A meta-analysis (McEachan et al., 2011) examining the effectiveness of the TPB in predicting behavioural outcomes reported that the TPB explained 19.3% of the variance in behaviour on average and about 44.3% in intent. However, the percentage explained in the variance of behaviour varied widely by the outcome behaviour. For physical activity, about 24% of the variance was explained, and for diet about 21% was explained employing the TPB. Behaviours such as safe sex and drug use were not as strongly predicted. Another meta-analysis by Cooke et al. (2014) examining alcohol consumption reported mixed support for different components of the TPB model.

Not unlike for the TTM, an editorial in *Health Psychology Review* by Sniehotta, Presseau and Araujo-Soares (2014) calls for the TPB to be retired. The authors point out that there is simply not enough support for it in the research literature and that when interventions have changed intentions, these changed intentions have not resulted in changed behaviour. When it comes down to it, the authors have a problem with the utility of the TPB. They suggest that it simply no longer has any utility in relation to interventions, designing experimental studies or theoretical development. A reply by Conner (2014) suggests that Sniehotta et al. are on the wrong track and that they have overlooked the ability of the TPB to explain considerable variance in many different outcome variables using only a few variables. Conner further suggests that the TPB should not simply be laid to rest because there are other, newer models out there. Conner has a point in that new models should clearly be shown to outperform older models before the older models can be considered for retirement.

Strengths

Like the HBM and TTM, the TPB is able to explain considerable variance in behaviour, be it somewhat less than the variance explained by the HBM. Thus the TPB supports research and healthcare interventions, providing a good framework for research and health programs. As there are no set standard measures to assess the different components of the TPB, it allows researchers to use the most appropriate measures for any given health behaviour outcome. Additionally, the TPB is not a closed model, which therefore allows for the inclusion of variables not originally specified and enables increased customisation.

Limitations

As with the TTM, strong cases have been made against the TPB, but again, as with the TTM, there are no strong alternative contenders. Thus, while no new or revised models exist that can provide the research and intervention foundational structure provided by the TPB and the TTM, there is no real case to put them to rest.

Mini case study 3.2

This mini case study was based on a recent interview with a PhD (psychology) student in his last year of study. The main theoretical focus of his PhD was on the use of the TPB in predicting environmental protest behaviour.

With hindsight he said that he should have included a broader theoretical framework than just the TPB, especially given the prediction he was after. He suggested that incorporating the theory of social inclusion (e.g. in-group and out-group) would have enabled him to explain the outcome more accurately. Another aspect that was very important was the research design aspect. The research design needs to incorporate a longitudinal design. A longitudinal design enables the researcher to assess the measures more than once with a set time interval; participants fill out questionnaires at Time 1 and Time 2 with maybe 2 months between the two time periods. A longitudinal design enables the researcher to examine the effects of Time 1 measures on Time 2 measures.

When using the TPB, questions have to be behaviour-specific and there are multiple questions to measure each component of the model (e.g. control beliefs, intentions, behavioural control). Additional measures can be added, such as past behaviour and demographics, to help increase the predictability of the model. The PhD student anticipates that the final model will explain more than 50% of the variance in the outcome measure.

Critical thinking question

Select two health-related outcome behaviours and consider them in relation to the TPB. What variables would you measure in addition to the variables that are already in the TPB model for each of your health behaviour outcomes?

Building better models of health behaviour

Three health behaviour models have been examined in this chapter. However, there are many other models which also describe assorted health behaviours. For instance, the precaution adoption process model (PAPM) is a stage model similar to the TTM, with comparable strengths and limitations. The protection motivation theory (PMT) focuses on factors such as rewards, costs, self-efficacy, fear and appraisal. The PMT is similar to the HBM, with comparable strengths and limitations. The coverage in this chapter will enable you to evaluate these other models and consider them in your future endeavours as researchers and/or healthcare professionals. As you have seen, most of these models share the same strengths and weaknesses and all of them will have many protagonists and antagonists. That said, there are many factors that need to be considered to maximise the utility of the model you are employing in any given project or intervention.

Explanatory power of models

Please note that just because the HBM, TTM and TPB do not explain 100% of the variance in the outcome behaviour, this in itself is not enough to lay any theory or model to rest. If this was the case, then few theories would remain. Furthermore, a criterion of 100% of variance explained would make theory improvements next to impossible if not simply an oxymoron. Simply stated, models that help explain behaviour should not be discarded unless an alternative model is better at predicting behaviour and has better utility than the old model.

It is a testament to these different models that they are not just used within health psychology. They are used widely in areas such as business (Wang & Ritchie, 2012), environmental psychology (Chan & Bishop, 2013; Hurlimann, Dolnicar & Meyer, 2009; Read et al., 2013), education (Moss et al., 2014) and medicine (Weber, Dwyer & Mummery, 2012).

Cultural differences

Is there an aspect to the health behaviour models covered in this chapter that needs to be considered from an Australian perspective? The answer to that is 'maybe'. However, given the flexibility of these models, it is relatively easy to incorporate any measures that assess some unique Australian variables or aspects. Many Australian researchers have employed these models successfully in the past. One longitudinal study into helmet use among cyclists contrasted TPB and HBM and reported strong predictive effects for both models (Quine, Rutter & Arnold, 1998).

Demographics

It is important to note that these models do not exclude the assessment of variables other than those listed for each model. They rely on the researcher incorporating other variables as needed to enable a clear understanding of the health behaviour in question. Thus different demographics will have different utility depending on the outcome behaviour in question.

Age

It is important to take age into account in any research and it is certainly important when predicting health-related behaviour. Childhood, for example, comes with a high chance of drowning and childhood diseases. Adolescence is associated with high incidences of motor vehicle accidents and risk-taking behaviour (e.g. experimenting with drugs). Older adults are more prone to accidents in relation to falls and certain illnesses such as heart disease and breast cancer. The norm being followed is also different from one age group to the next. Children have the immediate family as the norm while teenagers have moved away from the immediate family and onto the peer norm.

Sex

Being male or female will affect the risks associated with different illnesses. Females tend to have more health problems than males, such as gut disorders and non-fatal chronic diseases (e.g. arthritis, headaches, anaemia), and they tend to use more medication than males. However, males tend to have higher physiological reactivity, infant death rate, death rate from injury, smoking and drinking and, maybe not surprisingly, shorter life expectancy.

Beliefs about personal control

Different beliefs about personal control may impact how individuals appraise stressful situations and thus affect the coping mechanisms implemented to deal with the stressful situation in question. Research results from as early as 1969 suggested that a strong sense of personal control may reduce affective symptoms such as those associated with depression among college students, for instance (Abramowitz, 1969).

Self-efficacy

Bandura's concept of self-efficacy captures the individual's belief in himself or herself. This belief may include being able to reach a certain goal (e.g. start going to the gym, walking to work) or being able to do something such as quitting drinking alcohol. When it comes to smoking cessation, self-efficacy reflects the smoker's belief that she or he can actually quit. Self-efficacy seems a perfect match for any model meant to measure health-related behaviour, and research suggests that it is an important predictor of behaviour. Armitage et al. (2014) found that self-efficacy was a key predictor of weight loss for English women at high risk of breast cancer in a longitudinal study. In Victoria, parental self-efficacy in relation to oral health was a predictor of positive oral health behaviour such as brushing teeth twice a day (more than three times as likely) and visits to the dentist (more than four times as likely) in parents and their children (de Silva-Sanigorski et al., 2013). Maybe the key focus for healthcare professionals should be on the role self-efficacy may play in improving mental health. In the *Australian and New Zealand Journal of Psychiatry*, Castle (2013) suggests that the key to improved mental health may lie with self-efficacy. Castle proposes that healthcare professionals need to equip individuals who suffer from mental health problems and their families with the skills needed to live high-functioning lives. An Australian illness generic program called the Optimal Health Program (OHP) has been designed to do exactly this. This program is now used to teach and enhance self-efficacy (Gilbert et al., 2012). The OHP is a self-management intervention program that emphasises self-efficacy, coping, social support, goal setting and forward planning, and can be delivered along with routine care. Initial results for the OHP's effectiveness are promising, showing improvements in health (about half a standard deviation) and social functioning for adults with a mental illness as well as a significant reduction in cost to society of about $6000 per participant per annum (Gilbert et al., 2012).

Locus of control

The Rotter's locus of control measure (1966) focuses on internal and external locus of control whereby participants select between competing statements such as: 1. 'Many of the unhappy things in people's lives are partly due to bad luck' and 2. 'People's misfortunes result from the mistakes they make'. Agreement with the former statement and other statements like it suggest external locus of control, while agreement with the latter suggests internal locus of control. Thus individuals with high internal locus of control will tend to think that they can affect life events, while those that score high on external locus of control tend to think they cannot. A multidimensional health locus of control scale has been developed (Wallston, Stein & Smith, 1994; Wallston, Wallston & DeVellis, 1978) enabling locus of control measures of different illnesses. Self-efficacy and locus of control are not competing concepts but rather complementary ones. Even if you score high on internal locus of control, you may still have low self-efficacy in relation to behavioural changes you see as necessary, such as a change in diet. A review of self-efficacy and locus of control suggests that self-efficacy is a strong predictor of health behaviour, capable of explaining > 50% of the variance in question (AbuSabha & Achterberg, 1997). Locus of control was found to be a good predictor, but not as strong as self-efficacy.

Social support

The individual is affected by family and friends and their norms. These norms can help or hinder positive health behaviours such as smoking cessation or change in diet. If an individual goes to a GP or another healthcare professional and is told to change his or her diet and stop smoking, this will be made all the more difficult if friends and family view smoking and bad diet as a normal part of everyday life. This is where norms come into these models, as you have already seen. However, measuring social support can add to our understanding and enable the healthcare professional to see where support is lacking or where it is available and can be used to help with the behavioural change in question. There are many different useful measures of social support, such as the brief Social Support Questionnaire (Sarason et al., 1987) that evaluates both satisfaction with support and network size. Cohen et al. (1985) proposed a scale that measures 'functional' support dimensions: appraisal, belonging, tangible and self-esteem support. As with other concepts, researchers and healthcare professionals need to pick a reliable and valid scale that fits in with their research questions and theory and/or the intervention they are implementing or evaluating.

Social support is often proposed as a buffer or moderator of stress. What this means is that support is thought to reduce the impact of a stressful situation on health, so that individuals with high support levels experience stressful situations as less stressful than individuals with low support levels. Thus the former will experience no or less negative consequences as a result of the stressful situation. Consequently, having high social support levels will help these individuals maintain optimal health. If, for example, a student is looking for housing (stressful situation) and a friend helps them by finding a place to rent (informational support), then the support has reduced the impact of the stressful situation and will not cause any or as much mental distress (negative outcome measure) as if no support had been forthcoming.

Coping

Coping is the style or method of dealing with stressful situations. One way of coping is to seek social support; another coping example would be to take illicit drugs or lash out in anger (physically or verbally). Researchers tend to separate coping into maladaptive (negative) and adaptive (positive) behaviour. Seeking social support would usually be considered an adaptive coping behaviour, while illicit drug taking would be seen as maladaptive. One of the main problems with reliable and valid coping assessment has been the lack of a good definition of coping and thus reliable and valid measures of it when it comes to adults (Parker & Endler, 1992) and adolescents (Sveinbjornsdottir & Thorsteinsson, 2008). Two adolescent coping scales have been developed in Australia: the *Adolescent Coping Scale* (Frydenberg & Lewis, 1992) now in its second edition (ACS-2, 2012), and a scale called the measure of adolescent coping strategies (MACS; published by Sveinbjornsdottir & Thorsteinsson in 2014). MACS has been employed in several studies in Australia (e.g. Thorsteinsson, Ryan & Sveinbjornsdottir, 2013; Thorsteinsson et al., 2013), with findings suggesting the importance of positive adolescent coping for positive mental health outcomes.

Non-rational behaviour

It seems to be a part of the human condition to behave in ways that are, or at least seem to be, devoid of logic and reason; that is, behaviour that we call non-rational. We gamble when the odds are against us, we drink too much alcohol and soft drinks, we eat too much, and we eat too much of what we know is bad for us, such as sugar and processed food. Furthermore, we have unprotected sex and we smoke and do other drugs, be they legal or illegal. If humans were rational beings, we simply would not need models to explain health-related behaviour. When it came to smoking, for example, it would be a straightforward matter of presenting the logic and reasons for not smoking and the smoker would quit smoking – right? Given our non-rational behaviour tendencies, it is really surprising how much variance in health behaviour a model such as the HBM actually manages to explain. Non-rational behaviour cannot really be factored into these models; rather it makes up some of the error variance in these models, reducing the variance explained by the model in question.

That said, does non-rational behaviour really exist? Is there not always an explanation for behaviour no matter how irrational it may appear at first sight? What of the smoker who started smoking when medical doctors were used by tobacco companies to advertise and promote smoking? Thus the norms in the TPB model suggest that smoking is a logical outcome. Once the individual has started smoking, it will be difficult to quit even after the dangers are known; thus continuing to smoke makes sense according to the HBM, as the barriers to quitting are just too high. Furthermore, the smoker may simply ignore any information suggesting that he or she needs to change their behaviour and quit smoking. The smoker may also look for any information showing low risks of smoking or look for alternative reasons why smoking has been linked to cancer. This will, in the end, cause the smoker to be in a state of total denial about the negative consequences of smoking on health and see them trapped as a smoker.

Given the impact of the norms in society, irrational behaviour should also not be attached to the individual because the individual strives to be a part of society. To be an accepted part of society, the individual has to fit in and that means following existing norms. These norms are, in turn, influenced by community factors, discussed later this chapter.

So how do researchers and healthcare professionals deal with irrational behaviour? There are models that incorporate both rational and irrational processes to determine health-related outcomes. These approaches are called *dual-process theories of cognition*. One Australian study (Rooke & Hine, 2011) used this dual-process approach to predict **binge drinking** in adolescents and adults. The findings suggested that rational processes, such as benefits that are captured by traditional models, were important predictors, as were 'irrational' processes, such as memory associations with alcohol cue phrases, with 24% of the variance in binge drinking explained. These findings suggest that researchers and healthcare professionals who employ the traditional models might like to examine and incorporate 'irrational' process models into their work.

Socioeconomic status (SES)

Health correlates strongly with **socioeconomic status (SES)**. People with a low SES can be more likely to: have a lower birth weight; die in infancy or childhood; die before the age of 65; have negative health habits, attitudes and norms; develop a chronic disease and experience restricted activity; and have less knowledge about disease risk factors. SES is associated with physical and mental health outcomes, with greatest mortality and disease risks evident in the most SES-disadvantaged groups.

SES consists of education, income, occupation and job status. Children who are disadvantaged through social and material means have been found to have a higher risk of being diagnosed with a mental disorder later in life (Das-Munshi et al., 2013). A meta-analysis concluded that SES-disadvantaged children and adolescents were up to three times more likely to develop mental health problems than their non-disadvantaged counterparts (Reiss, 2013). A review of the relationship between SES and physical health also makes it clear that low SES is a risk factor for worse physical health (Adler et al., 1994). The suggestion is that SES affects mental and physical health through different means. Considering the different components of SES, it is not surprising that it affects mental and physical health. Access to education can lead to better employment and income prospects, which can enable you to look after your own and your family's mental and physical wellbeing (e.g. taking holidays and engaging in physical recreation). With a high SES, your workplace is also less likely to lead to exposure to dangerous environments, such as chemicals that may be carcinogenic. The relationship between SES and bad physical health is almost inevitable as occupation forms a part of your SES. If you have a job that exposes you to physical risk, such as an asbestos miner, then you have a low SES. That said, workers in the mining industry are well paid in Australia. Thus it is an occupation that has a low status but a high salary, resulting in a mixed SES effect depending on its definition. If salary is weighted highly and job status less so, the resulting SES for Australian miners will increase.

The many differences between low and high SES individuals may also help explain any differences in health status. In this regard, consider a Danish study that found that individuals with low SES were more likely to be smokers, be obese, have low job security and have a higher risk of exposure to dangerous chemicals (Borg & Kristensen, 2000). A meta-analysis (Pinquart & Sörensen, 2000) summarising 286 studies found that high SES was related to high life satisfaction.

Community factors

If health behaviour models incorporate non-rational behaviour as error variance, how do they then deal with political, corporate and religious pressures and realities? For example, how can these models incorporate factors to predict smoking behaviour if the social norms about smoking are dictated by the tobacco industry through advertising, sponsorships and legislative influence? A model like the TPB indirectly takes these into account through any measures to deal with norms, and the HBM potentially through the barrier component. If healthcare professionals want to change health behaviour, they have to become familiar or engage with different community factors. The symptoms of negative health behaviour may manifest within the individual but the causes cannot be tied to the individual without examining their community.

Healthcare services

Some communities have limited access to healthcare and health-related education, thus restricting any preventative healthcare measures that can be enacted or evaluated. Health inequities are real and have to be considered carefully by healthcare professionals. Healthcare inequities are covered in Chapter 12.

Political, corporate, religious and cultural influences

To improve the physical and mental health of individuals in any particular country, the political system has to support the healthcare system with the right policy and legal framework. Healthcare professionals and researchers cannot ignore this structure as they have to work within it in order to work effectively. For example, a researcher trying to understand smoking rates and behaviour in Indonesia and then comparing these to smoking rates and behaviour in Australia has to understand the policy and legal framework in both countries. In this example, one important difference is that Indonesia has no or very little restriction on cigarette advertising while Australia has some of the strictest anti-smoking laws in the world.

If the healthcare framework is the responsibility of the political system, how will corporations influence affect policymaking? Where corporations have free rein, smoking rates are high due to pro-smoking advertising campaigns, lack of prohibitive laws that would limit smoking to specified areas, and low prices and easy access to tobacco products (e.g. outside school gates). Given this scenario, it is no surprise that the rate of smoking among Indonesian physicians is 22% for males (Ng et al., 2007) and that Indonesia has one of the highest smoking rates in the world for males at 67% (Centers for Disease Control and Prevention, 2011). Indonesia is facing disastrous health consequences in the next decade due to high smoking rates that are caused by the reasons listed above as well as cultural and religious acceptance of male smoking.

Another example you can examine further is condom use. To improve condom use to help reduce the spread of sexually transmitted infections, researchers and healthcare professionals have to take into account aspects related to religion and culture (Shaw & El-Bassel, 2014; Varga, 1997). Furthermore, the decision not to use a condom may be based on perceptions of trust, infidelity and lack of hygiene (Varga, 1997).

In Australia there is a major health issue that successive governments have not been willing to tackle seriously: alcohol consumption. The damage done by alcohol consumption in Australia every year includes about 3000 deaths, about 65 000 hospital submissions, and more than $15 billion in costs. This is not surprising given that 8% of Australians drink daily, 41% drink weekly and 90% of 14 year olds have tried alcohol (Australian Government Department of Health, 2008; NHMRC, 2015). Given how successful we have been in reducing smoking in Australia, we need to start tackling alcohol using the methods that were used to reduce smoking rates, such as banning alcohol advertisements and countering the current cultural acceptance of binge drinking and drinking in general. A cultural change is needed; a change where the valued outcome is less or no drinking, the same as for tobacco consumption.

As a final note of caution, students should realise that the models discussed are being used to try to help people improve their health and take back control of their lives. That said, these same models could be (and possibly are) used by corporations to understand how they can increase the sale of tobacco and alcohol by manipulating societal norms and reducing barriers to promoting and selling the product in question.

Critical thinking question

What criteria would you use to select a model to use in your research and intervention?

Summary

- The basic building blocks of the models have been presented, including how the benefits and barriers may help or hinder and how self-efficacy is important, and how different stages of change may help healthcare professionals identify what information is needed to assist individuals to the next stage of change and towards a better health outcome.
- The models discussed provide a strong framework for researchers to build on in order to enhance our understanding of behaviour. Furthermore, they can help healthcare professionals deliver more effective and flexible health behaviour interventions. These models are limited because they do not have a set list of standardised measures to assess the different concepts they use. Also, they don't explain 100% of the variance in the outcome behaviour and don't seem to incorporate irrational behaviour effectively.
- Depending on the research question or healthcare behaviour intervention, there are many variables that need to be taken into account when building a clear understanding of the health behaviours in question. This understanding can then be used to provide a foundation for interventions and to reduce or increase the health-related behaviours in question.

Suggested weblinks

Refer to the companion website at www.cambridge.edu.au/academic/healthpsychology for a list of suggested weblinks.

References

Abramowitz, S. I. (1969). Locus of control and self-reported depression among college students. *Psychological Reports*, *25*, 149–50. doi: http://dx.doi.org/10.1037/h0037048

AbuSabha, R. & Achterberg, C. (1997). Review of self-efficacy and locus of control for nutrition- and health-related behavior. *Journal of the American Dietetic Association*, *97*, 1122–32. doi: http://dx.doi.org/10.1016/S0002-8223(97)00273-3

Adler, N. E., Boyce, T., Chesney, M. A., Cohen, S., Folkman, S., Kahn, R. L. & Syme, S. L. (1994). Socioeconomic status and health: the challenge of the gradient. *American Psychologist*, *49*, 15–24. doi: http://dx.doi.org/10.1037/0003-066X.49.1.15

Armitage, C. J., Wright, C. L., Parfitt, G., Pegington, M., Donnelly, L. S. & Harvie, M. N. (2014). Self-efficacy for temptations is a better predictor of weight loss than motivation and global self-efficacy: evidence from two prospective studies among overweight/obese women at high risk of breast cancer. *Patient Education and Counseling*, *95*, 254–8. doi: http://dx.doi.org/10.1016/j.pec.2014.01.015

Australian Government Department of Health. (2008). National binge drinking campaign backgrounder: the costs (Fact sheet: Don't turn a night out into a nightmare). Retrieved from: http://www.drinkingnightmare.gov.au/internet/drinkingnightmare/publishing.nsf/Content/B2D387C687D03FC9CA2574FD007CA91C/$File/The%20costs.pdf

Borg, V. & Kristensen, T. S. (2000). Social class and self-rated health: Can the gradient be explained by differences in life style or work environment? *Social Science & Medicine*, *51*, 1019–30. doi: http://dx.doi.org/10.1016/S0277-9536(00)00011-3

Buglar, M. E., White, K. M. & Robinson, N. G. (2010). The role of self-efficacy in dental patients' brushing and flossing: testing an extended Health Belief Model. *Patient Education and Counseling*, *78*, 269–72. doi: http://dx.doi.org/10.1016/j.pec.2009.06.014

Carpenter, C. J. (2010). A meta-analysis of the effectiveness of health belief model variables in predicting behavior. *Health Communication*, *25*, 661–9. doi: http://dx.doi.org/10.1080/10410236.2010.521906

Castle, D. J. (2013). Where to for Australian mental health services? Promoting self-efficacy. *Australian and New Zealand Journal of Psychiatry*, *47*, 699–702. doi: http://dx.doi.org/10.1177/0004867413494484

Centers for Disease Control and Prevention. (2011). *Global Adult Tobacco Survey: Fact Sheet Indonesia 2011*. Retrieved from: http://nccd.cdc.gov/GTSSData

Chan, L. & Bishop, B. (2013). A moral basis for recycling: extending the theory of planned behaviour. *Journal of Environmental Psychology*, *36*, 96–102. doi: http://dx.doi.org/10.1016/j.jenvp.2013.07.010

Cohen, S., Mermelstein, R., Kamarck, T. & Hoberman, H. M. (1985). Measuring the functional components of social support. In: I. G. Sarason & B. R. Sarason (eds), *Social Support: Theory, Research and Applications* (Vol. Series D, 24, pp. 73–94). Dordrecht: Martinus Nijhoff Publishers.

Conner, M. (2014). Extending not retiring the theory of planned behaviour: a commentary on Sniehotta, Presseau and Araújo-Soares. *Health Psychology Review*, 1–5. doi: http://dx.doi.org/10.1080/17437199.2014.899060

Cooke, R., Dahdah, M., Norman, P. & French, D. P. (2014). How well does the theory of planned behaviour predict alcohol consumption? A systematic review and meta-analysis. *Health Psychology Review*, 1–20. doi: http://dx.doi.org/10.1080/17437199.2014.947547

Das-Munshi, J., Clark, C., Dewey, M. E., Leavey, G., Stansfeld, S. A. & Prince, M. J. (2013). Does childhood adversity account for poorer mental and physical health in second-generation Irish people living in Britain? Birth cohort study from Britain (NCDS). *BMJ Open*, *3*. doi: http://dx.doi.org/10.1136/bmjopen-2012-001335

de Silva-Sanigorski, A., Ashbolt, R., Green, J., Calache, H., Keith, B., Riggs, E. & Waters, E. (2013). Parental self-efficacy and oral health-related knowledge are associated with parent and child oral health behaviors and self-reported oral health status. *Community Dentistry and Oral Epidemiology*, *41*, 345–52. doi: http://dx.doi.org/10.1111/cdoe.12019

Frydenberg, E. & Lewis, R. (1992). The short form of the Adolescent Coping Scale: a brief measure of coping. *Psychological Test Bulletin*, *5*, 122–9.

Gilbert, M. M., Chamberlain, J. A., White, C. R., Mayers, P. W., Pawsey, B., Liew, D., … Castle, D. J. (2012). Controlled clinical trial of a self-management program for people with mental illness in an adult mental health service – the Optimal Health Program (OHP). *Australian Health Review*, *36*, 1–7. doi: http://dx.doi.org/10.1071/AH11008

Herzog, T. A. (2005). When popularity outstrips the evidence: comment on West (2005). *Addiction*, *100*, 1040–1; author reply 1048–50. doi: http://dx.doi.org/10.1111/j.1360-0443.2005.01171.x

Hurlimann, A., Dolnicar, S. & Meyer, P. (2009). Understanding behaviour to inform water supply management in developed nations – a review of literature, conceptual model and research agenda. *Journal of Environmental Management*, *91*, 47–56. doi: http://dx.doi.org/10.1016/j.jenvman.2009.07.014

Larabie, L. (2005). To what extent do smokers plan quit attempts? *Tobacco Control*, *14*, 425–8. doi: http://dx.doi.org/10.1136/tc.2005.013615

Marshall, S. J. & Biddle, S. J. (2001). The transtheoretical model of behavior change: a meta-analysis of applications to physical activity and exercise. *Annals of Behavioral Medicine*, *23*, 229–46. doi: http://dx.doi.org/10.1207/S15324796ABM2304_2

McEachan, R. R. C., Conner, M., Taylor, N. J. & Lawton, R. J. (2011). Prospective prediction of health-related behaviours with the Theory of Planned Behaviour: a meta-analysis. *Health Psychology Review*, *5*, 97–144. doi: http://dx.doi.org/10.1080/17437199.2010.521684

Moss, N. D., Hamilton, K., White, K. M. & Hansen, J. (2014). The changing motivations of students' use of lecture podcasts across a semester: an extended theory of planned behaviour approach. *Innovations in Education and Teaching International, (ahead-of-print)*, 1–11. doi: http://dx.doi.org/10.1080/14703297.2012.746513

NHMRC. (2015). *Alcohol and Health in Australia*. Canberra: National Health & Medical Research Council. Retrieved from: http://www.nhmrc.gov.au/your-health/alcohol-guidelines/alcohol-and-health-australia

Ng, N., Prabandari, Y. S., Padmawati, R. S., Okah, F., Haddock, C. K., Nichter, M., … Pyle, S. A. (2007). Physician assessment of patient smoking in Indonesia: a public health priority. *Tobacco Control*, *16*, 190–6. doi: http://dx.doi.org/10.1136/tc.2006.018895

Noroozi, A., Jomand, T. & Tahmasebi, R. (2011). Determinants of breast self-examination performance among Iranian women: an application of the health belief model. *Journal of Cancer Education*, *26*, 365–74. doi: http://dx.doi.org/10.1007/s13187-010-0158-y

O'Connor, P. J., Martin, B., Weeks, C. S. & Ong, L. (2014). Factors that influence young people's mental health helpseeking behaviour: a study based on the Health Belief Model. *Journal of Advanced Nursing*, *70*, 2577–87. doi: http://dx.doi.org/10.1111/jan.12423

Olsen, S., Smith, S., Oei, T. & Douglas, J. (2008). Health belief model predicts adherence to CPAP before experience with CPAP. *European Respiratory Journal*, *32*, 710–7. doi: http://dx.doi.org/10.1183/09031936.00127507

Parker, J. D. A. & Endler, N. S. (1992). Coping with coping assessment: a critical review. *European Journal of Personality*, *6*, 321–44. doi: http://dx.doi.org/10.1002/per.2410060502

Pinquart, M. & Sörensen, S. (2000). Influences of socioeconomic status, social network, and competence on subjective well-being in later life: a meta-analysis. *Psychology and Aging*, *15*, 187–224. doi: http://dx.doi.org/10.1037/0882-7974.15.2.187

Prochaska, J. O. & DiClemente, C. C. (1986). Toward a comprehensive model of change. In: W. R. Miller & N. Heather (eds), *Treating Addictive Behaviors: Processes of Change (Advances in Behavioral Biology)* (Vol. 13, pp. 3–27). US: Springer.

Prochaska, J. O., Redding, C. A. & Evers, K. E. (2008). Transtheoretical model and stages of change. In: K. Glanz, B. K. Rimer & K. Viswanath (eds), *Health Behavior and Health Education: Theory, Research, and Practice* (4th edn) (pp. 97–117). San Francisco, CA: John Wiley & Sons.

Quine, L., Rutter, D. R. & Arnold, L. (1998). Predicting and understanding safety helmet use among schoolboy cyclists: a comparison of the theory of planned behaviour and the health belief model. *Psychology and Health*, *13*, 251–69. doi: http://dx.doi.org/10.1080/08870449808406750

Read, D., Brown, R. F., Thorsteinsson, E. B., Morgan, M. & Price, I. (2013). The theory of planned behaviour as a model for predicting public opposition to wind farm developments. *Journal of Environmental Psychology*, *36*, 70–6. doi: http://dx.doi.org/10.1016/j.jenvp.2013.07.001

Reiss, F. (2013). Socioeconomic inequalities and mental health problems in children and adolescents: a systematic review. *Social Science & Medicine*, *90*, 24–31. doi: http://dx.doi.org/10.1016/j.socscimed.2013.04.026

Rooke, S. E. & Hine, D. W. (2011). A dual process account of adolescent and adult binge drinking. *Addictive Behaviors*, *36*, 341–6. doi: http://dx.doi.org/10.1016/j.addbeh.2010.12.008

Rotter, J. B. (1966). Generalized expectancies for internal versus external control of reinforcement. *Psychological Monographs: General and Applied*, *80*, 1–28. doi: http://dx.doi.org/10.1037/h0092976

Sarason, I. G., Sarason, B. R., Shearin, E. N. & Pierce, G. R. (1987). A brief measure of social support: practical and theoretical implications. *Journal of Social and Personal Relationships*, *4*, 497–510. doi: http://dx.doi.org/10.1177/0265407587044007

Shaw, S. A. & El-Bassel, N. (2014). The influence of religion on sexual HIV risk. *AIDS and Behavior*, *18*, 1569–94. doi: http://dx.doi.org/10.1007/s10461-014-0714-2

Smith, P. J., Humiston, S. G., Marcuse, E. K., Zhao, Z., Dorell, C. G., Howes, C. & Hibbs, B. (2011). Parental delay or refusal of vaccine doses, childhood vaccination coverage at 24 months of age, and the Health Belief Model. *Public Health Reports*, *126*, 135–46.

Sniehotta, F. F., Presseau, J. & Araujo-Soares, V. (2014). Time to retire the theory of planned behaviour. *Health Psychology Review*, *8*, 1–7. doi: http://dx.doi.org/10.1080/17437199.2013.869710

Sveinbjornsdottir, S. & Thorsteinsson, E. B. (2008). Adolescent coping scales: a critical psychometric review. *Scandinavian Journal of Psychology*, *49*, 533–48. doi: http://dx.doi.org/10.1111/j.1467-9450.2008.00669.x

—— (2014). Psychometric properties of the Measure of Adolescent Coping Strategies (MACS). *Psychology*, *5*, 142–7. doi: http://dx.doi.org/10.4236/psych.2014.52022

Thorsteinsson, E. B., Ryan, S. & Sveinbjornsdottir, S. (2013). The mediating effects of social support and coping on the stress-depression relationship in rural and urban adolescents. *Open Journal of Depression*, *2*, 1–6. doi: http://dx.doi.org/10.4236/ojd.2013.21001

Thorsteinsson, E. B., Sveinbjornsdottir, S., Dintsi, M. & Rooke, S. E. (2013). Negative life events, distress, and coping among adolescents in Botswana. *Australian Journal of Educational & Developmental Psychology*, *13*, 75–86.

Varga, C. A. (1997). The condom conundrum: barriers to condom use among commercial sex workers in Durban, South Africa. *African Journal of Reproductive Health*, 74–88.

Walker, K. & Jackson, R. (2015). The Health Belief Model and determinants of oral hygiene practices and beliefs in preteen children: a pilot study. *Pediatric Dentistry*, *37*, 40–5.

Wallston, K. A., Stein, M. J. & Smith, C. A. (1994). Form C of the MHLC scales: a condition-specific measure of locus of control. *Journal of Personality Assessment*, *63*, 534–53. doi: http://dx.doi.org/10.1207/s15327752jpa6303_10

Wallston, K. A., Wallston, B. S. & DeVellis, R. (1978). Development of the Multidimensional Health Locus of Control (MHLC) scales. *Health Education Monographs*, *6*, 160–70. doi: http://dx.doi.org/10.1177/109019817800600107

Wang, J. & Ritchie, B. W. (2012). Understanding accommodation managers' crisis planning intention: an application of the theory of planned behaviour. *Tourism Management*, *33*, 1057–67. doi: http://dx.doi.org/10.1016/j.tourman.2011.12.006

Weber, A., Dwyer, T. & Mummery, K. (2012). Morphine administration by paramedics: an application of the theory of planned behaviour. *Injury*, *43*, 1393–6. doi: http://dx.doi.org/10.1016/j.injury.2010.12.006

West, R. (2005). Time for a change: putting the Transtheoretical (Stages of Change) Model to rest. *Addiction*, *100*, 1036–9. doi: http://dx.doi.org/10.1111/j.1360-0443.2005.01139.x

4

Understanding presentation of research in health: research designs, figures and statistics

Learning outcomes

After reading this chapter, you should be able to:

- understand key concepts, designs and statistical techniques in epidemiology and health research
- recognise and understand analysis of the occurrence of health-related events including relative risk and odds ratios
- recognise and understand analysis of the time to health-related events (survival analysis).

Introduction

> Epidemiology is the study of the distribution and determinants of health-related states or events (including disease), and the application of this study to the control of diseases and other health problems.
>
> (WHO, http://www.who.int/topics/epidemiology/en/)

All disciplines have their own *languages*, or their own preferred ways of communicating, with specific concepts, research designs, statistical methods and presentation techniques (e.g. use of figures and tables). Health psychology is informed by a number of disciplines, particularly epidemiology. In this multidisciplinary context, the health psychologist must be fluent in the languages of not only health psychology, but also its related disciplines. Our undergraduate training in the science of psychology teaches us about hypothesis-driven research, and covers designs that range from observational to experimental. Rarely do we have time to focus on the specifics of designs most frequently used in population-based studies of health. Further, the majority of undergraduate curricula in psychology research methods include analytic approaches such as correlations, analysis of variance and regression for continuous dependent variables. Leafing through many psychology research methods texts for undergraduates reveals the absence of a number of methods that are very common in the broader health literature. These methods are used to investigate factors related to the occurrence of disease or health event, which is often recorded as a binary variable (yes/no; or presence/absence). Binary outcome variables can be examined using **odds ratios** or **relative risks**. Further, we are frequently interested not only in whether a disease or event occurs but in how long it takes to occur. In this situation, we can use **survival analysis**. This chapter will: discuss common terms used in epidemiology; outline the key features of study designs in health; and explain odds ratios, relative risk and survival analyses. Rather than focus on computation, the intention of the chapter is to equip you to understand these concepts and techniques, and the way in which they are presented, so that you may more easily interpret a wider range of articles in the healthcare literature.

Epidemiology in brief for health psychology students

There has been much discussion in the literature about the importance of transdisciplinary research, and the important links between the social sciences and the health sciences, epidemiology in particular, for solving large and complex health problems (Bhopal et al., 2011; Rosenfield, 1992). It has been argued that combining the strengths of epidemiology in research at the population level with the frequent focus from psychology on the individual provides a very robust approach (McBeth & Cordingley, 2009). Moreover, rather than focusing on the differences between the disciplines, recent researchers have suggested that in answering increasingly large and complex questions, disciplines such as epidemiology are evolving as a result of collaboration with others, including the social sciences (Bhopal et al., 2011). There has never been a better time to work at the intersection between disciplines, using the strengths from numerous approaches to develop the best approach to answer the difficult questions. However, the challenge in transdisciplinary study is that, like other disciplines, epidemiology 'has its special techniques of data collection and interpretation, and its necessary jargon of technical terms' (Rose & Barker, 1978, p. 803). For those with psychology training, it is useful to understand a number of important concepts in the epidemiological literature.

Key concepts in health research

Epidemiology is concerned with the frequency of and reasons for disease in different groups of people, as well as the evaluation of prevention strategies and treatment (Coggon, Barker & Rose, 2009). In describing health in a certain group, epidemiologists may use the word **mortality**, which refers to death, or the word **morbidity**, which refers to a disease that may not in and of itself cause death, but that may cause subsequent health issues that may be fatal (Ragin, 2014). For example, injuries are associated with high morbidity, often leading to secondary conditions (e.g. osteoarthritis) and/or general long-term dysfunction. Similarly, mental health is one of the Australian national health priority areas, as one of the foremost contributors to morbidity in this country (ABS, 2012). Mental health issues, such as depression, are a principal risk factor for many diseases, including coronary artery disease (Milani et al., 2011; Rozanski et al., 2005).

Table 4.1 shows the most common long-term conditions in 2011 (data from AIHW, 2014a). You can see in the 'persons' column of this table that depression affected 2 143 100 people during this time. In other words, there were 2 143 100 cases. While this number seems large, in isolation it is somewhat difficult to determine what it really means. This has been referred to as a *floating numerator* problem (Rose & Barker, 1978). Therefore, as is done in the table, it is very common for mortality and morbidity statistics to be presented as both raw data and as rates. The **rate** expresses the number of people affected as a proportion of the **population at risk** (the group of people who would be counted as a **case** if they were diagnosed with the disease of interest) (Coggon et al., 2009). When the number of cases of depression is expressed as a percentage of the population, the impact of the disease is more easily understood: depression affected nearly 10% of the Australian population in 2011. Expression as a rate helps us to understand the public health impact of this disease. This approach is even more important when comparing populations. For example, the **prevalence** of depression has been estimated to be 3% in Japan and 9% in the US (Demyttenaere et al., 2004; Lépine & Briley, 2011). We can see from these rates that the proportion of people affected (or at least, the proportion of people with a recorded diagnosis) is similar in Australia and the US.

Table 4.1 Most common long-term conditions in Australia in 2011

Common long-term conditions in 2011–2012	Persons	% of population
arthritis	3 265 400	14.8
back pain, problems or disc disorders	2 805 500	12.7
hypertension	2 262 000	10.2
asthma	2 254 600	10.2
depression	2 143 100	9.7

Source: data from AIHW, 2014a

It is often important to distinguish new cases from existing cases, in order to understand how the impact of a disease in a population may change over time. This is done by examining the **incidence** of a disease, which refers to the number of new cases over a specific time period in a particular population. For example, in 2011 there were 53 300 Australians who began using insulin to treat diabetes, which suggests an incidence of 53 300 cases during this year (AIHW, 2014b). During the same time period, it was estimated that there were 917 000 Australian adults (≥ 18 years) who had diabetes (AIHW, 2014b). This suggests that the prevalence was 917 000.

In epidemiology and public health, researchers are often interested in calculating the **burden of disease**. This is done using data from many sources. It frequently includes the cost of medical care. In an ideal situation, this estimate would also include other, broader costs, such as those incurred through lost time at work, extra support services or products required to assist with the condition, and education costs (Mathers, Fat & Boerma, 2008; Rehm et al., 2009). However, these can be difficult to measure. When reading literature focusing on estimates of burden or cost, it is useful to understand how the investigators have defined and measured these concepts. Calculating different aspects of the economic burden of disease allows investigators to help people to understand the magnitude of the impact; for example, in Australia, 'The total health system cost for conditions attributed to sleep disorders in 2010 was estimated to be $544 million' and 'indirect financial costs associated with sleep disorders and conditions attributable to them were estimated to be $4.3 billion in 2010' (SHF, 2011, p. iv). You can see how these sorts of statements can be important clues to disease impact and are often cues to action.

In addition to the economic cost, it is critical to consider the wider burden of the disease for society. This is typically done by investigating changes in life expectancy – not simply as a function of years lived (or put another way, **years of life lost** to a disease: YLL), but also as a function of 'healthy' years lived. A useful summary measure is **disability-adjusted life years (DALY)**, which is the difference between a person's life expectancy and the number of years that they can expect to live free of disability or ill health. One DALY represents one lost year of health. This metric allows us to estimate the combined impact of diseases that tend to cause loss of life without lengthy disability (e.g. measles), and those that tend to result in lengthy disability without loss of life (e.g. cataracts resulting in blindness) (Mathers et al., 2008). This type of burden of disease measure enables health researchers to make powerful statements such as 'DALYs in Africa are at least two times higher than in any other region' (p. 40) and 'children bear more than half of the disease burden in low-income countries' (p. 42) (Mathers et al., 2008).

Common designs in health research

There are two primary types of research designs in health research: **observational studies**, which involve examination of naturally developing differences in health without investigator interference; and **intervention studies**, which focus on comparing health outcomes in two or more groups to determine whether a particular action in one group (e.g. drug administration) is associated with favourable outcomes relative to the group(s) receiving different or no action.

Observational studies

Cross-sectional studies involve sampling at a single time point, and are often used to investigate whether there are differences in the prevalence of a disease or other health outcome in different, pre-existing exposure groups. This type of study is typically faster and cheaper to run than other health-related study types. However, a primary disadvantage is that since there is only single-point-in-time measurement, causality cannot be inferred and incidence cannot be measured. Cross-sectional studies are not efficient for collecting data on rare conditions. These studies are useful as evidence for hypothesis generation (Carneiro & Howard, 2011; Ragin, 2014). For example, a cross-sectional study may include a population survey designed to investigate whether there are differences in the prevalence of cardiovascular disease according to occupational stress level (high versus low stress).

Case-control studies involve targeted sampling of individuals with particular health outcomes (conditions) and then retrospective assessment of exposure. These studies are particularly efficient when investigating rare conditions or events, for investigations of disease outbreak, or when the time period between exposure and disease is very lengthy. The retrospective nature of case-control studies leaves results vulnerable to recall bias (Carneiro & Howard, 2011; Ragin, 2014). For example, a case-control study may investigate risk factors for deep vein thrombosis (DVT), which has a low incidence (Heit et al., 2000). Another example of a very influential case-control study is the INTERHEART study, which compared patients with myocardial infarction (MI, n = 12 461) to matched controls (n = 24 637). Patients came from 52 countries (Yusuf et al., 2004). We will discuss some of the results of this important study later in the chapter.

Cohort studies recruit a group of participants who do not have the outcome of interest, and follow them over time, with repeated measurements, in order to record who develops the outcome during the study and to identify factors that may predict the outcome. These studies are typically lengthy and expensive, and are also open to issues of participant drop-out (or death). The benefit of this design is the ability to infer causality (Carneiro & Howard, 2011; Ragin, 2014). One example of an influential cohort study is the Framingham Heart Health Study from the US, which began in 1949, and still continues (Mahmood et al., 2014). We will see some of the results from the Framingham study later in the chapter.

Intervention studies

Non-randomised intervention studies may involve comparing results in a treatment group to a historical (pre-existing) control group. This approach has clear limitations, given the lack of temporal synchrony in data collection, and is potentially open to sampling biases within each group. Other non-randomised studies include simple before-and-after studies, or pre-test/post-test studies, where people are measured before and after a particular treatment and, in this way, act as their own controls (Carneiro & Howard, 2011; Ragin, 2014). While statistically powerful, since they limit the influence of individual differences, these too can have limitations, particularly in terms of participant expectation biases (where individual expectations of the treatment effects can influence outcome measures) (Delgado-Rodriguez & Llorca, 2004), inability to rule out placebo effects (where a patient's condition may improve simply due to their belief that it will) (Shapiro, 1960), and regression to the mean (if a measure is particularly high or low when it is first measured, it is likely that it will tend towards average when measured again) (Shephard, 2003).

Randomised clinical trials (RCT) are the gold standard intervention study design used to measure the impact of intervention in one or more treatment groups compared to a control group, with measurements taken within groups over time. As the name suggests, a key feature of the RCT is the randomisation. Participants are recruited into the study and are randomised to condition; each has an equal chance of ending up in any group (Moher et al., 2010; Peto et al., 1976; Ragin, 2014). This reduces selection bias and increases the chances that confounders are equally distributed across groups. Examples of RCTs include studies to evaluate the effects of therapies on depression and related health outcomes (Berk et al., 2015; Kiosses et al., 2015). There are a number of sets of guidelines for reporting of RCTs. Perhaps the most widely used is the Consolidated Standards of Reporting Trials (CONSORT), which provides a checklist and flow diagram indicating the minimum standards of reporting to allow sufficient scientific scrutiny (Moher et al., 2010).

It has been argued that the 'whole of medicine depends on the transparent reporting of clinical trials' (Rennie, 2001, p. 206). However, it is important to acknowledge the potential limitations of the RCT. First, not every research question is answerable by, or needs to be answered by, an RCT. In a lovely illustration of this, Smith and Pell (2003) published a systematic review of RCTs investigating the life- and injury-saving benefits of parachute use in response to 'gravitational challenge' (i.e. falling from the sky). Here is the author's summary of their logic from this paper, published in the *British Medical Journal* (p. 1460).

- Parachutes are widely used to prevent death and major injury after gravitational challenge.
- Parachute use is associated with adverse effects due to failure of the intervention and iatrogenic injury.
- Studies of free fall do not show 100% mortality.
- No randomised controlled trials of parachute use have been undertaken.
- The basis for parachute use is purely observational, and its apparent efficacy could potentially be explained by a 'healthy cohort' effect.
- Individuals who insist that all interventions need to be validated by a randomised controlled trial need to come down to earth with a bump.

Not only is it not always appropriate or necessary to conduct an RCT, but it must be understood that biases around publication can result in misleading conclusions.

> Medical decisions are based on an understanding of publicly reported clinical trials. If the evidence base is biased, then decisions based on this evidence may not be the optimal decisions. For example, selective publication of clinical trials, and the outcomes within those trials, can lead to unrealistic estimates of drug effectiveness.
>
> (Turner et al., 2008, p. 253)

Turner and colleagues (2008) examined the US Food and Drug Administration's (FDA) records of studies of 12 types of antidepressants and compared them to the published literature. They found that 31% of the 74 FDA-recorded trials were not published. The authors found evidence of biases in the publication of the studies, such that more trials with positive results appeared in the published literature, while trials with negative or null findings were less frequently published, or published in a way that was potentially misleading (Table 4.2). This led to the appearance from the published literature that 91% of studies were positive, whereas the proportion of positive studies that were run was actually closer to 50%. This work has fuelled an important debate about the

Table 4.2 Summary of results of publication bias analyses

	Positive results	Negative or questionable results
Published	37	3
Not published	1	22
Published in potentially misleading way	0	11

Source: Turner et al., 2008

importance of considering publication bias in decisions to prescribe antidepressants. There are many potential reasons for publication bias, which include the perception that null findings will not be interesting to journals and/or readers and the tendency to prioritise preparation and publication of articles with clear, positive findings, as well as more controversial arguments involving pharmaceutical companies and pressure to avoid publication of evidence that interventions are not efficacious. Of course, these factors apply not just in the case of antidepressants but in medical research more broadly. For these reasons, publication bias should always be a consideration in interpreting the published literature.

Statistical techniques in health research

With the study designs discussed so far in mind, let us consider the statistical techniques that are routinely included in our training in undergraduate psychology. As you already know, the statistical testing we typically focus on gives us a probability, specifically, of how likely it is that the finding would occur by luck alone. The alpha level (our cut-off for significance) is often 0.05, indicating that such findings would have occurred by chance alone less than 5% of the time. On this basis, we either fail to reject our null hypothesis (H_0: which is typically that there is no difference between groups, or no relationship between two variables), or we accept our alternate hypothesis (H_1: that there is a difference – often that a treatment will result in better outcomes, or a relationship). In the context of each study, we make decisions about which technique to apply based on the scale of measurement of our independent and dependent variables, and the aim of our data analysis. This is summarised in Table 4.3, which shows the majority of statistical tests that are most frequently included in our undergraduate training and found in many of our textbooks (e.g. Aron, Coups & Aron, 2011; Gravetter & Wallnau, 2013; Morling, 2012; Shaughnessy, Zechmeister & Zechmeister, 2012). For example, if we have a continuous dependent variable (can take on any value from its minimum to maximum) and a categorical independent variable with two levels, and we aim to compare the means between the two categories, then we would probably select a *t*-test (assuming the basic assumptions were met, of course).

The majority of techniques in Table 4.3 are for single-point-in-time designs (with the exception of the repeated measures analysis of variance, ANOVA) and continuous

Table 4.3 Review of common statistical tests covered in undergraduate psychology programs (DV = dependent variable; MANOVA = multivariate analysis of variance; ANOVA = analysis of variance)

DV scale of measurement	IV scale of measurement	Aim of data analysis	Statistical technique
categorical	categorical	compare proportions between categories	contingency table (cross tabs) chi square
continuous	one categorical (with two levels)	compare means between categories	*t*-test
continuous	one categorical (> 2 levels)	compare means between categories	one-way ANOVA
continuous	two or more categorical	compare means between categories	factorial ANOVA (two-way, three-way etc.)
continuous	time	compare means over time	repeated measures ANOVA
multiple continuous	categorical	compare means between categories on a number of DVs	MANOVA
continuous	continuous (or dichotomous)	determine linear relationship	correlation regression
continuous	multiple continuous or dichotomous	determine linear relationships	multiple regression

dependent variables (with the exception of the basic chi square). This is potentially limiting when we come to read literature involving the designs we discussed earlier, which include repeated measurements over time (e.g. cohort studies, RCT), and have binary dependent variables (i.e. disease exposure or outcome, yes/no). Indeed, there are a number of extensions to our already familiar statistical methods that we need to understand in order to properly interpret health literature. Some of us may have come across them in our study of research methods, but just in case, we will consider them in this chapter. In particular, we will consider why they are so relevant in studies of health, and how they are typically reported.

Dealing with longitudinal data

An issue for the majority of techniques that we learn, such as basic regression and ANOVA, is that they rely on the assumption that each observation is independent. That is, that each person appears once and only once in each model. However, when we measure people multiple times, as is typical in health designs, multiple observations for each person will be related to each other. That is, if you take measurements from me over a period of time, there will be a relationship between these measurements, by virtue of the fact that they all come from me. This is known as **serial correlation** in the data. We are taught a version of the ANOVA, the repeated measures (RM) ANOVA, which goes some way to dealing with this problem. It allows for multiple observations per person, assessing differences in grand means per time point (and over time per group if there are between-subjects effects, for example). However, there are a number of assumptions of the RM ANOVA that limit its use in studies of health. Specifically, there are assumptions of *sphericity* (having constant variance across time points, and constant correlation between any two time points), where the order of points is unimportant, and complete case analysis (no missing values) (Ma, Mazumdar & Memtsoudis, 2012). In addition, RM ANOVA may under or overestimate the effects of group/intervention due to the effects of individual differences at baseline and in response to treatment (Van Dongen et al., 2004). In health studies where we follow people over periods of time, there is always potential for drop-out, missed measurements, and uneven spacing and relationship between measurements. There are often differences in measurement at baseline and response to treatment. In addition, it is frequently the case that the order of measurements is important (Ma et al., 2012; Van Dongen et al., 2004). There are several techniques that can appropriately account for such limitations.

For example, **linear mixed-model regression** (or ANOVA) is able to deal with missing observations, non-constant time structure and individual differences. It allows for the specification of fixed effects (typically the primary independent variables) and random effects (which are assumed to arise as a product of sampling) (Ma et al., 2012; Van Dongen et al., 2004). It is very common to specify the participant as a random effect (Baayen, Davidson & Bates, 2008). Doing so in a linear model allows each participant to have their own baseline or starting value in the model (i.e. their own intercept, or starting point for their line), and/or to have their own trajectory of response to treatment (i.e. their own slope for their line). The overall model parameters (regression coefficients) are estimated, accounting for these individual differences. There is also the possibility to specify in the model *that* the order of observations is important, and *how* the order is important. What do we mean by this? If you measure a participant's sleepiness levels every week for a year, they are likely to be related in some way. This is referred to as the *covariance structure* in these data. It may be that the relationship between responses is fairly constant over time (known as an exchangeable structure), or it may be that measurements on week 2 are most highly related to week 1, and week 3 to week 2, and week 4 to week 3, etc. (a type of autoregressive structure). These covariance structures, and many more, can be specified (Ma et al., 2012). The good news is that despite the apparent complexity of such models, they can be interpreted in much the same way as an ordinary regression. Regression coefficients are typically reported alongside their standard errors or confidence intervals, frequently with associated significance tests. We will also review the basics of reporting of regression later in the chapter.

Another approach for dealing with longitudinal data is referred to as **generalised estimating equations (GEE)**. This approach can be used with continuous dependent variables, as for the linear mixed models discussed previously. However, it is more commonly used with discrete dependent variables. This technique allows the experimenter to specify different types of dependent variables with non-linear relationships via a *link function* (e.g. logistic for binary data, Poisson for count data) (Ma et al., 2012). It also allows specification of the covariance structure, referred to in this context as *within-cluster correlation*, to describe how the repeated measurements are related to each other (Carlin et al., 1999; Liang & Zeger, 1986; Ma et al., 2012). Again, the good news is that despite the complexity, the model outputs can generally be interpreted in a similar way to simple regressions, in that parameter estimates that describe the relationship between the predictor and dependent variable are reported, alongside related significance tests. In the case of GEE with binary dependent variables, the parameter estimates (or exponentiated versions) can be interpreted as odds ratios. We will discuss odds ratios in a later section of this chapter.

Messing with the null hypothesis

For RCT, we are typically testing the hypothesis (H_1) that a treatment group will have more positive outcome measures than a control group, compared to the null hypothesis (H_0) that there is no difference between groups. We are familiar with this approach to structuring our null and alternate hypotheses. However, there are times in health research when investigators are not seeking to test whether one treatment is better than a control, or even better than another treatment (we can refer to this as superiority testing). Rather, the emphasis is on providing evidence that the new treatment has similar effects to an old one (Ware & Antman, 1997). In an example of this type of study, researchers were testing whether telepsychiatry was equivalent to face-to-face psychiatry (O'Reilly et al., 2007). In such studies, researchers may be simply interested in demonstrating that one treatment is no worse than another (i.e. they don't care so much about whether it is better). This is referred to as **non-inferiority testing**. Alternatively, researchers may want to test whether one treatment is no worse and no better than another. This is referred to as **equivalence testing**.

In these trials it is usual for a team of clinicians to decide on some reasonable limits of agreement, referred to as the *equivalence margin* (δ, in an equivalence trial), or the *non-inferiority margin* (in a non-inferiority trial), which is the minimum clinically important difference in measures (e.g. a change in blood pressure of 5 mmHg, or a shift in tiredness of two points on an 11-point scale). Interestingly, in equivalence trials the null and alternative hypotheses are effectively reversed. The null hypothesis is that a difference of at least δ exists. Therefore, the focus is on whether the evidence supports acceptance of the alternative hypothesis that there is no clinically important difference (Jones et al., 1996). Caution has been advised when designing and interpreting these sorts of trials. For example, the exact definition of δ, which is often somewhat subjective, can have a very large impact on the findings. Also, just because you demonstrate that two treatments are equivalent does not mean that either is beneficial. Nevertheless, when the intent is to demonstrate non-inferiority or equivalence, traditionally conceptualised null and alternative hypotheses are not appropriate and these designs are required (Ebbutt & Frith, 1998; Jones et al., 1996; Stegner, Bostrom & Greenfield, 1996; Ware & Antman, 1997).

Drawing statistical conclusions across multiple studies

A critical imperative in healthcare is the requirement to synthesise results across a series of studies to come to a conclusion about the effects of an exposure (risk factor) or treatment. **Meta-analysis** is a cluster of methods that are designed to statistically combine results across studies, to understand the size and significance of the effect being observed. One way to conceptualise meta-analysis is simply by thinking about studies, rather than participants, as the unit of observation (Lipsey & Wilson, 2001). In this way, meta-analysis has been described as 'doing research about research'.

When done well, meta-analysis is a statistically powerful approach to combine studies and estimate overall effects with greater precision than each single study alone (Mak et al., 2010). This approach works on the principle that methodologically similar studies should all be tapping into a common underlying effect, but that there may be measurement error in individual studies. The focus of meta-analysis is often to derive a pooled estimate across studies, which allows the investigator to overcome this measurement error and get closer to the true effect. In order to do this, effect sizes (e.g. Cohen's d, an effect size for the difference between two means, Pearson's r, an effect size for the relationship between two variables [Cohen, 1992] and odds ratio, described below) are typically calculated or harvested from the individual studies. These effect sizes make it possible to describe the effect independent of the particulars of the study from which the data is harvested (Capraro, 2004). Rather than simply averaging the effect size across studies, estimates from individual studies are weighted to most appropriately reflect their contribution to the overall pooled estimate. Weightings may be calculated using simple sample size, sampling variance, study quality or other factors deemed important. In some cases, authors may access the original data from the individual studies and run a new combined analysis. Combining studies may result in increased statistical power to enable detection of effects that may have been overlooked in the individual studies (Capraro, 2004; Lipsey & Wilson, 2001; Mak et al., 2010; Garg, Hackman & Tonelli, 2008).

In many (but not all) cases, a critical grounding for meta-analysis is **systematic review**, which involves a transparent, replicable process for selecting and appraising research studies in order to answer a clear, focused research question. The role of the systematic review in meta-analysis is to provide evidence that study selection was comprehensive and unbiased (Garg et al., 2008). The number and quality of meta-analysis publications has increased in the last 50 years (Mak et al., 2010). One contributor to this increase in quality is Cochrane, an international network that publishes state-of-the-art, comprehensive, systematic reviews, providing an evidence base for medical decisions (http://www.cochranelibrary.com/).

There are several limitations to meta-analysis that must be acknowledged. The quality of a meta-analysis is completely dependent on the quality and availability of eligible studies, the quality of their review and the quality of the statistical combinatory techniques employed. Studies must be sufficiently similar in terms of methodology in order to appropriately pool the effects. The smaller the sample size of the individual studies, the larger the potential for a greater influence of sampling error. Publication bias must be considered and reported appropriately. There are also statistical techniques for estimating the potential impact of bias in meta-analysis. If there are shortcomings in any of these areas, then meta-analyses can create a false sense of rigour and be more convincing than correct. If there are insufficient studies, where there are highly variable methods, where answering a targeted research question is not the goal, when there are evolving concepts or controversy, when a story-based approach is more informative, then narrative review may be more appropriate (Collins & Fauser, 2005).

Coping with binary dependent variables

Health psychology frequently uses binaries (McBeth & Cordingley, 2009), such as the presence or absence of disease, exposure to a particular risk factor (yes/no), or the occurrence of a disease-related event (such as a heart attack), or death. Statistical methods used for dealing with this type of variable are often absent from training in research methods in psychology (although we can't fit everything in!) However, such methods are important to understand for those with a particular interest in health psychology – we must be able to read and interpret the broader health literature. The following two sections will focus on common statistical methods for analysis with binary dependent variables. The first will examine risk and odds, and the second will discuss survival analysis. We will focus on the concepts, as well as how the analyses are presented in research articles.

Mini case study 4.1

Consider this snippet from the abstract of an article by Andersson et al. (2013) that investigated the impact of an internet-delivered cognitive behaviour therapy (ICBT, $n = 33$) compared to live group therapy ($n = 36$) on self-ratings of depression.

> Measures were completed before and after the intervention to assess depression, anxiety and quality of life. Follow-ups were conducted at one-year and three-years after the treatment had ended. Data were analysed on an intention-to-treat basis using linear mixed-effects regression analysis. Results on the self-rated version of the Montgomery–Åsberg Depression Scale showed significant improvements in both groups across time indicating non-inferiority of guided ICBT.
>
> (Andersson et al., 2013, p. 986)

Critical thinking questions

1. Why would these authors have used a non-inferiority design for this study?
2. Why would they have used linear mixed-effects regression for their analysis?
3. What did their study find?

Analysing the occurrence of health-related events: risk and odds

Binary variables can be treated in a number of ways. On the most basic level, we can count the number of people with or without a disease, exposure or event. In the first section of this chapter, we discussed the way in which **rates** are used to provide context for understanding these counts. Table 4.4 provides a summary of rate calculations. You can see the calculations for prevalence and incidence, which we talked about earlier. Also in the table is **risk** – also referred to as cumulative incidence – which describes the number of new cases in an at-risk population over a period of time. In other words, it refers to the likelihood that a person (who hasn't already) will develop a particular health outcome (Carneiro & Howard, 2011). For example, if we studied a sample of 200 race car drivers for one racing season and found that 120 of our sample were injured in a crash, then the risk of crash-related injury in this group would be 60% over a season. The final row of Table 4.3 shows the calculation for **odds**, which describes the number of new cases divided by the number of people who did not become a case during a period of time (Carneiro & Howard, 2011; Ragin, 2014). Considering our race car driver example, the odds of crash-related injury over a season would be 1.5:1 (Carneiro & Howard, 2011; Ragin, 2014).

Table 4.4 Examples of common rate calculations

Rate	Calculation
prevalence	(number of cases at one time point) / (number of people in the particular population at that time point)
incidence	(number of new cases during a time period) / (number of people in the particular population during that time period)
risk	(number of new cases during a time period) / (number of people in the population at risk at the start of that time period)
odds	(number of new cases during a time period) / (number of people who did not become a case during that time period)

The odds ratio and relative risk

Relative measures are types of rate calculations that allow us to describe relationships between exposure to a particular risk and disease outcomes. We will now take the basic concepts of risk and odds, and show how we can use them as relative measures in a hypothetical example study. Table 4.5, part (a), shows our hypothetical study, which measured the relationship between smoking (exposure) and lung cancer (outcome). There

Table 4.5 *Hypothetical study 1: Odds ratio and relative risk of lung cancer in smokers compared to non-smokers.* Part (a) shows data from a hypothetical study examining smoking (exposure) as a risk factor for lung cancer (outcome). Part (b) shows the way in which you would calculate the odds ratio and the relative risk for these data.

(a) Exposure (e.g. smoking)	Outcome (e.g. lung cancer)			
		Yes	No	Total
Smoking	Yes	308	154	462
No smoking	No	142	709	851
	Total	450	863	1313

(b) Odds ratio (OR)			Relative risk (RR)		
Smoking	$=\frac{\text{cancer}}{\text{no cancer}}$	$=\frac{308}{154}$	**Smoking**	$=\frac{\text{cancer}}{\text{total}}$	$=\frac{308}{462}$
No smoking	$=\frac{\text{cancer}}{\text{no cancer}}$	$=\frac{142}{709}$	**No smoking**	$=\frac{\text{cancer}}{\text{total}}$	$=\frac{142}{851}$
OR	$=\frac{\text{smoking}}{\text{no smoking}}$	= 10	**RR**	$=\frac{\text{smoking}}{\text{no smoking}}$	= 4

are many studies that have investigated the relationship between smoking and cancer incidence (Risch et al., 1993; Stewart, Kleihues & Cancer, 2003). In this hypothetical study, 1313 people were studied for 10 years. The sample consisted of 462 people who identified as smokers and 851 who identified as non-smokers. Over the period of the study, 450 participants were diagnosed with cancer.

Part (b) shows the calculation for the odds ratio (OR, left) and relative risk (RR, right) for the relationship between smoking and lung cancer in this study. The OR is the odds of cancer for those who smoke, divided by the odds for those who do not. The odds of cancer in this study are nearly 10 times greater for those who smoke. The RR is the risk of cancer for those who smoke divided by the risk for those who do not (Bland & Altman, 2000). The risk is four times greater in this study for those who smoke. Note that these statistics (OR and RR) demonstrate the same relationship between exposure and outcome, but may give different impressions of the magnitude of the relationship. Indeed, at low probabilities OR and RR tend to be close, but they are further apart at higher magnitudes (Davies, Crombie & Tavakoli, 1998). A summary of how to interpret OR and RR is presented in Table 4.6.

Other useful risk measures

The example just discussed gives a situation where we are interested in the *increase* in risk of an outcome (cancer) given an exposure (smoking). In many cases, we are interested in the *decrease* in risk of a negative outcome (e.g. death) given a treatment (e.g. drug).

Table 4.6 Summary of how to interpret odds ratios and relative risks

	Odds ratio (OR)	Relative risk (RR)
Tells you	odds of an event related to exposure	risk of an event related to exposure
1	no difference in odds	no difference in risk
< 1	decrease in odds	decrease in risk
> 1	increase in odds	increase in risk
e.g. 1.25	25% increase in odds	25% increase in risk

For example, in a study of people with diagnosis of a particular disease, if mortality was 15% in a group taking a drug, compared to 45% in a control group, then the RR would be 0.33. We can also think about this in terms of the relative risk reduction (RRR) in the drug group compared to the controls, which would be 77% (i.e. 1 – 0.33). Another way of presenting this is the absolute risk reduction (ARR), which would be 30% (45% – 15%) (Irwig et al., 2008).

With an ARR of 30%, this means that if 100 people received the drug, 30 lives would be saved. Another very useful way of conceptualising risk reduction is in terms of **number needed to treat (NNT)**. With 30 people benefiting for every 100 treated, this means that 3.3 people would need to be treated for one single person to benefit (100/30), NNT = 3.3 (Irwig et al., 2008). NNT is particularly useful, as it is an indicator not only of statistical change, but also of meaningful change to a healthcare professional who is making clinical decisions. It is important, since the actual impact of a reduction in risk may not be the same for people with different baseline levels of risk (Cook & Sackett, 1995). An example that has received much attention in academic and community publications is the use of statins (which lower cholesterol) for reducing heart attack risk. There is clear evidence that statins can lower cholesterol, but whether this actually results in a reduction in likelihood of heart attack may depend on the pre-existing level of heart attack risk for each patient (Pignone et al., 2006; Ridker & Cook, 2013). In a report in *Businessweek* (28 January 2008), it was argued, based on the numbers, that for people who have not been diagnosed with heart disease the benefits, in terms of heart attack risk, of taking statins will only be evident for 1 in every 100 people, or an NNT of 100. This is a critical consideration given the potential side effects of statins, which include muscle pain, liver damage and increased blood sugar levels (Buettner et al., 2008; Zhao et al., 2004). Consideration of ARR, NNT and side effects are summarised nicely in a quote from Professor Jerome R. Hoffman in the report.

> What if you put 250 people in a room and told them they would each pay $1000 a year for a drug they would have to take every day, that many would get diarrhea and muscle pain, and that 249 would have no benefit? And that they could do just as well by exercising? How many would take that?
>
> (*Businessweek*, 28 January 2008, p. 54)

This highlights the benefits of understanding the many different measures with which risk is represented in the medical literature. Slightly different calculations can result in important differences in the clarity and direction of the story told by a single dataset.

Binary logistic regression

To generalise the odds ratio beyond a simple relationship between two binary variables, **binary logistic regression** models (BLR) are used (Bland & Altman, 2000). These models estimate the relationship between one or more continuous or categorical predictor variables and a binary dependent variable (Dodson, Hammett & Klerx, 2014; Harrell Jr, 2001). There are many parallels between **multiple regression (MR)**, with which you are already familiar, and BLR (Table 4.7). We will review these in turn.

- *What are we predicting?* Rather than predicting values of the dependent variable (Y) for increasing values of your predictor variable as in MR, in BLR, we predict the probability of Y occurring, where Y is an event (1 = yes; 0 = no).
- *How well does our model describe our dependent variable?* In order to understand how well our MR model describes Y, we might look at the R^2 value, to see how much variance we are explaining. There is no exact equivalent for R^2 in BLR; however, there are estimated values that can be obtained that are based on the log-likelihood of the fitted model compared to the null model (with only an intercept term). These may be corrected (since the R^2 value can never = 1 even if the residuals are zero, rescaled values try to account for this) (Nagelkerke, 1991). It is important to note, however, that trying to interpret proportion of variance accounted for in BLR models is controversial, and some investigators think it is meaningless (Shtatland, Kleinman & Cain, 2002). Therefore, in BLR, it is common to simply review the log-likelihood value.
- *What do our parameter estimates mean?* In MR, we compare whether our model is a better description of our dependent variable (Y) than our 'best guess', which is typically the mean value. A similar comparison is done for BLR using the most frequently occurring value of Y. The parameter estimates can be thought of in a similar way. For MR our regression parameters are beta weights, which tell us the unit change in Y for every unit change in the predictor, with the effects of the other predictors held constant. For BLR, we take the exponent of our parameter estimates, which gives us an odds ratio describing the change in odds of Y for every unit increase in our predictor, with the effects of the other predictors held constant (Field, 2009).
- *What are our effect size estimates?* As already discussed, we look at R^2 for MR but this is controversial for BLR. Luckily, our odds ratios are effect sizes.
- *What are the assumptions?* Both methods assume no *multicollinearity* (i.e. none of your variables in the model are so closely related to each other that you are really just entering the same variable twice), and independence of errors (model leftovers). While MR assumes a linear relationship between predictor and Y, BLR assumes a linear relationship between predictor and the logit of Y (Field, 2009).

Table 4.7 Similarities between multiple and binary logistic regression

	Multiple regression	Binary logistic regression
Predict	values of Y	probability of Y occurring
Goodness-of-fit	focus on R^2	log-likelihood
Comparing model to 'best guess'	mean	most frequently occurring category
Parameter estimates	beta values, B_x: amount of change in Y for each unit change in X with the effects of other predictors held constant	$\exp(B_x)$, (conditional) odds ratio: estimate of the odds ratio between Y and X with the effects of other predictors held constant
Effect size	R^2	odds ratio
Assumptions	no multicollinearity, independence of errors, linearity (relationship between variables)	no multicollinearity, independence of errors, linearity (relationship between variable and logit of outcome)

Reporting binary logistic regression

Given the similarities, it is not surprising that the basics of how BLR is reported are similar to any regression. For each predictor variable, you will usually see values for the parameter estimate (OR) and an indicator of the variability in the parameter estimate (standard error or confidence intervals). An indicator of whether the value is significant will usually accompany the OR. This may be done with a significance test or by observing the confidence intervals (typically 95%) to see whether they cross one (referred to as unity). That is, we know that if the OR is above one, the odds of *Y* increase with increasing values of our predictor. If the confidence intervals cross one, then sometimes the OR will be positive (increasing the odds) and sometimes negative (decreasing the odds). This means we cannot be confident in the direction of the relationship between our predictor and *Y*. The other factors you may see reported include tests of overall model fit and/or an estimate of R^2.

Reporting BLR in text

An example of how BLR results may be presented in text is shown in this extract from the results section of a paper (Dorrian et al., 2006).

> Logistic regression analysis indicated that sleep duration was a significant predictor of error/near error occurrence ($\beta = -0.319$, S.E. $\beta = 0.123$, Wald's $\chi^2 = 6.739$, df = 1, p = 0.009). … The odds ratio for sleep duration ($e^{\beta} = 0.727$) indicated a 27.3% reduction in odds of error with every hour of sleep. Overall, the model fit was good (model $\chi^2 = 8.650$, df = 1, p = 0.003, 94% correct classification). It accounted for approximately 7% of the variance (Nagelkerke $R^2 = 0.07$).

This pilot study followed a group of nurses for one month and investigated the relationship between prior sleep and errors. You can see that in this study, parameter estimates (β) are reported with their standard error and Wald's χ^2 test to see whether the parameter estimate is significant. The exponent of the parameter estimate (e^{β}) is reported, representing the OR, which is less than one, indicating that for every hour of sleep (i.e. a unit increase in the predictor), there was a 27.3% reduction in the odds of error; that is, $(1 - 0.727) \times 100$. You can also see a model χ^2 reported for overall model fit and a Nagelkerke estimate for R^2.

Reporting BLR in a table

Alternatively, results of BLR can be presented in a table. An example extract from a table from (Dorrian et al., 2008) is shown in Table 4.8. This was a follow-up study from the pilot described in the previous section, investigating the relationship between sleep, shift length and ratings of exhaustion on reports of struggling to remain awake at work in nurses followed for one month. In this example, OR are reported with their 95% confidence intervals (CI). As the CI do not cross unity, you can see that these predictors are significant. Every increasing point on the exhaustion scale was associated with a 63% increase, and every hour on shift a 46% increase, in the odds of reporting struggling to remain awake at work. Every hour of sleep was associated with an 8% decrease in odds. Also presented in the table are the model χ^2 and significance level for overall model fit.

Table 4.8 Example table from a study examining the odds of struggling to remain awake at work in a group of nurses

DV	χ^2	p	Predictors	OR	–95% CI	+95% CI
Struggling to remain awake	64.73	< 0.01	exhaustion	1.63	1.38	1.91
			sleep in prior 24 hours	0.92	0.85	0.98
			shift length	1.46	1.24	1.71

Source: Dorrian et al., 2008

The two studies just described (Dorrian et al., 2006; Dorrian et al., 2008) involved longitudinal datasets and used generalised estimating equations (GEE), described earlier, to account for the serial correlation in the data. Notably, however, the presentation techniques are the same for BLR with GEE and ordinary BLR. This is an illustration of how your knowledge of basic multiple and binary logistic regression can allow you to expand your understanding to interpret results of studies for quite complex datasets. As mentioned earlier, this principle also applies to your reading of studies including linear mixed-model regression. You are simply interpreting versions of regression modelling, with relatively consistent reporting practices; however, the investigators are using more complex forms of these techniques to appropriately deal with the repeated measurements for individuals across time.

Reporting BLR using figures

RR and OR are also frequently presented in figures. Figure 4.1 displays data from studies that have been used to examine the relationship between psychosocial factors and coronary artery disease. Part (a) shows RR for cardiac-related death. The traditional risk factors (age, hypertension, smoking, diabetes and cholesterol) are from the long and influential Framingham Cohort Study discussed earlier in the chapter (Mahmood et al., 2014). The estimates for depressed mood and clinical depression are from a meta-analysis (Rugulies, 2002), and they were displayed together in an excellent review by Rozanski et al. (2005). In the figure, the markers denote the RR value, and the whiskers show the 95% CI around the estimate. One (unity) is marked on the figure with the vertical grey line. Since none of the whiskers crosses unity, we can see that these RR are significant. You can see from the figure that smoking resulted in a 71% increase in risk of death (RR = 1.71; 95% CI = 1.39 – 2.10). Compared to this commonly understood risk factor, depressed mood resulted in a fairly similar increase of 49% (RR = 1.49; 95% CI = 1.16 – 1.92). Perhaps even more interestingly, clinical depression was associated with the highest RR at 2.69. It is important to note the large confidence intervals around this estimate (1.63–4.43), indicating that not only was it the highest increase in risk, but it was also associated with the biggest variability.

Part (b) shows data from the large INTERHEART Case-Control Study we talked about previously (Yusuf et al., 2004). This figure is set up in a similar way to part (a); however, in this figure the markers denote OR estimates for the risk of heart attack (acute MI) and the whiskers represent 99% CI. This figure also shows separate estimates for females (filled markers) and males (open markers). This study collected the traditional risk factors for MI and also included a *psychologic* index, which is a measure that combines information regarding depression, locus of control, perceived stress at home, perceived stress at work, financial stress and adverse life events. Again, one (unity) is marked with the vertical grey line, and the fact that the whiskers do not cross this line indicates that the OR are significant. Another interesting aspect of this figure is that it includes predictors that increase the odds (OR > 1), as well as predictors that decrease the odds (OR < 1). So, while smoking *increases* the odds of MI for females (OR = 2.86; 99% CI = 2.36 – 3.48) and males (OR = 3.05; 99% CI = 0.48 – 0.71), eating fruits and vegetables *decreases* the odds of MI for females (OR = 0.58; 99% CI = 2.36 – 3.48) and males (OR = 0.74; 99% CI = 0.66 – 0.83). The *psychologic* index (indicating experiencing psychosocial sources of stress) was associated with an increase in odds for females (OR = 3.49; 99% CI = 2.41 – 5.04) and males (OR = 2.58; 99% CI = 2.11 – 3.14). Overall, results of studies in parts (a) and (b) demonstrate that psychosocial factors result in increases in cardiac-related risk and odds at similar magnitudes to traditional risk factors such as smoking and hypertension.

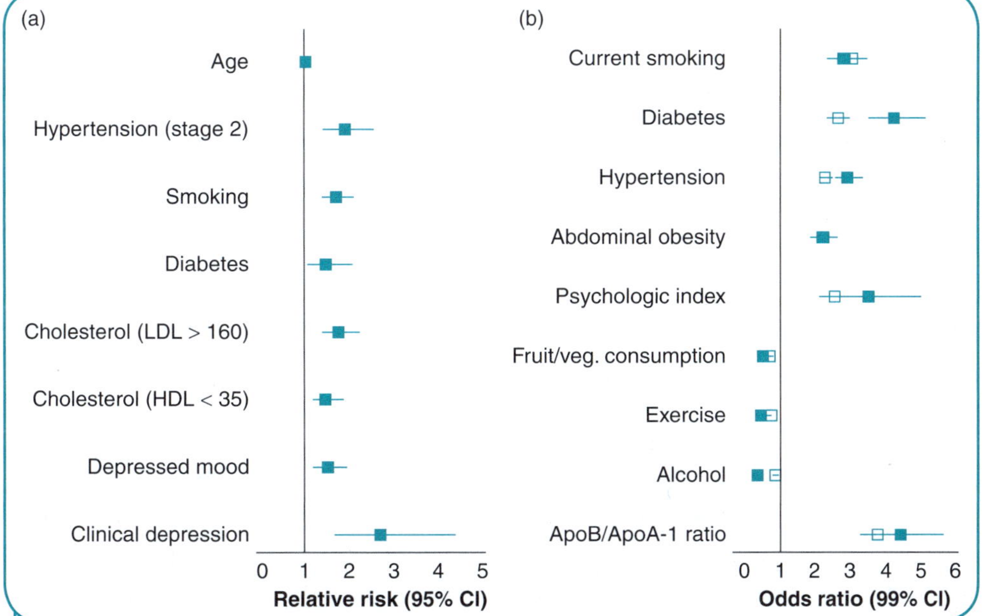

Figure 4.1 Examples of figures showing relative risk (RR) and odds ratio (OR). Part (a) shows RR combined from several studies to illustrate RR of cardiac-related death due to age, hypertension, smoking, diabetes, cholesterol (LDL = low-density lipoprotein; HDL = high-density lipoprotein), depressed mood and clinical depression. Markers show RR with whiskers indicating 95% CI.
Part (b) shows OR from an international case-control study investigating odds of acute myocardial infarction resulting from smoking status, diabetes, hypertension, abdominal obesity, psychologic index (including questions regarding depression, locus of control, perceived stress at home, perceived stress at work, financial stress and adverse life events), fruit and vegetable consumption, exercise, alcohol consumption and blood apolipoproteins (Apo). Markers show OR with whiskers indicating 99% CI for females (filled squares) and males (open squares).
Source: adapted from Rozanski et al., 2005

Mini case study 4.2

Consider this snippet from the abstract of an article by Walters et al. (2014), which is an example of a cohort study using odds ratios to describe the relationship between risk factors and depression in 803 patients with coronary heart disease.

> Factors independently associated with this diagnosis [depression] were problems living alone (OR 5.49, 95% CI 2.11–13.30), problems carrying out usual activities (OR 3.71, 95% CI 1.93–7.14), experiencing chest pain (OR 3.27, 95% CI 1.58–6.76), other pains or discomfort (OR 3.39, 95% CI 1.42–8.10), younger age (OR 0.95 per year 95% CI 0.92–0.98). Problems living alone, chest pain and disability are important predictors of depression in this population.
>
> (Walters et al., 2014, p. 1)

continued ›

Mini case study 4.2 continued ›

Critical thinking questions

1. From this abstract, which risk factor results in the greatest increase in the odds of diagnosis of depression? How would you describe this increase in odds? What do the confidence intervals (CI) tell you about this increase?
2. How does younger age influence the odds of diagnosis of depression?

Analysing time to event: survival analysis

There are many cases in healthcare when we are concerned not only with whether a disease, or a particular health-related event, occurs, but also with the time until that event. This is very frequently the case, for example, in analysing data from randomised clinical trials, where we may be interested in how long patients survive following a particular treatment. Alternatively, we may be interested in how quickly a treatment works (time to recovery) (Greenhouse, Stangl & Bromberg, 1989). In these cases, it would be tempting to think we could use traditional multiple regression models to examine differences between treatment groups, with time as a dependent variable. However, there are several problems with this, which means that we need a specialised approach. Perhaps the most important of these is the fact that some individuals will not experience the event of interest (e.g. death or recovery) during the time that they are followed in our study. We refer to this as the problem of **censoring** (Bull & Spiegelhalter, 1997). It may be that participants drop out before they experience the event, or that they are yet to experience it.

Let's consider another hypothetical example study. We have a group of 32 patients who have been diagnosed with obstructive sleep apnoea (OSA), which is a disorder that involves collapse of the airway and a reduction in blood oxygen levels during sleep (see Chapter 6 Sleep, sleep loss, safety and health for more information). OSA is an independent risk factor for cardiovascular disease, systemic hypertension, stroke, impaired glucose metabolism and diabetes (Punjabi, 2008; Sharafkhaneh & Grogan, 2015). In our hypothetical study, patients are randomly assigned to one of two treatment groups. One receives treatment with continuous positive airway pressure (CPAP), which involves a mask fitted over the nose delivering filtered room air at pressure to help to keep the airways open during sleep. The other group is treated using mandibular advancement splints, which are worn during sleep to draw the mandible forward to prevent airway collapse (Sharafkhaneh & Grogan, 2015). These groups are followed for 10 years (120 months), and patient mortality is recorded.

Data from our study are shown in Table 4.9. Our time-to-event variable (time), in months is shown, alongside our status variable (1 = death recorded; 0 = censored). For example, ID #1 died at 32 months, whereas ID #9 was alive at the end of the study (120 months). In the CPAP group, 7/16 (44%) died during the study, compared to 11/16 (69%) splint group. However, this way of summarising the data is flawed, since it does

Table 4.9 *Hypothetical study 2: Survival time in a group receiving CPAP therapy compared to those using mandibular advancement splints.* Data shows participant ID, time to death in months and status (1 = death; 0 = censored).

CPAP group			Mandibular splint group		
ID	Time (months)	Status	ID	Time (months)	Status
1	32	1	17	11	1
2	32	1	18	12	1
3	38	1	19	20	1
4	40	1	20	22	1
5	48	1	21	22	1
6	50	1	22	24	0
7	88	0	23	30	1
8	91	1	24	32	0
9	120	0	25	35	1
10	120	0	26	37	1
11	120	0	27	40	1
12	120	0	28	40	1
13	120	0	29	90	1
14	120	0	30	120	0
15	120	0	31	120	0
16	120	0	32	120	0

not account for the fact that one person in the CPAP group (#7) and two people in the splint group (#22, #24) exited the study early (they were censored). If we simply omit the censored patients from our proportions, then we lose the potential contribution that these patients have for the study (i.e. remaining for a certain time, event free). Survival analysis allows us to overcome these issues, including information in our analysis about both the length of time in the study (which may be different for each participant) and whether the event of interest occurred during the study.

Reporting survival analysis using figures

One of the most common ways that survival analyses are presented is through a cumulative survival plot, or **survival curve**. The survival curve illustrates the cumulative proportion of participants in the study that are 'surviving' or as yet free of the event (*y*-axis) at each time point (*x*-axis). A Kaplan–Meier (non-parametric) survival curve from our hypothetical dataset (Table 4.9) is plotted in Figure 4.2. The proportion at Time 0 is 1.0 for both groups, since all are alive at the study start. Following the lines, you can see that the first two participant deaths in the CPAP group occurred at 32 months (the line begins to drop at this time point and continues to drop as more patients die), and at the end of the study (120 months) the proportion is 0.56 (or 56%). In contrast, at the end of the study, the proportion surviving in the splint group is 0.23 (or 23%).

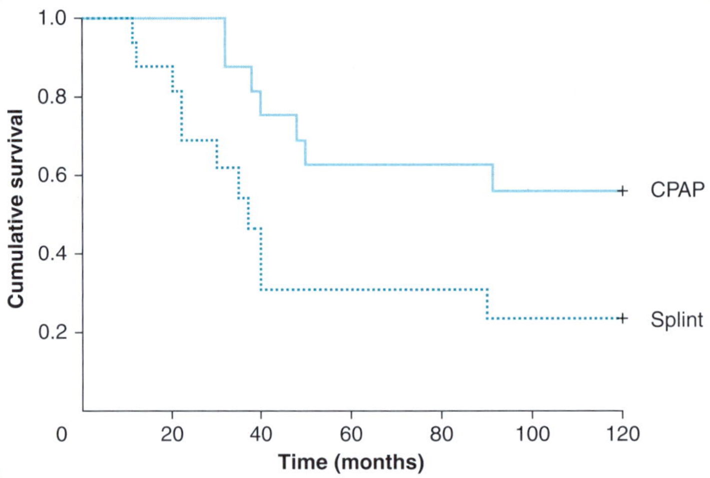

Figure 4.2 Survival plot from hypothetical study 2 (data in Table 4.9).

Reporting survival analysis in text

Results are typically reported as mean (or the median), ±standard error in survival time for each group (Greenhouse et al., 1989). It is also possible to statistically test for significant differences between groups. There are several tests for this, but one common one is referred to as the Mantel–Cox or logrank test (Greenhouse et al., 1989). In our study, the mean survival time was 88.0±9.5 months in the CPAP group and 54.1±10.9 months in the splint group. This difference was significant ($\beta_1^2 = 5.23$, $p = 0.022$).

Extensions of basic survival analysis

The results of another good study (Lespérance et al., 2002) are shown in Figure 4.3. This study recruited 896 patients who had experienced MI (or heart attack). Based on their scores on the Beck Depression Inventory (BDI), they were grouped into one of four severity groups. Investigators then followed up their 5-year survival based on Medicare records. You can see from Figure 4.3 that the slope of the survival plots is progressively steeper for each step-increase in BDI group. This study suggests a dose–response relationship between depression during hospital admission and survival for patients who have experienced MI. A further interesting aspect of this study is that it used a slightly different approach to test differences between groups. Lespérance and colleagues used a Cox proportional hazards model, which allowed them to control for a number of covariates related to the severity of cardiac disease. They were then able to conclude that the impact of depression at hospitalisation remained significant after controlling for these potential confounders.

It is also interesting to note that survival analysis can be extended, not only to include covariates, as mentioned previously (Bull & Spiegelhalter, 1997), but also to account for multiple observations in the same people over time (Hosmer, Lemeshow & May, 2008; Mario et al., 2008).

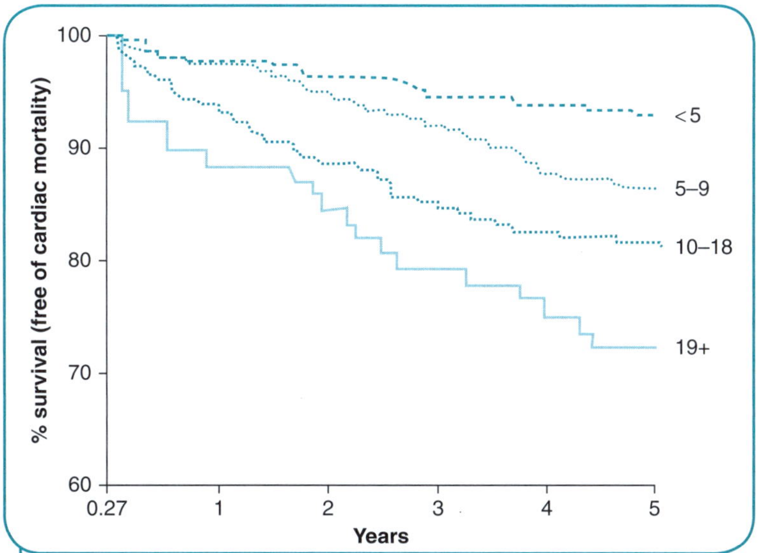

Figure 4.3 Example of survival analysis shows % survival over 5 years in patients who have experienced a heart attack, grouped according to their scores on the Beck Depression Inventory (< 5; 5–9; 10–18; 19+). *Source:* adapted from Lespérance et al., 2002

Mini case study 4.3

Consider this snippet from the abstract of an article by Baine et al. (2011), which is an example of a study using survival analysis to describe the relationship between marital status and survival in patients with pancreatic cancer (pancreatic ductal adenocarcinoma):

> OS [overall survival] for these patients was plotted using the Kaplan–Meier method. Comparative risks of mortality were evaluated by using univariate and multivariate-adjusted Cox regression models. Using Kaplan–Meier analysis, we found that the median overall survival of patients was 4 months and 3 months ($p < 0.001$) for married and unmarried patients, respectively. Subgroup analysis on patients with cancer-directed surgery showed that the median survival was 16 months and 13 months ($P < 0.0005$) for married and unmarried groups, respectively. Multivariate analysis adjusting for age, race, sex, stage, year of diagnosis, radiation therapy and cancer-directed surgery showed that patients who were married at the time of diagnosis had a significantly decreased risk of death at both 2 months (15% risk reduction) and 3 years (13% risk reduction) post diagnosis.
>
> (Baine et al., 2011, p. 1)

Critical thinking questions

1. What was the median survival for married patients? How did it compare to unmarried patients? How were these values different in the subgroup who had cancer-directed surgery?
2. Which tests were done using Kaplan–Meier analyses, and which using Cox? Why do you think the researchers chose these methods in each case?

Summary

- Epidemiology focuses on the magnitude and reasons behind disease occurrence as well as intervention and treatment. Understanding what is meant by terms such as mortality (death), morbidity (non-fatal health issues), population at risk (people who would be cases if they were diagnosed with the disease of interest), prevalence (number of cases in a population) and incidence (number of new cases in a population over a period of time) is important.
- Observational designs such as cross-sectional studies (sampling at a single time point), case-control studies (targeted sampling of individuals with a particular outcome with retrospective assessment of exposure) and cohort studies (recruiting a cohort of participants with an outcome of interest and following them over time) are common. Treatment studies are also common. The randomised clinical trial (RCT) is the gold standard approach for evaluating treatment efficacy.
- These designs may involve repeated measurements over time (requiring extensions to basic regression such as mixed-effects linear regression and generalised estimating equations), deviations from traditional conceptualisations of the null hypothesis (for equivalence or non-inferiority testing), and binary dependent variables (e.g. the presence/absence of disease or health event).
- In a study investigating the risk between two binary variables of 1. exposure (yes/no) and 2. outcome (yes/no), the relative risk is the risk (number of new cases in a time period/number of people at risk at the start of the time period) of the outcome (e.g. lung cancer) for those in the exposure group (e.g. smokers) divided by the risk for those not exposed (e.g. non-smokers). The odds ratio is the odds (number of new cases in a time period/number of people who did not become a case) of the outcome (e.g. lung cancer) for those in the exposure group (e.g. smokers) divided by the odds for those not exposed (e.g. non-smokers). In a study with a binary outcome and several predictors, the binary logistic regression can be used to calculate the odds ratio for each predictor and the outcome. Binary logistic regressions have many similarities to basic multiple regression. We considered how to read results presented in text, tables and figures.
- Survival analysis allows us to analyse time-to-event in datasets where not everyone will experience that event before they are lost to follow up or the study ends. The most common way to present results is through a survival curve, which illustrates the cumulative proportion of participants in the study who are 'surviving' or as yet free of the event (y-axis) at each time point (x-axis). Differences between exposure groups can be tested using non-parametric (Kaplan–Meier) or parametric (Cox) models.

Suggested weblinks

Refer to the companion website at www.cambridge.edu.au/academic/healthpsychology for a list of suggested weblinks.

References

ABS. (2012). *Year Book Australia*. Canberra: Australian Bureau of Statistics.

AIHW. (2014a). *Australia's Health 2014. Australia's health series no. 14*. Cat. no. AUS 178. Canberra: Australian Institute of Health and Welfare.

—— (2014b). Cardiovascular disease, diabetes and chronic kidney disease – Australian facts: prevalence and incidence. *Cardiovascular, Diabetes and Chronic Kidney Disease Series no. 2*. Cat. no. CDK 2. Canberra: Australian Institute of Health and Welfare.

Andersson, G., Hesser, H., Veilord, A., Svedling, L., Andersson, F., Sleman, O., … Zetterqvist, V. (2013). Randomised controlled non-inferiority trial with 3-year follow-up of internet-delivered versus face-to-face group cognitive behavioural therapy for depression. *Journal of Affective Disorders*, *151*(3), 986–94.

Aron, A., Coups, E. J. & Aron, E. (2011). *Statistics for the Behavioral and Social Sciences: A Brief Course*. New Jersey: Prentice Hall.

Baayen, R. H., Davidson, D. J. & Bates, D. M. (2008). Mixed-effects modeling with crossed random effects for subjects and items. *Journal of Memory and Language*, *59*(4), 390–412.

Baine, M., Sahak, F., Lin, C., Chakraborty, S., Lyden, E. & Batra, S. K. (2011). Marital status and survival in pancreatic cancer patients: a SEER based analysis. *PLoS ONE*, *6*(6), e21052.

Berk, L. S., Bellinger, D. L., Koenig, H. G., Daher, N., Pearce, M. J., Robins, C. J., … King, M. B. (2015). Effects of religious vs. conventional cognitive-behavioral therapy on inflammatory markers and stress hormones in major depression and chronic medical illness: a randomized clinical trial. *Open Journal of Psychiatry*, *5*(03), 238.

Bhopal, R., Macfarlane, G. J., Smith, W. C. & West, R. (2011). What is the future of epidemiology? *The Lancet*, *378*(9790), 464–5.

Bland, J. M. & Altman, D. G. (2000). The odds ratio. *British Medical Journal*, *320*(7247), 1468.

Buettner, C., Davis, R. B., Leveille, S. G., Mittleman, M. A. & Mukamal, K. J. (2008). Prevalence of musculoskeletal pain and statin use. *Journal of General Internal Medicine*, *23*(8), 1182–6.

Bull, K. & Spiegelhalter, D. J. (1997). Tutorial in biostatistics survival analysis in observational studies. *Statistics in Medicine*, *16*(9), 1041–74.

Capraro, R. M. (2004). Statistical significance, effect size reporting, and confidence intervals: best reporting strategies. *Journal for Research in Mathematics Education*, 35(1), 57–62.

Carlin, J. B., Wolfe, R., Coffey, C. & Patton, G. C. (1999). Analysis of binary outcomes in longitudinal studies using weighted estimating equations and discrete-time survival methods: prevalence and incidence of smoking in an adolescent cohort. *Statistics in Medicine*, *18*(19), 2655–79.

Carneiro, I. & Howard, N. (2011). *Introduction to Epidemiology*. Maidenhead, Berkshire: Open University Press.

Coggon, D., Barker, D. & Rose, G. (2009). *Epidemiology for the Uninitiated*. New York: John Wiley & Sons.

Cohen, J., (1992). A power primer. *Psychological Bulletin*, *112*(1), 155.

Collins, J.A. & Fauser, B.C. (2005). Balancing the strengths of systematic and narrative reviews. *Human Reproduction Update*, *11*(2), 103–4.

Cook, R. J. & Sackett, D. L. (1995). The number needed to treat: a clinically useful measure of treatment effect. *British Medical Journal*, *310*(6977), 452.

Davies, H. T. O., Crombie, I. K. & Tavakoli, M. (1998). When can odds ratios mislead? *BMJ*, *316*(7136), 989–91.

Delgado-Rodriguez, M. & Llorca, J. (2004). Bias. *Journal of Epidemiology and Community Health*, *58*(8), 635–41.

Demyttenaere, K., Bruffaerts, R., Posada-Villa, J., Gasquet, I., Kovess, V., Lépine, J., … Morosini, P. (2004). Prevalence, severity, and unmet need for treatment of mental disorders in the World Health Organization World Mental Health Surveys. *The Journal of the American Medical Association*, *291*(21), 2581–90.

Dodson, B., Hammett, P. C. & Klerx, R. (2014). Binary Logistic Regression. *Probabilistic Design for Optimization and Robustness for Engineers*, 202–24.

Dorrian, J., Lamond, N., Van Den Heuvel, C., Pincombe, J., Rogers, A. E. & Dawson, D. (2006). A pilot study of the safety implications of Australian nurses' sleep and work hours. *Chronobiology International*, *23*(6), 1149–63.

Dorrian, J., Tolley, C., Lamond, N., van den Heuvel, C., Pincombe, J., Rogers, A. E. & Drew, D. (2008). Sleep and errors in a group of Australian hospital nurses at work and during the commute. *Applied Ergonomics*, *39*(5), 605–13.

Ebbutt, A. & Frith, L. (1998). Practical issues in equivalence trials. *Statistics in Medicine*, *17*(15–16), 1691–701.

Field, A. (2009). *Discovering Statistics Using SPSS*. London: Sage.

Garg A. X., Hackam, D. & Tonelli, M. (2008). Systematic review and meta-analysis: when one study is just not enough. *Clinical Journal of the American Society of Nephrology: CJASN*, *3*(1).
Gravetter, F. & Wallnau, L. (2013). *Essentials of Statistics for the Behavioral Sciences*. Belmont: Cengage Learning.
Greenhouse, J. B., Stangl, D. & Bromberg, J. (1989). An introduction to survival analysis: statistical methods for analysis of clinical trial data. *Journal of Consulting and Clinical Psychology*, *57*(4), 536.
Harrell Jr, F. E. (2001). Chapter 9: Binary logistic regression. *Regression Modeling Strategies* (pp. 215–67). New York: Springer.
Heit, J. A., Silverstein, M. D., Mohr, D. N., Petterson, T. M., O'Fallon, W. M. & Melton, L. J. (2000). Risk factors for deep vein thrombosis and pulmonary embolism: a population-based case-control study. *Archives of Internal Medicine*, *160*(6), 809–15.
Hosmer, D. W., Lemeshow, S. & May, S. (2008). *Applied Survival Analysis*. Hoboken, NJ: Wiley.
Irwig, L., Irwig, J., Trevena, L. et al. (2008). Chapter 18: Relative risk, relative and absolute risk reduction, number needed to treat and confidence intervals. *Smart Health Choices: Making Sense of Health Advice*. London: Hammersmith Press. Available from: http://www.ncbi.nlm.nih.gov/books/NBK63647
Jones, B., Jarvis, P., Lewis, J. & Ebbutt, A. (1996). Trials to assess equivalence: the importance of rigorous methods. *British Medical Journal*, *313*(7048), 36–9.
Kiosses, D. N., Ravdin, L. D., Gross, J. J., Raue, P., Kotbi, N. & Alexopoulos, G. S. (2015). Problem adaptation therapy for older adults with major depression and cognitive impairment: a randomized clinical trial. *Journal of the American Medical Association Psychiatry*, *72*(1), 22–30.
Lépine, J.-P. & Briley, M. (2011). The increasing burden of depression. *Neuropsychiatric Disease and Treatment*, *7*(Suppl 1), 3.
Lespérance, F., Frasure-Smith, N., Talajic, M. & Bourassa, M. G. (2002). Five-year risk of cardiac mortality in relation to initial severity and one-year changes in depression symptoms after myocardial infarction. *Circulation*, *105*(9), 1049–53.
Liang, K.-Y. & Zeger, S. L. (1986). Longitudinal data analysis using generalized linear models. *Biometrika*, 13–22.
Lipsey, M. W. & Wilson, D. B. (2001). *Practical meta-analysis*. Thousand Oaks, CA: Sage.
Ma, Y., Mazumdar, M. & Memtsoudis, S. G. (2012). Beyond repeated measures ANOVA: advanced statistical methods for the analysis of longitudinal data in anesthesia research. *Regional Anesthesia and Pain Medicine*, *37*(1), 99.
Mahmood, S. S., Levy, D., Vasan, R. S. & Wang, T. J. (2014). The Framingham Heart Study and the epidemiology of cardiovascular disease: a historical perspective. *The Lancet*, *383*(9921), 999–1008.
Mak, A., Cheung, M. W., Fu, E. H. & Ho, R. (2010). Meta-analysis in medicine: an introduction. *International Journal of Rheumatic Diseases*, 13(2), 101–4.
Mario, C., Gould, W. W., Gutierrez, R. G. & Marchenko, Y. (2008). An introduction to survival analysis using Stata. College Station, TX: Stata Press.
Mathers, C., Fat, D. M. & Boerma, J. T. (2008). *The Global Burden of Disease: 2004 Update*: Geneva: World Health Organisation.
McBeth, J. & Cordingley, L. (2009). Current issues and new direction in psychology and health: epidemiology and health psychology – please bridge the gap. *Psychology and Health*, *24*(8), 861–5.
Milani, R. V., Lavie, C. J., Mehra, M. R. & Ventura, H. O. (2011). Impact of exercise training and depression on survival in heart failure due to coronary heart disease. *The American Journal of Cardiology*, *107*(1), 64–8.
Moher, D., Hopewell, S., Schulz, K. F., Montori, V., Gøtzsche, P. C., Devereaux, P., … Altman, D. G. (2010). CONSORT 2010 explanation and elaboration: updated guidelines for reporting parallel group randomised trials. *Journal of Clinical Epidemiology*, *63*(8), e1–37.
Morling, B. (2012). *Research Methods in Psychology: Evaluating a World of Information*. New York: Norton.
Nagelkerke, N. J. (1991). A note on a general definition of the coefficient of determination. *Biometrika*, *78*(3), 691–2.
O'Reilly, R., Bishop, J., Maddox, K., Hutchinson, L., Fisman, M. & Takhar, J. (2007). Is telepsychiatry equivalent to face-to-face psychiatry? Results from a randomized controlled equivalence trial. *Psychiatric Services*, *58*(6), 836–43.
Peto, R., Pike, M., Armitage, P., Breslow, N., Cox, D., Howard, S. V., … Smith, P. (1976). Design and analysis of randomized clinical trials requiring prolonged observation of each patient. I. Introduction and design. *British Journal of Cancer*, *34*(6), 585.

Pignone, M., Earnshaw, S., Tice, J. A. & Pletcher, M. J. (2006). Aspirin, statins, or both drugs for the primary prevention of coronary heart disease events in men: a cost–utility analysis. *Annals of Internal Medicine*, 144(5), 326–36.

Punjabi, N. M. (2008). The epidemiology of adult obstructive sleep apnea. *Proceedings of the American Thoracic Society*, *5*(2), 136–43.

Ragin, D. F. (2014). *Health Psychology: An Interdisciplinary Approach to Health*. Pearson Higher Ed.

Rehm, J., Mathers, C., Popova, S., Thavorncharoensap, M., Teerawattananon, Y. & Patra, J. (2009). Global burden of disease and injury and economic cost attributable to alcohol use and alcohol-use disorders. *The Lancet*, *373*(9682), 2223–33.

Rennie, D. (2001). CONSORT revised – improving the reporting of randomized trials. *Journal of the American Medical Association*, *285*(15), 2006–7.

Ridker, P. M. & Cook, N. R. (2013). Statins: new American guidelines for prevention of cardiovascular disease. *The Lancet*, *382*(9907), 1762–5.

Risch, H. A., Howe, G. R., Jain, M., Burch, J. D., Holowaty, E. J. & Miller, A. B. (1993). Are female smokers at higher risk for lung cancer than male smokers? A case-control analysis by histologic type. *American Journal of Epidemiology*, *138*(5), 281–93.

Rose, G. & Barker, D. (1978). What is epidemiology? *British Medical Journal*, *2*(6140), 803–4.

Rosenfield, P. L. (1992). The potential of transdisciplinary research for sustaining and extending linkages between the health and social sciences. *Social Science & Medicine*, *35*(11), 1343–57.

Rozanski, A., Blumenthal, J. A., Davidson, K. W., Saab, P. G. & Kubzansky, L. (2005). The epidemiology, pathophysiology, and management of psychosocial risk factors in cardiac practice: the emerging field of behavioral cardiology. *Journal of the American College of Cardiology*, *45*(5), 637–51.

Rugulies, R. (2002). Depression as a predictor for coronary heart disease: a review and meta-analysis. *American Journal of Preventive Medicine*, *23*(1), 51–61.

Shapiro, A. K. (1960). A contribution to a history of the placebo effect. *Behavioral Science*, *5*(2), 109–35.

Sharafkhaneh, A. & Grogan, W. A. (2015). Neurocognitive functions in patients with obstructive sleep apnea hypopnea syndrome. In: R. R. Watson (ed.), *Modulation of Sleep by Obesity, Diabetes, Age, and Diet* (pp. 63–8). London: Elsevier.

Shaughnessy, J. J., Zechmeister, E. B. & Zechmeister, J. S. (2012). *Research Methods in Psychology*. New York: McGraw-Hill.

Shephard, R. J. (2003). Regression to the mean. *Sports Medicine*, *33*(8), 575–84.

SHF. (2011). Re-awakening Australia: the economic cost of sleep disorders in Australia, 2010. Canberra: Economics, Deloitte Access.

Shtatland, E. S., Kleinman, K. & Cain, E. M. (2002). One more time about R2 measures of fit in logistic regression. *NESUG 15 Proceedings*, *15*, 222–6.

Smith, G. C. S. & Pell, J. P. (2003). Parachute use to prevent death and major trauma related to gravitational challenge: systematic review of randomised controlled trials. *BMJ*, *327*, 1459–61.

Stegner, B. L., Bostrom, A. G. & Greenfield, T. K. (1996). Equivalence testing for use in psychosocial and services research: an introduction with examples. *Evaluation and Program Planning*, *19*(3), 193–8.

Stewart, B. W., Kleihues, P. & Cancer, I. A. f. R. o. (2003). *World Cancer Report*. 57. Lyon: IARC Press.

Turner, E. H., Matthews, A. M., Linardatos, E., Tell, R. A. & Rosenthal, R. (2008). Selective publication of antidepressant trials and its influence on apparent efficacy. *New England Journal of Medicine*, *358*(3), 252–60.

Van Dongen, H. P., Olofsen, E., Dinges, D. F. & Maislin, G. (2004). Mixed-model regression analysis and dealing with interindividual differences. *Methods in Enzymology*, *384*, 139–71.

Walters, P., Barley, E. A., Mann, A., Phillips, R. & Tylee, A. (2014). Depression in primary care patients with coronary heart disease: baseline findings from the UPBEAT UK study. *PLoS ONE*, 12 June, *9*(6).

Ware, J. H. & Antman, E. M. (1997). Equivalence trials. *New England Journal of Medicine*, *337*(16), 1159–61.

Yusuf, S., Hawken, S., Ôunpuu, S., Dans, T., Avezum, A., Lanas, F., ... Varigos, J. (2004). Effect of potentially modifiable risk factors associated with myocardial infarction in 52 countries (the INTERHEART study): case-control study. *The Lancet*, *364*(9438), 937–52.

Zhao, X. Q., Morse, J. S., Dowdy, A. A., Heise, N., DeAngelis, D., Frohlich, J., ... & Brown, B. G. (2004). Safety and tolerability of simvastatin plus niacin in patients with coronary artery disease and low high-density lipoprotein cholesterol (The HDL Atherosclerosis Treatment Study). *The American Journal of Cardiology*, *93*(3), 307–31.

5

Nutrition, exercise and health

Learning outcomes

After reading this chapter, you should be able to:

- explain key benefits and risks associated with nutrition and different types of diet
- critically analyse different types of nutritional and exercise recommendations and claimed health benefits
- identify limitations in the existing scientific research and how that impacts on the generalisability of said research findings
- understand issues surrounding eating disorders
- evaluate barriers to increased physical activity levels.

Introduction

This chapter focuses on scientific findings and theory surrounding nutrition and exercise and how the right nutrition and exercise can improve health-related outcomes. Nutrition and diet will be examined synonymously, and this examination will cover controversial areas such as saturated fat, cholesterol, salt, alcohol, fibre, sugar, fast food and some of the diets on offer. This chapter should provide you with an understanding of diet, exercise, weight gain and eating disorders. This means that we will try to delve into the many complex motivators for food selection and consumption.

If there was ever an area in science that has been regarded as difficult, contentious and full of 'gurus' who preach 'the truth', that might be the science of nutrition, and especially how the food we ingest has the power to affect our health. Given our current state of knowledge, it seems safe to say that anyone trying to sell you the perfect diet is really only selling the *idea* of a perfect diet and not the perfect diet per se.

So how do we know what to eat, what not to eat and how much to eat? What can the research literature tell us? When we implement interventions to change the diet of a particular population, we need to base such interventions on scientific evidence and knowledge and we need to monitor what effects such changes have on the health of the population in question. We can also examine animal-based studies to see what extreme diets can do to our health. The question is: Can we improve our consumption patterns in Australia and, if so, how?

When it comes to exercise the findings are clear, at least in comparison to nutrition research. The take-home message is that we all need to make sure we get adequate levels of exercise. How *adequate* is defined, however, is another matter. We need to broaden the definition of exercise to include any physical activity in order to get a better idea of how we can increase individuals' physical activity. Different health psychology models can help us identify barriers and opportunities to increasing physical activity.

Nutrition

Health psychology research into **nutrition** is varied and covers research into the effects that different types of food can have on our behaviour, what we eat, why we eat the food we eat, and how we can change our behaviour when it comes to selecting the food that makes up our **diet**. We need to know what to eat and how much. There are some 'magic' numbers that people often discuss with respect to diet, such as '8700 kJ'. This number is the amount of energy that the average person needs from food per day. However, no two individuals are the same and our daily energy needs will obviously vary. Children and adolescents will have very different energy needs compared to adults. Our activity levels (e.g. **exercise**), as governed by our lifestyle, will obviously affect our energy needs as well. The National Health and Medical Research Council (NHMRC, 2015b) has published dietary guidelines for Australians with the aim of improving **health** and **wellbeing**. These guidelines are also intended to act as a preventative tool to reduce the impact of diseases such as type 2 diabetes.

The NHMRC's summary report suggests that *most* Australians need to *consume more* vegetables and fruit, highlighting the fact that we need to consume more green, orange, and red vegetables (2013). We also need to eat *more* wholegrain foods, preferably high in fibre when possible, as well as consume *more* lean meats, poultry, fish, eggs, nuts, seeds and legumes. The summary report also suggests that most Australians should *reduce* their consumption of pies and sausage rolls as well as chips, both fried and crisps. Furthermore, we are eating too much when it comes to sweets such as cakes, confectionery, chocolate and desserts, and we drink too many sugar-sweetened beverages (e.g. soft drinks and sport-type drinks) and alcoholic drinks. To put it bluntly, we are no longer eating enough 'proper' meals but rather consuming anything that will satisfy our craving for sweets. The report also suggests that we need to reduce our consumption of full-fat dairy (e.g. full-fat milk, butter and cream). In this chapter we will examine these summary guidelines more carefully, especially about fat, in light of the evidence.

One of the key NHMRC reports (2011) reviews the evidence for the recommendations that are then reflected in the guidelines. The guidelines are based largely on meta-analysis, reviews and randomised control trials from the US and Europe, and are mostly based on samples from adult populations. The strength of the evidence behind different recommendations varies but it seems clear that the consumption of fruit, vegetables, dairy, fruit and nuts, and fish as part of a regular diet will act as a protective factor against diseases such as **cardiovascular disease (CVD)** and cancer.

Fruit and vegetables

An NHMRC (2011) review of studies that examined the effects of *fruit* consumption on health suggested that fruit is a protective factor against: 1. CVD (i.e. coronary heart disease [CHD] and stroke); 2. obesity and weight gain; and 3. cancer (gastric, lung, oesophageal, oral and nasopharyngeal). Citrus fruit was noted as a protective factor for pancreatic cancer. Fruit consumption was not associated with type 2 diabetes or several types of cancer. Vegetables were found to be a protective factor against: 1. CVD; 2. weight gain; and 3. several types of cancer (i.e. gastric cancer, lung and nasopharyngeal). Tomato consumption was found to be a protective factor against prostate cancer. Vegetable consumption was not linked to type 2 diabetes or several types of cancer. Studies that examined the combined effects of *fruits and vegetables* on health found that fruits and vegetables protected against CVD. The findings for the combined effects of fruits and vegetables were consistent with the findings for fruit and vegetables when examined as separate factors.

The underlying causes of the health benefits of fruits and vegetables need to be examined carefully. Van Duyn and Pivonka (2000) suggest several factors that could explain the relationship between fruit and vegetable consumption and health. One of these factors is the antioxidant properties of many fruits and vegetables, which may reduce your chances of developing cancer and potentially reduce cancer growth. Other factors to consider include phytochemicals (compounds in plants; phyto = plant) including flavonoids (e.g. quercetin, kaempterol, tangeretin), carotenoids (e.g. betacarotene, lutein), phytoestrogens (e.g. genistein), capsaicin and resveratrol. Different types of sulphides may also help fight cancer cells or potential cancer cells through anticancer enzymes (Van Duyn & Pivonka, 2000). Liu (2003) asks whether purified phytochemical (think supplements) have the same effect as whole foods (think apples, oranges, kale and so on), suggesting that whole foods are needed rather than supplements due to the interaction among the numerous phytochemicals in whole foods.

So do we consume enough fruit and vegetables in Australia? The statistics for the Indigenous population suggest that about 42% get an adequate amount of fruit on a daily basis. However, when it comes to vegetables only 5% of the Indigenous population gets enough on a daily basis (Australian Indigenous HealthInfoNet, 2015). Females are more likely to consume enough fruit (44% versus 40%) and vegetables (7% versus 4%) than males. The numbers are much better for children (2 to 14 years of age), with 78% eating enough fruit and 16% enough vegetables. Being employed predicted more fruit and vegetable consumption, while sex, area lived in (remote versus non-remote) and education had limited or mixed effects on consumption. This consumption pattern is reflected in the non-Indigenous population.

So how many serves of fruit and vegetables are we to consume per day and what types of fruit and vegetables? Given the situation in Australia, it is probably safe to say that you should increase your consumption, especially of vegetables. Try to eat what is in season, thus it will be fresh and at a fair price. Eat maybe two types or more of vegetables with every meal on average. Snack on bananas, apples, carrots and so on rather than sweets or chips. Measure your current consumption of fruit and vegetables and try to keep it above 500 g per day or about five serves per day of vegetables and two of fruit for an adult. A *serve* of vegetables is generally considered to be a ½ cup of cooked vegetables or one cup of salad while a serve of fruit is a medium-sized fruit such as a medium-sized apple, two small apples or one cup of fruit (NHMRC, 2013).

Saturated fat

If you want to find a topic within nutrition that polarises people, then saturated fat would be a good candidate. Fat, and especially saturated fat, has conventionally been linked to increased risk of CVD. We certainly see the evidence every time we go to the supermarket to buy food as the shelves are stacked with products that claim, as virtue, that they are X% fat free. Fat-free food is everywhere in the Western world, yet the obesity epidemic is worse than ever. And if anyone should challenge this wisdom and cite data showing a diet high in fat to be associated with low CVD, then such data is labelled as a paradox and thus explained away as the exception that proves the rule. But before we get too far ahead of ourselves, why would we think that saturated fat is linked to CVD? To answer this question, we need to go back to the middle of the 20th century and look at the work by Ancel Keys. Keys was a scientist who examined the effects of diet on health. He focused particularly on the effects of fat on cardiovascular disease and published influential work in this area. He looked at the rates of CHD and fat consumption in six countries. His data suggested that as the ratio of fat in the diet increased, so did the rate of CHD (Smith, 2014). Keys' data was gathered after World War II when there was a food shortage in some of the countries studied, biasing the findings. This bias is as nothing to Keys' ability to select data points (Smith, 2014), suggesting that his findings can be dismissed. When it comes to reliable and comprehensive research findings, the link between saturated fat and CVD all but evaporates. A meta-analysis based on epidemiological studies (5- to 23-year follow-up) found no link between the intake of saturated fat and CHD, stroke, or CVD (Siri-Tarino et al., 2010). However, this meta-analysis has not been without its critics. One of the best observations of this meta-analysis comes from Katan et al. (2010), who point out that 'lower intake of saturated fat implies an increased intake of some other source of calories to maintain caloric balance' (p. 459). Other criticism of the meta-analysis tends to be related to limitations of the studies examined and the way they were aggregated, something that speaks more to the lack of studies into this area than to the quality of the meta-analysis. Even with its limitations, the research is now clearly showing that fat was framed.

The history of diet research is, sadly, littered with vested interests and very efficient lobby groups. To make a long story short, at one stage fat, and especially saturated fat, was demonised while trans fats were glorified. Now trans fats are banned by the US Food and Drug Administration (FDA) and saturated fats are starting to make a comeback, given both the lack of evidence against them and the use of fraudulent evidence (Smith, 2014). A recent animal study further supports the notion that fat is not to blame for obesity, concluding that obesity and cognitive impairment are caused by diet quality and not fat (Blaisdell et al., 2014).

So what about the situation in Australia? What does the NHMRC (2011) report say about fat? The report suggests that fats (**trigycerides**) and **oils** may protect your health. Consumption of **polyunsaturated fatty acids** reduces the risk of CVD while omega-3 polyunsaturated fatty acids may improve triglyceride levels. Polyunsaturated fatty acids may improve infant lipid profile while short-chain fatty acids and high total fat intake protects children from CVD. Dementia risks can be attenuated (reduced) through the consumption of omega-3 long-chain polyunsaturated fatty acids. Furthermore, fat consumption is *not* associated with type 2 diabetes, hypertension or cancer.

Overall, the take-home message is that the saturated fat in your diet may simply be good for you, or at least neutral, when it comes to disease. So if you reduce the fat in your diet, consider what you will be replacing it with. Just because fat is called fat does not mean it will make you fat. If you replace some of the fat in your diet with sugar, for instance, then you may be worse off than you were to begin with.

Cholesterol

Cholesterol levels are generally reported based on levels of low-density lipoprotein (LDL), levels of high-density lipoprotein (HDL) and the ratio between LDL and HDL. These different levels and ratios have been under close examination for some time, with studies suggesting that high LDL levels are a risk factor for CVD. As a result, thousands of Australians are on cholesterol-lowering drugs (e.g. statins). However, the use of such drugs is under question given their overprescription by doctors and proven lack of effectiveness.

When it comes to the effectiveness of cholesterol-lowering drugs, it is essential to keep in mind that what you are after is not lower cholesterol but reduced mortality and morbidity rates. Cholesterol-lowering drugs are not to be taken lightly (puns intended) as the maths shows (Carey, 2008). Even targeted use of statins (for pre-existing CHD) shows limited effectiveness (**number needed to treat (NNT)** = 21), in protecting against a major vascular event (Cholesterol Treatment Trialists' [CTT] Collaborators, 2005). The higher the NNT, the smaller the chances are that any one individual will benefit from the treatment in question. With NNT = 21, only one in 21 will benefit after years of adhering to the treatment. Any treatment also has to be evaluated against potential side effects. A meta-analysis into statin-related side effects suggested that there were some potential side effects such as myopathy, increased levels of liver enzymes and increased risk of diabetes (Macedo et al., 2014).

A meta-analysis conducted by Yu-Poth et al. (1999) evaluated the effects of cholesterol education programs on resulting cholesterol levels. The authors suggest that education programs promoting a low-fat diet and increased exercise may reduce cholesterol levels. Exercise and reduced fat intake were both associated with lower LDL cholesterol levels. However, the role played by any reduction in sugar or total carbohydrate intake could not be examined or controlled for. A diet incorporating legumes (e.g. soy) may act as a protective factor for lower total and LDL cholesterol as well as breast and prostate cancer. Consumption of nuts and seeds (high fat) is also related to lower cholesterol levels and not to weight gain (NHMRC, 2011).

The current state of the research literature in relation to cholesterol suggests that we have only just started to understand cholesterol. This is reflected in changes over time, as seen in amendments to recommendations made by healthcare professionals. Once upon a time, egg consumption was considered bad as eggs are high in cholesterol. However, the latest recommendations suggest that egg consumption is *not* related to CHD or cancer and may in fact reduce the risk of stroke (NHMRC, 2011).

Cholesterol may not be the negative causal factor it is made out to be; it may simply be an indicator of an underlying problem such as inflammation. After all, cholesterol is essential to the cells in our body and to normal healthy life. More research is needed to clarify the role of cholesterol in health.

Salt

The NHMRC (2011) report suggests that we need to reduce the *sodium* (salt) intake in our diet. Note that typical table salt is about 40% sodium and 60% chloride. Restrictions on sodium intake in hypertensive adults helps reduce systolic blood pressure by about 5 mmHg and diastolic blood pressure by about 3 mmHg. Such interventions will also lower blood pressure in healthy adults, but only by about 2 mmHg systolic and 1 mmHg diastolic. Therefore, reducing sodium intake may reduce the risk of CVD among pre-hypertensive adults. Postmenopausal women may also want to consider their sodium intake in order to improve bone health.

This raises a question about the effectiveness of interventions restricting sodium intake. Brunner et al. (1997) conducted a meta-analysis examining randomised control trials of primary **prevention** dietary interventions of 3 months or more aimed at reducing fat and sodium intake. They found that there were only very modest reductions in risk indictors such as blood pressure and cholesterol. A recent meta-analysis by Taylor et al. (2011) evaluated behavioural interventions to reduce salt intake, examining seven randomised control trials. They reported minimal reduction in blood pressure and no effect on CVD morbidity.

Fibre

Research findings clearly show that dietary fibre has the potential to act as primary and secondary prevention for many diseases and complications. These include CVD, type 2 diabetes, cancers (e.g. gastric, oesophageal), obesity and gastrointestinal disorders

(Anderson et al., 2009). Fibre may reduce the risk of CVD, including stroke, through mechanisms such as lowered blood pressure, and type 2 diabetes and obesity through improved glucose homeostasis. High-fibre diets are also more filling than low-fibre diets and this may help individuals control their food consumption and fight obesity. Brown et al. (1999) conducted a meta-analysis of 67 randomised control trials examining the effects of dietary fibre on cholesterol levels and triacylglycerol. They reported that soluble fibre reduced LDL cholesterol levels. The authors suggest that increased fibre consumption may translate into a 4% reduction in coronary artery disease, suggesting that modest increases in fibre consumption can have huge benefits for society. Other reviews have suggested that fibre acts as a protective factor against CVD and cancer mortality (Huang & Zhang, 2015). Cereal consumption, especially when high in whole grains and fibre, is associated with a reduced risk of colorectal cancer, CVD, weight gain and type 2 diabetes (NHMRC, 2011). Fibre consumption is generally conceived as too low in countries like the US, the UK and Australia, with fibre consumption less than half its recommended levels in the US (Anderson et al., 2009). Daily consumption of fibre should be about 28 g and 36 g per day for adult women and men, respectively (Anderson et al., 2009).

Meat

In the NHMRC (2011) report *red meat* is defined as the fresh muscle from animals such as cattle, kangaroo, sheep and rabbit. The report suggests that consuming red fresh meat is *not* associated with different types of cancer (i.e. bladder, pancreatic, prostate, breast). However, the report's findings state that meat is a risk factor for cancers such as lung, renal and colorectal. That said, this report does not provide consistent findings or high effect sizes and thus the findings are tenuous. Fish consumption (about two serves per week) may reduce the risk of CVD, dementia, age-related macular degeneration, and stroke. According to this report, fish consumption is not linked to depression, breast cancer, colorectal cancer, prostate cancer or renal cell cancer.

Dairy

Examining the effects of dairy (excluding butter) consumption on health, findings suggest that dairy consumption is related to better bone mineral density (NHMRC, 2011). However, the NHMRC report states that consuming less than the equivalent of 240 mL of milk per day is not related to osteoporotic or hip fracture. Regular dairy consumption may *reduce* the risk of hypertension, stroke, type 2 diabetes, **metabolic syndrome**, and some cancers (i.e. colorectal and rectal). Furthermore, the report has found that dairy consumption is not related to **body mass index (BMI)** in childhood. Also, dairy consumption is not associated with renal cell or breast cancer. However, it is related to an increased risk of prostate cancer.

Carbohydrates

Carbohydrates (the hydrates of carbon) are contained in many different types of food, such as rice, pasta, sugar, bread, grain, fruit and vegetables. So are there good and bad carbohydrates? To answer that question it is important to consider two indices: **glycaemic load (GL)** and **glycaemic index (GI).** The GI tells you how fast the food in question is digested, absorbed and metabolised. The lower the GI, the slower this process is and the better it is for your blood glucose and insulin levels. A GI of 55 or less is considered low. Furthermore, food with a low GI should help reduce appetite through feeling fuller longer. GL tells you how much your glucose levels will rise after eating the food in question. It is derived from GI using the formula GL = (GI × carbohydrates in grams)/100. An apple might have about a GI of 38 and 16 g of carbohydrates, giving it a GL equal to 6 ([38 × 16]/100); a GL of > 20 is considered to be high. A 60 g Mars bar will have a GI of 62 and 40 g of carbohydrate, giving it a GL of 25. Search 'banana' on http://www.glycemicindex.com/ and you will see that the GL for a banana will vary from 6 to 16, with under-ripe bananas scoring the lowest due to lower GI and carbohydrates per banana.

One correlational study suggests that BMI may be more strongly related to GI than carbohydrate intake or GL (Ma et al., 2005). A large epidemiologic study suggested that a diet high in GI, high in GL and low in cereal fibre is a risk factor for type 2 diabetes (Bhupathiraju et al., 2014). Thus there certainly seem to be better and worse sources of carbohydrates. Legumes are good, with a low GI and high fibre content. The same goes for cereals such as muesli, oats and bran.

Consumption of *sugars* was also examined in the (NHMRC, 2011) report. *Sucrose* was not found to be associated with cancer, but the evidence was not overwhelming. Sugars were associated with increased risk of dental cavities, especially in infants and young children. Reducing sugar consumption was associated with a decreased chance of weight gain. When it comes to sugar, most of the attention has been on sugar-sweetened beverages, covered later in this chapter. A lot of attention has also been paid to high fructose corn syrup (HFCS), with a recent review suggesting that there is insufficient evidence to conclude that HFCS affects the health of your liver (Chung et al., 2014). However, the authors suggest that any potential effects may be masked as the overall energy intake in the different samples is too high.

Fast food

Fast food, also known as junk food, may actually cause serious negative health effects. One experimental study (Blaisdell et al., 2014) compared a group of female rats after a 6-month junk food diet with a group of rats after 6 months on a normal food diet. The results suggest that junk food diet will make you fat, lazy, sedentary, obese and fatigued (for news coverage of this study, see Wolpert, 2014). Furthermore, task performance is impeded both in terms of quality and how long you take to complete a task as a result of a junk food diet. More seriously, giving the junk food rats a normal diet for nine days did not reverse the damage done to the rats by the junk food diet.

Supplements

The evidence for any potential benefits or harm from the use of supplements (e.g. vitamins) is less than conclusive. Correlational studies that find an association or a link between a high supplement intake and increased risk of cancer tend to suffer typical problems associated with correlational studies. The explanations for a supplement-related relationship could be: 1. a causal link where a high supplement intake causes an increased risk of cancer; 2. a causal link where family history of cancer (genetic risk) drives behaviour such as consumption of supplements in the hope that supplements will reduce the genetic risk of cancer; and 3. diagnosis of cancer, causing increased consumption of supplements in the hope that they will reduce the impact of the cancer and help slow its progression. Other explanations are possible too, such as the limited availability of fresh fruits and vegetables due to environmental factors.

Examination of randomised control trials show mixed results for the effects of supplements on health. Bjelakovic et al. (2007) reported that betacarotene and vitamins A and E seemed to increase the risk of mortality, while the effects on mortality of vitamin C and selenium needed further examination. On a more positive note, another review of randomised control trials reported beneficial effects of both dietary folic acid and vitamin B_{12}, through reduced blood homocysteine concentrations (Homocysteine Lowering Trialists' Collaboration, 1998). Bischoff-Ferrari et al. (2005) examined the literature and reported that vitamin D supplements can act as a protective factor against fractures in individuals 60 years of age or older. The dose had to be 700 to 800 IU per day to be effective. Vitamin D supplements have also been associated with a reduction in total mortality (Autier & Gandini, 2007), especially vitamin D_3. Given the importance of sun exposure and cholesterol in vitamin production in your body, you might be surprised to learn that about a quarter of Indigenous and non-Indigenous Australians are vitamin D deficient, with little difference between the two populations (Australian Indigenous HealthInfoNet, 2015).

It seems that supplements should generally not be taken unless recommended by a healthcare professional and only if no dietary or behavioural (e.g. correct amount of sun exposure) measures can be taken to address the issue in question.

Drinks

Making health recommendations about what drinks to consume is easy, at least compared to diet recommendations. Given a clean source, tea and water are the clear favourites, while alcoholic and sugar-sweetened drinks are clearly bad choices.

Water

This is going to be a short section but necessary in order to clarify any misunderstanding and myths. We need to be clear that there is no scientific evidence for the notion that you need to drink eight glasses of water a day. Obviously you need to stay hydrated, while avoiding **hyponatremia**, but how much water/fluid you need depends on your activity, diet and environmental factors.

Tea and coffee

According to the Australian Bureau of Statistics (ABS, 2014b) about 46% of the Australian population drinks coffee, consuming about 330 mL per day on average. Coffee consumption takes off in the 14- to 18-year age group (with more than 10% drinking coffee) while more than 50% of Australians older than 30 consume coffee. About 38% of Australians drink tea, consuming about 400 mL per day on average. Conservative estimates show that tea consumption increases steadily with age, with more than 50% of Australians older than 50 drinking tea.

The evidence suggests that coffee consumption increases your chances of getting gastric, lung and bladder cancer (NHMRC, 2011). However, the same report suggested that coffee consumption was *negatively* associated with hepatocellular and endometrial cancer and reduces the risk of type 2 diabetes. Also, coffee consumption was *not* associated with breast, ovarian or colorectal cancer. The evidence for any effects of coffee on CVD was mixed, with coffee consumption *not* being associated with CHD, while coffee consumption was found to be associated with increased blood pressure.

Given these mixed findings for coffee one might expect tea (e.g. green and black) to also have mixed results, but tea consumption was not associated with any type of cancer examined. Tea consumption was found to *reduce* the risk of stroke. Other reviews suggest that black tea reduces blood pressure (Greyling et al., 2014) and the overall risk of CVD (Gardner, Ruxton & Leeds, 2007). Furthermore, green tea has recently been associated with reduced risk of endometrial cancer (Yang et al., 2015). One of tea's potential health benefits may come from the flavonoid catechin, an antioxidant.

Soft drinks (sugar-sweetened beverages)

The consumption of soft drinks in Australia shows a steep rise from a young age with a peak in the 14- to 18-year-olds. In this age group, about 50% of males and 40% of females consumed a soft drink the day before answering the survey. Worryingly, about 5% of males and females in the 2- to 3-year-old age group had consumed a soft drink the day before the survey. The early introduction to soft drinks and the high proportion of children and young adults who drink soft drinks is worrying given that soft drinks and other sugar-based drinks (excluding fruit juice) increase the risk of weight gain in both adults and children. Furthermore, these drinks are associated with worse bone strength and worse dental health (NHMRC, 2011; WHO, 2003).

It is interesting to examine the findings from different meta-analyses examining the effects of sugar-sweetened beverages on weight. A study by Forshee, Anderson and Storey (2008) reported an almost zero correlation between the consumption of sugar-sweetened beverages and BMI in children and adolescents. However, Malik, Willett and Hu (2009) pointed out shortcomings in this meta-analysis, including potential conflicts of interest regarding funding. Malik et al. (2013) went on to conduct their own meta-analysis incorporating all of the studies from the study by Forshee et al. (2008). Malik et al. (2013) found that there was a clear association between sugar-sweetened beverages and BMI in both children and adults. A previous meta-analysis by Vartanian, Schwartz and Brownell (2007) supports the negative health effects of sugar-sweetened beverages. This analysis found that sugar-sweetened beverages increased energy intake, body weight, and risk of type 2 diabetes (for the effects on type 2 diabetes see also Malik et al., 2010; Schulze et al., 2004) while lowering intake of nutrients such as calcium. The authors also suggested that the negative effects of sugar-sweetened beverages were generally lower in studies funded by the food industry than in studies not funded by industry. Furthermore, animal studies indicate that different components of addiction can be associated with sugar (Avena, Rada & Hoebel, 2008), possibly through its effects on opioids and dopamine.

Overconsumption of sugar-sweetened beverages, especially caffeine-'enhanced' ones, may be deadly. In 2013 the New Zealand coroner took on the makers of Coca-Cola, arguing that a 30-year-old woman died due to her large Coca-Cola consumption (Fairfax NZ, 2013). In Australia, caffeine toxicity was blamed for the death of a 35-year-old man who consumed more than 640 mg of caffeine per day, mostly from drinking four cans (2 L in total) of an energy drink (Burke, 2014). This amount of caffeine is more than three times the maximum caffeine consumption limit according to the Australian Beverages Council (2013).

What about low-calorie sweetened (diet) soft drinks? Could they replace the sugar-sweetened soft drink? A systematic review found that diet drinks were associated with minor weight loss based on randomised control trial studies (Miller & Perez, 2014). However, artificial sweeteners may have negative health effects (e.g. Collison et al., 2012). That said, replacing standard soft drinks with water would be the best solution, assuming safe drinking water is easily accessible.

Fruit and vegetable juice

About a quarter of Australians drink fruit and vegetable juice (ABS, 2014b), with most of these being fruit-based juices. According to the NHMRC (2011), fruit and vegetable juice will not increase the risk of weight gain in children, though the evidence is limited. Given the high consumption of fruit juice among young male and female Australians (more than 40% of 2- to 3-year-olds and more than 30% of 14- to 18-year-olds), it is important to study the potential health effects of fruit and vegetable juice. Clearly, fruit and vegetable juices cannot replace whole fruit and vegetables from your diet as juices tend to lack fibre and have a higher sugar concentration.

Alcohol

It is essential to examine the effects of alcohol on health given its strong cultural hold in Australia. Data for 2011–2012 from the ABS (2014a) found that 32% of participants had consumed alcohol the day before the survey. The data suggests that drinking starts in the 9- to 13-year-old group (1.3%), then increases sharply from the 14- to 18-year-old group (6.5%) to the 19- to 30-year-old group (29.1%), peaks in the 51- to 70-year-old group (45.4%) and stays high in the 71 and older group (43.5%).

When consumed, alcohol starts by acting as a depressant on the central nervous system (e.g. loss of inhibition, relaxation). However, as consumption continues, the individual starts experiencing drowsiness and nausea, which can end in inhibition of breathing and death. When it comes to moderate alcohol consumption (1 to 3 standard drinks per day), the evidence suggests that it may have some limited health benefits, such as increased HDL cholesterol, reduced dementia in older adults, less chance of renal cancer and non-Hodgkin's lymphoma, while it appears *not* to be related to type 2 diabetes or ovarian cancer (NHMRC, 2011). However, trying to justify alcohol consumption based on health benefits is not a good idea as even low alcohol consumption *increases* your risk of breast, colon, oesophagus, oral cavity, pharynx, larynx, rectal and liver cancer; high alcohol consumption is associated with pancreatic cancer.

According to the NHMRC (2015a), daily drinking rates in Australia were at 6.5% in 2013 with rates currently falling in comparison with 2010 rates of 7.2%. This is in line with an increasing number of Australians abstaining from alcohol. These alcohol consumption trends are in the right direction but more needs to be done to reduce alcohol consumption given the impact it has on individuals and society as a whole. Thus alcohol consumption is a risk factor for 'a wide range of health and other harms including being the major cause of road and other accidents, domestic and public violence, crime, liver disease and brain damage, and contributes to family breakdown and broader social dysfunction' (NHMRC, 2015a).

The annual alcohol cost in Australia has been estimated at $14.4 billion. Lost productivity makes up about 42.1% of this cost, the criminal justice system about 20.6%, healthcare about 11.7%, and traffic accidents about 25.5%. According to the Australian Government Department of Health (2008), we can attribute about 3000 deaths and 65 000 hospitalisations every year to our 'love' of alcohol. The good news is that Australian adolescents are smartening up, with more abstaining from alcohol and delaying when they first try alcohol; the average starting age was 14.4 years in 1998 but in 2013 it was 15.7 (NHMRC, 2015a).

Diets

The findings reported so far in this chapter should give you ample resources to start critically examining different types of diets. Healthcare professionals are always willing to recommend a healthy diet and an active lifestyle. This sounds like good advice, but how do we achieve it? After all, what is a 'healthy diet' and what is an 'active lifestyle'? If we consider our diet and compare it to the diet of our friends we find significant differences, caused by factors such as variations in cultural background, family dynamics, ethics, religion and environmental concerns. As an individual moves further outside his or her own culture and closest environment, he or she will find that the differences increase.

Diet for weight loss

If you want to go on a diet there are plenty of options, such as the Atkins diet, the Paleo diet and the Dukan diet – the list goes on. But what does it mean when we say we 'go on a diet'? Generally, we go on a diet to try to reduce our weight before we go back to our old dietary habits. However, diets are not necessarily about reducing weight. Body builders, for example, may want to increase muscle mass and so weight loss or gain as a result of the diet may not be a key concern. Diets can also be associated with religious beliefs such as a kosher diet. Views towards animals may contribute to adopting vegan or vegetarian diets. We also have short diet-type interventions such as detoxes. Whatever diet an individual is on, it will have an impact on their health.

To evaluate a diet and diet change, you need to consider outcome measures other than just weight loss and metabolic health. You also need to consider wellbeing, adherence rates and any other factors that may be relevant to individual studies – all with your clients' interests at heart. Typically, diet studies compare several different diets. Dansinger et al. (2005) ran a **randomised control trial** to compare four diets (i.e. Atkins, Ornish, Weight Watchers and Zone) with 40 participants in each group. The participants were overweight or obese and the outcomes examined were weight loss and reduction in cardiac risk factors after 1 year. The results indicated that all four diets were associated with reduced weight and waist circumference and reduction in cardiac risk factors such as cholesterol and insulin levels. However, all of the diets had low adherence. There was no practical difference between the four diets. Another diet comparison study (Gardner et al., 2007) found that for premenopausal overweight and obese women, the Atkins diet contributed to greater weight loss and better metabolic outcome over a 12-month period than the Zone, Ornish or LEARN diets.

A better diet: barriers and enablers

As a healthcare professional you can talk all you like to your clients to try to convince them of the benefits of changing their diet with all the scientific evidence on your side, but they still might not change it. You may also have stories to scare your clients with (the proverbial stick), and of course success stories (the proverbial carrot) to try to get them to change their ways. So, you may well ask why don't clients change their ways? Well the answer may lie outside the individual and in his or her environment, as you may already have suspected. To change an individual's diet, you may well need to get the support of family and friends and change the diet of the whole family, or at least your closest family and friends. A diet does not just appear for one individual; it should be seen as being handed down from one generation to the next. Therefore, if an individual's diet needs change then chances are that their family's diet needs to change. If you and your client have the family, or at least key members of the family (i.e. in charge of buying and preparing food), 'on-board' then you have a much better chance of implementing the changes needed.

Obesity

In the media, we see headlines such as 'Doctors succumb to obesity epidemic' (Fair, 2015), where we learn that medical doctors are becoming overweight and obese at the about the same rate as the rest of us. We find out about the logistical challenges the obese and overweight population pose for hospital staff from articles such as 'Obesity epidemic weighs down hospitals' (Stark, 2015) and 'The heavy cost of obesity and how NSW health workers are responding' (Browne, 2015). The ABS (2013b) suggests that obesity is clearly a problem. Looking at Australians over the age of 18 years in 2011–2012, the ABS reports that 35.3% are overweight and 27.5% are obese. Not only is weight a problem for more than 62% of Australians in and of itself, but being overweight or obese is a risk factor for chronic illnesses such as CVD (e.g. hypertension) and type 2 diabetes.

Chronic illnesses are a huge burden not just on the individuals in question but on their families and society in general, so any sensible measures that can be taken to reduce the obesity epidemic should be considered carefully. Given that more of us are becoming overweight and obese every year, we need to act on this problem. In 1995, about 56% of Australians were overweight or obese, in 2007–2008 more than 61%, and in 2011–2012 more than 62% (ABS, 2013b). So what are the risk factors for becoming overweight or obese? What are we doing wrong?

In the NHMRC (2011) dietary guidelines, *television* watching was evaluated and found to be a risk factor for obesity and being overweight. However, the evidence was contradictory and a longitudinal study did not support this relationship. Given the changes in our interaction with television, where *internet screen time* has really replaced television time, one has to wonder if there is not a need to redefine the research into television viewing and expand it to screen time. The evidence was clearer when it came to risk factors such as *smoking during pregnancy* and *obesity status of parents*. If you are born to a mother who smoked during pregnancy, then you are at an increased risk of becoming overweight or obese. You are also at an increased risk of becoming overweight or obese if one or both of your parents are overweight or obese. The higher the *education* levels of your parents, especially your mother, the less likely you are to become overweight or obese. This is consistent with studies showing a relationship between low *socioeconomic status* and being overweight or obese. The NHMRC (2011) report also found that family-based behavioural interventions are effective in combating obesity. The report identified *sleep* as a potential risk factor for being overweight or obese; more sleep during childhood protects the individual against becoming overweight or obese later in life. Other issues to consider include low resting metabolic rate (a risk factor for increased weight gain), side effects from medication, and binge eating.

Motivators for food selection and consumption

In Australia we have identified factors such as time constraints, cost, and health issues (Betts et al., 1995; Lockie et al., 2002) as motivators for food selection and consumption. Students' consumption of fruit and vegetables has been found to be related to their parents' consumption (Young, Fors & Hayes, 2004). Families with young children may find that the consumption of fish and omega-3 enriched food will be influenced by taste and the preferences of younger family members (Rahmawaty et al., 2013). The more parents allow their children to influence food selection, the more vegetable consumption is going to decrease (Russell, Worsley & Liem, 2015). This will effectively make vegetables 'extinct' from the dining table. Parents driven by natural and ethical choices in food selection are more likely to have children who favour vegetables. Given that parents seem to be influenced strongly by food's health and nutrition values, there is hope yet for vegetable consumption in Australia.

Food producers need to examine the role of ethical and environmental motivators for food selection as consumers get better informed. Ethical treatment of the environment, including animals and plants, is likely to be strongly associated with consumers' environmental concerns. Combine this with for-profit food production and conflicts will inevitably occur. The popularity of organic food has met with scepticism about any health benefits and any environmental benefits have been met with arguments suggesting that organic food cannot feed the growing number of humans in the world. When it comes to the scare campaigns regarding population growth, it is recommended that you examine the work by Hans Rosling on the overpopulation myth and watch some of his documentaries. As for the lack of food production, that is clearly a myth as well; check out overpopulationisamyth.com. If you expand your research further, you will find that in the so-called developed countries we throw away 40 to 60% of produced food. The solution to feeding the world is better education, better access to healthcare, sustainable food production, equitable food distribution and regeneration of both land and sea.

Weight indices and health

There are a few weight indices available to researchers and healthcare professionals. The body mass index (BMI; weight/height^2 as in kg/m^2) has been used extensively in research and is easy to ascertain even without seeing your participants in person, by getting them to report their height and weight. However, self-reporting of height and weight is problematic for the BMI (Gorber et al., 2007), though the accuracy of self-report weight measures other than the BMI are also obviously going to be contested. It has been suggested that the BMI is not as good a predictor as other weight-related ratios such as the waist–hip ratio (WHR) and waist circumference. The WHR requires two measures, the waist below navel (no sucking in that stomach) and hips where largest, both measured in the same unit (e.g. cm). Divide the waist measure by the hip measure (waist/hip) and you have the WHR.

Would the obesity problem go away if we used a different index? The answer is 'no'. However, obesity rates vary depending on the index used (see Table 5.1). An Australian study (Dalton et al., 2003) examining more than 11 000 Australians (≥ 25 years) reported that using BMI, obesity was 19% for males and 22% for females, with WHR it was 10%

Table 5.1 Weight-related indices and observations associated with them (BMI = body mass index (kg/m^2); WHR = waist–hip ratio)

Observation	BMI (kg/m^2)	WHR	Waist circumference (cm)
overweight men	25.0 to 29.9	0.90 to 0.99	94 to 101.9
overweight women	25.0 to 29.9	0.80 to 0.84	80 to 87.9
obese men	≥ 30	≥ 1.00	≥ 102.0
obese women	≥ 30	≥ 0.85	≥ 88.0

Source: WHO, 2000

for males and 22% for females, and with waist circumference it was 27% for males and 34% for females. Examination of the association between the three weight measures and health outcomes (e.g. diabetes, hypertension) showed that all three weight measures have similar associations when adjusting for age. However, when unadjusted measures were used, the WHR had the strongest association with the different health outcomes. That said, the research findings did not conclude that any one of the three weight measures should no longer be used.

Nutrition summary

The evidence presented here backs up the NHMRC summary guidelines fairly strongly except maybe for fat and especially fat in dairy products, where the evidence is not strong enough to recommend low-fat options over standard full-fat dairy products. Furthermore, the benefits of tea (black and green) seem downplayed given recent research findings. That said, overall, the work by the NHMRC is very valuable and should help guide you in your role as a healthcare professional. The information presented, along with your own examination of the latest scientific evidence, should enable you to help your clients towards better nutritional selection. It is worthwhile examining how specific populations respond to different interventions, such as how the population of those with a CVD respond to reduced salt intake in their diet and how the population of those with type 2 diabetes respond to increased fibre in their diet. Furthermore, how do we answer questions about the underlying causal factors that give fruits and vegetables their protective edge when it comes to our health?

Mini case study 5.1

Given the negative effects of alcohol on people's health and society in general, you would be justified in wondering why people drink. Imagine that you are a healthcare professional or a researcher and that you have been asked to explain to an audience of concerned parents in a small (about 7000 inhabitants) rural community why their children drink alcohol.

Critical thinking questions

1. How would you approach this task? Consider what you need to know about the problem, what answers your audience is looking for and what actions they might be able to take.
2. Apply models such as the health belief model to try to understand and predict if someone is likely to start drinking. You can also consider yourself and your friends in relation to your approach to alcohol consumption and examine the influences you experienced for the approach you have taken. Make sure you consider factors such as social and cultural, peer influence/pressure, norms, genetics and price of alcohol. When it comes to the price of alcohol consider an Australian study by Byrnes et al. (2013) examining the effects of price on alcohol consumption patterns.

Mini case study 5.2

Imagine that you are a health psychologist and that you need to get your client to change her diet. All you know at this stage is that the client has just had an operation following a cardiovascular incident and that there is a clear need for her to stop smoking, change her diet and increase her activity levels. You also know that her diet before the operation consisted of a high-sugar cereal with milk for breakfast, pies and other quick snack type foods from cafes for lunch, and then a takeaway meal for dinner. Your client is not overweight and has no family close by where she lives and works.

Critical thinking questions

1. Where would you start with this client? How do you move from a limited lifestyle picture to a more complete lifestyle picture?
2. How will you try to maximise adherence to your recommendations (hint: food diary apps)?

Eating disorders

While having a good diet may help reduce the risk of illness, an inadequate diet will increase the risk of illness and death. It is estimated that about 9% of Australians are affected by **eating disorders** such as bulimia and anorexia nervosa (National Eating Disorders Collaboration, 2014). Eating disorders are a mental illness that is sometimes mistakenly portrayed as a lifestyle choice. Eating disorders increase the risk of death (e.g. suicide and medical issues) more than sixfold and cost Australia more than $69 billion per year according to the National Eating Disorders Collaboration (2014). Affective disorders and substance abuse are **comorbid** with eating disorders. The risk factors for eating disorders are: being female, Caucasian and adolescent; dieting; and having a distorted body image (Striegel-Moore & Bulik, 2007). However, generalising across all types of eating disorders risks hiding important relationships such as the fact that onset of bulimia and anorexia nervosa after adolescence is unlikely, anorexia nervosa is linked to socioeconomic status (i.e. affluence) and females may have higher rates of bulimia nervosa than males as the diagnostic criteria may have an 'inbuilt' sex bias. Future research needs to examine the interaction between genes and environment to understand eating disorders. A longitudinal Australian study of adolescents by Patton et al. (1999) suggests that dieting is an important risk factor for eating disorders while exercise is less so. Eight percent of the 15-year-old girls in this sample showed a severe level of dieting while 60% showed moderate levels of dieting.

Causes

So what might cause eating disorders? Theories about eating disorders being caused by sexual abuse have not been supported (Stice, 2002), and other theories and suggestions (such as perfectionism) and family-related measures (such as function and interaction) have not been found to be risk factors (Jacobi et al., 2004). Studies into the causes of eating disorders tend to suffer from various limitations such as being **cross-sectional** rather than longitudinal, having limited sample sizes, high dropout levels, and varying definitions of eating disorders or inconsistent inclusion of different eating disorders. As a result, future researchers will have plenty of opportunity to improve on our understanding of eating disorders, such as causes, prevention, progression and treatment. Future studies could combine biological and psychological factors to help get a more complete picture of eating disorders.

Anorexia nervosa

Anorexia nervosa is a mental disorder whereby the sufferer restricts his or her food consumption, largely refusing to eat and sometimes exercising to the extreme to promote weight loss. The mortality rates for sufferers of anorexia nervosa are higher than for the general population, with a **standardised mortality ratio (SMR)** of 5.86 (95% CI, 4.17, 8.26) suggesting that the mortality rate is 486% higher among those suffering anorexia nervosa than those without anorexia nervosa (Arcelus et al., 2011). The age of seeking treatment is a strong predictor of mortality: under 15 years of age, SMR = 3; 15 to 19 years of age, SMR = 10; 20 to 29 years of age, SMR = 18; and then a big drop for those older than 29 years of age, SMR = 6.

One of the problems with treating mental illness is the large number of comorbid disorders the client suffers and the complex and early history of some of these disorders. Childhood anxiety disorders, for instance, may well be a risk factor for developing anorexia later in life. Kaye et al. (2004) reported that out of 97 anorexia sufferers, 55% had at least one anxiety disorder, 35% had obsessive-compulsive disorder and 22% had social phobia.

Bulimia nervosa

Bulimia nervosa is characterised by binge eating behaviour that is then followed by behaviours trying to 'compensate' for the binge such as purging (e.g. vomiting, laxatives). The risk of mortality associated with bulimia nervosa has been reported as SMR = 1.93, suggesting an increase in mortality rate among bulimia nervosa sufferers 93% higher than in the comparison group (Arcelus et al., 2011). Bulimia nervosa may have its roots in childhood anxiety disorders, not unlike anorexia. Individuals who suffer bulimia are likely to suffer from anxiety and obsessive-compulsive disorder (Kaye et al., 2004); of 282 bulimia sufferers 68% had at least one anxiety disorder, 40% had obsessive-compulsive disorder and 16% had social phobia.

Body image

Our body image captures our thoughts, both negative and positive, about our physical appearance. When building a healthy body image, children and adolescents need to stay away from the array of magazines that present images of airbrushed celebrities as impossible models of perfection. Children and adolescents should have a healthy appreciation for the amount of work done by professionals to make celebrities look anything but human. But is the media to blame? A news report by Roxby (2014) suggests that we should not just look at the 'body perfect' in magazines or in TV programs/movies but also at social media, where children and adolescents today are inundated by information shaping their perception of body image. There have been calls for body image lessons in school in the UK. These body image interventions have been evaluated and found to show some promising results for body esteem and thin-ideal internalisation (Sharpe et al., 2013). In 2011, the Australian government developed the Respect Every Body information kit that could be incorporated into the curriculum (Rout, 2011). The Australian Medical Association (AMA, 2009) sees the popular media as a clear culprit in distorting body image, especially for children and adolescents. It seems clear that children start to worry about body image early (Australian Institute of Family Studies, 2014), potentially leading to anxiety and other disorders such as anorexia, bulimia and obsessive-compulsive disorder.

Treatments

An evaluation of treatments by the Australian Psychological Society (2010) shows that eating disorders are among the mental illnesses hardest to treat. That said, for adults several interventions have a good rating; the higher the rating level the better the evidence for the efficiency of the intervention. When it comes to treating anorexia nervosa in adults, cognitive behavioural therapy (CBT) has a level III-2 'rating'. However, for bulimia nervosa and binge eating CBT has a level I rating. For anorexia nervosa, both family therapy as well as psychodynamic therapy have a level II rating. Other interventions for bulimia that have good evidential support include interpersonal psychotherapy (level III-3), dialectical behaviour therapy (level II) and self-help (level II). For binge eating, dialectical behaviour therapy (level II) and self-help (level I) have been supported.

When it comes to treating anorexia nervosa, bulimia nervosa and binge eating in children and adolescents, CBT has insufficient evidence (IE rating). This is worrying as these are the times when these disorders are likely to cause the greatest harm mentally and physically. The only intervention for anorexia nervosa in children and adolescence that has enough evidence is family intervention, but it only has a level I rating. For bulimia nervosa, only two treatments have enough evidence to be rated: family and self-help, both with level II(A) rating. When it comes to binge eating, all of the treatments reviewed have an IE rating.

Recent studies suggest that mindfulness may help deal with eating disorders such as body image (Alberts, Thewissen & Raes, 2012) and binge eating (Katterman et al., 2014). Furthermore, interventions based on CBT may have even stronger outcomes than mindfulness when it comes to binge eating (Vocks et al., 2010). In adolescents and adults, CBT has been found to be more effective than treatment based on medication for bulimia based on outcomes such as binge and purge behaviours, depression, and eating attitudes (Whittal, Agras & Gould, 2000).

Mini case study 5.3

Consider a situation in which researchers start reporting the negative effects of certain food products (e.g. fast food, soft drinks). Presumably, the companies involved will want to defend their market share and the products in question. Imagine that you work as a researcher publishing in this area and a healthcare professional advising your clients about their diet.

Critical thinking questions

1. Consider the mini case study. If you were dealing with companies with a vested interest, what would you expect these companies to be doing to undermine the research findings in question, including yours, and what would these companies be doing to present a positive image to governments and the public? Should you fight back? How would you fight back?
2. Consider the mini case study and critical thinking questions in terms of other products, such as tobacco and sugar.

Exercise

We call physical activity that requires effort and is conducted to improve or maintain physical health 'exercise'. A definition like this implies that exercise is planned and structured and probably not much fun. Maybe we need to examine this definition a bit more closely. If an activity helps to maintain physical health, then does it matter if it is planned or not? And what about the perception of effort? What if your parents work hard in their garden and walk regularly? Is that exercise? Does it matter if your parents do not plan these activities or even consider them an effort? Start thinking about exercise and consider the definition carefully. Consider effort and two of your friends, one who is physically fit and the other who is not physically fit. Clearly the same activity, such as a 1 km walk, could be considered exercise for the unfit friend, at least in relation to effort, while for your fit friend such an activity could hardly be called exercise as it involves little to no effort. However, if the outcome (i.e. improved physical health) defines exercise then maybe neither could be said to have exercised. The 1 km walk may not have any benefits for your fit friend but it may have damaging effects on your unfit friend, as the latter put in too much effort, which overexerted them. The take-home message is that when you are conducting research into exercise you need to have a clear **operationalisation** of exercise. As a healthcare professional, you might like to incorporate a broad definition of exercise. This may help you empower your clients to reconsider and increase their activity levels. For example, when assessing your clients' activity levels, you might like to include an everyday walking and gardening activity. Even if such activities are not deliberately conducted to improve physical health, they are still contributing to improved physical and mental health. This will, in turn, help your clients realise that they can incorporate physical activity (exercise, if you like) into their daily life. This may also help your clients overcome obstacles towards increasing their physical activity levels, especially by overcoming any set ideas that exercise can only happen in a gym or a similarly structured environment.

Health benefits of exercise

Physically fit and active individuals have a clear advantage over their unfit counterparts when it comes to mental and physical health. Australian cross-sectional studies show these benefits (Brown et al., 2000) as well as Australian intervention studies (Bretland & Thorsteinsson, 2015). The question is no longer *if* physical activity improves health but rather what underlying factors explain the causal relationship between physical activity and health. Many factors have been suggested, with the main emphasis on biological factors such as reduced blood pressure, reduced inflammation and improved levels/ homeostasis of lipoprotein, triglyceride, glucose and insulin. Psychological factors associated with exercise may also play an important role, increasing levels of wellbeing and reducing stress and depression. These psychological factors may, in turn, affect and be affected by endorphin levels.

Physical health

Exercise has clear physical health benefits. In a review by Warburton, Nicol and Bredin (2006), a strong case is made for the health benefits of both physical activity and being physically fit. The corresponding danger of being inactive and unfit is also clear. The terms 'physically active' and 'physically fit' are used interchangeably in this chapter, but when you read research reports remember that self-report measures are generally used to assess physical activity while various objective measures are generally used to assess fitness.

The research literature consistently shows that being unfit, as compared with being fit, means that you have a higher risk of all causes of death, premature death, death due to CVD and death due to cancer (e.g. breast and colon). The risk to your health from being unfit are similar to the risks associated with being a smoker or being obese (Warburton et al., 2006). Thus being fit is clearly an effective *primary prevention* when it comes to your health.

The good news is that even limited improvement in fitness will see your risks reduced. As a healthcare professional, you can pass this knowledge on to your clients, thus empowering them to gradually improve their fitness through increases in physical activity and to set realistic goals. Remind your clients that being fit is an effective primary prevention for ill-health such as CVD. However, clients with CVD will also benefit from improved fitness, thus providing a *secondary prevention* for ill-health. Gone are the days when patients with CVD were told to take it easy and never exert themselves. Being physically fit and active can halt disease progression and even help reverse some disease progression, not just for those suffering from CVD but also type 2 diabetes or those at risk of developing type 2 diabetes (Warburton et al., 2006). For type 2 diabetes sufferers, simply walking 2 hours per week will reduce the risk of any cause of premature death.

Mental health

Exercise has not just physical health benefits; it also has psychological (i.e. mental) health benefits. Physical exercise can help reduce both state and trait anxiety (Petruzzello et al., 1991). An Australian exercise intervention study has shown exercise to have positive psychological effects, such as increased wellbeing and accomplishment, while reducing distress, emotional exhaustion and burnout (Bretland & Thorsteinsson, 2015). A large-scale survey from Canada shows clear benefits where being physically active not only directly improves mental and physical health but also helps to reduce the impact of stressful events (e.g. stressful work settings), leading to overall better mental and physical health (Iwasaki, Zuzanek & Mannell, 2001).

As a secondary prevention, exercise has been found to reduce cancer-related fatigue in cancer patients (Brown et al., 2011), depression in depressive patients (Josefsson, Lindwall & Archer, 2014) and depression in patients suffering a chronic illness (Herring et al., 2012). The link between increased exercise and reduced depression may partly be explained by serotonin levels, as exercise may lead to increased 'effectiveness' of serotonin levels.

Promoting exercise

So given the clear health benefits of being fit, what is the level of physical activity in Australia? Data from the ABS (2013a) suggests that children (5 to 17 years) spend about 1½ hours per day being physically active. At the same time, more than 2 hours per day were spent on activity that involved watching a screen; only 6 minutes per day were spent on homework-related activity. Overall, more than 75% of children have 1 hour or more of daily sedentary screen time. The balance between screen time and physical activity time changes across the age groups, with physical activity decreasing while screen time increases. This trend, though not based on longitudinal data, is worrying, as being physically fit will improve academic performance along with personal and social responsibility (Bauman et al., 2002).

Currently, children over the age of 10 and adolescents don't seem to get enough physical activity and we need to find out why in order to improve the situation. We need to make sure that children not only maintain but increase the time spent being physically active. We also need more research to examine how positive peer pressure can be directed in ways that increase activity levels. Are children and adolescents in Australia dropping out of organised sport because of its competitive nature? How can we direct the focus away from competition with others and towards improving oneself and enjoying the activity? Organised sports in Australia help to keep physical activity levels high among young Australians but more needs to be done to help maintain these levels of activity and to make sure the activity is enjoyable.

Barriers to exercise

A survey of Australian students (median age = 20 years) suggests some predictors of lack of fitness (Leslie et al., 1999). Inactivity, for males and females, was associated with lack of social support from family and friends and also with lack of enjoyment of activity. If you started playing soccer because your friend was playing, would you stop if they stopped going and you no longer had a friend to walk with to and from practice and matches? Australian cities and towns need to be planned to enable their inhabitants to walk in aesthetically pleasing environments (e.g. Ball et al., 2001; Humpel et al., 2004). Furthermore, people seem to need companionship on their walks, be it from a dog or another person.

Motivation

As a healthcare professional, you might expect your clients to be motivated to exercise or to keep physically fit if they have intrinsic autonomous regulation motives for exercising; in plain English, clients exercise because they like it. There is some support for this notion (Schutte & McNeil, 2015; Wilson & Rodgers, 2004), suggesting that you need to find physical activity that your clients like. This is not exactly surprising and the take-home message is that you need to work with your clients to find multiple ways to increase their activity levels.

Mini case study 5.4

Imagine that you are a healthcare professional and that you have a client who works in an office in front of a computer screen all day, 'slumped down' in an office chair. This client gets very few breaks at work. After work the client spends hours studying in a small room; think student accommodation.

Critical thinking questions

1. What steps would you take to help the client to become more active? (**Hint**: Consider all the 'tools' you have available, such as apps for mobiles, wrist activity bands/trackers, HBM and CBT.)
2. If you recommend to your clients that they use activity bands, how would you enable them to get the most out of using such technology?
3. When you imagined your client, did you imagine a male or a female client? Consider the questions above again, but this time change the sex of your client from what you imagined before. Did your recommendations change?

Research

The future of research into nutrition, exercise and health is clearly going to be linked to technology, especially the use of devices associated with smartphones, such as smart watches. Currently, apps are being used in relation to mood disorders (Torous & Powell, 2015), and there are plenty of smartphone apps and hardware that can collect physiological readings such as blood pressure and heart rate (Withings, 2015). As a future researcher or healthcare professional, you need to note that in order to gather and use physiological data you need reliable and valid hardware and software, and much of what is on offer has not been validated (O'Riordan, 2015). Thus there are many apps available with great potential, but they are in need of independent validation. In the future, your health app may even tell you that you are about to have a stroke or a heart attack and suggest what action you might like to take while you wait for the ambulance that your health app has already called for and to which it has communicated health information.

When it comes to conducting research into the effects of diets, you will find that everyone is an expert or has an opinion. The headlines speak clearly of the importance of diet research and the importance of separating fact from fiction. Headlines such as 'Are some diets "mass murder"?' (Smith, 2014) are not from the newspapers but the *British Medical Journal* (*BMJ*). Smith explains in plain English the difficulties faced by diet researchers when the variation between individuals' diets is so great, and the difficulty involved in trying to isolate individual food compounds such as saturated fats, sugar or fibre in order to support some sort of causal relationship with health. We need more well-designed longitudinal human studies and longitudinal animal experimental studies, with the latter designed to span generations.

In **quasi-experimental studies**, researchers are comparing existing groups such as individuals who drink alcohol in moderation compared to individuals who abstain from drinking alcohol. Drawing conclusions from such comparison studies in isolation from other evidence (e.g. experimental studies) is problematic because the groups may exist as a result of different factors that can in turn affect (or confound) the outcome. For example, if you were evaluating a study of alcohol consumption that compared the health of drinkers (moderate) versus non-drinkers, you might find that the drinkers are healthier than the non-drinkers. However, you cannot draw the conclusion that drinking alcohol has health benefits based on this outcome. Why not? Well, what if you looked in the participant section of the report and discovered that the participants are from a country where moderate alcohol consumption is the norm from an early age? You should then ask yourself, why are there non-drinkers in this country? Then you might find that the participants that are in the non-drinking group had been ordered by their medical doctor not to drink alcohol because of ill-health. Now the findings are not so clear. The non-drinkers were already suffering ill-health before they quit drinking so the comparison between the two groups for this study is meaningless at best, misleading at worst.

Summary

- What we can agree on is that for improved health, the population generally needs to increase its consumption of vegetables, fruit and fibre while reducing its consumption of sugar-sweetened beverages, alcohol and fast food.
- The benefits of exercise to mental and physical health seem clear, but when it comes to nutrition there are still plenty of limitations to our knowledge.
- One of the key limitations is a lack of well-designed human longitudinal studies and longitudinal animal experimental studies that can be designed to span generations.
- Eating disorders are deadly mental disorders that are difficult to treat; however, the sooner the diagnosis, the better the prognosis. These mental disorders seem to share common causal roots in anxiety and distorted body image.
- Healthcare professionals need to help activate social networks to get their clients off the couch and on their feet, at least for a walk or a spot of gardening.

Suggested weblinks

Refer to the companion website at www.cambridge.edu.au/academic/healthpsychology for a list of suggested weblinks.

References

ABS. (2013a). *Australian Health Survey: Physical Activity, 2011–12*. Cat no. 4364.0.55.004. Canberra: Australian Bureau of Statistics. Retrieved from: http://www.abs.gov.au/ausstats/abs@.nsf/lookup/462FBA87B642FCA4CA257BAC0015F3CE?opendocument#Bauman_0

—— (2013b). *Overweight and Obesity. Australian Health Survey: Updated Results, 2011–2012*. Cat. no. 4364.0.55.003. Canberra: Australian Bureau of Statistics. Retrieved from: http://www.abs.gov.au/AUSSTATS/abs@.nsf/2f762f95845417aeca25706c00834efa/33C64022ABB5ECD5CA257B8200179437?opendocument

—— (2014a). *Australian Health Survey: Nutrition First Results – Foods and Nutrients, 2011–12 (alcoholic beverages)*. Cat. no. 4364.0.55.007. Canberra: Australian Bureau of Statistics. Retrieved from: http://www.abs.gov.au/ausstats/abs@.nsf/Lookup/by%20Subject/4364.0.55.007~2011–12~Main%20Features~Alcoholic%20beverages~729

—— (2014b). *Australian Health Survey: Nutrition First Results – Foods and Nutrients, 2011–12 (non-alcoholic beverages)*. Cat. no. 4364.0.55.007. Canberra: Australian Bureau of Statistics. Retrieved from: http://www.abs.gov.au/ausstats/abs@.nsf/Lookup/by%20Subject/4364.0.55.007~2011–12~Main%20Features~Non-alcoholic%20beverages~701

AIHW. (2011). Natural Health Priority Areas. Canberra: Australian Institute of Health and Welfare. Retrieved from http://www.aihw.gov.au/health-priority-areas

Alberts, H. J. E. M., Thewissen, R. & Raes, L. (2012). Dealing with problematic eating behaviour. The effects of a mindfulness-based intervention on eating behaviour, food cravings, dichotomous thinking and body image concern. *Appetite*, *58*, 847–51. doi: http://dx.doi.org/10.1016/j.appet.2012.01.009

AMA. (2009). *Body image and health – 2002. Revised 2009*. Canberra, Australia: Australian Medical Association. Retrieved from: https://ama.com.au/position-statement/body-image-and-health-2002-revised-2009.

Anderson, J. W., Baird, P., Davis, R. H., Ferreri, S., Knudtson, M., Koraym, A., … Williams, C. L. (2009). Health benefits of dietary fiber. *Nutrition Reviews*, *67*, 188–205. doi: http://dx.doi.org/10.1111/j.1753-4887.2009.00189.x

Arcelus, J., Mitchell, A. J., Wales, J. & Nielsen, S. (2011). Mortality rates in patients with anorexia nervosa and other eating disorders: a meta-analysis of 36 studies. *Archives of General Psychiatry*, *68*, 724–31. doi: http://dx.doi.org/10.1001/archgenpsychiatry.2011.74

Australian Beverages Council. (2013). Caffeine – the facts. Retrieved from: http://australianbeverages.org/for-consumers/caffeine-facts/

Australian Government Department of Health. (2008). National binge drinking campaign backgrounder: the costs (Fact sheet: Don't turn a night out into a nightmare). Retrieved from: http://www.drinkingnightmare.gov.au/internet/drinkingnightmare/publishing.nsf/Content/B2D387C687D03FC9CA2574FD007CA91C/$File/The%20costs.pdf

Australian Indigenous HealthInfoNet. (2015). Overview of Australian Indigenous health status, 2014. Retrieved from: http://www.healthinfonet.ecu.edu.au/uploads/docs/overview_of_indigenous_health_2014.pdf

Australian Institute of Family Studies. (2014). Primary school children concerned with body image. Retrieved from: https://aifs.gov.au/media-releases/primary-school-children-concerned-body-image

Australian Psychological Society. (2010). *Evidence-based Psychological Interventions in the Treatment of Mental Disorders: A Literature Review (3rd edn)*. Melbourne: APS.

Autier, P. & Gandini, S. (2007). Vitamin D supplementation and total mortality: A meta-analysis of randomized controlled trials. *Archives of Internal Medicine*, *167*, 1730–7. doi: http://dx.doi.org/10.1001/archinte.167.16.1730

Avena, N. M., Rada, P. & Hoebel, B. G. (2008). Evidence for sugar addiction: behavioral and neurochemical effects of intermittent, excessive sugar intake. *Neuroscience & Biobehavioral Reviews*, *32*, 20–39. doi: http://dx.doi.org/10.1016/j.neubiorev.2007.04.019

Ball, K., Bauman, A., Leslie, E. & Owen, N. (2001). Perceived environmental aesthetics and convenience and company are associated with walking for exercise among Australian adults. *Preventive Medicine*, *33*, 434–40. doi: http://dx.doi.org/10.1006/pmed.2001.0912

Bauman, A., Bellew, B., Vita, P., Brown, W. & Owen, N. (2002). *Getting Australia Active: Towards Better Practice for the Promotion of Physical Activity*. Melbourne: National Public Health Partnership.

Betts, N. M., Amos, R. J., Georgiou, C., Hoerr, S. L., Ivaturi, R., Keim, K. S., … Voichick, J. (1995). What young adults say about factors affecting their food intake. *Ecology of Food and Nutrition*, *34*, 59–64. doi: http://dx.doi.org/10.1080/03670244.1995.9991447

Bhupathiraju, S. N., Tobias, D. K., Malik, V. S., Pan, A., Hruby, A., Manson, J. E., … Hu, F. B. (2014). Glycemic index, glycemic load, and risk of type 2 diabetes: results from 3 large US cohorts and an updated meta-analysis. *The American Journal of Clinical Nutrition*, ajcn. 079533. doi: http://dx.doi.org/10.3945/ajcn.113.079533

Bischoff-Ferrari, H. A., Willett, W. C., Wong, J. B., Giovannucci, E., Dietrich, T. & Dawson-Hughes, B. (2005). Fracture prevention with vitamin D supplementation: a meta-analysis of randomized controlled trials. *Journal of the American Medical Association*, *293*, 2257–64. doi: http://dx.doi.org/10.1001/jama.293.18.2257

Bjelakovic, G., Nikolova, D., Gluud, L. L., Simonetti, R. G. & Gluud, C. (2007). Mortality in randomized trials of antioxidant supplements for primary and secondary prevention: systematic review and meta-analysis. *JAMA*, *297*, 842–57. doi: http://dx.doi.org/10.1001/jama.297.8.842

Blaisdell, A. P., Lau, Y. L. M., Telminova, E., Lim, H. C., Fan, B., Fast, C. D., … Pendergrass, D. C. (2014). Food quality and motivation: A refined low-fat diet induces obesity and impairs performance on a progressive ratio schedule of instrumental lever pressing in rats. *Physiology & Behavior*, *128*, 220–5. doi: http://dx.doi.org/10.1016/j.physbeh.2014.02.025

Bretland, R. J. & Thorsteinsson, E. B. (2015). Reducing workplace burnout: the relative benefits of cardiovascular and resistance exercise. *PeerJ*, *3*, e891. doi: http://dx.doi.org/10.7717/peerj.891

Brown, J. C., Huedo-Medina, T. B., Pescatello, L. S., Pescatello, S. M., Ferrer, R. A. & Johnson, B. T. (2011). Efficacy of exercise interventions in modulating cancer-related fatigue among adult cancer survivors: a meta-analysis. *Cancer Epidemiology Biomarkers & Prevention*, *20*, 123–33. doi: http://dx.doi.org/10.1158/1055–9965.EPI-10–0988

Brown, L., Rosner, B., Willett, W. W. & Sacks, F. M. (1999). Cholesterol-lowering effects of dietary fiber: a meta-analysis. *The American Journal of Clinical Nutrition*, *69*, 30–42.

Brown, W. J., Mishra, G., Lee, C. & Bauman, A. (2000). Leisure time physical activity in Australian women: relationship with well being and symptoms. *Research Quarterly for Exercise and Sport*, *71*, 206–16. doi: http://dx.doi.org/10.1080/02701367.2000.10608901

Browne, R. (2015, June 13). The heavy cost of obesity and how NSW health workers are responding. *Sydney Morning Herald*. Retrieved from: http://www.smh.com.au/nsw/the-heavy-cost-of-obesity-and-how-nsw-health-workers-are-responding-20150613-ghmxbu.html

Brunner, E., White, I., Thorogood, M., Bristow, A., Curle, D. & Marmot, M. (1997). Can dietary interventions change diet and cardiovascular risk factors? A meta-analysis of randomized controlled trials. *American Journal of Public Health*, *87*, 1415–22. doi: http://dx.doi.org/10.2105/AJPH.87.9.1415

Burke, L. (2014). Did energy drinks kill Mick Clarke? Grieving mum calls for ban. news.com.au. Retrieved from: http://www.news.com.au/lifestyle/health/health-problems/did-energy-drinks-kill-mick-clarke-grieving-mum-calls-for-ban/news-story/d38b6d434cf5d62adf392ed11cd5a239

Byrnes, J., Shakeshaft, A., Petrie, D. & Doran, C. (2013). Can harms associated with high-intensity drinking be reduced by increasing the price of alcohol? *Drug and Alcohol Review*, *32*, 27–30. doi: http://dx.doi.org/10.1111/j.1465-3362.2012.00482.x

Carey, J. (2008). Do cholesterol drugs do any good? *BusinessWeek*, 52–9. Retrieved from: http://einarbthorsteinsson.blogspot.com.au/2015/05/health-psychology.html

Cholesterol Treatment Trialists' (CTT) Collaborators. (2005). Efficacy and safety of cholesterol-lowering treatment: prospective meta-analysis of data from 90 056 participants in 14 randomised trials of statins. *The Lancet*, *366*, 1267–78. doi: http://dx.doi.org/10.1016/S0140-6736(05)67394-1

Chung, M., Ma, J., Patel, K., Berger, S., Lau, J. & Lichtenstein, A. H. (2014). Fructose, high-fructose corn syrup, sucrose, and nonalcoholic fatty liver disease or indexes of liver health: a systematic review and meta-analysis. *The American Journal of Clinical Nutrition*, *100*, 833–49. doi: http://dx.doi.org/10.3945/ajcn.114.086314

Collison, K. S., Makhoul, N. J., Zaidi, M. Z., Saleh, S. M., Andres, B., Inglis, A., ... Al-Mohanna, F. A. (2012). Gender dimorphism in aspartame-induced impairment of spatial cognition and insulin sensitivity. *PloS ONE*, *7*, e31570. doi: http://dx.doi.org/10.1371/journal.pone.0031570

Dalton, M., Cameron, A., Zimmet, P., Shaw, J., Jolley, D., Dunstan, D. & Welborn, T. (2003). Waist circumference, waist–hip ratio and body mass index and their correlation with cardiovascular disease risk factors in Australian adults. *Journal of Internal Medicine*, *254*, 555–63. doi: http://dx.doi.org/10.1111/j.1365-2796.2003.01229.x

Dansinger, M. L., Gleason, J. A., Griffith, J. L., Selker, H. P. & Schaefer, E. J. (2005). Comparison of the Atkins, Ornish, Weight Watchers, and Zone diets for weight loss and heart disease risk reduction: a randomized trial. *Journal of the American Medical Association*, *293*, 43–53. doi: http://dx.doi.org/10.1001/jama.293.1.43

Fair, K. (2015, July 11). Doctors succumb to obesity epidemic. *Sydney Morning Herald*. Retrieved from: http://www.smh.com.au/nsw/doctors-succumb-to-obesity-epidemic-20150711-gi99o3.html

Fairfax NZ. (2013, February 13). Is Coke addictive? Coroner takes on soft drinks giant. *Sydney Morning Herald*. Retrieved from: http://www.smh.com.au/world/is-coke-addictive-coroner-takes-on-soft-drinks-giant-20130212-2ebor

Forshee, R. A., Anderson, P. A. & Storey, M. L. (2008). Sugar-sweetened beverages and body mass index in children and adolescents: a meta-analysis. *The American Journal of Clinical Nutrition*, *87*, 1662–71.

Gardner, C. D., Kiazand, A., Alhassan, S., Kim, S., Stafford, R. S., Balise, R. R., ... King, A. C. (2007). Comparison of the Atkins, Zone, Ornish, and LEARN diets for change in weight and related risk factors among overweight premenopausal women: the A TO Z Weight Loss Study: A randomized trial. *Journal of the American Medical Association*, *297*, 969–77. doi: http://dx.doi.org/10.1001/jama.297.9.969

Gardner, E., Ruxton, C. & Leeds, A. (2007). Black tea – helpful or harmful? A review of the evidence. *European Journal of Clinical Nutrition*, *61*, 3–18. doi: http://dx.doi.org/10.1038/sj.ejcn.1602489

Gorber, S. C., Tremblay, M., Moher, D. & Gorber, B. (2007). A comparison of direct vs. self-report measures for assessing height, weight and body mass index: a systematic review. *Obesity Reviews*, *8*, 307–26. doi: http://dx.doi.org/10.1111/j.1467-789X.2007.00347.x

Greyling, A., Ras, R. T., Zock, P. L., Lorenz, M., Hopman, M. T., Thijssen, D. H. & Draijer, R. (2014). The effect of black tea on blood pressure: a systematic review with meta-analysis of randomized controlled trials. *PLoS ONE*, *9*, e103247. doi: http://dx.doi.org/10.1371/journal.pone.0103247

Herring, M. P., Puetz, T. W., O'Connor, P. J. & Dishman, R. K. (2012). Effect of exercise training on depressive symptoms among patients with a chronic illness: a systematic review and meta-analysis of randomized controlled trials. *Archives of Internal Medicine*, *172*, 101–11. doi: http://dx.doi.org/10.1001/archinternmed.2011.696

Homocysteine Lowering Trialists' Collaboration. (1998). Lowering blood homocysteine with folic acid based supplements: meta-analysis of randomised trials. *BMJ*, *316*, 894–8.

Huang, T. & Zhang, X. (2015). Dietary fiber intake and mortality from all causes, cardiovascular disease, cancer, infectious diseases and others: a meta-analysis of 42 prospective cohort studies with 1,752,848 participants. *North American Journal of Medicine and Science*, *8*, 59–67. doi: http://dx.doi.org/10.7156/najms.2015.0802059

Humpel, N., Owen, N., Leslie, E., Marshall, A. L., Bauman, A. E. & Sallis, J. F. (2004). Associations of location and perceived environmental attributes with walking in neighborhoods. *American Journal of Health Promotion*, *18*, 239–42.

Iwasaki, Y., Zuzanek, J. & Mannell, R. C. (2001). The effects of physically active leisure on stress-health relationships. *Canadian Journal of Public Health*, *92*, 214–18.

Jacobi, C., Hayward, C., de Zwaan, M., Kraemer, H. C. & Agras, W. S. (2004). Coming to terms with risk factors for eating disorders: Application of risk terminology and suggestions for a general taxonomy. *Psychological Bulletin*, *130*, 19–65. doi: http://dx.doi.org/10.1037/0033-2909.130.1.19

Josefsson, T., Lindwall, M. & Archer, T. (2014). Physical exercise intervention in depressive disorders: meta-analysis and systematic review. *Scandinavian Journal of Medicine & Science in Sports*, *24*, 259–72. doi: http://dx.doi.org/10.1111/sms.12050

Katan, M. B., Brouwer, I. A., Clarke, R., Geleijnse, J. M. & Mensink, R. P. (2010). Saturated fat and heart disease. *The American Journal of Clinical Nutrition*, *92*, 459–60.

Katterman, S. N., Kleinman, B. M., Hood, M. M., Nackers, L. M. & Corsica, J. A. (2014). Mindfulness meditation as an intervention for binge eating, emotional eating, and weight loss: a systematic review. *Eating Behaviors*, *15*, 197–204. doi: http://dx.doi.org/10.1016/j.eatbeh.2014.01.005

Kaye, W. H., Bulik, C. M., Thornton, L., Barbarich, N., Masters, K. & Group, P. F. C. (2004). Comorbidity of anxiety disorders with anorexia and bulimia nervosa. *American Journal of Psychiatry*, *161*, 2215–21. doi: http://dx.doi.org/10.1176/appi.ajp.161.12.2215

Leslie, E., Owen, N., Salmon, J., Bauman, A., Sallis, J. F. & Lo, S. K. (1999). Insufficiently active Australian college students: perceived personal, social, and environmental influences. *Preventive Medicine*, *28*, 20–7. doi: http://dx.doi.org/10.1006/pmed.1998.0375

Liu, R. H. (2003). Health benefits of fruit and vegetables are from additive and synergistic combinations of phytochemicals. *The American Journal of Clinical Nutrition*, *78*, 517S–20S.

Lockie, S., Lyons, K., Lawrence, G. & Mummery, K. (2002). Eating 'green': motivations behind organic food consumption in Australia. *Sociologia Ruralis*, *42*, 23–40. doi: http://dx.doi.org/10.1111/1467-9523.00200

Ma, Y., Olendzki, B., Chiriboga, D., Hebert, J. R., Li, Y., Li, W., ... Ockene, I. S. (2005). Association between dietary carbohydrates and body weight. *American Journal of Epidemiology*, *161*, 359–67. doi: http://dx.doi.org/10.1093/aje/kwi051

Macedo, A. F., Taylor, F. C., Casas, J. P., Adler, A., Prieto-Merino, D. & Ebrahim, S. (2014). Unintended effects of statins from observational studies in the general population: systematic review and meta-analysis. *BMC Medicine*, *12*, 51. doi: http://dx.doi.org/10.1186/1741-7015-12-51

Malik, V. S., Pan, A., Willett, W. C. & Hu, F. B. (2013). Sugar-sweetened beverages and weight gain in children and adults: a systematic review and meta-analysis. *The American Journal of Clinical Nutrition*, *98*, 1084–102. doi: http://dx.doi.org/10.3945/ajcn.113.058362

Malik, V. S., Popkin, B. M., Bray, G. A., Després, J.-P., Willett, W. C. & Hu, F. B. (2010). Sugar-sweetened beverages and risk of metabolic syndrome and type 2 diabetes: a meta-analysis. *Diabetes Care*, *33*, 2477–83. doi: http://dx.doi.org/10.2337/dc10-1079

Malik, V. S., Willett, W. C. & Hu, F. B. (2009). Sugar-sweetened beverages and BMI in children and adolescents: reanalyses of a meta-analysis. *The American Journal of Clinical Nutrition*, *89*, 438–9.

Miller, P. E. & Perez, V. (2014). Low-calorie sweeteners and body weight and composition: a meta-analysis of randomized controlled trials and prospective cohort studies. *The American Journal of Clinical Nutrition*, *100*, 765–77. doi: http://dx.doi.org/10.3945/ajcn.113.082826

National Eating Disorders Collaboration. (2014). Eating disorders in Australia. Retrieved from: http://www.nedc.com.au/eating-disorders-in-australia

NHMRC. (2011). *A Review of the Evidence to Address Targeted Questions to Inform the Revision of the Australian Dietary Guidelines*. Canberra: National Health and Medical Research Council. Retrieved from: http://www.nhmrc.gov.au/_files_nhmrc/file/publications/n55d_australian_dietary_guidelines_evidence_report.pdf

—— (2013). *Eat for Health: Australian Dietary Guidelines Summary*. Retrieved from: http://www.nhmrc.gov.au/_files_nhmrc/publications/attachments/n55a_australian_dietary_guidelines_summary_131014.pdf

—— (2015a). *Alcohol and Health in Australia*. Retrieved from: http://www.nhmrc.gov.au/your-health/alcohol-guidelines/alcohol-and-health-australia

—— (2015b). *Australian Dietary Guidelines (2013)*. Retrieved from: http://www.nhmrc.gov.au/guidelines-publications/n55

O'Riordan, M. (2015, January 5). Smartphone apps for BP popular, useful, but unvalidated. *Medscape*. Retrieved from: http://www.medscape.com/viewarticle/837525

Patton, G. C., Selzer, R., Coffey, C., Carlin, J. B. & Wolfe, R. (1999). Onset of adolescent eating disorders: population based cohort study over 3 years. *BMJ*, *318*, 765–8. doi: http://dx.doi.org/10.1136/bmj.318.7186.765

Petruzzello, S. J., Landers, D. M., Hatfield, B. D., Kubitz, K. A. & Salazar, W. (1991). A meta-analysis on the anxiety-reducing effects of acute and chronic exercise. *Sports Medicine*, *11*, 143–82. doi: http://dx.doi.org/10.2165/00007256-199111030-00002

Rahmawaty, S., Charlton, K., Lyons-Wall, P. & Meyer, B. J. (2013). Factors that influence consumption of fish and omega–3-enriched foods: a survey of Australian families with young children. *Nutrition & Dietetics*, *70*, 286–93. doi: http://dx.doi.org/10.1111/1747-0080.12022

Rout, M. (2011, July 19). Schools campaign puts body image issues on the line. *The Australian*. Retrieved from: http://www.theaustralian.com.au/national-affairs/schools-campaign-puts-body-image-issues-on-the-line/story-fn59niix-1226097136896

Roxby, P. (2014, October 13). *Does social media impact on body image? BBC News*. Retrieved from: http://www.bbc.com/news/health-29569473

Russell, C. G., Worsley, A. & Liem, D. G. (2015). Parents' food choice motives and their associations with children's food preferences. *Public Health Nutrition*, *18*, 1018–27. doi: http://dx.doi.org/10.1017/S1368980014001128

Schulze, M. B., Manson, J. E., Ludwig, D. S., Colditz, G. A., Stampfer, M. J., Willett, W. C. & Hu, F. B. (2004). Sugar-sweetened beverages, weight gain, and incidence of type 2 diabetes in young and middle-aged women. *Journal of the American Medical Association*, *292*, 927–34. doi: http://dx.doi.org/10.1001/jama.292.8.927

Schutte, N. S. & McNeil, D. G. (2015). Athletic identity mediates between exercise motivation and beneficial outcomes. *Journal of Sport Behavior*, *38*, 234–52.

Sharpe, H., Schober, I., Treasure, J. & Schmidt, U. (2013). Feasibility, acceptability and efficacy of a school-based prevention programme for eating disorders: cluster randomised controlled trial. *The British Journal of Psychiatry*, *203*, 428–35. doi: http://dx.doi.org/10.1192/bjp.bp.113.128199

Siri-Tarino, P. W., Sun, Q., Hu, F. B. & Krauss, R. M. (2010). Meta-analysis of prospective cohort studies evaluating the association of saturated fat with cardiovascular disease. *The American Journal of Clinical Nutrition*, *91*, 535–46. doi: http://dx.doi.org/10.3945/ajcn.2009.27725.1

Smith, R. (2014). Are some diets 'mass murder'? *BMJ*, *349*, g7654.

Stark, J. (2015, May 31). Obesity epidemic weighs down hospitals. *Sydney Morning Herald*. Retrieved from: http://www.smh.com.au/national/health/obesity-epidemic-weighs-down-hospitals-20150530-ghcfqr.html

Stice, E. (2002). Risk and maintenance factors for eating pathology: A meta-analytic review. *Psychological Bulletin*, *128*, 825–48. doi: http://dx.doi.org/10.1037//0033-2909.128.5.825

Striegel-Moore, R. H. & Bulik, C. M. (2007). Risk factors for eating disorders. *American Psychologist*, *62*, 181–98. doi: http://dx.doi.org/10.1037/0003-066X.62.3.181

Taylor, R. S., Ashton, K. E., Moxham, T., Hooper, L. & Ebrahim, S. (2011). Reduced dietary salt for the prevention of cardiovascular disease: a meta-analysis of randomized controlled trials (Cochrane Review). *American Journal of Hypertension*, *24*, 843–53. doi: http://dx.doi.org/10.1038/ajh.2011.115

Torous, J. & Powell, A. C. (2015). Current research and trends in the use of smartphone applications for mood disorders. *Internet Interventions*, *2*, 169–73. doi: http://dx.doi.org/10.1016/j.invent.2015.03.002

Van Duyn, M. A. S. & Pivonka, E. (2000). Overview of the health benefits of fruit and vegetable consumption for the dietetics professional: selected literature. *Journal of the American Dietetic Association*, *100*, 1511–21.

Vartanian, L. R., Schwartz, M. B. & Brownell, K. D. (2007). Effects of soft drink consumption on nutrition and health: a systematic review and meta-analysis. *American Journal of Public Health*, *97*, 667–75. doi: http://dx.doi.org/10.2105/AJPH.2005.083782

Vocks, S., Tuschen-Caffier, B., Pietrowsky, R., Rustenbach, S. J., Kersting, A. & Herpertz, S. (2010). Meta-analysis of the effectiveness of psychological and pharmacological treatments for binge eating disorder. *International Journal of Eating Disorders*, *43*, 205–17. doi: http://dx.doi.org/10.1002/eat.20696

Warburton, D. E., Nicol, C. W. & Bredin, S. S. (2006). Health benefits of physical activity: the evidence. *Canadian Medical Association Journal*, *174*, 801–9. doi: http://dx.doi.org/10.1503/cmaj.051351

Whittal, M. L., Agras, W. S. & Gould, R. A. (2000). Bulimia nervosa: a meta-analysis of psychosocial and pharmacological treatments. *Behavior Therapy*, *30*, 117–35. doi: http://dx.doi.org/10.1016/S0005-7894(99)80049-5

WHO. (2000). *Obesity: Preventing and Managing the Global Epidemic – Report of a WHO Consultation (WHO Technical Report Series 894)*. Geneva: World Health Organisation. Retrieved from: http://www.who.int/nutrition/publications/obesity/WHO_TRS_894/en/

—— (2003). *Diet, Nutrition and the Prevention of Chronic Diseases*. Geneva: World Health Organisation. Retrieved from: http://whqlibdoc.who.int/trs/WHO_TRS_916.pdf?ua=1

Wilson, P. M. & Rodgers, W. M. (2004). The relationship between perceived autonomy support, exercise regulations and behavioral intentions in women. *Psychology of Sport and Exercise*, *5*, 229–42. doi: http://dx.doi.org/10.1016/S1469-0292(03)00003-7

Withings. (2015). Wireless blood pressure monitor. Retrieved from: http://www2.withings.com/us/en/products/blood-pressure-monitor

Wolpert, S. (2014). Does a junk food diet make you lazy? UCLA psychology study offers answer. Retrieved from: http://newsroom.ucla.edu/portal/ucla/does-a-junk-food-diet-make-you-271793.aspx

Yang, T. O., Crowe, F., Cairns, B. J., Reeves, G. K. & Beral, V. (2015). Tea and coffee and risk of endometrial cancer: cohort study and meta-analysis. *The American Journal of Clinical Nutrition*, *101*, 570–8. doi: http://dx.doi.org/10.1007/s00404-015-3811-1

Young, E. M., Fors, S. W. & Hayes, D. M. (2004). Associations between perceived parent behaviors and middle school student fruit and vegetable consumption. *Journal of Nutrition Education and Behavior*, *36*, 2–12. doi: http://dx.doi.org/10.1016/S1499-4046(06)60122-X

Yu-Poth, S., Zhao, G., Etherton, T., Naglak, M., Jonnalagadda, S. & Kris-Etherton, P. M. (1999). Effects of the National Cholesterol Education Program's Step I and Step II dietary intervention programs on cardiovascular disease risk factors: a meta-analysis. *The American Journal of Clinical Nutrition*, *69*, 632–46.

6

Sleep, sleep loss, safety and health

Learning outcomes

After reading this chapter, you should be able to:

- describe sleep and circadian rhythms and how they are measured
- describe the stages of sleep
- describe the consequences of inadequate sleep
- explain why sleep is so important in healthcare
- describe actions you can take to improve sleep quantity and quality.

Introduction

> Trust no one, my prince. Not your chainless maester, not your false father, not the gallant Duck or the lovely Lemore nor these other fine friends who grew you up from a bean. Above all, trust not the cheese monger, nor the Spider, nor this little dragon queen you mean to marry. All this mistrust will sour your stomach and keep you awake at night, 'tis true, but better that than the long sleep that does not end.
>
> (Tyrion VI, Chapter 22, *A Dance with Dragons*)

We are designed to sleep for approximately one-third of our lives. We know that, as described in the quote above, when basic needs are not met, sleep is lost. Sleep deprivation is extremely common. Many groups, including those working long and irregular hours (Åkerstedt, 2003; Rajaratnam & Arendt, 2001), those who report high levels of stress and emotional disturbance (Hall et al., 2015; Lee et al., 2015), new parents (Doan et al., 2007; Gay, Lee & Lee, 2004), and, of course, students (Lack, 1986; Marhefka, 2011; Ming et al., 2011) get less sleep than they need.

A primary focus of health psychology is to look at behaviour patterns and try to encourage people to behave in ways that better equip them for positive health outcomes. In Australia, as in other developed countries today, the primary reasons for medical treatment and death are chronic illness and accidents. Current health priority areas in Australia include cancer, cardiovascular disease, diabetes, mental health, obesity and injury prevention/control (AIHW, 2011). The risk factors for these health priorities are a complex interaction of physical, behavioural and social factors. Key behavioural risk factors that are an important research focus include poor diet, lack of exercise, smoking and excessive alcohol consumption (Amoroso et al., 2009; Bennett, 1995; Crouch, Wilson & Newbury, 2011; Flicker, Lautenschlager & Almeida, 2006). At the same time, we have an increasing body of evidence highlighting the negative impact of sleep loss for performance, safety and health (Bohle et al., 2004; Caruso, 2014; Folkard & Tucker, 2003; Rajaratnam & Arendt, 2001). However, sleep is frequently left out of discussions about healthcare. This chapter will: discuss sleep and circadian rhythms and how scientists define and understand sleep based on measurement of our body and brain; discuss the consequences of sleep loss for performance, safety and health, focusing on one example group who is very frequently sleep deprived (shiftworkers); and describe simple recommendations for maximising sleep.

Understanding sleep and circadian rhythms

What is sleep?

> Sleep is a reversible behavioral state of perceptual disengagement from and unresponsiveness to the environment.
>
> (Carskadon & Dement, 2011, p. 6)

The above definition of **sleep** captures a major property of sleep: a change in consciousness or environmental awareness. Sleep is also typically associated with physical inactivity, closed eyes and reclined posture (Carskadon & Dement, 2011). Why do we sleep? Interestingly, this is something about which researchers find it difficult to agree (Kavanau, 2005; Krueger, Obál & Fang, 1999; Nicolau et al., 2000). A large body of research has focused on understanding sleep from a physiological perspective, measuring what happens in our brains and bodies while we sleep to identify patterns. These patterns are used to define sleep and classify it into a series of stages. We will discuss sleep measurement and staging in the following section of this chapter. Many studies in sleep research have focused on what happens to physiology and behaviour when sleep is reduced, or removed altogether, for periods of time. Our mainstream understanding of the importance of sleep comes from what we know about what happens to us when we are sleep deprived. We will discuss the effects of sleep loss later in the chapter.

Measuring sleep

In 1930 the development of the electroencephalogram, a non-invasive, objective sleep-recording instrument, changed the general conception that sleep was an elementary, passive state. This technological advance, involving the application of electrodes to the face and scalp to record brainwaves and muscle movement, allowed scientists to discover that sleep consists of specific patterns of brain and body activity. What was astonishing was that even in the deepest sleep, the brain is extremely active. Figure 6.1 shows someone who is 'wired-up' for basic sleep monitoring. They have **electroencephalogram (EEG)** electrodes on top of their head to monitor brainwaves, **electro-oculogram (EOG)** electrodes next to their eyes to measure eye movements and **electromyogram (EMG)** electrodes under their chin to measure muscle tone. In part (b) of Figure 6.1, you can see our sleep research participant lying in bed, with all of her electrodes plugged into a headbox. This box will conduct the signals via leads to our computers outside her bedroom, where we can watch her brainwaves, eye movements and muscle tone while she sleeps.

(a)

(b)

Figure 6.1 Sleep study participant 'wired-up' for sleep measurement: (a) participant with electroencephalogram (EEG), electro-oculogram (EOG) and electromyogram (EMG) electrodes for measuring (b) brainwaves, eye movements and muscle tone while she sleeps

Figure 6.2 shows the signals we would see on our computer screens. In each part the top two traces are the brainwaves or EEG, the middle two traces show eye movements or EOG and the lower trace shows muscle tone or EMG from the chin. Wake is displayed in

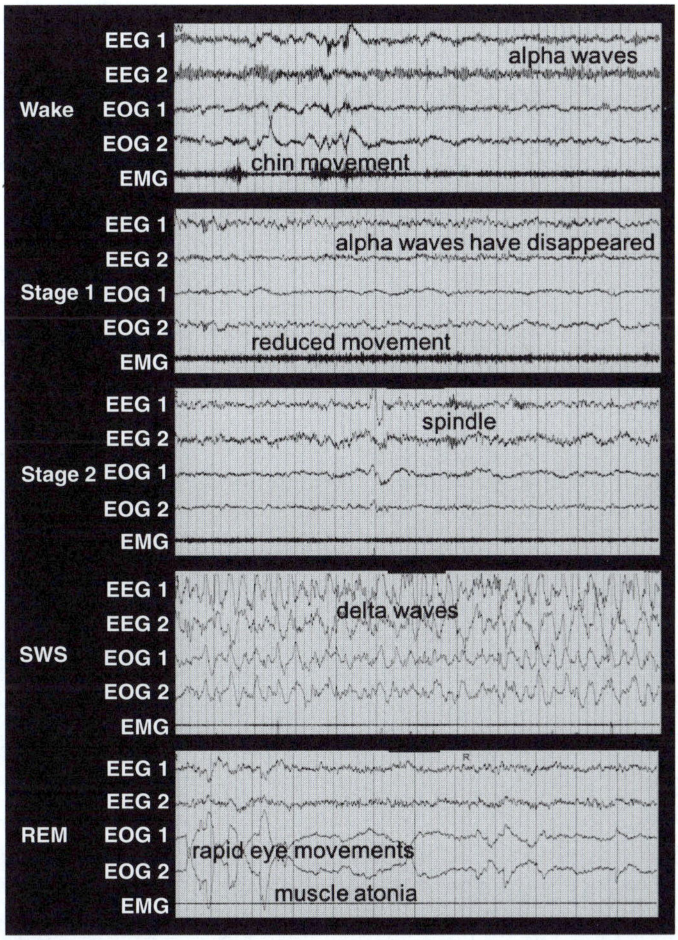

Figure 6.2 View of measurement traces for scoring sleep

the top panel. The EEG show lots of high-frequency activity, referred to as alpha waves; the eyes show a little bit of movement, as does the chin. You can see that this pattern contrasts with the patterns in the lower four panels, which illustrate the different stages of sleep. Based on the patterns observed in the brain and muscles, sleep is categorised into two contrasting substates: non-rapid eye movement (NREM) and **rapid eye movement (REM)**. Panels show brainwave, eye and chin signals in wake, Stage 1, Stage 2, slow wave sleep (SWS) (Stages 3 and 4) and REM sleep.

NREM sleep has been divided into four stages. Stage 1 is considered to be a transitional stage, somewhere between sleep and wakefulness, only occurring for a short time. It is characterised by low amplitude EEG activity, slow rolling eye movements and a low arousal threshold (it is easy to rouse someone from Stage 1). Stage 2 is generally recognised as the onset of true sleep, and is the most prevalent sleep stage. It is associated with EEG spindles (waves of 12 to 14 Hz, lasting for 0.5 to 1.5 seconds), and K complexes (a sharp negative incline followed by a positive wave, lasting for 0.5 seconds). Stages 3 and 4 are collectively known as **slow wave sleep (SWS)**, colloquially referred to as deep sleep. This stage is marked by the occurrence of high amplitude, slow wave (delta) activity. The arousal threshold is high (it is difficult to wake people from SWS) and individuals tend to be unable to recall awakenings, which are often very brief (Carskadon & Rechtschaffen, 1994; Zee & Turek, 1999). Interestingly, the EOG during this stage makes it look as if the eyes are moving around all over the place. However, you can see that the pattern in the eye traces closely resembles the pattern in the EEG. The eyes are actually quite still during SWS; the electrical activity in the brain is so large that artefact from the EEG is being picked up in the EOG signals. Among other functions, SWS is associated with the secretion of growth hormone, and for this reason has been implicated in growth and tissue repair (Zee & Turek, 1999).

REM sleep, discovered by Aserinsky and Kleitman in 1953, is characterised by: prominent rapid eye movements; fast, desynchronised wave forms of low amplitude; and loss of muscle tone (Carskadon & Rechtschaffen, 1994; Hobson, 1999). While there is a high level of brain activation, the body is in a state of flaccid paralysis (loss of muscle tone). For this reason, it is also referred to as paradoxical sleep (Zee & Turek, 1999). REM is associated with irregularities in temperature, heart rate and respiration, and intermittent muscle twitches. A large proportion of dreaming is thought to occur in REM sleep, since individuals awoken during this stage report detailed story-like dreams and vivid hallucinations (Carskadon & Rechtschaffen, 1994). It has been suggested that one of the important roles of the loss of muscle tone during REM sleep is to stop people from physically acting out their dreams. Indeed, REM behaviour disorder is characterised by loss of normal muscle atonia during REM sleep, and is associated with motor activity while dreaming (Boeve et al., 2007). Numerous possible functions of REM sleep have been suggested. It has been implicated in maintenance of sustained attention (Siegel & Rogawski, 1988), motivation and mood (Vogel et al., 1980), and facilitation of learning and memory (Stickgold, 2005; Stickgold et al., 2001).

NREM and REM sleep alternate in periodic cycles. A healthy individual will typically experience four to five alternating NREM/REM cycles of approximately 90 minutes' duration during a nocturnal sleep period. With each cycle, the amount of REM sleep increases, and the amount of NREM sleep decreases (Zee & Turek, 1999). This means that we get the majority of our SWS during the first half of the night, and the majority of our REM later in the sleep period. This is illustrated in Figure 6.3, which shows a sleep hypnogram. We refer to the pattern of sleep stages across the night as sleep architecture. When we consider healthy sleep, we are interested not only in duration, but also in architecture. It is important to get enough sleep of sufficient quality to maintain performance and health. Time of day is on the *x*-axis and sleep stage is on the *y*-axis. SWS (Stages 3 and 4) is highlighted by the blue boxes and REM sleep is highlighted by the black boxes. Sleep stages are experienced in cycles, with the majority of SWS early in the night, and the majority of REM later in the sleep period.

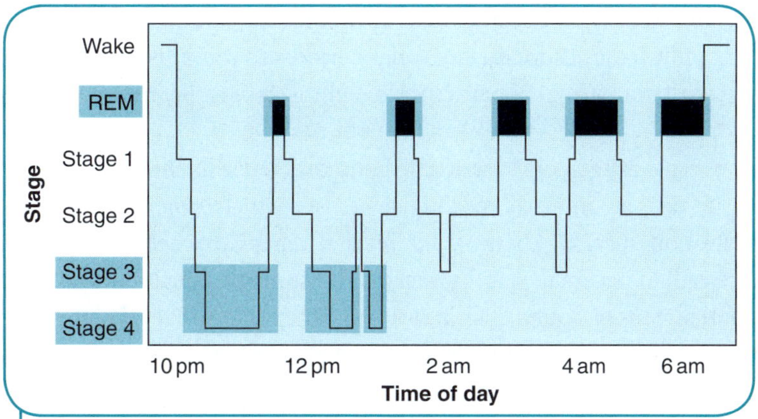

Figure 6.3 Hypnogram of healthy adult sleep

Circadian rhythms

Humans are diurnal, which means that they remain active by day and at rest at night. This sleep/wake cycle is one of the many human functions that follow what is referred to as a **circadian rhythm** (Glazner, 1991). The term 'circadian rhythm' was first used by Halberg to refer to rhythms that roughly follow a 24-hour cycle (Webb & Levy, 1982). It comes from the Latin *circa diem*, meaning 'about a day' (Zee & Turek, 1999). Circadian rhythms can be observed in many physiological and psychological functions, including hormone levels, body temperature, performance, alertness and sleepiness/sleep propensity (Czeizler et al., 1980; Kleitman, 1963; Lack & Lushington, 1995).

Externally, the main zeitgeiber (time giver, or signal) that synchronises internal body rhythms to the 24-hour day is the light/dark cycle (Czeisler et al., 1981). Although their influence may not be as strong, cues such as meal times and social events also act as zeitgeibers (Duffy, Kronauer & Czeisler, 1996; Minors & Waterhouse, 1981). In the absence of external time cues, circadian rhythms revert to what is known as a 'free-running' state. Experiments have demonstrated that in many cases, free-running rhythms maintain a period (referred to as *tau*) which is slightly greater than 24 hours. One of the earliest studies of this type was conducted in a cave in an attempt to provide an environment free of time cues, particularly light. During the 61-day experimental period, the single subject telephoned experimenters to tell them his retiring and waking times, and measured his pulse rate. Despite the lack of external zeitgeibers, the subject's sleep/wake cycle and pulse rate exhibited constant rhythmicity, with cycles of approximately 24.5 hours (Halberg et al., 1965 in Minors & Waterhouse, 1981).

Since then, numerous studies have demonstrated that the rest/activity cycle and body temperature maintain a distinct, near 24-hour circadian period. Experiments have typically involved long-term isolation of subjects, essentially creating a similar environment to that of Halberg's cave study. That is, the subject is isolated from time cues including clocks, outdoor light and television. Social contact is minimised, and limited to interaction with experimenters only. In addition, during wake periods, to minimise the influence of room light on the circadian rhythms of participants, light is kept at a constant low level (usually < 50 lux).

Without external zeitgeibers such as the light/dark cycle to entrain our bodily rhythms to the 24-hour day, an internal mechanism exists which synchronises these rhythms to the near 24-hour period; there is an internal circadian pacemaker (Czeizler et al., 1999). The circadian pacemaker in humans is the suprachiasmatic nucleus (SCN) of the anterior hypothalamus. Located just above the optic chiasm (see Figure 6.4), the SCN receives photic input (light), primarily via the retino-hypothalamic tract, which appears to provide the information about the light/dark cycle necessary for the entrainment, or synchronisation, of rhythms to the 24-hour day (Schwartz, 1995). The neurons in the SCN activate in an oscillating pattern, generating a circadian signal. This signal influences the sleep/wake cycle and neuroendocrine function via projections from the SCN to the relevant areas of the hypothalamus (Dijk & Edgar, 1999; Moore, 1999).

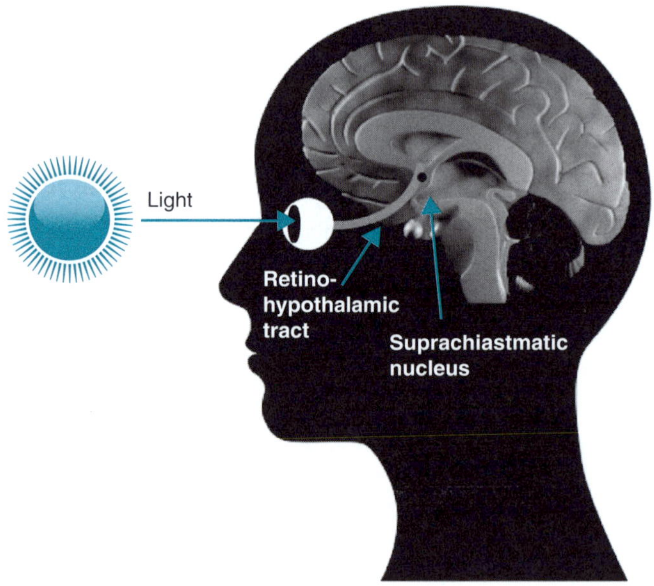

Figure 6.4 The suprachiasmatic nucleus (SCN)

Evidence for the connection between this area of the brain in humans and the timing of circadian rhythms has been found in medical investigations. For example, Schwartz, Busis and Hedley-Whyte (1986) describe a patient with a tumour in the hypothalamus, above the optic chiasm. Although, over 24 hours, their average temperature (taken orally) didn't change, the researchers noticed that the rhythm became abnormal. Thus it was suggested that pressure from the hypothalamic tumour was causing abnormalities in the circadian rhythms of the individual. Similar changes in the normal circadian body rhythms have been found in other patient groups. For example, Wang et al. (1997) studied 100 patients with acute cerebrovascular disorders. While 48 patients retained normal fluctuations, 52 showed abnormal blood pressure rhythms. There was a strong negative correlation between the likelihood of developing an abnormal rhythm and the distance between the hypothalamus and the lesion.

Markers of circadian phase: melatonin and core body temperature

Melatonin is synthesised primarily in the pineal gland, but also in the retina. Its production is controlled by the SCN (Schwartz, 1995). It is secreted nocturnally in humans, such that it is produced in low levels during the daytime and in high levels during the normal sleep period. Melatonin levels start to increase in the evening (11.00 pm to midnight), peaking during the early morning hours and returning to basal levels by dawn (Burgess & Dawson, 1999). Functionally, it has been argued that melatonin may serve as a circadian timekeeper, providing information about the light/dark cycle, and thus day length, to the SCN (Dawson & Armstrong, 1996). Indeed, a high concentration of melatonin receptors are found in the circadian pacemaker (Weaver et al., 1993). Melatonin, mediated by the circadian clock, is highly lipid-soluble (it dissolves easily into fatty substances), and is detectable in the blood, urine, saliva and cerebrospinal fluid (Shanahan, 1995). As such, it has been suggested that SCN acts as a messenger, relaying circadian information to systems throughout the body.

Since melatonin production is regulated by the SCN, it is strongly influenced by the light/dark cycle. Light is measured in lux. Normal indoor room light is typically around 180 lux (Boivin & Czeisler, 1998). It has been demonstrated that bright light administration (2500 lux) can suppress melatonin secretion (Lewy et al., 1980). Furthermore, exposure to moderate to bright intensity light (1200–3000 lux) has been shown to shift the melatonin rhythm (Bougrine et al., 1995). However, while melatonin production is affected by bright light, the melatonin rhythm does not seem to be masked by dim light, sleep or activity. Melatonin rhythms persist in 'free-running conditions' (Czeizler et al., 1999, described above), and in the absence of sleep (Morris, Lack & Barrett, 1990). As such, the timing of the onset of melatonin production under dim lighting conditions (< 50 lux) is considered an effective marker of circadian phase (Lewy, 1999). Specifically, time shifts in dim light melatonin onset (DLMO) are interpreted as shifts in circadian phase. Thus in many studies, including those involving sleep deprivation or shifts in the sleep/wake cycle, the onset time of melatonin secretion has been used as a circadian phase marker.

Another marker used to measure circadian phase is core body temperature. There is a temporal relationship between core body temperature and melatonin such that they are synchronised, but peak at different time points (Refinetti, 1999). In entrained diurnal animals, the rhythm in core body temperature is smooth and symmetrical and resembles a sine wave. Core body temperature is lowest in the early morning (2.00 am to 6.00 am), gradually increasing across the day to reach a maximum during the afternoon (4 pm to 6 pm) (Refinetti, 1999). As previously discussed, the rhythm persists even in situations of temporal isolation (Czeizler et al., 1999). The commencement of the early morning increase in body temperature usually starts before people wake in the morning. It has been suggested that this helps to ready the body to react appropriately to environmental hazards on waking (Moore-Ede, 1986).

Sleep homeostasis, circadian rhythms and the sleep/wake cycle

Circadian factors constitute only one element that influences the sleep/wake cycle. The other is the homeostatic drive for sleep. Sleep homeostasis refers to the sleep/wake-dependent aspect of sleep regulation. In situations of sleep deprivation, the homeostatic sleep drive serves to increase sleep propensity; when sufficient or excess sleep occurs, it serves to decrease sleep propensity (Borbély & Achermann, 1994). The longer we are awake, the more we want to sleep. In addition, when people are deprived of sleep, their subsequent sleep tends to be longer (Borbély & Achermann, 1994) and deeper (Dijk et al., 1990).

The relationship between circadian rhythms and the homeostatic sleep drive is both competitive and additive. One functional role of the SCN in humans is to compete with the homeostatic sleep drive, maintain wakefulness and promote the continuance of activity over the day, despite increasing time awake. Put simply, the homeostatic drive for sleep builds across the day and dissipates during sleep. At the same time, the circadian-modulated drive for wakefulness increases over the day and decreases during the night. The term 'opponent processes' was coined by Edgar and colleagues to describe the conflicting forces of the homeostatic sleep drive and the SCN (Dijk & Edgar, 1999). The homeostat and the circadian system act in opposition to produce a rhythm in sleepiness that peaks during the early hours of the morning. In addition, there is a less marked mid-afternoon peak (Lavie, 1986), which has been referred to as the 'post-prandial' or 'post-lunch' dip (Carrier & Monk, 1999). The 'opponent processes' of the homeostatic sleep drive and the circadian drive for wake are shown in Figure 6.5. This figure illustrates the way in which these processes interact to produce our rhythm of sleepiness across the day. Part (a) shows that our homeostatic drive for sleep increases across the day with increasing time awake. At the same time, the circadian drive for wakefulness is working in opposition, to keep us awake. As we reach habitual sleep time, our circadian drive for wake starts to drop, allowing our homeostatic sleep drive to put us to sleep. During sleep, our homeostatic drive dissipates and our circadian drive for wake plunges lower, to reach a low point between 4 am and 6 am, and keeps us asleep through the night.

We function best when the 24-hour rhythms in our body and behaviour (e.g. sleep) are synchronised with the outside world. However, humans are one of the few species who are able to exert some level of control over their diurnal rhythms. Thus, we have the ability to engage in activities that are counter to our innate rhythms, such as **shiftwork** and transmeridian travel (crossing time zones). We know that when we do this, we experience negative consequences for our alertness, performance and health. For example,

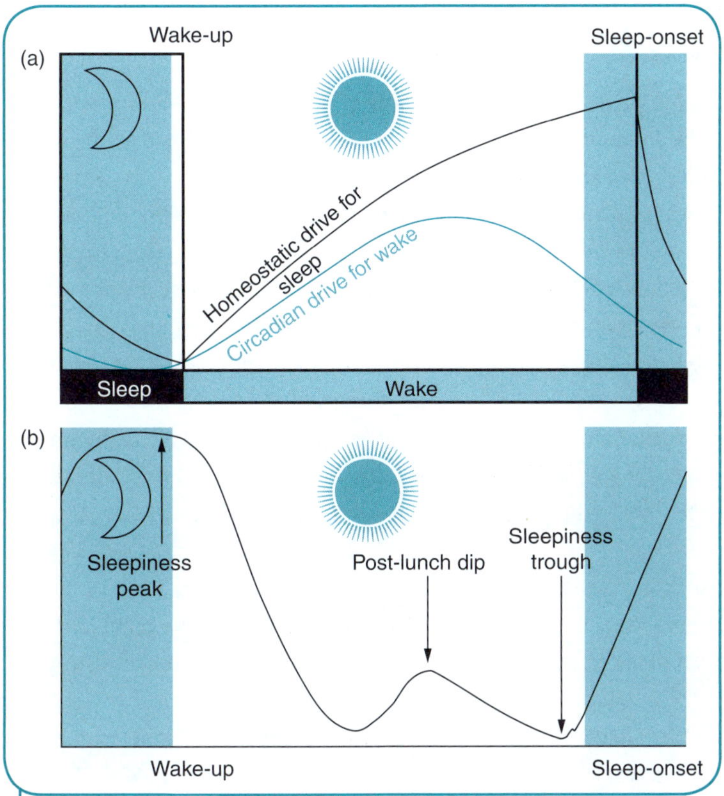

Figure 6.5 The interaction of homeostatic and circadian processes to produce our daily sleepiness rhythm

when we travel across time zones, our internal circadian rhythms no longer match the light/dark cycle at our destination. We may then experience difficulty sleeping, excessive sleepiness while we're trying to remain awake, problems with attention and concentration, fluctuations in mood, feelings of disorientation, appetite loss and gastrointestinal issues. Collectively, we refer to these symptoms as jet lag (Lagarde & Doireau, 1997; Manfredini et al., 1998). Similarly, the irregular working hours of shiftworkers conflict with circadian body rhythms and the normal sleep/wake cycle. The continuous pressure on the shiftworker to adjust to new schedules despite competing social and environmental cues provides a constant source of stress for the body. Not surprisingly, this has a negative influence on health and performance. Immediate effects of this stress manifest in a phenomenon that has been coined 'shift-lag' syndrome. That is, the worker experiences a set of symptoms similar to jet lag (Folkard, Waterhouse & Minors, 1985). We will further explore the implications of sleep loss and circadian disruption for shiftworkers later in this chapter.

Mini case study 6.1

It's 9.00 pm. Ten-year-old Sam has been asleep since 8.00 pm. His brother, five-year-old Henry, is in the room next door and can't get to sleep – he is afraid of the dark. Henry runs into Sam's room and whispers 'Sam, help, I'm afraid of the dark'. Sam does not wake up. Henry goes back into his room and manages to get some sleep, until he wakes up again at 3.00 am, feeling scared. He runs back into Sam's room and whispers 'Sam, help, I'm afraid of the dark'. This time Sam does wake up. Sam says, 'Why are you waking me Henry? I was dreaming about a room full of yummy doughnuts!' Sam lets Henry climb into bed with him. Henry tosses and turns, and Sam doesn't get much more sleep that night.

The next day is Saturday. Sam is playing computer games with his friend. He notices that he is not playing as well as he usually does and after lunch, he finds it hard to stay awake. He feels a bit grumpy and can't wait to go to bed that night.

Critical thinking questions

1. Why is Henry likely to find it difficult to wake Sam early in the night?
2. Why was it easier to wake Sam at 3.00 am, and why did he tell that story when he woke?
3. Why does Sam have trouble playing computer games? Why is he grumpy? Why does he struggle to stay awake after lunch?

The effects of sleep loss

> I spend several days at a time without enough sleep. At first, normal activities become annoying. When you are too tired to eat, you really need some sleep. A few days later, things become strange. Loud noises become louder and more startling, familiar sounds become unfamiliar, and life reinvents itself as a surrealist dream.
>
> (Henry Rollins, *LA Weekly*, 27 October 2011)

We have well over a century of research demonstrating that sleep loss results in performance impairment (Dorrian & Dinges, 2005; Kleitman, 1963). The impairment we see is driven by the homeostatic drive for sleep, and by our circadian rhythms, as described in the previous section. In Figure 6.6, part (a) (performance during a single night awake) shows impairment on a performance task, in this case response time on a vigilance measure, across 28 hours awake (i.e. a full night awake) (Lamond & Dawson, 1999). As you can see from the figure, performance is relatively stable during the day, starts to drop after habitual bedtime in the late evening and then reaches a low point (nadir) in the early morning. After that, the circadian drive for wake is acting to prepare us for the day, and performance starts to improve again. Also, in this study, participants knew that they were about to

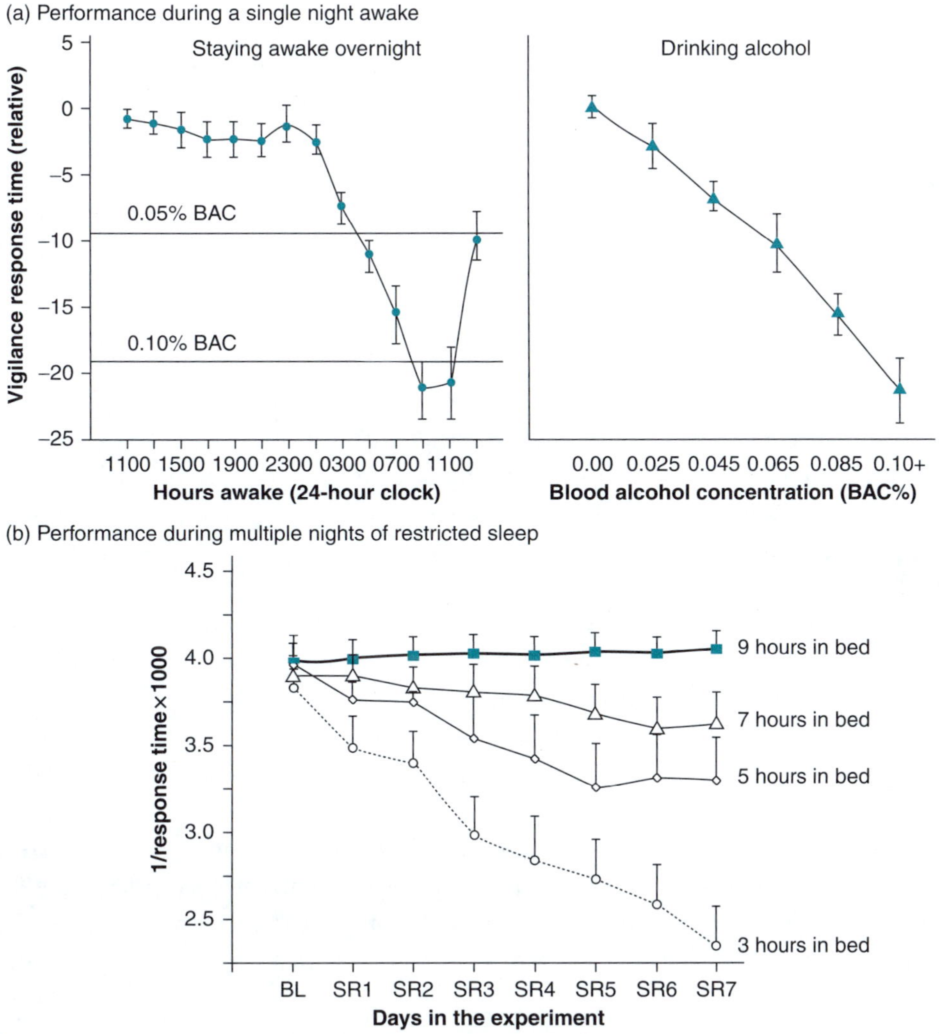

Figure 6.6 The effects of sleep loss are similar to those of alcohol intoxication and add up over a series of days.
Source: adapted from Belenky et al., 2003; Lamond & Dawson, 1999

finish the experiment, so the improvement in the last test could be due to an 'end-of-test effect'. On the right of part (a), you can see the same participants undergoing an alcohol condition, where they had an alcoholic drink every hour and had their blood alcohol concentration measured (BAC%). You can see that performance gets worse with a higher BAC%. Researchers found that performance in the morning following 19 hours awake was equivalent to performance at 0.05% BAC, which is the legal driving limit in Australia. After about 24 hours, it was equivalent to twice the legal driving limit (Lamond & Dawson, 1999). This study is one example of a series of studies that have equated the impairment resulting from sleep loss and alcohol intoxication (Dawson & Reid, 1997; Roach et al., 2001; Williamson et al., 2001). These studies demonstrate that the effects of sleep loss are not only measurable, but also meaningful. After a single night awake, performance impairment reaches levels that we would consider to be concerning from an operational perspective, and that we would specifically legislate against.

However, you don't have to stay awake all night to experience the effects of sleep loss. Figure 6.6 part (b) (performance during multiple nights of restricted sleep) shows the results from an influential study demonstrating that sleep restriction is associated with impairment, which accumulates across a week in a dose-response manner (Belenky et al., 2003). In this study, participants were given 9 hours (average sleep = 7.9 hours), 7 hours (average sleep = 6.3 hours), 5 hours (average sleep = 4.7 hours) or 3 hours (average sleep = 2.9 hours) time in bed for a week. The figure shows mean reciprocal of performance on a psychomotor vigilance task during a baseline (BL) day and seven sleep restriction (SR) days. Results suggest that sleep restriction, even by small amounts, adds up across a week to produce cumulative impairment. In another similar study also conducted in 2003, participants were given 8 hours, 6 hours or 4 hours in bed for 14 days (Van Dongen et al., 2003). Again, performance impairment accumulated across days. Remarkably, after 2 weeks, performance impairment of participants in the 6 hours in-bed condition was equivalent to the performance of a group of participants who had remained awake for two full nights. These studies demonstrate that when sleep is lost, even at relatively mild (and commonly experienced) levels, impairment accumulates over a series of days and can add up over time to levels that are of concern.

These effects are not only observable in controlled laboratory situations such as the studies just discussed. We also observe the negative impact of sleep loss (and also the disruption to circadian rhythms) in a number of groups in the community. A clear example of this is for shiftworkers, who have schedules that conflict with our natural rhythms.

Sleep loss and shiftwork

We live in an around-the-clock society, with growing requirement for continuous services (Härmä, 1998). Increasing pressures on industry for extended hours of operation are not only a reflection of customer demand, but also the result of technological and commercial concerns. For example, certain manufacturing processes must be run continuously to avoid product deterioration. In addition, many services now rely on expensive machinery that must be run continuously to be cost effective (Monk, 2000). These factors have led to a move away from the traditional 9.00 am to 5.00 pm, 40-hour work week to more complex and diverse shift schedules, referred to broadly as shiftwork. Indeed, shiftwork has been operationally defined as: 'any regularly taken employment outside the day working window, defined arbitrarily as the hours between 7.00 am and 6.00 pm' (Monk & Folkard, 1992). As such, shifts may differ in terms of length and time of day (morning, afternoon, evening), and the number of consecutive shifts scheduled may vary.

Estimates suggest that 20 to 25% of all employees are engaged in some type of shiftwork (Monk, 2000; Rajaratnam & Arendt, 2001). Not only are more employees working at different times of day, there is also a growing tendency for employees to work longer hours (Rosa, 1995). While longer and more varied work hours provide societal and economic benefits, they come at a high cost to the workers. Shiftwork is associated with sleep loss (Åkerstedt, 1995, 2003). Shiftwork, and night work in particular, requires the employee to live outside the normal human sleep/activity schedule. The irregular working hours conflict with circadian body rhythms and the normal sleep/wake cycle. Shiftworkers may work hours that vary from day to day, they may work nights or they may be crossing time zones, as in the case of pilots. Due to the fact that internal circadian mechanisms are robust and only adjust slowly, such changes to the normal sleep/wake schedule cause desynchronisation of internal mechanisms, relative to external signals. The sleep/wake schedule and the internal circadian rhythms will be out of phase.

In addition, shiftwork schedules often result in reduced opportunity for sleep and rest, and alter the timing of rest periods. Since the worker often sleeps at times when they would usually be awake, they experience sleep of reduced quality and quantity. The sleep of night shiftworkers may be shortened by as much as 4 hours between shifts (Åkerstedt, 1991, 1995). As a consequence, shiftworkers generally report higher levels of sleepiness and fatigue than day workers (Åkerstedt & Torsvall, 1978; Verhaegen, Maasen & Meers, 1981). This sleepiness has important consequences for performance and safety.

Shiftwork and performance

We've seen in the early sections of this chapter that sleepiness and performance are influenced by how long we've been awake, how much sleep we've had and the time of day. The studies we've looked at so far have been conducted in the laboratory, under controlled conditions, with basic performance tests. However, there are many studies that have demonstrated the same effects with more complex tasks in more complex settings. These studies demonstrate that staying awake for long periods, getting reduced sleep and performing during the night are associated with sleepiness and performance impairment for people at work. Some example studies, all conducted in Australia, are shown in Figure 6.7. Part (a) shows a cohort of 20 professional and 20 non-professional drivers who completed a 30-minute driving simulation 3–4 hourly for 24 hours. Variation in speed (left) and lane position (right) increased with increasing time awake, indicating poorer driving performance (Howard et al., 2014). Part (b) shows performance on a sustained response time task, completed by 35 mining operators at the beginning and end of their work shifts. Performance was worst on shifts with less sleep, and was worse at the end of night shifts compared to the start of night shifts or the start or end of day shifts (Ferguson et al., 2011). Part (c) shows fuel use in 50

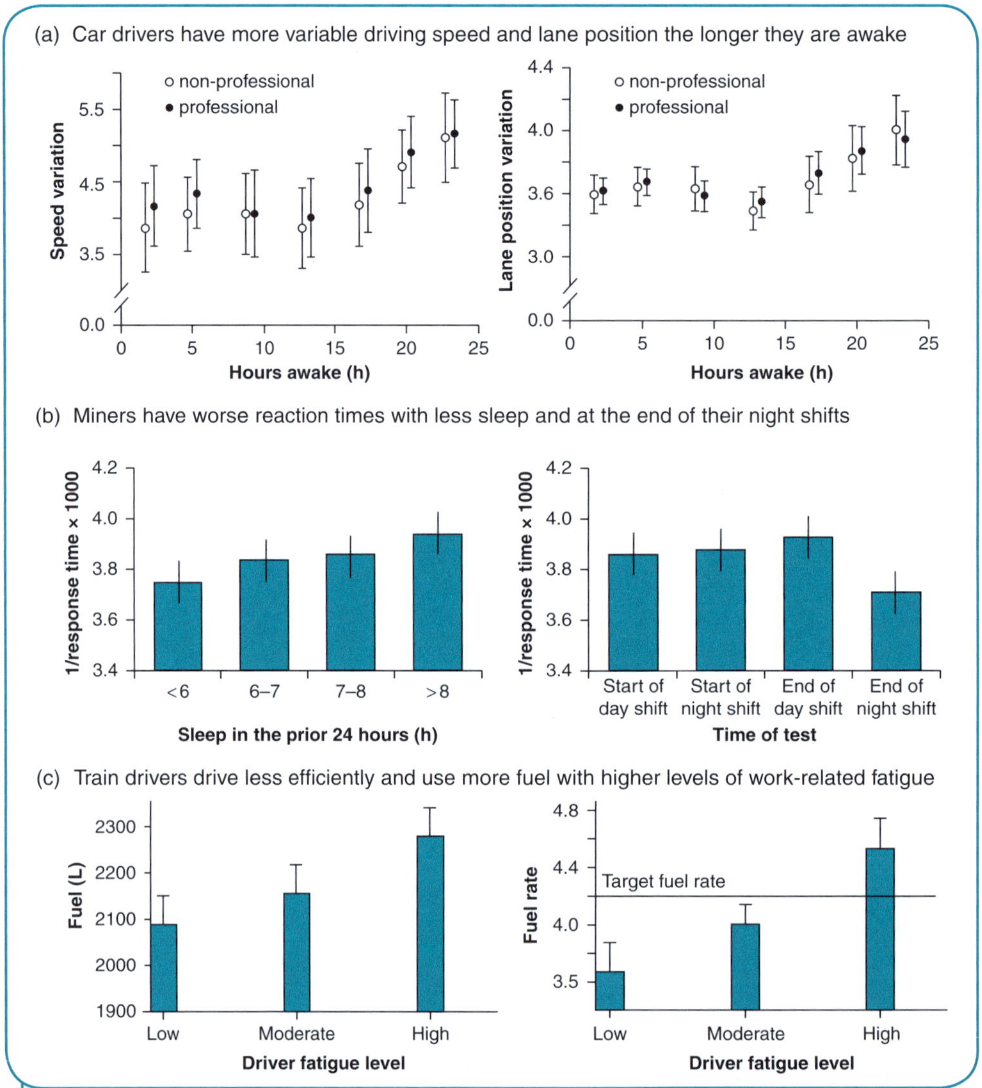

Figure 6.7 Long wake times, short sleep times and time of day influence performance at work
Source: adapted from Dorrian et al., 2007; Ferguson et al., 2011; Howard et al., 2014

freight trains operating on a single non-metropolitan rail corridor. With increasing work-related fatigue, drivers were less efficient and used more fuel (left). Drivers at a high level of fatigue had fuel use levels above the cut-off set by the operator – they were using more fuel than expected for this trip. High-fatigue drivers used 9% more fuel, which was estimated to cost the company an extra \$3500 per week, or \$180 000 per year, just for this single corridor (Dorrian, Hussey & Dawson, 2007). Given these clear examples of performance impairment, it is not surprising that there is also a relationship between how long you've been awake, how much sleep you've had, time of day and risk of incident and accident.

Shiftwork and accidents

Sleep loss has often been ignored, and definitely understated, as a factor contributing to accidents in the workplace and on the roads, often because other causes, such as drugs or alcohol, are more easily identified (Åkerstedt, 1995; Leger, 1994). Nevertheless, we have significant evidence that sleep-related accidents are both prevalent and costly. Investigations have revealed an association between sleep loss and fatigue and human error in major operational catastrophes. For example, the report on the grounding of the oil tanker *Exxon Valdez* identified human error as the cause, and stated that longer work hours and shorter sleep duration had resulted in an increased level of fatigue (National Transport Safety Board, 1990). The investigation into the Challenger Space Shuttle disaster revealed a connection between causal error, sleep loss and fatigue (The Presidential Commission, 1986).

Consistent with our understanding of the circadian rhythm in sleepiness and performance, peak times for road accidents coincide with the biological peaks in sleepiness (Figure 6.5), such that a large number occur during the early morning hours (12.00 am to 6.00 am), with a secondary, post-lunch peak (Figure 6.8) (Folkard, 1997). The relative risk of incidents and accidents increases with time on shift (Figure 6.9(a)), across successive day shifts (Figure 6.9(b)) and across successive night shifts (Figure 6.9(c)). Relative risk is also higher on night and afternoon shift than on morning shift (Figure 6.9(d)) (Folkard & Tucker, 2003).

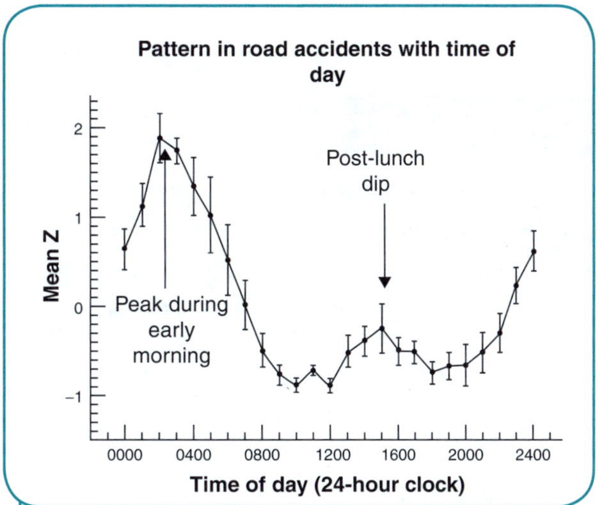

Figure 6.8 Circadian pattern in road accidents. Summary across a series of studies investigating time of day and road accidents. There is a peak during the early morning hours, and a secondary peak after lunch.
Source: adapted from Folkard, 1997, p. 418

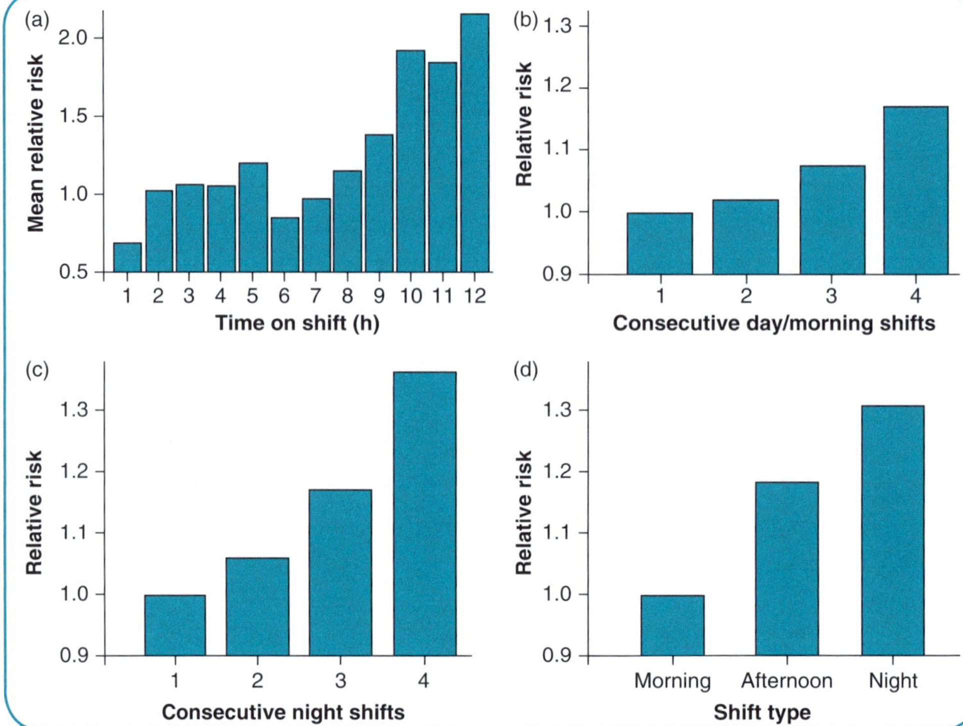

Figure 6.9 Pattern in relative risk of incident and accident varies as a function of schedule-related factors. Risk increases with time on shift (a), consecutive day shifts (b), consecutive night shifts (c) and on night and afternoon shifts relative to morning shifts (d).
Source: adapted from Folkard & Tucker, 2003, pp. 97–8

Mini case study 6.2

At 2.30 am on 25 May 2013, a Union Pacific (UP) and a BNSF freight train were heading towards Rockview Junction in Chafee, Missouri. The UP train had 2 locomotives and 60 cars; the BNSF had 3 locomotives and 75 cars. Crew members on the UP train failed to respond to a stop signal that should have prevented them crossing the junction. As the BNSF train was in the junction, the UP train struck it, derailing 13 cars of the BNSF train and 2 locomotives and 11 cars from the UP train. Fuel spilled and caught fire. The train cars hit bridge supports and parts of the bridge collapsed. Following this, two motor vehicles hit the damaged bridge. The engineer, conductor and five occupants of the motor vehicles were taken to hospital. The estimated damage was more than $11 million. In the days leading up to the accident, the UP crew were working variable schedules, which caused circadian disruption. The train driver had undiagnosed obstructive sleep apnoea.

Critical thinking question

Can you identify the factors in this accident description that point to sleep loss and fatigue as contributing factors?

Sleep loss in healthcare

> Sleep that knits up the ravell'd sleeve of care,
> The death of each day's life, sole labour's bath,
> Balm of hurt minds, Great nature's second course,
> Chief nourisher in life's feast.
>
> (William Shakespeare, *Macbeth*, Act 2, Scene 2)

So far in this chapter we've discussed sleep and circadian rhythms, and explored some of the evidence for sleep loss being a workplace hazard, with clear implications for performance and safety. We then examined one group of people who commonly experience sleep loss and disruption to their daily rhythms: shiftworkers. All of this has important implications for healthcare for several reasons. First, shiftwork predominates in healthcare. The majority of nurses and doctors, for example, are shiftworkers. Medical attention is required around the clock and so are those who work in healthcare. Second, adequate sleep is necessary for good health. We see increased risk of health problems among the sleep deprived. Finally, health issues specifically related to sleep (sleep disorders) are increasingly common. The following section will consider sleep loss in the healthcare system: in healthcare professionals and their patients.

Sleep loss and medical error

As previously discussed, those with disrupted sleep and daily rhythms are at increased risk of performance impairment, error and accident. This is also true for healthcare professionals. In the last 15 years, there has been a focus on reducing medical error in hospitals from the perspective of managing sleep loss and fatigue. According to Australian Productivity Commission records, in 2012 there were 107 'sentinel events' (serious medical errors) in Australian hospitals. These included procedures involving the wrong patient or the wrong body part, leaving instruments inside patients during surgery and incorrect drug administration. The magnitude of this issue in US hospitals has recently been estimated, with one report suggesting that between 210 000 and 400 000 deaths each year may be associated with preventable harm (James, 2013).

The Harvard Work Hours, Health and Safety Group has published a series of studies demonstrating the link between long work hours, time of day and error. For example, trainee doctors in the US showed an increase in medical errors after being at work longer than 16 hours, had double the attentional failures during night shift and double the risk of a car crash when driving home from a work period of 24 hours or longer. They found that the levels of performance impairment exhibited by trainees were equivalent to what would be expected at blood alcohol concentrations of 0.05 to 0.10% (Lockley et al., 2007). This group demonstrated that imposing limits on work hours reduced performance deficits (Landrigan et al., 2004).

In another set of studies from the University of Pennsylvania School of Nursing, Rogers and her colleagues studied a large, random sample of US hospital nurses, following them for a month and collecting daily diaries with information about work, sleep and error.

These studies showed that long work hours were associated with increased risk of medical error (Rogers et al., 2004; Scott et al., 2006). Work from this group also showed that drowsy driving, common for these nurses, increased with shorter sleep and working at night (Scott et al., 2007). Data collected by Rogers and colleagues is shown in Figure 6.10. On the *x*-axis is the amount of sleep nurses had in the 24 hours and 48 hours prior to starting shifts, and the number of hours they had been awake. On the *y*-axis is probability of error. This figure shows a clear relationship between sleep, wake and error, such that as sleep reduces and wake increases, error probability increases.

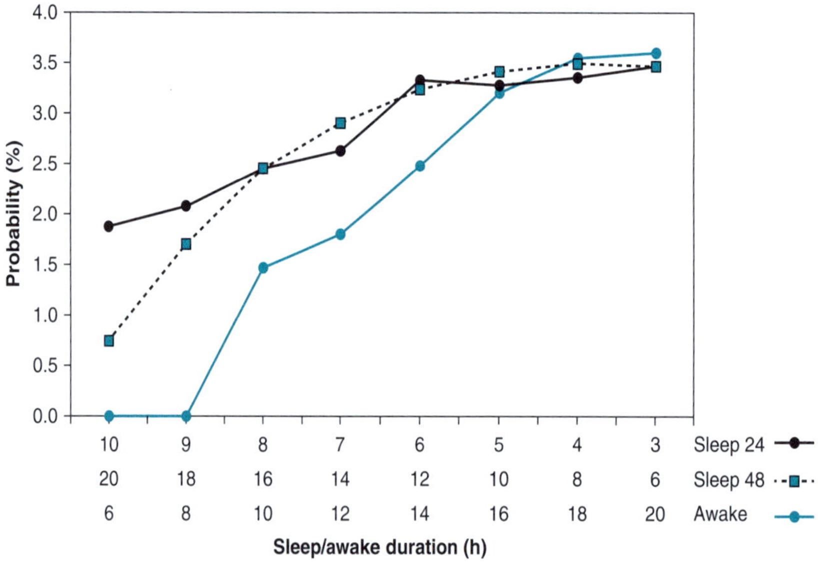

Figure 6.10 Probability of nursing error as a function of prior sleep and hours awake. Error probability increases as sleep in the prior 24 hours and 48 hours reduces, and as time awake increases.
Source: data from Rogers et al., 2004

The study design used in the University of Pennsylvania studies was adapted and used in studies of Australian hospital nurses. Results indicated that Australian nurses reported moderate to high levels of sleepiness and stress, and struggled to remain awake on one in three work shifts. Findings also suggested that less sleep was associated with an increased likelihood of making an error, but also a decreased likelihood of catching an error made by a colleague (Dorrian et al., 2006). This has implications for teamwork, which is particularly important in multidisciplinary, team-based environments such as hospital healthcare. The studies also showed an increase in reports of extreme drowsiness or near accident during the commute following night shifts (Dorrian et al., 2008). Taken together, results suggest that work-related sleep loss and associated impairment are a concern for healthcare professionals and their patients, at work and on the roads during the commute.

It's not only sleep loss and safety risk that are a concern. There is also mounting evidence to suggest that these factors can have negative implications for health. This is explored in the next section.

Sleep loss and health

> That we are not much sicker and much madder than we are is due exclusively to that most blessed and blessing of all natural graces, sleep.
>
> (Aldous Huxley)

Sleep and mental health are inexorably linked (Harrington, 2001). Sleep and mood share hormonal pathways (Meltzer & Nash Jr, 1988). The amount of sleep we have influences our mood (Paterson et al., 2011), and our mood, in particular when we experience disorders such as depression or anxiety, can change our sleep (Åkerstedt 1990). As you may have experienced yourselves, university students are frequently sleep deprived (Lund et al., 2010; Wolfson & Carskadon, 2003). Mood disturbance is also common among students. A study in Australian university students found that three-quarters reported sleep quality measures that were indicative of poor sleep, and one in three reported depression measures that were indicative of depressed mood (Valpiani et al., 2011). This study also found that sleep quality was a mediator of the relationship between depressed mood and fatigue. A number of studies have found relationships between sleep, mood and measures of impaired daytime functioning, including fatigue and academic performance (Thacher, 2008; Wolfson & Carskadon, 2003). For example, Thacher (2008) found that 60% of students had pulled an 'all-nighter' during their studies, and that this was associated with poorer academic outcomes and a trend for increased depression. Have you stayed up all night to finish an assignment? How did you feel the next day? How did you feel about the quality of your work?

Indeed, a useful way of understanding the effects of sleep loss on health is to examine the health profiles of sleep-deprived groups such as students. As discussed previously, shiftworkers also commonly experience sleep loss. In this group, chronic changes in sleep have been associated with changes in physical and mental health.

> Shiftwork is probably bad for the heart, almost certainly bad for the head and definitely bad for the gut.
>
> (Monk & Folkard, 1992)

Shiftwork is a risk factor for indigestion and gastrointestinal ulcers (Minors, Scott & Waterhouse, 1986), cardiovascular disease (Åkerstedt & Knutsson, 1997), overweight, obesity (Givens et al., 2015) and type 2 diabetes (particularly for males and those working rotating shifts) (Gan et al., 2014). Female nightshift workers may be at increased risk of reproductive health problems (Axelsson, Rylander & Molin, 1989). In several groups of shiftworkers, including nurses, studies have indicated a higher incidence of breast cancer (Davis, Mirik & Stevens, 2001; Schernhammer et al., 2001). However, it should be noted that these findings, particularly in cancer research, are new and inconsistent (Wang et al., 2011). More studies are needed to understand the relationship between sleep, circadian disruption, fatigue and physical health. Anxiety and depressive disorders are also commonly reported by shiftworkers (Cavallo, Jaskiewicz & Ris, 2002; Scott, Monk & Brink, 1997). Studies suggest that shiftwork increases the risk of symptoms of depression (Driesen et al., 2010), stress, anger, tension, anxiety and poorer mental health more generally (Srivastava, 2010).

So why do shiftworkers experience these changes in physical and mental health? The answer is complex. There are a number of behavioural, social and physiological mechanisms that are probably interacting with the sleep loss and circadian disruption to produce the observed effects for health. These are summarised in Figure 6.11.

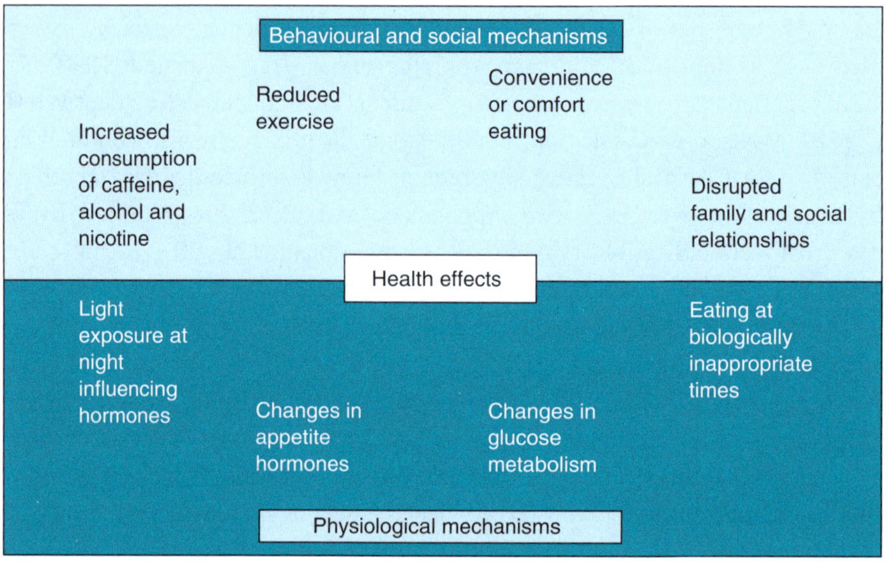

Figure 6.11 Behavioural, social and physiological mechanisms that contribute to the negative health effects seen in shiftworkers

- *Behavioural and social mechanisms.* Shiftworkers often engage in behavioural strategies to promote alertness while at work, and sleep during time off, particularly when these are in conflict with their natural circadian rhythms. This includes use of stimulants, such as caffeine and nicotine (Knauth & Hornberger, 2003; Richardson, Miner & Czeisler, 1989), and use of sleep aids such as prescription medication and alcohol (Dorrian et al., 2011; Knauth & Hornberger, 2003). Due to the fact that their work hours may include times of high social value, such as evenings and weekends, shiftworkers may be unable to participate in regular community events, such as team sport (Atkinson et al., 2008). This may contribute to lower exercise levels among shiftworkers. There are also several suggestions for dietary changes in shiftworkers. For example, shiftworkers may choose foods that are quick and/or convenient, since they may have reduced time for meals, or may eat at atypical times (Persson & Mårtensson, 2006; Waterhouse et al., 2003). Shiftworkers may also experience cravings for high-fat or sugary foods (Persson & Mårtensson, 2006). It has been suggested that this may be a strategy to cope with elevated sleepiness and fatigue.

- *Physiological mechanisms.* One of the physiological mechanisms suggested for the changes in health, particularly in relation to the evidence of increased cancer risk, is that light exposure at night (particularly for those on night shift), alters hormone production, which may in turn increase risk (Davis & Mirick, 2006). Through sleep loss and circadian disruption, shiftworkers may also experience changes in hormones connected with appetite (leptin, ghrelin), changing feelings of hunger and/or satiety (Suwazono et al., 2008). Glucose metabolism is also negatively impacted, so that the body processes food differently when eating occurs at non-optimal circadian times or when sleep is restricted (Banks et al., 2015).

Taken together, this constellation of changes in behaviour and physiology arising from sleep loss and circadian disruption puts pressure on shiftworker health.

Sleep disorders

In 2010, estimates suggested that there were approximately 9% of Australians with sleep disorders, with a total cost to the health system for sleep disorder-related conditions of $544 million. The most common sleep disorders are obstructive sleep apnoea, affecting nearly 5% of Australians and costing $408.5 million, and insomnia, affecting 3% of Australians and costing $118.7 million (SHF, 2011).

Obstructive sleep apnoea

Obstructive sleep apnoea (OSA) is characterised by pauses in breath (apnoea) during sleep. It is a type of sleep-disordered breathing that is often, but not always, accompanied by snoring. Apnoeas are typically associated with reductions in blood oxygen saturation and interruptions to sleep. Due to sleep disruption and hypoxia, people with OSA are often excessively sleepy, experience cognitive impairment and are at increased risk of depressed mood (Hillman et al., 2006; Millman et al., 1989; Thorpy, 2011). OSA is frequently associated with high BMI, obesity and having a thicker neck (Sharafkhaneh & Grogan, 2015). It is diagnosed through an overnight sleep study using sleep monitoring, as described previously (EEG, EOG, EMG), along with respiratory measures including airflow and blood oxygen saturation. OSA is primarily treated using continuous positive airway pressure (CPAP). This involves wearing a mask that fits over the nose and delivers filtered room air at pressure into the airways. CPAP acts like an airway splint, to keep the airways open during sleep, preventing collapse or obstruction and, in turn, associated apnoea. Other treatments for OSA include oral appliances, such as mandibular advancement splints, which hold the lower mandible forward during sleep, and surgery (Sharafkhaneh & Grogan, 2015).

In the context of the growing obesity epidemic, the association between obesity and OSA has led to concern over increasing OSA prevalence. OSA has a number of serious ancillary health effects: it is an independent risk factor for cardiovascular disease, systemic hypertension, stroke, impaired glucose metabolism and diabetes (Punjabi, 2008;

Sharafkhaneh & Grogan, 2015). Overall, people with OSA can experience a feedback loop where apnoea can lead to sleepiness, performance impairment and depressed mood and further health complications such as stroke and diabetes. These consequences of OSA can then lead to changes in behaviour, such as reduced physical activity or changes in diet that can further exacerbate weight gain. The result is a negative cycle that must be broken with interventions (see Figure 6.12).

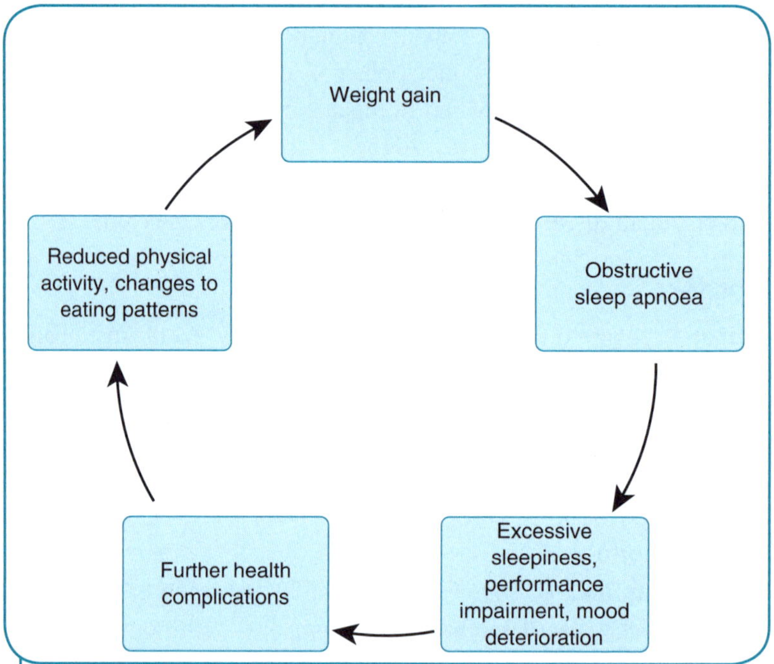

Figure 6.12 Potential cycle of impairment associated with obstructive sleep apnoea (OSA)

As Figure 6.12 shows, weight gain increases the risk of developing OSA, which often results in excessive sleepiness and impaired performance and mood. In addition, further health complications can arise. Together, these factors can lead to reductions in physical activity and changes in diet. These can result in further weight gain, exacerbating the problem.

Insomnia and sleep hygiene

Insomnia is indicated by problems going to sleep or staying asleep. It may be primary (not attributable to another cause) or secondary (where it is comorbid with other disorders such as sleep apnoea). It may be acute or chronic (having symptoms at least three nights per week for more than a month). Primary insomnia can be triggered by trauma or emotional distress. It can also be triggered by illness. Insomnia may be treated with behavioural therapies, including cognitive behavioural therapy and biofeedback. Stimulants may be used to help with sleepiness, and sometimes drugs are prescribed to assist with sleep (soporific) or underlying issues with the circadian rhythm (chronobiotic) (Chesson Jr et al., 1999; Güneş, 2015; Hillman et al., 2006; Thorpy, 2011).

In the International Classification of Sleep Disorders (ICSD-3, 2014), 'inadequate sleep hygiene' is specified as an insomnia subtype. Sleep hygiene refers to environmental or behavioural recommendations with the goal of promoting sleep, or avoiding behaviour that disrupts sleep (Stepanski & Wyatt, 2003). While these were originally aimed at managing insomnia, they are useful general guidelines for achieving a 'good night's sleep'. In the ICSD-3, inadequate sleep hygiene is identified by a series of characteristics, addressed in turn as follows (ICSD-3, 2014, p. 27).

- *Practices such as daytime napping.* While naps have been demonstrated to be useful countermeasures to fatigue under conditions of sleep loss, such as during shiftwork (Driskell & Mullen, 2005), under normal conditions napping during the day can have a negative impact on the main sleep period that night. Napping can lead to a longer time taken to fall asleep and a reduction in deep sleep during the night-time sleep period (Werth et al., 1996). For this reason, it is generally recommended to monitor naps and use them strategically, keeping in mind the potential effect on subsequent sleep.
- *Maintaining a highly variable sleep schedule.* As discussed early in this chapter, when timing of sleep and wake becomes out of sync with our circadian rhythms, such as often happens for shiftworkers, sleep tends to be shorter and of poorer quality (Åkerstedt, 2003). Keeping a consistent bedtime and wake time helps to keep all of our rhythms in synchrony and facilitates better sleep.
- *Routinely using sleep-disruptive products (caffeine, tobacco, alcohol) too close to bedtime.* Caffeine, particularly when used close to bedtime, can have a negative impact on night-time sleep (Drake et al., 2013). As with napping, studies have demonstrated that caffeine can be used as an effective countermeasure for sleepiness and performance impairment (Rogers, Dorrian & Dinges, 2003). The benefits of caffeine use should be weighed against potential effects on subsequent sleep. Nicotine, in tobacco, has been connected with sleep changes. Withdrawal results in sleep fragmentation and people who are in the process of quitting frequently report insomnia (Jaehne et al., 2014). Alcohol has sedative effects and can make it easier to fall asleep. However, it can fragment sleep, particularly later in the sleep period. It is not recommended for use as a sleep aid (Dorrian et al., 2015).
- *Engaging in mentally or physically activating or emotionally upsetting activities too close to bedtime.* There is inconsistent literature investigating the relationship between exercise and sleep. While having a consistent exercise routine can improve sleep, exercising very close to bedtime may result in taking longer to fall asleep (Dzierzewski et al., 2014; Kredlow et al., 2015). Working late into the evening may result in problems getting to sleep. Having a television in the bedroom has also been shown to negatively impact on sleep. With increasing access to screens on computers and smartphones, and the portability of these devices leading to use in the bedroom, the potential impact of screen time on sleep is a big issue at present. Emerging research is indicating the potential for screen time, particularly in the hours before bed, to disrupt sleep (Lanaj, Johnson & Barnes, 2014; Lemola et al., 2014). This includes engaging with social

media, which may provoke emotional responses during the time that we would ideally use to wind down and prepare for sleep.

- *Routinely using the bed and bedroom for activities other than sleep.* This is based on the idea that creating and maintaining strong associations between the bedroom and sleep can make it easier to fall asleep and stay asleep. Having a regular routine and connecting the bedroom with sleep only can help your brain to automatically begin to prepare for sleep upon entering the room. Using the bedroom for other purposes, such as work, may not only break this association, but also introduce the possibility that the bedroom will become associated with something stressful. Stress is the enemy of sleep (Åkerstedt, 2006).
- *Failing to maintain a comfortable environment for sleep.* The sleep environment is important. Studies with shiftworkers have shown that something as simple as covering bedroom windows with black plastic to block out light can have benefits for sleep (Eastman et al., 1995). Noise can also disrupt sleep (Basner et al., 2014). The best sleep environment has a moderate ambient temperature (18–24 °C), and is dark and quiet (Stepanski & Wyatt, 2003).

Mini case study 6.3

John has just graduated with his nursing degree and has been working in his new hospital job for two months. He works rotating shifts. His roster usually consists of two morning shifts (7.00 am to 3.00 pm), then two afternoon shifts (3.00 pm to 11.00 pm) and then two night shifts (11.00 pm to 7.00 am) followed by four days off. He has noticed that he feels very tired. He has been drinking lots of coffee, especially on night shift, to try to stay awake, and often finds himself at the hospital vending machines, buying chocolate bars and caffeinated soft drinks. When he gets home from night shift, he still feels jittery from the caffeine and has trouble falling asleep. He has trouble staying asleep during the day too – the sun shines straight through his bedroom window, and his housemates are noisy. When his shifts fall on weekends, he is unable to play for his soccer team, and has missed the last few parties held by his friends because he had to work.

Critical thinking question

With what you now know about sleep, circadian rhythms and shiftwork, what would you recommend for John to help him cope with his new work hours?

Summary

- Sleep is measured using electrodes that capture patterns in brainwaves, eye movements and muscle tone. On the basis of these patterns, we decide whether people are awake or asleep, and which stage of sleep they are in. Circadian rhythms are near-24 hour rhythms in functioning. These rhythms are controlled by the pacemaker in our brain, and synchronised to the Earth day by light. Our circadian rhythms prime us to be awake and performing during the day and to be asleep at night.
- Sleep is classified into five stages: Stage 1 (transition), Stage 2 (first proper stage of sleep), Stages 3 and 4 (slow wave, or deep sleep) and rapid eye movement (REM) sleep (dreaming sleep).
- When we are sleep deprived, we often feel moody and have trouble making decisions. Our response times are slower and we make more errors. We are also more likely to experience incident or accident. There is increasing evidence that chronic sleep loss and circadian disruption also results in negative impacts for health.
- Understanding sleep is important for healthcare professionals and for clients. Sleep is critical for performance, safety and health, yet sleep is frequently left out of discussions about healthcare. Due to their work schedules, shiftworkers frequently experience sleep loss and circadian disruption. Shiftwork is extremely common for healthcare professionals, including nurses and doctors. Sleep disorders affect 1 in every 11 Australians. The most common sleep disorders are obstructive sleep apnoea and insomnia.
- Napping should be used strategically, and potential consequences for the following main sleep period should be considered. A consistent sleep schedule, with regular sleep and wake times, is best for sleep. Avoid use of caffeine, tobacco and alcohol in the hours before bedtime. Use that time to wind down, and avoid activities that are too mentally or physically intense or emotional. Use the bedroom for sleep (and intimacy) only. The best sleep environment is of moderate ambient temperature and is dark and quiet.

Suggested weblinks

Refer to the companion website at www.cambridge.edu.au/academic/healthpsychology for a list of suggested weblinks.

References

AIHW. (2011). National health priority areas. Canberra: Australian Institute of Health and Welfare. Retrieved from http://www.aihw.gov.au/health-priority-areas/

Åkerstedt, T. (1990). Psychological and psychophysiological effects of shift work. *Scandinavian Journal of Work, Environment & Health*, *16 Suppl 1*, 67–73.

—— (1991). Sleepiness at work: effects of irregular work hours. In: T. H. Monk (ed.), *Sleep, Sleepiness and Performance* (pp. 131–52).

—— (1995). Work hours and sleepiness. *Clinical Neurophysiology*, *25*(6), 367–75. doi: http://dx.doi.org/10.1016/0987-7053(96)84910-0

—— (2003). Shift work and disturbed sleep/wakefulness. *Occupational Medicine* (Oxford, England), *53*(2), 89–94.

—— (2006). Psychosocial stress and impaired sleep. *Scandinavian Journal of Work, Environment & Health*, 493–501.

Åkerstedt, T. & Knutsson, A. (1997). Cardiovascular disease and shift work. *Scandinavian Journal of Work, Environment and Health*, *23*, 241–2.

Åkerstedt, T. & Torsvall, L. (1978). Experimental changes in shift schedules – their effects on wellbeing. *Ergonomics*, *21*, 849–56.

Amoroso, C., Harris, M. F., Ampt, A., Laws, R. A., McKenzie, S., Williams, A. M., … Powell Davies, G. (2009). The 45-year-old health check – feasibility and impact on practices and patient behaviour. *Australian Family Physician*, *38*(5), 358–62.

Atkinson, G., Fullick, S., Grindey, C. & Maclaren, D. (2008). Exercise, energy balance and the shift worker. *Sports Medicine*, *38*(8), 671–85.

Axelsson, G., Rylander, R. & Molin, I. (1989). Outcome of pregnancy in relation to irregular and inconvenient work schedules. *British Journal of Industrial Medicine*, *46*, 393–8.

Banks, S., Dorrian, J., Grant, C. & Coates, A. (2015). Circadian misalignment and metabolic consequences: shiftwork and altered meal times. In: R. Watson (ed.), *Modulation of Sleep by Obesity, Diabetes, Age and Diet* (pp. 155–62). London: Elsevier.

Basner, M., Babisch, W., Davis, A., Brink, M., Clark, C., Janssen, S. & Stansfeld, S. (2014). Auditory and non-auditory effects of noise on health. *The Lancet*, *383*(9925), 1325–32. doi: http://dx.doi.org/10.1016/S0140-6736(13)61613-X

Belenky, G., Wesensten, N. J., Thorne, D. R., Thomas, M. L., Sing, H. C., Redmond, D. P., … Balkin, T. J. (2003). Patterns of performance degradation and restoration during sleep restriction and subsequent recovery: a sleep dose-response study. *Journal of Sleep Research*, *12*(1), 1–12.

Bennett, S. (1995). Cardiovascular risk factors in Australia: trends in socioeconomic inequalities. *Journal of Epidemiology & Community Health*, *49*(4), 363–72.

Boeve, B., Silber, M., Saper, C., Ferman, T., Dickson, D., Parisi, J., … Caselli, R. (2007). Pathophysiology of REM sleep behaviour disorder and relevance to neurodegenerative disease. *Brain*, *130*(11), 2770–88.

Bohle, P., Quinlan, M., Kennedy, D. & Williamson, A. (2004). Working hours, work-life conflict and health in precarious and 'permanent' employment. *Revista de Saúde Pública*, *38*, 19–25. doi: http://dx.doi.org//10.1590/S0034-89102004000700004

Boivin, D. B. & Czeisler, C. A. (1998). Resetting of circadian melatonin and cortisol rhythms in humans by ordinary room light. *Neuroreport*, *9*(5), 779–82.

Borbély, A. A. & Achermann, P. (1994). Sleep homeostasis and models of sleep regulation. In: M. H. Kryger, T. Roth & W. C. Dement (eds), *Principles and Practices of Sleep Medicine* (pp. 309–20). Philadelphia: W. B. Saunders Company.

Bougrine, S., Mollard, R., Ignazi, G. & Coblentz, A. (1995). Appropriate use of bright light promotes a durable adaptation to night-shifts and accelerates readjustment during recovery after a period of night-shifts. *Work Stress*, *9*(2–3), 314–26.

Burgess, H. J. & Dawson, D. (1999). Melatonin: its physiological effects and clinical applications. *Journal of the British Menopause Society, September*, 122–6.

Carrier, J. & Monk, M. (1999). Effects of sleep and circadian rhythms on performance. In: F. W. Turek & P. C. Zee (eds), *Regulation of Sleep and Circadian Rhythms* (pp. 527–56). New York: Marcel Dekker Inc.

Carskadon, M. A. & Dement, W. C. (2011). Monitoring and staging human sleep. In: M. H. Kryger, T. Roth & W. C. Dement (eds), *Principles and Practice of Sleep Medicine* (5th edn), (pp. 16–26). St. Louis: Elsevier Saunders.

Carskadon, M. A. & Rechtschaffen, A. (1994). Monitoring and staging human sleep. In: M. H. Kryger, T. Roth & W. C. Dement (eds), *Principles and Practices of Sleep Medicine*. Philadelphia: W. B. Saunders Company.

Caruso, C. C. (2014). Negative impacts of shiftwork and long work hours. *Rehabilitation Nursing*, *39*(1), 16–25. doi: http://dx.doi.org/10.1002/rnj.107

Cavallo, A., Jaskiewicz, J. & Ris, M. D. (2002). Impact of night-float rotation on sleep, mood, and alertness: the resident's perception. *Chronobiology International*, *19*(5), 893–902.

Chesson Jr, A. L., Anderson, W., Littner, M., Davila, D., Hartse, K., Johnson, S., ... Rafecas, J. (1999). Practice parameters for the nonpharmacologic treatment of chronic insomnia. An American Academy of Sleep Medicine report. Standards of Practice Committee of the American Academy of Sleep Medicine. *Sleep*, *22*(8), 1128–33.

Crouch, R., Wilson, A. & Newbury, J. (2011). A systematic review of the effectiveness of primary health education or intervention programs in improving rural women's knowledge of heart disease risk factors and changing lifestyle behaviours. *International Journal of Evidence-Based Healthcare*, *9*(3), 236–45. Retrieved from: http://onlinelibrary.wiley.com/doi/10.1111/j.1744-1609.2011.00226.x/abstract

Czeisler, C. A., Duffy, J. F., Shanahan, T. L., Brown, E. N., Mitchell, J. F., Rimmer, D. W., ... Kronauer, R. E. (1999). Stability, precision, and near-24-hour period of the human circadian pacemaker. *Science*, *284*(25 June), 2177–81.

Czeisler, C. A., Richardson, G. S., Zimmerman, J. C., Moore-Ede, M. & Weitzman, E. D. (1981). Entrainment of human circadian rhythms by light/dark cycles: a reassessment. *Photochemistry and Photobiology*, *34*, 239–47.

Czeisler, C. A., Weitzman, E. D., Moore-Ede, M. C., Zimmerman, J. C. & Knauer, R. S. (1980). Human sleep: its duration and organisation depend on its circadian phase. *Science*, *210*(12 December), 1264–7.

Davis, S. & Mirick, D. K. (2006). Circadian disruption, shift work and the risk of cancer: a summary of the evidence and studies in Seattle. *Cancer Causes & Control*, *17*(4), 539–45.

Davis, S., Mirick, D. K. & Stevens, R. G. (2001). Night shift work, light at night, and risk of breast cancer. *Journal of the National Cancer Institute*, *93*(20), REPORTS 1557–62.

Dawson, D. & Armstrong, S. M. (1996). Chronobiotics: drugs that shift rhythms. *Pharmacology and Therapeutics*, *69*, 15–36.

Dawson, D. & Reid, K. (1997). Fatigue, alcohol and performance impairment. *Nature*, *388*(6639), 235. doi: http://dx.doi.org/10.1038/40775

Dijk, D. & Edgar, D. M. (1999). Circadian and homeostatic control of wakefulness and sleep. In: F. W. Turek & P. C. Zee (eds), *Regulation of Sleep and Circadian Rhythms* (pp. 111–47). New York: Marcel Dekker Inc.

Dijk, D. J., Brunner, D. P., Beersma, D. G. & Borbély, A. A. (1990). Electrogram power density and slow wave sleep as a function of prior waking and circadian phase. *Sleep*, *13*, 430–40.

Doan, T., Gardiner, A., Gay, C. L. & Lee, K. A. (2007). Breast-feeding increases sleep duration of new parents. *Journal of Perinatal & Neonatal Nursing*, *21*(3), 200–6. doi: http://dx.doi.org/10.1097/01.JPN.0000285809.36398.1b

Dorrian, J., Coates, A., Heath, G. & Banks, S. (2015). Patterns of alcohol consumption and sleep in shiftworkers. In: R. Watson (ed.), *Modulation of Sleep by Obesity, Diabetes, Age and Diet* (pp. 353–62). London: Elsevier.

Dorrian, J. & Dinges, D. F. (2005). Sleep deprivation and its effects on cognitive performance. *Sleep: A Comprehensive Handbook*, 139–44.

Dorrian, J., Hussey, F. & Dawson, D. (2007). Train driving efficiency and safety: examining the cost of fatigue. *Journal of Sleep Research*, *16*(1), 1–11. doi: http://dx.doi.org/10.1111/j.1365-2869.2007.00563.x

Dorrian, J., Lamond, N., van den Heuvel, C., Pincombe, J., Rogers, A. E. & Dawson, D. (2006). A pilot study of the safety implications of Australian nurses' sleep and work hours. *Chronobiology International*, *23*(6), 1149–63. doi: http://dx.doi.org/10.1080/07420520601059615

Dorrian, J., Paterson, J., Dawson, D., Pincombe, J., Grech, C. & Rogers, A. E. (2011). Sleep, stress and compensatory behaviors in Australian nurses and midwives. *Revista de Saúde Pública*, *45*(5), 922–30.

Dorrian, J., Tolley, C., Lamond, N., van den Heuvel, C., Pincombe, J., Rogers, A. E. & Drew, D. (2008). Sleep and errors in a group of Australian hospital nurses at work and during the commute. *Applied Ergonomics*, *39*(5), 605–13. doi: http://dx.doi.org/10.1016/j.apergo.2008.01.012

Drake, C., Roehrs, T., Shambroom, J. & Roth, T. (2013). Caffeine effects on sleep taken 0, 3, or 6 hours before going to bed. *Journal of Clinical Sleep Medicine*, *9*(11), 1195.

Driesen, K., Jansen, N. W., Kant, I., Mohren, D. C. & van Amelsvoort, L. G. (2010). Depressed mood in the working population: associations with work schedules and working hours. *Chronobiology International*, *27*(5), 1062–79.

Driskell, J. E. & Mullen, B. (2005). The efficacy of naps as a fatigue countermeasure: a meta-analytic integration. *Human Factors: The Journal of the Human Factors and Ergonomics Society*, *47*(2), 360–77.

Duffy, J., Kronauer, R. & Czeisler, C. (1996). Phase-shifting human circadian rhythms: influence of sleep timing, social contact and light exposure. *The Journal of Physiology*, *495*(1), 289–97.

Dzierzewski, J. M., Buman, M. P., Giacobbi, P. R., Roberts, B. L., Aiken-Morgan, A. T., Marsiske, M. & McCrae, C. S. (2014). Exercise and sleep in community-dwelling older adults: evidence for a reciprocal relationship. *Journal of Sleep Research*, *23*(1), 61–8.

Eastman, C. I., Boulos, Z., Terman, M., Campbell, S. S., Dijk, D.-J. & Lewy, A. J. (1995). Light treatment for sleep disorders: consensus report VI. Shift work. *Journal of Biological Rhythms*, *10*(2), 157–64.

Ferguson, S. A., Paech, G. M., Dorrian, J., Roach, G. D. & Jay, S. M. (2011). Performance on a simple response time task: is sleep or work more important for miners? *Applied Ergonomics*, *42*(2), 210–13. doi: http://dx.doi.org/10.1016/j.apergo.2010.06.010

Flicker, L., Lautenschlager, N. T. & Almeida, O. P. (2006). Healthy mental ageing. *The Journal of the British Menopause Society*, *12*(3), 92–6. doi: http://dx.doi.org/10.1258/136218006778234011

Folkard, S. (1997). Black times: temporal determinants of transport safety. *Accident Analysis and Prevention*, *29*(4), 417–30.

Folkard, S. & Tucker, P. (2003). Shift work, safety and productivity. *Occupational Medicine* (Oxford, England), *53*(2), 95–101.

Folkard, S., Waterhouse, J. M. & Minors, D. S. (1985). Chronobiology and shiftwork: current issues and trends. *Chronobiologia*, *12*, 31–54.

Gan, Y., Yang, C., Tong, X., Sun, H., Cong, Y., Yin, X., … Gong, Y. (2014). Shift work and diabetes mellitus: a meta-analysis of observational studies. *Occupational and Environmental Medicine*, oemed-2014–102150.

Gay, C. L., Lee, K. A. & Lee, S. Y. (2004). Sleep patterns and fatigue in new mothers and fathers. *Biological Research for Nursing*, *5*(4), 311–18.

Givens, M. L., Malecki, K. C., Peppard, P. E., Palta, M., Said, A., Engelman, C. D., … Nieto, F. J. (2015). Shiftwork, sleep habits, and metabolic disparities: results from the Survey of the Health of Wisconsin. *Sleep Health*, *1*(2), 115–120. doi: http://dx.doi.org/10.1016/j.sleh.2015.04.014

Glazner, L. K. (1991). Shiftwork: its effect on workers. *AAOHN Journal*, *39*(9), 416–21.

Güneş, Z. (2015). The effects of nutrition on sleep and sleep complaints among elderly persons. In: R. Watson (ed.), *Modulation of Sleep by Obesity, Diabetes, Age and Diet* (pp. 255–61). London: Elsevier.

Hall, M. H., Casement, M. D., Troxel, W. M., Matthews, K. A., Bromberger, J. T., Kravitz, H. M., … Buysse, D. J. (2015). Chronic stress is prospectively associated with sleep in midlife women: the SWAN sleep study. *Sleep*. *38*(10), 1645–54.

Härmä, M. (1998). New work times are here – are we ready? *Scandinavian Journal of Work, Environment and Health*, *24*(suppl 3), 3–6.

Harrington, J. M. (2001). Health effects of shift work and extended hours of work. *Occupational and Environmental Medicine*, *58*(1), 68–72.

Hillman, D. R., Murphy, A. S., Antic, R. & Pezzullo, L. (2006). The economic cost of sleep disorders. *Sleep*, *29*(3), 299.

Hobson, A. (1999). Neural control of sleep. In: F. W. Turek & P. C. Zee (eds), *Regulation of Sleep and Circadian Rhythms* (pp. 81–110). New York: Marcel Dekker Inc.

Howard, M. E., Jackson, M. L., Swann, P., Berlowitz, D. J., Grunstein, R. R. & Pierce, R. J. (2014). Deterioration in driving performance during sleep deprivation is similar in professional and nonprofessional drivers. *Traffic Injury Prevention*, *15*(2), 132–7.

ICSD-3. (2014). *International Classification of Sleep Disorders – Third edition (ICSD-3)*. Darien, IL: American Academy of Sleep Medicine.

Jaehne, A., Unbehaun, T., Feige, B., Cohrs, S., Rodenbeck, A. & Riemann, D. (2014). Sleep changes in smokers before, during and 3 months after nicotine withdrawal. *Addiction Biology*, *20*(4), 747–55.

James, J. T. (2013). A new, evidence-based estimate of patient harms associated with hospital care. *Journal of Patient Safety*, *9*(3), 122–8.

Kavanau, J. L. (2005). Evolutionary approaches to understanding sleep. *Sleep Medicine Reviews*, *9*(2), 141–52.

Kleitman, N. (1963). Deprivation of sleep. In: N. Kleitman (ed.), *Sleep and Wakefulness* (pp. 215–29). Chicago: University of Chicago Press.

Knauth, P. & Hornberger, S. (2003). Preventive and compensatory measures for shift workers. *Occupational Medicine* (Oxford, London), *53*(2), 109–16.

Kredlow, M. A., Capozzoli, M. C., Hearon, B. A., Calkins, A. W. & Otto, M. W. (2015). The effects of physical activity on sleep: a meta-analytic review. *Journal of Behavioral Medicine*, *38*(3), 427–49.

Krueger, J. M., Obál, F. & Fang, J. (1999). Why we sleep: a theoretical view of sleep function. *Sleep Medicine Reviews*, *3*(2), 119–29.
Lack, L. C. (1986). Delayed sleep and sleep loss in university students. *Journal of American College Health*, *35*(3), 105–10. doi: http://dx.doi.org/10.1080/07448481.1986.9938970
Lack, L. C. & Lushington, K. (1995). The rhythms of human sleep propensity and core body temperature. *Journal of Sleep Research*, *5*, 1–11.
Lagarde, D. & Doireau, P. (1997). [Jet lag]. *Médecine Tropicale*, *57*(4 Bis), 489–92.
Lamond, N. & Dawson, D. (1999). Quantifying the performance impairment associated with fatigue. *Journal of Sleep Research*, *8*(4), 255–62.
Lanaj, K., Johnson, R. E. & Barnes, C. M. (2014). Beginning the workday yet already depleted? Consequences of late-night smartphone use and sleep. *Organizational Behavior and Human Decision Processes*, *124*(1), 11–23.
Landrigan, C. P., Rothschild, J. M., Cronin, J. W., Kaushal, R., Burdick, E., Katz, J. T., ... Bates, D. W. (2004). Effect of reducing interns' work hours on serious medical errors in intensive care units. *New England Journal of Medicine*, *351*(18), 1838–48.
Lavie, P. (1986). Ultrashort sleep-waking schedule. III. 'Gates' and 'forbidden zones' for sleep. *Electroencephalography and Clinical Neurophysiology*, *63*(5), 414–25.
Lee, C. Y., Chen, H. C., Meg Tseng, M. C., Lee, H. C. & Huang, L. H. (2015). The relationships among sleep quality and chronotype, emotional disturbance, and insomnia vulnerability in shift nurses. *Journal of Nursing Research*. *23*(3), 225–35. doi: http://dx.doi.org/10.1097/jnr.0000000000000095
Leger, D. (1994). The cost of sleep-related accidents: a report for the National Commission on Sleep Disorders Research. *Sleep*, *17*(1), 84–93.
Lemola, S., Perkinson-Gloor, N., Brand, S., Dewald-Kaufmann, J. F. & Grob, A. (2014). Adolescents' electronic media use at night, sleep disturbance, and depressive symptoms in the smartphone age. *Journal of Youth and Adolescence*, *44*(2), 405–18.
Lewy, A. J. (1999). Melatonin as a marker and phase-resetter of circadian rhythms in humans. *Advances in Experimental Medicine and Biology*, *460*, 425–34.
Lewy, A. J., Wehr, T. A., Goodwin, F. K., Newsome, D. A. & Markey, S. P. (1980). Light suppresses melatonin secretion in humans. *Science*, *210*(4475), 1267–9.
Lockley, S. W., Barger, L. K., Ayas, N. T., Rothschild, J. M., Czeisler, C. A. & Landrigan, C. P. (2007). Effects of health care provider work hours and sleep deprivation on safety and performance. *Joint Commission Journal on Quality and Patient Safety*, *33*(Sup. 1), 7–18.
Lund, H. G., Reider, B. D., Whiting, A. B. & Prichard, J. R. (2010). Sleep patterns and predictors of disturbed sleep in a large population of college students. *Journal of Adolescent Health*, 46(2), 124–32.
Manfredini, R., Manfredini, F., Fersini, C. & Conconi, F. (1998). Circadian rhythms, athletic performance, and jet lag. *British Journal of Sports Medicine*, *32*(2), 101–6.
Marhefka, J. K. (2011). Sleep deprivation: consequences for students. *Journal of Psychosocial Nursing and Mental Health Services*, *49*(9), 20–5. doi: http://dx.doi.org/10.3928/02793695-20110802-02
Meltzer, H. & Nash Jr, J. (1988). Serotonin and mood: neuroendocrine aspects In: D. Ganten & D. Pfaff (eds) *Current Topics in Neuroendocrinology: Neuroendocrinology of Mood* (pp. 183–210). Berlin: Springer.
Millman, R. P., Fogel, B. S., McNamara, M. E. & Carlisle, C. C. (1989). Depression as a manifestation of obstructive sleep apnea: reversal with nasal continuous positive airway pressure. *Journal of Clinical Psychiatry*, 50(9), 348–51.
Ming, X., Koransky, R., Kang, V., Buchman, S., Sarris, C. E. & Wagner, G. C. (2011). Sleep insufficiency, sleep health problems and performance in high school students. *Clinical Medicine Insights: Circulatory, Respiratory and Pulmonary Medicine*, *5*, 71–9. doi: http://dx.doi.org/10.4137/CCRPM.S7955
Minors, D. S., Scott, A. R. & Waterhouse, J. M. (1986). Circadian arrhythmia: shiftwork, travel and health. *Journal of the Society of Occupational Medicine, 36*, 39–44.
Minors, D. S. & Waterhouse, J. M. (1981). *Circadian Rhythms and the Human*. Bristol: Wright.
Monk, T. H. (2000). What can the chronobiologist do to help the shift worker? *Journal of Biological Rhythms*, *15*(2), 86–94.
Monk, T. H. & Folkard, S. (1992). *Making Shiftwork Tolerable*. London: Taylor & Francis.
Moore, R. Y. (1999). A clock for the ages. *Science*, *284*, 2102–3.
Moore-Ede, M. C. (1986). Physiology of the circadian timing system: predictive versus reactive homeostasis. *American Journal of Physiology*, *250*(5 Pt 2), R737–52.

Morris, M., Lack, L. & Barrett, J. (1990). The effect of sleep/wake state on nocturnal melatonin excretion. *Journal of Pineal Research*, *9*(2), 133–8.

National Transportation Safety Board (NTSB) (1990). Grounding of U.S. Tankship Exxon Valdez on Bligh Reef, Prince William Sound Near Valdez, AK March 24, 1989. Report Number: MAR-90-04. Washington: NTSB.

Nicolau, M., Akaarir, M., Gamundı, A., Gonzalez, J. & Rial, R. (2000). Why we sleep: the evolutionary pathway to the mammalian sleep. *Progress in Neurobiology*, *62*(4), 379–406.

Paterson, J. L., Dorrian, J., Ferguson, S. A., Jay, S. M., Lamond, N., Murphy, P. J., ... Dawson, D. (2011). Changes in structural aspects of mood during 39–66 h of sleep loss using matched controls. *Applied Ergonomics*, *42*(2), 196–201. doi: http://dx.doi.org/10.1016/j.apergo.2010.06.014

Persson, M. & Mårtensson, J. (2006). Situations influencing habits in diet and exercise among nurses working night shift. *Journal of Nursing Management*, *14*(5), 414–23.

Punjabi, N. M. (2008). The epidemiology of adult obstructive sleep apnea. *Proceedings of the American Thoracic Society*, *5*(2), 136–43.

Rajaratnam, S. M. & Arendt, J. (2001). Health in a 24-h society. *The Lancet*, *358*(9286), 999–1005. doi: http://dx.doi.org/10.1016/S0140-6736(01)06108-6

Refinetti, R. (1999). *Circadian Physiology*. New York: CRC Press.

Richardson, G. S., Miner, J. D. & Czeisler, C. A. (1989). Impaired driving performance in shiftworkers: the role of the circadian system in a multifactorial model. *Alcohol Drugs, and Driving: Abstracts and Reviews*, *5–6*(4-1), 265–73.

Roach, G. D., Dorrian, J., Fletcher, A. & Dawson, D. (2001). Comparing the effects of fatigue and alcohol consumption on locomotive engineers' performance in a rail simulator. *Journal of Human Ergology*, *30*(1–2), 125–30.

Rogers, A. E., Hwang, W.-T., Scott, L. D., Aiken, L. H. & Dinges, D. F. (2004). The working hours of hospital staff nurses and patient safety. *Health Affairs*, *23*(4), 202–12.

Rogers, N. L., Dorrian, J. & Dinges, D. F. (2003). Sleep, waking and neurobehavioural performance. *Frontiers in Bioscience*, *8*, s1056–67.

Rosa, R. R. (1995). Extended workshifts and excessive fatigue. *Journal of Sleep Research*, *4*(S2), 51–6.

Schernhammer, E. S., Laden, F., Speizer, F. E., Willett, W. C., Hunter, D. J., Kawachi, I. & Colditz, G. A. (2001). Rotating nights shifts and risk of breast cancer in women participating in the nurse's health study. *Journal of the National Cancer Institute*, *93*(20), REPORTS 1563–8.

Schwartz, W. J. (1995). Suprachiasmatic nucleus of the hypothalamus. In: M. A. Carskadon, A. Rechtschaffen, G. Richardson, T. Roth & J. Siegel (eds), *The Encyclopaedia of Sleep and Dreaming* (pp. 606–8). New York: Simon & Schuster/Macmillan.

Schwartz, W. J., Busis, N. A. & Hedley-Whyte, E. T. (1986). A discrete lesion of ventral hypothalamus and optic chiasm that disturbed the daily temperature rhythm. *Journal of Neurology*, *233*(1), 1–4.

Scott, A., Monk, T. & Brink, L. (1997). Shiftwork as a risk factor for depression: a pilot study. *International Journal of Occupational and Environmental Health*, *3*(Sup. 2), S2–9.

Scott, L. D., Hwang, W.-T., Rogers, A. E., Nysse, T., Dean, G. E. & Dinges, D. F. (2007). The relationship between nurse work schedules, sleep duration, and drowsy driving. *Sleep*, *30*(12), 1801.

Scott, L. D., Rogers, A. E., Hwang, W.-T. & Zhang, Y. (2006). Effects of critical care nurses' work hours on vigilance and patients' safety. *American Journal of Critical Care*, *15*(1), 30–7.

Shanahan, T. L. (1995). Melatonin. In: M. A. Carskadon, A. Rechtschaffen, G. Richardson, T. Roth & J. Siegel (eds), *The Encyclopaedia of Sleep and Dreaming* (pp. 359–60). New York: Simon & Schuster/Macmillan.

Sharafkhaneh, A. & Grogan, W. A. (2015). Neurocognitive functions in patients with obstructive sleep apnea hypopnea syndrome. In: R. Watson (ed.), *Modulation of Sleep by Obesity, Diabetes, Age and Diet* (pp. 63–8). London: Elsevier.

SHF. (2011). *Re-awakening Australia: The Economic Cost of Sleep Disorders in Australia, 2010.* Canberra: Deloitte Access Economics.

Siegel, J. M. & Rogawski, M. A. (1988). A function of REM sleep: regulation of nonadrenergic receptor sensitivity. *Brain Research*, *13*, 213–33.

Srivastava, U. R. (2010). Shift work related to stress, health and mood states: a study of dairy workers. *Journal of Health Management*, *12*(2), 173–200.

Stepanski, E. J. & Wyatt, J. K. (2003). Use of sleep hygiene in the treatment of insomnia. *Sleep Medicine Reviews*, *7*(3), 215–25.

Stickgold, R. (2005). Sleep-dependent memory consolidation. *Nature*, *437*(7063), 1272–8.

Stickgold, R., Hobson, J. A., Fosse, R. & Fosse, M. (2001). Sleep, learning, and dreams: off-line memory reprocessing. *Science*, *294*(5544), 1052–7.

Suwazono, Y., Dochi, M., Sakata, K., Okubo, Y., Oishi, M., Tanaka, K., … Nogawa, K. (2008). A longitudinal study on the effect of shift work on weight gain in male Japanese workers. *Obesity* (Silver Spring), *16*(8), 1887–93.

Thacher, P. V. (2008). University students and the 'all nighter': correlates and patterns of students' engagement in a single night of total sleep deprivation. *Behavioral Sleep Medicine*, 6(1), 16–31.

The Presidential Commission (1986). *Report of the Presidential Commission on the Space Shuttle Challenger Accident*. Washington: US Government Printing Office.

Thorpy, M. J. (2011). Classification of sleep disorders. *Principles and Practice of Sleep Medicine*, *5*, 680–93.

Valpiani, E. M., Brown, R. F., Thorsteinsson, E. B. & Hine, D. W. (2011). Poor sleep quality mediates between affective symptoms and fatigue in a university student sample. *Psychology and Education*, *48*, 59–71.

Van Dongen, H. P., Maislin, G., Mullington, J. M. & Dinges, D. F. (2003). The cumulative cost of additional wakefulness: dose-response effects on neurobehavioral functions and sleep physiology from chronic sleep restriction and total sleep deprivation. *Sleep*, *26*(2), 117–29.

Verhaegen, P., Maasen, A. & Meers, A. (1981). Health problems in shiftworkers. In: L. C. Johnson, D. J. Tepas, W. P. Colquhoun & M. J. Colligan (eds), *Biological Rhythms and Shift Work* (pp. 271–82). New York: Spectrum.

Vogel, G. W., Vogel, F., McAbee R. S. & Thurmond, A. (1980). Improvement of depression by REM sleep deprivation. *Archives of General Psychiatry*, *37*, 247–53.

Wang, T. L., Chiang, F. T., Hsu, K. I., Tseng, C. D., Lee, T. K. & Tseng, Y. Z. (1997). Abnormal circadian blood pressure changes in patients with acute cerebrovascular disorders. *Journal of the Formos Medical Association*, *96*(9), 710–17.

Wang, X., Armstrong, M., Cairns, B., Key, T. & Travis, R. (2011). Shift work and chronic disease: the epidemiological evidence. *Occupational Medicine* (Oxford, England), *61*(2), 78–89.

Waterhouse, J., Buckley, P., Edwards, B. & Reilly, T. (2003). Measurement of, and some reasons for, differences in eating habits between night and day workers. *Chronobiology International*, *20*(6), 1075–92.

Weaver, D. R., Stehle, J. H., Stopa, E. G. & Reppert, S. M. (1993). Melatonin receptors in human hypothalamus and pituitary: implications for circadian and reproductive responses to melatonin. *The Journal of Clinical Endocrinology and Metabolism*, *76*(2), 295–301.

Webb, W. & Levy, C. (1982). Age, sleep deprivation and performance. *Psychophysiology*, *19*(3), 272–6.

Werth, E., Dijk, D., Achermann, P. & Borbély, A. A. (1996). Dynamics of the sleep EEG after an early evening nap: experimental data and simulations. *American Journal of Physiology-Regulatory, Integrative and Comparative Physiology*, *271*(3), R501–10.

Williamson, A. M., Feyer, A. M., Mattick, R. P., Friswell, R. & Finlay-Brown, S. (2001). Developing measures of fatigue using an alcohol comparison to validate the effects of fatigue on performance. *Accident Analysis and Prevention*, *33*(3), 313–26.

Wolfson, A. R. & Carskadon, M. A. (2003). Understanding adolescents' sleep patterns and school performance: a critical appraisal. *Sleep Medicine Reviews*, 7(6), 491–506.

Zee, P. C. & Turek, F. W. (1999). Introduction to sleep and circadian rhythms. In: F. W. Turek & P. C. Zee (eds), *Regulation of Sleep and Circadian Rhythms* (pp. 1–17). New York: Marcel Dekker Inc.

7

Health risk behaviours: alcohol, drugs and smoking

Learning outcomes

After reading this chapter, you should be able to:

- describe the primary risk factors for health in Australia today
- explain behavioural risk factors that meet diagnostic criteria for substance use disorders
- explain why drivers of health risk behaviours are often complex, personal and emotionally laden
- describe the prevalence and impact of, and treatments for, excessive alcohol use and tobacco smoking
- describe the risk factors, treatment barriers and predictors of relapse for excessive alcohol use and tobacco smoking.

Introduction

Historically, healthcare has primarily focused on infectious diseases. In recent times, in developed countries such as Australia there has been a shift towards chronic illness and accidents. Indeed, the current health priority areas in Australia are cancer, cardiovascular disease, diabetes, mental health, obesity, injury prevention/control, arthritis/musculoskeletal conditions and asthma (AIHW, 2011b). Risk factors for these priorities involve complex behavioural and social interactions. This chapter outlines some of the most common behaviours that are considered risk factors for health. An additional intricacy when considering health risk behaviours is that they are often associated with social disapproval or stigma. This can itself become a barrier to behaviour change, and ultimately treatment. In order to be effective agents of positive behaviour change, health psychologists need to understand the many factors that predispose an individual to health risk behaviours, as well as the barriers to change. In this chapter, we discuss alcohol dependence and tobacco smoking as examples of the complex reasons for behaviour that go beyond conscious 'choice'. These two behaviours are primary risk factors for the common chronic illnesses (or 'lifestyle diseases') that are putting a large burden on the healthcare system.

Behavioural risk factors for health

The Australian Institute of Health and Welfare (AIHW, 2015) has compiled a list of risk factors to health, summarised in Table 7.1. These risk factors fall into five categories: behavioural, genetic, biomedical, environmental and demographic. As health psychologists, we are particularly interested in the behavioural risk factors, as they are potentially modifiable through targeted interventions at the individual and societal level. Further, many of the behavioural risk factors influence biomedical risks; for example, poor diet and nutrition can lead to obesity (Wyatt, Winters & Dubbert, 2006). Indeed, if you examine the most common chronic illnesses placing the largest burden on the healthcare system in Australia and other developed countries (e.g. cardiovascular disease, diabetes, cancer), the behavioural risk factors in that list, in particular smoking, excessive alcohol consumption, poor diet and physical inactivity, are critical for all. Excessive sun exposure is also important in Australia as we have the highest rate of skin cancers in the world (Lomas, Leonardi-Bee & Bath-Hextall, 2012). Skin cancer is primarily caused by ultraviolet radiation from the sun and can be prevented through sun protection behaviours (AIHW, 2014b; Chen, Halliday & Damian, 2013). Many communicable diseases and sexually transmitted infections are also highly preventable by following recommended vaccination schedules and through the adoption of safe sex practices respectively (Christenson et al., 2001; Holmes, Levine & Weaver, 2004; Omer et al., 2009). Addressing behavioural risk factors and promoting health behaviour can have a significant impact on health and wellbeing. Sleep loss and disruption to daily rhythms should also be considered a risk factor (see Chapter 6).

Further, when we consider this list of behavioural risk factors, it is important to note that the drivers of these behaviours are complex, personal and emotionally laden. Figure 7.1 displays results of a study where informants were asked to rank 18 conditions in terms of **stigma**, or social disapproval. Alcoholism, positive HIV status and drug addiction were in the top four most stigmatised conditions, along with having a criminal record for burglary (Room, 2005).

Similarly, in a recent review of stigma and tobacco smoking, Graham (2012) found descriptions of smokers across studies that included terms such as 'malodorous', 'selfish', 'unattractive', 'outcasts', 'lepers' and 'excessive users of public services'. While it has been suggested that public disapproval of such behaviours can aid in their reduction, it has also been clearly argued that even policies that are originally intended for health promotion can result in marginalisation and vilification of certain groups. A frequently cited example is the public health action during the HIV/AIDS epidemic, which deepened the disparities and **discrimination** around gender and sexuality (Graham, 2012). Further, stigma and marginalisation can result in the breakdown of relationships with family, friends and healthcare providers, which can exacerbate engagement in behavioural risk factors and act as barriers to treatment (Carr, 2011; Crothers & Dorrian, 2011; Dorrian, 2010, 2012). This challenging landscape of emotions, relationships, behaviour and health is where health psychologists can play a critical role.

Table 7.1 Risk factors to health

Behavioural	Biomedical
• tobacco smoking	• overweight and obesity
• excessive alcohol consumption	• high blood pressure
• poor diet and nutrition	• high blood cholesterol
• physical inactivity	• impaired glucose tolerance
• excessive sun exposure	**Environmental**
• insufficient vaccination	• social, economic, cultural and political
• unprotected sexual activity	• physical, chemical and biological
Genetic	**Demographic**
• single gene disorders	• age
• chromosomal abnormalities	• sex
• multifactorial diseases	• population subgroups

Source: AIHW, 2015

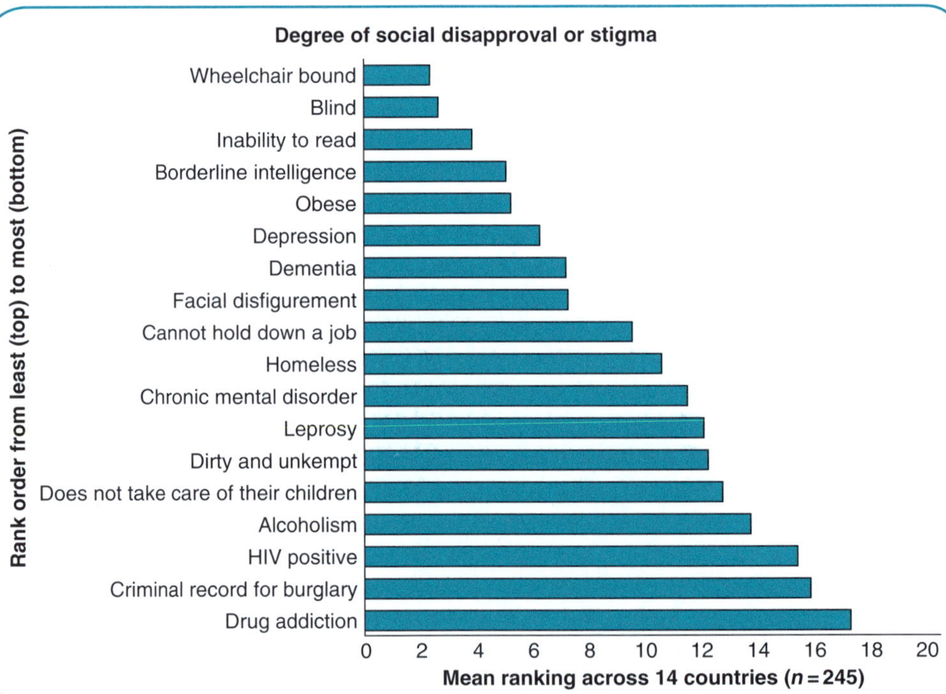

Figure 7.1 Data from a World Health Organisation (WHO) study on the degree of stigma of 18 conditions, ranked by key informants across 14 countries (Canada, China, Egypt, Greece, India, Japan, Luxembourg, the Netherlands, Nigeria, Romania, Spain, Tunisia, Turkey and the UK)
Source: adapted from Room, 2005

The first two risk factors in Table 7.1 are tobacco smoking and excessive alcohol consumption. These come with the added complication of the potential for addiction. Indeed, patterns of tobacco and alcohol consumption may be particularly problematic when they take on characteristics of *impaired control*, *social impairment* and *risky use*, and there is evidence of *tolerance*, and *withdrawal effects* upon use cessation. When these occur, consumption may reach the diagnostic criteria for 'Substance-related and addictive disorders' (American Psychiatric Association, 2013). This is discussed further in the following section.

Substance-related risk behaviours and disorders

> The essential feature of a substance use disorder is a cluster of cognitive, behavioral, and physiological symptoms indicating that the individual continues using the substance despite significant substance-related problems ... An important characteristic of substance use disorders is an underlying change in brain circuits that may persist beyond detoxification, particularly in individuals with severe disorders.
>
> (American Psychiatric Association, 2013, p. 483)

The *Diagnostic and Statistical Manual of Mental Disorders*, 5th edition (DSM-5), published by the American Psychiatric Association, represents a primary diagnostic reference for mental disorders, not only in the US but also in Australia. The latest edition, published in 2013, includes disorders of **alcohol** and **tobacco** use among the 10 classes of drugs in the DSM-5's chapter on substance-related disorders. The other classes include: **cannabis** (also known as marijuana); **hallucinogens** (e.g. phencyclidine or other arylcyclohexylamines, with common names such as PCP, angel dust or ketamine); **inhalants** (e.g. glue, petrol, nitrous oxide); **opioids** (e.g. morphine, heroin); **sedatives**, **hypnotics** and **anxiolytics** (e.g. barbiturates, benzodiazepines); and **stimulants** (e.g. amphetamines, cocaine).

While the mechanisms for each substance are different, all classes activate reward systems in the brain (including GABA [gamma aminobutyric acid], glutamate, opiate and dopamine systems), which are involved with behavioural reinforcement through processing reward and pleasure (Carr, 2011; American Psychiatric Association, 2013). Reward system activation may be so strong that a focus on obtaining and using the substance may occur, leading to *impaired control* over the substance use (Criteria 1 to 4, Table 7.2). Day-to-day activities may be overlooked, leading to *social impairment* (Criteria 5 to 7, Table 7.2) and use of the substance may continue despite knowledge that use is potentially hazardous or harmful, referred to as *risky use* (Criteria 8 to 9, Table 7.2). The *pharmacological* criteria (Criteria 10 to 11, Table 7.2) occur with many substance use disorders (e.g. alcohol), but are not necessary or sufficient for diagnosis. Indeed, these criteria have been at the centre of a long-standing debate that has resulted in changes to the terminology in DSM-5 (O'Brien, 2011).

Table 7.2 Diagnostic criteria for substance use disorders from the DSM-5. There are 11 criteria in total, split into four themes (impaired control, social impairment, risky use, pharmacological criteria). An individual must exhibit at least two of these criteria in a 12-month period. In the DSM-5, specific criteria are given for each disorder in each class of drugs. However, as a general rule, you can understand how these criteria apply to each drug by substituting the particular drug (e.g.'alcohol') in place of '[substance]'.

Impaired control (Criteria 1–4)
This may be characterised by a strong desire for the substance, with time spent accessing it or recovering from its effects. It may also be associated with ingesting more than intended and/or thoughts about cutting down use.
Social impairment (Criteria 5–7)
This may be characterised by continued or recurrent use that results in problems with work, study, domestic or social life.
Risky use (Criteria 8, 9)
This may be characterised by continued or recurrent use that results in physical risk and/or consumption that continues even though it is causing or exacerbating a known psychological or physical health problem.
Pharmacological criteria (Criteria 10, 11)
Tolerance refers to the phenomenon seen with many drugs whereby chronic use results in the requirement for more to achieve the same effect (e.g. level of intoxication). Withdrawal refers to the spectrum of negative physical and psychological consequences associated with cessation of use.

Source: adapted from American Psychiatric Association, 2013, pp. 483–4

That is, when a previous version of the DSM (DSM-III) was being revised in the mid-1980s, there was debate about whether to use the word 'addiction', or 'dependence'. Some argued that the word 'addiction' was denigratory, and resulted in marginalisation of the patients. On the other hand, others argued that the word 'dependence' was already used to describe tolerance and withdrawal, which were standard, non-pathologic responses to many substances. This would make use of 'dependence' in this context confusing. Apparently, in a final vote the word 'dependence' was chosen by the smallest of margins. In previous versions of the DSM, you will see the word 'dependence' used to describe uncontrolled drug-seeking. One of the adverse outcomes of this was that doctors were reluctant to prescribe pain medications, such as opioids, because the normal tolerance to the drug and rebound effects when discontinued could be considered to be indicative of 'addiction' (American Psychiatric Association, 2013; O'Brien, 2011).

For the current DSM, many were in favour of going back to the word 'addiction', but as a more neutral compromise you will see that the current label is 'substance use disorders', under the broader heading of 'Substance-related and addictive disorders' (American Psychiatric Association, 2013). What this debate highlights is the importance of the words we use and the recognition, even in this central mechanism by which we medically define

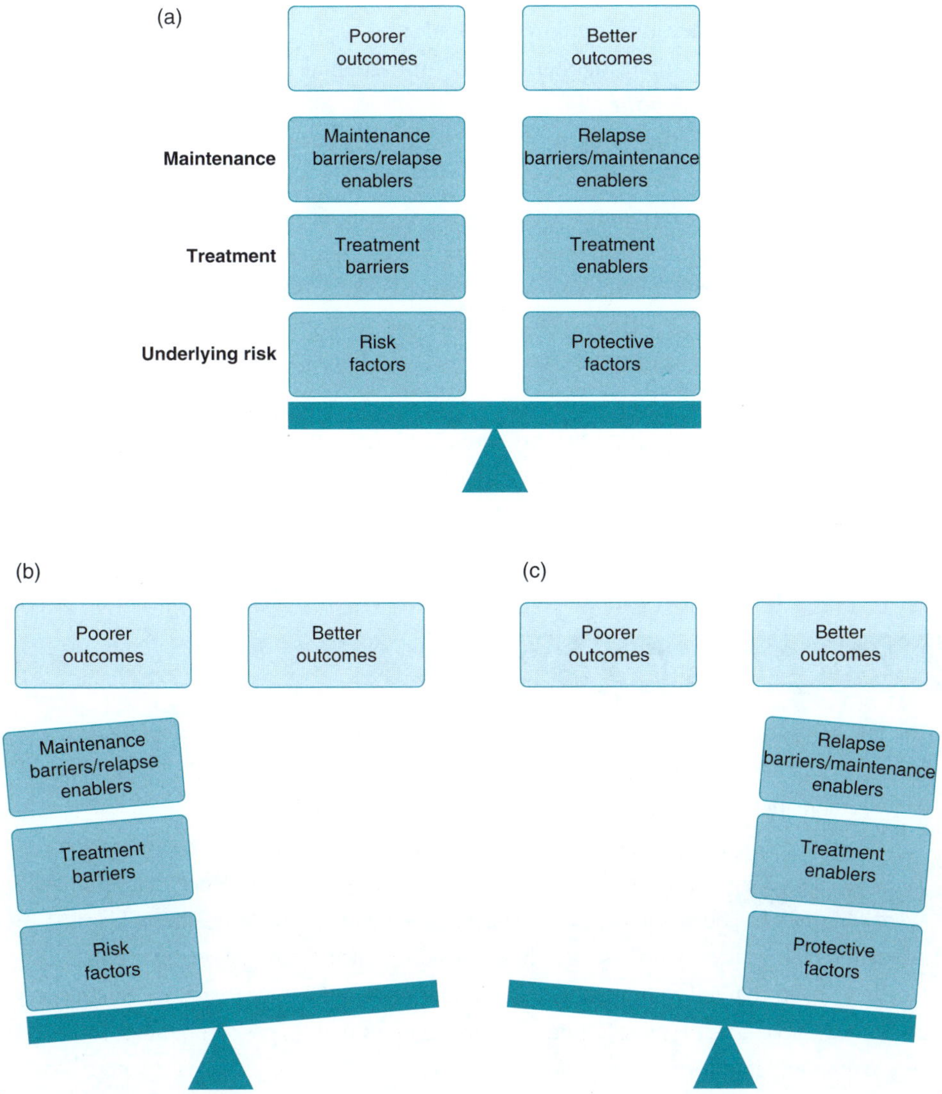

Figure 7.2 Drivers of outcomes in substance use disorders. Part (a) shows the drivers of poorer outcomes and better outcomes that will be the focus for the rest of the chapter – specifically the underlying risk, treatment and maintenance. When weight shifts towards risk and barriers to treatment and maintenance, poorer outcomes are more likely (b). When the opposite occurs, the balance shifts towards better outcomes (c).

these disorders, that the way we talk about health risk behaviours can have important effects. These effects include stigma, marginalisation, discrimination and barriers to support and treatment. This understanding is fundamental for everyone working in the area of health-related behaviour.

It is important to note that, when considering substances such as alcohol, it is possible to consume it in amounts that may have a negative impact on health even without meeting the criteria for disorder. For example, the National Health and Medical Research Council (NHMRC) guidelines for alcohol consumption recommend no more than four drinks in 24 hours to minimise risk of injury, and no more than two drinks per day to minimise risk of lifetime harm (NHMRC, 2009). However, what is particularly useful about looking at the diagnostic criteria for substance use disorders is that it is clear that the idea that someone simply *chooses* to take or not to take a substance is far too simplistic. The following sections consider this in more detail, focusing on two common health risk behaviours: alcohol consumption and tobacco smoking. We will discuss each of these behaviours in relation to underlying risk, treatment and maintenance, as outlined in Figure 7.2.

Mini case study 7.1

The following is a conversation between two healthcare professionals, John and Jane, regarding a patient, Mr Smith. While this mini case study is hypothetical, the situation and conversation are based on real events.

Mr Smith is 50 years old and has a history of chronic alcohol use and heavy smoking. Five years ago, Mr Smith's wife and son were killed in a car accident. Since that traumatic event Mr Smith has been admitted to the hospital many times due to health problems associated with heavy alcohol use (e.g. falls, accidents, gastrointestinal issues). John and Jane have been charged with his care on a number of his visits. A year ago, Mr Smith was diagnosed with cancer. He has just been given the news that his condition has become very serious and that he may not have long to live.

John: 'Sad about Mr Smith.'

Jane: 'Yeah, I suppose, but it's his own fault really.'

John: 'I guess he was warned.'

Jane: 'It's not like people don't know that smoking and heavy drinking can cause cancer. He was told enough times.'

John: 'It's still sad – he's a nice guy.'

Jane: 'Yeah, but I find it hard to feel sorry for him. I can't help thinking he deserves it. But then I remember how he lost his family.'

John: 'That was horrific. He's never recovered from that.'

Jane: 'True. He's been in here almost every time he's had too much to drink and done more damage to himself. I feel like we patch him up just to go out and hurt himself again, and now look what's happened.'

John: 'Yeah, I feel a bit like that too. Why couldn't he just stop? Didn't he see what he was doing to himself?'

Jane: 'Well, I guess he's paying for it now – learning his lesson.'

John: 'I guess . . . Hey, do you know if he ever got treatment for his alcohol problem?'

Jane: 'Don't know. Don't think so.'

Critical thinking questions

1. How do you feel after reading this?
2. What do you think about John's attitude towards Mr Smith? What do you think about Jane's comments?
3. Do you think John and Jane's attitudes may have influenced their interactions with Mr Smith? What about his quality of care?

Alcohol consumption and alcohol-use disorder (AUD)

> The harmful use of alcohol results in approximately 2.5 million deaths each year, with a net loss of life of 2.25 million, taking into account the estimated beneficial impact of low levels of alcohol use on some diseases in some population groups … Alcohol consumption is the world's third largest risk factor for disease and disability; in middle-income countries, it is the greatest risk. Alcohol is a causal factor in 60 types of diseases and injuries and a component cause in 200 others. Almost 4% of all deaths worldwide are attributed to alcohol, greater than deaths caused by HIV/AIDS, violence or tuberculosis. Alcohol is also associated with many serious social issues, including violence, child neglect and abuse, and absenteeism in the workplace.
>
> (WHO, 2011, pp. 10–11)

In many countries, alcohol is a notable part in the social and economic fabric. In Australia, think about our wine industry alone, which is considered to be among the top 10 in the world (australia.gov.au, 2007). In 2012–2013, 1.75 million tonnes of grapes were crushed, with 487.7 million litres of wine sold domestically for $2369.2 million (ABS, 2013b). Wine is frequently used for relaxation, celebration and condolence (NAS, 2006).

Globally, most people either don't drink alcohol or do so at levels that would not be considered harmful (WHO 2011). However, when consumed to excess, alcohol can have serious negative consequences. Of those who drink, it has been estimated that 10% engage in **heavy episodic drinking**, which refers to the consumption of approximately five or more standard drinks on a single occasion. Heavy episodic drinking increases risk of accident and injury. As with all measures of alcohol consumption, men outnumber women: men are four times more likely to engage in heavy episodic drinking (WHO, 2011). Globally, alcohol is among the top 12 risk factors for disease burden (NAS, 2006), accounting for approximately 4% of deaths and 4.6% of disability life years, which take into account years lost through early death as well as years lived with disability (Rehm et al., 2009).

The proportion of the Australian adult population drinking at levels indicative of lifetime harm (NHMRC, 2009) is around 20% (ABS, 2013b). The proportion consuming alcohol at risk levels for harm on a single occasion (NHMRC, 2009) is approximately 45% (AIHW, 2014a). In Australia, alcohol-related social issues have been estimated to cost $7.6 million in a single year (1998–1999), affecting workplace participation and productivity and contributing to road accidents, crime, lost production in the home and health costs (NAS, 2006). In Australia, more than other drugs, alcohol consumption has been cited as the greatest serious community concern (AIHW, 2011a).

Underlying risk

As with other mental illness, risk factors for developing alcohol-use disorder (AUD) include family history, social learning experience (including early exposure to drinking behaviours and violence or trauma), and mood or anxiety disorders. Trauma in adulthood can also act as a triggering event. These are discussed in turn.

Family history

The heritability rate for AUD has been estimated at up to 60% (Eve, 1989; Ginter & Simko, 2009). Genetic factors can predispose people to developing AUD, as evidenced by genetic (Ginter & Simko, 2009; Hansell et al., 2009) and adoptee studies (Morrison et al., 2008). As we know, however, when we ask questions in psychology about whether nature or nurture is responsible for certain outcomes, the answer is almost universally 'both'! This is also true for development of AUD.

Family and social learning experience

Research has suggested that early experience may enable the expression of related genes (Agrawal et al., 2009). Many studies have demonstrated the importance of early exposure to alcohol-related behaviours for development of drinking patterns in later life (Fergusson, Boden & Horwood, 2008). For example, one study suggested that alcohol exposure before age six doubled the likelihood of frequent, heavy or problem drinking during teenage years (Fergusson, Lynskey & Horwood, 1994). Other studies have indicated that parental drinking patterns (Eve 1989), violence between parents (Fergusson & Horwood, 1998), and maltreatment and abuse during childhood (Gilbert et al., 2009; Magnusson et al., 2011) also elevate the likelihood of later development of problematic drinking patterns.

Mood and anxiety disorders

AUD is frequently comorbid with depression (Fowler, 2006), anxiety and post-traumatic stress (Carr, 2011). Comorbidity between alcohol problems, depression and suicide among adolescents has been estimated at 73% (Ganz & Sher, 2009). It has been suggested that people may use alcohol to self-medicate (Ganz & Sher, 2009) in situations where they are nervous (Swendsen et al., 2000), depressed (Deykin, Levy & Wells, 1986), experiencing distress resulting from sexual assault (Miranda et al., 2002), or anxious because of social phobia (Carrigan & Randall, 2003). Such studies may indicate that negative mood states may encourage alcohol consumption (Young-Wolff et al., 2009). However, there have been suggestions that this relationship could have the opposite causal direction: that changes in alcohol consumption may result in mood change. Indeed, withdrawal or detoxification are often associated with symptoms of depression and anxiety. It has also been argued that alcohol use and mood disorders may have the same underlying risk factors, and that AUD may appear to be the predisposing factor in this relationship because it has an earlier onset (Swendsen et al., 2000).

Triggering events in adulthood

AUD has been connected to unpleasant or traumatic events (Johnson, 2010; Sacks & Keks, 1998), such as disaster, witnessing grotesque death, physical and sexual abuse in later life, and military combat (Stewart, 1996). Alcohol problems can also be triggered (Byrne, Raphael & Arnold, 1999), or exacerbated (Dorrian, 2010) by the loss of a spouse.

Treatment

Treatment for AUD can be applied at a societal and/or individual level.

- *Societal level.* In a comprehensive review of the evidence for alcohol and harm-related policies and programs, it was argued that more rigorous mechanisms must be put in place to prevent further increases in harms resulting from alcohol at a global level (Anderson, Chisholm & Fuhr, 2009). Such mechanisms include reducing availability of alcohol, price increases, increasing the proportion of alcohol that is taxed, placing further restrictions on alcohol advertising, and legally enforced drink-driving penalties and countermeasures (Anderson et al., 2009; Rehm et al., 2009; Room, Babor & Rehm, 2005).
- *Individual level.* Given the levels of stigma surrounding AUD, it is not surprising that a central tenet in treatment is the maintenance of a non-judgemental attitude (Sacks & Keks, 1998), giving consideration to the person's biology and social and family history (Morrison et al., 2008). Care is multilayered and ongoing. Not only is assistance required during the planning and intervention phase, but detoxification and withdrawal symptoms can be very serious in AUD. Symptoms include headache, anxiety, sleep issues, nausea, very high heart rate, high blood pressure, impaired thermoregulation, sweating, tremors, seizures, delirium and shaking (*delirium tremens*). In some cases, these symptoms themselves are life threatening (Carr, 2011). Current best practice involves a comprehensive approach to care, including education, therapy (individual and/or group), and attention to potential comorbid mental illness. Where possible, involving family and other social supports can be vital (Carr, 2011; Sacks & Keks, 1998). Pharmacological interventions such as **naltrexone** may be used to assist with reducing dependence. However, these are recommended as only one part of the approach: psychological aspects of dependence must also be treated (Garbutt et al., 1999; Graham, Wodak & Whelan, 2002).

A pivotal component of current treatments is readiness and willingness to change. This influences treatment engagement, compliance and outcomes (Catalbiano, Sarafino & Byrne, 2008; Ekendahl, 2007; Erickson et al., 1995; Holmwood, 2002; Sacks & Keks, 1998). One critical problem with this focus on readiness to change is that the effects of alcohol on the brain make it very difficult for some people to make the decision to change and to engage with treatment. Specifically, alcohol damages the **frontal lobe**, resulting in issues with motivation, energy, planning and decision-making (Moselhy, Georgiou & Kahn, 2001). This is explored further below. In addition, some researchers have found that treatment may be unsuccessful, even when initial readiness to change is high (Yonas et al., 2005). These factors have led to the argument that 'waiting for the addict to "be ready" for treatment can be dangerous' (Clay, Allen & Parran 2008, p. 1).

Another central tenet of many treatments is **abstinence**. There is an ongoing debate about whether individuals who have been diagnosed with AUD may be able to progress to a point where they are able to consume alcohol again at safe levels (Catalbiano et al., 2008). It has been suggested that this may be appropriate for younger people with fewer associated issues (McMurran, 1991). It may be important to acknowledge that abstinence may not be realistic for everyone, and relapse is common (Graham et al., 2002; Sacks & Keks, 1998). For example, individuals with concomitant chronic illness and AUD are frequently on a number of medications that may interact with alcohol. Facilitating open discussion about alcohol consumption in these cases can help with safe and effective management of the medications, and the illness more broadly (Dorrian, 2010).

Treatment barriers

Brain damage

Alcohol has wide-ranging negative effects on the brain. One area of focus has been the frontal lobe, with research in people with alcohol-use problems revealing lower glucose utilisation in this area of the brain (Kopelman, 2008; Moselhy et al., 2001) and impaired performance on tasks designed to measure frontal lobe function (Kopelman, 2008). Autopsy has identified loss of volume and reduced frontal lobe neuronal counts in people with chronic alcohol use (Kopelman, 2008). A list of the characteristics of impairment experienced by individuals with frontal lobe impairment is summarised in Table 7.3. Frontal lobe dysfunction can manifest in increased risk-taking (e.g. impulsivity, disinhibition, reduced attention), communication and relationship difficulties (e.g. abnormalities of emotion, apathy, shallowness), and reduction in the ability to engage with behaviour change and treatment more broadly (e.g. decrease in will and energy, problems with planning and problem-solving, poor motivation and decision-making).

Illness, disease and injury

Chronic alcohol problems have been linked with a 200 to 300% increase in likelihood of premature death. Common causes include cirrhosis of the liver, cancer (head, neck, oesophagus, breast, gastrointestinal), cardiovascular disease, stroke and accidents (e.g. burns, falls, drowning) (Carr, 2011; Schuckit, 2009). Excessive alcohol use impairs

Table 7.3 Characteristics of frontal lobe impairment

Characteristics of frontal lobe dysfunction		
• disorders of categorising • decrease in voluntary motor behaviour • difficulty in response shifting • abnormalities in emotion • apathy • indifference • shallowness • difficulty in creative thinking	• decrease in will and energy • perseverative behaviour • short-term memory problems • problem-solving difficulties • impulsivity • disinhibition • poor motivation • problems with decision-making	• reduced artistic expression • poor spatial working memory • poor language and motor control • reduced ability to sustain attention • reduced capacity to plan future actions

Source: adapted from Moselhy et al., 2001

endocrine function, and can cause reduced sex drive and reproductive capability (Carr, 2011). Another key impact is interference with absorption of vitamins and minerals. **Thiamine** deficiency is common, and may result in **Wernicke's encephalopathy**. It is also associated with changes to balance and gait, confusion and memory loss. In severe cases, **Korsakoff's syndrome** can also result, which is characterised by the inability to create new memories (**anterograde amnesia**). When changes in gait and anterograde amnesia are seen together, the combination is commonly referred to as **Wernicke-Korsakoff Syndrome** (Carr, 2011; Schuckit, 2009). AUD can exacerbate the risks associated with concomitant illnesses, including psychiatric disorders (Schuckit, 2009). Alcohol can interact with medications, making it difficult to titrate appropriate doses, and negatively impact on memory, making adherence to medication schedules difficult (Dorrian, 2010). Complications following surgery, such as bleeding and infection, are also more likely (Carr, 2011).

Family and social effects

As mentioned earlier, AUD is associated with high social disapproval and stigma. This can cause breakdown of relationships with family and friends. Stereotypic views of people with AUD include ideas that they are 'scruffy', 'derelict', 'amoral' and 'weak-willed' (Carr, 2011; Catalbiano et al., 2008). In a review of population studies, it was concluded that:

> People suffering from alcohol dependence (and from other addictions) are particularly severely stigmatized. They are less frequently regarded as mentally ill, they are held much more responsible for their condition, they provoke more social rejection and more negative emotions and they are at a particular risk of being structurally discriminated against.
>
> (Schomerus et al. 2011, p. 109)

AUD affects a wide spectrum of the population, across age, gender and socioeconomic groups (Catalbiano et al., 2008; Huerta & Borgonovi, 2010). As discussed in the earlier section on underlying risk, research has led to an understanding of multiple factors that can predispose someone to developing AUD, including genetics and family history, early exposure to patterns of drinking in the home, mood and anxiety disorders and trauma. Stigma and negative stereotypes persist despite this increasing understanding. This may be due, at least in part, to the disinhibited behaviour that frequently accompanies such disorders and may put the individual, and others, at risk. A large Australian survey ($n > 26000$) (AIHW, 2011a) asked respondents to identify certain behaviours that they had engaged in while intoxicated during the preceding year, and revealed that:

- 13% cent reported that they had driven a vehicle
- 6% reported engaging in verbal abuse
- 5% reported going to work
- 4% reported that they created a disturbance, damaged or stole goods
- 1% reported engaging in physical abuse
- 20% reported engaging in at least one potentially harmful activity while intoxicated.

The same survey asked respondents to identify behaviours that they had experienced during the preceding year from others who were intoxicated, and revealed that:

- 24% over 14 years of age had been verbally abused
- 8% had been physically abused
- 14% had been put in fear by someone under the influence of alcohol.

As with other disorders involving addiction, AUD is frequently associated with deceit, shame and guilt (Shaffer et al., 2004). At the same time, frontal lobe deficits (Table 7.3), can cause indifference, shallowness and apathy, as well as difficulties in understanding cues such as speech intonation, emotional content of facial expressions and humour (Uekermann & Daum, 2008). All of these factors contribute to relationship breakdown and isolation for people with AUD.

Interactions with healthcare professionals

As with the population more generally, healthcare professionals are also vulnerable to negative stereotype and stigma in relation to people with AUD.

> Historically, we have attributed addictive illness, including alcoholism, to wilful misconduct, character flaws, weak will, moral turpitude, or just bad people. Science does not support these outdated stereotypes. In 1956, the American Medical Association declared alcoholism an illness. Hampered by prejudice, misinformation, and an outdated sense of hopelessness at our supposed inability to effect meaningful intervention, the medical community has been slow to respond. Even today, most medical students and residents complete training without benefit of a rudimentary working knowledge of addictive illness; an illness they will see in their office almost daily for the rest of their careers.
>
> (Carr, 2011, pp. 9–10)

Literature highlights the importance of supportive, positive, non-judgemental interactions with healthcare professionals as fundamental to effective care (Sacks & Keks, 1998). Research in this area has been conducted with doctors and nurses in general, and emergency department staff in particular, as being among the front line workers treating patients with AUD. This work suggests that:

- attitudes of healthcare professionals towards patients with AUD may be negative (Clay et al., 2008; Durand, 1994)
- perceived barriers to care include lack of training, expertise and time (Durand, 1994; Geirsson, Bendtsen & Spak, 2005), the view that the patient will be unmotivated to engage in treatment (Indig et al., 2009) and that treatment will be ineffective (Carr, 2011) and unrewarding (Crothers & Dorrian, 2011)
- healthcare professionals in areas with specialised drug and alcohol programs tend to have more positive attitudes towards patients with AUD (Allen, 1993)
- training and knowledge are predictors of positive attitudes and intention to care (Allen, 1993; Crothers & Dorrian, 2011; Geirsson et al., 2005; Talbot, Dorrian & Chapman, 2015)
- healthcare professionals may not diagnose or treat AUD (Gordon, Fahey & Sanson-Fisher, 1988), potentially as a result of lack of screening or systematic procedures (Anderson et al., 2001; Indig et al., 2009), or due to a focus on more immediate, life-threatening aspects of patient presentation, with a lack of follow-up in longer term care (Baird, Burge & Grant, 1989; Dorrian, 2010)
- there is a clear need for and interest in alcohol-related training across all areas of healthcare studied (Anderson et al., 2001; Indig et al., 2009; Owens, Gilmore & Pirmohamed, 2000).

Treatment seeking

It has been estimated that only 25% of people with alcohol dependency will seek and/or pursue treatment (Schuckit, 2009), and that only 13% will be specifically treated for their addiction (Carr, 2011). Barriers to treatment seeking may include concern about healthcare professionals maintaining confidentiality (Gordon et al., 2011), worry over the treatment (Durand, 1994) and, importantly, the negative stereotypes, stigma and prejudice from the general community, healthcare professionals, family and friends. AUD-related brain damage (Table 7.3), which can reduce the capacity to perceive risk, plan and engage in behaviour change may also represent a key hurdle. This impairment of personal agency has been referred to as a reduced capacity to 'choose health' and is a critical oversight in treatment approaches and also in public policy (Dorrian, 2010, 2012; Williamson, 2009a, 2009b).

Maintenance

> People living with dependency problems must strive for recovery (often relapsing along the way) within communities and families which often despise them and/or their condition.
>
> (Williamson, 2009a, p. 9)

As we have discussed in this chapter, there is a biopsychosocial spectrum of consequences of AUD, including physical damage, associated disease, increased personal risk, cognitive and psychological impairment, and family and social injury. These are summarised in Figure 7.3. These consequences serve not only as barriers to treatment, but also as drivers bio —— psycho —— social

Physical damage	Associated diseases	Risk	Cognitive/psychological	Family/social
Brain	Cancers	Motor vehicle accident	Frontal lobe dysfunction	Family deprivation
Gastrointestinal system	Epilepsy	Falls	Unipolar depressive disorders	Unintentional injury
Cardiovascular system	Cardiovascular disorders	Drowning	Suicidal ideation	Interpersonal violence
Endocrine system	Gastrointestinal disease	Poisoning	Anxiety	Injury/fatality caused through drink-driving
Vitamin and nutrient absorption	Diabetes mellitus	Trauma	Korsakoff's psychosis	Reduced job performance
Immune system	Wernicke's encephalopathy	Burns	Confusion	Absenteeism
Dehydration	Infections		Hallucinations	Spread of sexually transmitted infections (STI)
Blood thinning				Maternal and perinatal disorders
				Judgements from others

Figure 7.3 The biopsychosocial spectrum: summary of negative physical consequences, associated disease and illness, risks, cognitive and psychological issues, and family and social problems associated with alcohol-use disorders.
Source: adapted from Dorrian, 2012

for relapse. Relapse in AUD is common (Graham et al., 2002; Sacks & Keks, 1998). It has even been suggested that the detoxification process itself may result in reduced **brain plasticity** and longer timeframes required for healing frontal lobe damage, such that repeated relapse makes treatment increasingly difficult (Loeber et al., 2010).

Indeed, the spectrum of consequences of AUD has been conceptualised as a self-perpetuating feedback loop, where each aspect of the disease reduces the capacity to engage and to comply with treatment (Figure 7.4). At the centre of the loop are the psychosocial risk factors, which predispose the individual to developing problematic drinking behaviours. Around the outside are the consequences of AUD that have been discussed in this chapter: family/social damage, frontal lobe damage, loss of independence, negative interactions with healthcare professionals, alcohol interactions with other medications, and alcohol-related illness and injury. These consequences not only magnify the negative impact of the disease, but also make it more and more difficult for the individual to engage in behaviour change. The more serious and long-term the AUD, the more likely that an individual will have progressed further in this cycle. Arguably, at a certain point, individuals may no longer have the capacity to 'choose health', and current treatments that focus on readiness to change will no longer be of value. A key question for healthcare and public policy is: what do we do then?

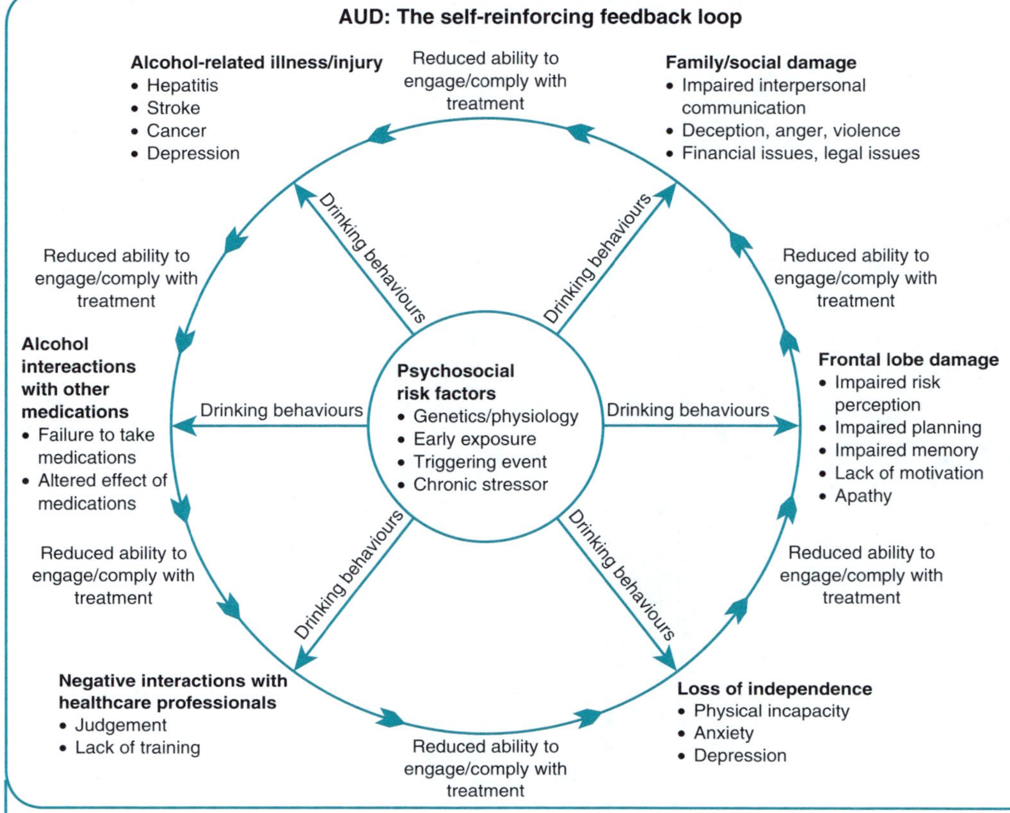

Summary points

- The importance of support from friends, family and the wider community for those with AUD cannot be overstated ... and is required at times when these relationships are put under particular strain. Stigma and stereotypes of individuals with AUD must be addressed at a community level, and among healthcare professionals, as they are outdated, unhelpful and present barriers for treatment.
- Education for healthcare professionals in evidence-based identification, treatment and follow-up for individuals with AUD is absolutely required and desired by the professionals themselves.
- This education must emphasise the importance of positive, supportive, non-judgemental interactions and provide a clear understanding of alcohol addiction as a relapsing brain disease, with recognised biological and social risk factors.
- Education will also facilitate increased routine screening for patients, particularly those who may be identifiable as 'at-risk' (e.g. older, bereaved individuals; those with frequent hospital admissions for burns, falls or common alcohol-related chronic illness).
- Public-level policies and education may be demonstrably effective, as may current treatments with a central focus on readiness to change, but these may have limited influence for those with impaired cognitive capacity who may not be able to '*choose health*'. We cannot overlook the most ill patients with alcohol-use disorders, and dedicated and innovative research and development of treatments and support systems for those who have reduced agency is crucial.

Figure 7.4 Summary diagram: AUD as a self-reinforcing (positive) feedback loop (left) and summary points
Source: Dorrian, 2012, pp. 15–16

Mini case study 7.2

The following details are summarised from a case study (Spilsbury, 2012) of Mr B, a 54-year-old man who had gingivitis. A blood test by his GP revealed markers of impaired liver function. This alerted his doctor to his AUD. Mr B reports that he started drinking when he was 14, and at 17 he left home and school and began to drink daily. He reports a violent family environment when he was growing up; his father would fly into alcohol-fuelled rages and assault members of his family. His brother attempted to protect him during one of his father's rages, and ended up hurting his father so badly that hospitalisation was required. Mr B was himself imprisoned for 5 years for manslaughter after killing someone with a lump of wood while drunk. He has a history of turbulent relationships, and his most recent relationship had just broken down. He is absent from work frequently, which has put his job at risk. He reported that he 'found life without alcohol colourless and his work was boring'. He was having trouble getting out of bed and 'distracting himself from dark thoughts'. He had a history of major depression, which included two attempts at suicide. At the time of his interview, Mr B was living alone and had remained abstinent from alcohol for one week. He had experienced shivering and shaking.

Critical thinking questions

1. From the short case description, can you identify possible underlying risk factors for AUD for Mr B?
2. Can you identify some physical and social/family consequences of AUD for Mr B?
3. Can you identify signs that indicate that Mr B had experienced withdrawal symptoms?
4. What do you think about the link between AUD and depression in Mr B's case?

Tobacco use

> The tobacco epidemic is one of the biggest public health threats the world has ever faced, killing around 6 million people a year. More than 5 million of those deaths are the result of direct tobacco use while more than 600 000 are the result of non-smokers being exposed to second-hand smoke.
>
> (WHO, 2015)

Tobacco use is associated with increased risk of chronic diseases including coronary heart disease, stroke, respiratory disease and cancer. Tobacco accounts for 20 to 30% of cancer cases in Australia, making it the most preventable cause of ill health and mortality (AIHW, 2014b). Smoking during pregnancy also has serious consequences, including increased risk of an ectopic pregnancy, miscarriage and low birth weight, placing the baby at risk of a range of health problems throughout their life. Therefore, smoking tobacco has significant health, social and economic costs to the community and has been the focus of numerous public health campaigns to improve health and quality of life at the individual and population level. The consequences of smoking tobacco are summarised in Figure 7.5.

bio —— psycho —— social

Physical damage	Associated diseases and health outcomes	Cognitive/ psychological	Family/social
DNA damage Inflammation Oxidative stress Respiratory system Cardiovascular system Immune system	Cancers (e.g. oesophagus, lung, larynx) Cardiovascular disorders (e.g. heart disease, stroke) Respiratory diseases (e.g. chronic obstructive pulmonary disease, tuberculosis) Reproductive effects (fertility problems, premature menopause) Type 2 diabetes Rheumatoid arthritis Male sexual dysfunction Eye disease (age-related macular degeneration) Fractures Pregnancy complications (ectopic pregnancy, low birth weight) Sudden infant death syndrome	(Evidence for a causal relationship between smoking and cognitive and psychological outcomes is mixed)	Relationship issues related to fertility and/or sexual function Judgements from others Financial cost of tobacco products Absenteeism Social and economic costs of ill health

Figure 7.5 The biopsychosocial spectrum: summary of negative physical consequences, associated disease and illness, risks, cognitive and psychological issues and family and social problems associated with smoking
Source: AIHW, 2015; Patel & Hirsch, 2014; US Department of Health and Human Services, 2010, 2014.

Tobacco consumption involves using a range of products including (but not limited to) cigarettes, pipes, cigars, waterpipes, chewing tobacco and snuff. Smoking cigarettes has been adopted globally and the consequences for health are well documented. Therefore, this section will focus primarily on smoking cigarettes.

The National Drug Strategy Household Survey conducted in Australia in 2013 found that 15.8% of adults reported smoking daily. Twenty years earlier this was 29.1% (AIHW, 2014a), indicating a substantial decline. Furthermore, the number of cigarettes smoked per week decreased between 2010 and 2013 (AIHW, 2014a). It is encouraging that the number of smokers has steadily declined over time (ABS, 2013a). Reducing rates of smoking by encouraging current smokers to quit, and by prevention of people taking up smoking, is of critical importance. Reductions in smoking lead to reduced population rates of chronic disease, and in turn, the associated burden on the healthcare system.

Underlying risk

Although it is promising that the number of daily smokers has declined significantly, it is important to understand which groups have the highest risk of smoking. Smoking rates are higher in Indigenous populations, those living in remote regions, those with low socioeconomic status and people who are unemployed. Men are also more likely to smoke than women (ABS, 2013a; AIHW, 2014a).

Socioeconomic status

Interventions have been successful in reducing smoking; however, the impact has been greatest in middle- and high-income groups. The number of cancer deaths due to tobacco is higher in low and middle-income groups than in high-income groups (Jemal et al., 2014), highlighting considerable health inequities related to tobacco.

Indigenous populations

More than half of the disease burden in Indigenous Australians is attributable to the health gap between Indigenous and non-Indigenous Australians. Tobacco has been reported to make the largest contribution to the burden of disease in Indigenous Australians and to the health gap (Vos et al., 2009). Rates of smoking in Indigenous Australian communities are double those of the general population and as high as 77% in remote communities (Clough, Robertson & Maclaren, 2009). These differences are not restricted to Australia, with smoking prevalence significantly higher in Māori than non-Māori populations in New Zealand (Blakely et al., 2015).

Age

Fewer young people are smoking than in the past and the vast majority of Australian teenagers (95%) report never having smoked. Rates of daily smoking are highest in adults in their late 20s and in their 40s (AIHW, 2014a), indicating that these groups are at greatest risk of tobacco-related harm.

Mental health

People with a mental illness have higher rates of smoking than the general population. A study of South Australian adults found that smoking rates were 1.5 times higher in people with mental illness (26%) compared with adults without mental illness (19%). Alarmingly, the rate in adults with a severe mental illness was 51% (Bowden, Miller & Hiller, 2011). It isn't clear whether mental illness results in higher rates of smoking (e.g. as a way to cope with symptoms) or smoking results in higher rates of mental illness. Alternatively, there may be other common factors that result in higher rates of both smoking and mental health problems. Either way, it is important to address the emotional and physical needs of those with mental illness, including smoking and associated health concerns.

Family and social environment

Consistent with alcohol use, smoking has been shown to have a nature and nurture component; approximately one-third of the variance in smoking is thought to be due to genetic influences (Boardman, Blalock & Pampel, 2010). However, both genetic predisposition and the social environment play an important role (Chen et al., 2014). In terms of the social environment, friends and family have been shown to have a significant influence on smoking uptake. Adolescents who smoke tend to choose friends who also smoke. However, friends also influence their friends' behaviour; that is, those who are friends with smokers are more likely to start smoking themselves (Go et al., 2012). These processes of selection and influence can be summarised with two common sayings: 'birds of a feather flock together' and 'like breeds like'. Living or working with other smokers also increases the likelihood of smoking (Holahan et al., 2013). Smoking with others has been shown to lead to a greater perceived reward associated with smoking in university students. For this reason, it is possible that designated smoking areas actually encourage smoking in those who already smoke by enhancing the reward associated with smoking together (Lochbihler, Miller & Etcheverry, 2014). The importance of the environment was further highlighted by a study by Conklin et al. (2013), who found that participants had increased cravings to smoke when they saw pictures of people with whom they usually smoke; that is, people can serve as cues for smoking. Overall, the people you spend time with at home, at work and in social settings play an important role in promoting or discouraging smoking.

Multiple health risk behaviours

There is evidence that risky health behaviours tend to cluster together, with strong evidence for an association between alcohol consumption and smoking. Socioeconomic disadvantage has also been associated with greater engagement in risky health behaviours in general (Noble et al., 2015). Therefore, it is important for interventions targeting smoking to address the broader social context as well as multiple health behaviours, particularly addictive behaviours that are likely to co-occur.

Treatment

Individual approaches

The health consequences of smoking are well known, prompting many smokers to make attempts to quit. Health benefits, increased fitness, pregnancy and acting on advice from a doctor are common reasons for quitting (AIHW, 2014a; Buczkowski et al., 2014). The cost of cigarettes, the unpleasant smell of cigarette smoke and restrictions on smoking at work or home have also been shown to motivate cessation attempts (Buczkowski et al., 2014). Individual approaches to quitting smoking include nicotine replacement therapy, the use of electronic cigarettes as an alternative to traditional cigarettes, telephone counselling, psychological interventions, and online/mobile interventions (see Table 7.4).

Nicotine replacement therapy (NRT) involves delivery of nicotine to the body by means other than traditional cigarettes. This includes the use of transdermal nicotine patches in which nicotine is delivered through the skin, and nicotine gum or lozenges in which it is delivered orally. Nasal sprays and inhalers are also available. NRT aims to address nicotine cravings and withdrawal symptoms without the use of tobacco, thereby

Table 7.4 Summary of individual and population or public health approaches to reducing smoking prevalence

Individual approaches	Population or public health approaches
• nicotine replacement therapy	• taxing tobacco products
• telephone counselling/Quitline services	• restrictions on smoking (creation of smoke-free environments)
• psychological/behavioural interventions (e.g. CBT, MI)	• banning advertising and promotion
	• health warnings on cigarette packaging
	• plain packaging
	• education through media campaigns
	• prevention programs (e.g. delivered to families, schools)

supporting the transition from smoking to abstinence. In addition, the harmful effects of smoking are avoided. NRT has been shown to support both reductions in smoking and smoking cessation (Begh, Lindson-Hawley & Aveyard, 2015; Silagy et al., 2000; Stead et al., 2012; Stead et al., 2008). Other pharmacological approaches to smoking cessation that have been shown to be effective include **bupropion** (an atypical antidepressant) and **varenicline** (Aubin, Luquiens & Berlin, 2014; Mendelsohn, Kirby & Castle, 2015; Wilkes, 2008). These drugs reduce the reward and withdrawal symptoms associated with nicotine.

Electronic nicotine delivery systems, also known as an electronic cigarette or **e-cigarette**, are designed to simulate tobacco smoking and present an alternative to smoking traditional cigarettes. These devices do not contain tobacco but produce an aerosol containing propylene glycol, flavouring agents and sometimes, but not always, nicotine (AIHW, 2014a; Section on Tobacco Control, 2015). The vapour produced is inhaled and sometimes called 'vaping'. Youth and young adults more readily adopt e-cigarettes than other products (Hildick-Smith et al., 2015; Section on Tobacco Control, 2015). Although e-cigarettes are not a tobacco product, the use of e-cigarettes is of concern due to the addictive and toxic nature of nicotine (Section on Tobacco Control, 2015). Furthermore, there is some evidence that adolescents and young adults who use e-cigarettes are at risk of progressing to traditional cigarette smoking (Primack et al., 2015). E-cigarette use has been shown to be higher in young adults, low socioeconomic groups and those who currently smoke cigarettes. This may be due to the adoption of e-cigarettes as a strategy to reduce tobacco use with the eventual goal of quitting smoking (Huang, Kim, Vera & Emery, 2015).

E-cigarettes provide an appealing alternative for current smokers as they resemble traditional cigarettes and are less harmful (Farsalinos & Le Houezec, 2015). It has been argued that the adoption of e-cigarettes as a replacement for smoking tobacco will result in health benefits for respiratory patients who smoke (Polosa, Campagna & Caponnetto,

2015). However, this advice remains controversial due to mixed evidence in terms of health outcomes. Importantly, long-term longitudinal studies are lacking (Begh et al., 2015). There are relatively few studies examining outcomes from electronic cigarette use in terms of quitting; some studies have found no significant differences between electronic cigarette users and placebo groups, possibly due to a lack of power, and others have found different results related to the type of e-cigarette used (Begh et al., 2015). A recent study examining outcomes from an Australian Quitline indicated that e-cigarettes neither reduced cravings nor increased success in quitting smoking, providing little confidence in e-cigarettes as a means of quitting (Maksimovic et al., 2015). The number of participants in this study was small and further research evaluating outcomes is clearly needed. Although e-cigarettes may provide a useful approach for those who have been unsuccessful in quitting using evidence-based approaches, they are rarely recommended due to a lack of current knowledge about long-term outcomes (Bullen, 2014).

Behavioural interventions and psychological support are likely to increase the probability of quitting when using NRT or pharmacological interventions (Silagy et al., 2000). They are also commonly used independently by people attempting to quit smoking. For example telephone counselling, often delivered through a Quitline, provides smokers with support and advice. These services are widespread and frequently evaluated. Telephone counselling has been shown to increase quit rates, although the relative increase when used in conjunction with medication is small. Two or more contacts with a Quitline, often delivered through call-back services, also increase success (Stead et al., 2013). Interventions including a motivational component, cognitive behaviour therapy or addressing the **transtheoretical stages of change** (precontemplation, contemplation, preparation, action and maintenance) have yielded positive outcomes, although evidence for long-term change is lacking (Stanton & Grimshaw, 2013).

Mobile or smart phone applications have been used to assist people in quitting. These include quit services delivered via text messages, telephone counselling and online resources. Promising results have been found for systems providing tailored messages (Head et al., 2013; Whittaker et al., 2012). However, further research is needed to accurately evaluate the effectiveness of these strategies (Ghorai et al., 2014; Whittaker et al., 2012). Internet-based interventions have been employed to reach young smokers and often feature tailored advice, feedback and multimedia components such as video and interactive tools including online discussions and journals. One advantage of internet-based interventions is their widespread accessibility. Park and Drake (2015) concluded that these internet-based approaches, particularly those with tailored education, are useful in promoting smoking cessation in adolescents and young adults.

Online and phone-based interventions have the potential to reach remote populations including Indigenous groups. However, there is little evidence supporting their use in these settings (Brusse et al., 2014). Few interventions have been adapted for use with Indigenous populations. Tailoring approaches for this group may be particularly important for those who do not access mainstream services or have exposure to public health messages. Cultural issues, cost of smoking and interventions, provision of support and addressing specific barriers are particularly important considerations for the design and implementation of smoking interventions with Indigenous Australians (DiGiacomo et al., 2011).

Public health approaches

In addition to individual approaches to reducing tobacco use, public health interventions and policies have had a significant impact on smoking at a population level (see Table 7.4). Public health approaches not only target current smokers but also aim to prevent smoking and smoking-related diseases by providing education or implementing change at a community or national level. The World Health Organisation Framework Convention on Tobacco Control is a treaty describing an internationally coordinated effort to address the issue of tobacco consumption globally. Strategies include increased taxation on tobacco products, banning the advertising and promotion of tobacco, creation of smoke-free environments and placing health warnings on packaging (Jemal et al., 2014). There are currently 180 parties to the Convention committed to reducing tobacco consumption.

Policy and legislative changes have made a significant contribution to the reduction in smoking rates. Banning smoking in restaurants, in cars carrying children and in a variety of public spaces has influenced individuals' smoking behaviour as well as the social acceptability of smoking cigarettes. Graphic health warnings and plain packaging have also been employed to discourage smoking. Cigarette packets display prominent warnings about the impact of smoking on one's health and are often accompanied by graphic pictures. Plain packaging has also reduced the extent to which specific brands can be identified.

Mass media campaigns have also been used and typically promote negative and highly emotional messages evoking fear, sadness or disgust in relation to smoking and ill health. These campaigns have been associated with a reduction in the number of young people starting to smoke as well as an increase in the number of adults quitting (Wakefield, Loken & Hornik, 2010).

Smoking prevention efforts are most effective when media campaigns are combined with school or community-based programs (Wakefield et al., 2010). These interventions address the broader social context in which smoking behaviour occurs, acknowledging the significant influence of family and school environments on the smoking status of youth and young adults. A review of family-based interventions in families with children and adolescents found that these interventions led to an estimated reduction of between 16 and 32% in adolescent smoking (Thomas et al., 2015). Successful family-based interventions were characterised by teaching authoritative parenting skills which were characterised by care and concern as well as rule setting. School-based interventions have been found to reduce smoking uptake by 12%. However, this was only observed for long-term outcomes, 1 year after the interventions (Thomas, McLellan & Perera, 2013). Successful interventions focused on social competence and social influence. Efforts that combine general information from media campaigns with specific skills related to an individual's school and home environment hold the most promise in preventing smoking uptake.

Barriers to treatment

Data from the Australian Institute of Health and Welfare indicate that 30% of smokers attempted to quit in the previous year but were unsuccessful (AIHW, 2014a). There are many barriers that make it difficult to give up the habit. Common barriers to quitting include associating smoking with enjoyment and stress relief and associating quitting with irritability, withdrawal symptoms and possible weight gain (Twyman et al., 2014). Several social and environmental factors also support smoking and therefore act as a barrier to quitting; the social acceptability of smoking, cultural norms and smoke-friendly living environments make quitting more difficult. Some people also lack access to quitting resources such as those outlined earlier. Quit attempts are less successful in vulnerable groups including Indigenous populations, people with a mental illness and those who are socioeconomically disadvantaged (Twyman et al., 2014).

Specific groups have additional barriers to health behaviour change. People with mental illness have identified symptom management, motivation and identity as additional concerns related to quitting. Indigenous Australian populations have also reported racism and cultural values related to identity, health, privacy and independence as impacting on smoking cessation and help-seeking behaviour. While barriers to smoking cessation in Indigenous young adults include social influences, social exclusion and stress management, several factors have been identified as motivating Indigenous Australians to quit smoking. The cost of cigarettes, the detrimental impact on sporting performance and pregnancy may be factors that can help overcome barriers to seeking assistance (Cosh et al., 2014; Dawson et al., 2012). Interventions targeting sports groups and pregnant women may have higher rates of success with Indigenous young Australians. Pregnancy may represent a **teachable moment**; that is, an opportunity for behaviour changes due to the mother's desire to protect her own health and the health of her baby.

Maintenance

Despite the best of intentions, many smokers commence smoking again after abstaining from smoking cigarettes for a period of time. The reasons for this vary, but include the perceived need to smoke to relieve stress, the perceived pleasure associated with smoking, and exposure to other smokers at home, work or in social situations (Buczkowski et al., 2014). Relapse can occur at any time during or following a quit attempt. Therefore, many studies assessing intervention outcomes are relevant in terms of relapse. However, some studies have specifically addressed long-term outcomes, at least 6 months after commencing treatment. There is not strong evidence for any approach in terms of maintaining treatment effects. A recent review found insufficient evidence for behavioural interventions, and in terms of pharmacological approaches, found some support for extended treatment with varenicline but not bupropion (Hajek et al., 2013). These results reflect the difficulty of achieving lasting behaviour change and the limitations of existing evidence, with few studies examining NRT or intensive interventions.

In order to reduce the social, health and economic burden of smoking cigarettes, a multifaceted approach is needed that includes prevention, treatment and relapse prevention. These efforts are most likely to be successful when they address barriers to change, are relevant to at-risk populations (including Indigenous and lower socioeconomic groups) and take into account the importance of cultural issues and the influence of family and friends. Furthermore, health education and legislation are needed to supplement individual treatments in order to create lasting change at an individual and societal level.

Mini case study 7.3

The advertising and marketing of tobacco products was significantly restricted during the 1980s and 1990s due to the significant negative consequences of smoking on people's health and longevity. As a result, cigarette packets themselves became a medium for promotion of smoking in general as well as advertising specific brands and products (Smith et al., 2015).

In late 2012, Australia introduced the *Tobacco Plain Packaging Act 2011* (Cwlth). requiring tobacco products to be sold in plain packaging with prominent health warnings. The aim of this public health initiative was to reduce the appeal of smoking while making graphic health warnings more prominent. Removal of marketing information and branding from cigarette packets, including logos, brand colours, images and fonts, reduces the extent to which cigarette packaging itself can promote smoking behaviour.

The implementation of plain packaging has led to backlash from the tobacco industry, including legal challenges, media campaigns and claims that these laws have not led to a decrease in smoking. However, research conducted with smokers before and after the regulations were applied indicated that graphic warnings had a greater impact on smokers than plain packaging, calls to smoking Quitlines increased, cigarette sales decreased (Smith et al., 2015; Young et al., 2014) and smokers reported that smoking held less appeal (Wakefield et al., 2013). The World Health Organisation stated that standardised packaging was a 'legitimate and effective tobacco control measure' (WHO, 2014). Australia was the first country to enact this legislation. Ireland introduced plain packaging laws in 2014 and similar regulations are now being considered around the world.

Critical thinking questions

1. In your view, what has made plain packaging a successful strategy for smoking reduction and prevention in Australia?
2. How do plain packaging laws affect smokers?
3. How do plain packaging laws affect young people considering taking up smoking?
4. Are there any potential unintended consequences of this initiative?

Summary

- Health-related risk factors can be categorised as behavioural, genetic, biomedical, environmental and demographic. Modifiable risk factors are of particular interest to health psychologists as they offer the potential to decrease risk of chronic diseases including cancer, cardiovascular disease and diabetes. Behavioural risk factors that may be modified to reduce risk include reducing alcohol consumption and tobacco smoking, increasing physical activity and having a healthy diet.
- Impaired control over substance use, social impairment and risky use of the substance are outlined in the DSM-5 definition of substance use disorders.
- Health risk behaviours are often associated with stigma, social disapproval and discrimination. The situation is further complicated by the fact that people often receive criticism from their friends or family when trying to change their health behaviour if the risky behaviour (e.g. smoking or drinking) is considered normal by their social network.
- Many view alcohol consumption as a prominent part of Australian culture. Approximately 20% of the population drink at levels associated with lifetime alcohol-related harm and 40% drink at levels considered risky in terms of harm on a single occasion. Smoking prevalence has decreased considerably in the past few decades. It is estimated that 16% of Australian adults currently smoke.
- Both excessive alcohol use and tobacco smoking have a significant impact on the health of Australians, and have been associated with cancers and cardiovascular diseases, among many other health concerns. However, the impact is not limited to physical health and extends to psychological and social consequences. Individual and societal approaches have been used to address these health risk behaviours.
- Social factors such as the behaviours and attitudes of friends, family and colleagues can facilitate behaviour change or act as a barrier to treatment. Other barriers include lack of access to resources, reluctance to seek help, a non-supportive environment and personal beliefs. An individual's beliefs about the benefits of alcohol or smoking can contribute to relapse. For example, beliefs that alcohol and/or smoking will reduce stress or result in social acceptance increase the chance of relapse.

Suggested weblinks

Refer to the companion website at www.cambridge.edu.au/academic/healthpsychology for a list of suggested weblinks.

References

ABS. (2013a). *Profiles of Health, Australia, 2011–2013*. Canberra: Australian Bureau of Statistics. Retrieved from: http://www.abs.gov.au/ausstats/abs@.nsf/Lookup/by%20Subject/4338.0~2011-13~Main%20 Features~Tobacco%20smoking~10008

—— (2013b). *Australian Wine and Grape Industry, 2012–13*. Canberra: Australian Bureau of Statistics.

Agrawal, A., Sartor, C. E., Lynskey, M. T., Grant, J. D., Pergadia, M. L., Grucza, R., ... Heath, A. C. (2009). Evidence for an interaction between age at first drink and genetic influences on DSM-IV alcohol dependence symptoms. *Alcoholism: Clinical & Experimental Research*, *33*(12), 2047–56. doi: http://dx.doi.org/10.1111/j.1530-0277.2009.01044.x

AIHW. (2011a). *2010 National Drug Strategy Household Survey Report. Drug Statistics Series*. Canberra: Australian Institute of Health and Welfare.

—— (2011b). National Health Priority Areas. Canberra: Australian Institute of Health and Welfare. Retrieved from: http://www.aihw.gov.au/health-priority-areas/

—— (2014a). *National Drug Strategy Household Survey detailed report 2013. Drug statistics series no. 28*. Cat. no. PHE 183. Canberra: Australian Institute of Health and Welfare.

—— (2014b). *Cancer in Australia 2014: An Overview*. Canberra: Australian Institute of Health and Welfare.

—— (2015). Risk factors to health. Canberra: Australian Institute of Health and Welfare. Retrieved from: http://www.aihw.gov.au/risk-factors/

Allen, K. (1993). Attitudes of registered nurses toward alcoholic patients in a general hospital population. *International Journal of the Addictions*, *28*(9), 923–30.

American Psychiatric Association. (2013). *Diagnostic and Statistical Manual of Mental Disorders: DSM-5* (5th edn). Arlington: American Psychiatric Press.

Anderson, P., Chisholm, D. & Fuhr, D. C. (2009). Effectiveness and cost-effectiveness of policies and programmes to reduce the harm caused by alcohol. *The Lancet*, *373*(9682), 2234–46. doi: http://dx.doi.org/10.1016/s0140-6736(09)60744-3

Anderson, S. (2012). Judgemental attitudes to addiction. *Nursing New Zealand* (Wellington, NZ: 1995), *18*(1), 5; author reply 5.

Anderson, S., Eadie, D. R., MacKintosh, A. M. & Haw, S. (2001). Management of alcohol misuse in Scotland: the role of A&E nurses. *Accident and Emergency Nursing*, *9*(2), 92–100. doi: http://dx.doi.org/10.1054/aaen.2000.0210

Aubin, H. J., Luquiens, A. & Berlin, I. (2014). Pharmacotherapy for smoking cessation: pharmacological principles and clinical practice. *British Journal of Clinical Pharmacology*, *77*(2), 324–36. doi: http://dx.doi.org/10.1111/bcp.12116

australia.gov.au. (2007). Australia's wine industry. Retrieved from: http://www.australia.gov.au/about-australia/australian-story/australias-wine-industry

Baird, M. A., Burge, S. K. & Grant, W. D. (1989). A scheme for determining the prevalence of alcoholism in hospitalized patients. *Alcoholism: Clinical and Experimental Research*, *13*(6), 782–5. doi: http://dx.doi.org/10.1111/j.1530-0277.1989.tb00421.x

Begh, R., Lindson-Hawley, N. & Aveyard, P. (2015). Does reduced smoking if you can't stop make any difference? *BMC Medicine*, *13*, 257. doi: http://dx.doi.org/10.1186/s12916-015-0505-2

Blakely, T., Cobiac, L. J., Cleghorn, C. L., Pearson, A. L., van der Deen, F. S., Kvizhinadze, G., ... Wilson, N. (2015). Health, health inequality, and cost impacts of annual increases in tobacco tax: multistate life table modeling in New Zealand. *PLoS Medicine*, *12*(7), e1001856. doi: http://dx.doi.org/10.1371/journal.pmed.1001856

Boardman, J. D., Blalock, C. L. & Pampel, F. C. (2010). Trends in the genetic influences on smoking. *Journal of Health and Social Behavior*, *51*(1), 108–23.

Bowden, J. A., Miller, C. L. & Hiller, J. E. (2011). Smoking and mental illness: a population study in South Australia. *Australian & New Zealand Journal of Psychiatry*, *45*(4), 325–31. doi: http://dx.doi.org/10.3109/00048674.2010.536904

Brusse, C., Gardner, K., McAullay, D. & Dowden, M. (2014). Social media and mobile apps for health promotion in Australian Indigenous populations: scoping review. *Journal of Medical Internet Research*, *16*(12), e280. doi: http://dx.doi.org/10.2196/jmir.3614

Buczkowski, K., Marcinowicz, L., Czachowski, S. & Piszczek, E. (2014). Motivations toward smoking cessation, reasons for relapse, and modes of quitting: results from a qualitative study among former and current smokers. *Patient Preference and Adherence*, *8*, 1353–63. doi: http://dx.doi.org/10.2147/PPA.S67767

Bullen, C. (2014). Electronic cigarettes for smoking cessation. *Current Cardiology Reports*, *16*(11), 538. doi: http://dx.doi.org/10.1007/s11886-014-0538-8

Byrne, G. J. A., Raphael, B. & Arnold, E. (1999). Alcohol consumption and psychological distress in recently widowed older men. *Australian and New Zealand Journal of Psychiatry*, *33*, 740–7.

Carr, G. D. (2011). Alcoholism: a modern look at an ancient illness. *Primary Care: Clinics in Office Practice*, *38*(1), 9–21, v. doi: http://dx.doi.org/10.1016/j.pop.2010.11.002

Carrigan, M. H. & Randall, C. L. (2003). Self-medication in social phobia: a review of the alcohol literature. *Addictive Behaviors*, *28*(2), 269–84. doi: http://dx.doi.org/10.1016/s0306-4603(01)00235-0

Catalbiano, M. L., Sarafino, E. P. & Byrne, D. G. (2008). *Health Psychology: Biopsychosocial Interactions* (2nd Australasian edn). Australia: John Wiley & Sons.

Chen, A. C., Halliday, G. M. & Damian, D. L. (2013). Non-melanoma skin cancer: carcinogenesis and chemoprevention. *Pathology*, *45*(3), 331–41. doi: http://dx.doi.org/10.1097/PAT.0b013e32835f515c

Chen, L. S., Baker, T. B., Piper, M. E., Smith, S. S., Gu, C., Grucza, R. A., ... Bierut, L. J. (2014). Interplay of genetic risk (CHRNA5) and environmental risk (partner smoking) on cigarette smoking reduction. *Drug and Alcohol Dependence*, *143*, 36–43. doi: http://dx.doi.org/10.1016/j.drugalcdep.2014.06.027

Christenson, B., Lundbergh, P., Hedlund, J. & Ortqvist, A. (2001). Effects of a large-scale intervention with influenza and 23-valent pneumococcal vaccines in adults aged 65 years or older: a prospective study. *The Lancet*, *357*(9261), 1008–11. doi: http://dx.doi.org/10.1016/S0140-6736(00)04237-9

Clay, S. W., Allen, J. & Parran, T. (2008). A review of addiction. *Postgraduate Medicine*, *120*(2), E01–7. doi: http://dx.doi.org/10.3810/pgm.2008.07.1802

Clough, A. R., Robertson, J. A. & Maclaren, D. J. (2009). The gap in tobacco use between remote Indigenous Australian communities and the Australian population can be closed. *Tobacco Control*, *18*(4), 335–6. doi: http://dx.doi.org/10.1136/tc.2009.030577

Conklin, C. A., Salkeld, R. P., Perkins, K. A. & Robin, N. (2013). Do people serve as cues to smoke? *Nicotine & Tobacco Research*, *15*(12), 2081–7. doi: http://dx.doi.org/10.1093/ntr/ntt104

Cosh, S., Hawkins, K., Skaczkowski, G., Copley, D. & Bowden, J. (2014). Tobacco use among urban Aboriginal Australian young people: a qualitative study of reasons for smoking, barriers to cessation and motivators for smoking cessation. *Australian Journal of Primary Health*. doi: http://dx.doi.org/10.1071/PY13157

Crothers, C. & Dorrian, J. (2011). Determinants of nurses' attitudes toward the care of patients with alcohol problems. *International Scholarly Research Notices*, 1–11. doi: http://dx.doi.org/10.5402/2011/821514

Dawson, A. P., Cargo, M., Stewart, H., Chong, A. & Daniel, M. (2012). Aboriginal health workers experience multilevel barriers to quitting smoking: a qualitative study. *International Journal for Equity in Health*, *11*, 27. doi: http://dx.doi.org/10.1186/1475-9276-11-27

Deykin, E. Y., Levy, J. C. & Wells, V. (1986). Adolescent depression, alcohol and drug abuse. *American Journal of Public Health*, *76*, 178–82.

DiGiacomo, M., Davidson, P. M., Abbott, P. A., Davison, J., Moore, L. & Thompson, S. C. (2011). Smoking cessation in Indigenous populations of Australia, New Zealand, Canada, and the United States: elements of effective interventions. *International Journal of Environmental Research and Public Health*, *8*(2), 388–410. doi: http://dx.doi.org/10.3390/ijerph8020388

Dorrian, J. (2010). Alcoholism: disease or symptom? The challenges of managing advanced alcoholism and chronic illness. *Medical Journal of Australia*, *192*(11), 661–2.

—— (2012). Alcoholism: the self-reinforcing feedback loop. In: G. Rossi (ed.), *Psychology – Selected Papers*, Croatia: InTech.

Durand, M. A. (1994). General practice involvement in the management of alcohol misuse: dynamics and resistances. *Drug and Alcohol Dependence*, *35*(3), 181–9.

Ekendahl, M. (2007). Will and skill – an exploratory study of substance abusers' attitudes towards lifestyle change. *European Addiction Research*, *13*(3), 148–55. doi: http://dx.doi.org/10.1159/000101551

Erickson, J. R., Stevens, S., McKnight, P. & Figueredo, A. J. (1995). Willingness for treatment as a predictor of retention and outcomes. *Journal of Addictive Diseases*, *14*(4), 135–50. doi: http://dx.doi.org/10.1300/J069v14n03_11

Eve, S. I. (1989). A psychotherapeutic approach to treatment of a population at high risk for alcoholism: adult children of alcoholics. *Medicine and Law*, *8*(4), 357–63.

Farsalinos, K. E. & Le Houezec, J. (2015). Regulation in the face of uncertainty: the evidence on electronic nicotine delivery systems (e-cigarettes). *Risk Management and Healthcare Policy*, *8*, 157–67. doi: http://dx.doi.org/10.2147/RMHP.S62116

Fergusson, D. M., Boden, J. M. & Horwood, L. J. (2008). The developmental antecedents of illicit drug use: evidence from a 25-year longitudinal study. *Drug and Alcohol Dependence*, *96*(1–2), 165–77. doi: http://dx.doi.org/10.1016/j.drugalcdep.2008.03.003

Fergusson, D. M. & Horwood, L. J. (1998). Exposure to interparental violence in childhood and psychosocial adjustment in young adulthood. *Child Abuse & Neglect*, *22*(5), 339–57.

Fergusson, D. M., Lynskey, M. T. & Horwood, L. J. (1994). Childhood exposure to alcohol and adolescent drinking patterns. *Addiction*, *89*(8), 1007–16.

Fowler, T. L. (2006). Alcohol dependence and depression: advance practice nurse interventions. *Journal of the American Academy of Nurse Practitioners*, *18*(7), 303–8. doi: http://dx.doi.org/10.1111/j.1745-7599.2006.00135.x

Ganz, D. & Sher, L. (2009). Suicidal behavior in adolescents with comorbid depression and alcohol abuse. *Minerva Pediatrica*, *61*(3), 333–47.

Garbutt, J. C., West, S. L., Carey, T. S., Lohr, K. N. & Crews, F. T. (1999). Pharmacological treatment of alcohol dependence. *The Journal of the American Medical Association*, *281*(14), 1318–25. doi: http://dx.doi.org/10.1001/jama.281.14.1318

Geirsson, M., Bendtsen, P. & Spak, F. (2005). Attitudes of Swedish general practitioners and nurses to working with lifestyle change, with special reference to alcohol consumption. *Alcohol and Alcoholism*, *40*(5), 388–93. doi: http://dx.doi.org/10.1093/alcalc/agh185

Ghorai, K., Akter, S., Khatun, F. & Ray, P. (2014). mHealth for smoking cessation programs: a systematic review. *Journal of Personalized Medicine*, *4*(3), 412–23. doi: http://dx.doi.org/10.3390/jpm4030412

Gilbert, R., Widom, C. S., Browne, K., Fergusson, D., Webb, E. & Janson, S. (2009). Burden and consequences of child maltreatment in high-income countries. *The Lancet*, *373*(9657), 68–81. doi: http://dx.doi.org/10.1016/S0140-6736(08)61706-7

Ginter, E. & Simko, V. (2009). Alcoholism: recent advances in epidemiology, biochemistry and genetics. *Bratisl Lek Listy*, *110*(5), 307–11.

Go, M. H., Tucker, J. S., Green, H. D., Jr., Pollard, M. & Kennedy, D. (2012). Social distance and homophily in adolescent smoking initiation. *Drug and Alcohol Dependence*, *124*(3), 347–54. doi: http://dx.doi.org/10.1016/j.drugalcdep.2012.02.007

Gordon, A. J., Ettaro, L., Rodriguez, K. L., Mocik, J. & Clark, D. B. (2011). Provider, patient, and family perspectives of adolescent alcohol use and treatment in rural settings. *The Journal of Rural Health*, *27*(1), 81–90. doi: http://dx.doi.org/10.1111/j.1748-0361.2010.00321.x

Gordon, J. J., Fahey, P. & Sanson-Fisher, R. W. (1988). Interns' identification of patients' health risks in a casualty department. *Medical Journal of Australia*, *148*(12), 615–19.

Graham, H. (2012). Smoking, stigma and social class. *Journal of Social Policy*, *41*(01), 83–99.

Graham, R., Wodak, A. D. & Whelan, G. (2002). New pharmacotherapies for alcohol dependence. *Medical Journal of Australia*, *177*(2), 103–7.

Hajek, P., Stead, L. F., West, R., Jarvis, M., Hartmann-Boyce, J. & Lancaster, T. (2013). Relapse prevention interventions for smoking cessation. *Cochrane Database of Systematic Reviews*, *8*, CD003999. doi: http://dx.doi.org/10.1002/14651858.CD003999.pub4

Hansell, N. K., Agrawal, A., Whitfield, J. B., Morley, K. I., Gordon, S. D., Lind, P. A., … Martin, N. G. (2009). Can we identify genes for alcohol consumption in samples ascertained for heterogeneous purposes? *Alcoholism: Clinical & Experimental Research*, *33*(4), 729–39. doi: http://dx.doi.org/10.1111/j.1530-0277.2008.00890.x

Head, K. J., Noar, S. M., Iannarino, N. T. & Harrington, N. G. (2013). Efficacy of text messaging-based interventions for health promotion: a meta-analysis. *Social Science & Medicine*, *97*, 41–8. doi: http://dx.doi.org/10.1016/j.socscimed.2013.08.003

Hildick-Smith, G. J., Pesko, M. F., Shearer, L., Hughes, J. M., Chang, J., Loughlin, G. M. & Ipp, L. S. (2015). A practitioner's guide to electronic cigarettes in the adolescent population. *Journal of Adolescent Health*. doi: http://dx.doi.org/10.1016/j.jadohealth.2015.07.020

Holahan, C. K., Holahan, C. J., Li, X. & Jung, S. (2013). Social influences on smoking in American workers: the role of the presence of smokers in the workplace and in the home. *American Journal of Health Promotion*, *28*(2), 105–7. doi: http://dx.doi.org/10.4278/ajhp.120604-ARB-283

Holmes, K. K., Levine, R. & Weaver, M. (2004). Effectiveness of condoms in preventing sexually transmitted infections. *Bulletin of the World Health Organization*, *82*(6), 454–61.

Holmwood, C. (2002). Alcohol-related problems in Australia: is there a role for general practice? *Medical Journal of Australia*, *177*(2), 102–3.

Huang, J., Kim, Y., Vera, L. & Emery, S. L. (2015). Electronic cigarettes among priority populations: role of smoking cessation and tobacco control policies. *American Journal of Preventative Medicine*. doi: http://dx.doi.org/10.1016/j.amepre.2015.06.032

Huerta, M. C. & Borgonovi, F. (2010). Education, alcohol use and abuse among young adults in Britain. *Social Science & Medicine*, *71*(1), 143–51. doi: http://dx.doi.org/10.1016/j.socscimed.2010.03.022

Indig, D., Copeland, J., Conigrave, K. M. & Rotenko, I. (2009). Attitudes and beliefs of emergency department staff regarding alcohol-related presentations. *International Emergency Nursing*, *17*(1), 23–30. doi: http://dx.doi.org/10.1016/j.ienj.2008.08.002

Jemal, A., Vineis, P., Bray, F., Torre, L. & Forman, D. (eds) (2014). *The Cancer Atlas* (2nd edn). Atlanta, GA: American Cancer Society.

Johnson, B. A. (2010). Medication treatment of different types of alcoholism. *American Journal of Psychiatry*, *167*(6), 630–9. doi: http://dx.doi.org/10.1176/appi.ajp.2010.08101500

Kopelman, M. D. (2008). Alcohol and frontal lobe impairment: fascinating findings. *Addiction*, *103*(5), 736–7. doi: http://dx.doi.org/10.1111/j.1360-0443.2008.02225.x

Lochbihler, S. L., Miller, D. A. & Etcheverry, P. E. (2014). Extending animal models to explore social rewards associated with designated smoking areas on college campuses. *Journal of American College Health*, *62*(3), 145–52. doi: http://dx.doi.org/10.1080/07448481.2013.865624

Loeber, S., Duka, T., Welzel Marquez, H., Nakovics, H., Heinz, A., Mann, K. & Flor, H. (2010). Effects of repeated withdrawal from alcohol on recovery of cognitive impairment under abstinence and rate of relapse. *Alcohol and Alcoholism*, *45*(6), 541–7. doi: http://dx.doi.org/10.1093/alcalc/agq065

Lomas, A., Leonardi-Bee, J. & Bath-Hextall, F. (2012). A systematic review of worldwide incidence of nonmelanoma skin cancer. *British Journal of Dermatology*, *166*(5), 1069–80. doi: http://dx.doi.org/10.1111/j.1365-2133.2012.10830.x

Magnusson, Å., Lundholm, C., Göransson, M., Copeland, W., Heilig, M. & Pedersen, N. L. (2011). Familial influence and childhood trauma in female alcoholism. *Psychological Medicine*, 1–9. doi: http://dx.doi.org/10.1017/s0033291711001310

Maksimovic, L., Frame, A., & Sparrow, A. (2015). E-cigarette use among Quitline clients: who is using them and what for? Paper presented at the Oceania Tobacco Control Conference, Perth, Australia.

McMurran, M. (1991). Young offenders and alcohol-related crime: what interventions will address the issues? *Journal of Adolescence*, *14*(3), 245–53.

Mendelsohn, C. P., Kirby, D. P. & Castle, D. J. (2015). Smoking and mental illness. An update for psychiatrists. *Australasian Psychiatry*, *23*(1), 37–43. doi: http://dx.doi.org/10.1177/1039856214562076

Miranda, R., Meyerson, L., Long, P., Marx, B. & Simpson, S. (2002). Sexual assault and alcohol use: exploring the self-medication hypothesis. *Violence and Victims*, *17*(2), 205–17.

Morrison, V., Bennett, P., Butow, P., Mullan, B. & White, K. (2008). *Introduction to Health Psychology in Australia*. Sydney: Pearson Education.

Moselhy, H. F., Georgiou, G. & Kahn, A. (2001). Frontal lobe changes in alcoholism: a review of the literature. *Alcohol and Alcoholism*, *36*(5), 357–68.

NAS. (2006). *National Alcohol Strategy 2006–2009*. Canberra: Commonwealth of Australia.

NHMRC. (2009). *Australian Guidelines to Reduce Health Risks from Drinking Alcohol* (pp. 1–179). Canberra: National Health and Medical Research Council.

Noble, N., Paul, C., Turon, H. & Oldmeadow, C. (2015). Which modifiable health risk behaviours are related? A systematic review of the clustering of Smoking, Nutrition, Alcohol and Physical activity ('SNAP') health risk factors. *Preventative Medicine*, *81*, 16–41. doi: http://dx.doi.org/10.1016/j.ypmed.2015.07.003

O'Brien, C. (2011). Addiction and dependence in DSM-V. *Addiction*, *106*(5), 866–7.

Omer, S. B., Salmon, D. A., Orenstein, W. A., deHart, M. P. & Halsey, N. (2009). Vaccine refusal, mandatory immunization, and the risks of vaccine-preventable diseases. *New England Journal of Medicine*, *360*(19), 1981–8. doi: http://dx.doi.org/10.1056/NEJMsa0806477

Owens, L., Gilmore, I. T. & Pirmohamed, M. (2000). General practice nurses' knowledge of alcohol use and misuse: a questionnaire survey. *Alcohol Alcoholism*, *35*(3), 259–62.

Park, E. & Drake, E. (2015). Smoking Cessation treated with pharmacologic agents. *International Journal of Child and Adolescent Health*, *47*(1), 43–50. doi: http://dx.doi.org/10.1111/jnu.12104

Patel, D.R., & Hirsch, D. (2014). Smoking cessation treated with pharmacologic agents. *International Journal of Child and Adolescent Health*, *7*(4), 275–292.

Polosa, R., Campagna, D. & Caponnetto, P. (2015). What to advise to respiratory patients intending to use electronic cigarettes. *Discovery Medicine*, *20*(109), 155–61.

Primack, B. A., Soneji, S., Stoolmiller, M., Fine, M. J. & Sargent, J. D. (2015). Progression to traditional cigarette smoking after electronic cigarette use among US adolescents and young adults. *JAMA Pediatrics*, 1–7. doi: http://dx.doi.org/10.1001/jamapediatrics.2015.1742

Rehm, J., Mathers, C., Popova, S., Thavorncharoensap, M., Teerawattananon, Y. & Patra, J. (2009). Global burden of disease and injury and economic cost attributable to alcohol use and alcohol-use disorders. *The Lancet*, *373*(9682), 2223–33. doi: http://dx.doi.org/10.1016/s0140-6736(09)60746-7

Rehm, J. & Room, R. (2009). A case study in how harmful alcohol consumption can be. *The Lancet*, *373*(9682), 2176–7. doi: http://dx.doi.org/10.1016/s0140-6736(09)61170-3

Room, R. (2005). Stigma, social inequality and alcohol and drug use. *Drug and Alcohol Review*, *24*(2), 143–55.

Room, R., Babor, T. & Rehm, J. (2005). Alcohol and public health. *The Lancet*, *365*, 519–30.

Sacks, T. L. & Keks, N. A. (1998). Alcohol and drug dependence: diagnosis and management. *Medical Journal of Australia*, *168*(7), 355–60.

Schomerus, G., Lucht, M., Holzinger, A., Matschinger, H., Carta, M. G. & Angermeyer, M. C. (2011). The stigma of alcohol dependence compared with other mental disorders: a review of population studies. *Alcohol and Alcoholism*, *46*(2), 105–12.

Schuckit, M. A. (2009). Alcohol-use disorders. *The Lancet*, *373*(9662), 492–501. doi: http://dx.doi.org/10.1016/s0140-6736(09)60009-x

Section on Tobacco Control. (2015). Electronic nicotine delivery systems. *Pediatrics*. doi: http://dx.doi.org/10.1542/peds.2015-3222

Shaffer, H. J., LaPlante, D. A., LaBrie, R. A., Kidman, R. C., Donato, A. N. & Stanton, M. V. (2004). Toward a syndrome model of addiction: multiple expressions, common etiology. *Harvard Review of Psychiatry*, *12*, 367–74.

Silagy, C., Mant, D., Fowler, G. & Lancaster, T. (2000). Nicotine replacement therapy for smoking cessation. *Cochrane Database of Systematic Reviews* (2), CD000146. doi: http://dx.doi.org/10.1002/14651858.CD000146

Smith, C. N., Kraemer, J. D., Johnson, A. C. & Mays, D. (2015). Plain packaging of cigarettes: do we have sufficient evidence? *Risk Management and Healthcare Policy*, *8*, 21–30. doi: http://dx.doi.org/10.2147/RMHP.S63042

Spilsbury, G. (2012). Solution-focused brief therapy for depression and alcohol dependence: A case study. *Clinical Case Studies*, 1534650112450506.

Stanton, A. & Grimshaw, G. (2013). Tobacco cessation interventions for young people. *Cochrane Database of Systematic Reviews*, *8*, CD003289. doi: http://dx.doi.org/10.1002/14651858.CD003289.pub5

Stead, L. F., Hartmann-Boyce, J., Perera, R. & Lancaster, T. (2013). Telephone counselling for smoking cessation. *Cochrane Database of Systematic Review*, *8*, CD002850. doi: http://dx.doi.org/10.1002/14651858.CD002850.pub3

Stead, L. F., Perera, R., Bullen, C., Mant, D., Hartmann-Boyce, J., Cahill, K. & Lancaster, T. (2012). Nicotine replacement therapy for smoking cessation. *Cochrane Database of Systematic Reviews*, *11*, CD000146. doi: http://dx.doi.org/10.1002/14651858.CD000146.pub4

Stead, L. F., Perera, R., Bullen, C., Mant, D. & Lancaster, T. (2008). Nicotine replacement therapy for smoking cessation. *Cochrane Database of Systematic Reviews*, *1*, CD000146. doi: http://dx.doi.org/10.1002/14651858.CD000146.pub3

Stewart, S. H. (1996). Alcohol abuse in individuals exposed to trauma: a critical review. *Psychological Bulletin*, *120*(1), 83–112.

Swendsen, J. D., Tennen, T., Carney, M. A., Affleck, G., Willard, A. & Hromi, A. (2000). Mood and alcohol consumption: an experience sampling test of the self-medication hypothesis. *Journal of Abnormal Psychology*, *109*(2), 198–204.

Talbot, A.-L., Dorrian, J. & Chapman, J. (2015). Using the theory of planned behaviour to examine enrolled nursing students' intention to care for patients with alcohol dependence: a survey study. *Nurse Education Today*.

Thomas, R. E., Baker, P. R., Thomas, B. C. & Lorenzetti, D. L. (2015). Family-based programmes for preventing smoking by children and adolescents. *Cochrane Database of Systematic Reviews*, *2*, CD004493. doi: http://dx.doi.org/10.1002/14651858.CD004493.pub3

Thomas, R. E., McLellan, J. & Perera, R. (2013). School-based programmes for preventing smoking. *Cochrane Database of Systematic Reviews*, *4*, CD001293. doi: http://dx.doi.org/10.1002/14651858.CD001293.pub3

Twyman, L., Bonevski, B., Paul, C. & Bryant, J. (2014). Perceived barriers to smoking cessation in selected vulnerable groups: a systematic review of the qualitative and quantitative literature. *BMJ Open*, *4*(12), e006414. doi: http://dx.doi.org/10.1136/bmjopen-2014-006414

Uekermann, J. & Daum, I. (2008). Social cognition in alcoholism: a link to prefrontal cortex dysfunction? *Addiction*, *103*(5), 726–35. doi: http://dx.doi.org/10.1111/j.1360-0443.2008.02157.x

U.S. Department of Health and Human Services. (2010). How Tobacco Smoke Causes Disease: The Biology and Behavioral Basis for Smoking-Attribute Disease: A Report of the Surgeon General. Atlanta, GA: U.S. Department of Health and Human Services, Centers for Disease Control and Prevention, National Centre for Chronic Disease Prevention and Health Promotion, Office of smoking and Health.

—— (2014). The Health Consequences of Smoking: 50 Years of Progress. A Report of the Surgeon General. Atlanta, GA: U.S. Department of Health and Human Services, Centers for Disease Control and Prevention, National Centre for Chronic Disease Prevention and Health Promotion, Office of smoking and Health.

Vos, T., Barker, B., Begg, S., Stanley, L. & Lopez, A. D. (2009). Burden of disease and injury in Aboriginal and Torres Strait Islander Peoples: the Indigenous health gap. *International Journal of Epidemiology*, *38*(2), 470–7. doi: http://dx.doi.org/10.1093/ije/dyn240

Wakefield, M. A., Hayes, L., Durkin, S. & Borland, R. (2013). Introduction effects of the Australian plain packaging policy on adult smokers: a cross-sectional study. *BMJ Open*, *3*(7). doi: http://dx.doi.org/10.1136/bmjopen-2013-003175

Wakefield, M. A., Loken, B. & Hornik, R. C. (2010). Use of mass media campaigns to change health behaviour. *The Lancet*, *376*(9748), 1261–71. doi: http://dx.doi.org/10.1016/S0140-6736(10)60809-4

Whittaker, R., McRobbie, H., Bullen, C., Borland, R., Rodgers, A. & Gu, Y. (2012). Mobile phone-based interventions for smoking cessation. *Cochrane Database of Systematic Reviews*, *11*, CD006611. doi: http://dx.doi.org/10.1002/14651858.CD006611.pub3

WHO. (2011). *Global Status Report on Alcohol and Health 2011*. Geneva: World Health Organisation.

—— (2014). *Statement of the World Health Organization in Relation to the Issue of Standardized Tobacco Product Packaging*. Geneva: World Health Organisation. Retrieved from: http://www.who.int/fctc/mediacentre/news/2014/WHOSTATEMENTWTOTRIPSOCT2014.pdf?ua=1

—— (2015). *Tobacco*. Geneva: World Health Organisation. Retrieved from: http://www.who.int/mediacentre/factsheets/fs339/en/

Wilkes, S. (2008). The use of bupropion SR in cigarette smoking cessation. *International Journal of Chronic Obstructive Pulmonary Disease*, *3*(1), 45–53.

Williamson, L. (2009a). Alcohol dependence in public policy: towards its (re)inclusion. *Clinical Ethics*, *4*, 74–8. doi: http://dx.doi.org/10.1258/ce.2008.008043

—— (2009b). Public policy on alcohol in the United Kingdom: towards a safety net for the alcohol-dependent. *Journal of Law and Medicine*, *17*(3), 386–99.

Wyatt, S. B., Winters, K. P. & Dubbert, P. M. (2006). Overweight and obesity: prevalence, consequences, and causes of a growing public health problem. *The American Journal of the Medical Sciences*, *331*(4), 166–74.

Yonas, M., Baker, D., Cornwell, E. E., 3rd, Chang, D., Phillips, J., Paradise, J., ... Elihu, A. (2005). Readiness to change and the role of inpatient counseling for alcohol/substance abusing youth with major trauma. *Journal of Trauma*, *59*(2), 466–9.

Young, J. M., Stacey, I., Dobbins, T. A., Dunlop, S., Dessaix, A. L. & Currow, D. C. (2014). Association between tobacco plain packaging and Quitline calls: a population-based, interrupted time-series analysis. *Medical Journal of Australia*, *200*(1), 29–32.

Young-Wolff, K. C., Kendler, K. S., Sintov, N. D. & Prescott, C. A. (2009). Mood-related drinking motives mediate the familial association between major depression and alcohol dependence. *Alcoholism: Clinical and Experimental Research*, *33*(8), 1476–86. doi: http://dx.doi.org/10.1111/j.1530-0277.2009.00978.x

8

Stress and managing stress

Learning outcomes

After reading this chapter, you should be able to:

- describe what is meant by 'stress' and the 'stress response'
- describe factors that cause stress (stressors)
- explain how people cope with stress
- describe how people manage stress
- explain what is meant by the terms 'mindfulness' and 'mindfulness meditation'.

Introduction

> Everyone knows what stress is and nobody knows what it is.
>
> (Selye, 1973, p. 692)

If you search for the term 'stress' on the internet, you will get over half a billion results. This highlights the ubiquity of stress. Stress is something that most people can relate to – especially students. Stress is a controversial concept and some have even denied its existence. However, stress is a major focus of health psychology. *But what is stress?* The term 'stress' has its origins in physics and in that discipline means the force or tension needed to bend or break an object. In psychology, stress is a multifaceted concept. It includes a stimulus, a cognitive evaluation of the stimulus and a physiological response (Van Reeth et al., 2000). Stress can be caused by major life events (stimuli) such as getting married, illness, natural disasters such as bushfires, or even everyday hassles and the ever-constant demands that are placed on us. Stress can also be a response to trauma or abuse. Stress can be either acute – sudden and short-lived – or chronic. In our daily lives, people are expected to do many and varied tasks. Many demands are placed on our time and attention: deadlines; meetings to attend; appointments; chores to be done; attending work, school or university; emails to respond to; assignments to write; studying for exams; meeting friends; or caring for loved ones. Sometimes these events and ever-present demands are more than we can handle or cope with; we can feel as if we are under pressure to perform or to get everything done. Sometimes we can get overwhelmed by the constant demands on our time. The way we think about these demands can also contribute to our sense of pressure or stress. The more important we deem an outcome, the more overwhelmed we can become about not succeeding, or failing. For instance, if you highly value passing all of your exams and assignments and believe that failure is unacceptable, this can add to your sense of pressure and need to succeed. This relates to the sometimes unrealistic expectations we place on ourselves.

Responding to the stress-invoking event (the stimulus), or stressor, may involve emotional arousal, cognitions and behaviours in an attempt to cope with the stressor and to reduce its negative effects. This chapter will: describe the physiological and psychological components of the stress response; discuss the effects of chronic stress and illness; review factors that are known to invoke a stress response; discuss the various strategies people use to cope with and manage stress; and finally provide an example of the much-researched stress-reducing **coping** mechanisms known as **mindfulness** and mindfulness meditation. Let's begin with the physiological changes that occur during acute stress.

The stress response

According to Lazarus (1966), 'stress arises when individuals perceive that they cannot adequately cope with the demands being made on them or with threats to their wellbeing'. Using this definition, stress is a transaction between the individual and their environment. **Stress** involves a physiological (bodily) and psychological (cognitive) response to an external or internal experience that taxes our ability to manage or deal with the situation. This combined response is also referred to as *strain* (Selye, 1956). Therefore, stress involves a biological response: a transaction between factors inside the person and the outer environment, and the individual's own perception about how they can deal with a situation.

A physiological model of stress

Stress can be considered a bodily reaction, an orchestrated physiological response. This response is triggered by the brain when it perceives and evaluates an event or situation as potentially harmful or threatening to the individual. So stress involves a bodily response to an environmental stimulus. For example, if you are walking along a darkly lit street at night by yourself and suddenly you hear footsteps approaching from behind, you might perceive that as an impending or possible dangerous situation. You may believe that you could be attacked or mugged. During this evaluation, you may notice that your heart rate suddenly increases, your chest starts to thump, your breathing rate increases, your senses become heightened, you become more alert and attentive, and you may have a sudden urge to run away. You may also notice some tension in your body, particularly your muscles. The potential threat activates this bodily response, which is commonly referred to as the fight-or-flight response, or the acute stress response. In response to danger, most animals will run away or stay and fight the danger. This response is activated by a part of the peripheral nervous system known as the *autonomic nervous system*, which controls the **sympathetic nervous system (SNS)**. The SNS is responsible for stimulating and arousing the body and prepares it for action or movement by mobilising energy resources. This process is automatic. The brain, without our conscious directive, triggers this neurobiological response; however, as will be discussed at the end of this chapter, we can learn to moderate this response. The SNS involves a series of connected parts of the nervous and endocrine systems, known as the hypothalamic–pituitary–adrenal axis, more commonly referred to as the **HPA axis**.

Can you think of a recent time you were in danger? Perhaps you were driving and a car suddenly pulled out in front of you and almost collided with your car. Were you aware of any changes in your body? Did you get a sudden surge of energy?

Fight-or-flight response

Two scientists and researchers made significant contributions to our understanding of the physiological (stress) response: Walter Cannon and Hans Selye. Cannon (1929) was a physiologist who studied human and animal bodily responses to danger, which he termed the **fight-or-flight response**. This is the body's response to acute stress. It can also be triggered by anger or aggression and is in essence an emotional reaction to an external event. When confronted by danger, the brain automatically begins to prepare the body for action by activating the neuroendocrine system: both the SNS and the endocrine system. The latter is the body's system for releasing hormones into the bloodstream. A subcortical structure in the brain known as the *hypothalamus* releases corticotrophin-releasing hormone (CRH), which triggers the (anterior) *pituitary gland*, also known as the master gland, to release adrenocorticotropic hormone (ACTH). These hormones belong to a class of chemicals known as *catecholamines*. ACTH then travels via the bloodstream to the adrenal glands, which are located in the adrenal cortices on top of each of our kidneys. Once stimulated, the adrenals release two hormones: **cortisol** and **adrenalin**. These are classes of chemical compounds called *glucocorticoids or corticosteroids*. Cortisol is commonly referred to as the 'stress hormone'. It has a chemical effect on various bodily tissues, as well as on the brain. In the brain it attaches to glucocorticoid receptors, particularly in the hypothalamus. The function of cortisol is to increase blood pressure and blood glucose through a process known as *gluconeogenesis*, which means the creation or release of glucose (Padgett & Glaser, 2003). Glucose is a sugar, which all cells in the body need for the production of energy. Glucose can either be ingested via one's diet, usually as the compound sucrose, or it can be metabolised from complex carbohydrates, proteins or fats. Glucose is stored in our liver and muscles as a glycogen until it is needed to produce energy (Johnson et al., 2002). Glucose is akin to petrol in a car. Cortisol also suppresses the immune system and decreases bone formation (Hoehn & Marieb, 2010). Excess or chronic secretion of cortisol, as in chronic stress, can lead to illnesses such as cardiovascular disease and can cause atrophy of the *hippocampus*, an important subcortical structure in the brain involved in the formation and storage of new memories.

Adrenalin, also known as epinephrine, is both a hormone and a neurotransmitter. It is also secreted by the adrenal glands. During the fight-or-flight response, the effect of adrenalin is to increase blood pressure and heart rate, dilate respiratory vessels in the lungs, thus enabling them to take in more oxygen, dilate the pupils, redirect blood away from the digestive system to muscles, and increase blood glucose levels by releasing glycogen from the liver and muscles. This process happens very rapidly, within seconds of the brain detecting the stressful event or danger. When the acute stress has passed, these stress hormones return to non-stress levels, as do blood pressure, heart rate and respiration. This also occurs in a feedback loop or regulation. The brain detects higher levels of cortisol in the bloodstream and stops sending signals for CRH to be released by the hypothalamus. However, in situations such as chronic stress this feedback mechanism ceases to function properly, which is known as *dysregulation*. The fight-or-flight response is adaptive. It has contributed to our survival as a species during times of danger; however, as previously mentioned, chronic exposure to stress can lead to severe illnesses (Cohen et al. 2007). Chronically elevated levels of cortisol can be indicative of chronic stress.

An alternative, female-oriented response to threat is known as 'tend and befriend'. This model, proposed by Taylor et al. (2000), states that females will seek to protect their offspring (tend) and build social networks to aid defence against stress (befriend).

General adaptation syndrome

Selye (1936, 1956, 1976) also made significant contributions to our understanding of the stress response, in particular exposure to chronic stress. He was attributed with first using the term 'stress' to describe this phenomenon. Selye observed people who were ill and also conducted experiments on animals and exposed them to various prolonged stressful situations such as X-rays, extremes of temperature and extended exercise. Through his investigations of the effect of stress hormones, he developed a theory known as the **general adaptation syndrome (GAS)**. The theory describes both an acute and chronic response to stress. Selye proposed that the GAS has three stages: alarm, resistance and exhaustion.

During the first stage, *alarm*, cortisol and adrenalin are released. The SNS is activated and numerous physiological changes occur that prepare the body for action. They include the following: dilation of pupils; increased lung capacity; increased heart rate, breathing and blood pressure; direction of blood towards muscles from the gastrointestinal tract; reduced saliva flow and digestive functions; inhibition of the bladder and excretory functions; increased release of glucose into the bloodstream; and activation of sweat glands. This stage is time limited: it occurs only for a short time.

The body may then enter the second stage, *resistance*. The parasympathetic nervous system, which largely functions in opposition to the SNS, takes over. The main function of the parasympathetic nervous system is to calm the body down, to reverse the effects of the SNS activation. Usually only one of these systems can be activated at any one time.

If the SNS is like the accelerator in a car, then the parasympathetic nervous system is like the brakes: it slows the body back down. Respiration returns to a normal rate, as do heart rate and blood pressure. However, adrenalin and cortisol remain high, as do blood glucose levels, because they take longer to return to pre-stress levels. The body is in a state of heightened alert and arousal, but is slowly adapting to elevated levels of stress. If the body remains in this state for extended periods, which occurs during chronic stress, it is vulnerable to illness.

During the final stage of the GAS, the body will enter the stage known as *exhaustion*; this occurs if the resistance stage is prolonged. The body becomes increasingly vulnerable to more serious life-threatening conditions. The heart is one of the more affected organs during this stage.

Chronic stress and its effects

Chronic stress can have a wear and tear effect on the body. Chronic stress has been defined as 'feelings of fatigue, lack of energy, irritability, demoralisation and hostility' (Flier et al., 1998, p. 172), and it occurs when we are exposed to environmental stressors repeatedly and over a lengthy period. A **stressor** is an event or situation that can cause stress. The bodily effect of chronic stress, referred to as *allostatic load*, can lead to serious mental health issues such as depression or anxiety. Stress, depression and anxiety are highly correlated. The more stressed someone feels, the more likely they are to experience depression. Chronic stress can also have an impact on physical health. High levels of stress are associated with insomnia or sleep disturbances, which can then lead to feeling tired and fatigued after nights of constant poor-quality sleep. This can then impair concentration and can also lead to depression if the chronic stress and insomnia continue for a lengthy period. As mentioned, chronic stress has been associated with more serious physical health issues such as heart disease, cancer and stroke (Cohen et al., 2007). You can read more about cardiovascular disease in the chapter on chronic illness (Chapter 9). Prolonged stress has also been shown to impair the immune system. Studies have found that participants under chronic stress were more likely to show a poorer antibody response to an influenza vaccine than participants not under this condition (Kiecolt-Glaser et al., 1995). This may explain why many students are vulnerable to colds, influenza or glandular fever during times of increased academic stress such as the exam period. Similar studies have shown that chronic stress has been found to interfere with healing of a punch biopsy wound. Wound healing took significantly longer in women caring for a family member with dementia compared to women not caring for a family member with dementia or other chronic illness (Kiecolt-Glaser et al., 1995). Thus, carers are at an increased risk of the ill effects of chronic stress. Chronic stress has also been linked to the development of insulin resistance, a risk factor for type 2 diabetes (Raikkonen et al., 1996).

During chronic stress, the neurobiological mechanism, via the HPA axis, is dysregulated. Cortisol levels remain chronically elevated. So too can blood pressure or blood glucose levels. Chronic activation of the stress response, or the allostatic load, over a lifetime may cause the allostatic systems to wear out or become exhausted (Seeman & Robbins, 1994). Allostatic systems are responsible for maintaining stability in the body (e.g. HPA axis activation that occurs to deal with a stressor). An example of the harmful effects of allostatic load is on the cardiovascular system. The risk of heart disease is increased if there is a lack of job control (Bosma et al., 1997), which can result in increased blood pressure (Schnall et al., 1992) and increased atherosclerosis (Everson et al., 1997).

Chronic stress and the brain

In recent years, stress and brain researchers have given us new insight into how stress affects our brain. Chronic stress can alter brain structures in ways that can later predispose individuals to mental illnesses (Chetty et al., 2014). A key brain structure involved in the regulation of the response of the HPA axis to stress is the hippocampus (Duman & Monteggia, 2006; Jacobson & Sapolsky, 1991). The hippocampus plays a key role in the formation of verbal memory and memory of context of strongly emotionally charged events, and in our experiences of stress. As mentioned, chronic stress can damage the hippocampus. A theory known as the 'glucocorticoid cascade hypothesis' speculates that wear and tear on the hippocampus results in dysregulation of the HPA axis and also memory impairment (Flier et al., 1998; Sapolsky, 1992; Sapolsky, Krey & McEwen, 1986). The hippocampus has high concentrations of cortisol receptors. Cortisol attaches itself to these receptors (Duman, 2004). Repeated stress affects the normal function of the hippocampus (Flier et al., 1998; McEwen, De Kloet & Rostene, 1986). For instance, the consistency and validity of contextual memories will be less accurate if there is any impairment to the hippocampus. The hippocampus plays a key role in deciding whether a situation is threating; therefore, if the hippocampus is damaged the stress response may be intensified where normally it would not (Flier et al., 1998; Sapolsky, 1990). During acute stress, the increase in cortisol secretion impairs the normal function of the hippocampus and so impairs short-term memory (McEwen & Sapolsky, 1995). Repeated stress causes atrophy in certain areas of the hippocampus (McEwen et al., 1995), which is reversible if the stress is acute; however, chronic stress can permanently destroy nerve cells in the hippocampus (Sapolsky, 1992). Once destroyed, any memories stored in those cells are also destroyed.

Chronic stress and depression

Magnetic resonance imaging (MRI) has shown that stress-related disorders such as recurrent depressive illness are associated with atrophy of the hippocampus (Flier et al., 1998). Stress also causes atrophy to other areas of the limbic system that regulate mood, emotion and cognition, including the amygdala and the prefrontal cortex, which are all neurologically connected to the hippocampus (Duman & Monteggia, 2006). This means that stress can change the structure of the brain, and therefore the way it functions; this can lead to psychological disorders such as depression. The volume of the hippocampus has been found to be decreased in people with depression (Duman, 2004). Suicide is one of the results of severe depression and chronic stress.

Chronic stress and sleep disturbance

Our sleep habits may change when we are feeling stressed. Some people might sleep more than usual. Some people may be unable to sleep and eventually develop sleep disorders such as insomnia. Insomnia is when people have trouble getting to sleep, staying asleep or waking up a few hours more than their usual wake-up time. The HPA axis also plays a role in our sleep-wake cycles. Our biological circadian rhythm, which controls sleep, is intimately linked to the system that regulates the stress response. Therefore, acute and chronic stress can disrupt sleep. Sleep deprivation can also activate the stress response, leading to elevated cortisol levels and cognitive impairment (Van Reeth et al., 2000).

What happens when we experience stress?

When we experience stress, and feelings of stress are experienced by almost everyone at some point in their lives, emotionally we may feel tense, anxious, angry, irritable or even depressed. Generally, stress is perceived as a negative experience. Our way of thinking, our cognition, tends to change. We may have trouble concentrating, we may become forgetful and we may find it hard to make decisions. We may also become apathetic and have a sense of hopelessness or despair. In order to cope with these thoughts and feelings our behaviour may also change. Some people cope with the stress they are experiencing by using unhealthy coping mechanisms such as self-medicating with legal drugs (e.g. caffeine, alcohol, tobacco, prescription drugs) or non-legal drugs (e.g. cannabis). This behaviour is also referred to as *maladaptive coping*. Some people can even self-medicate by using food. Studies have found a link between chronic stress and diet. People under stress tend to eat more sugary or fatty fried foods, which can then lead to weight gain and other associated health problems (Dallman et al., 2003) that can exacerbate the stress. The increase in food intake happens for two main reasons. The first is that these foods trigger the reward centres in our brain and increase our sense of pleasure, which can temporarily negate the negative experiences associated with stress. The second is that stress causes signals in our brains that entice us to eat more of these foods so that more fat can be stored in our fat cells (adipose tissue), especially in the abdominal regions (Warne & Dallman, 2007). Some people can become more accident prone or develop obsessive-compulsive behaviours or anxiety. Some people may gamble. Gambling can be become so problematic that it can develop into an addiction.

Not all experiences of stress are negative. Some stress helps us to get motivated. This is known as *eustress*. Some people find stress challenging. They find it a positive motivating experience. An optimal level of stress has been shown to enhance performance. It gets us aroused to an optimum level. However, if we experience too much stress our performance may be impaired, sometimes referred to as *distress*. This relationship between arousal and performance was first described by Yerkes and Dodson (1908) and is known as the Yerkes–Dodson Law. Recent studies have confirmed this relationship between stress and cognition (Lupien et al., 2007).

Mini case study 8.1

Joe Smith recently moved from a small country town to a large capital city to study at one of the major universities. It is the first time he has lived away from home. He lives in student housing. He shares with a roommate who is also from a country town. Joe is studying law and has a very heavy course load. He has also just started to work part-time at the local fast-food shop. He finds his new environment very different from the open spaces he loved at home. He misses his mum, dad, sisters and brother, and also his football friends. His apartment can be very noisy and he finds it hard to study and concentrate. He also sometimes struggles to find the time to study. He constantly worries about failing his course. He did not do as well as he expected with his first few assignments. He is starting to have trouble sleeping, he constantly feels uptight and edgy, and he has trouble relaxing. He would like to join the university's football team but does not believe he would have the time to go to training. Consequently, he is starting to become unfit and has gained weight. When he lived at home, the family members all shared the cooking and he ate well-balanced healthy meals. Now he mostly eats meals in the student cafeteria or meals from the takeaway shop where he works. He is also drinking more sugary and caffeinated drinks so he can stay awake and study, although he constantly feels extremely tired. He has made a few new friends but he has not spoken to anyone, including his family, about his concerns. He comes from a traditional Anglo-Australian farming community where people do not express their emotions or concerns, where the words 'she'll be right, mate' are often heard. When Joe goes out with friends, he drinks more alcohol than he used to back at home and is starting to use drugs such as valium, which he obtains illegally, to help him relax.

Critical thinking questions

1. Can you identify potential sources of stress for Joe?
2. What are the signs that Joe is experiencing stress?
3. Can you identify evidence that Joe is engaging in maladaptive coping?

Factors that cause stress (stressors)

The stress response initially evolved to help humans and other animals escape real danger such as lions and tigers. Although our modern world has evolved dramatically from the life of our cavemen ancestors, our stress response has not. The same stress response is evoked when we perceive external events or situations as dangerous or harmful to our physical and also our psychological selves. These stress-evoking events include many positive or joyful life events such as getting married, starting a new job, moving home, having a baby. Likewise, life events that we could describe as unpleasant or negative such as losing a job, divorce, losing our home, the death of a loved one, suffering a major injury, developing a chronic condition (e.g. asthma), being a carer for someone with an illness, sitting an exam or failing an exam can also cause stress. Psychiatrists Holmes and Rahe (1967) developed a life events scale known as the Social Readjustment Rating Scale, or the Holmes and Rahe Stress Scale, to measure these stress-inducing events. They were interested in the link between life events and illness. Holmes and Rahe found small positive correlations between the number of life events or stressors listed on their scale and an increased risk of illness. You can assess your own risk of experiencing stress by evaluating your current life events risk levels at www.stress.org using the Holmes and Rahe Stress Scale. The work of Holmes and Rahe led to much research in the area of stress, major life events and illness (Dohrenwend, 2006). Major life events can contribute to the experience of stress; however, not everyone will experience stress in relation to them.

Experiences such as poverty, homelessness, harassment, persecution, war, trauma, abuse, discrimination, racism, homophobia, bullying, domestic violence or threats of terrorism can be major sources of stress. So too can interpersonal problems, arguments or conflict with others, as well as events that are considered daily hassles, such as being stuck in traffic, finding a car park and having to pay bills. Our modern 21st-century lifestyles, the internet, mobile phones, computers and other screen devices have created new sources of stress. We are now 'connected' 24/7 to these devices, emails and social media. Paid work is no longer primarily conducted between the hours of 9.00 am and 5.00 pm, Monday to Friday. The internet and information technology allow us to be connected to our workplaces virtually anywhere, anytime. Increasingly, there is no disconnection between the workplace and the rest of our lives, and therefore no downtime or time for rest and relaxation. During the last few decades, this dramatic change in social and work circumstances has seen a substantial rise in reports of work-related stress caused by increasing work demands and a lack of control. Work-related chronic stress is strongly related to a higher incidence of heart disease (Chandola et al., 2008). The experience of stress involves a complex interaction between the stressor, our perception of how harmful or threatening it will be and our ability to cope with the situation.

Stress perception: a psychological model of stress

Lazarus and Eriksen (1952) noted that people varied in their ability to tolerate stressful situations. For some people their performance was greatly impaired by stressful situations; for others it either improved or was unaffected. In 1966, Lazarus developed the *transactional model of stress*, which was later refined by Lazarus and Folkman (1984). This model is analogous to a balloon and the amount of air being pumped into it.

If the balloon is thin, it will burst more readily than a balloon that is thick. A thicker balloon is able to withstand more pressure. However, even with the thicker balloon, if you pump in enough air it too will eventually burst. Each of us will have a point at which we experience stress, but where this point is depends on our coping skills, our available coping resources, many personal factors and our past life experiences of stressful events.

According to the Lazarus model (1966), stress is based on one's perception and *cognitive appraisal*. Cognitive appraisal involves the mental evaluation of a situation. Stress occurs if an individual perceives that their environmental demands exceed the coping resources available to deal effectively with them. If someone believes that they have enough resources to cope with the environmental demands, then they will not experience feelings of stress. They may even find the situation challenging. Some people thrive on higher demands, while others are overly taxed by them; therefore, our response to various stressors is individual and unique. If we do not believe that we have the coping resources to manage the stressor, then we will experience the physiological and psychological (subjective) sensations of stress described earlier.

The Lazarus and Folkman (1984) transactional model of stress has two stages. The first involves a **primary appraisal** or evaluation of the situation. Is the situation threatening, challenging or irrelevant? Will it involve harm or loss? Lazarus (1993) defines 'harm' as a loss that involves psychological damage to the individual, 'threat' as the anticipation of impending harm, and 'challenge' as a feeling of confidence that comes from successfully dealing with a demanding situation. If a situation is appraised as threatening or harmful, we must decide how to deal with it. An example could be being fired from your job. Losing a job also involves losing an income, losing an identity and losing connectedness with colleagues and friends. However, you may dislike your job or your manager, and therefore view the firing as an opportunity to find a job you will like. How you initially appraise the situation will determine how you will respond to it. **Secondary appraisal** occurs if the event or situation is perceived as threatening or dangerous. The individual then determines whether they have personal resources available to cope with the event. If not, this will result in a perception and feelings of stress. In the previous example, if you lose your job and are confident you will find another job easily, you are less likely to experience stress. If, on the other hand, you are overly concerned about finding another job because you may think you will never find one, then you are more likely to experience stress. In this model of stress, primary and secondary appraisal can occur concurrently. Stress can also arise in the absence of any cognitive appraisal, such as during a natural disaster. According to this model, the person can regulate the impact of the stressor by using various coping strategies. Lazarus (1966) defined stress as 'the psychological state which derives from people's appraisals of their adaptation to the demands which are made of them'. The transactional model of stress is useful to explain the stress perception process, but it does not take into account the many factors the influence one's self-perception or our individual experiences of stress in terms of biological response.

Individual and situation factors

Individuals can respond to stress and stressors very differently. Our response depends on many different individual factors such as our attitudes and beliefs, our personality, our approach to life, our past life experiences with stress, and our coping style. Emerging research knowledge is demonstrating that children who experience stress have brains that have developed differently from those of children who have not. This can then affect their future response to stressors and can result in a heightened reactivity to stress. That is, their response to stressors will be intensified compared to those who did not experience stress early in life. Research has found that the brains of young children and the elderly are more vulnerable to the biological effects of stress (Lupien et al., 2009). In animal studies, the developing brain of embryos in utero is susceptible to a mother's stress as glucocorticoids can cross the placenta, activating the embryo's HPA axis and altering the development of the brain (Koehl et al., 1999). Elevated or suppressed glucocorticoid levels affect the development and functioning of the brain (Lupien et al., 2009).

The way we generally think about events in our lives can also affect our stress response. Some people tend to have an optimistic attributional style, while others are more pessimistic. The latter could be related to *learned helplessness* (Seligman, 1972). How we usually experience anxiety can affect our stress perception and stress response. Those who rate highly on neuroticism tend to experience more stress. Other personality factors such as hardiness (Maddi & Kobassa, 1984) and self-efficacy (Bandura, 1982) are related to resilience and an increased ability to tolerate and cope with stress and stressful situations.

Some situations or stressors have a more severe impact than others. Catching a cold before an exam would probably not elicit the same stress response as being involved in a serious car accident. Our sense of *control* over these situations and how *predicable* these situations are also contribute to stress. The more uncontrollable or unpredictable the situation, usually the more stress provoking it will be. The duration of an event can also impact on our experience of stress. That car accident could involve lengthy stays in hospital, time away from loved ones or work, a long rehabilitation period or even loss of functioning such as not being able to walk again. These are all factors that contribute to our ability to cope with a potentially stressful situation.

Mini case study 8.2

John is 42 years old and very overweight. He is a high-flying executive who works 70 hours per week. He is married with two young children. He often works late and during the weekend. He has little spare time for exercise and often eats at restaurants for business dinners or lunches, during which he drinks a few glasses of wine. He rarely eats breakfast and has many takeaway meals. Although he thrives on his demanding job, he spends little time with his family or friends, is often sleep deprived, and feels immense pressure and tension. He often suffers from headaches, neck tension, and insomnia, and is unable to relax and unwind without the use of alcohol or other drugs. John sometimes uses amphetamines to stay alert during waking hours. In recent years he has developed high blood pressure, high cholesterol and impaired blood sugar control. He also smokes up to 30 cigarettes per day. His GP recommended that he quit smoking, take up at least 30 minutes of moderate exercise per day, such as brisk walking, and that he cut back on his alcohol intake. John has a large mortgage and intends to seek promotion to become an executive manager at his company. He does not believe he is at risk of a heart attack as suggested by his GP. However, six months later John has a massive heart attack that requires quadruple bypass surgery. He has been unable to work for the past two months, and has now developed major depression.

Critical thinking questions

1. Can you identify potential sources of stress for John?
2. Can you identify evidence that Joe is engaging in maladaptive coping?
3. Can you identify potential short- and long-term health consequences for John?

Coping with stress

Coping is how we behaviourally and cognitively try to deal, manage or struggle with problems or situations that could cause stress. Lazarus, Averill and Opton (1974) defined 'coping' as the 'problem-solving efforts made by an individual when the demands of a given situation tax adaptive resources' (p. 15). The objective of these efforts by the individual is to reduce the negative effects of strain. According to Lazarus (1993) there are two main outcomes of this effort. One changes the person's relationship with their environment so that the stress is likely to be eliminated or reduced. The other only changes how the situation is perceived. These efforts are referred to as problem-solving or emotion-focused coping, respectively.

Coping strategies

The behavioural and cognitive resources that people use when confronted with threatening or harmful situations are known as coping strategies. Folkman and Lazarus

(1988) developed a scale, the Ways of Coping Questionnaire, to measure various coping strategies. Following primary appraisal, problem- or emotion-focused strategies are applied depending on the circumstance. Problem-focused coping tends to be used if the situation is under the person's control or is predictable. Examples of problem-focused coping strategies are problem-solving, being organised, effective time management, assertive communication and instrumental social support. When a situation is beyond the person's control then emotion-focused coping is used to reduce the negative emotional responses associated with stress such as embarrassment, fear, anxiety, excitement or frustration. Examples of emotion-focused coping are avoiding or denying the situation to take your mind off it, venting to others, praying, ignoring the problem, or distraction (e.g. watching TV or eating). These strategies do not remove or minimise the stressor and so are often less effective than problem-focused coping strategies. Studies have found that those who used denial while sick got worse than those who faced their problems (Epping-Jordan, Compas & Howell, 1994).

Coping resources

Coping resources are various existing resources that are available to us before the occurrence of a stressful event and that allow us to manage the situation more effectively (Matheny et al., 1993). We can use these during stressful situations. According to one model, there are five main groups of coping resources: cognitive, social, emotional, spiritual/philosophical and physical (Hammer & Martin, 1988). Cognitive coping refers to being optimistic, having a positive sense of self-worth and viewing others positively. Social coping relates to the social support we derive from our social networks during stressful events. Emotional coping refers to the ability to express and accept our range of emotions. Spiritual/philosophical coping relates to the value we derive from religious, familial or cultural tradition or personal philosophies that guide our behaviours. Physical coping relates to health-promoting behaviours such as engaging in regular exercise that increase physical wellbeing. Coping resources help to manage the stressful situation by reducing the intensity of feelings associated with stress and by increasing the recovery rate from the stress-inducing situation (Hammer & Martin, 1988).

Managing stress

It is virtually impossible to eliminate stress from our lives; therefore, developing effective coping skills and learning how to manage, reduce or control our stress is desirable to avoid its harmful effects. While genetics or hereditary factors do not seem to play a large role in one's response to stress, our perception of an event or situation and our general state of physical health, which is determined not only by genetic factors but also by behavioural and lifestyle choices, generally determine our susceptibility. The effects of acute and chronic stress may be exacerbated or reduced by lifestyle behaviours such as diet, drug use, physical activity and sleep habits. Taking control of our lives is an important step towards managing many potentially stressful situations.

Stress involves a physiological response and a cognitive appraisal of a situation. How one person experiences stress is very different to another, therefore stress management should be tailored to individual needs and circumstances. Psychotherapy is used for people needing cognitive coping mechanisms whereas physiological strategies are used for people who respond to these best. Both can help combat stress and assist in coping with future stressful situations. This section describes factors such as healthy lifestyle behaviours that are known to reduce stress.

Physical activity

Many studies have found that physical activity and being physically fit are important factors in minimising the impact of stress in our lives. A meta-analytic review of aerobic fitness and response to a psychosocial stress found that aerobically fit participants had a reduced stress response compared to controls (Crews & Landers, 1987). Kobasa, Maddi and Puccetti (1982) were among the first researchers to study the effects of exercise as a buffer in the stress–illness relationship. Faced with stressful events, participants who exercised were less likely to become ill. Exercise reduces stress hormones such as cortisol and increases feel-good hormones such as endorphins, the body's natural morphine. Exercise reduces blood pressure, resting heart rate and blood glucose levels, helps reduce insomnia, relaxes the body, relieves tension, increases energy levels and helps maintain a healthy weight (Penedo & Dahn, 2005).

Diet

Numerous studies have found that certain types of diets contribute to overall health (Sofi et al., 2010). While there is often some conjecture as to what constitutes a healthy diet and dietary guidelines may change over time, a few consistencies can be observed. Studies have repeatedly found that a diet high in plant foods and vegetables, fruits, nuts and seeds confers many health benefits (Sofi et al., 2010). These foods contain nutrients and biochemicals that the body and brain need for optimal functioning, such as vitamins and minerals. Diets high in processed foods and added sugar contribute to various chronic illnesses, such as type 2 diabetes, and exacerbate the effects of stress, such as high blood pressure (Shultze et el., 2004). Furthermore, poor health itself can be a source of stress and can exacerbate existing stress.

Sleep

Both too little and too much sleep are associated with a greater risk of death, cardiovascular disease, type 2 diabetes, hypertension and obesity (Cappuccio et al., 2010). Sleep deprivation is a stressor and induces a stress response (McEwan, 2006). Shiftworkers naturally have disrupted sleep cycles. They tend to have poorer quality and amount of sleep, increased anxiety and depression, and poorer heart health (Harrington, 2001). Adequate sleep is important for good optimum health.

Time management

Time management, plus behaviours and strategies intended to increase productivity and to reduce stress, are often used together as a stress management strategy. Time management includes goal setting, planning ahead and prioritising tasks. A study involving university students found that time management was strongly inversely correlated to academic stress and stress reaction. The associations were stronger in female participants (Misra & McKean, 2000).

Critical thinking questions

1. Describe how regular exercise can alleviate and reduce stress.
2. Discuss the role of diet and stress.
3. Why is sleep important for managing stress?

Mini case study 8.3

Jane is a non-smoking woman who is 45 years of age and of average weight for her height and build. She is a successful manager of a small business and works 50 hours per week. She employs 20 people. She strongly believes that the good physical and mental health of her employees and herself is vital to business success and prosperity. She aims to have a workplace that minimises stress and emphasises health and wellbeing. Jane is married with two teenage children. She has eliminated highly processed food such as packaged snack foods, sweets, bottled sauces and dressings from her home environment. The family maintains a vegetable and fruit garden, they shop weekly at local food produce markets, and each member of the family cooks a nightly meal consisting of whole, real, unprocessed food that is high in vegetables. Highly nutritious homemade lunches are packed the night before. Each member of the family engages in regular team sports such as netball. Where possible, the family avoids using the car for transport and walks, cycles or catches public transport instead. Jane and her husband drink alcohol in moderation according to the national guidelines of 1 to 2 glasses of wine per day, and two alcohol-free days per week. No one in the family smokes or takes any other drugs. In the workplace, healthy food choices are encouraged and once a week there is a team lunch where everyone brings healthy food such as salads, casseroles, homemade dips, vegetable crudités or a fruit platter. Workers are encouraged to go for a walk for at least 30 minutes every day. The office has a health conscious plan and layout. There are standing desks and one even has a walking treadmill underneath it. Once a week there is a group mindfulness meditation session.

continued ›

Mini case study 8.3 continued ›

Critical thinking questions

1. Compare and contrast the lifestyles of John and Jane.
2. What factors could protect Jane from health risks?
3. What factors increase John's health risks?
4. In what ways could John change his lifestyle to minimise ill effects of stress?

Mindfulness meditation

It is easier to understand what mindfulness is not: listening and paying attention to the constant chatter in our minds and not paying attention to the world around us; not fully listening when others are talking, instead mentally preparing our response; eating while watching TV or during other activities; being constantly 'busy'; drinking excessive alcohol, taking mind-altering drugs or engaging in problem gambling; and constantly checking or playing with a mobile phone or screen device. Mindfulness is the opposite of these mind-distracting behaviours. It is paying purposeful attention without judgement (examples of judgemental thoughts include: 'this is bad', 'this is good', 'this is useless', 'this is a waste of time'). Mindfulness is being fully aware of the current moment, rather than being caught up in our thoughts or emotions, and fully focusing our attention on the current moment (Davis & Hayes, 2011). For example, if I go for a walk my mind could be distracted by thinking about work matters, the list of things I need to do or the argument I had with my best friend this morning. In such a distracted state of mind, I am not being mindful. Instead, if I notice the sounds I hear such as passing cars, birds singing, the sound of leaves rustling in the trees overhead; if I pay attention to the various sights on my walk such as houses, children playing, the colours of plants; if I feel the sun warming my skin, a light breeze blowing across my skin, the feel of my leg muscles as I take a step, the feel of my feet inside my shoes; if I notice the perfumed air or the smell of pollution then I am fully in the present moment, fully attending and experiencing my walk and being totally mindful. Mindfulness is a choice, but it is also a habit, as are many human behaviours. We can choose when and where we focus our mind, our awareness.

Benefits and consequences of mindfulness

Being mindful is an opportunity for the brain (and body) to experience 'downtime' or being 'offline'. It is an opportunity to allow our brain and body to recharge. As well as reducing stress, mindfulness has many known physical and mental health benefits. It can: improve mental health; reduce stress, anxiety and depression; reduce blood pressure;

increase focus, concentration, memory and attention; increase positivity, happiness and wellbeing; increase relaxation; improve sleep quality; increase self-esteem, which is how we feel about ourselves; and increase empathy and compassion (Davis & Hayes, 2011). Many mindfulness resources, including apps, are now freely available (see http://www.healthline.com/health/mental-health/top-meditation-iphone-android-apps#5 for some examples).

A mindfulness exercise

The following is an exercise to introduce you to mindfulness. Breathing is something we all do (otherwise we're in trouble!), so one of the easiest ways to practise mindfulness is by doing a mindfulness meditation focusing on the breath. *Are you aware of what happens when you breathe?*

1. Sit up straight in your chair, feet uncrossed, parallel on ground.
2. Rest your arms and hands on your lap.
3. Eyes should be closed or half-closed.
4. Let thoughts gently come and go through your mind as you focus.
5. Bring your full attention to your breath going in and out of your lungs.
6. You do not need to change your rate of breathing.
7. Focus on the breath going in and out of your nostrils.
8. Notice the colder air going in and warmer air going out as you breathe.
9. Bring your attention to your chest; notice how it rises and falls as you breathe in and out.
10. Now bring your attention to your abdomen and notice how it expands and contracts as you breathe in and out.
11. Now bring your attention to your shoulders and notice how they gently rise and fall as you breathe in and out.

Expand the exercise to focus your attention fully on sounds, then back to breathing, then smells, then back to breathing, then air on skin, then back to breathing, the physical sensations of sitting in chair: from your feet, legs, bottom, back and all the way up to your head, then go back to focusing on your breathing.

The final step is to be fully aware of being in the space you are in and gently opening your eyes.

Critical thinking question

1. What is mindfulness?
2. How would mindfulness help to alleviate or prevent stress?

Summary

- The terms 'stress' and 'stress response' are defined and the various physiological changes that occur during the stress response and the underlying neurobiological mechanism responsible for these changes outlined. A description of Hans Selye's GAS, the negative effects of stress, and the effects of chronic stress on the body and the contributing role of chronically elevated cortisol levels are given.
- Various factors and events that are able to induce a stress response are described. Lazarus and Folkman's transactional model of stress and primary and secondary appraisals are discussed as well as how personality factors and situational factors can contribute to stress.
- The meaning of the term 'coping' as it relates to stress is given. As people cope with stress very differently from each other, the difference between emotion-focused coping and problem-focused coping, and coping strategies and coping resources are outlined.
- There are various healthy means of managing stress. The positive effects of a healthy lifestyle are defined in terms of diet, physical activity and adequate sleep.
- The terms 'mindfulness' and 'mindfulness meditation' are defined and a mindfulness meditation exercise given that you can use to manage your own stress.

Suggested weblinks

Refer to the companion website at www.cambridge.edu.au/academic/healthpsychology for a list of suggested weblinks.

References

Bandura, A. (1982). Self-efficacy mechanism in human agency. *American Psychologist*, *44*, 1175–84. Retrieved from: http://www.uky.edu/~eushe2/Bandura/Bandura1982AP.pdf

Bosma, H., Marmot, M. G., Hemingway, H., Nicholson, A. C., Brunner, E. & Stansfeld, S. A. (1997). Low job control and risk of coronary heart disease in Whitehall II (prospective cohort) study. *British Medical Journal*, *314*, 558–65. doi: http://dx.doi.org/10.1136/bmj.314.7080.558

Cannon, W. B. (1929). *Bodily Changes in Pain, Hunger, Fear and Rage*. New York: D. Appleton & Co. Retrieved from: https://archive.org/stream/cu31924022542470#page/n11/mode/2up

Cappuccio, F. P., D'Elia, L., Strazzullo, P. & Miller, M. A. (2010). Sleep duration and all-cause mortality: A systematic review and meta-analysis of prospective studies. *Sleep*, *33*, 585–92. Retrieved from: http://www.ncbi.nlm.nih.gov/pmc/articles/PMC2864873/pdf/aasm.33.5.585.pdf

Chandola, T., Britton, A., Brunner, E., Hemingway, H., Malik, M. … Marmot, M. (2008). Work stress and coronary heart disease: what are the mechanisms? *European Heart Journal*, *29*, 640–8. doi: http://dx.doi.org/10.1093/eurheartj/ehm584

Chetty, S., Friedman, A. R., Taravosh-Lahn, K., Kirby, E. D., Mirescu, C., … Kaufer, D. (2014). Stress and glucocorticoids promote oligodendrogenesis in the adult hippocampus. *Molecular Psychiatry*, 19, 1275–83. doi: http://dx.doi.org/10.1038/mp.2013.190

Cohen, S., Janicki-Deverts, D. & Miller, G. E. (2007). Psychological stress and disease. Commentary. *Journal of the American Medical Association*, *298*, 1685–7. doi: http://dx.doi.org/10.1001/jama.298.14.1685

Crews, D. J. & Landers, D. M. (1987). A meta-analytic review of aerobic fitness and reactivity to psychosocial stressors. *Medicine and Science in Sports and Exercise*, *19*, S114–20.

Dallman, M. F., Pecoraro, N., Akana, S. F., la Fleur, S. E., Gomez, F., ... Manalo, S. (2003). Chronic stress and obesity: a new view of 'comfort food'. *Proceedings of the National Academy of Science*, *100*, 11696–701. doi: http://dx.doi.org/10.1073/pnas.1934666100

Davis, D. M. & Hayes, J. A. (2011). What are the benefits of mindfulness? A practice review of psychotherapy-related research. *Psychotherapy*, *48*, 198–208. doi: http://dx.doi.org/10.1037/a0022062

Dohrenwend, B. P. (2006). Inventorying stressful life events as risk factors for psychopathology: toward resolution of the problem of intracategory variability. *Psychological Bulletin*, 132, 477–95. doi: http://dx.doi.org/10.1037/0033-2909.132.3.477

Duman, R. S. (2004). Role of neurotrophic factors in the etiology and treatment of mood disorders. *Neuromolecular Medicine*, *5*, 11–25. Retrieved from: http://link.springer.com/article/10.1385/NMM:5:1:011

Duman, R. S. & Monteggia, L. M. (2006). A neurotrophic model for stress-related mood disorders. *Biological Psychiatry*, *59*, 1116–27. doi: http://dx.doi.org/10.1016/j.biopsych.2006.02.013

Epping-Jordan, J. A., Compas, B. E. & Howell, D. C. (1994). Predictors of cancer progression in young adult men and women: avoidance, intrusive thoughts, and psychological symptoms. *Health Psychology*, *13*, 539–47. http://dx.doi.org/10.1037/0278-6133.13.6.539

Everson, S. A., Lynch, J. W., Chesney, M. A., et al. (1997). Interaction of workplace demands and cardiovascular reactivity in progression of carotid atherosclerosis: population-based study. *British Medical Journal*, *314*, 553–8. Retrieved from: http://www.ncbi.nlm.nih.gov/pubmed/9055713

Flier, J. S., Underhill, L. H., McEwen, B. S. & McEwen, B. S. (1998). Protective and damaging effects of stress mediators. *New England Journal of Medicine*, *338*, 171–9. doi: http://dx.doi.org/10.1056/NEJM199801153380307

Folkman, S. & Lazarus, R. S. (1988). *Manual for the Ways of Coping Questionnaire*. Palo Alto, CA: Consulting Psychologists Press.

Hammer, A. L. & Martin M. S. (1988). *Coping Resources Inventory Manual*. Palo Alto, CA: Consulting Psychologists.

Harrington, J. M. (2001). Health effects of shift work and extended hours of work. *Occupational & Environmental Medicine*, *58*, 68–72. Retrieved from: http://oem.bmj.com/

Hoehn, K. & Marieb, E. N. (2010). *Human Anatomy and Physiology*. San Francisco: Benjamin Cummings.

Holmes, T. H. & Rahe, R. H. (1967). The social readjustment rating scale. *Journal of Psychosomatic Research*, *11*, 213–18. doi: http://dx.doi.org/10.1016/0022-3999(67)90010-4

Jacobson, L. & Sapolsky, R. (1991). The role of the hippocampus in feedback regulation of the hypothalamic-pituitary-adrenocortical axis. *Endocrine Review*, *12*, 118–34. Retrieved from: http://www.ncbi.nlm.nih.gov/pubmed/2070776

Johnson, A., Alberts, B., Bray, D., Lewis, J., Roberts, K. & Raff, M. (2002). *Molecular Biology of the Cell* (4th edn). New York: Garland Science. Retrieved from: http://www.ncbi.nlm.nih.gov/books/NBK26882/

Kiecolt-Glaser, J. K., Marucha, P. T., Mercado, A. M., Malarkey, W. B. & Glaser, R. (1995). Slowing of wound healing by psychological stress. *The Lancet*, *346* (8984), 1194–6. doi: http://dx.doi.org/10.1016/S0140-6736(95)92899-5

Kobasa, S. C., Maddi, S. R. & Puccetti, M. C. (1982). Personality and exercise as buffers in the stress–illness-relationship. *Journal of Behavioral Medicine*, *5*, 391–404.

Koehl, M., Darnaudéry, M., Dulluc, J., Van Reeth, O., Le Moal, M. & Maccari, S. (1999). Prenatal stress alters circadian activity of hypothalamo-pituitary-adrenal axis and hippocampal corticosteroid receptors in adult rats of both gender. *Journal of Neurobiology*, *5*, 302–15. doi: http://dx.doi.org/10.1002/(SICI)1097-4695(19990905)40:3<302::AID-NEU3>3.0.CO;2-7

Lazarus, R. S. (1966). *Psychological Stress and the Coping Process*. New York: McGraw-Hill.

—— (1993). From psychological stress to emotions: a history of changing outlooks. *Annual Review of Psychology*, *44*, 1–21. Retrieved from: http://commonweb.unifr.ch/artsdean/pub/gestens/f/as/files/4660/18222_105619.pdf

Lazarus, R. S., Averill, J. R. & Opton, E. M. (1974). The psychology of coping: issues of research and assessment. In: G. V. Coelho, D. A. Hamburg & J. E. Adams (eds). *Coping and Adaptation*. Oxford: Basic Books.

Lazarus, R. S. & Eriksen, C. W. (1952). Effects of failure stress upon skilled performance. *Journal of Experimental Psychology*, *43*, 100–5.

Lazarus, R. S. & Folkman, S. (1984). *Stress, Appraisal, and Coping*. New York: Springer.

Lupien, S. J., Maheu, F., Tu, M., Fiocco, A. & Schramek, T. E. (2007). The effects of stress and stress hormones on human cognition: implications for the field of brain and cognition. *Brain & Cognition*, *65*, 209–37. doi: http://dx.doi.org/10.1016/j.bandc.2007.02.007

Lupien, S. J., McEwen, B. S., Gunnar, M. R. & Heim, C. (2009). Effects of stress throughout the lifespan on the brain, behaviour and cognition. *Nature Reviews Neuroscience*, *10*, 434–45. doi: http://dx.doi.org/10.1038/nrn2639

Maddi, S. R. & Kobasa, S. C. (1984). *The Hardy Executive: Health Under Stress*. Pacific Grove, CA: Brooks/Cole.

Matheny, K. B., Aycock, D. W., Curlette, W. L. & Junker, G. N. (1993). The coping resources inventory for stress: a measure of perceived resourcefulness. *Journal of Clinical Psychology*, *49*, 815–30. Retrieved from: http://www.ncbi.nlm.nih.gov/pubmed/8300870

McEwan, B. S. (2006). Sleep deprivation as a neurobiologic and physiologic stressor: allostasis and allostatic load. *Metabolism*, *55*, S20–3. doi: http://dx.doi.org/10.1016/j.metabol.2006.07.008

McEwen, B. S., Albeck, D., Cameron, H., Chao, H. M., Gould, E. & Hastings, N. (1995) Stress and the brain: a paradoxical role for adrenal steroids. *Vitamins & Hormones*, *51*, 371–402. doi: http://dx.doi.org/10.1016/0006-3223(92)90204-D

McEwen, B. S., De Kloet, E. R. & Rostene, W. (1986). Adrenal steroid receptors and actions in the nervous system. *Physiology Review*, *66*, 1121–88. Retrieved from: http://physrev.physiology.org/content/66/4/1121

McEwen, B. S. & Sapolsky, R. M. (1995). Stress and cognitive function. *Current Opinions in Neurobiology*, *5*, 205–16. doi: http://dx.doi.org/10.1016/0959-4388(95)80028-X

Misra, R. & McKean, M. (2000). College students' academic stress and its relation to their anxiety, time management, and leisure satisfaction. *American Journal of Health Studies*, *16*. Retrieved from: http://www.biomedsearch.com/article/College-students-academic-stress-its/65640245.html

Padgett, D. & Glaser, R. (2003). How stress influences the immune response. *Trends in Immunology*, *24*(8), 444–8. doi: http://dx.doi.org/10.1016/S1471-4906(03)00173-X

Penedo, F. & Dahn, J. R. (2005). Exercise and well-being: a review of mental and physical health benefits associated with physical activity. *Current Opinion in Psychiatry*, *18*, 189–93.

Raikkonen, K., Keltikangas-Jarvinen, L., Adlercreutz, H. & Hautenen, A. (1996). Psychosocial stress and the insulin resistance syndrome. *Metabolism*, *45*, 1533–8. doi: http://dx.doi.org/10.1016/S0026-0495(96)90184-5

Sapolsky, R. M. (1990). Stress in the wild. *Scientific American*, *262*, 116–23. Retrieved from: http://academic.reed.edu/biology/professors/srenn/pages/teaching/2008_syllabus/2008_readings/9_Sapolsky_1990.pdf

—— (1992). *Stress, the Aging Bain and the Mechanisms of Neuron Death*. Cambridge, MA: MIT Press.

Sapolsky, R. M., Krey, L. C. & McEwen, B. S. (1986). The neuroendocrinology of stress and aging: the glucocorticoid cascade hypothesis. *Endocrinology Review*, *7*, 284–301. doi: http://dx.doi.org/10.1210/edrv-7-3-284

Schnall, P. L., Schwartz, J. E., Landsbergis, P. A., Warren, K. & Pickering, T. G. (1992). Relation between job strain, alcohol, and ambulatory blood pressure. *Hypertension*, *19*, 488–94. doi: http://dx.doi.org/10.1161/01.HYP.19.5.488

Schulze, M. B., Manson, J. E., Ludwig, D. S., Colditz, G. A., Stampfer, M. J., Willett, W. C. & Hu, F. B. (2004). Sugar-sweetened beverages, weight gain, and incidence of type 2 diabetes in young and middle-aged women. *JAMA*, *292*, 927–34. doi: http://dx.doi.org/10.1001/jama.292.8.927

Seeman, T. E. & Robbins, R. J. (1994). Aging and hypothalamic–pituitary–adrenal response to challenge in humans. *Endocrine Reviews*, *15*, 233–60. doi: http://dx.doi.org/10.1210/edrv-15-2-233

Seligman, M. E. P. (1972). Learned helplessness. *Annual Review of Medicine*, *23*, 407–12.

Selye, H. (1936). A syndrome produced by diverse nocuous agents. *Nature*, *138*, 32. Retrieved from: http://www.lonkilgore.com/5093/selye_1936.pdf

—— (1956). *The Stress of Life*. New York: McGraw-Hill.

—— (1973). The evolution of the stress concept. *American Scientist*, *61*, 692–9.

—— (1976). *Stress in Health and Disease*. Boston, MA: Butterworth Inc. Retrieved from: https://books.google.com.au/books?hl=en&lr=&id=wrfYBAAAQBAJ&oi=fnd&pg=PP1&dq=hans+selye&ots=_imumjc8h6&sig=HuLqzrWvIjNFa7Fdh7nkeaoJpnc#v=onepage&q=hans%20selye&f=false

Sofi, F., Abbate, R., Gensini, G. & Casini, A. (2010). Accruing evidence on benefits of adherence to the Mediterranean diet on health: an updated systematic review and meta-analysis. *American Journal of Clinical Nutrition*, *92*, 1189–96. doi: http://dx.doi.org/10.3945/ajcn.2010.29673

Taylor, S. E., Klein, L. C., Lewis, B. P., Gruenewald, T. L., Gurung, R. A. R., Updegraff, J. A. (2000). Biobehavioral responses to stress in females: tend-and-befriend, not fight-or-flight. *Psychological Review*, *107*, 411–29. doi: http://dx.doi.org/10.1037/0033-295X.107.3.411

Van Reeth, O., Weibel, L., Spiegel, K., Leproult, R., Dugovic, C. & Maccari, S. (2000). Physiology of sleep (review) – Interactions between stress and sleep: from basic research to clinical situations. *Sleep Medicine Reviews*, *4*, 201–19, doi: http://dx.doi.org/10.1053/smrv.1999.0097

Warne, J. P. & Dallman, M. F. (2007). Stress, diet and abdominal obesity: Y? *Nature Medicine*, *13*, 781–3. doi: http://dx.doi.org/10.1038/nm0707-781

Yerkes, R. M. & Dodson, J. D. (1908). The relation of strength of stimulus to rapidity of habit-formation. *Journal of Comparative Neurology and Psychology 18*, 459–82. doi: http://dx.doi.org/10.1002/cne.920180503

9

Lifestyle-related chronic illnesses (CVD and T2D) and depression

Learning outcomes

After reading this chapter, you should be able to:

- describe cardiovascular disease (CVD), insulin resistance, and type 2 diabetes (T2D)
- describe the human cardiovascular system, the pancreas, the role of insulin and the metabolism of carbohydrates
- identify common causes of CVD and T2D
- explain the medical regimen for someone with T2D
- describe treatment and prevention strategies for CVD and T2D
- evaluate the interconnection between CVD, T2D and depression, how depression complicates CVD and T2D and suggest possible treatment regimens for lifestyle-related chronic illnesses and comorbid depression.

Introduction

Chronic illness, **depression** and lifestyle behaviours are strongly interrelated. Chronic illness, for the purposes of this chapter, will only refer to the lifestyle-related chronic illnesses (LRCI), namely **type 2 diabetes (T2D)** and **cardiovascular disease (CVD),** conditions strongly determined by lifestyle behaviours. There is well-established evidence that a diet lacking in nutrition and a lack of physical activity contribute to both illnesses (AIHW, 2014a). Moreover, both are associated with an increased risk of depression (National Heart Foundation of Australia [NHFA], 2013; Peyrot & Rubin, 1997).

The rate of depression associated with CVD or T2D is two to three times the rate found in the general population (Anderson et al., 2001; Musselman, Evans & Nemeroff, 1998), which is about 4.1 to 14.5% (ABS, 2008). Conversely, there is also well-established evidence that depression increases the risk for these illnesses, particularly CVD. Depression is also associated with an increase in unhealthy lifestyle behaviours, particularly inactivity, and conversely, unhealthy lifestyle behaviours can increase the risk for depression. These interrelated relationships are depicted in Figure 9.1.

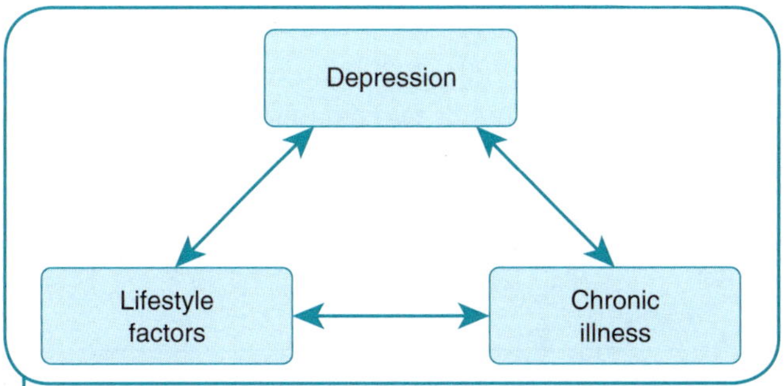

Figure 9.1 Bidirectional relationships between chronic illness, lifestyle behaviours and depression

This chapter will introduce you to CVD and T2D. The chapter begins with an overview of CVD and the human cardiovascular system. This will be followed by an introduction to the main types of CVD that are related to lifestyle behaviours, and includes a description of atherosclerosis, the leading underlying physiological cause of CVD. An introduction to T2D will follow, with a discussion of its precursor, insulin resistance. In this section the role of the pancreas, insulin and glucose metabolism will be briefly outlined. People who have T2D must follow a strict medical regimen and this will be outlined. The treatment and prevention of CVD and T2D will then be addressed concurrently, as both conditions are ameliorated with changes to lifestyle behaviours. The chapter concludes with an extended discussion on the interconnection between depression, lifestyle behaviours and LRCI. The difficulties diagnosing people with LRCI and depression will be mentioned, as well as possible treatments for depression associated with LRCI.

Cardiovascular disease

Cardiovascular disease (CVD) refers to any disease of the cardiovascular system. CVD is among the leading causes of death and loss of **disability-adjusted life years** worldwide. Rates of CVD have declined throughout the 20th century in developed countries (Yusuf et al., 2004) since the 1960s, largely due to decreases in smoking rates (ABS, 2002). Despite major improvements to cardiovascular health since then, CVD remains the leading cause of death in Australia (AIHW, 2006). The economic burden of CVD exceeds that of all other disease, costing $7.7 billion in 2008–2009 (AIHW, 2014a). In 2012, **coronary heart disease (CHD)**, a type of CVD, was still the leading cause of death of all Australians, accounting for 13.6% (20,046) of all deaths. CHD is also the leading cause of death in most Western countries (Gaziano et al., 2010).

The human cardiovascular system

The human **cardiovascular system (CVS)**, or circulatory system, is responsible for pumping blood throughout the body. The CVS includes the heart, blood vessels and blood

(Figure 9.2). Blood consists of plasma, red (erythrocytes) and white blood cells (leukocytes), and platelets. The heart consists of four chambers: the left and right atrium and the left and right ventricles. The CVS consists of two circuits: the pulmonary circulation system, passing through the lungs, and the systemic circulation system, which goes to the rest of the body. Oxygenated blood enters the left atrium from the pulmonary veins and then passes through the left mitral valve into the left ventricle. The heart then pumps the oxygenated

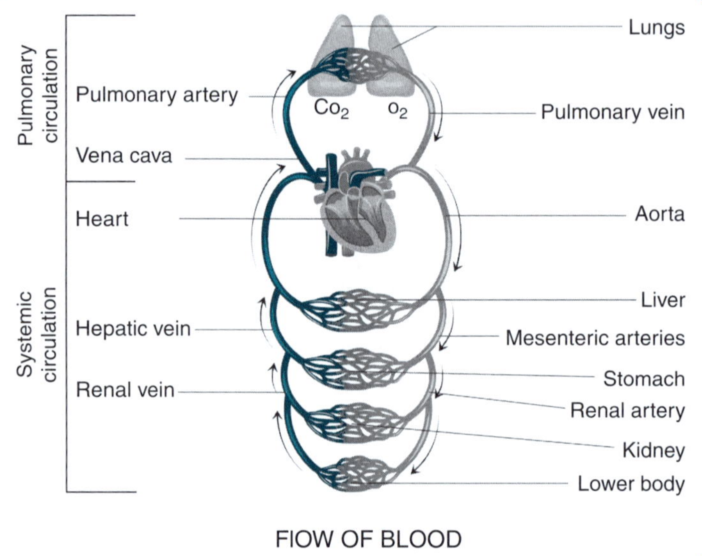

Figure 9.2 Human circulation system
Source: Getty Images/stock-shoppe

blood out via the aorta. At the base of the aorta is the aortic valve. Cardiac valves ensure that blood can only flow in a forward direction. The aorta branches out to form an arterial system that reaches every cell in the body. At the cellular level, arteries form a capillary system where oxygen and nutrients are exchanged for carbon dioxide and cellular waste products. These return to the heart and lungs via the body's venous system. Deoxygenated (venous) blood returns to the heart through the right atrium and passes through the right tricuspid valve into the right ventricle. The heart then pumps this deoxygenated blood to the lungs via the pulmonary artery. In the lungs, carbon dioxide is exchanged for oxygen.

Go to the following link to view an animation of the structure and function of the heart: https://www.youtube.com/watch?v=JA0Wb3gc4mE.

The coronary arteries supply the heart. These branch out from the aorta (McAlpine, 1975). Arteries are tubular, flexible and have a wall of outer tissue. Figure 9.3 shows a cross-section of an artery. Arteries are made up of layers of tissue. They contain smooth muscle tissue surrounded by both an external and internal elastic tissue membrane. The outermost layer is known as the tunica externa, or adventitia, and the innermost layer is the tunica intima.

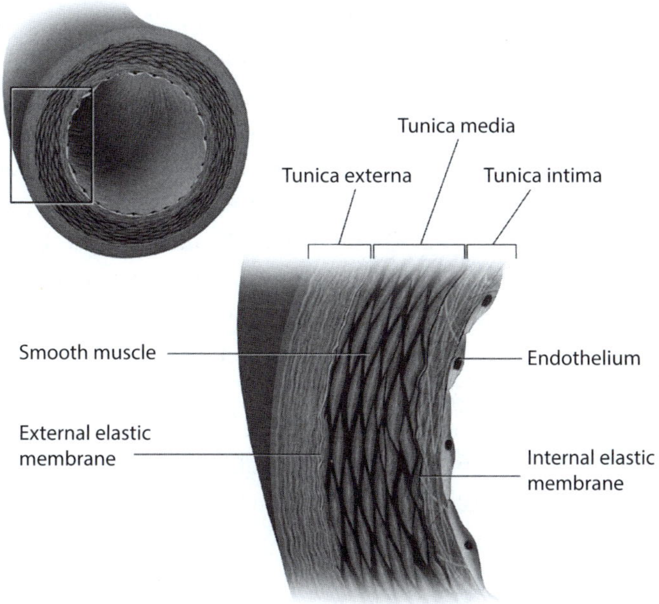

Figure 9.3 Cross-section of arterial wall
Source: Wikimedia Commons/Blausen Gallery 2014, Wikiversity Journal of Medicine http://dx.doi.org/10.15347/wjm/2014.010

Blood pressure is largely determined by the arteries. Blood pressure varies during a cardiac cycle; it is lowest when the heart dilates (systolic) and highest when the heart contracts (diastolic). Healthy blood pressure is about 120/80 mmHg. The upper number is the diastolic blood pressure and the lower number the systolic blood pressure. Blood pressure tends to increase as we age, mainly corresponding with an increase in body weight and a decrease in physical activity (AIHW, 2007). About 30% of Australians have **hypertension**, commonly referred to as high blood pressure (Heart Foundation, n.d.).

Arteries branch out to form thinner arterioles and then our smallest blood vessels, the capillaries. Arterioles contribute to blood pressure by contracting or dilating the smooth muscles in their walls. If arteries become 'hardened' (losing elasticity), blood pressure will increase (Purves, Augustine & Fitzpatrick, 2001).

Types of cardiovascular disease

Cardiovascular disease (CVD) is a term that refers to all diseases and conditions that can affect the heart and the blood vessels. The main types of CVD related to lifestyle factors are CHD (ischaemic heart disease or coronary arterial disease), **heart failure**, **stroke**, **cardiomyopathy** and **peripheral vascular disease** (AIHW, 2015a). Cardiomyopathy, a disease of the heart muscle, is when the heart cannot adequately supply blood throughout the body. The worse the cardiomyopathy becomes, the weaker the heart becomes. Symptoms of cardiomyopathy include fatigue, breathlessness and oedema of the legs and abdomen (due to a build-up of fluid). **Atherosclerosis**, an inflammatory disease, is the leading cause of CVD (Libby, Ridker & Maseri, 2002). Atherosclerosis ('hardening of the arteries') is a disease in which a plaque or **atheroma** forms on the tunica intima. The process begins as a fatty streak that contains macrophages and T lymphocytes (Epstein & Ross, 1999). The plaques consist of fatty tissue, cholesterol, calcium, leukocytes and **proinflammatory cytokines**. The plaques eventually reduce arterial blood flow and may completely occlude or block an artery, termed **ischaemia**. Depending on the site of the **occlusion**, this can then lead to an **acute myocardial infarction** (**AMI**, 'heart attack'), or **cerebral infarction**, a type of stroke. Both are serious life-threatening medical conditions (Hofmeijer et al., 2008). Plaques are thought to occur because of damage to the tunica intima (Buja & Krueger, 2013). Smoking, hypertension and dietary factors are all thought to cause damage and inflammation to arterial walls. The damage causes leukocytes to stick to the inner wall of the arteries (Figure 9.4). Proinflammatory cytokines are released, which are part of the inflammatory response. Plaques can also rupture and a blood clot can form around the rupture that can dislodge, move through the artery and occlude somewhere else in the circulation system, a common cause of AMI (Warrel, Cox & Firth, 2010).

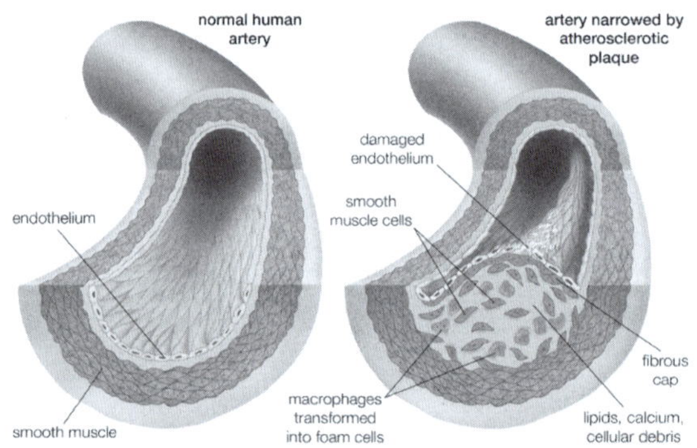

Figure 9.4 Disrupted atherosclerotic plaque causing thrombus
Source: Getty Images/Encyclopedia Britannica/UIG

The most common type of CVD is CHD. CHD is due to blockages of the coronary arteries. An AMI occurs every 10 minutes in Australia, equating to over 52 000 AMIs per year. An AMI occurs when there is a complete blockage of a coronary artery, usually due to a thrombotic atheroma. The blood supply and oxygen to that section of the heart stop and there is tissue damage and tissue death ('infarct'). The symptoms of an AMI vary especially from females to males. Common symptoms include: chest pain or discomfort; heaviness, tightness, pain or pressure in the upper body such as chest, neck, jaw, arms, shoulders or back; shortness of breath; light-headedness or dizziness; prolonged and unexplained fatigue; nausea or vomiting; or a cold sweat. About 33% of people who have an AMI experience no chest pain. They are more likely to be female, the elderly and people with diabetes. Some people have no symptoms (referred to as a silent heart attack). An AMI is an emergency. Anyone experiencing these symptoms should call 000 immediately (NHFA, 2015).

Angina is chest pain or discomfort caused by ischaemia. Angina is a symptom of CHD and usually occurs when someone physically exerts themselves, during severe emotional stress or following a big meal. The chest pain usually dissipates with rest, unlike in an AMI.

Cerebral infarction (ischaemic stroke) is the result of an occlusion of a cerebral artery. The most common cause is a blood clot (NHFA, 2015). Less common is a haemorrhagic stroke caused by bleeding into the brain following the rupture of a cerebral artery. This is usually due to chronic hypertension or arterial diseases (AIHW, 2013). When a cerebral artery is occluded, oxygen and glucose cannot reach the adjacent areas of the brain. This can result in brain tissue death (infarction). Symptoms of a stroke depend on which areas of the brain are damaged and can include unilateral paralysis, inability to speak or understand language, vertigo or partial loss of vision. Haemorrhagic strokes can be accompanied by severe headache. If symptoms of a stroke last less than 2 hours, this is known as a ('mini-stroke') **transient ischaemic attack** (AIHW, 2013). Strokes can be fatal. Although the rate of death following a stroke has fallen in Australia by 70% from 1979 to 2010, about 23 Australians die each day due to a stroke. The number of strokes over the same period has increased. Strokes usually occur in those over 65 years of age (AIHW, 2013).

Common causes of cardiovascular disease

The prevalence of LRCI is increasing in Western societies because of the rise of unhealthy lifestyle behaviours. These behaviours play a large role in the aetiology of LRCI. The main behavioural risk factors that contribute to CVD are smoking, unhealthy diet, physical inactivity and excessive alcohol intake. The main medical risk factors are hypertension, overweight and obesity, T2D and poor mental health (Nichols et al., 2014) and are also related to behavioural lifestyle factors. Once believed to be a leading cause of CVD, the role of high blood cholesterol and its contribution to CVD are increasingly controversial (Siri-Tarino et al., 2010).

Currently many Australians engage in unhealthy lifestyle behaviours that increase the risk for LRCI. For instance, 15% of Australians aged 14 years and over are daily smokers (AIHW, 2013) and 10% consume alcohol at risky levels. Only 28% of Australians aged 15 years and older engage in sufficient physical activity (AIHW, 2013). About 63% of Australian adults and 25% of Australian children are overweight (ABS, 2013). Unhealthy lifestyle behaviours increase the risk of LRCI, yet unlike other factors such as age, sex and genetics, modifiable lifestyle behaviours are largely within the control of the individual and society. While behavioural and medical risk factors for T2D and CVD are reasonably well known, it is less widely known that depression is a key risk factor for CHD and also for stroke (Nichols et al., 2014).

Yusuf and colleagues (2004) collected data from 52 countries (n = 30 000) of people with or without AMI. They concluded that 90% of all AMIs worldwide are associated with the following modifiable lifestyle factors, listed from highest to lowest risk for both genders across ages: smoking, abnormal lipid profile, diabetes, hypertension, psychosocial factors (including depression) and abdominal obesity. Protective lifestyle factors included consuming fruits, consuming vegetables, moderate alcohol intake three or more times per week and engaging in moderate or strenuous exercise for 4 or more hours per week. Moderate exercise was defined as walking, cycling or gardening, and strenuous exercise as jogging, football or vigorous swimming. A combination of risk factors was associated with greater overall risk for AMI. The more protective factors one engaged in and the risk factors avoided, the lower the odds ratio risk for AMI.

Current understanding is that atherosclerosis is caused by chronic damage to the inner lining of arteries resulting in inflammation. Recent research also suggests that a high sugar intake can also cause damage to arteries (Lavi et al., 2009). It was once believed that high cholesterol caused damaged to the arteries; however, the latest research suggests this may not be the case (Barter et al., 2007).

The role of dietary cholesterol and saturated fat as main risk factors for CVD is increasingly challenged (Siri-Tarino et al., 2010). See Chapter 5 for more detailed information about the relationship between saturated fat and sometimes fraudulent science. There is also currently much controversy as to what constitutes a healthy, balanced and nutritious diet. Recent studies of low-carbohydrate diets, which tend to be high in saturated fat, indicate that they do not cause an increase in blood cholesterol, but they can contribute to a healthier heart/blood profile. A meta-analysis of 17 low-carbohydrate diet trials (n = 1140 obese patients) found that low-carbohydrate diets were associated with significant decreases in: body weight, triglycerides, fasting glucose, blood pressure, body mass index, abdominal circumference, plasma insulin, and C-reactive protein; and an increase in high density lipoprotein (HDL) cholesterol. However, the low-carbohydrate diets had no effect on blood low-density lipoprotein cholesterol (Santos et al., 2012).

Mini case study 9.1

Peter is 42 years old and manages an IT company. He often spends up to 60 hours per week sitting in front of a computer. He has been living alone for the past 6 months. He usually eats at irregular times and almost always eats food from a fast-food chain. Peter also drinks a six-pack of beer on most nights. Peter's father and grandfather both died of heart attacks in their mid-50s. Due to his family history of heart disease, Peter does not believe that a heart attack is preventable. Peter has been smoking since he was 15 years old and he currently smokes 20 cigarettes per day. He does very little physical activity. He is overweight for his height, especially around his abdomen. Twelve months ago he was diagnosed with hypertension. Although his GP has prescribed anti-hypertensive medication for him, Peter takes his medication haphazardly. His job involves a high degree of stress and Peter often feels time-pressured. Recently he has been experiencing tightness in his chest and shortness of breath, but he has not visited his GP as he believes these symptoms might be due to the stress he is experiencing and not heart problems. Six months ago, Peter separated from his wife and he no longer sees his two children. This has caused him a great deal of psychological distress. Increasingly he has problems staying asleep, he is very irritable at work, he has increased his drinking and smoking, and he spends less time with friends and doing activities he usually enjoys, such as going to watch the football. He generally feels fatigued and has trouble concentrating.

Critical thinking questions

1. What lifestyle behaviours increase Peter's risk of CVD?
2. What psychosocial factors increase Peter's risk of CVD?

Type 2 diabetes

Type 2 diabetes (T2D), also known as diabetes mellitus or mature onset diabetes, is the fastest growing chronic illness worldwide, including Australia. Globally, 387 million people have T2D, more than the population of the US. In Australia the rate has more than doubled since 1989–1990 and has stabilised since 2007–2008. Over 1 445 000 Australians have T2D (AIHW, 2015b). The majority of people with T2D live in low- or middle-income countries (Diabetes Australia, 2015a). Sixty per cent of cases of T2D are preventable. It has been estimated that by 2033 approximately 3.3 million Australians will have T2D (Magliano et al., 2009). Every five minutes someone in Australia develops T2D. The risk of T2D increases with age. It is more common in men and it is more than twice as common in those from the lowest compared to the highest socioeconomic groups: 7.2% versus 3.2%, respectively (AIHW, 2015b).

The pancreas, insulin and insulin resistance

Human cells need glucose to produce energy. Ingested carbohydrates and simple sugars such as sucrose are broken down into glucose in the small intestine and rapidly absorbed into the bloodstream. When the brain registers an increase in blood glucose levels (BGLs, as well as amino acids), it sends chemical messages to cells in the pancreas, Islets of Langerhans, to release the hormone **insulin**. Insulin normally regulates BGLs, preventing levels from getting too high (hyperglycaemia) or too low (hypoglycaemia). Insulin attaches itself to the outside of muscle cells and allows these cells to absorb glucose. If there is more glucose in the blood than the body needs, then it is stored as glycogen in the liver or muscles or it may be converted to fat and stored in adipose tissue. When BGLs fall, glycogen is converted to glucose and is released into the bloodstream.

Chronic hyperglycaemia is toxic to arteries, capillaries and the body's organs and other structures (such as the eyes) and will lead to various health complications. Chronic hyperglycaemia due to high dietary levels of sugar, carbohydrate or saturated fat intake can lead to a condition known as insulin resistance (Insel et al., 2012), a precursor to T2D.

Insulin resistance

Insulin resistance is a condition in which skeletal muscle cells no longer respond to the normal action of insulin; the result is hyperglycaemia. In an effort to control BGLs, the pancreas produces more insulin, which results in high blood insulin levels. Insulin loses its ability to transport glucose into muscle cells, but is still able to convert glucose to fat for storage in adipose tissue. Because there is more insulin being released by the pancreas and an increase in food intake, there is a higher likelihood of weight gain, especially around the abdominal region (Holt et al., 2010). Weight gain then usually leads to a reduction in physical activity as it becomes more difficult and requires more effort to exercise and move (Insel et al., 2012), so there is a very high risk of developing T2D. Initially T2D can be treated with modifications to lifestyle, namely increasing physical activity and eating a healthy balanced diet that is low in added sugars and in refined and highly processed carbohydrates. Insulin sensitivity can be increased by as little as a single bout of aerobic exercise (30 to 60 minutes at approximately 60 to 70% of maximal oxygen consumption [VO_2max]). It is well established that exercise training can improve glucose tolerance and enhance skeletal muscle insulin sensitivity (Henriksen, 2002).

Mini case study 9.2

Tina is a 50-year-old successful business woman. She regularly works 60 to 80 hours per week. She has little time for structured physical activity and has a sedentary lifestyle. She arrives home late from work every night and works on most weekends. She rarely has home-cooked meals. Her diet largely consists of snacks such as chocolate and muesli bars. On most days she consumes fruit juice. She has progressively gained weight, especially around the midriff, for the past decade since her working hours have increased. She is now in the obese range for her height. Although she is highly driven and motivated to success in her chosen career, she is increasingly tired, has developed sleep apnoea and constantly feels hungry. Her mother and two sisters have T2D.

Critical thinking question

1. What are the factors that suggest Tina might have developed insulin resistance?
2. If Tina could make one lifestyle change to improve her health, what would you recommend and why?

What is type 2 diabetes?

Type 2 diabetes is when the body no longer produces enough insulin to maintain blood glucose within accepted normal levels, resulting in chronic hyperglycaemia. Although the symptoms of T2D can include increased thirst and hunger, frequent urination, weight loss, fatigue, blurred vision, slow-healing sores, frequent infections and areas of darkened skin, up to 500 000 Australians are undiagnosed (Diabetes Australia, 2015a). T2D is treated initially by modifying lifestyle behaviours, oral medications and ultimately subcutaneous injections of insulin and other drugs. However, it is well known that many of the medications used to treat T2D cause weight gain (Carver, 2006) and thus ultimately exacerbate the problem for people with T2D. Insulin, although used to treat T2D, largely removes glucose from the bloodstream and converts it to fat thus making people with T2D more overweight or obese. The best treatment for T2D is permanent changes to lifestyle behaviours; however, due to increasing obesogenic environments many people find this difficult to maintain.

Living with type 2 diabetes

Uncontrolled T2D can lead to serious and fatal health conditions that include atherosclerosis, CVD, renal disease and failure, retinopathy and blindness, gangrene and limb amputations, as well as an increased risk of mental illness (AIHW, 2011; Deshpande et al., 2008; Kannel & McGee, 1979). T2D is associated with an increased risk of depression. Therefore, it is critical that people with T2D manage their condition with diet, exercise and medication. The management of T2D involves daily blood glucose monitoring using a blood glucose monitor. BGLs should be maintained between 4 to 6 mmol/L (fasting) to prevent short-term and long-term complications (Diabetes Australia, 2015a). Currently T2D is a progressive disease. Insulin will become more resistant and increasing levels of insulin will be needed to maintain BGLs. Because of the complications that can arise due to chronic hyperglycaemia, people with T2D need to regularly have their eyes and feet checked for damage to capillaries in these areas. Severe damage to the retina can lead to blindness and severe damage to the feet can result in ulcers that can become gangrenous and then need amputation (Diabetes Australia, 2015b).

Treatment and prevention of CVD and T2D

Avoiding sedentary behaviour, increasing regular physical activity, engaging in moderate to strenuous exercise a few times per week, eating a diet high in vegetables and fruit and low in processed and sweetened foods, avoiding excessive alcohol intake, not smoking, maintaining good mental health, reducing and managing stress and getting adequate sleep are all beneficial to overall health and longevity (Diener & Chan, 2011; Insel et al., 2012). See Chapter 5 for more detailed information on nutrition, exercise and health. Regular exercise has anti-inflammatory properties and is protective against both CVD and T2D

(Petersen & Pedersen, 2005). The evidence also suggests that the more healthy lifestyle factors engaged in, the greater the reduction in risk of developing CVD, T2D or other chronic conditions. Such lifestyle choices will help to maintain a healthy muscle-to-fat ratio and will help prevent weight gain (Rippe, 2011). These healthy lifestyle choices can also help reduce further risk of CVD once CVD has occurred. However, many people are unable to make the lifestyle changes needed to maintain good health. Therefore, medication and/or surgery are needed to treat existing CVD. It is beyond the scope of this chapter to discuss such treatments.

Time for a change

Since 1989, Australians have reduced their smoking by about 40% (ABS, 2009). However, the reduction in smoking rates was not simply due to individuals changing their behaviour. In Australia, reductions in smoking rates were accompanied by major changes in public health policies and legislation surrounding the sale of tobacco products, smoking in public places and increased taxes on tobacco products (Scollo & Winstanley, 2015). The latest legislative change was the introduction of plain packaging, which has been successful at helping to further reduce smoking rates in Australia but has also been vehemently opposed by the tobacco industry (Australian Council on Smoking and Health, 2011; AIHW, 2014b; Mitchell, 2014).

As the research evidence continues to accumulate, it has become increasingly undeniable that the rising intake of sugar-laden processed food, sugared beverages and fast food has made an enormous contribution to the pandemic 'diabesity' crisis. Most countries that have adopted the typical Western diet have also seen increases in obesity, T2D and CVD, including China and India – the two most populous nations in the world (Popkin et al., 2001). Reversing this global trend is no longer simply within the grasp of the individual. Public health policy and legislative changes, which led to decreasing rates of tobacco smoking, are desperately needed to combat this global health crisis.

Mini case study 9.3

Jason is 47 years old. His is obese. Jason works erratically as a carpenter. He often has bouts of depression. During these times he feels irritable and fatigued, has trouble getting to sleep, tends to withdraw socially, eats more than usual and has trouble concentrating. Jason was diagnosed with hypertension and T2D a year ago. Initially he tried to lose weight and to increase his daily exercise, but his efforts lasted only a few weeks before he reverted to his usual habits of spending most of his day in front of the TV or computer, while regularly eating processed snack foods such as chips, chocolate bars and sugared drinks. His GP has prescribed him metformin, a drug that helps control blood sugar levels, and also referred him to a diabetes educator. However, Jason has not followed up on the referral. He takes his medication irregularly and does not regularly measure his blood glucose levels.

Critical thinking questions

1. What is the long-term prognosis for Jason if he does not modify his lifestyle behaviours?
2. How does depression affect Jason's ability to modify his behaviour?

The interconnection between CVD, T2D and depression

Defining depression

The *Diagnostic and Statistical Manual of Mental Disorders: DSM-5* (American Psychiatric Association, 2013) criteria for a major depression disorder (MDD) includes symptoms lasting at least 2 weeks and present on most days, and symptoms causing significant distress. Key symptoms must include either depressed mood or anhedonia (inability to feel pleasure from everyday experiences), and at least four of the following symptoms: weight changes, sleep changes, psychomotor agitation or retardation, fatigue, feelings of worthlessness or guilt, lack of concentration and reduced decision-making ability, and suicidal ideation. A milder form of depression (persistent depressive disorder) is diagnosed if two or more of the above symptoms are present, more days than not, over a 2-year period.

The DSM-5 uses a discrete categorical classification system: either you do or you do not have a depressive disorder. However, such a strict classification system is problematic in the context of LRCI and depression comorbidity. For example, a well-established observation reported in the cardiac literature is that depression does not have to be at the clinical level to have a detrimental effect on prognosis, particularly following an **acute coronary syndrome (ACS)**. The presence of only a few symptoms of depression has been found to be sufficient to be detrimental to prognosis following ACS (Sullivan et al., 1999; Ware & Sherbourne, 1992). When using depression scales, depression scores from four to nine have been associated with a mortality rate of 17% compared with a rate of 3% for those with depression scores of less than four (Bush et al., 2001).

As the rate and severity of depressive symptoms increases, so does the risk of mortality. For example, those post-AMI and those with angina who have a depression score of 10 or more have a marked increase in subsequent mortality compared with patients with depression scores of less than 10. Consequently, it has been argued that depression, particularly in cardiac populations, should be viewed along a continuum/spectrum rather than as a discrete/categorical entity (Di Benedetto et al., 2006; Kendler & Gardner, 1998). In the psychiatric literature there is some debate as to whether subclinical depression warrants treatment or attention; however, in cardiac populations, subclinical symptoms of depression are highly relevant and should not be ignored or trivialised.

Depressive symptoms are present in about 40% of those with a LRCI (AIHW, 2006). T2D significantly increases the risk of developing depression (Anderson et al., 2001). The odds of having a MDD are twice as high in those with T2D compared to those without T2D. In those with T2D, rates of MDD have varied from 11 to 20%, to 31% for those with subclinical depression (Anderson et al., 2001).

In the immediate months after an AMI, the prevalence of an MDD can vary from 16 to 45% of patients, depending on the measurement tool and the depression criteria (e.g. duration), with another 20% of patients having a minor form of depression (Carney et al., 1988).

Depression is often undetected or untreated in those with LRCI. For example, nursing staff and medical residents were only able to detect 1 of 9 cases of major depression and only 2 cases from 21 of those with a depression score greater than or equal to 10 in post-AMI inpatients (Ziegelstein et al., 2005). Other studies have reported that only about 10% of cardiac inpatients with depression are diagnosed and treated for depression (Strik, Honig & Maes, 2001). Somatic symptoms, fatigue and insomnia are common to both depression and (particularly) cardiac illnesses, and these can be incorrectly attributed to a patient's underlying cardiac problems and not to depression (Di Benedetto et al., 2006; Thornton, 2001). Further explanations for undiagnosed depression are that patients and doctors might believe that depression is normal in cardiac patients, a diagnosis of depression is stigmatising, patients might be reluctant to disclose depressive symptoms or doctors might not be asking their patients if they are depressed (Di Benedetto et al., 2006).

Depressive symptoms have a negative impact on healthy lifestyle behaviours and treatment. Depressed patients post-ACS are less likely to attend cardiac rehabilitation (Grace et al., 2005) and if they do they are more likely to drop out of cardiac rehabilitation programs, and less likely to adhere to treatment (Ziegelstein et al., 2000). Cardiac patients with depression have difficulty modifying and adhering to lifestyle changes to reduce further risk of CHD. They are less likely to: take prescribed medication (e.g. Carney et al., 1995; Ziegelstein et al., 2000); exercise regularly; reduce stress; increase social support (Ziegelstein et al., 2000); stop smoking (Havik & Maeland, 1988); or modify diet for disease risk factors such as hyperlipidaemia, hypercholesterolaemia, diabetes (Ziegelstein et al., 2000) or hypertension (Fogel, Fauerbach, Ziegelstein & Bush, 2004).

Individuals with comorbid depression and LRCI have significantly more burden in terms of premature mortality, morbidity (Carney et al., 1995; Musselman et al., 1998) and increased healthcare costs. Moreover, this comorbidity impacts on individuals' functioning and wellbeing (ABS, 2008). These individuals have poorer prognosis, diminished functioning, poorer control of symptoms, and a more severe course of comorbid psychiatric and medical conditions (Peyrot & Rubin, 1997). Studies have shown that those with a chronic illness have worse quality of life. Di Benedetto et al. (2010) found that in those with T2D, CVD or both illnesses, lower coping resources and higher levels of depression predicted worse quality of life as determined by mental and physical health status.

Mortality

Depression increases the risk of mortality, especially within the first 6 months following an AMI (Ahern et al., 1990; Bush et al., 2001; Silverstone 1987). Van Melle et al. (2004) completed a meta-analysis of 22 prospective studies of depression and prognostic outcome in hospitalised AMI patients from North America, Europe and Japan. Of note, in most of these studies depression was not related to cardiac disease severity. All of the studies used validated measures of depression and determined depression within three months post-AMI. There was an overall increased risk of 2 to 2.5 times for cardiac mortality or all-cause mortality in the depressed groups. Katon et al. (2005) examined 3-year-period death rates in those with T2D, and those who had no depression, minor depression or major depression. The rates were 8.3%, 13.6% and 11.9% for no depression, minor depression and major depression, respectively. Katon et al. also found that depression in T2D led to a 2.3-fold increase in levels of mortality when compared with the non-depressed T2D.

Morbidity

As with T2D, the presence of depression in CVD is linked to poor physical, social and emotional health. In those without depression, low levels of self-management and medication adherence leads to a higher presence of diabetic symptoms, complications and poor glycaemic control, resulting in a poorer quality of life and increased mortality rates (Barr et. al., 2006; Cherrington, Wallston & Rothman, 2010). For example, participants with higher levels of depression had lower levels of self-management of T2D in terms of diet, exercise, monitoring BGLs, foot care (to prevent ulcers) and medication adherence (Ciechanowski, Katon & Russo, 2000; Wagner, Tennen & Osbourn, 2010). If the T2D patient also has symptoms of depression, the negative impact of depression is even more detrimental to the individual. The presence of depression in those with T2D is associated with lower rates of self-management, which leads to higher levels of symptomology that are then associated with higher levels of morbidity and mortality.

Possible interventions for treating depression in comorbid chronic illness (theoretical and evidence based)

Despite the adverse consequences of depression associated with LRCI, as yet there is no firm consensus regarding the treatment of depression in those with LRCI. Few intervention studies for depression in chronic illness populations have been conducted.

When determining suitable interventions for depression in those with comorbid chronic illness, a number of factors should be considered such as physical activity and coping resources. As there is ample evidence of the interrelationships among lifestyle factors, LRCI and psychological symptoms of depression, it is highly likely that improvements in chronic illness management by adopting health-promoting lifestyle behaviours will also improve health outcomes and reduce depression in those with a chronic illness. Exercise has been demonstrated to possess anxiolytic (Long & van Stavel, 1995; Salmon, 2001) and antidepressant (Byrne & Byrne, 1993; North, McCullagh & Tran, 1990) properties, in addition to improvements in self-concept (Plante & Rodin, 1990), perceived coping ability (Moses et al., 1989) and general wellbeing (Cramer, Nieman & Lee, 1991).

Stress, coping and depression

In an ACS sample, Di Benedetto et al. (2007) found that people with higher levels of perceived stress and fewer coping resources had higher depression levels. The relationship between stress and coping has also been defined using Lazarus and Folkman's (1984) cognitive transactional model. Stress also occurs when the perceived pressure of the situation exceeds one's perceived ability to cope with the situation. In a separate analysis using an additional cardiac sample, Di Benedetto et al. (2010) found that low physical coping resources predicted higher levels of depression in a cardiac sample. Coping resources are existing and available resources that people bring to situations that enable them to deal with stressors more effectively during times of stress (Matheny et al., 1993). Individuals with more coping resources had higher levels of hardiness (Kobasa, 1979) and resilience (Kessler & Essex, 1982), whereas individuals with fewer resources had a higher vulnerability to stress (Kessler, 1979) and depression (Di Benedetto et al., 2006; 2007, 2010; Penninx et al., 1998). Coping resources have been found to negatively correlate with depression in those with LRCI (Di Benedetto et al., 2010).

An individual's level of coping, and the cognitive and behavioural mechanisms by which one manages stressful events, can play a key role in a patient's psychological adjustment to chronic illness diagnosis, symptomatology and management (Taylor, 1999). There is emerging evidence that coping is an important protective factor for depression in T2D and CVD populations. For example, Schroder (2004) examined *coping competence*, a stress resistance variable defined as a predisposition to cope effectively when exposed to a stressor, in three medical groups including those with a CVD. In the CVD sample, coping competence was found to inversely correlate with depression. Those with the highest stress levels and lowest coping competence had the highest levels of depression. Therefore, coping provides a stress-buffering effect and reduces the likelihood of depression. In a cardiac sample Di Benedetto et al. (2007) found that coping resources were the best predictor of depression 24 weeks following an ACS. Moreover, cognitive coping had the strongest loading on a coping construct, which predicted depression levels. Both cognitive and physical coping predicted the depression construct from the other coping resources variables. This may indicate that cognitive and physical coping resources play a more important role in preventing depression post-ACS (Di Benedetto et al., 2010).

Given that the link among stress, depression and coping is well established in the non-medical literature, the previously mentioned findings are not surprising.

Mindfulness could be considered both a cognitive and an emotional coping resource. It has been defined as the conscious allocation of attention in the service of non-judgemental awareness, a state of physiological hypo-arousal with the intention of enhancing present moment awareness and diminishing habitual patterns of cognitive, behavioural and physiological reactivity (Salmon et al., 2004). The emerging field of mindfulness-based practice would probably benefit those with an LRCI. Baer (2003) conducted a meta-analytic review of 21 studies using non-LRCI samples. In studies that used mindfulness-based stress reduction, participants had less stress and improved medical and other psychological symptoms. In studies that used mindfulness-based cognitive therapy, there were much lower relapse rates for those with three or more repeated episodes of depression. In another review, Hofmann et al. (2010) concluded that mindfulness-based therapies improved depressive symptoms across varying severities. More importantly, improvements were recorded even when there were co-morbidities with other disorders and medical problems. Although further studies are needed to determine the efficacy of mindfulness-based therapies for preventing and treating depression in those with LRCI, there is emerging evidence that mindfulness-based therapies may be helpful in treating depression in these populations.

Summary

- The various types of cardiovascular disease (CVD) and type 2 diabetes (T2D) include coronary heart disease, associated heart failure and cardiomyopathy.
- The human CVS consists of a central pumping organ, the heart, with vessels radiating from and returning to the central core to allow circulation of blood.
- The common risk factors leading to CVD and T2D are unhealthy lifestyle behaviours (e.g. a poor diet, physical inactivity, smoking or excessive alcohol intake), obesity and poor mental health.
- Lifestyle behaviour modification for CVD and T2D includes regular physical activity and a diet high in vegetables and some fruit and low in processed and sugar-laden foods.
- Prevention and treatment strategies for CVD and T2D include adherence to healthy lifestyle behaviours such as a balanced diet, adequate exercise and weight control, as well as medication and surgery in some circumstances.
- Carbohydrate metabolism is important in the development of T2D, which occurs when the pancreas cannot produce enough insulin and thus regulate blood glucose levels.
- Depression symptoms often co-occur with CVD and T2D, which has implications for treatment and recovery.

Suggested weblinks

Refer to the companion website at www.cambridge.edu.au/academic/healthpsychology for a list of suggested weblinks.

References

ABS. (2002). *Australian Social Trends, 2002*. Cat no. 4102.0. Canberra: Australian Bureau of Statistics. Retrieved from: http://www.abs.gov.au/AUSSTATS/abs@.nsf/DetailsPage/4102.02002?OpenDocument

—— (2008). *National Survey of Mental Health and Wellbeing: Summary of Results, 2007*. Cat no. 4326.0. Canberra: Australian Bureau of Statistics. Retrieved from: http://www.abs.gov.au/ausstats/abs@.nsf/Latestproducts/4326.0Main%20Features32007?opendocument&tabname=Summary&prodno=4326.0&issue=2007&num=&view=

—— (2009). *Australian Social Trends, Dec 2009: International Comparisons.* Cat no. 4102.0. Canberra: Australian Bureau of Statistics. Retrieved from: http://www.abs.gov.au/AUSSTATS/abs@.nsf/Lookup/4102.0Main+Features60Dec+2009

—— (2013). *Australian Health Survey: updated results, 2011–2012.* Cat no. 4364.0.55.003. Canberra: Australian Bureau of Statistics. Retrieved from: http://www.abs.gov.au/ausstats/abs@.nsf/Lookup/4364.0.55.003main+features12011-2012

Ahern, D. K., Gorkin, L., Anderson, J. L., Tierney, C., Hallstrom, A., ... Follick, M. (1990). Biobehavioural variables and mortality or cardiac arrest in the Cardiac Arrhythmia Pilot Study (CAPS). *American Journal of Cardiology*, *66*, 59–62.

AIHW. (2006). *Australia's Health 2006.* Cat. no. AUS 73. Canberra: Australian Institute of Health and Welfare. Retrieved from: http://www.aihw.gov.au/publications/index.cfm/title/10321

—— (2007). *Older Australians at a Glance* (4th edn). Cat. no. AGE 52. Canberra: Australian Institute of Health and Welfare. Retrieved from: http://www.aihw.gov.au/publication-detail/?id=6442468045

—— (2011). *Diabetes and Poor Mental Health and Wellbeing: an Exploratory Analysis.* Cat. no. CVD 55. Canberra: Australian Institute of Health and Welfare. Retrieved from: http://www.aihw.gov.au/publication-detail/?id=10737419252

—— (2013). *Stroke and its Management in Australia: an Update.* Cardiovascular disease series no. 37. Cat. no. CVD 61. Canberra: Australian Institute of Health and Welfare. Retrieved from: http://www.aihw.gov.au/publication-detail/?id=60129543613

—— (2014a). *Cardiovascular Disease, Diabetes and Chronic Kidney Disease: Australian Facts.* Cat. no. CVD 65. Canberra: Australian Institute of Health and Welfare. Retrieved from: http://www.aihw.gov.au/WorkArea/DownloadAsset.aspx?id=60129549107

—— (2014b). *National Drug Strategy Household Survey Detailed Report: 2013.* Cat. no. PHE 183. Canberra: Australian Institute of Health and Welfare. Retrieved from: http://www.aihw.gov.au/publication-detail/?id=60129549469

—— (2015a). *Cardiovascular Disease.* Canberra: Australian Institute of Health and Welfare. Retrieved from: http://www.aihw.gov.au/cardiovascular-disease/

—— (2015b). *How Many Australians Have Diabetes?* Canberra: Australian Institute of Health and Welfare. Retrieved from http://www.aihw.gov.au/how-common-is-diabetes/

American Psychiatric Association. (2013). *Diagnostic and Statistical Manual of Mental Disorders: DSM-5* (5th edn). Arlington: American Psychiatric Press.

Anderson, R. J., Freedland, K. E., Clouse, R. E. & Lustman, P. J. (2001). The prevalence of comorbid depression in adults with diabetes: a meta-analysis. *Diabetes Care*, *24*, 1069–78. Retrieved from: http://www.ncbi.nlm.nih.gov/pubmed/11375373

Australian Council on Smoking and Health. (2011). Media release: historic tobacco plain packaging will hasten end of smoking in Australia. Retrieved from: http://www.acosh.org/resources/110407_TOBACCO-PLAIN-PACKAGING-WILL-HASTEN-END-OF-SMOKING-IN-AUSTRALIA.pdf

Baer, R. A. (2003). Mindfulness training as a clinical intervention: a conceptual and empirical review. *Clinical Psychology: Science and Practice*, *10*(2), 125–43. doi: http://dx.doi.org/10.1093/clipsy.bpg015

Barr, E., Magliano, D., Zimmet, P., Polkinghorne, K., Atkins, R., Dunstan, D., Murray, S. & Shaw, J. (2006). *AusDiab 2005: The Australian Diabetes, Obesity and Lifestyle Study.* Melbourne: International Diabetes Institute. Retrieved from: https://www.bakeridi.edu.au/ausdiab/publications/

Barter, P., Gotto, A. M., LaRosa, J. C., Maroni, J., Szarek, M., Grundy, S. M., ... & Fruchart, J. C. (2007). HDL cholesterol, very low levels of LDL cholesterol, and cardiovascular events. *New England Journal of Medicine*, *357*(13), 1301–10. doi: http://dx.doi.org/10.1056/NEJMoa064278

Buja, L. M. & Krueger, G. R. F. (2013). *Netter's Illustrated Human Pathology Updated E.* Philadelphia PA: Elsevier.

Bush, D. E., Ziegelstein, R. C., Tayback, M., Richter, D., Stevens, S., ... Fauerbach, J. A. (2001). Even minimal symptoms of depression increase mortality risk after acute myocardial infarction. *American Journal of Cardiology*, *88*(4), 337–41. doi: http://dx.doi.org/10.1016/S0002-9149(01)01675-7

Byrne, A. & Byrne, D. G. (1993). The effect of exercise on depression, anxiety and other mood states: a review. *Journal of Psychosomatic Research*, *37*(6), 565–74. doi: http://dx.doi.org/10.1016/0022-3999(93)90050-P

Carney, R. M., Freedland, K. E., Eisen, S. A., Rich, M. W., Jaffe, A. S. (1995). Major depression and medication adherence in elderly patients with coronary artery disease. *Journal of Health Psychology*, *14*, 88–90. doi: http://dx.doi.org.ezproxy.lib.rmit.edu.au/10.1037/0278-6133.14.1.88

Carney, R. M., Freedland, K. E., Rich, M. W. & Jaffe, A. S. (1995). Depression as a risk factor for cardiac events in established coronary heart disease: a review of possible mechanisms. *Annals of Behavioral Medicine*, *17*(2), 142–9. doi: http://dx.doi.org/10.1007/BF02895063

Carney, R. M., Rich, M. W., Freedland, K. E., Saini, J., Tevelde, A., Simeone, C.& Clarke, K. (1988). Major depressive disorders predict cardiac events in patients with coronary artery disease. *Psychosomatic Medicine*, *50*, 627–33.

Carver, C. (2006). Insulin treatment and the problem of weight gain in type 2 diabetes. *The Diabetes Educator*, *32*(6), 910–17. doi: http://dx.doi.org/10.1177/0145721706294259

Cherrington, A., Wallston, K. A. & Rothman, R. L. (2010). Exploring the relationship between diabetes self-efficacy, depressive symptoms, and glycemic control among men and women with type 2 diabetes. *Journal of Behavioral Medicine*, *33*(1), 81–9. doi: http://dx.doi.org/10.1007/s10865-009-9233-4

Ciechanowski, P. S., Katon, W. J. & Russo, J. E. (2000). Depression and diabetes: impact of depressive symptoms on adherence, function, and costs. *Archives of Internal Medicine*, *160*(21), 3278–85. doi: http://dx.doi.org/10.1001/archinte.160.21.3278

Cramer, S. R., Nieman, D. C. & Lee, J. W. (1991). The effects of moderate exercise training on psychological well-being and mood state in women. *Journal of Psychosomatic Research*, *35*(4), 437–49. doi: http://dx.doi.org/10.1016/0022-3999(91)90039-Q

Deshpande, A. D., Harris-Hayes, M. & Schootman, M. (2008). Epidemiology of diabetes and diabetes-related complications. *Physical Therapy*, *88*(11), 1254–64. doi: http://dx.doi.org/10.2522/ptj.20080020

Di Benedetto, M., Burns, L., Lindner, H. & Kent, S. (2010). A biopsychosocial model for depressive symptoms following acute coronary syndromes. *Psychology & Health.* doi: http://dx.doi.org/10.1080/08870440903019535.

Di Benedetto, M., Lindner, H., Hare, D. L. & Kent, S. (2006). Depression following acute coronary syndromes: a comparison between the Cardiac Depression Scale and the Beck Depression Inventory-II. *Journal of Psychosomatic Research*, *60*, 13–20. doi: http://dx.doi.org/10.1016/j.jpsychores.2005.06.003

—— (2007). The role of coping, anxiety, and stress in depression post-acute coronary syndrome. *Psychology, Health & Medicine*, *12*, 460–9. doi: http://dx.doi.org/10.1080/13548500601109334

Diabetes Australia (2015a). Diabetes in Australia. Retrieved from: https://www.diabetesaustralia.com.au/diabetes-in-australia

—— (2015b). Preventing complications. Retrieved from: https://www.diabetesaustralia.com.au/preventing-complications

Diener, E. & Chan, M. Y. (2011). Happy people live longer: subjective well-being contributes to health and longevity. *Applied Psychology: Health and Well-Being*, *3*(1), 1–43. doi: http://dx.doi.org/10.1111/j.1758-0854.2010.01045.x

Epstein, F. H. & Ross, R. (1999). Atherosclerosis: an inflammatory disease. *New England Journal of Medicine*, *340*, 115–26. doi: http://dx.doi.org/10.1056/NEJM199901143400207

Fogel, J., Fauerbach, J. A., Ziegelstein, R. C. & Bush, D. E. (2004). Quality of life in physical health domains predicts adherence among myocardial infarction patients even after adjusting for depressive symptoms. *Journal of Psychosomatic Research*, *56*, 75–82. doi: http://dx.doi.org/10.1016/S0022-3999(03)00563-4

Gaziano, T. A., Bitton, A., Anand, S., Abrahams-Gessel, S. & Murphy, A. (2010). Growing epidemic of coronary heart disease in low-and middle-income countries. *Current Problems in Cardiology*, *35*(2), 72–115. doi: http://dx.doi.org/10.1016/j.cpcardiol.2009.10.002

Grace, S. L., Abbey, S., Pinto, R., Shnek, Z. M., Irvine, J. & Stewart, D. E. (2005). Longitudinal course of depressive symptomatology after a cardiac event: effects of gender and cardiac rehabilitation. *Psychosomatic Medicine*, *67*, 52–8. doi: http://dx.doi.org/10.1097/01.psy.0000151486.28349.70

Havik, O. E. & Maeland, J. G. (1988). Changes in smoking behaviour after a myocardial infarction. *Health Psychology*, *7*, 403–20. Retrieved from: http://www.ncbi.nlm.nih.gov/pubmed/3215153

Heart Foundation. (n.d.). High blood pressure statistics. Retrieved from: http://heartfoundation.org.au/about-us/what-we-do/heart-disease-in-australia/high-blood-pressure-statistics

Henriksen, E. J. (2002). Invited review: effects of acute exercise and exercise training on insulin resistance. *Journal of Applied Physiology*, *93*, 788–96. doi: http://dx.doi.org/10.1152/japplphysiol.01219.2001

Hofmann, S. G., Sawyer, A. T., Witt, A. A. & Oh, D. (2010). The effect of mindfulness-based therapy on anxiety and depression: a meta-analytic review. *Journal of Consulting and Clinical Psychology*, *78*(2), 169. doi: http://dx.doi.org/10.1037/a0018555

Hofmeijer, J., Algra, A., Kappelle, L. J. & Van Der Worp, H. B. (2008). Predictors of life-threatening brain edema in middle cerebral artery infarction. *Cerebrovascular Diseases*, *25*(1–2), 176–84. doi: http://dx.doi.org/10.1159/000113736

Holt, R. I., Cockram, C., Flyvbjerg, A. & Goldstein, B. J. (eds). (2010). *Textbook of Diabetes* (4th edn). United Kingdom: John Wiley & Sons.

Insel, P., Ross, D., Bernstein, M. & McMahon, K. (2012). *Discovering Nutrition* (4th edn). Massachusetts: Jones & Bartlett Publishers.

Kannel, W. B. & McGee, D. L. (1979). Diabetes and cardiovascular disease: the Framingham study. *JAMA*, *241*(19), 2035–8. doi: http://dx.doi.org/10.1001/jama.1979.03290450033020

Katon, W. J., Rutter, C., Simon, G., Lin, E. H., Ludman, E., Ciechanowski, P., ... & Von Korff, M. (2005). The association of comorbid depression with mortality in patients with type 2 diabetes. *Diabetes Care*, 28, 2668–72. doi: http://dx.doi.org/10.2337/diacare.28.11.2668

Kendler, K. S. & Gardner, C. O. (1998). Boundaries of major depression: an evaluation of DSM-IV criteria. *American Journal of Psychiatry*, *155*, 172–7. Retrieved from: http://ajp.psychiatryonline.org/doi/abs/10.1176/ajp.155.2.172

Kessler, R. C. (1979). A strategy for studying differential vulnerability to the psychological consequences of stress. *Journal of Health and Social Behavior*, *20*, 100–8. Retrieved from: http://www.jstor.org/stable/2136432?seq=1#page_scan_tab_contents

Kessler, R. C. & Essex, M. (1982). Marital status and depression: the importance of coping resources. *Social Forces*, *6*, 484–507. doi: http://dx.doi.org/10.2307/2578238

Kobasa, S. C. (1979). Stressful life events, personality, and health: an inquiry into hardiness. *Journal of Personality and Social Psychology*, *37*, 1–11. doi: http://dx.doi.org/10.1037/0022-3514.37.1.1

Lavi, T., Karakil, A., Koren-Morag, N. K., Kanety, H., Feinberg, M. S. & Shechter, M. (2009). The acute effect of various glycemic index dietary carbohydrates on endothelial function in nondiabetic overweight and obese subjects. *Journal of the American College of Cardiology*, *53*(24). doi: http://dx.doi.org/10.1016/j.jacc.2009.03.025

Lazarus, R. & Folkman, S. (1984). *Stress, Appraisal and Coping*. New York: Springer-Verlag.

Libby, P., Ridker, P. M. & Maseri, A. (2002). Inflammation and atherosclerosis. *Circulation*, *105*, 1135–43.

Long, B. C. & van Stavel, R. (1995). Effects of exercise training on anxiety. A meta-analysis. *Journal of Applied Sport Psychology*, *7*, 167–89. doi: http://dx.doi.org/10.1080/10413209508406963

Magliano, D. J., Peeters, A., Vos, T., Sicree, R., Shaw, J., Sindall, C., ... & Zimmet, P. Z. (2009). Projecting the burden of diabetes in Australia – what is the size of the matter? *Australian and New Zealand Journal of Public Health*, *33*(6), 540–3. doi: http://dx.doi.org/10.1111/j.1753-6405.2009.00450.x

Matheny, K. B., Aycock, D. W., Curlette, W. L. & Junker, G. N. (1993). The coping resources inventory for stress: a measure of perceived resourcefulness. *Journal of Clinical Psychology*, *49*, 815–30. Retrieved from: http://onlinelibrary.wiley.com/doi/10.1002/1097-4679%28199311%2949:6%3C815::AID-JCLP2270490609%3E3.0.CO;2-%23/abstract

McAlpine, W. A. (1975). *Heart and Coronary Arteries: An Anatomical Atlas for Clinical Diagnosis, Radiological Treatment and Surgical Intervention*. Berlin, Germany: Springer-Verlag.

Mitchell, B. (2014). A trail of misinformation and manipulation. Retrieved from: http://bilbo.economicoutlook.net/blog/?p=28206

Moses, J., Steptoe, A., Mathews, A. & Edwards, S. (1989). The effects of exercise training on mental well-being in the normal population: a controlled trial. *Journal of Psychosomatic Research*, *33*(1), 47–61. doi: http://dx.doi.org/10.1016/0022-3999(89)90105-0

Musselman, D. L., Evans, D. L. & Nemeroff, C. B. (1998). The relationship of depression to cardiovascular disease: epidemiology, biology, and treatment. *Archives of General Psychiatry*, *55*(7), 580–92. Retrieved from: http://www.qpdpanel.com/downloads/depression_cardiovascular.pdf

NHFA. (2013). *Heart disease patients face higher depression risk*. National Heart Foundation of Australia. Retrieved from: http://heartfoundation.org.au/news/heart-disease-patients-face-higher-depression-risk

—— (2015). Heart attack warning signs. National Heart Foundation of Australia. Retrieved from: http://www.heartfoundation.org.au/driving-change/warning-signs-heart-attack/Pages/welcome.aspx

Nichols, M., Peterson, K., Alston, L. & Allender, S. (2014). *Australian Heart Disease Statistics 2014*. Melbourne: National Heart Foundation of Australia.

North, T. C., McCullagh, P. & Tran, Z. V. (1990). Effect of exercise on depression. *Exercise and Sport Sciences Reviews*, *18*(1), 379–416. Retrieved from: http://journals.lww.com/acsm-essr/Citation/1990/01000/Effect_of_Exercise_on_Depression_.16.aspx

Penninx, B. W., van Tilburg, T., Boeke, A. J., Deeg, D. J., Kriegsman, D. M. & van Eijk, J. M. (1998). Effects of social support and personal coping resources on depressive symptoms: different for various chronic diseases? *Health Psychology*, *17*, 551–8. doi: http://dx.doi.org/10.1037/0278-6133.17.6.551

Petersen, A. W. & Pedersen, B. K. (2005). The anti-inflammatory effect of exercise. *Journal of Applied Physiology*, *98*, 1154–62 doi: http://dx.doi.org/10.1152/japplphysiol.00164.2004

Peyrot, M. & Rubin, R. R. (1997). Levels and risks of depression and anxiety symptomatology among diabetic adults. *Diabetes Care*, *20*, 585–90. Retrieved from: http://dx.doi.org/10.2337/diacare.20.4.585

Plante, T. G. & Rodin, J. (1990). Physical fitness and enhanced psychological health. *Current Psychology: Research and Reviews*, *9*, 3–24. doi: http://dx.doi.org/10.1007/BF02686764

Popkin, B. M., Horton, S., Kim, S., Mahal, A. & Shuigao, J. (2001). Trends in diet, nutritional status, and diet-related noncommunicable diseases in China and India: the economic costs of the nutrition transition. *Nutrition Reviews*, *59*(12), 379–90. doi: http://dx.doi.org/10.1111/j.1753-4887.2001.tb06967.x

Purves, D., Augustine, G. J. & Fitzpatrick, D. (eds) (2001). *Neuroscience* (2nd edn). Sunderland: Sinauer Associates Inc.

Rippe, J. M. (2011). *Encyclopedia of Lifestyle Medicine and Health*. US: SAGE Publications.

Salmon, P. (2001). Effects of physical exercise on anxiety, depression, and sensitivity to stress: a unifying theory. *Clinical Psychology Review*, *21*, 33–61.

Salmon, P., Sephton, S., Weissbecker, I., Hoover, K., Ulmer, C. & Studts, J. L. (2004). Mindfulness meditation in clinical practice. *Cognitive and Behavioral Practice*, *11*(4), 434–46. doi: http://dx.doi.org/10.1016/S1077-7229(04)80060-9

Santos, F. L., Esteves, S. S., da Costa Pereira, A., Yancy, W. S. & Nunes, J. P. (2012). Systematic review and meta-analysis of clinical trials of the effects of low carbohydrate diets on cardiovascular risk factors. *Obesity Reviews*, *13*, 1048–166. doi: http://dx.doi.org/10.1111/j.1467-789X.2012.01021.x

Schroder, K. E. E. (2004). Coping competence as predictor and moderator of depression among chronic disease patients. *Journal of Behavioural Medicine*, *27*, 123–43. doi: http://dx.doi.org/10.1023/B:JOBM.0000019848.84779.a9

Scollo, M. M. & Winstanley, M. H. (2015). *Tobacco in Australia: Facts and issues.* Melbourne: Cancer Council Victoria. Retrieved from http://www.TobaccoInAustralia.org.au

Silverstone, P. H. (1987). Depression and outcome in acute myocardial infarction. *British Medical Journal*, *294*, 219–20.

Siri-Tarino, P. W., Sun, Q., Hu, F. B. & Krauss, R. M. (2010). Meta-analysis of prospective cohort studies evaluating the association of saturated fat with cardiovascular disease. *American Journal of Clinical Nutrition*, *91*, 535–46. doi: http://dx.doi.org/10.3945/ajcn.2009.27725

Strik, J. J., Honig, A. & Maes, M. (2001). Depression and myocardial infarction: relationship between heart and mind. *Progress in Neuro-Psychopharmacology & Biological Psychiatry*, *25*, 879–92.

Sullivan, M., LaCroix, A., Russo, J. & Swords, E. (1999). Depression in coronary heart disease: what is the appropriate diagnostic threshold? *Psychosomatics*, *40*, 286–94.

Taylor, S. E. (1999). *Health Psychology* (4th edn). New York: McGraw Hill.

Thornton L. (2001). Depression in post-acute myocardial infarction patients. *Journal of the American Academy of Nurse Practice*, *13*, 364–7.

Van Melle, J. P., De Jonge, P., Spijkerman, T. A., Tijssen, J. G. P., Ormel, J., ... van den Berg M. P. (2004). Prognostic association of depression following myocardial infarction with mortality and cardiovascular events: a meta-analysis. *Psychosomatic Medicine*, *66*, 814–22.

Wagner, J. A., Tennen, H. & Osbourn, C. Y. (2010). Lifetime depression and diabetes self-management in women with type 2 diabetes: a case-control study. *Diabetes Medicine*, *27*, 713–17. doi: http://dx.doi.org/10.1111/j.1464-5491.2010.02996.x

Warrell, D. A., Cox, T. M. & Firth, J. D. (2010). *Oxford Textbook of Medicine* (vol. 2). Oxford: Oxford University Press.

Ware, J. E. & Sherbourne, C. D. (1992). The MDS Short-Form Health Survey (SF-36): conceptual framework and item selection. *Medical Care*, *30*, 473–83.

Yusuf, S., Hawken, S., Ounpuu, S., Dans, T., Avezum, A., Lanas, ... Lisheng, L. (2004). Effect of potentially modifiable risk factors associated with myocardial infarction in 52 countries (the INTERHEART study): case-control study. *Lancet*, *364*, 937–52.

Ziegelstein, R. C., Fauerbach, J. A., Stevens, S. S., Romanelli, J. & Richter, D. P. (2000). Patients with depression are less likely to follow recommendations to reduce cardiac risk during recovery from a myocardial infarction. *Archives of Internal Medicine*, *160*, 1818–23.

Ziegelstein, R. C., Kim, S. Y., Kao, D., Fauerbach, J., Thombs, B., McCann, U., Colburn, J. & Bush, D. E. (2005). Can doctors and nurses recognize depression in patients hospitalized with an acute myocardial infarction in the absence of formal screening? *Psychosomatic Medicine*, *67*, 393–7.

10

Experiencing cancer: an acute and chronic condition

Learning outcomes

After reading this chapter, you should be able to:

- describe the nature of cancer and its prevention
- critically examine factors leading to poor adherence to cancer screening programs
- explain the psychological, emotional and social challenges facing cancer patients at each stage of their cancer journey
- outline intervention approaches used to address psychological, emotional and social challenges associated with cancer
- describe how cancer can affect the family.

Introduction

> Time is shortening. But every day that I challenge this cancer and survive is a victory for me.
>
> (Ingrid Bergman)

This chapter explores the impact that cancer has on our lives. What does cancer mean to you? What do you think and feel when you contemplate cancer? In this chapter we will look first at cancer as a disease, its prevalence and how it is typically treated. Improvements in treatment and the ability to detect some cancers at an early stage mean that a number of people diagnosed with cancer will live many years following initial diagnosis. These cancer survivors are living with what is essentially a chronic condition, albeit one that may entail living with residual treatment side effects, and for which uncertainty about recurrence remains. Consequently, we can think of cancer as having phases, ranging from individuals who are not yet diagnosed but are at an increased risk of developing cancer, through to cancer diagnosis and treatment, survivorship, cancer recurrence, palliative care and end of life. Importantly, not everyone will experience all phases, or in the order that we outline. This chapter highlights how each phase presents unique challenges to the affected individual in terms of coping and psychological adjustment. Also, cancer is not just a 'me' disease, as a diagnosis typically will impact on other family members and close friends, requiring adjustment and coping responses from all concerned. After gaining insight into the key challenges that cancer presents, we will explore some of the interventions that have been developed to facilitate coping with cancer.

Why examine cancer as a specific condition? Despite medical advances, the cure for cancer largely remains elusive, yet to a great extent cancer is a lifestyle disease, a consequence of the way we lead our lives. Cancer does not discriminate: it affects individuals of all ages, and across all societies. The global burden of cancer is increasing due to ageing and population growth, along with increasing adoption of cancer-causing behaviours, particularly smoking, in economically developing countries (Jemal et al., 2011). Given that in Australia alone the lifetime risk for cancer is 1 in 2 for men and 1 in 3 for women, in all likelihood health professionals working in psychological and counselling practices will encounter many clients who have been touched by cancer, either directly or as a close family member or friend. It is important that practitioners understand the cancer context in order to be able to respond effectively to clients' concerns, and provide appropriate and sensitive care.

Cancer and its prevalence

Cancer begins when cells in our bodies start dividing uncontrollably. It is not just one disease but many, with the type of cancer determined by the organ in which the cancer starts, the kind of cell from which it is derived, as well as the appearance of the cancer cells. Sarcoma refers to cancer of the connective tissue, cartilage, bone and muscle, and carcinoma is cancer of the epithelial (lining) cells. When cells from the primary cancer site break off they can lodge elsewhere in the body and grow into secondary cancer, commonly known as metastatic cancer. However, not all metastatic cancer has a known starting point. This cancer of unknown primary (CUP) is the eighth most common cancer in men and the ninth most common in women (AIHW, 2012). The extent to which we can provide effective treatment varies dramatically from cancer to cancer. The predicted 5-year survival rate for individuals with cancers such as testicular, melanoma, breast and prostate exceeds 80% of cases; yet with other cancers for which treatment is less effective, such as lung, pancreatic and brain cancers, fewer than 20% of diagnosed individuals are expected to live beyond 5 years from diagnosis (American Cancer Society, 2014b; AIHW, 2014; Cancer Research UK, 2014a, 2014b). In Australia, cancer accounts for 19% – the highest percentage – of the total disease burden (AIHW, 2015b). With increasingly effective cancer treatment approaches, we are seeing a corresponding rise in the number of individuals who survive cancer in the long term (DeSantis et al., 2014).

Cancer is highly prevalent in Australia and other Western countries. By 2020 it is estimated that 150 000 Australians a year will receive a diagnosis of cancer (AIHW, 2014). The incidence and mortality rates of most cancers (e.g. lung, colorectal, breast, prostate) are decreasing in many Western countries, including Australia and New Zealand (Jemal et al., 2011), yet incidence is increasing in less developed and emerging economies (such as China, India and Brazil). These changes in health status in developing countries are most likely a consequence of the adoption of unhealthy Western lifestyles (including smoking and sedentary behaviour) and consumption of calorie-dense food (Jemal et al., 2011). Unfortunately, due to a combination of later stage diagnosis and limited access to standard cancer treatment, mortality rates in developing countries are often higher than those in developed nations. A substantial proportion of the worldwide burden of cancer could be prevented through implementing prevention programs (e.g. tobacco control, vaccination for liver and cervical cancers), and in more widespread early detection and treatment, as well as public health campaigns promoting physical activity and a healthier dietary intake (Jemal et al., 2011).

Understanding the phases of cancer

The cancer experience is characterised by a number of phases. For most people, their cancer journey starts at the point of diagnosis, through to a phase of active treatment, and then survivorship. Unfortunately, not everyone can receive treatment for cancer, due to extensive disease, and other people will experience cancer recurrence where the cancer becomes advanced and spreads throughout the body. Palliative care may be offered to best manage symptoms in this end-of-life phase. Some people who are diagnosed with advanced cancer are immediately offered palliative care and have a relatively short estimated time to live. People with a strong family history of cancer are at increased genetic risk of developing the disease. Irrespective of the specific phase of cancer, there are unique physical, psychological and social challenges facing the affected individual. We have conceptualised these cancer phases in Figure 10.1, which also outlines the likely activities/experiences at each phase.

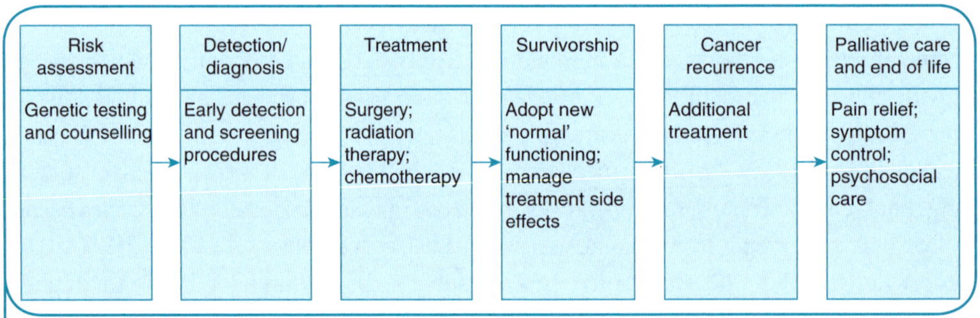

Figure 10.1 Conceptualisation of cancer phases

Diagnosis

For most people, their cancer journey starts at the time of diagnosis, typically entailing a number of procedures, which can be uncomfortable, embarrassing and anxiety-provoking (Mitsonis et al., 2011). For example, endoscopy to examine the upper digestive system (including the oesophagus) entails the insertion of an endoscopic tube through the mouth and down into the upper digestive system. This procedure has been described as painful, yet it is a necessary step in diagnosis of gastrointestinal conditions (Shah et al., 2002). Early detection programs that screen for common cancers, including breast, cervical and bowel, are widely available. Unfortunately, the very thought of undergoing these procedures can deter some people from being screened (Hawkins et al., 2013; Jones et al., 2010; Todd & Stuifbergen, 2011). Anticipated embarrassment, pain and fear of the procedure itself are common reasons for not participating in bowel, cervical and breast cancer screening (Bukowska-Durawa & Luszczynska, 2014; Feldstein et al., 2011; Jones et al., 2010). Not surprisingly, fear of being diagnosed is a major deterrent for participating in cancer screening. Perceiving that you are too young and healthy, or that you are unlikely to get cancer (low perceived risk) and discounting symptoms that you are experiencing as unimportant, also act as barriers to undergoing diagnostic tests (Katapodi et al., 2004). This can translate into delays in being diagnosed and in seeking appropriate medical care. These findings are consistent with several models of health behaviour, including the health belief model. One successful public health campaign run in the UK by the National Health Service (NHS) directly taps into perceived susceptibility as a barrier to seeking medical advice for smokers, who are at increased risk of developing lung cancer (see Figure 10.2). The approach makes people question their beliefs about lung cancer vulnerability and their corresponding discounting of symptoms. By challenging these beliefs, the campaign aims to encourage people to get checked by a medical professional.

Figure 10.2 Public health campaign run by the NHS
Source: NHS Cumbria

Mini case study 10.1

Senya (55 years) and her partner James (57 years) live in suburban Adelaide. They are both active people working in full-time jobs and enjoy regular exercise. Senya plays tennis once a week and walks every other day, and James is an avid golfer, playing once a week on weekends. They love their food and are both a little overweight. After a regular check-up by the GP, both Senya and James have been advised that because of their age they are now at an increased risk of developing bowel cancer. The GP has recommended that each of them undertakes a simple screening test every year from now on. He has given them each a kit so that they can start their screening this year. The kit involves a simple swab of faecal matter that gets sent off to a lab for testing. That was 6 months ago. Both kits are sitting unopened in the bedroom cabinet.

Critical thinking questions

1. Why do you think Senya and James have decided not to use their bowel cancer screening kits?
2. What can we do to improve the participation of people like Senya and James in cancer screening services?

In summary, detecting cancer is the first step in managing and treating this condition. There are many psychosocial barriers to participation in cancer screening programs, and that decrease the likelihood of symptoms being acted upon by seeking medical advice. Cognitions (such as low perceived vulnerability and lack of salience of symptoms) and emotions (including fear and embarrassment) are common barriers. Interventions to change attitudes are an effective wide-scale approach to enhancing cancer screening participation and encouraging individuals to recognise symptoms and promptly seek medical advice. We now look at how people typically respond to being diagnosed.

Response to initial cancer diagnosis

Despite improvements in treatment and survival rates for most cancers, negative attitudes towards cancer prevail (Cho et al., 2013; Keeney et al., 2010). Fatalistic beliefs regarding the inability to treat cancer effectively and stereotypes of individuals with cancer as having a death sentence remain, and create a stigma for those affected by this disease (Chen et al., 2006; Cho et al., 2013). These negative attitudes are particularly evident among individuals with lower education levels (Schernhammer et al., 2010). The most common initial response to being given a diagnosis of cancer is shock, as most people take good health for granted. This is typified by being stunned, behaving automatically and feeling detached (Shontz, 1975). Initial responses are described by Shontz (1975) as 'encounter', characterised by feelings of loss, helplessness and being overwhelmed by the enormity of the diagnosis, and 'retreat', entailing denial and disengagement. Over time most people with cancer will come to terms with their diagnosis, adjusting slowly to its meaning and impact. However, continued denial can be harmful, as it may interfere with important treatment decision-making (Leighl et al., 2008).

At the time of diagnosis, individuals need to process a large amount of information concerning recommendations for treatment and their overall prognosis. Not surprisingly, making decisions while at the same time experiencing shock and anxiety is very difficult (Arnaboldi et al., 2014). The time-pressured nature of the decision-making makes it even more challenging, as surgery may be recommended within weeks of diagnosis (Wright et al., 2010). The key challenges at this point of diagnosis then are to make effective decisions based on a clear understanding of the treatment options. How can we help people through this pressured time?

Provision of information is certainly a key requirement of informed and effective decision-making (Peate et al., 2012). However, not everyone responds to information in the same way, nor does everyone have the same optimal level of requisite information prior to making a decision (Miller, 1995; Roussi & Miller, 2014). We can facilitate treatment-related decision-making by providing cancer patients with decision aids that provide information, and by taking into account individual values and preferences (Sheehan & Sherman, 2012; Stacey et al., 2014). Decision aids have been developed for a variety of cancer conditions, including prostate cancer screening (Ilic et al., 2015) and treatment (Lin et al., 2009), breast reconstruction (Sherman et al., 2014) and fertility for younger breast cancer patients (Peate et al., 2011, 2012). Decision aids for cancer patients provide benefits in terms of reduced decisional conflict (Banegas et al., 2013), improved knowledge and the perception of having made a more effective choice (Chabrera et al., 2015; Vodermaier et al., 2011), and enhanced satisfaction with information about the decision options (Sherman et al., 2014). The psychological benefits of decision aids for making cancer treatment-related decisions have been reported up to 12 months after receipt of the aid (Vodermaier et al., 2011).

During active treatment

Cancer treatment often entails initial surgery (for solid tumours), followed by **radiation therapy** (used to kill cancer cells with high energy beams) and/or **chemotherapy** (which kills cancer cells or damages cells to stop them reproducing) (Siegel et al., 2012). Neo-adjuvant chemotherapy, which is given prior to surgery, is being increasingly used. For some cancers (e.g. breast, prostate) hormonal treatments may be prescribed for several years post-surgery to help prevent further cancer cell growth. The type of treatment varies according to the site of the cancer, the stage of diagnosis and other factors, such as whether the lymph nodes have been affected with cancer.

The initial phase of shock and disbelief may be followed by a period of anxiety and depressive symptoms (Massie, Gagnon & Holland, 1994), with the threat to an individual's mortality a raw memory, and the threat of unpleasant and possibly painful treatments looming. Compared with healthy individuals, cancer patients report higher levels of anxiety, depression and negative affect and lower levels of positive affect and current happiness (Markovitz et al., 2015; Mitchell et al., 2013). Distress responses to the diagnosis tend to coincide with fear of the treatment itself and of possible treatment side effects (Hess & Chen, 2014). Surgical intervention may be disfiguring, leading to negative effects on self-esteem and body image (Collins et al., 2011; Fallbjork et al., 2013; Fingeret, Teo & Epner, 2014). Radiation therapy, which is typically administered for 4 to 6 weeks, can lead to skin changes, including blistering, peeling, dryness and itching, and fatigue (Di Franco et al., 2013; Jereczek-Fossa, Marsiglia & Orecchia, 2002). Depending on the location of the cancer, radiation therapy can cause further problems such as dry mouth, difficulty swallowing, joint problems, urinary/bladder symptoms and swelling (Lind et al., 2011; National Cancer Institute, 2012). Prior to receiving radiation therapy, fear of the unknown, of getting burnt, of damaging internal parts and of fatigue are commonly reported patient concerns (Halkett, Kristjanson & Lobb, 2008). A systematic review (Hess & Chen, 2014) identified that for most patients the heightened anxiety experienced prior to the first radiation treatment peaks during the treatment cycle, and then gradually diminishes. Depression, however, tends to increase once the radiation treatment commences, and for many individuals remains after the conclusion of this treatment (Hess & Chen, 2014).

Chemotherapy also has many and varied side effects. Nausea, vomiting, loss of appetite, mouth sores, painful gums and throat, diarrhoea/constipation and low blood cell counts are commonly experienced (Breen et al., 2015). Hair loss is a noticeable side effect of many types of chemotherapy that impacts on the cancer patient's sense of identity and body image (Choi et al., 2014). For younger men and women diagnosed with cancer, reproductive issues may arise as chemotherapy commonly renders individuals temporarily or permanently infertile (Lambertini et al., 2013). Prior to commencing chemotherapy, 50% of patients experience anxiety and 25% report depressive symptoms (Breen et al., 2009). Although depression may decrease in the months following chemotherapy, anxiety often increases, and is associated with poorer perceived social support, increased intrusive thoughts and younger age (Hipkins et al., 2004).

Specific coping strategies adopted by individuals following cancer diagnosis can impact on their wellbeing throughout the active phases of treatment. Some would argue that these negative emotional responses are normal and expected for a highly stressful situation (American Cancer Society, 2014a). Seeking information (Halkett et al., 2008), emotional repression (Zachariae et al., 2004) and managing fears by trying not to worry about them, and avoiding being overwhelmed by emotional reactions (Drageset, Lindstrom & Underlid, 2010) are common coping approaches in the early days following cancer diagnosis. However, persistent anxiety and depression symptoms will impede the overall adjustment post-cancer and lead to diminished quality of life (Brown et al., 2010).

Internal resources may help buffer the stress of cancer diagnosis. Resilience, the capacity to adapt and overcome stress and adversity while maintaining normal psychological and physical functioning (Wu et al., 2013), provides protective effects on the wellbeing of cancer patients. Markovitz et al. (2015) compared the emotional responses of women recently diagnosed with breast cancer who then received surgical treatment with healthy age-matched controls. They found that cancer patients reported greater anxiety, depression and negative affect, and less happiness and positive affect than the control group. However, women with higher levels of resilience also reported better emotional adjustment, suggesting that resilience may protect against emotional distress in the diagnostic and early treatment phases.

Fatigue during cancer treatment is another common concern. This can arise from disturbed sleep, and as a direct consequence of cancer treatment (i.e. chemotherapy, radiotherapy). Interventions addressing fatigue and sleep quality concerns include pharmacologic and non-pharmacologic approaches (Mitchell et al., 2014). Physical exercise and yoga can reduce fatigue, as can psychosocial interventions entailing psychoeducation (Tomlinson et al., 2014). Cognitive behavioural therapies for insomnia, pain, and depression, and mindfulness-based stress reduction, and interventions such as anticipatory guidance, psychosocial support, energy conservation and activity management show promise for addressing cancer-related fatigue during treatment and beyond.

For many cancer-affected individuals, the end of active treatment does not automatically bring about better psychological functioning (Andrykowski, Lykins & Floyd, 2008). During active treatment, patients have regular and intensive interactions with the medical care team that are reassuring (Foster & Fenlon, 2011). Once active treatment concludes, there is less interaction with the team and some patients find this stressful due to loss of the support network from staff and patients, even experiencing a sense of abandonment (Foster & Fenlon, 2011). Coupled with this is the ongoing uncertainty about the efficacy of the treatment once it is completed.

Survivorship

Definitions of survivorship vary, with some referring to a cancer survivor as anyone who has been diagnosed (Burton et al., 2007; Hughes, 2000). A more common definition is to describe survivors as individuals who have completed their active treatment and are now looking to resume their lives post-cancer (Feuerstein, 2007; Hudson et al., 2003). There are several aspects that characterise survivorship, not least being the physical health of the individual concerned. At this stage there are inevitable questions about the efficacy of treatment now that it is completed, and whether there are residual treatment side effects. Some side effects, such as hair loss following chemotherapy, are apparent early in the treatment cycle and tend to be temporary (Ramirez et al., 2009). Other side effects, such as lymphoedema (chronic swelling of a limb due to excessive lymph fluid accumulation) and pain after radiotherapy, may manifest months or years following treatment completion (Peeters et al., 2005; Petrek et al., 2001). After treatment has finished, many patients expect to be healthy, and think positively about the future (Clark et al., 2003). Resuming a pre-cancer life is a top priority for many survivors, yet the reality is that aiming for a prior level of functioning may be an unrealistic goal. Patients may need to adopt a new 'normal' functioning. Psychological support can be very beneficial at this stage, particularly the opportunity to explore the likely limits of a newly functioning self. Approaches such as medical crisis counselling (Koocher et al., 2001), based on the normalising premise that serious medical conditions are stressful for everyone, focus on finding ways for cancer survivors to modify their lives to optimise functioning and enjoyment within the confines of the cancer.

The depressive symptoms commonly experienced in the early stages following cancer diagnosis and during treatment tend to dissipate over time for most individuals (Fann et al., 2008). However, approximately 12% of cancer patients experience depression well beyond completion of their active treatment (Mitchell et al., 2013). Having a poor prognosis, lack of confidence in coping with cancer, self-blame and fear of cancer recurrence are risk factors for experiencing cancer-related depression (Beutel et al., 2015; Fann et al., 2008; Philip et al., 2013). Fortunately, there are evidence-based interventions that assist cancer patients who experience depression. Pharmacological interventions are commonly prescribed and tend to reduce depressive symptoms in at least half of cancer survivors (Fann et al., 2008). Non-pharmacological interventions, such as psychological therapies, are also effective and can be used alone or in conjunction with pharmacological approaches in the short term. Cognitive behavioural interventions are the most effective psychotherapeutic approach to decreasing depressive symptoms (Chien et al., 2014; Hart et al., 2012; Naaman et al., 2009). These can be provided one-on-one or in group settings, the latter being more cost-effective, and may decrease patients' feelings of alienation through interacting with others in similar circumstances (McKiernan et al., 2010). Another depression management approach is mindfulness-based stress reduction interventions that teach people to more positively address experiences by encouraging present awareness of feelings, thoughts and bodily sensations (Garland et al., 2013; Lengacher et al., 2012; Sharplin et al., 2010; Wurtzen et al., 2015). However, meta-analyses indicate that the effect of cognitive behavioural interventions on depressive symptoms is stronger than that of mindfulness-based approaches (Hart et al., 2012; Naaman et al., 2009; Piet, Wurtzen & Zachariae, 2012). Moreover, there is emerging evidence that cognitive behavioural stress management interventions administered after initial surgery may improve psychological adaptation to cancer, and provide mortality benefit (Stagl et al., 2015).

Sleep problems and cancer-related fatigue are common post-treatment concerns that have long-lasting and serious impacts on a survivor's quality of life and day-to-day functioning (Brown & Kroenke, 2009; Curt et al., 2000). These concerns may occur co-morbidly with depression. Chemotherapy and hormonal treatments can directly impact on sleep quality, as can residual treatment side effects such as pain and lymphoedema (Brown & Kroenke, 2009; Ridner, 2009). As with the treatment approaches for depression, psychosocial interventions are effective at addressing cancer-related sleep problems and fatigue. Cognitive behavioural therapies for insomnia, pain, depression;

mindfulness-based stress reduction; psychoeducational interventions, such as anticipatory guidance, psychosocial support and energy conservation; and activity management have all demonstrated efficacy in reducing fatigue in cancer survivors (Mitchell et al., 2014).

Creative-based intervention approaches for cancer survivors are a promising alternative to more traditional psychosocial approaches. A meta-analysis of music interventions has demonstrated that they are effective at reducing anxiety, depression, pain and fatigue in cancer survivors (Tsai et al., 2014). Perhaps not surprisingly, the age of the patient and the choice of music are important factors influencing the effectiveness of music interventions. Adults are most responsive, particularly when they choose their own music. Other creative-based interventions, including art and dance therapy, have demonstrated improvements in anxiety and depression, quality of life, coping, stress, anger and mood in adult cancer survivors (Archer, Buxton & Sheffield, 2015).

Managing fear of recurrence

Of critical importance for an individual diagnosed and treated for cancer, even if the treatment is successful and the individual is cancer free, is the threat that the cancer may return at some time in the future. Fear of recurrence is the greatest concern (Ness et al., 2013; Simard et al., 2013) for up to 50% of all cancer survivors (Savard & Ivers, 2013). In general, individuals with greater fear of recurrence have a poorer prognosis and more advanced cancer (Savard & Ivers, 2013). Head and neck cancer patients, in particular, are likely to fear recurrence (Ghazali et al., 2013; Savard & Ivers, 2013), as do younger patients (Brennan et al., 2014). Individuals with helpless/hopeless and avoidance-oriented coping styles and lower levels of perceived social support may be more likely to report fear of recurrence anxieties (Smith et al., 2015; Stanton, Danoff-Burg & Huggins, 2002). Fear of recurrence may become a chronic way of responding to cancer survivorship, and over time these fears negatively impact on the quality of life of these patients (Koch et al., 2014). Despite the high incidence of fear of recurrence, and the perception that it is challenging to manage, individuals with high levels of these concerns are not routinely referred for psychosocial support (Thewes et al., 2014). Clearly interventions are needed to reduce the likelihood of these fears developing in the first instance, and in effectively managing them once they arise.

Mini case study 10.2

Josh was 31 when he found a dark mole on his back. It was mid-summer and he had spent the last month down at the beach surfing for hours on end. This is his favourite pastime and he has been surfing since his childhood: pretty much an all-year-round activity for this Queensland resident. His girlfriend, Nicole, had noticed a fast-growing dark mole and convinced Josh to have it checked by the GP. Less than a week after seeing the doctor, Josh was in hospital having a melanoma removed. The tumour was large and he needed a skin graft as well as radiation treatment.

continued ›

Mini case study 10.2 continued ›

After completing treatment, Josh was told by his cancer specialist that there was no evidence of cancer in his body. Josh needs to visit the specialist every few months for the next 5 years to check that the cancer hasn't returned. The specialist is optimistic that it is unlikely to return. Nevertheless, Josh cannot get out of his mind the recurring thought that the cancer will be back. He feels very fearful of this possibility and he sometimes lies awake at night thinking the worst. One of the most difficult aspects of his cancer is that there is no certainty. Doctors cannot for certain say that he has been cured, but at the same time they cannot say for certain that the cancer will return. All they can provide are the statistics that suggest that, because of his young age and the good response to the treatment, it is unlikely that the cancer will return.

Critical thinking questions

1. How would you describe Josh's ongoing response to his experience of cancer?
2. Based on what you've read, would you consider this to be a common response?
3. How might Josh's ongoing thoughts about cancer impact on his ability to resume 'normal life' after cancer?

Body image and sexuality

Many cancer treatments cause changes to an individual's physical appearance. Consequently, these treatments and their associated side effects can significantly and negatively impact a patient's body image; that is, the perception of (Collins et al., 2011; Helms, O'Hea & Corso, 2008) and attitudes towards (Cash, Melnyk & Hrabosky, 2004; Moreira, Silva & Canavarro, 2010) one's physical appearance. Body image difficulties have been identified in patients with breast, cervical, colorectal, head and neck, haematological, melanoma, ovarian, prostate, renal and testicular cancers (Campolmi et al., 2015; Carpentier & Fortenberry, 2010; Denlinger & Barsevick, 2009; Fingeret, Nipomnick, et al., 2014; Foster & Stern, 2014; Harrington, Jones & Badger, 2009; Taylor-Ford et al., 2013). For example, the partial or complete removal of the breast following breast cancer can result in breast asymmetry, extensive scarring or the need for prostheses, any of which can negatively affect a woman's identity and body image (Collins et al., 2011; Helms et al., 2008; Gopie et al., 2013). Approximately 30% of breast cancer patients experience body image difficulties (Falk Dahl et al., 2010). Head and neck cancer and melanoma treatment can also result in highly visible scarring and changes in appearance (Campolmi et al., 2015; Fingeret, Nipomnick, et al., 2014), and functional difficulties such as with eating, chewing, drinking, breathing and speaking, that compound the negative effects of visible changes in appearance (Fingeret et al., 2013; Semple et al., 2004). Up to 75% of head and neck cancer patients experience body image difficulties (Fingeret, Nipomnick, et al., 2014; Fingeret et al., 2012). Generally, radiation therapy may cause skin discolouration and chemotherapy may lead to hair loss, both highly visible changes to an individual's physical appearance. Body image concerns are typically most evident in the period immediately following surgery and treatment (Cororve Fingeret, Teo & Epner, 2014), but can last years into cancer survivorship (Falk Dahl et al., 2010). There is some evidence that younger age, greater body mass index and more extensive, invasive surgery are potential risk factors for cancer patients to experience body image disturbance (Cororve Fingeret et al., 2014). Along with changes to physical appearance, it is common for cancer survivors to experience heightened psychological distress (depression, anxiety, stress) associated with these body appearance and functional changes (Begovic-Juhant et al., 2012; Gopie et al., 2013).

As is the case for managing depressive symptoms in cancer survivors, cognitive behavioural therapy interventions have demonstrated efficacy in improving body image and reducing concerns in the short and long term (Fingeret, Teo, et al., 2014). Other intervention approaches, including couples-based psychosexual interventions (Kalaitzi et al., 2007) and psychoeducation (Helgeson et al., 1999), may also be effective in reducing body image concerns.

Mini case study 10.3

How does cancer impact on how we feel about our bodies? Consider the following quotations from individuals with cancer.

- 'I only have sex with my shirt on. I am really worried that my partner won't find me attractive anymore.' (woman, 35, breast cancer diagnosis)
- 'I don't really go out much anymore, you know, socially. My wife and I used to enjoy going out to the local sports club but I feel too ashamed of my incontinence and needing to wear those awful, obvious incontinence pads.' (man, 68, prostate cancer diagnosis)
- 'I can't stand looking in the mirror each morning. It's bad enough as we get older, but after the surgery for my throat cancer I look like a freak. I don't even think about meeting my friends for coffee at the local café. I'm too ashamed with how I look … I have difficulty eating and swallowing. I don't want people staring at me. My friends … they are all so glamorous … they wouldn't understand.' (woman, 56, ex-smoker, throat cancer diagnosis)

Critical thinking questions

1. Are these reactions to be expected?
2. What can we do to minimise these concerns about physical appearance?

Sexual dysfunction is another common concern after cancer diagnosis and treatment. It is strongly associated with changes in physical appearance and consequent body image difficulties, and is exacerbated by physical side effects of treatment such as vaginal dryness, low libido and impotence (Bartula & Sherman, 2013). While sexuality and intimacy can help minimise emotional distress associated with cancer (Sadovsky et al., 2010), sexual difficulties may lead to relationship and emotional problems, which can negatively impact on coping and psychological adjustment (Taylor et al., 2011; Tierney, 2008). These difficulties may arise because of the cancer itself, its treatment and side effects, psychological distress associated with cancer, and even changes within the couple's relationship (Tierney, 2008).

One of the greatest challenges regarding sexual dysfunction is being able to identify that this is a concern. For many patients, and even health professionals, this is a taboo subject, one to be avoided despite ongoing difficulties (Vermeer et al., 2015). Successful intervention approaches for managing sexual dysfunction acknowledge the role of the cancer patient's partner and address the psychosocial concerns held by each member of the couple (Kalaitzi et al., 2007). Validated measures have been developed to assess body image concerns and sexual dysfunction in cancer patients (e.g. Bartula & Sherman, 2013, 2015). These tools can be used by healthcare teams to gain an understanding of the difficulties of most concern, and as a conversation starter with cancer patients.

In summary, cancer and its treatment can have a profound effect on the physical, emotional, psychological and social functioning of the affected individual. These negative impacts can continue beyond the initial point of diagnosis and treatment, well into survivorship. Clearly there is a need for psychological support to be available to cancer patients to help guide them through each of the challenges they face along their cancer journey. Forewarning patients and educating them about what to expect in terms of changes to their physical functioning and appearance may facilitate adaptive coping and adjustment to these changing circumstances. Moreover, proactively providing cancer patients with contacts for relevant community-based resources and mental health specialists should further assist this adjustment process and ensure that appropriate support is available when, and if, it is needed (Fingeret, Teo, et al., 2014).

Cancer recurrence and end-of-life

> The cancer just keeps coming back. I've been treated twice already. Each time it seemed to go away, only for it to rear its ugly head again. It's a bit like having a chronic disease, going in and out of acute phases and treatment and then into a time of remission.
>
> (Jeff, 72, bladder cancer diagnosis)

Even after patients are reassured by the medical team that they have 'got the all clear' and that the scans and tests show no evidence of cancer, there are sometimes residual cancer cells that remain after treatment concludes. Over time these residual cells may multiply, leading to a return of the cancer, known as *cancer recurrence*. The cancer may return to where it first started (e.g. in the bowel) or to somewhere else in the body (e.g. bowel cancer cells affecting the liver). Return of the cancer typically means more treatment, which may be a repeat of initial adjuvant treatments, or a new treatment regimen. Whatever the course of action recommended, it means that both physically and psychologically the cancer patient needs to summon up the resources to cope with treatment all over again.

Responses to cancer recurrence vary from one individual to the next. Feeling less hopeful and more psychologically distressed are common responses (Acquaye et al., 2015), but so too are feelings of anger (Thornton et al., 2014).

For others, recurrence is an indicator that the cancer has not responded well, and that it has progressed. Generally, active treatment for cancer will continue until it is mutually agreed between the healthcare team and the patient that this is no longer effective and a rapid decline in health has commenced (Murray et al., 2005). The patient then enters the palliative phase of their cancer care, where the objective is pain relief and symptom control, as well as psychosocial care, rather than curing the cancer (Sepúlveda et al., 2002). Importantly, the objective of palliative care is also to provide psychosocial support for the carer of the cancer patient. Up to this point in the cancer experience, the carer will have shared with the patient their changes in physical and psychological wellbeing since diagnosis. Moving to the palliative care phase signals to the carer a new sequence of unpredictable challenges with the certainty of death, and for many carers this can be deeply distressing (Schofield et al., 2006).

Approximately 40% of Australians diagnosed with cancer are not expected to survive beyond 5 years after their initial diagnosis (AIHW, 2014). For individuals entering the palliative phase of cancer care, the physical and psychological burdens change. Anxiety tends to increase as thoughts turn to limited life expectancy and likely death (Roth & Massie, 2007). Patients may experience anger, disappointment and even a sense of betrayal that the medical treatments have been ineffective at controlling their disease (Thornton et al., 2014). For those whose cancer is regarded as incurable, their illness trajectory is usually characterised by rapid decline in the months prior to death (Murray et al., 2005). This decline in physical capacity and increased physical symptoms such as pain, shortness of breath and incontinence will usually be associated with heightened psychological distress (Bruera & Hui, 2010).

Intrusive and recurrent thoughts about fear of pain and death are common, as are concerns about losing independence and being dependent on others for care (Roth & Massie, 2007). Physical symptoms may fuel anxious feelings, blurring the line between anxiety arising from somatic causes and anxiety that is psychological in nature (Roth & Massie, 2007). Another common response to the end-of-life phase is demoralisation, a condition that arises from existential conflict (Robinson et al., 2015), and is characterised by feelings of hopelessness and helplessness, and a loss of purpose and meaning in life (Robinson et al., 2015). Unfortunately, demoralisation may further enhance the cancer patient's desire for death. Individuals who have poorly controlled pain and other physical symptoms, who are concurrently experiencing anxiety or depression, and those with diminished social functioning, are more likely to experience feelings of demoralisation (Robinson et al., 2015).

Despite the inherent difficulties in providing psychosocial support for the end-stage cancer patient, due to their overarching poor health and the uncertainty surrounding their health state, there are several intervention approaches that are being developed to address these supportive care needs. One approach showing promise has been developed for advanced lung cancer patients and their carers and entails a six-session, telephone-based dyadic psychosocial intervention. Based on self-determination theory, the intervention emphasises the importance of self-efficacy, autonomy and relatedness (Badr et al., 2015). Preliminary evidence suggests that both the patient and the carer benefit in terms of decreased depression and anxiety, as well as the carer feeling less burdened by their role. One of the greatest challenges facing carers is that there is an increasing trend for end-stage cancer patients to remain at home for as long as possible, placing high responsibility for the welfare of the patient on the carer, particularly in monitoring the patient's physical state, yet many carers are ill-prepared and poorly supported to manage patient symptoms at home (Chih et al., 2013). Researchers in the US have developed a system whereby carers can email their concerns directly to the healthcare team. If the symptom distress is registered over a predetermined threshold, this triggers alerts to the clinicians, who then provide an immediate response for managing these new symptoms (Chih et al., 2013). Carers using this communication system have reported experiencing fewer negative mood symptoms than carers without access to this system (Chih et al., 2013).

Cancer and the family

Cancer is not just a 'me' disease, it is very much a 'we' disease. A cancer diagnosis will have a ripple effect, impacting on the family caregivers and close friends. Regardless of the gender, type of cancer, treatment chosen, prognosis or external support systems, the partners of individuals diagnosed with cancer are particularly affected, as they usually take on the role of the primary caregiver and are responsible for most of the patient's support (Sherman, Kasparian & Mireskandari, 2010). Berg and Upchurch (2007) provide a conceptual model for understanding the role of the cancer patient's partner in the experience of cancer (see Figure 10.3) (Berg & Upchurch, 2007).

Embedded within the sociocultural context, the relationship quality and the specific characteristics of the disease, the patient and their partner form a dyad in which the process of appraisal, coping and adjustment occur at both the individual and the dyadic levels. Over time, the couple's relationship tends to be defined by both behavioural and psychological interdependence, placing considerable strain on the relationship when one partner is affected by serious illness, such as cancer (Berg & Upchurch, 2007). Rolland's model (Rolland, 2005) provides a similar approach, this time focusing more broadly on family systems, rather than just the dyad. In Rolland's model, illnesses are classified according to their psychosocial demand, taking into account the onset, course and outcomes of the illness, including whether it is progressive, acute or gradual and incapacitating. The strengths and weaknesses in family functioning in relation to the illness are considered in this model at different phases over the illness life course. What is common to these models is the acknowledgement that the cancer experience encompasses more people than just the patient, and that in aiming to facilitate psychological adjustment of the patient, we need to consider more broadly how the patient's family may be impacted by the diagnosis and what can be done to assist them.

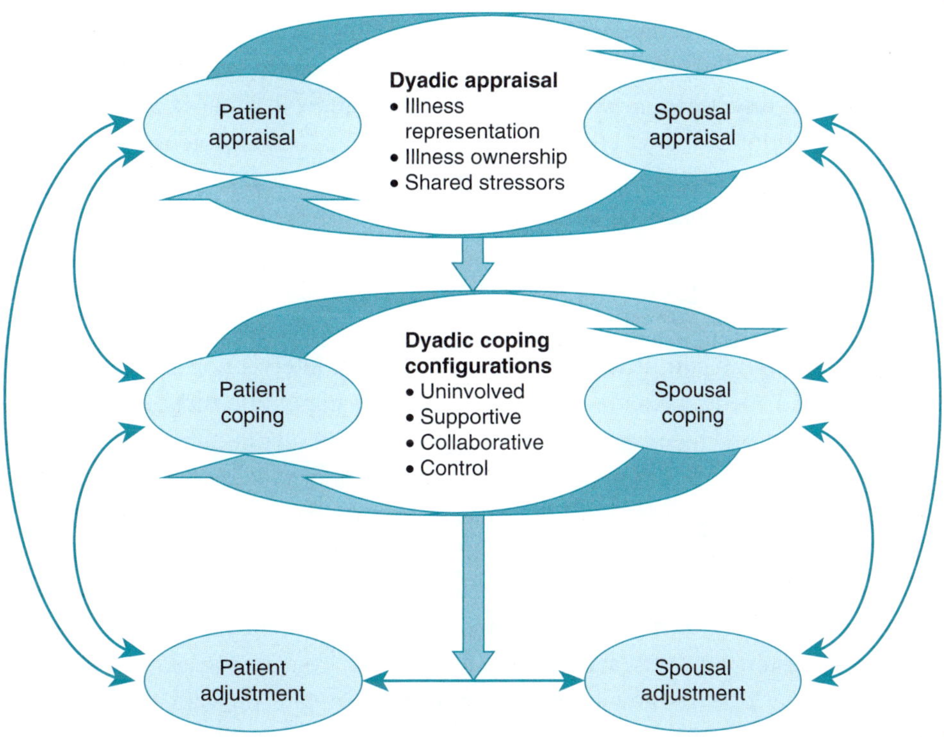

Figure 10.3 Dyadic appraisal, coping and adjustment in couples
Source: Berg & Upchurch, 2007 © American Psychological Association. Published by the American Psychological Association. Reprinted/adapted with permission.

Family members are implicitly expected to be well informed about the cancer diagnosis and to understand symptoms. They typically provide both instrumental support (such as transport to medical appointments) and reassurance and psychosocial support to the patient. Clearly a diagnosis of cancer has the potential to disrupt the usual familial relationships. Most individuals change from being independent members of a family to becoming highly dependent on others, particularly in the acute initial phases of treatment, and then during the palliative care and end-of-life stages. This requires considerable adjustment from all family members, with the partner most affected (Sherman et al., 2010). The timing of a cancer diagnosis will have an impact on overall adjustment. As people age, we generally anticipate that they will be diagnosed with chronic and serious conditions, hence the diagnosis of a 70-year-old man with bowel cancer would be 'on time', as opposed to a 35-year-old man with the same diagnosis. The more 'inappropriately timed' the diagnosis, the more stressful it will be, as it is unlikely that the individual concerned and their family will have had time to plan for this eventuality. Support from peers may also be lacking due to their inability to fully understand and accept the situation (Berg & Upchurch, 2007).

A cancer diagnosis of one's partner has the potential to impact on diverse aspects of the 'well' partner's life, including role changes within the dyad and the family more broadly (Schubart, Kinzie & Farace, 2008). Relational distress, sexual dysfunction and communication difficulties between partners are common (Bartula & Sherman, 2013; Manne et al., 2006; Ussher et al., 2012; Yu & Sherman, 2015). Moreover, the stress of managing physical symptoms and functional disability, and being the primary provider of instrumental and emotional support, can take its toll on the 'well' partner (Segrin et al., 2007). For these reasons, it is important to develop and implement psychological interventions for couples coping with cancer; that is, interventions addressing the dyadic aspects.

Systematic reviews and meta-analysis of psychosocial interventions for these couples have identified benefits in terms of improvements to communication, dyadic coping, quality of life and psychological distress, as well as overall marital satisfaction (Brandão, Schulz & Matos, 2014; Li & Loke, 2014). Most interventions focus on patient caregiving and self-care of the caregiver (Li & Loke, 2014). CanCope is a multi-session cognitive behavioural intervention that was developed for women diagnosed with breast cancer and their partners (Scott, Halford & Ward, 2004). It seeks to clarify each partner's understanding of the patient's diagnosis and treatments, to enhance coping skills and prevent relationship concerns, such as sexual problems, from arising (Scott et al., 2004). A version of CanCope has now been developed for men with prostate cancer and their partners (Elliott et al., 2015).

Having dependent children living with you at the time of a cancer diagnosis adds further strain to the challenges facing couples. Adolescent children, and girls in particular, appear to be at risk of psychological morbidity (Huizinga et al., 2005; Krattenmacher et al., 2013). Having a parent with cancer is a family experience, with the children's adjustment reflecting the nature of the parent's cancer, the quality of the support network of the parents and the family structure generally (Huizinga et al., 2005). Clearly, intervention approaches are needed that provide a family-oriented and child-focused approach to managing the psychosocial needs of the family unit.

Mini case study 10.4

Anna, a 38-year-old mother of two young children under five, and married to Simon, 40, has just been diagnosed with breast cancer. She has a busy, full-time job and has up until her recent diagnosis been exercising three times a week at her local gym, but has been feeling very fatigued after doing this.

Critical thinking question

What are the possible impacts of this diagnosis on: Anna? Simon? Their children?

When cancer runs in the family

Genetic risk

Since the human genome sequence was released in 2001, genetic tests for a number of hereditary conditions have been developed (Lander et al., 2001). **Genetic testing** can identify specific gene mutations (or faults) known to increase risk for some cancers, including breast, ovarian, melanoma, bowel and prostate (Bancroft, 2010; Sherman & Cameron, 2015). Identification of a gene mutation means that the individual has an increased risk of developing the cancer, and several options may be presented to them for reducing their risk, including heightened surveillance, and prophylactic options, such as surgery and chemoprevention.

The decision to undergo genetic testing is not necessarily straightforward, and interest in such testing may be motivated by factors including the degree to which the condition is perceived as being preventable and treatable (Sherman et al., 2015). An assumption of providing genetic risk assessment for cancer is that this may motivate risk-reduction strategies. Provision of genetic test result feedback has been found to promote greater understanding of the cancer risk and to enhance the personal salience of prevention recommendations (Taber et al., 2015). Receipt of positive mutation results indicating the presence of a genetic fault has also been linked with increased intention to undergo preventive surgery for breast cancer (Miller et al., 2005).

While genetic testing for cancer susceptibility is mostly offered for disorders associated with single genes, most cancers result from some contributions from genetic susceptibility combined with environmental factors (Moore et al., 2012; Nickels et al., 2013; Richiardi, Pettersson & Akre, 2007). Research suggests that receiving information about the gene–environment interactions may not encourage preventive behaviours to as great an extent as genetic risk information alone (Weinberg et al., 2014). These findings bring into question the efficacy of genetic risk information in promoting favourable healthcare behaviour.

There is evidence that receiving genetic testing information does not diminish perceived control over risk-reducing behaviours, such as sun protection for melanoma prevention (Taber et al., 2015), and that brief messages enhancing illness coherence by explaining how certain actions can reduce genetic risks may promote beliefs motivating protective action (Cameron et al., 2012). However, there are individual differences in the way in which genetic risk information is interpreted, with one study reporting that for individuals belonging to high breast cancer risk families, their risk comprehension and risk management approaches were largely influenced by intuition, rather than objective risk information provided by genetic testing (Heiniger et al., 2015). Moreover, race differences are evident in responses to genetic risk information, with Caucasian people being more likely than non-Caucasian to view risk feedback as a prompt to undertake cancer screening, and for non-Caucasians to be more likely to report feeling anxiety about the likelihood of being diagnosed with cancer (Myers et al., 2015).

Childhood cancer

Cancer affects people of all ages, and unfortunately this includes children. Each year, 950 children in Australia (AIHW, 2015a), and 175 000 children worldwide (American Cancer Society, 2013), are diagnosed with cancer, with the most common cancers affecting fast-growing tissues such as blood, lymph, bone marrow, nervous tissues, muscles, kidney, liver and bone (Cancer Australia, 2015). Treatment for childhood cancer is similar to adult treatment approaches, and may also include stem cell transplants for children with blood cancer (e.g. leukaemia) (Cancer Australia, 2015).

Research has demonstrated that strategies such as acceptance, cognitive reappraisal and positive methods of cognitive and behavioural distraction help children cope with cancer and adapt to the stress associated with their diagnosis (Compas et al., 2014). There is also some support for art interventions in reducing anxiety, fear and pain in childhood cancer patients (Derman & Deatrick, 2015). Following treatment, childhood cancer survivors must contend with a myriad of medical and psychosocial vulnerabilities, and hence a number of interventions have sought to alleviate adverse outcomes in this population. A recent systematic review indicates that current interventions successfully address health (e.g. bone and sun safety behaviour, knowledge of smoking-related risks, physical activity), neurocognitive (e.g. attention, processing speed) and psychosocial (e.g. internalising problems, social skills, quality of life) outcomes (Brier, Schwartz & Kazak, 2015).

Summary

- Cancer begins when cells in our bodies start dividing uncontrollably. The cancer experience can be characterised by a number of phases, from initial risk assessment, through to diagnosis, treatment, survivorship, cancer recurrence, and palliative care and end of life. Importantly, not everyone will experience all these phases, or in this order. Cancer is highly prevalent in Australia and other Western countries. While the incidence and mortality rates of most cancers are decreasing in many Western countries (including Australia and New Zealand), incidence is increasing in less developed and emerging economies.
- There are many barriers that decrease participation in cancer screening programs, and decrease the likelihood of symptoms being acted upon by seeking medical advice. Cognitions, such as low perceived vulnerability, lack of salience of symptoms and affective responses – including fear (of being diagnosed) and embarrassment – are common barriers.
- Common responses to a cancer diagnosis include shock, 'encounter' (i.e. feelings of loss, helplessness and feeling overwhelmed) and 'retreat' (i.e. denial and disengagement). During active treatment, many patients report anxious and depressive symptoms in the context of unpleasant and possibly painful treatment approaches. During survivorship, individuals must

contend with longer-term side effects, including issues with body image and sexuality. They must also manage fear of cancer recurrence.

- When cancer recurs, patients face further treatment and must summon up the mental and physical resources to cope with this. For individuals entering the palliative phase of cancer care, anxiety may increase as thoughts turn to limited life expectancy and likely death. Patients may experience anger, disappointment and even a sense of betrayal that the medical treatments have been ineffective at controlling their disease. Intrusive and recurrent thoughts about fear of pain and death are common, as are concerns about losing independence and being dependent on others for care.
- Decision aids can be used to facilitate treatment-related decision-making when patients receive their cancer diagnosis. Several interventions have also been shown to be efficacious in managing treatment side effects, including cognitive behavioural therapy, mindfulness therapy and pharmacological approaches.
- Several intervention approaches are also being developed to address supportive care needs for the end-stage cancer patient (e.g. a telephone-based dyadic intervention) and their carer(s) (e.g. existential behavioural therapy).
- Cancer is not just a 'me' disease; it is very much a 'we' disease. A cancer diagnosis will have a ripple effect, impacting on the family caregivers and close friends. The partners of individuals diagnosed with cancer are particularly affected, as they usually take on the role of the primary caregiver and are responsible for most of the patient's support.

Suggested weblinks

Refer to the companion website at www.cambridge.edu.au/academic/healthpsychology for a list of suggested weblinks.

References

Acquaye, A. A., Lin, L., Vera-Bolanos, E., Gilbert, M. R. & Armstrong, T. S. (2015). Hope and mood changes throughout the primary brain tumor illness trajectory. *Neuro-Oncology*. doi: http://dx.doi.org/10.1093/neuonc/nov101

AIHW. (2012). *Cancer Survival and Prevalence in Australia: Period Estimates from 1982 to 2010*. Canberra: Australian Institute of Health and Welfare.

—— (2014). *Cancer in Australia: An Overview, 2014*. Canberra: Australian Institute of Health and Welfare.

—— (2015a). 0–19 years incidence data. Canberra: Australian Institute of Health and Welfare. Retrieved from: http://www.aihw.gov.au/acim-books

—— (2015b). Burden of disease due to cancer. Canberra: Australian Institute of Health and Welfare. Retrieved from: http://www.aihw.gov.au/cancer/cancer-in-australia-overview-2012/ch7/

American Cancer Society. (2013). *Cancer Facts & Figures 2013*. Atlanta GA: American Cancer Society.

—— (2014a). Coping with cancer in everyday life. Retrieved from: http://www.cancer.org/treatment/treatmentsandsideeffects/emotionalsideeffects/copingwithcancerineverydaylife/a-message-of-hope-emotional-impact-of-cancer

—— (2014b). Pancreatic cancer survival by stage. Retrieved from: http://www.cancer.org/cancer/pancreaticcancer/detailedguide/pancreatic-cancer-survival-rates

Andrykowski, M. A., Lykins, E. & Floyd, A. (2008). Psychological health in cancer survivors. *Seminars in Oncology Nursing, 24*(3), 193–201. doi: http://dx.doi.org/10.1016/j.soncn.2008.05.007

Archer, S., Buxton, S. & Sheffield, D. (2015). The effect of creative psychological interventions on psychological outcomes for adult cancer patients: a systematic review of randomised controlled trials. *Psycho-Oncology, 24*(1), 1–10. doi: http://dx.doi.org/10.1002/pon.3607

Arnaboldi, P., Lucchiari, C., Santoro, L., Sangalli, C., Luini, A. & Pravettoni, G. (2014). PTSD symptoms as a consequence of breast cancer diagnosis: clinical implications. *SpringerPlus, 3*, 392. doi: http://dx.doi.org/10.1186/2193-1801-3-392

Badr, H., Smith, C. B., Goldstein, N. E., Gomez, J. E. & Redd, W. H. (2015). Dyadic psychosocial intervention for advanced lung cancer patients and their family caregivers: results of a randomized pilot trial. *Cancer, 121*(1), 150–8.

Bancroft, E. K. (2010). Genetic testing for cancer predisposition and implications for nursing practice: narrative review. *Journal of Advanced Nursing, 66*(4), 710–37. doi: http://dx.doi.org/10.1111/j.1365-2648.2010.05286.x

Banegas, M. P., McClure, J. B., Barlow, W. E., Ubel, P. A., Smith, D. M., Zikmund-Fisher, B. J., ... Fagerlin, A. (2013). Results from a randomized trial of a web-based, tailored decision aid for women at high risk for breast cancer. *Patient Education and Counseling, 91*(3), 364–71. doi: http://dx.doi.org/10.1016/j.pec.2012.12.014

Bartula, I. & Sherman, K. A. (2013). Screening for sexual dysfunction in women diagnosed with breast cancer: systematic review and recommendations. *Breast Cancer Research and Treatment, 141*(2), 173–85. doi: http://dx.doi.org/10.1007/s10549-013-2685-9

—— (2015). Development and validation of the Female Sexual Function Index adaptation for breast cancer patients (FSFI-BC). *Breast Cancer Research and Treatment, 152*(3), 477–88. doi: http://dx.doi.org/10.1007/s10549-015-3499-8

Begovic-Juhant, A., Chmielewski, A., Iwuagwu, S. & Chapman, L. A. (2012). Impact of body image on depression and quality of life among women with breast cancer. *Journal of Psychosocial Oncology, 30*(4), 446–60. doi: http://dx.doi.org/10.1080/07347332.2012.684856

Berg, C. A. & Upchurch, R. (2007). A developmental-contextual model of couples coping with chronic illness across the adult life span. *Psychological Bulletin, 133*(6), 920–54.

Beutel, M. E., Fischbeck, S., Binder, H., Blettner, M., Brähler, E., Emrich, K., ... Zeissig, S. R. (2015). Depression, anxiety and quality of life in long-term survivors of malignant melanoma: a register-based cohort study. *PLoS ONE, 10*(1), e0116440. doi: http://dx.doi.org/10.1371/journal.pone.0116440

Brandão, T., Schulz, M. S. & Matos, P. M. (2014). Psychological intervention with couples coping with breast cancer: a systematic review. *Psychology & Health, 29*(5), 491–516. doi: http://dx.doi.org/10.1080/08870446.2013.859257

Breen, S., Ritchie, D., Schofield, P., Hsueh, Y.-s., Gough, K., Santamaria, N., ... Aranda, S. (2015). The Patient Remote Intervention and Symptom Management System (PRISMS) – a Telehealth-mediated intervention enabling real-time monitoring of chemotherapy side-effects in patients with haematological malignancies: study protocol for a randomised controlled trial. *Trials, 16*, 472. doi: http://dx.doi.org/10.1186/s13063-015-0970-0

Breen, S. J., Baravelli, C. M., Schofield, P. E., Jefford, M., Yates, P. M. & Aranda, S. K. (2009). Is symptom burden a predictor of anxiety and depression in patients with cancer about to commence chemotherapy? *Medical Journal of Australia, 190*(7 Suppl), S99–104.

Brennan, M. E., Butow, P., Spillane, A. J. & Boyle, F. (2014). Patient-reported quality of life, unmet needs and care coordination outcomes: moving toward targeted breast cancer survivorship care planning. *Asia-Pacific Journal of Clinical Oncology*, 12(2), e323–31. doi: http://dx.doi.org/10.1111/ajco.12254

Brier, M. J., Schwartz, L. A. & Kazak, A. E. (2015). Psychosocial, health-promotion, and neurocognitive interventions for survivors of childhood cancer: a systematic review. *Health Psychology, 34*(2), 130–48. doi: http://dx.doi.org/10.1037/hea0000119

Brown, L. F. & Kroenke, K. (2009). Cancer-related fatigue and its associations with depression and anxiety: a systematic review. *Psychosomatics, 50*(5), 440–7. doi: http://dx.doi.org/10.1176/appi.psy.50.5.440

Brown, L. F., Kroenke, K., Theobald, D. E., Wu, J. & Tu, W. (2010). The association of depression and anxiety with health-related quality of life in cancer patients with depression and/or pain. *Psycho-Oncology*, *19*(7), 734–41. doi: http://dx.doi.org/10.1002/pon.1627

Bruera, E. & Hui, D. (2010). Integrating supportive and palliative care in the trajectory of cancer: establishing goals and models of care. *Journal of Clinical Oncology*, *28*(25), 4013–17.

Bukowska-Durawa, A. & Luszczynska, A. (2014). Cervical cancer screening and psychosocial barriers perceived by patients: a systematic review. *Contemporary Oncology*, *18*(3), 153–9. doi: http://dx.doi.org/10.5114/wo.2014.43158

Burton, A. W., Fanciullo, G. J., Beasley, R. D. & Fisch, M. J. (2007). Chronic pain in the cancer survivor: a new frontier. *Pain Medicine*, *8*(2), 189–98. doi: http://dx.doi.org/10.1111/j.1526-4637.2006.00220.x

Cameron, L. D., Marteau, T. M., Brown, P. M., Klein, W. M. & Sherman, K. A. (2012). Communication strategies for enhancing understanding of the behavioral implications of genetic and biomarker tests for disease risk: the role of coherence. *Journal of Behavioral Medicine*, *35*(3), 286–98. doi: http://dx.doi.org/10.1007/s10865-011-9361-5

Campolmi, E., Mugnai, F., Riccio, M., Grifoni, R., Gunnella, S., Fortunato, S., ... Pimpinelli, N. (2015). Body image and awareness in patients with advanced stage melanoma. *Giornale Italiano di Dermatologia e Venereologia*.

Cancer Australia. (2015). What is children's cancer? Retrieved from: http://childrenscancer.canceraustralia.gov.au/about-childrens-cancer/what-childrens-cancer

Cancer Research UK. (2014a). Brain, other CNS and intracranial tumours survival statistics. Retrieved from: http://www.cancerresearchuk.org/health-professional/cancer-statistics/statistics-by-cancer-type/brain-tumours/survival#heading-Zero

—— (2014b). Lung cancer survival statistics. Retrieved from: http://www.cancerresearchuk.org/health-professional/cancer-statistics/statistics-by-cancer-type/lung-cancer/survival#heading-Zero

Carpentier, M. Y. & Fortenberry, J. D. (2010). Romantic and sexual relationships, body image, and fertility in adolescent and young adult testicular cancer survivors: a review of the literature. *Journal of Adolescent Health*, *47*(2), 115–25. doi: http://dx.doi.org/10.1016/j.jadohealth.2010.04.005

Cash, T. F., Melnyk, S. E. & Hrabosky, J. I. (2004). The assessment of body image investment: an extensive revision of the appearance schemas inventory. *Internal Journal of Eating Disorders*, *35*(3), 305–16. doi: http://dx.doi.org/10.1002/eat.10264

Chabrera, C., Zabalegui, A., Bonet, M., Caro, M., Areal, J., Gonzalez, J. R. & Font, A. (2015). A decision aid to support informed choices for patients recently diagnosed with prostate cancer: a randomized controlled trial. *Cancer Nursing*, *38*(3), E42–50. doi: http://dx.doi.org/10.1097/ncc.0000000000000170

Chen, H. M., Tan, W. H., Tan, W. C., Yu, C. K., Lim, T. H., Tay, M. H. & See, H. T. (2006). Attitudes towards cancer survivors: a small survey. *Singapore Medical Journal*, *47*(2), 143–6.

Chien, C. H., Liu, K. L., Chien, H. T. & Liu, H. E. (2014). The effects of psychosocial strategies on anxiety and depression of patients diagnosed with prostate cancer: a systematic review. *International Journal of Nursing Studies*, *51*(1), 28–38. doi: http://dx.doi.org/10.1016/j.ijnurstu.2012.12.019

Chih, M. Y., DuBenske, L. L., Hawkins, R. P., Brown, R. L., Dinauer, S. K., Cleary, J. F. & Gustafson, D. H. (2013). Communicating advanced cancer patients' symptoms via the Internet: a pooled analysis of two randomized trials examining caregiver preparedness, physical burden, and negative mood. *Palliative Medicine*, *27*(6), 533–43.

Cho, J., Smith, K., Choi, E. K., Kim, I. R., Chang, Y. J., Park, H. Y., ... Shim, Y. M. (2013). Public attitudes toward cancer and cancer patients: a national survey in Korea. *Psycho-Oncology*, *22*(3), 605–13. doi: http://dx.doi.org/10.1002/pon.3041

Choi, E. K., Kim, I. R., Chang, O., Kang, D., Nam, S. J., Lee, J. E., ... Cho, J. (2014). Impact of chemotherapy-induced alopecia distress on body image, psychosocial well-being, and depression in breast cancer patients. *Psycho-Oncology*, *23*(10), 1103–10. doi: http://dx.doi.org/10.1002/pon.3531

Clark, J. A., Inui, T. S., Silliman, R. A., Bokhour, B. G., Krasnow, S. H., Robinson, R. A., ... Talcott, J. A. (2003). Patients' perceptions of quality of life after treatment for early prostate cancer. *Journal of Clinical Oncology*, *21*(20), 3777–84. doi: http://dx.doi.org/10.1200/jco.2003.02.115

Collins, K. K., Liu, Y., Schootman, M., Aft, R., Yan, Y., Dean, G., ... Jeffe, D. B. (2011). Effects of breast cancer surgery and surgical side effects on body image over time. *Breast Cancer Research and Treatment, 126*(1), 167–76. doi: http://dx.doi.org/10.1007/s10549-010-1077-7

Compas, B. E., Desjardins, L., Vannatta, K., Young-Saleme, T., Rodriguez, E. M., Dunn, M., ... Gerhardt, C. A. (2014). Children and adolescents coping with cancer: self- and parent reports of coping and anxiety/depression. *Health Psychology, 33*(8), 853–61. doi: http://dx.doi.org/10.1037/hea0000083

Cororve Fingeret, M., Teo, I. & Epner, D. E. (2014). Managing body image difficulties of adult cancer patients. *Cancer, 120*(5), 633–41.

Curt, G. A., Breitbart, W., Cella, D., Groopman, J. E., Horning, S. J., Itri, L. M., ... Vogelzang, N. J. (2000). Impact of cancer-related fatigue on the lives of patients: new findings from the Fatigue Coalition. *Oncologist, 5*(5), 353–360.

Denlinger, C. S. & Barsevick, A. M. (2009). The challenges of colorectal cancer survivorship. *Journal of the National Comprehensive Cancer Network: JNCCN, 7*(8), 883–94. Retrieved from: http://www.ncbi.nlm.nih.gov/pmc/articles/PMC3110673/

Derman, Y. E. & Deatrick, J. A. (2015). Promotion of well-being during treatment for childhood cancer: a literature review of art interventions as a coping strategy. *Cancer Nursing*. doi: http://dx.doi.org/10.1097/ncc.0000000000000318

DeSantis, C. E., Lin, C. C., Mariotto, A. B., Siegel, R. L., Stein, K. D., Kramer, J. L., ... Jemal, A. (2014). Cancer treatment and survivorship statistics, 2014. *CA: A Cancer Journal for Clinicians, 64*(4), 252–71. doi: http://dx.doi.org/10.3322/caac.21235

Di Franco, R., Sammarco, E., Calvanese, M. G., De Natale, F., Falivene, S., Di Lecce, A., ... Ravo, V. (2013). Preventing the acute skin side effects in patients treated with radiotherapy for breast cancer: the use of corneometry in order to evaluate the protective effect of moisturizing creams. *Radiation Oncology (London, England), 8*, 57. doi: http://dx.doi.org/10.1186/1748-717X-8-57

Drageset, S., Lindstrom, T. C. & Underlid, K. (2010). Coping with breast cancer: between diagnosis and surgery. *Journal of Advanced Nursing, 66*(1), 149–58. doi: http://dx.doi.org/10.1111/j.1365-2648.2009.05210.x

Elliott, K.-E. J., Scott, J. L., Monsour, M. & Nuwayhid, F. (2015). Profiles of dyadic adjustment for advanced prostate cancer to inform couple-based intervention. *Psychology & Health, 30*(11), 1259–73. doi: http://dx.doi.org/10.1080/08870446.2015.1043301

Falk Dahl, C. A., Reinertsen, K. V., Nesvold, I. L., Fossa, S. D. & Dahl, A. A. (2010). A study of body image in long-term breast cancer survivors. *Cancer, 116*(15), 3549–57. doi: http://dx.doi.org/10.1002/cncr.25251

Fallbjork, U., Rasmussen, B. H., Karlsson, S. & Salander, P. (2013). Aspects of body image after mastectomy due to breast cancer – a two-year follow-up study. *European Journal of Oncology Nursing, 17*(3), 340–5. doi: http://dx.doi.org/10.1016/j.ejon.2012.09.002

Fann, J. R., Thomas-Rich, A. M., Katon, W. J., Cowley, D., Pepping, M., McGregor, B. A. & Gralow, J. (2008). Major depression after breast cancer: a review of epidemiology and treatment. *General Hospital Psychiatry, 30*(2), 112–26. doi: http://dx.doi.org/10.1016/j.genhosppsych.2007.10.008

Feldstein, A. C., Perrin, N., Rosales, A. G., Schneider, J., Rix, M. M. & Glasgow, R. E. (2011). Patient barriers to mammography identified during a reminder program. *Journal of Women's Health, 20*(3), 421–8. doi: http://dx.doi.org/10.1089/jwh.2010.2195

Feuerstein, M. (2007). Defining cancer survivorship. *Journal of Cancer Survivorship, 1*(1), 5–7. doi: http://dx.doi.org/10.1007/s11764-006-0002-x

Fingeret, M. C., Hutcheson, K. A., Jensen, K., Yuan, Y., Urbauer, D. & Lewin, J. S. (2013). Associations among speech, eating, and body image concerns for surgical patients with head and neck cancer. *Head & Neck, 35*(3), 354–60. doi: http://dx.doi.org/10.1002/hed.22980

Fingeret, M. C., Nipomnick, S., Guindani, M., Baumann, D., Hanasono, M. & Crosby, M. (2014). Body image screening for cancer patients undergoing reconstructive surgery. *Psycho-Oncology, 23*(8), 898–905. doi: http://dx.doi.org/10.1002/pon.3491

Fingeret, M. C., Teo, I. & Epner, D. E. (2014). Managing body image difficulties of adult cancer patients: lessons from available research. *Cancer, 120*(5), 633–41. doi: http://dx.doi.org/10.1002/cncr.28469

Fingeret, M. C., Yuan, Y., Urbauer, D., Weston, J., Nipomnick, S. & Weber, R. (2012). The nature and extent of body image concerns among surgically treated patients with head and neck cancer. *Psycho-Oncology*, *21*(8), 836–44. doi: http://dx.doi.org/10.1002/pon.1990

Foster, C. & Fenlon, D. (2011). Recovery and self-management support following primary cancer treatment. *British Journal of Cancer*, *105*(Suppl 1), S21–8. doi: http://dx.doi.org/10.1038/bjc.2011.419

Foster, R. H. & Stern, M. (2014). Peer and romantic relationships among adolescent and young adult survivors of childhood hematological cancer: a review of challenges and positive outcomes. *Acta Haematologica*, *132*(3–4), 375–82. doi: http://dx.doi.org/10.1159/000360239

Garland, S. N., Tamagawa, R., Todd, S. C., Speca, M. & Carlson, L. E. (2013). Increased mindfulness is related to improved stress and mood following participation in a mindfulness-based stress reduction program in individuals with cancer. *Integrative Cancer Therapies*, *12*(1), 31–40. doi: http://dx.doi.org/10.1177/1534735412442370

Ghazali, N., Cadwallader, E., Lowe, D., Humphris, G., Ozakinci, G. & Rogers, S. N. (2013). Fear of recurrence among head and neck cancer survivors: longitudinal trends. *Psycho-Oncology*, *22*(4), 807–13. doi: http://dx.doi.org/10.1002/pon.3069

Gopie, J. P., Mureau, M. A., Seynaeve, C., Ter Kuile, M. M., Menke-Pluymers, M. B., Timman, R. & Tibben, A. (2013). Body image issues after bilateral prophylactic mastectomy with breast reconstruction in healthy women at risk for hereditary breast cancer. *Family Cancer*, *12*(3), 479–87. doi: http://dx.doi.org/10.1007/s10689-012-9588-5

Halkett, G. K., Kristjanson, L. J. & Lobb, E. A. (2008). 'If we get too close to your bones they'll go brittle': women's initial fears about radiotherapy for early breast cancer. *Psycho-Oncology*, *17*(9), 877–84. doi: http://dx.doi.org/10.1002/pon.1298

Harrington, J. M., Jones, E. G. & Badger, T. (2009). Body image perceptions in men with prostate cancer. *Oncology Nursing Forum*, *36*(2), 167–72. doi: http://dx.doi.org/10.1188/09.onf.167–172

Hart, S. L., Hoyt, M. A., Diefenbach, M., Anderson, D. R., Kilbourn, K. M., Craft, L. L., ... Stanton, A. L. (2012). Meta-analysis of efficacy of interventions for elevated depressive symptoms in adults diagnosed with cancer. *Journal of the National Cancer Institute*, *104*(13), 990–1004. doi: http://dx.doi.org/10.1093/jnci/djs256

Hawkins, N. A., Benard, V. B., Greek, A., Roland, K. B., Manninen, D. & Saraiya, M. (2013). Patient knowledge and beliefs as barriers to extending cervical cancer screening intervals in Federally Qualified Health Centers. *Preventative Medicine*, *57*(5), 641–5. doi: http://dx.doi.org/10.1016/j.ypmed.2013.08.021

Heiniger, L., Butow, P. N., Charles, M. & Price, M. A. (2015). Intuition versus cognition: a qualitative exploration of how women understand and manage their increased breast cancer risk. *Journal of Behavioral Medicine*, *38*(5), 727–39. doi: http://dx.doi.org/10.1007/s10865-015-9632-7

Helgeson, V. S., Cohen, S., Schulz, R. & Yasko, J. (1999). Education and peer discussion group interventions and adjustment to breast cancer. *Archives of General Psychiatry*, *56*(4), 340–7.

Helms, R. L., O'Hea, E. L. & Corso, M. (2008). Body image issues in women with breast cancer. *Psychology, Health & Medicine*, *13*(3), 313–25. doi: http://dx.doi.org/10.1080/13548500701405509

Hess, C. B. & Chen, A. M. (2014). Measuring psychosocial functioning in the radiation oncology clinic: a systematic review. *Psycho-Oncology*, *23*(8), 841–54. doi: http://dx.doi.org/10.1002/pon.3521

Hipkins, J., Whitworth, M., Tarrier, N. & Jayson, G. (2004). Social support, anxiety and depression after chemotherapy for ovarian cancer: a prospective study. *British Journal of Health Psychology*, *9*(Pt 4), 569–81. doi: http://dx.doi.org/10.1348/1359107042304542

Hudson, M. M., Mertens, A. C., Yasui, Y., Hobbie, W., Chen, H., Gurney, J. G., ... Oeffinger, K. C. (2003). Health status of adult long-term survivors of childhood cancer: a report from the Childhood Cancer Survivor Study. *JAMA*, *290*(12), 1583–92. doi: http://dx.doi.org/10.1001/jama.290.12.1583

Hughes, M. K. (2000). Sexuality and the cancer survivor: a silent coexistence. *Cancer Nursing*, *23*(6), 477–82.

Huizinga, G. A., Visser, A., van der Graaf, W. T., Hoekstra, H. J., Klip, E. C., Pras, E. & Hoekstra-Weebers, J. E. (2005). Stress response symptoms in adolescent and young adult children of parents diagnosed with cancer. *European Journal of Cancer*, *41*(2), 288–95.

Ilic, D., Jammal, W., Chiarelli, P., Gardiner, R. A., Hughes, S., Stefanovic, D. & Chambers, S. K. (2015). Assessing the effectiveness of decision aids for decision making in prostate cancer testing: a systematic review. *Psycho-Oncology*. doi: http://dx.doi.org/10.1002/pon.3815

Jemal, A., Bray, F., Center, M. M., Ferlay, J., Ward, E. & Forman, D. (2011). Global cancer statistics. *CA: A Cancer Journal for Clinicians*, *61*(2), 69–90. doi: http://dx.doi.org/10.3322/caac.20107

Jereczek-Fossa, B. A., Marsiglia, H. R. & Orecchia, R. (2002). Radiotherapy-related fatigue. *Critical Reviews in Oncology/Hematology*, *41*(3), 317–25.

Jones, R. M., Devers, K. J., Kuzel, A. J. & Woolf, S. H. (2010). Patient-reported barriers to colorectal cancer screening: a mixed-methods analysis. *American Journal of Preventive Medicine*, *38*(5), 508–16. doi: http://dx.doi.org/10.1016/j.amepre.2010.01.021

Kalaitzi, C., Papadopoulos, V. P., Michas, K., Vlasis, K., Skandalakis, P. & Filippou, D. (2007). Combined brief psychosexual intervention after mastectomy: effects on sexuality, body image, and psychological well-being. *Journal of Surgical Oncology*, *96*(3), 235–40. doi: http://dx.doi.org/10.1002/jso.20811

Katapodi, M. C., Lee, K. A., Facione, N. C. & Dodd, M. J. (2004). Predictors of perceived breast cancer risk and the relation between perceived risk and breast cancer screening: a meta-analytic review. *Preventative Medicine*, *38*(4), 388–402. doi: http://dx.doi.org/10.1016/j.ypmed.2003.11.012

Keeney, S., McKenna, H., Fleming, P. & McIlfatrick, S. (2010). Attitudes to cancer and cancer prevention: what do people aged 35–54 years think? *European Journal of Cancer Care*, *19*(6), 769–77. doi: http://dx.doi.org/10.1111/j.1365-2354.2009.01137.x

Koch, L., Bertram, H., Eberle, A., Holleczek, B., Schmid-Hopfner, S., Waldmann, A., … Arndt, V. (2014). Fear of recurrence in long-term breast cancer survivors-still an issue. Results on prevalence, determinants, and the association with quality of life and depression from the cancer survivorship – a multi-regional population-based study. *Psycho-Oncology*, *23*(5), 547–554. doi: http://dx.doi.org/10.1002/pon.3452

Koocher, G., Curtiss, E., Pollin, I. & Patton, K. (2001). Medical crisis counselling in a health maintenance organization: preventive intervention. *Professional Psychology: Research and Practice*, *32*, 52–8. Retrieved from: http://dx.doi.org/10.1037/0735-7028.32.1.52

Krattenmacher, T., Kuhne, F., Fuhrer, D., Beierlein, V., Brähler, E., Resch, F., … Moller, B. (2013). Coping skills and mental health status in adolescents when a parent has cancer: a multicenter and multi-perspective study. *Journal of Psychosomatic Research*, *74*(3), 252–9.

Lambertini, M., Anserini, P., Levaggi, A., Poggio, F. & Del Mastro, L. (2013). Fertility counseling of young breast cancer patients. *Journal of Thoracic Disease*, *5*(Suppl 1), S68–80. doi: http://dx.doi.org/10.3978/j.issn.2072-1439.2013.05.22

Lander, E. S., Linton, L. M., Birren, B., Nusbaum, C., Zody, M. C., Baldwin, J., … Chen, Y. J. (2001). Initial sequencing and analysis of the human genome. *Nature*, *409*(6822), 860–921.

Leighl, N. B., Shepherd, F. A., Zawisza, D., Burkes, R. L., Feld, R., Waldron, J., … Tattersall, M. H. N. (2008). Enhancing treatment decision-making: pilot study of a treatment decision aid in stage IV non-small cell lung cancer. *British Journal of Cancer*, *98*(11), 1769–73. doi: http://dx.doi.org/10.1038/sj.bjc.6604395

Lengacher, C. A., Reich, R. R., Post-White, J., Moscoso, M., Shelton, M. M., Barta, M., … Budhrani, P. (2012). Mindfulness based stress reduction in post-treatment breast cancer patients: an examination of symptoms and symptom clusters. *Journal of Behavioral Medicine*, *35*(1), 86–94. doi: http://dx.doi.org/10.1007/s10865-011-9346-4

Li, Q. & Loke, A. Y. (2014). A systematic review of spousal couple-based intervention studies for couples coping with cancer: direction for the development of interventions. *Psycho-Oncology*, *23*(7), 731–9. doi: http://dx.doi.org/10.1002/pon.3535

Lin, G. A., Aaronson, D. S., Knight, S. J., Carroll, P. R. & Dudley, R. A. (2009). Patient decision aids for prostate cancer treatment: a systematic review of the literature. *CA: A Cancer Journal for Clinicians*, *59*(6), 379–90. doi: http://dx.doi.org/10.3322/caac.20039

Lind, H., Waldenström, A. C., Dunberger, G., al-Abany, M., Alevronta, E., Johansson, K. A. … Åvall-Lundqvist, E. (2011). Late symptoms in long-term gynaecological cancer survivors after radiation therapy: a population-based cohort study. *British Journal of Cancer*, *105*(6), 737–45. doi: http://dx.doi.org/10.1038/bjc.2011.315

Manne, S. L., Ostroff, J. S., Norton, T. R., Fox, K., Goldstein, L. & Grana, G. (2006). Cancer-related relationship communication in couples coping with early stage breast cancer. *Psycho-Oncology*, *15*(3), 234–47.

Markovitz, S. E., Schrooten, W., Arntz, A. & Peters, M. L. (2015). Resilience as a predictor for emotional response to the diagnosis and surgery in breast cancer patients. *Psycho-Oncology*, 24(12), 1639–45. doi: http://dx.doi.org/10.1002/pon.3834

Massie, M. J., Gagnon, P. & Holland, J. C. (1994). Depression and suicide in patients with cancer. *Journal of Pain and Symptom Management, 9*(5), 325–40.

McKiernan, A., Steggles, S., Guerin, S. & Carr, A. (2010). A controlled trial of group cognitive behavior therapy for Irish breast cancer patients. *Journal of Psychosocial Oncology*, *28*(2), 143–56. doi: http://dx.doi.org/10.1080/07347330903570511

Miller, S. M. (1995). Monitoring versus blunting styles of coping with cancer influence the information patients want and need about their disease. Implications for cancer screening and management. *Cancer*, *76*(2), 167–77. Retrieved from: http://www.ncbi.nlm.nih.gov/pubmed/8625088

Miller, S. M., Fleisher, L., Roussi, P., Buzaglo, J. S., Schnoll, R., Slater, E., ... Popa-Mabe, M. (2005). Facilitating informed decision making about breast cancer risk and genetic counseling among women calling the NCI's Cancer Information Service. *Journal of Health Communication*, *1*, 119–36.

Mitchell, A. J., Ferguson, D. W., Gill, J., Paul, J. & Symonds, P. (2013). Depression and anxiety in long-term cancer survivors compared with spouses and healthy controls: a systematic review and meta-analysis. *The Lancet Oncology*, *14*(8), 721–32. doi: http://dx.doi.org/10.1016/s1470-2045(13)70244-4

Mitchell, S. A., Hoffman, A. J., Clark, J. C., DeGennaro, R. M., Poirier, P., Robinson, C. B. & Weisbrod, B. L. (2014). Putting evidence into practice: an update of evidence-based interventions for cancer-related fatigue during and following treatment. *Clinical Journal of Oncology Nursing*, *18*, 38–58. doi: http://dx.doi.org/10.1188/14.cjon.s3.38–58

Mitsonis, C., Dimopoulos, N., Zavrou, M., Psarra, V., Giofkos, C., Fiorakis, C., ... Papavassiliou, E. (2011). Panic attack during elective gastrointestinal endoscopy. *Gastroenterology Research and Practice*, *2011*, 162574. doi: http://dx.doi.org/10.1155/2011/162574

Moore, E. E., Wark, J. D., Hopper, J. L., Erbas, B. & Garland, S. M. (2012). The roles of genetic and environmental factors on risk of cervical cancer: a review of classical twin studies. *Twin Research and Human Genetics*, *15*(1), 79–86. doi: http://dx.doi.org/10.1375/twin.15.1.79

Moreira, H., Silva, S. & Canavarro, M. C. (2010). The role of appearance investment in the adjustment of women with breast cancer. *Psycho-Oncology*, *19*(9), 959–66. doi: http://dx.doi.org/10.1002/pon.1647

Murray, S. A., Kendall, M., Boyd, K. & Sheikh, A. (2005). Illness trajectories and palliative care. *BMJ: British Medical Journal*, *330*(7498), 1007–11. Retrieved from: http://www.ncbi.nlm.nih.gov/pmc/articles/PMC557152/

Myers, R. E., Ruth, K., Manne, S. L., Cocroft, J., Sifri, R., Ziring, B., ... Weinberg, D. S. (2015). Effects of genetic and environmental risk assessment feedback on colorectal cancer screening adherence. *Journal of Behavioral Medicine, 38*(5), 777–786. doi: http://dx.doi.org/10.1007/s10865-015-9626-5

Naaman, S. C., Radwan, K., Fergusson, D. & Johnson, S. (2009). Status of psychological trials in breast cancer patients: a report of three meta-analyses. *Psychiatry*, *72*(1), 50–69. doi: http://dx.doi.org/10.1521/psyc.2009.72.1.50

National Cancer Institute. (2012). Radiation therapy and you. National Cancer Institute, US Department of Health and Human Services, National Institutes of Health. Retrieved from http://www.cancer.gov/publications/patient-education/radiationttherapy.pdf

Ness, S., Kokal, J., Fee-Schroeder, K., Novotny, P., Satele, D. & Barton, D. (2013). Concerns across the survivorship trajectory: results from a survey of cancer survivors. *Oncology Nursing Forum*, *40*(1), 35–42. doi: http://dx.doi.org/10.1188/13.onf.35–42

Nickels, S., Truong, T., Hein, R., Stevens, K., Buck, K., Behrens, S., ... Chang-Claude, J. (2013). Evidence of gene-environment interactions between common breast cancer susceptibility loci and established environmental risk factors. *PLoS Genetics*, *9*(3), e1003284. doi: http://dx.doi.org/10.1371/journal.pgen.1003284

Peate, M., Meiser, B., Cheah, B. C., Saunders, C., Butow, P., Thewes, B., ... Friedlander, M. (2012). Making hard choices easier: a prospective, multicentre study to assess the efficacy of a fertility-related decision aid in young women with early-stage breast cancer. *British Journal of Cancer*, *106*(6), 1053–61. doi: http://dx.doi.org/10.1038/bjc.2012.61

Peate, M., Meiser, B., Friedlander, M., Saunders, C., Martinello, R., Wakefield, C. E. & Hickey, M. (2011). Development and pilot testing of a fertility decision aid for young women diagnosed with early breast cancer. *The Breast Journal*, *17*(1), 112–14. doi: http://dx.doi.org/10.1111/j.1524-4741.2010.01033.x

Peeters, K. C., van de Velde, C. J., Leer, J. W., Martijn, H., Junggeburt, J. M., Kranenbarg, E. K., ... Marijnen, C. A. (2005). Late side effects of short-course preoperative radiotherapy combined with total mesorectal excision for rectal cancer: increased bowel dysfunction in irradiated patients – a Dutch colorectal cancer group study. *Journal of Clinical Oncology*, *23*(25), 6199–206. doi: http://dx.doi.org/10.1200/jco.2005.14.779

Petrek, J. A., Senie, R. T., Peters, M. & Rosen, P. P. (2001). Lymphedema in a cohort of breast carcinoma survivors 20 years after diagnosis. *Cancer*, *92*(6), 1368–77.

Philip, E. J., Merluzzi, T. V., Zhang, Z. & Heitzmann, C. A. (2013). Depression and cancer survivorship: importance of coping self-efficacy in post-treatment survivors. *Psycho-Oncology*, *22*(5), 987–94. doi: http://dx.doi.org/10.1002/pon.3088

Piet, J., Wurtzen, H. & Zachariae, R. (2012). The effect of mindfulness-based therapy on symptoms of anxiety and depression in adult cancer patients and survivors: a systematic review and meta-analysis. *Journal of Consulting and Clinical Psychology*, *80*(6), 1007–20. doi: http://dx.doi.org/10.1037/a0028329

Ramirez, L. Y., Huestis, S. E., Yi Yap, T., Zyzanski, S., Drotar, D. & Kodish, E. (2009). Potential chemotherapy side effects: what do oncologists tell parents? *Pediatric Blood & Cancer*, *52*(4), 497–502. doi: http://dx.doi.org/10.1002/pbc.21835

Richiardi, L., Pettersson, A. & Akre, O. (2007). Genetic and environmental risk factors for testicular cancer. *International Journal of Andrology*, *30*(4), 230–40. doi: http://dx.doi.org/10.1111/j.1365-2605.2007.00760.x

Ridner, S. H. (2009). The psycho-social impact of lymphedema. *Lymphatic Research and Biology*, *7*(2), 109–12. doi: http://dx.doi.org/10.1089/lrb.2009.0004

Robinson, S., Kissane, D. W., Brooker, J. & Burney, S. (2015). A systematic review of the demoralization syndrome in individuals with progressive disease and cancer: a decade of research. *Journal of Pain and Symptom Management*, *49*(3), 595–610.

Rolland, J. S. (2005). Cancer and the family: an integrative model. *Cancer*, *104*(11 Suppl), 2584–95.

Roth, A. J. & Massie, M. J. (2007). Anxiety and its management in advanced cancer. *Current Opinion in Support and Palliative Care*, *1*(1), 50–6.

Roussi, P. & Miller, S. M. (2014). Monitoring style of coping with cancer-related threats: a review of the literature. *Journal of Behavioral Medicine*, *37*(5), 931–54. doi: http://dx.doi.org/10.1007/s10865-014-9553-x

Sadovsky, R., Basson, R., Krychman, M., Morales, A. M., Schover, L., Wang, R. & Incrocci, L. (2010). Cancer and sexual problems. *Journal of Sexual Medicine*, *7*, 349–73. doi: http://dx.doi.org/10.1111/j.1743-6109.2009.01620.x

Savard, J. & Ivers, H. (2013). The evolution of fear of cancer recurrence during the cancer care trajectory and its relationship with cancer characteristics. *Journal of Psychosomatic Research*, *74*(4), 354–60. doi: http://dx.doi.org/10.1016/j.jpsychores.2012.12.013

Schernhammer, E., Haidinger, G., Waldhor, T., Vargas, R. & Vutuc, C. (2010). A study of trends in beliefs and attitudes toward cancer. *Journal of Cancer Education*, *25*(2), 211–16. doi: http://dx.doi.org/10.1007/s13187-010-0104-z

Schofield, P., Carey, M., Love, A., Nehill, C. & Wein, S. (2006). 'Would you like to talk about your future treatment options'? Discussing the transition from curative cancer treatment to palliative care. *Palliative Medicine*, *20*(4), 397–406.

Schubart, J. R., Kinzie, M. B. & Farace, E. (2008). Caring for the brain tumor patient: family caregiver burden and unmet needs. *Neuro-Oncology*, *10*(1), 61–72. doi: http://dx.doi.org/10.1215/15228517-2007-040

Scott, J. L., Halford, W. K. & Ward, B. G. (2004). United we stand? The effects of a couple-coping intervention on adjustment to early stage breast or gynecological cancer. *Journal of Consulting and Clinical Psychology, 72*(6), 1122–35.

Segrin, C., Badger, T., Dorros, S. M., Meek, P. & Lopez, A. M. (2007). Interdependent anxiety and psychological distress in women with breast cancer and their partners. *Psycho-Oncology*, *16*(7), 634–43.

Semple, C. J., Sullivan, K., Dunwoody, L. & Kernohan, W. G. (2004). Psychosocial interventions for patients with head and neck cancer: past, present, and future. *Cancer Nursing*, *27*(6), 434–41.

Sepúlveda, C., Marlin, A., Yoshida, T. & Ullrich, A. (2002). Palliative care: the World Health Organization's global perspective. *Journal of Pain and Symptom Management, 24*(2), 91–6. doi: http://dx.doi.org/http://dx.doi.org/10.1016/S0885-3924(02)00440-2

Shah, S. G., Brooker, J. C., Thapar, C., Williams, C. B. & Saunders, B. P. (2002). Patient pain during colonoscopy: an analysis using real-time magnetic endoscope imaging. *Endoscopy*, *34*(6), 435–40. doi: http://dx.doi.org/10.1055/s-2002–31995

Sharplin, G. R., Jones, S. B., Hancock, B., Knott, V. E., Bowden, J. A. & Whitford, H. S. (2010). Mindfulness-based cognitive therapy: an efficacious community-based group intervention for depression and anxiety in a sample of cancer patients. *Medical Journal of Australia*, *193*(5 Suppl), S79–82.

Sheehan, J. & Sherman, K. A. (2012). Computerised decision aids: a systematic review of their effectiveness in facilitating high-quality decision-making in various health-related contexts. *Patient Education and Counseling, 88*(1), 69–86. doi: http://dx.doi.org/10.1016/j.pec.2011.11.006

Sherman, K., Shaw, L. K., Champion, K., Caldeira, F. & McCaskill, M. (2015). The effect of disease risk probability and disease type on interest in clinic-based versus direct-to-consumer genetic testing services. *Journal of Behavioral Medicine*, *38*(5), 706–14.

Sherman, K. A. & Cameron, L. D. (2015, Oct). Current directions in behavioral medicine research on genetic testing for disease susceptibility: introduction to the special section. *Journal of Behavioral Medicine*, *38*(5), 701–5. doi: http://dx.doi.org/10.1007/s10865-015-9674-x.

Sherman, K. A., Harcourt, D. M., Lam, T. C., Shaw, L. K. & Boyages, J. (2014). BRECONDA: development and acceptability of an interactive decisional support tool for women considering breast reconstruction. *Psycho-Oncology*, *23*(7), 835–8. doi: http://dx.doi.org/10.1002/pon.3498

Sherman, K. A., Kasparian, N. A. & Mireskandari, S. (2010). Psychological adjustment among male partners in response to women's breast/ovarian cancer risk: a theoretical review of the literature. *Psycho-Oncology*, *19*(1), 1–11.

Shontz, F. C. (1975). *The Psychological Aspects of Physical Illness and Disability*. New York: Macmillan.

Siegel, R., DeSantis, C., Virgo, K., Stein, K., Mariotto, A., Smith, T., ... Ward, E. (2012). Cancer treatment and survivorship statistics, 2012. *CA: A Cancer Journal for Clinicians*, *62*(4), 220–41. doi: http://dx.doi.org/10.3322/caac.21149

Simard, S., Thewes, B., Humphris, G., Dixon, M., Hayden, C., Mireskandari, S. & Ozakinci, G. (2013). Fear of cancer recurrence in adult cancer survivors: a systematic review of quantitative studies. *Journal of Cancer Survivorship*, *7*(3), 300–22. doi: http://dx.doi.org/10.1007/s11764-013-0272-z

Smith, A., Thewes, B., Turner, J., Gilchrist, J., Fardell, J., Sharpe, L., ... Butow, P. (2015). Pilot of a theoretically grounded psychologist-delivered intervention for fear of cancer recurrence (Conquer Fear). *Psycho-Oncology*, *24*(8), 967–70. doi: http://dx.doi.org/10.1002/pon.3775

Smith, A. B., Butow, P., Olver, I., Luckett, T., Grimison, P., Toner, G. C., ... King, M. T. (2015). The prevalence, severity, and correlates of psychological distress and impaired health-related quality of life following treatment for testicular cancer: a survivorship study. *Journal of Cancer Survivorship*. doi: http://dx.doi.org/10.1007/s11764-015-0468-5

Stacey, D., Legare, F., Col, N. F., Bennett, C. L., Barry, M. J., Eden, K. B., ... Wu, J. H. (2014). Decision aids for people facing health treatment or screening decisions. *Cochrane Database of Systematic Reviews*, *1*, Cd001431. doi: http://dx.doi.org/10.1002/14651858.CD001431.pub4

Stagl, J. M., Lechner, S. C., Carver, C. S., Bouchard, L. C., Gudenkauf, L. M., Jutagir, D. R., ... Antoni, M. H. (2015). A randomized controlled trial of cognitive-behavioral stress management in breast cancer: survival and recurrence at 11-year follow-up. *Breast Cancer Research and Treatment*, *154*(2), 319–28. doi: http://dx.doi.org/10.1007/s10549-015-3626-6

Stanton, A. L., Danoff-Burg, S. & Huggins, M. E. (2002). The first year after breast cancer diagnosis: hope and coping strategies as predictors of adjustment. *Psycho-Oncology*, *11*(2), 93–102.

Taber, J. M., Aspinwall, L. G., Stump, T. K., Kohlmann, W., Champine, M. & Leachman, S. A. (2015). Genetic test reporting enhances understanding of risk information and acceptance of prevention recommendations compared to family history-based counseling alone. *Journal of Behavioral Medicine, 38*(5), 740–53.

Taylor, S., Harley, C., Ziegler, L., Brown, J. & Velikova, G. (2011). Interventions for sexual problems following treatment for breast cancer: a systematic review. *Breast Cancer Research and Treatment, 130*, 711–24. doi: http://dx.doi.org/10.1007/s10549-011-1722-9

Taylor-Ford, M., Meyerowitz, B. E., D'Orazio, L. M., Christie, K. M., Gross, M. E. & Agus, D. B. (2013). Body image predicts quality of life in men with prostate cancer. *Psycho-Oncology, 22*(4), 756–61. doi: http://dx.doi.org/10.1002/pon.3063

Thewes, B., Brebach, R., Dzidowska, M., Rhodes, P., Sharpe, L. & Butow, P. (2014). Current approaches to managing fear of cancer recurrence: a descriptive survey of psychosocial and clinical health professionals. *Psycho-Oncology, 23*(4), 390–6. doi: http://dx.doi.org/10.1002/pon.3423

Thornton, L. M., Levin, A. O., Dorfman, C. S., Godiwala, N., Heitzmann, C. & Andersen, B. L. (2014). Emotions and social relationships for breast and gynecologic patients: a qualitative study of coping with recurrence. *Psycho-Oncology, 23*(4), 382–9. doi: http://dx.doi.org/10.1002/pon.3429

Tierney, K. D. (2008). Sexuality: a quality of life issue for cancer survivors. *Seminars in Oncology Nursing, 24*(2), 71–9. doi: http://dx.doi.org/10.1016/j.soncn.2008.02.001

Todd, A. & Stuifbergen, A. (2011). Barriers and facilitators related to breast cancer screening: a qualitative study of women with multiple sclerosis. *International Journal of MS Care, 13*(2), 49–56. doi: http://dx.doi.org/10.7224/1537-2073-13.2.49

Tomlinson, D., Diorio, C., Beyene, J. & Sung, L. (2014). Effect of exercise on cancer-related fatigue: a meta-analysis. *American Journal of Physical Medicine & Rehabilitation, 93*(8), 675–86. doi: http://dx.doi.org/10.1097/phm.0000000000000083

Tsai, H. F., Chen, Y. R., Chung, M. H., Liao, Y. M., Chi, M. J., Chang, C. C. & Chou, K. R. (2014). Effectiveness of music intervention in ameliorating cancer patients' anxiety, depression, pain, and fatigue: a meta-analysis. *Cancer Nursing, 37*(6), E35–50. doi: http://dx.doi.org/10.1097/ncc.0000000000000116

Ussher, J. M., Perz, J. & Gilbert, E. (2012). Changes to sexual well-being and intimacy after breast cancer. *Cancer Nursing, 35*(6), 456–65. doi: http://dx.doi.org/10.1097/NCC.0b013e3182395401

Vermeer, W. M., Bakker, R. M., Kenter, G. G., Stiggelbout, A. M. & Ter Kuile, M. M. (2015). Cervical cancer survivors' and partners' experiences with sexual dysfunction and psychosexual support. *Support Care Cancer*. doi: http://dx.doi.org/10.1007/s00520-015-2925-0

Vodermaier, A., Caspari, C., Wang, L., Koehm, J., Ditsch, N. & Untch, M. (2011). How and for whom are decision aids effective? Long-term psychological outcome of a randomized controlled trial in women with newly diagnosed breast cancer. *Health Psychology, 30*(1), 12–19. doi: http://dx.doi.org/10.1037/a0021648

Weinberg, D. S., Myers, R. E., Keenan, E., Ruth, K., Sifri, R., Ziring, B., ... Manne, S. L. (2014). Gene environment risk assessment and colorectal cancer screening in an average risk population: a randomized, controlled trial. *Annals of Internal Medicine, 161*(8), 537–45. doi: http://dx.doi.org/10.7326/M14-0765

Wright, G. P., Wong, J. H., Morgan, J. W., Roy-Chowdhury, S., Kazanjian, K. & Lum, S. S. (2010). Time from diagnosis to surgical treatment of breast cancer: factors influencing delays in initiating treatment. *The American Surgeon, 76*(10), 1119–22.

Wu, G., Feder, A., Cohen, H., Kim, J. J., Calderon, S., Charney, D. S. & Mathé, A. A. (2013). Understanding resilience. *Frontiers in Behavioral Neuroscience, 7*, 10. doi: http://dx.doi.org/10.3389/fnbeh.2013.00010

Wurtzen, H., Dalton, S. O., Christensen, J., Andersen, K. K., Elsass, P., Flyger, H. L., ... Johansen, C. (2015). Effect of mindfulness-based stress reduction on somatic symptoms, distress, mindfulness and spiritual wellbeing in women with breast cancer: results of a randomized controlled trial. *Acta Oncologica, 54*(5), 712–19. doi: http://dx.doi.org/10.3109/0284186x.2014.997371

Yu, Y. & Sherman, K. A. (2015). Communication avoidance, coping and psychological distress of women with breast cancer. *Journal of Behavioral Medicine, 38*(3), 565–77.

Zachariae, R., Jensen, A. B., Pedersen, C., Jorgensen, M. M., Christensen, S., Lassesen, B. & Lehbrink, M. (2004). Repressive coping before and after diagnosis of breast cancer. *Psycho-Oncology, 13*(8), 547–61. doi: http://dx.doi.org/10.1002/pon.772

11

Pain and its optimal management

Learning outcomes

After reading this chapter, you should be able to:

- understand the basic physiology underlying the experience of pain
- describe the biopsychosocial perspective of pain
- understand the problems that arise when acute pain becomes chronic/persistent
- understand the psychological theory associated with the psychosocial management of chronic pain
- have a basic understanding of current evidence-based psychosocial approaches for the management of chronic pain
- know what is needed in the field of pain management, from a health psychology perspective, to optimise treatment and public healthcare resources.

Introduction

Pain is a highly complex, universal phenomenon that at some point in our lives nearly all of us have experienced. At its core, pain is adaptive and is as essential to our everyday existence as being able to see, hear, touch, taste and smell; the reason is that pain entails a 'withdrawal' function designed to prevent and/or minimise harm to our body. Rare individuals who are born with a congenital insensitivity to pain experience an abnormal number of injuries, such as cuts, burns and infections, due to their inability to perceive and respond appropriately to painful stimuli, and they usually die young. Such individuals do not know how to avoid activities that cause harm, and are unable to report when they are feeling ill (Melzack & Wall, 1982).

Most often, especially when we are young and relatively healthy, pain naturally diminishes as the source (i.e. the injury of whatever form) heals. However, in some cases, pain persists beyond the normal or expected healing time, and pain becomes chronic. Chronic pain is pain that extends for at least 3 to 6 months (depending on the classification system used), and it affects hundreds of millions of individuals worldwide (Task Force on Taxonomy, IASP, 1994). It is not only associated with critically high financial costs, but also carries with it a tremendous emotional, social and psychological burden. Health psychologists have an important role in helping to effectively rehabilitate individuals with acute pain following injury. However, in today's healthcare setting (where medical interventions such as surgery and medication are typically the go-to choice in acute pain), health psychologists are more typically called to intervene at the point at which pain becomes chronic. Thus, chronic pain will be the primary focus of this chapter. Health psychologists work collaboratively with individuals to help them develop a nonpharmacological skill set that they can use to effectively cope with and manage daily ongoing chronic pain.

The physiology of pain

The now widely held understanding of the role the brain plays in actively processing pain has been a relatively recent scientific development. Mounting evidence documenting the important role of cognition and emotion in pain culminated in a tipping point of dissatisfaction with the reductionistic, mechanistic, biomedical conceptualisation. In the mid-1960s, a revolutionary theory in the area of pain was proposed by Melzack and Wall (Melzack & Wall, 1965, 1982). This unified pain theory, the **gate control theory**, took into account the unique and highly interconnected role of neurophysiological pathways, thoughts, emotions and behaviour in determining the experience we call 'pain'.

Historical and theoretical conceptualisations

Historically, the biomedical model dominated illness and pain conceptualisation for almost 300 years, right up until approximately midway through the last century (Thorn, 2004). The biomedical approach, which describes pain purely in physical terms, originates from the 17th century when Descartes promoted mind–body dualism; that is, that the mind and body were separate entities, and while the body was under the auspices of scientific investigation, the mind and the brain were not. In this approach, the brain was considered to play a passive, receptive role for pain signals, and psychosocial factors were considered essentially irrelevant. However, with the emergence of numerous documented cases where the amount of tissue damage was not a 1:1 predictor of the experience of pain, this understanding came to be viewed with growing scepticism. For example, athletes will often play through a game with a severe injury, a parent will run through intense fire to rescue their child from a burning house and when yogis are in deep meditation they do not feel pain.

In their revolutionary gate control theory of pain, Melzack and Wall (1965, 1982) first proposed that the brain is actively involved in the interpretive processing of the sensory pain experience, as opposed to being a passive recipient of pain signals from a peripheral pain generator (i.e. the identified 'source' of injury/pain). They emphasised that cognitive and emotional activity played a key determinative function in the amount of pain signals processed in the brain and, associated with this, the amount of pain perceived. According to this model, the immediate experience of pain entails three fundamental, highly interconnected neurological brain mechanisms: 1. sensory; 2. evaluative; and 3. affective/ motivational. Thus, there are unique somatosensory pathways for pain and each of these three components is processed simultaneously within a pain network within the brain. This network is referred to as the 'neuromatrix' of pain by Melzack and Wall (Melzack, 2001, 2005). The gate control theory (also now known as the neuromatrix model of pain; Melzack, 2001, 2005) paved the way for an ensuing body of research that has found strong support for the idea that cognitive and emotional factors can amplify pain signals and rewire the brain circuitry that is specific to the perception of pain.

Pain in the brain

It is now widely accepted that pain is the result of supraspinal (i.e. above the spine) activity. The process of pain perception, termed nociception, has four primary elements: 1. transduction (the process by which pain receptors detect painful stimuli and convert them to an electrical message); 2. transmission (the delivery of the electrical pain message to the spinal column and brain); 3. modulation (specific parts of the brain, including cognitive and emotional processing areas, are directly involved in sending inhibitory signals that modulate the experience of pain); and 4. perception (the result of the neuromatrix of pain-processing areas in the brain that process the pain signal, causing perception of pain). These four elements, from the peripheral pain receptor to the cerebral cortex of the brain, encapsulate specialised neuronal pathways termed the nociceptive system, which is part of the larger somatosensory system (Schnitzler & Ploner, 2000). Extensive data emerging from human and animal research using anatomical and electrophysiological methodology has converged to paint a comprehensive, reliable picture of understanding of how the nociceptive system functions and how pain is perceived and processed primarily in the brain (Jensen, 2010).

The transition from acute to chronic pain

An important line of research is examining the factors that might explain why pain persists and becomes chronic for a subset of individuals. Research has found that the neurological and psychological foundation for long-term pain may be in place within hours of the initial injury (Carr & Goudas, 1999). An emerging body of literature has identified that the initial brain response to an inciting event (i.e. judgements of the intensity, quality and meaning of the pain) may set off a cascade of neurological changes that for some individuals spark a slow reorganisation of the central nervous system, including structural changes, an increase in the number of pain receptors in the spinal cord and a reduction in brain modulation processes (Apkarian, Baliki & Farmer, 2013; Woolf & Salter, 2000). Further, as pain persists, it leads to changes in pain processing and associated connections, as well as in general brain function; however, there are also structural, anatomical brain changes that have been consistently observed in the presence of persistent, ongoing pain. Specifically, a loss in cortical regional grey matter volume has been found for a number of chronic pain conditions (Kim et al., 2008; Luerding et al., 2008; Rodriguez-Raecke et al., 2009; Schmidt-Wilcke et al., 2006). This loss has been found to increase with longer duration of pain, higher intensity of pain and as a function of the interaction between these factors (Apkarian et al., 2004; Geha et al., 2008; Kuchinad et al., 2007). Although the loss in grey matter volume may be an indicator of neuronal death in the context of chronic pain, some research has found that these volume decreases are reversible when pain is relieved (Gwilym et al., 2010; Obermann et al., 2009; Rodriguez-Raecke et al., 2009). This finding, that structural brain changes in the context of pain are reversible once adequate pain relief is achieved, is certainly promising.

Mini case study 11.1

This mini case study is based on a client, HM, who attended the rehabilitation unit of a major trauma hospital in Seattle, in the US. HM was a 24-year-old male who had been in a motorcycle accident 8 months earlier, and as a result had his left leg amputated above the knee. HM met with a member of the multidisciplinary treatment team each day he was on the unit as he reported intense pain that was refractory to pain medication and that was interfering with his ability to fully engage in the rehabilitation program. HM reported that worst of all was the pain he felt in the toes of his left foot, which he felt were always 'scrunched up under my foot', despite this foot having been amputated.

Pain in the body part that has been amputated is referred to as phantom pain and occurs in 50 to 80% of people with amputations, irrespective of whether the amputation was the result of a traumatic experience or performed for a medical reason (Ephraim et al., 2005; Houghton et al., 1994). Biomedical models, which conclude that the amount of pain is equal to the amount of tissue damage, fail to explain this phenomenon, as the tissue that is damaged no longer exists! To view a YouTube video demonstrating mirror therapy, which is a clever intervention designed to alleviate phantom limb pain, access the following link: https://www.youtube.com/watch?v=YL_6OMPywnQ. This is the intervention that was delivered for HM, and it was tremendously successful, allowing him to engage in his therapies and successfully return to using his prosthesis to walk again.

Critical thinking question

How is it possible that HM feels pain in the toes of his left foot after experiencing amputation of his left leg?

A biopsychosocial understanding of pain

Almost 40-years ago, Engel proposed the biopsychosocial model, which redefined illness (including but not specific to pain) as an entity that was not independent of psychological, social and behavioural forces (Engel, 1977). Engel proposed that when these factors amalgamate, in certain contexts, then outward, manifest illness would result. The **biopsychosocial perspective of pain** aligned perfectly with Melzack and Wall's 'gate control theory' (Melzack & Wall, 1965). Together, these two models fuelled a zeitgeist in the way pain was assessed and treated such that cognitive, emotional and behavioural factors were considered central to case conceptualisation and effective treatment.

Cognitive factors

Chronic pain is a stressor and therefore, in accordance with the transactional model of stress described in Chapter 8 (Lazarus & Folkman, 1984), is influenced by the meaning ascribed to the pain (primary appraisals) and perceptions of whether the pain is controllable and whether one has the resources to cope with it (what Lazarus and Folkman termed secondary appraisals). Lazarus and Folkman (1984) described three forms of primary appraisals, based on which pain may be judged as a: 1. *threat*, which represents the belief that pain is a danger that outweighs one's ability to cope; 2. *loss/harm*, where pain is viewed as representing damage and/or a loss of some form; or 3. *challenge*, where one perceives that he/she has the resources to cope. Of the three forms of primary appraisals stemming from Lazarus and Folkman's model, threat appraisals have been found to be perhaps the most common within the context of coping with pain (Unruh & Richie, 1998). Threat appraisals have been proposed to impact pain via heightening one's attention or vigilance towards painful sensations, which may give rise to anxiety/fear and avoidance of activity (Crombez et al., 2013). Following on from this, fear–avoidance beliefs have been shown to predict disability in daily or occupational activity, and to negatively impact treatment outcomes and return-to-work rates (Pfingsten et al., 2000; Poiraudeau et al., 2006; Waddell et al., 1993).

Pain catastrophising is by far the most researched and documented cognitive factor associated with the experience of pain. Pain catastrophising refers to an exaggerated negative mental set about actual or anticipated pain (Sullivan et al., 2001), and is consistently associated with higher pain severity, disability and worse mood (e.g. depression and anxiety) (Day & Thorn, 2010; Geisser et al., 1994; Sullivan et al., 2001). Beliefs related to pain control and self-efficacy are typically considered within the secondary appraisal domain (Thorn, 2004), and a large body of research has shown these factors to have a protective role in fostering adaptive coping and adjustment to pain (Altmaier et al., 1993; Jensen, Turner & Romano, 2001; Keefe et al., 2004; Rudy et al., 2003). In the last decade, an increasing amount of research has demonstrated the potentially protective role of the cognitive approaches of mindfulness and pain acceptance in coping with pain, and promising interventions have been developed to target these adaptive ways of coping (Kabat-Zinn, 1990; McCracken & Eccleston, 2003; McCracken, Vowles & Eccleston, 2004).

Emotions and pain

Pain may entail a range of emotional experiences; however, for most people it is an aversive experience and therefore emotional responses to coping with pain are predominantly negative. Mirroring this, the bulk of the research to date has focused on understanding the influence of negative emotions on pain and associated disability and rehabilitation. Within chronic pain populations, rates of comorbid depressive disorders have been found to be approximately 40 to 50% (Banks & Kerns, 1996; Dersh et al., 2006; Romano & Turner, 1985), and poorer outcomes are associated with the treatment of pain when comorbid depression goes untreated (Shmuely et al., 2001). Although epidemiological data on the rates of anxiety in pain populations is limited, one large-scale study reported that 44 to 51% of individuals with fibromyalgia pain experienced anxiety symptoms (Wolfe et al., 1990). Anxiety-related fear of pain, fear of movement (kinesiophobia) and fear of re-injury is particularly debilitating (Vlaeyen & Linton, 2000). There are many reasons why a person living with chronic pain might feel anger (ranging from slight irritation or frustration up to fury), including anger towards self, significant other, healthcare providers, employers, insurance companies, the person who caused the accident and so on. Indeed, Okifuji and colleagues found that approximately 98% of patients seen at a multidisciplinary pain management centre reported feeling some degree of anger at the time of their assessment, and for most this anger was directed towards themselves (74%) (Okifuji, Turk & Curran, 1999). This is a significant cause for concern, as research has consistently found that anger-related variables are associated with higher pain intensity ratings, longer pain duration, increased analgesic medication intake and increased impaired functioning (Gatchel et al., 2007; Greenwood et al., 2003; Trost et al., 2012).

More recent research has shifted to understanding the role of positive emotions and resilience, which may serve a protective function and buffer the stress associated with living with chronic pain. Research suggests that positive emotions may foster recovery after pain flare-ups (Zautra et al., 2001). Subjective happiness has also been found to correlate with improved general health perception in individuals with low back pain (Takeyachi et al., 2003). Finally, humour and laughter (while obviously including cognitive, behavioural and social components) are typically associated with pleasant emotions, and the use of humour has been shown to improve pain thresholds (Mahony, Burroughs & Hieatt, 2001) and pain intensity (Tse et al., 2010), and lead to the release of endorphins, natural pain killers, in the brain (Haig, 1988).

Behavioural and social factors

The behavioural and social effects of pain are most pronounced when pain persists and becomes chronic, and for these individuals the effects are devastating. The World Health Organisation (WHO) reported data from the International Association for the Study of Pain (IASP) that one in three people with chronic pain are unable or less able to maintain an independent lifestyle due to its effects (WHO, 2004). In terms of the day-to-day living, the WHO reported that approximately one-half to two-thirds of individuals are less able or unable to engage in physical exercise, enjoy normal sleep, attend to household chores, participate in social activities, drive a car, walk or have sexual relations (WHO, 2004). Thus, chronic pain has a profound effect on one's work and level of independence, what one can 'do' in their spare time and/or for hobbies, and also often places a strain on one's relationships. Reviews of the pain literature now show compelling support for a disability model based on fear and maladaptive behavioural avoidance activity patterns, with fear underlying avoidance behaviour, leading to disuse and disability (Asmundson, Norton & Vlaeyen, 2004; Vlaeyen & Linton, 2000). Many people who live with chronic pain report it to be an isolating experience and feel their experience is not understood by family and friends; for many, an important part of being involved in a group-delivered multidisciplinary pain treatment is learning that they are not alone and that their experiences are commonly shared by others living with pain (Day, Thorn & Kapoor, 2011).

Mini case study 11.2

This mini case study is based on the reports from H. K. Beecher, who served as a physician in the US Army during World War II (Beecher, 1946). Beecher noticed that of the many soldiers he treated who had lost limbs through combat or who had experienced compound fractures or penetrating wounds to the abdomen or other typically intensely painful injuries, the majority (as many as 75%) reported no to moderate pain and required far less pain medication than civilians with comparable injuries. Moreover, only those individuals who were alert and otherwise functioning normally were included in Beecher's report. Due to their injuries, the soldiers were evacuated and were returned to the US for recuperation; the civilians, on the other hand, left the hospital to return to their war-torn homeland, and often experienced loss of wages due to an inability to return to work.

Critical thinking questions

1. What factors might explain why the soldiers reported less pain and required less medication compared to the civilians, who had similar injuries?
2. Consider what thoughts, emotions and behavioural responses the soldiers might have been experiencing compared to the civilians.

Psychosocial pain management approaches: theory and evidence

An abundance of brain imaging research has clearly demonstrated that the experience of pain, and particularly chronic pain, is intimately linked to areas of the brain that process not only the pain stimuli, but also emotions, cognition and motivation, and that these factors modulate the felt sensation of pain (Apkarian, Baliki & Geha, 2009; Jensen, 2010). Psychological processes actually shape the way painful stimuli are interpreted, and this provides a convincing rationale as to why psychological approaches to pain management are viable treatments. We saw in the previous section, that emotions, behaviours/social factors and cognition all play a role in the experience of pain, and therefore treatment can intervene at any one (or more) of these levels. Health psychologists play an important role in the management of pain by giving clients *skills they can use* to manage their persistent condition, thereby allowing them to step out of a passive patient role and to become an active participant in the management of their pain.

Behavioural approaches

Wilbert E. Fordyce is considered by many to be the founding father of multidisciplinary pain treatment. Fordyce (1976) was the first to apply psychological principles within the realm of pain management through his application of behavioural technology that stemmed from operant conditioning principles (developed by B. F. Skinner). He hypothesised that certain interpersonal and social consequences of chronic pain create powerful environmental contingencies that operantly condition increased maladaptive pain behaviours (e.g. guarding, grimacing, pain-contingent resting) and decreased adaptive behaviours (e.g. paced physical activity, social interaction), which leads to increased disability and worsening functioning over time. This approach recognised the importance of learning theory and environmental context, as others in the client's surrounding environment may unwittingly play an important role in reinforcing maladaptive pain behaviours (i.e. by providing solicitous responses and attending to the behaviour), which serves to sustain the behaviour. Thus, Fordyce's model programs were based on analysing pain behaviours and their function, and subsequently applying contingency management and reinforcement principles to shape an increase in adaptive well behaviour, and a decrease in maladaptive pain behaviour to improve adjustment to chronic pain. Although this strictly behavioural approach is not currently still widely used, the understanding and treatment of pain to this day is still influenced by operant behavioural principles and research supports the efficacy of this approach (Keefe & Lefebvre, 1999; Ostelo et al., 2005).

More recently, behavioural treatments have focused on incorporating respondent conditioning principles (as opposed to the operant conditioning principles that were the focus of Fordyce's model) and exposure-based techniques that are explicitly designed to target fear of pain. Within the fear-avoidance model, fear of pain is considered a classically conditioned response that leads to increased avoidance behaviour, which ultimately leads to more rest time, deconditioning of muscles and heightened disability (Vlaeyen & Linton, 2000). Based on this model, graded exposure techniques have been designed to reduce fear of pain and associated avoidance behaviour (Leeuw et al., 2007; Vlaeyen et al., 2001). A rapidly building body of evidence supports this exposure-based approach to pain treatment, with data showing that this treatment results in significant improvements in pain, fear of pain, catastrophising, disability and return-to-work rates (Linton et al., 2008; Staal et al., 2006; Sullivan et al., 2006; Vlaeyen et al., 2002; Woods & Asmundson, 2008). Although behavioural approaches represent an excellent treatment option for many people with pain, Linton and colleagues suggested that such approaches may not be an adequate standalone measure, as they found in their study that many participants had additional issues beyond just fear of pain (i.e. maladaptive cognitive beliefs, family issues, workplace changes) that needed to be acknowledged and targeted (Linton et al., 2008). One of the advantages of integrated cognitive and behavioural approaches is that these issues, along with maladaptive behaviours, can be addressed concurrently.

Cognitive behavioural therapy

Cognitive behavioural therapy (CBT) represented a paradigm shift in the management of pain (Turk, Meichenbaum & Genest, 1983), where the focus of treatment was broadened beyond extinguishing maladaptive behaviours to also include a focus on targeting maladaptive thoughts, beliefs and perceptions (Day, Thorn & Burns, 2012). The initial empirical investigations into the CBT approach for chronic pain by leaders in the field such as Turk, Turner, Kerns and others demonstrated its tremendous potential (Kerns et al., 1986; Turner, 1982; Turner & Clancy, 1988). Three decades later, CBT has become the first-line, gold standard psychosocial treatment for chronic pain (Ehde, Dillworth & Turner, 2014). Theoretically, the cognitive aspect of CBT for pain is designed to target changing unhelpful, maladaptive thoughts and beliefs. Primarily through the use of cognitive restructuring (although other cognitive techniques may also be applied), unhelpful thoughts and beliefs are identified, the evidence for their 'truth' and helpfulness examined, and then unhelpful or overly rigid and maladaptive thoughts/beliefs are challenged and restructured to be more helpful and adaptive. Behavioural techniques are also taught – such as relaxation, biofeedback, assertiveness training, expressive writing (or another form of emotional expression), setting and working towards behavioural goals (such as increasing physical activity), behavioural activation and guidance on activity pacing (Turner & Romano, 2001) – to enhance stress management and increase well behaviours. Cognitive and behavioural homework exercises are assigned to further develop client ownership of pain self-management skills, and often include thought records, coping self-statement cards, guided relaxation exercises, working towards behavioural goals and many others (Thorn, 2004; Turner & Romano, 2001).

The efficacy of CBT has been documented in a proliferation of randomised controlled trials, as well as in meta-analyses and systematic reviews (Ehde et al., 2014). Research has shown that this approach leads to short- and long-term reduction of pain intensity, interference in daily activities due to pain, pain catastrophising, function and mood (Aggarwal et al., 2011; Andrasik, 2007; Ehde et al., 2014; Hoffman et al., 2007; Williams,

Eccleston & Morley, 2012). Further, research suggests that CBT for heterogeneous chronic pain conditions is at least as efficacious as medically based treatments such as surgery and medication management (Eccleston et al., 2009). Prolific research in the area of CBT for pain is continuing, with more recent efforts focusing on understanding how this approach engenders beneficial outcomes and for whom this approach is most suited (Day, Ehde & Jensen, 2015; Jensen, 2011; Thorn & Burns, 2011).

Mindfulness and acceptance-based interventions

An exciting, relatively recent development in pain treatment has been the successful development and application of mindfulness-based as well as acceptance-based interventions for pain self-management. Mindfulness is defined as 'the awareness that emerges through paying attention on purpose, in the present moment, and non-judgmentally to the unfolding of experience, moment by moment' (Kabat-Zinn, 1990, p. 145). Interventions based on mindfulness meditation as a primary means to cultivate this quality include mindfulness-based stress reduction (MBSR) and mindfulness-based cognitive therapy (MBCT). In mindfulness-based approaches the aim is to engender a shift in cognitive processes or one's relationship to thoughts and pain such that they are mindfully perceived and accepted (Day et al., 2014). Homework includes guided meditation, yoga and, in MBCT, a selection of cognitive therapy-oriented exercises. Although still preliminary, a steadily growing body of research is supporting the efficacy of mindfulness-based approaches for pain. Most of the trials conducted to date have compared MBSR or MBCT to standard care and found these approaches to be beneficial with respect to pain intensity, pain coping, pain interference, and measures of affect immediately post-treatment and also at follow-up (Day et al., 2014; Fjorback et al., 2011; Grossman et al., 2004; Keng, Smoski & Robins, 2011; Parra-Delgado & Latorre-Postigo, 2013).

Acceptance-based approaches such as acceptant and commitment therapy (ACT) focus on modification of the function, rather than the symptoms, of chronic pain (Hayes, 2004; McCracken, MacKichan & Eccleston, 2007). Hayes (the developer of ACT) emphasises that the changing of thoughts should not be a treatment focus; rather he argues that the critical issue is to increase psychological flexibility and to either change or persist in behaviour in such a way that behaviour serves valued ends (Hayes, 2004). Within ACT, Hayes suggests that many traditional behaviour therapy change methods can be assigned as homework (e.g. exposure, goal setting), and that all homework assignments should be linked to short-, medium- and long-term behavioural change goals so that the client lives a life that is progressively more consistent with what is valued. An emerging body of evidence examining the efficacy of ACT for chronic pain conditions has found significant positive outcomes associated with this approach, including improved physical performance and fewer sick days, as well as reduced pain intensity, medical utilisation, daytime rest, distress, depression and pain-related anxiety (Dahl et al., 2005; McCracken et al., 2007; McCracken & Vowles, 2014; McCracken & Vowles, 2008; Vowles, McCracken & O'Brien, 2011; Vowles et al., 2014).

Mini case study 11.3

This mini case study is based on a high-achieving 35-year-old-female, JG, who was married with one 2-year-old son. JG started to experience intense headaches in her late 20s that recently had started to become more frequent. Notably, the most frequently identified headache trigger is stress (Nash & Thebarge, 2006). JG was working in an incredibly high-pressured position as the chief executive officer within a company that was struggling financially to stay afloat, and had recently had to lay a lot of people off work. Although opioid pain medication had previously been effective, due to tolerance effects the same dose of medication was no longer working and JG found that higher doses interfered with her ability to think and concentrate. I saw JG for brief therapy (10 sessions) to equip her with CBT pain coping skills, which is recommended by many professional headache organisations alongside pharmacotherapy (Penzien, 2009).

In our first session together, JG said that due to her headaches, she felt her thinking was 'groggy' and that she was falling behind at work, 'no matter how much harder I keep pushing myself'. JG described 'feeling under the pump as the buck stops with me' and reported often feeling anxious and irritated with herself and the headaches. JG reported having extremely high standards for herself in her work, and she considered needing to take breaks at work a 'sign of weakness', so she typically tried to 'fight through the pain'. JG has recently been prioritising working at night in an effort to keep up, at the expense of her exercise routine and 'play time' with her son. She reported this was also having a negative effect on her relationship with her husband, and increasingly they were having arguments. She felt the headaches 'came out of the blue' and she felt helpless as to how to control them.

Critical thinking questions

1. Essential to delivering CBT effectively is to collaboratively formulate a case conceptualisation which is then used to target treatment. The case conceptualisation should include potential environmental triggers (i.e. stressful situations), emotional and behavioural responses to the pain, unhelpful thoughts that might be triggering the headaches, and personal strengths or resources of the client that might be enhanced. In the case of JG, what factors in each of these domains can you see that might be impacting her pain?
2. What specific cognitive and behavioural techniques might you implement to address these identified treatment targets?

Needed future directions

Although CBT is considered the gold standard psychological approach to pain management, effect sizes are modest and not everyone responds to this treatment (Morley, 2011). The growing enormity of the problem of chronic pain drives the critical need to streamline and optimise psychosocial approaches for its management. To meet the challenge of chronic pain, experts in the broad psychotherapy (Kazdin, 2009) as well as pain literature (Jensen, 2011; Thorn & Burns, 2011) have emphasised the need to examine treatment mechanisms; that is, to investigate treatment mediators (*how* does a treatment work?) and moderators (for *whom* does the treatment work?).

Streamlining psychological pain treatments: a focus on mediation

Unfortunately, too few studies have systematically evaluated both specific and common factors (including those variously described as placebo effects) to determine their unique and potentially synergistic effects in mediating psychosocial treatments for chronic pain. Carefully constructed research trials that examine these factors are needed before we can conclude how our treatments are exerting effects (Day et al., 2012). In terms of pain treatment mediators, Jensen (2011) proposed an overarching framework to organise the key factors that might be of influence: 1. the environment/social variables; 2. brain states; 3. cognitive content; 4. cognitive coping (also known as cognitive processes); and 5. behaviour. This model was recently updated to also include another factor: 6. emotion and affect (Day et al., 2014). Burns and colleagues (Burns et al., 2015) proposed an alternative theoretical framework in which two potential competing models were thought to explain treatment effects: 1. the specific mechanism model, in which treatments work primarily via the mediators/reasons specified by theory (e.g. change in maladaptive thoughts during CBT); or 2. the general mechanism model, where treatments work via a widespread network of shared, not necessarily theory-specific, mechanisms (e.g. change in maladaptive thoughts during a psychoeducation about pain program). Support for both proposed models has been found. Some studies have found pain catastrophising underlies improvement in CBT (consistent with the specific mechanism model) (Thorn et al., 2007), whereas other research has found change in both pain catastrophising *and* pain acceptance (a theorised mechanism of ACT) jointly account for improvement in outcome during CBT-based interventions (supporting a general mechanism model) (Baranoff et al., 2013).

A fundamental difficulty in examining either of these theoretical frameworks is that any test of these models rests on the assumption that we have 'pure', valid, psychometrically sound measures of the mediators specific to the various psychological theories to begin with. Currently, however, this is not the case. Many measures contain items that assess a combination of purported mechanisms and therefore the sum scores of these measures (which are used in mediation analyses) do not accurately represent the construct purportedly 'uniquely' assessed. For example, both the pain catastrophising scale (Sullivan, Bishop & Pivik, 1995) and the Chronic Pain Acceptance Questionnaire (McCracken et al., 2004) are widely used in mechanism studies to assess cognitive content and cognitive process, respectively; however, *both* of these measures are comprised of items that assess cognitive content, cognitive process and emotions. Thus, it is not surprising that research implementing these measures would show that statistically they mediate outcomes across a 'mix' of theoretically unique treatments that are theorised to primarily target one of these domains (thereby inadvertently, and inaccurately, supporting the general mechanism model). It is critical that *pure*, validated measures of the key mechanisms of the most widely used treatments be developed in future research. Without this, premature conclusions about how pain treatments work may be drawn and consequently the future streamlining of treatments to include only those 'active' components will be biased due to these method factors, and will not be based on the *actual* importance of the various constructs (supposedly assessed).

Advancing patient-treatment matching: identifying treatment moderators

When two active treatments are compared, on average they show the same relative effects (Day et al., 2012). While determining whether this is achieved via the same mediational pathways is important, it is also critical to determine *who* within these group level comparisons is improving (and staying the same or getting worse) with treatment, and what are the defining characteristics of that person (Day et al., 2015). In a recent review of the moderation research within the area of pain, Day et al. (2015) found that baseline psychosocial variables of somatisation, perceived stress, emotional distress and pain control beliefs have been shown to influence outcomes in some psychosocial pain treatment clinical trials (Blanchard et al., 2006; Gale & Funch, 1984; Litt, Shafer & Kreutzer, 2010; McCracken & Turk, 2002; Sinclair & Wallston 2001; Tota-Faucette et al., 1993; Turk et al., 1996). However, the review by Day et al. (2015) also identified that to date, most moderation research within the pain literature has focused on client weaknesses as moderating factors, and has been conducted in an exploratory, *post hoc* manner. As such, past research has not led to an *a priori* theoretical framework upon which to build systematic hypotheses.

To address this gap in the literature, Day et al. have proposed the 'limit, activate and enhance model of moderating effects in psychosocial pain management' (2015). This model makes specific predictions about which clients should benefit from which treatments, and accounts for both client weaknesses (i.e. responses that are either maladaptive and need to be 'limited', or deficits in the use of an adaptive coping strategy that needs to be 'activated') as well as strengths (i.e. strengths, skills and resources that could facilitate the efficacy of treatment, and therefore are factors that need to be recognised, utilised and 'enhanced'). Figure 11.1 from Day et al. (2015) illustrates these predictions.

Research into the treatment moderator questions proposed in this model is limited, although preliminary research supports the tenets of the theory (Day et al., 2015). Ultimately, the answers to the questions proposed in this model will allow us in the future to develop algorithms so that we can match clients to the treatment that is most likely to be of optimal benefit. This will limit the burden that therapy may place on the client, while also maximising the use of limited healthcare resources.

Final considerations

The role of health and rehabilitation psychologists in improving pain management is a critical one, and to optimise our role within the current healthcare system there are a number of additional future directions that we will need to address. First, we

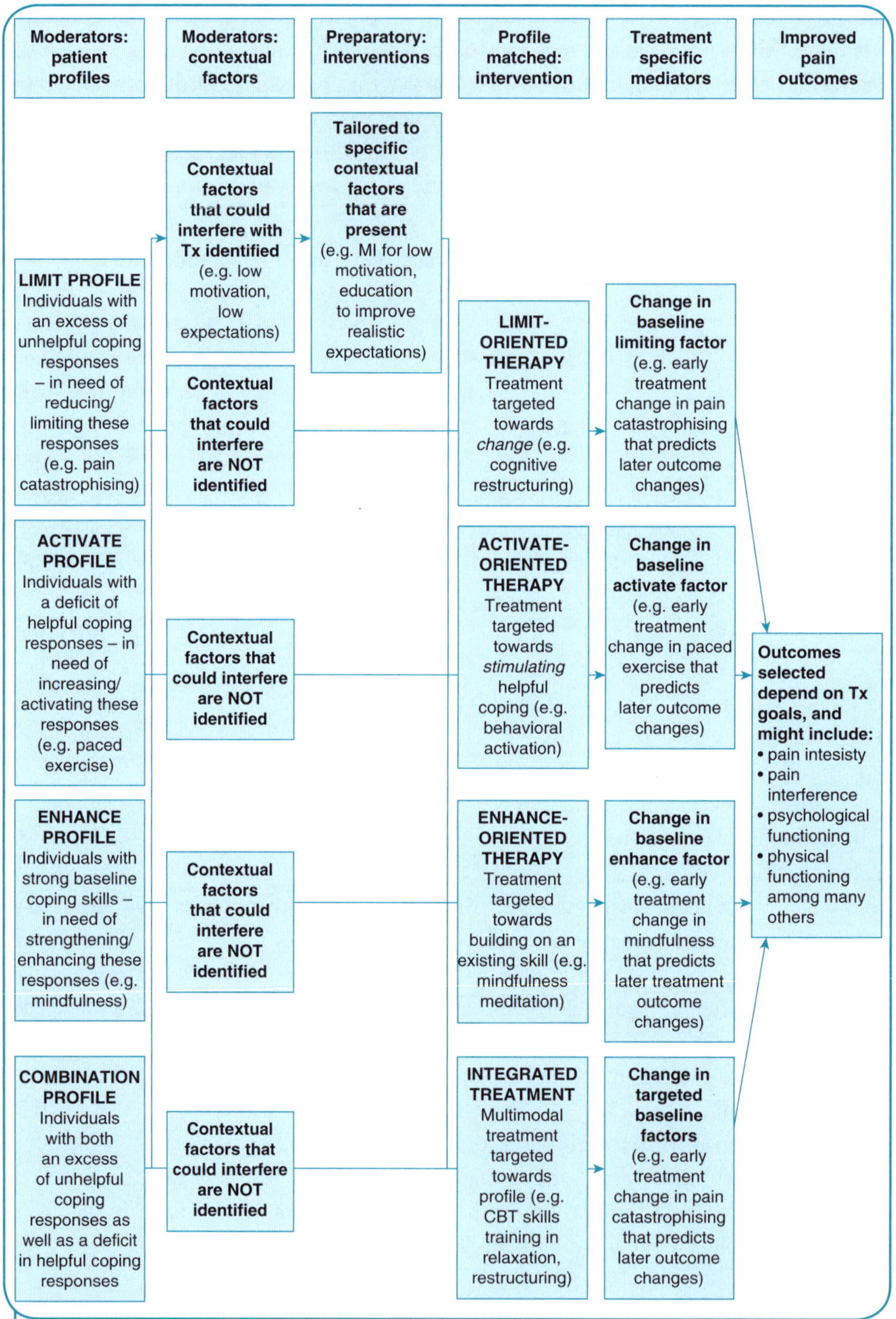

Figure 11.1 The limit, activate and enhance model of moderating effects in psychosocial pain management (Tx = treatment)
Source: Day et al., 2015

have shown that a number of psychological interventions are effective; however, we do not yet know 'how much is enough' in terms of the optimal dose of treatment for a given individual. Related to this, we also have limited knowledge regarding client engagement in treatment, and the degree of engagement in between-session activities that is necessary and sufficient for clinically meaningful change. Second, although we know that pain is underdiagnosed and undertreated (Institute of Medicine, 2011), we have not established effective means to overcome the barriers underlying these circumstances. Barriers exist in the form of geographical location (i.e. large areas of Australia are rural and therefore access to services is limited), financial constraints, cultural factors (i.e. most treatments have been developed for Caucasian, relatively high socioeconomic status individuals, and have not been appropriately adapted for minorities and low-literacy individuals), and obstructions within the healthcare system (i.e. providers may not be familiar with the role of health psychologists in pain management and therefore don't refer for services such as CBT). Innovative research by Thorn and colleagues (Eyer & Thorn, 2015; Thorn, 2015) is attempting to overcome these barriers by adapting CBT for pain to reduce the cognitive demands, be culturally sensitive and be accessible for low-literacy, minority individuals (to view Thorn's CBT manual, access the following link: http://bthorn.people.ua.edu/literacy-adapted-cbt-manual-for-chronic-pain.html), and research investigating this approach is promising (Thorn et al., 2011). Other research (summarised by Ehde et al., 2014) has shown that internet-delivered, interactive voice-response technology, video conferencing and web-based programs may also all be effective in overcoming barriers to treatment access. To address healthcare system barriers, health psychologists will need to educate other healthcare providers and advocate for psychological approaches to become mainstream treatments for pain within the medical system. Finally, while in the research setting we have strong evidence for psychosocial therapies for pain, historically there has been a gap in translating this research into clinical practice to improve pain management. Thorn (and others) have engaged in a community-based participatory research (Viswanathan et al., 2004) agenda to collaboratively involve key community stakeholders within a research program in efforts to more effectively disseminate and sustain the identified pain management approaches that have demonstrated real-world feasibility, use, applicability and effectiveness (Eyer & Thorn, 2015). Clearly, in the past several decades much improvement and advancement has been achieved in the area of chronic pain management; and equally as clearly, we still have more work to do.

Summary

- The process of pain perception, termed nociception, has four primary elements: 1. transduction; 2. transmission; 3. modulation; and 4. perception. The gate control theory of pain (and the subsequent neuromatrix model) proposed by Melzack and Wall emphasised that cognitive and emotional activity in the brain plays an active role in the modulation and felt experience of pain.
- Within the biopsychosocial perspective, pain is conceptualised as the result of a convergence of a multitude of internal and external, biological, psychological, emotional, social and behavioural influences. Effective treatment can intervene at any of these levels.
- Chronic pain is associated with substantial economic as well as personal and social costs, therefore advancing our capacity to prevent the transition from acute to chronic pain is critical. The way pain is processed by the brain has been shown to change as a function of pain duration, and critical differences between the brain in acute versus chronic pain have been identified. Promising research suggests that brain-related changes observed in the transition from acute to chronic pain may be reversible once adequate pain relief is achieved.
- Behaviourally oriented techniques are typically now combined with cognitive techniques within an integrated CBT treatment package, which is the current gold standard treatment for pain. More recent interventions have been developed to include mindfulness- and acceptance-based principles, and these innovative approaches show great promise.
- A variety of 'standalone' behavioural interventions, such as exposure-based therapy, have been shown to be effective for pain. However, CBT has the largest evidence base demonstrating its efficacy and therefore is typically the first-line treatment of choice.
- Research extrapolating *how* and for *whom* treatments work will in the future lead to streamlined protocols that can be effectively matched to individual client needs. Innovative modes of treatment delivery will hopefully address barriers to receiving adequate care. Health and rehabilitation psychologists have a key role to play if we are to continue to advance and optimise treatment for chronic pain, and to establish psychological pain treatment approaches within mainstream healthcare.

Suggested weblinks

Refer to the companion website at www.cambridge.edu.au/academic/healthpsychology for a list of suggested weblinks.

References

Aggarwal, V. R., Lovell, K., Peters, S., Javidi, H., Joughin, A. & Goldthorpe, J. (2011). Psychosocial interventions for the management of chronic orofacial pain. *Cochrane Database of Systematic Reviews, 11*.

Altmaier, E. M., Russell, D. W., Kao, C. F., Lehmann, T. R. & Weinstein, J. N. (1993). Role of self-efficacy in rehabilitation outcome among chronic low back pain patients. *Journal of Counseling Psychology, 40*(3), 335–9.

Andrasik, F. (2007). What does the evidence show? Efficacy of behavioural treatments for recurrent headaches in adults. *Neurological Sciences, 28*, S70–7.

Apkarian, A. V., Baliki, M. N. & Farmer, M. A. (2013). Predicting transition to chronic pain. *Current Opinion in Neurology, 26*(4), 360–7.

Apkarian, A. V., Baliki, M. N. & Geha, P. Y. (2009). Towards a theory of chronic pain. *Progress in Neurobiology, 87*(2), 81–97.

Apkarian, A. V., Sosa, Y., Sonty, S., Levy, R. M., Harden, R. N., Parrish, T. B. & Gitelman, D. R. (2004). Chronic back pain is associated with decreased prefrontal and thalamic gray matter density. *The Journal of Neuroscience 24*(46), 10410–15.

Asmundson, G. J., Norton, P. & Vlaeyen, J. W. (2004). Fear-avoidance models of chronic pain: an overview. In: G. J. Asmundson, J. W. Vlaeyen & G. Crombez (eds), *Understanding and Treating Fear of Pain* (pp. 3–24). Oxford: Oxford University Press.

Banks, S. M. & Kerns, R. D. (1996). Explaining high rates of depression in chronic pain: a diathesis-stress framework. *Psychological Bulletin, 119*, 95–110.

Baranoff, J., Hanrahan, S. J., Kapur, D. & Connor, J. P. (2013). Acceptance as a process variable in relation to catastrophizing in multidisciplinary pain treatment. *European Journal of Pain, 17*, 101–10.

Beecher, H. K. (1946). Pain in men wounded in battle. *Annals of Surgery, 123*(1), 96–105.

Blanchard, E. B., Lackner, J. M., Gusmano, R., Gudleski, G. D., Sanders, K., Keefer, L., Krasner, S. (2006). Prediction of treatment outcome among patients with irritable bowel syndrome treated with group cognitive therapy. *Behaviour Research and Therapy, 44*, 317–37.

Burns, J., Nielson, W. R., Jensen, M. P., Heapy, A., Czlapinski, R. & Kerns, R. D. (2015). Does change occur for the reasons we think it does? A test of specific therapeutic operations during cognitive-behavioral treatment of chronic pain. *Clinical Journal of Pain, 31*, 603–11.

Carr, D. B. & Goudas, L. C. (1999). Acute pain. *The Lancet, 353*, 2051–8.

Crombez, G., Van Ryckeghem, D. M. L., Eccleston, C. & van Damme, S. (2013). Attentional bias to pain-related information: a meta-analysis. *Pain, 154*, 497–510.

Dahl, J. C., Wilson, K. G., Luciano, C. & Hayes, S. C. (2005). *Acceptance and Commitment Therapy for Chronic Pain*. Reno, NV: Context Press.

Day, M. A., Ehde, D. M. & Jensen, M. P. (2015). Psychosocial pain management moderation: the limit, activate and enhance model. *The Journal of Pain, 16*(10), 947–60.

Day, M. A., Jensen, M. P., Ehde, D. M. & Thorn, B. E. (2014). Towards a theoretical model for mindfulness-based pain management. *Journal of Pain, 15*(7), 691–703.

Day, M. A. & Thorn, B. E. (2010). The relationship of demographic and psychosocial variables to pain-related outcomes in a rural chronic pain population. *Pain, 151*(2), 467–74.

Day, M. A., Thorn, B.E. & Burns, J. (2012). The continuing evolution of biopsychosocial interventions for chronic pain. *Journal of Cognitive Psychotherapy: An International Quarterly, 26*(2), 114–29.

Day, M. A., Thorn, B. E. & Kapoor, S. (2011). A qualitative analysis of a randomized controlled trial comparing a cognitive-behavioral treatment with education. *Journal of Pain, 12*(9), 941–52.

Day, M. A., Thorn, B. E., Ward, L. C., Rubin, N., Hickman, S. D., Scogin, F. & Kilgo, G. R. (2014). Mindfulness-based cognitive therapy for the treatment of headache pain: a pilot study. *Clinical Journal of Pain, 22*(2), 278–85.

Dersh, J., Gatchel, R. J., Mayer, T. G., Polatin, P. B. & Temple, O. W. (2006). Prevalence of psychiatric disorders in patients in patients with chronic disabling occupational spinal disorders. *Spine, 31*, 1156–62.

Eccleston, C., Palermo, T. M., Williams, A. C., Lewandowski, A. & Morley, S. (2009). Psychological therapies for the management of chronic and recurrent pain in children and adolescents. *Cochrane Database of Systematic Reviews* (2), CD003968.

Ehde, D. M., Dillworth, T. M. & Turner, J. A. (2014). Cognitive behavioural therapy for individuals with chronic pain: efficacy, innovations and directions for research. *American Psychologist, 69*(2), 153–66.

Engel, G. L. (1977). The need for a new medical model: a challenge for biomedicine. *Science*, *196*(4286), 129–36.
Ephraim, P. L., Wegener, S. T., MacKenzie, E. J., Billingham, T. R. & Pezzin, L. E. (2005). Phantom pain, residual limb pain, and back pain in amputees: results of a national survey. *Archives of Physical Medicine and Rehabilitation*, *86*(10), 1910–19.
Eyer, J. C. & Thorn, B. E. (2015). The Learning About My Pain study protocol: reducing disparities with literacy-adapted psychosocial treatments for chronic pain, a comparative behavioral trial. *Journal of Health Psychology*, 1–12.
Fjorback, L. O., Arendt, M., Ornbol, E., Fink, P. & Walach, H. (2011). Mindfulness-based stress reduction and mindfulness-based cognitive therapy: a systematic review of randomized controlled trials. *Acta Psychiatrica Scandinavica*, *124*(2), 102–19.
Fordyce, W. E. (1976). *Behavioral Methods for Chronic Pain and Illness*. St. Louis: Mosby.
Gale, E. N. & Funch, D.P. (1984). Factors associated with successful outcome from behavioral therapy for temporomandibular joint (TMJ) pain. *Journal of Psychosomatic Research*, *28*, 441–8.
Gatchel, R. J., Peng, Y. B., Peters, M. L., Fuchs, P. N. & Turk, D. C. (2007). The biopsychosocial approach to chronic pain: scientific advances and future directions. *Psychological Bulletin*, *133*(4), 581–624.
Geha, P. Y., Baliki, M. N., Harden, R. N., Bauer, W. R., Parrish, T. B. & Apkarian, A. V. (2008). The brain in chronic CRPS pain: abnormal gray-white matter interactions in emotional and autonomic regions. *Neuron*, *60*, 570–81.
Geisser, M. E., Robinson, M. E., Keefe, F. J. & Weiner, M. L. (1994). Catastrophizing, depression and the sensory, affective and evaluative aspects of chronic pain. *Pain*, *59*(1), 79–83.
Greenwood, K. A., Thurston, R., Rumble, M., Waters, S. J. & Keefe, F. J. (2003). Anger and persistent pain: current status and future directions. *Pain*, *103*, 1–5.
Grossman, P., Niemann, L., Schmidt, S. & Walach, H. (2004). Mindfulness-based stress reduction and health benefits. A meta-analysis. *Journal of Psychosomatic Research*, *57*, 35–43.
Gwilym, S. E., Fillipini, N., Douaud, G., Carr, A. J. & Tracey, I. (2010). Thalamic atrophy associated with painful osteoarthritis of the hip is reversible after arthroplasty: a longitudinal voxel-based-morphometric study. *Arthritis and Rheumatism*, *62*, 2930–40.
Haig, R. A. (1988). *The anatomy of humor*. Springfield, IL: Charles C. Thomas.
Hayes, S. C. (2004). Acceptance and commitment therapy, relational frame theory, and the third wave of behavioral and cognitive therapies. *Behavior Therapy*, *35*, 639–64.
Hoffman, B. M., Papas, R. K., Chatkoff, D. K. & Kerns, R. D. (2007). Meta-analysis of psychological interventions for chronic low back pain. *Health Psychology*, *26*(1), 1–9.
Houghton, A. D., Nicholls, G., Houghton, A. L., Saadah, E. & McColl, L. (1994). Phantom pain: natural history and association with rehabilitation. *Annals of the Royal College of Surgeons of England*, *76*, 22–5.
Institute of Medicine. (2011). *Relieving Pain in America: A Blueprint for Transforming Prevention, Care, Education, and Research*. Washington, DC: The National Academics Press.
Jensen, M., Turner, J. A. & Romano, J. M. (2001). Changes in beliefs, catastrophizing and coping are associated with improvement in multidisciplinary pain treatment. *Journal of Consulting and Clinical Psychology*, *69*, 655–62.
Jensen, M. P. (2010). A neuropsychological model of pain: research and clinical implications. *Journal of Pain*, *11*, 2–12.
—— (2011). Psychosocial approaches to pain management: an organizational framework. *Pain*, *152*(4), 717–25.
Kabat-Zinn, J. (1990). *Full Catastrophe Living: Using the Wisdom of your Body and Mind to Face Stress, Pain and Illness*. New York: Delacourt.
Kazdin, A. E. (2009). Understanding how and why psychotherapy leads to change. *Psychotherapy Research*, *19*(4–5), 418–28.
Keefe, F. J. & Lefebvre, J. C. (1999). Behavior therapy. In: R. Melzack & P. D. Wall (eds), *Textbook of Pain* (pp. 1445–61). London: Churchill Livingstone.
Keefe, F. J., Rumble, M. E., Scipio, C. D., Giordano, L. A. & Perri, L. M. (2004). Psychological aspects of persistent pain: current state of the science. *Journal of Pain*, *5*(4), 195–211.
Keng, S. L., Smoski, M. J. & Robins, C. J. (2011). Effects of mindfulness on psychological health: a review of empirical studies. *Clinical Psychology Review*, *31*(6), 1041–56.
Kerns, R. D., Turk, D. C., Holzman, A. D. & Rudy, T. E. (1986). Comparison of cognitive-behavioral and behavioral approaches to the outpatient treatment of chronic pain. *Clinical Journal of Pain*, *1*, 195–203.

Kim, J. H., Suh, S. I., Seol, H. Y., Oh, K., Seo, W. K., Yu, S. W., … Koh, S. B. (2008). Regional grey matter changes in patients with migraine: a voxel-based morphometry study. *Cephalagia*, *28*, 598–604.

Kuchinad, A., Schweinhardt, P., Seminowicz, D. A., Wood, P. B., Chizh, B. A. & Bushnell, M. C. (2007). Accelerated brain gray matter loss in fibromyalgia patients: premature aging of the brain? *The Journal of Neuroscience*, 27(15), 4004–7.

Lazarus, R. S. & Folkman, S. (1984). *Stress, appraisal, and coping*. New York: Springer.

Leeuw, M., Goossens, M. E., Linton, S. J., Crombez, G., Boersma, K. & Vlaeyen, J. W. (2007). The fear-avoidance model of musculoskeletal pain: current state of scientific evidence. *Journal of Behavioral Medicine*, *30*, 77–94.

Linton, S. J., Boersma, K., Jansson, M., Overmeer, T., Lindblom, K. & Vlaeyen, J. W. (2008). A randomized controlled trial of exposure in vivo for patients with spinal pain reporting fear of work-related activities. *European Journal of Pain*, *12*(6), 722–30.

Litt, M. D., Shafer, D. M. & Kreutzer, D. L. (2010). Brief cognitive-behavioral treatment for TMD pain: long-term outcomes and moderators of treatment. *Pain*, *151*(1), 110–16.

Luerding, R., Weigand, T., Bogdahn, U. & Schmidt-Wilcke, T. (2008). Working memory performance is correlated with local brain morphology in the medial frontal and anterior cingulate cortex in fibromyalgia patients: structural correlates of pain-cognition interaction. *Brain*, *131*, 3222–31.

Mahony, D. L., Burroughs, D. L. & Hieatt, A. C. (2001). The effects of laughter on discomfort thresholds: does expectation become reality? *Journal of General Psychology*, *128*(2), 217–26.

McCracken, L. M. & Eccleston, C. (2003). Coping or acceptance: what to do about chronic pain? *Pain*, *105*, 197–204.

McCracken, L. M. & MacKichan, F. & Eccleston, C. (2007). Contextual cognitive-behavioral therapy for severely disabled chronic pain sufferers: effectiveness and clinically significant change. *European Journal of Pain*, *11*(3), 314–22.

McCracken, L. M. & Turk, D.C. (2002). Behavioral and cognitive-behavioral treatment for chronic pain: outcome, predictors of outcome, and treatment process. *Spine*, *27*, 2564–73.

McCracken, L. M. & Vowles, K. E. (2008). A prospective analysis of acceptance of pain and values-based action in patients with chronic pain. *Health Psychology*, *27*(2), 215–20.

—— (2014). Acceptance and commitment therapy and mindfulness for chronic pain: model, process, and progress. *American Psychologist*, *69*(2), 178–87.

McCracken, L. M., Vowles, K. E. & Eccleston, C. (2004). The Chronic Pain Acceptance Questionnaire. *Pain*, *107*(1), 271–7.

Melzack, R. (2001). Pain and the neuromatrix in the brain. *Journal of Dental Education*, *65*, 1378–82.

—— (2005). Evolution of the neuromatrix theory of pain. The Prithvi Raj Lecture: presented at the third World Congress of World Institute of Pain, Barcelona 2004. *Pain Practice*, *5*, 85–94.

Melzack, R. & Wall, P. D. (1965). Pain mechanisms: a new theory. *Science*, *150*(699), 971–9.

—— (1982). *The Challenge of Pain*. New York: Basic Books.

Morley, S. (2011). Efficacy and effectiveness of cognitive behaviour therapy for chronic pain: progress and some challenges. *Pain*, *152*(3 Suppl), S99–106.

Nash, J. M. & Thebarge, R. W. (2006). Understanding psychological stress, its biological processes, and impact on primary headache. *Headache*, *46*(9), 1377–86.

Obermann, M., Nebel, K., Schumann, C., Holle, D., Gizewski, E. R., Maschke, M., Goadsby, P. J., Dienar, H. C., Katsarava, Z. (2009). Grey matter changes related to chronic posttraumatic headache. *Neurology*, *73*, 978–83.

Okifuji, A., Turk, D. C. & Curran, S. L. (1999). Anger in chronic pain: investigations of anger targets and intensity. *Journal of Psychosomatic Research*, *47*, 1–12.

Ostelo, R. W., van Tulder, M. W., Vlaeyen, J. W., Linton, S. J., Morley, S. J. & Assendelft, W. J. (2005). Behavioural treatment for chronic low-back pain. *Cochrane Database of Systematic Reviews, 1*, CD002014.

Parra-Delgado, P. M. & Latorre-Postigo, J. M. (2013). Effectiveness of mindfulness-based cognitive therapy in the treatment of fibromyalgia: a randomised trial. *Cognitive Therapy Research*, *37*, 1015–26.

Penzien, D. B. (2009). Stress management for migraine: recent research and commentary. *Headache*, *49*(9), 1395–8.

Pfingsten, M., Kroner-Herwig, B., Leibing, E., Kronshage, U. & Hildebrandt, J. (2000). Validation of the German version of the Fear-Avoidance Beliefs Questionnaire (FABQ). *European Journal of Pain*, *4*, 259–66.

Poiraudeau, S., Rannou, F., Baron, G., Le Henanff, A., Coudeyre, E., Rozenberg, S., … Ravaud, P. (2006). Fear-avoidance beliefs about back pain in patients with subacute low back pain. *Pain*, *124*, 305–11.

Rodriguez-Raecke, R., Niemeier, A., Ihle, K., Ruether, W. & May, A. (2009). Brain grey matter decrease in chronic pain is the consequence and not the cause of pain. *The Journal of Neuroscience*, *29*, 13746–50.

Romano, J. & Turner, J. A. (1985). Chronic pain and depression: does the evidence support a relationship? *Psychological Bulletin*, *97*, 18–34.

Rudy, T. E., Lieber, S. J., Boston, J. R., Gourley, L. M. & Baysal, E. (2003). Psychosocial predictors of physical performance in disabled individuals with chronic pain. *Clinical Journal of Pain*, *19*, 18–30.

Schmidt-Wilcke, T., Leinisch, E., Ganssbauer, S., Draganski, B., Bogdahn, U., Altmeppen, J. & May, A. (2006). Affective components and intensity of pain correlate with structural differences in gray matter in chronic back pain patients. *Pain*, *125*(1–2), 89–97.

Schnitzler, A. & Ploner, M. (2000). Neurophysiology and functional neuroanatomy of pain perception. *Journal of Clinical Neurophysiology*, *17*(6), 592–603.

Shmuely, Y., Baumgarten, M., Rovner, B. & Berlin, J. (2001). Predictors of improvement in health-related quality of life among elderly patients with depression. *International Psychogeriatrics*, *13*, 63–73.

Sinclair, V. G., Wallston, K. A. (2001). Predictors of improvement in a cognitive-behavioral intervention for women with rheumatoid arthritis. *Annals of Behavioral Medicine*, *23*, 291–7.

Staal, J. B., Hlobil, H., Köke, A. J., Twisk, J. W., Smid, T. & van Mechelen, W. (2006). Graded activity for workers with low back pain: who benefits most and how does it work. *Arthritis and Rheumatism*, *59*, 642–9.

Sullivan, M., Adams, A., Rhodenizer, T. & Stanish, W. (2006). A psychosocial risk factor targeted intervention for the prevention of chronic pain and disability following whiplash injury. *Physical Therapy*, *86*, 8–18.

Sullivan, M. J., Rodgers, W. M. & Kirsch, I. (2001). Catastrophizing, depression and expectancies for pain and emotional distress. *Pain*, *91*(1–2), 147–54.

Sullivan, M. J., Thorn, B., Haythornthwaite, J. A., Keefe, F., Martin, M., Bradley, L. A. & Lefebvre, J. C. (2001). Theoretical perspectives on the relation between catastrophizing and pain. *Clinical Journal of Pain*, *17*(1), 52–64.

Sullivan, M. J. L., Bishop, S. & Pivik, J. (1995). The pain catastrophizing scale: development and validation. *Psychological Assessment*, *7*, 524–32.

Takeyachi, Y., Konno, S., Otani, K., Yamauchi, K., Takahashi, I., Suzukamo, Y. & Kikuchi, S. (2003). Correlation of low back pain with functional status, general health perception, social participation, subjective happiness and patient satisfaction. *Spine*, *28*(13), 1461–7.

Task Force on Taxonomy, IASP. (1994). *Classification of Chronic Pain* (2nd edn). Seattle, WA: IASP Press.

Thorn, B. E. (2004). *Cognitive therapy for chronic pain: a step-by-step guide*. New York: Guilford Press.

—— (2015). Reducing the cognitive demands of psychosocial treatments for chronic pain: clinical research. *The California Psychologist*, *48*(3), 11–16.

Thorn, B. E. & Burns, J. W. (2011). Common and specific treatment mechanisms in psychosocial pain interventions: the need for a new research agenda. *Pain*, *152*(4), 705–6.

Thorn, B. E., Day, M. A., Burns, J., Kuhajda, M. C., Gaskins, S. W., Sweeney, K., … Cabbil, C. (2011). Randomized trial of group cognitive behavioral therapy compared with a pain education control for low-literacy rural people with chronic pain. *Pain*, *152*(12), 2710–20.

Thorn, B. E., Pence, L. B., Ward, L. C., Kilgo, G., Clements, K. L., Cross, T. H., Davis, A.M. Tsui, P. W. (2007). A randomized clinical trial of targeted cognitive behavioral treatments to reduce catastrophizing in chronic headache sufferers. *The Journal of Pain*, *8*(12), 938–49.

Tota-Faucette, M., Gil, K. M., Williams, D. A., Keefe, F. J., Goli, V. (1993). Predictors of response to pain management treatment: the role of family environment and changes in cognitive processes. *Clinical Journal of Pain*, *9*, 115–23.

Trost, Z., Vangronsveld, K., Linton, S. J., Quartana, P. J. & Sullivan, M. J. L. (2012). Cognitive dimensions of anger in chronic pain. *Pain*, *153*, 515–17.

Tse, M., Lo, A., Cheng, T., Chan, E., Chan, A. & Chung, H. (2010). Humor therapy: relieving chronic pain and enhancing happiness for older adults. *Journal of Aging Research*, *2010*, 1–9.

Turk, D. C., Meichenbaum, D. & Genest, M. (1983). *Pain and Behavioral Medicine: a Cognitive-Behavioral Perspective*. New York: Guilford Press.

Turk, D. C., Rudy, T. E., Kubinski, J. A., Zaki, H. S. & Greco, C. M. (1996). Dysfunctional patients with temporomandibular disorders: evaluating the efficacy of a tailored treatment protocol. *Journal of Consulting and Clinical Psychology*, *64*, 139–46.

Turner, J. A. (1982). Comparison of group progressive-relaxation training and cognitive-behavioral group therapy for chronic low back pain. *Journal of Consulting and Clinical Psychology*, *50*(5), 757–65.

Turner, J. A. & Clancy, S. (1988). Comparison of operant behavioral and cognitive-behavioral group treatment for chronic low back pain. *Journal of Consulting and Clinical Psychology*, *56*, 261–6.

Turner, J. A. & Romano, J. M. (2001). Cognitive-behavioral therapy for chronic pain. In: J. D. Loeser & J. J. Bonica (eds), *Bonica's Management of Pain* (3rd edn), pp. 1751–1758). Philadelphia, PA: Lippincott, Williams & Wilkins.

Unruh, A. M. & Richie, J. A. (1998). Development of the pain appraisal inventory: psychometric properties. *Pain*, *65*, 105–10.

Viswanathan, M., Ammerman, A., Eng, E., Gartlehner, G., Lohr, K. N., Griffith, D., ... Whitener, L. (2004). *Community-Based Participatory Research: Assessing the Evidence. Evidence Report/Technology Assessment No. 99*. Rockville, MD: Agency for Healthcare Research and Quality. Prepared by RTI–University of North Carolina Evidence-based Practice Center.

Vlaeyen, J. W., de Jong, J., Geilen, M., Heuts, P. H. & van Breukelen, G. (2001). Graded exposure in vivo in the treatment of pain-related fear: a replicated single-case experimental design in four patients with chronic low back pain. *Behaviour Research and Therapy*, *39*(2), 151–66.

—— (2002). The treatment of fear of movement/(re)injury in chronic low back pain: further evidence on the effectiveness of exposure in vivo. *Clinical Journal of Pain*, *18*(4), 251–61.

Vlaeyen, J. W. S. & Linton, S. J. (2000). Fear-avoidance and its consequences in chronic musculoskeletal pain: a state of the art review. *Pain*, *85*, 317–32.

Vowles, K. E., McCracken, L. M. & O'Brien, J. Z. (2011). Acceptance and values-based action in chronic pain: a three-year follow-up analysis of treatment effectiveness and process. *Behaviour Research and Therapy*, *49*(11), 748–55.

Vowles, K. E., Witkiewitz, K., Sowden, G. & Ashworth, J. (2014). Acceptance and commitment therapy for chronic pain: evidence of mediation and clinically significant change following an abbreviated interdisciplinary program of rehabilitation. *Journal of Pain*, *15*(1), 101–13.

Waddell, G., Newton, M., Henderson, I., Somerville, D. & Main, C. J. (1993). A Fear Avoidance Beliefs Questionnaire (FABQ) and the role of fear-avoidance beliefs in chronic low back pain and disability. *Pain*, *52*, 157–68.

WHO. (2004). World Health Organization supports global effort to relieve chronic pain. Geneva: World Health Organisation. Retrieved from: http://www.who.int/mediacentre/news/releases/2004/pr70/en/

Williams, A. C., Eccleston, C. & Morley, S. (2012). Psychological therapies for the management of chronic pain (excluding headache) in adults. *Cochrane Database of Systematic Reviews*, *11*, CD007407.

Wolfe, F., Smythe, H. A., Yunus, M. B., Bennett, R. M., Bombardier, C., Sheon, R. P. (1990). The American College of Rheumatology 1990 criteria for the classification of fibromyalgia: Report of the Multicenter Criteria Committee. *Arthritis and Rheumatism*, *33*, 160–72.

Woods, M. P. & Asmundson, G. J. (2008). Evaluating the efficacy of graded in vivo exposure for the treatment of fear in patients with chronic back pain: a randomized controlled clinical trial. *Pain*, *136*, 271–80.

Woolf, C. J. & Salter, M. W. (2000). Neuronal plasticity: increasing the gain in pain. *Science*, *288*, 1765–8.

Zautra, A. J., Smith, B., Affleck, G. & Tennen, H. (2001). Examinations of chronic pain and affect relationships: applications of a dynamic model of affect. *Journal of Consulting and Clinical Psychology*, *69*, 786–95.

12

Health inequalities

Learning outcomes

After reading this chapter, you should be able to:

- explain how society's norms may contribute to health inequalities
- critically evaluate different contributing factors to health inequalities
- evaluate barriers to reduced health inequalities
- identify limitations in the existing scientific research and how these impact on the generalisability of said research findings.

Introduction

There has probably never been a human society without health **inequalities**. Human societies tend to have a clear power-based hierarchy. With increased power comes increased influence and access to wealth generation and health expertise and services. Such human societies will have health inequalities. You can capture society's health inequality by examining the profile of the ruling class. In typical Western societies, the ruling class tends to be Caucasian, heterosexual, male and well educated, with good social networks and a well-paid prestigious job. Clearly the **ruling class** has a high socioeconomic status (SES) and it certainly does not have any stigma associated with its status. Stigma is about perceptions and perceptions matter, as we will see in the present chapter. When it comes to your health, it all matters: SES, employment status, occupation, marital status, education, isolation (e.g. social support), sex (male, female), unemployment, culture, sexual orientation, religion or lack thereof, race (e.g. Indigenous), living in an urban versus rural community, and **health literacy**.

Different factors that capture your standing in society affect your health but it can be difficult to discover exactly how they do so. These factors do not exist in a vacuum. If you are homeless, you are also likely to be poor with a low-paying job, if you even have a job, and it will likely be in a low prestigious occupation requiring low education levels. Does your birth status, courtesy of your parents, determine the rest of your life? The answer is 'no, not 100%, but to some extent'. Thus it is up to society to make sure that the factors we can control, such as education and healthcare access, are as equal as possible across all Australians to make sure that we have a population that is as healthy as possible.

Socioeconomic status

By measuring levels of education, income and job status, we capture an individual's or a group's SES (e.g. social status or class). Research into the health effects of SES show similar patterns of findings. Low SES is associated with increased risk of negative health outcome. In London (the Whitehall II study), low SES from birth to middle age may increase, almost double, your chances of developing type 2 diabetes, partly through increased inflammation (Stringhini et al., 2013). Furthermore, being a smoker was predicted by low levels of education, occupation and overall low SES. Physical inactivity and unhealthy diet were predicted by low level occupation and overall low SES. In India, low SES partly explains worse health outcomes for Indigenous versus non-Indigenous groups and within groups as well (Subramanian, Davey Smith & Subramanyam, 2006). The effects of low SES in the Indigenous groups were especially pertinent when it came to alcohol use, with Indigenous status more than doubling the risk of alcohol use. Meanwhile, a twin study in the US showed that differences among twins in relation to occupation affects health; a higher occupation class was associated with better health, but differences in education levels were *not* associated with blood pressure or cholesterol profile (Krieger et al., 2005). A meta-analysis of studies from England, Ireland, Scotland, Canada, New Zealand and Sweden found that low SES reduces your chances of undergoing lung cancer treatment (Forrest et al., 2013). Even if treatment was free, those with low SES were less likely to undergo treatment, suggesting that factors such as occupation and education may explain health inequities between low and high SES groups.

In Australia, the higher your SES the better your health (ABS, 2010; AIHW, 2004). Indigenous children are at a higher risk of mortality than non-Indigenous children (AIHW, 2014). Some of this difference may be attributed to family-related factors such as access to water and food of adequate standards, education, healthcare services and employment. Each of these factors, or any combination of them, can have detrimental effects on the individual's health, both physical and mental. A large meta-analysis examining studies from several countries found that being in a low SES group means that you have higher chances of suffering from depression or persistent depression (Lorant et al., 2003).

Education

The more educated will generally enjoy better health (Furnée, Groot & van Den Brink, 2008). However, this does not necessarily suggest that education in and of itself is a health protective factor. This relationship between health and education may simply suggest that children brought up in families that value education also enjoy better health norms. Better health norms should deliver the individual a better diet, reduced chances of drug use (e.g. smoking, alcohol), and increased physical activity through sport and recreation.

In a large US survey, education was found to be related to better health (Sturm & Gresenz, 2002). However, more education may not always mean better health. Findings from Europe suggest that making education compulsory for longer causes only a small improvement in health (Ljungdahl & Bremberg, 2015). That said, even if compulsory education does not improve health by much, it may do so for specific populations. Furthermore, what is being taught needs to be examined, as changing behaviour through health education is effective in improving health (Kok, van den Borne & Mullen, 1997). As a future researcher or healthcare professional, you need to also understand that the relationship between education and health may be skewed, as education levels may inflate and deflate reports of illness (Mackenbach, Looman & Van der Meer, 1996). Education may also be very important in increasing mental health literacy and reducing stigma associated with mental illness.

A national survey from Australia shows that factors such as sex (being a female), education (higher), age (lower), geographic location (remote), living condition (alone) and marital status (separated) predict your chances of visiting a psychologist in relation to mental health (Parslow & Jorm, 2000). Findings like these can be interpreted in different ways. Seeking social support or help is an important coping skill and being able to identify what support you may need is a vital part of this approach. It is not surprising that being female is a predictor of seeking professional help, as females tend to have better mental health literacy than males (Gibbons, Thorsteinsson & Loi, 2015). The second predictor, higher education, may suggest again the importance of mental health literacy and education in general. Higher education may contribute to your: 1. ability to accept that you may need to seek professional help; 2. mental health literacy; and 3. awareness of services available. Lower age, the third predictor, may suggest that younger individuals are more accepting and aware of mental health issues. Mental health issues are better understood and there is now less stigma and discrimination. Factors such as being separated and living alone in a remote area may interact to create an environment where the individual needs to seek professional help to deal with the pressures associated with their life.

Occupation and income

A large US survey found a strong relationship between income and health, showing that the higher your income, the better your physical and mental health (Sturm & Gresenz, 2002). Reviews of the literature suggested that the greater the income difference is in a society, the worse the overall health will be in that society (Kondo et al., 2009; Wilkinson & Pickett, 2006). However, income is only part of the story when it comes to work. Job satisfaction is a strong predictor of mental health, explaining more than 16% of the variance in mental health disorders such as depression, anxiety and burnout (Faragher, Cass & Cooper, 2005). The effects of job satisfaction on physical health are also strong, explaining more than 8% of the variance. The implications of findings like these are that employers need to make sure that income levels are adequate and that job satisfaction is high. Fulfilling both of these requirements should help reduce sick days and increase productivity.

Social determinants of health inequalities

It is all well and good to examine SES and its impact on health, but how should researchers and healthcare professionals approach the assessment of inequalities and the factors (social determinants) that contribute to these health differences in the first place? Health inequalities exist between and within countries (Marmot, 2005), suggesting that even though some countries may have an advantage over others when it comes to morbidity and mortality rates, there are options within each country to beat these odds if the social determinants are in your favour.

Parents

The perceptions society has of your parents and their status starts affecting your health before you are even born. The status of your parents in society will affect the healthcare options available to them and thus to you. Their **diet** will affect your health as will their **body mass index (BMI)**. Their smoking and drinking status will affect your birth weight and cognition. So the story of your health advantages and disadvantages begins with your parents. According to the Australian National Health and Medical Research Council (NHMRC, 2011), your chances of becoming obese or overweight are increased if your parents are obese, in a low SES group or smoke. Combine all of these risk factors for obesity and you increase your risks even further. If you end up being overweight or obese, you will increase your chances of developing type 2 diabetes and, importantly, increase your chances of being stigmatised, for example, with respect to appearance.

The sexual orientation of your parents may also affect the healthcare you receive. A survey of Australian medical and nursing students in 2010 found that some of these students had negative attitudes towards same-sex couples, especially gay male couples (Chapman et al., 2012). Furthermore, the findings of a small Australian study suggest that a minority of healthcare professionals and bureaucracies have negative attitudes towards same-sex couples (Chapman et al., 2012). These findings are backed up by a review by Shields et al. (2012). Negative attitudes and discrimination, while relatively rare, may well decrease the chances of same-sex couples seeking important early medical intervention for their children. Medical schools need to address any prejudice among the minority of their students. Some medical schools may think this issue is too difficult to handle. However, education about same-sex couples and all gender types is essential for any educational institution that wants to produce good healthcare professionals. Education also needs to be backed up by law and policy under which discrimination by healthcare professionals, both through action and inaction, is illegal.

With your parents or guardians come privileges or the lack thereof. Privilege means that you have an advantage when it comes to education (better schools, free university education (your parents pay the bills)) and upper-class networks which can increase the prospect of a better job (e.g. higher prestige, pay and safety). Those who are privileged in life tend not to notice their status while those who are not privileged certainly do notice their lack of advantage. Being privileged is equivalent to a 100 metre runner starting the race 10 metres closer to the finishing line than the other runners.

Your parents live and die by their own diet and so will you, at least while you let your parents do the shopping and cooking. A parental norm of eating junk food and not eating fruit and vegetables will become your norm. If you are a male with low SES, you are less likely than your high SES counterparts to eat or even like fruit (Pechey et al., 2015).

Females and males

Females live longer than males no matter the culture or country. Given that this difference is not limited to human mammals, researchers have examined its potential biological bases (Regan & Partridge, 2013). Research by Viña et al. (2005) suggests that the difference may be at least partly attributed to the higher hydrogen peroxide (H_2O_2) production in male mitochondria. This may help explain the higher oxidative mitochondrial damage present in males compared to females (i.e. higher oxidative stress in males) and suggests that activation of oestrogen receptors might help reduce mitochondria-free radical production.

Males are also more vulnerable to diseases linked to the X chromosome as they only have one while females have two X chromosomes providing added protection (Regan & Partridge, 2013). The mitochondria are inherited from the mother and may be optimised for female energy needs, thus leaving males at a disadvantage and even more prone to 'energy'-related disease (Regan & Partridge, 2013). The male immune system may also be weaker than that of females with testosterone being a potential causal factor; males with reduced testosterone production live longer than their high-testosterone counterparts, even as long as females. For females, menopause will increase the risk of cardiovascular disease (CVD) due to reduced oestrogen production. However, when it comes to the effects of hormones on health, few things are clear cut and any risk-to-benefit assessment needs to take into account multiple biological factors.

When it comes to mental health, females tend to have a worse outcome than males both in New Zealand (Ministry of Health, 2002) and in Australia (ABS, 2011c). In Australia, the results are not that straightforward, though. Australian figures for 16- to 85-year-old participants in 2007 indicated that about 17.6% of males had a mental disorder in the last year while for females the figure was 22.3%. The higher percentage for females may be attributed to a higher rate of post-traumatic stress disorder (PTSD) and anxiety disorder. However, the pattern of findings is reversed when it comes to any lifetime mental disorder, with 48.1% of males and 43.0% of females being affected (ABS, 2011c). This is attributed to higher substance use in males (35%) compared to females (14%). Future research needs to examine and try to explain why there are these differences between males and females. Are certain disorders more accepted for one sex? Are there disorders associated with certain occupations that are in turn generally filled by males or females? Mental health literacy is changing along with attitudes towards mental illness improving detection and the acceptance of seeking professional help.

Mental disorders

The high rates of any lifetime mental disorder, one or more, among males and females in Australia (48.1% and 43.0%, respectively) suggest that potentially almost half the population is affected by health inequalities due to mental disorders of one type or another. Mental disorders are also associated with lost income and degraded protective social support networks. The cost of mental disorders is large, not only for the individual but for society as a whole, with the estimated cost in Australia being $20 billion every year (ABS, 2011c). Caring for those with mental disorders is also costly for society. There are more than 2.7 million unpaid carers (ABS, 2013) with 777 000 of these being primary carers. Carers are at an increased risk of having a disability themselves and many of them are younger than 18 (Carers Australia, 2012). Being a carer does not just affect their job and education options; it affects their mental health as well.

Mental disorders reach well beyond the individual directly affected. Partners are on the 'front line' in care taking and this can have serious health implications for them too. An Australian study into veterans with post traumatic stress disorder (PTSD) shows that their disorder affects their partners' dyadic (marital/relationship) adjustment, mental health and life satisfaction (MacDonell et al., 2014). The key factors that contribute to this relationship between veterans' PTSD and their partners' mental health include sleep problems, hypervigilance, social isolation, financial and intimacy problems, and exhaustion. Furthermore, sleep seems to be related to SES, with longer sleep predicting being unemployed, having low education status and being young (Carrillo-Larco et al., 2014).

Geographical factors

What about geographic factors? Is it better to live in an urban area (i.e. major city) than in a regional or remote (i.e. non-major city) area? If you live in a remote area, you are more likely to have reduced access to: 1. healthcare services and healthcare professionals (e.g. surgery options, dental services, specialised medical and psychological health); 2. education opportunities (e.g. universities); and 3. healthy food options. According to the ABS (2011a), living outside a major city puts people at risk in relation to various factors. Women are 50% more likely to be daily smokers than their major city-dwelling counterparts; the respective figure for men is 15%. High-level consumption and binge drinking is higher with binge drinking at its highest for 25- to 34-year-old males, with 72% engaging in binge drinking in the last 12 months. Being overweight or obese is 13% more prevalent in women and 8% more prevalent in men. When it comes to exercise, however, city and non-city areas are fairly evenly matched. The results for stress were mixed and thoughts or plans of suicide were similar between city and non-city dwellers. Mental disorder rates in the last

12 months were similar, but the lifetime mental disorder rate was 8% higher outside major cities. On the bright side for non-city dwellers, the consumption of fruit and vegetables is higher. Unfortunately, though, higher fruit and vegetable consumption does not make up for the other risk factors that are unfavourable, and as a result life expectancy is about 4 years lower outside major cities. Thus if you live outside a major city, you are more likely than your city counterpart to die from causes such as ischaemic heart disease, stroke, hypertensive diseases, heart failure and transport accidents.

The ABS (2010) has classified and compared the most to least disadvantaged areas in Australia. Examining these numbers, you find that those in the most disadvantaged areas have an increased risk for various negative health factors, such as being a current smoker, having smoked and being obese. Healthcare practitioners, such as generalist medical and dental practitioners, are also less likely to work in the most disadvantaged areas. Despite the lack of specialists, the need is greater in these areas, where about 15% consult their GP at least once per month; which is twice the rate of those in the most advantaged areas. However, given the cost associated with dental practitioners, the ratio is reversed when examining visits in the last 12 months to a dentist, with those in disadvantaged areas half as likely to visit as those in the most advantaged areas.

Disability

Having a disability means that you have a mental or physical condition that puts restrictions on your life. A woman who becomes blind in her late thirties has a disability as her movements and senses have been affected. Physical and mental disability may lead to fewer educational opportunities resulting in restricted job options, thus lowering income, which in turn will reduce good housing alternatives and access to transport, and thus jobs and education. Disability seems to come with limited options and having to rely on public housing or living in cheaper areas due to a small income (e.g. pension, few working hours). Having a disability does not have to mean that you are living in poverty or without medical care. It might be better to consider having a disability as a risk factor for worse health outcomes, as being disabled seems to have compounding effects such as leading to living in disadvantaged areas (ABS, 2010); that is, living in areas that lack adequate infrastructure and services. Your chances of being profoundly or severely disabled are more than double if we compare the most disadvantaged areas with the least disadvantaged areas. If you live in a disadvantaged area, educational and employment opportunities may be restricted, further compounding risk of low SES and poorer health.

In 2012, about 4.2 million Australians were affected by a disability according to a discussion paper by the Australian Human Rights Commission (AHRC, 2015). Of these, 2.2 million were of prime working age (15 to 64 years old) with about 52.8% having had some labour force participation; this is compared with 82.5% by Australians without a disability in the same age range. The unemployment rate was 9.4% for those with disability versus 4.9% for those without disability. Increasing the employment rate of those with disability has benefits for the individuals in question as well as society as a whole. Individuals will increase their income and potentially improve their psychological and physical health. Employers benefit from good employees who may, on average, have better retention and attendance at work. Furthermore, employees with a disability seem to have fewer health and safety incidents than their 'able' counterparts. Government and researchers in Australia are collaborating to help disabled workers return to employment by examining the influence of supervisors, co-workers (see Dunstan et al., 2015) and employees themselves. Workers disabled with chronic pain can benefit from multidisciplinary interventions to help them return to work, improving their psychological and physical health (Dunstan & Covic, 2006, 2007). The economic impact of increasing work participation rates has been estimated to be $50 billion in added GDP (AHRC, 2015) if Australia moved from the 21st OECD spot into the top eight in terms of disabled participation rate in the workforce.

If you are disabled, your access to services (e.g. healthcare, education) may be limited due to distance and lack of appropriate transport. Furthermore, you are more likely to live in a disadvantaged area and thus access to services is further limited as the healthcare services needed may simply not be in your area. Access to services for Indigenous Australians is generally worse in remote areas (versus urban), with the lack of access compounded by barriers to utilising services. For Indigenous populations in Australia, the key barriers to accessing services, when they can be accessed, are lack of English language skills, public transport, and communication such as internet access (ABS, 2011d). If you have limited access to childcare services, this may reduce your options for work and education, compounding issues such as poverty.

Poverty

To try to understand poverty better, we can look at the income distribution using the Gini coefficient within different countries. The Gini coefficient ranges theoretically from zero, where all income is distributed equally, to one, where only one individual has all the income (Kondo et al., 2009); this is sometimes also reported as a percentage (100 × Gini coefficient). Using Gini, income has been found to be related to health, suggesting that there might be a threshold (Gini = 0.3) for income distribution where health inequality becomes an issue (Kondo et al., 2009). When examining income distribution, it is important to look beyond the Gini index, as two countries or states with the same Gini score could be facing very different underlying causal factors driving the Gini. Lack of income and the poverty that results can put individuals and families under additional stress. Such additional stressors can push those with borderline mental disorders to breaking point or lead to drug abuse and possibly homelessness. Poverty that leads to homelessness will thus compound the difficulties individuals and families face, and place them at a further disadvantage.

Homelessness

Being without a home is a disadvantage and creates many different problems. Having a roof over one's head is not enough to call it a home. About half a percent of Australians are homeless and their numbers are increasing (ABS, 2012): about 44% are female, 25% are Indigenous, 30% were born outside Australia, 17% are younger than 12 and 6% are older than 64. There are many factors and combinations of factors that contribute to homelessness, such as breakup of families due to domestic violence and abuse, and mental illness and poverty (Crane et al., 2005; Rota-Bartelink & Lipmann, 2007). If you are homeless, you have a reduced chance of getting or maintaining a job because keeping up appearances (e.g. good clothes and hygiene) can be a problem and getting to and from an interview or your workplace is a challenge with limited funds. Again, attending school while homeless is obviously a challenge involving logistics like transport, study space and money for essentials. Even if services are made available, they may not be the right fit for the homeless. For example, homeless women who have been victims of domestic violence may find it hard to be in shelters where they are in close proximity to men and where they cannot have private lockable sleeping quarters.

Health policies

A health policy details what actions are planned to reach certain health-related goals. In Australia, the Department of Health (2015) has a very broad vision statement capturing its health policy goals: 'Better health and wellbeing for all Australians, now and for future generations'. The goal is clearly directed at reducing health inequalities and making healthcare accessible to all. The right healthcare policies can help address the distribution of resources in relation to factors such as race and location. Policies that attract healthcare professionals to remote locations could help deal with staff shortages. Such policies could include tax concessions in the form of lower tax rates for healthcare professionals who live and work in remote communities. Such policies could be extended to other sectors, encouraging more Australians to consider living in rural communities. It is clearly not just up to the healthcare sector to address health inequities (Woodward & Kawachi, 2000). Governments must and are using their control over health funding and health policies to build a more equitable society. Governments, in cooperation with healthcare professionals, must help set goals to reduce health inequalities by, for example, helping the disadvantaged access appropriate healthcare. By supporting the right projects, governments can help build healthier societies; for example, better bicycling paths to and from schools and workplaces can help fight childhood obesity and the general lack of physical activity in society (Scally, 2013). The Australian Federal Government introduced plain packaging laws for cigarettes, thus helping to reduce the appeal of smoking and the uptake of smoking among young people (Germain, Wakefield & Durkin, 2010). These laws will also help older adults as it will reduce the appeal of smoking (e.g. less satisfying) and even increase the desire to quit (Wakefield et al., 2013). The plain packaging laws in Australia are an initiative supported by the international Framework Convention on Tobacco Control (FCTC) to target the advertising and promotion of tobacco products (Freeman, Chapman & Rimmer, 2008). These Australian laws will hopefully become international standards in the near future.

Health literacy

If you are able to obtain, understand and utilise health-related information and services to the benefit of your health, then your health literacy is good. Good health literacy enables individuals to improve their diet and activity levels and seek appropriate healthcare. A survey into health literacy in Australia shows that only about 40% of males and females reach the minimum skill level (level 3) or above (ABS, 2006). This survey also found that high health literacy scores are predicted by: the high education level of individuals and their parents, being employed, having higher income and prestige of occupation, high societal group participation, and being born in an English-speaking country. Living in a remote area reduces health literacy but only to a small extent. There are no real surprises in this list of health literacy predictors and the list is similar to the predictors of good health. Good health literacy is not just important for the individual in question but also for their friends and family, as it can help them seek the correct help. Australians generally tend to have good mental health literacy for depression, such as postnatal depression (Thorsteinsson, Loi & Moulynox, 2014), though males tend to have poorer mental health literacy skills than females (Gibbons et al., 2015).

Indigenous Australians

The Indigenous (Aboriginals and Torres Strait Islander) population of Australia in 2014 was approximately 713 600, with about 30% living in New South Wales and another 30% in the Northern Territory. About a third of the Indigenous population lives in a capital city and their health tends to be worse than non-Indigenous Australians (Australian Indigenous Health*InfoNet*, 2015). CVD is a leading cause of death (about a quarter of all deaths), a rate 1.7 times higher than that of the non-Indigenous population. The death rate from lung and breast cancer is 1.4 times that of the non-Indigenous population, while diabetes rates are 3.3 times higher with the death rate 7.0 times higher. Blindness and tuberculosis rates are 6.2 and 11.1 times higher respectively. Addressing issues such as eye health in the Indigenous population makes not only humanitarian sense but economic sense as well. Implementing adequate eye healthcare could mean a return of $2.50 for every additional $1.00 of taxpayer funds spent (Taylor, 2015).

When it comes to psychological illness, the comparison again is not favourable for the Indigenous Australians. This population has a stress rate 2.6 times higher and a suicide rate 2.4 times more than that of the non-Indigenous population. Given these differences in physical and mental health outcomes, it is not surprising to see a gap in life expectancy.

Based on 2005 to 2007 figures, Indigenous males can expect to live for 67.2 years and females 72.9 years while their non-Indigenous counterparts can expect to live for 78.7 and 82.6 years, respectively (ABS, 2011b). The gap between non-Indigenous and Indigenous populations ranges from 7.5 years for females in New South Wales to 14.2 years for males in the Northern Territory.

On a positive note, the infant mortality rate in the Indigenous population has been dropping, from 23 per 1000 in 1991 to 10 per 1000 in 2010 in South Australia and the Northern Territory. However, a comparison of Indigenous and non-Indigenous death rates by age in Figure 12.1 shows that too many deaths are occurring among the young and middle aged in the Indigenous population (AIHW, 2014). Contributing factors to the gap in life expectancy between these populations in Australia, according to this report, are chronic diseases such as CVD, diabetes and cancer. However, the report also points to disadvantages caused by lack of education, employment and lower income. Furthermore, Indigenous Australians tend to live in low SES areas (ABS, 2010). When Indigenous people in low SES areas are compared with their non-Indigenous counterparts, they are more likely to suffer poorer health. Behavioural factors contribute to this gap as well. For example, more than 40% of adults in the Indigenous population are smokers, about double the smoking rate for the non-Indigenous population (Australian Indigenous Health*InfoNet*, 2015; MacRae et al., 2013). There are also low rates of fruit and vegetable consumption and high rates of physical inactivity.

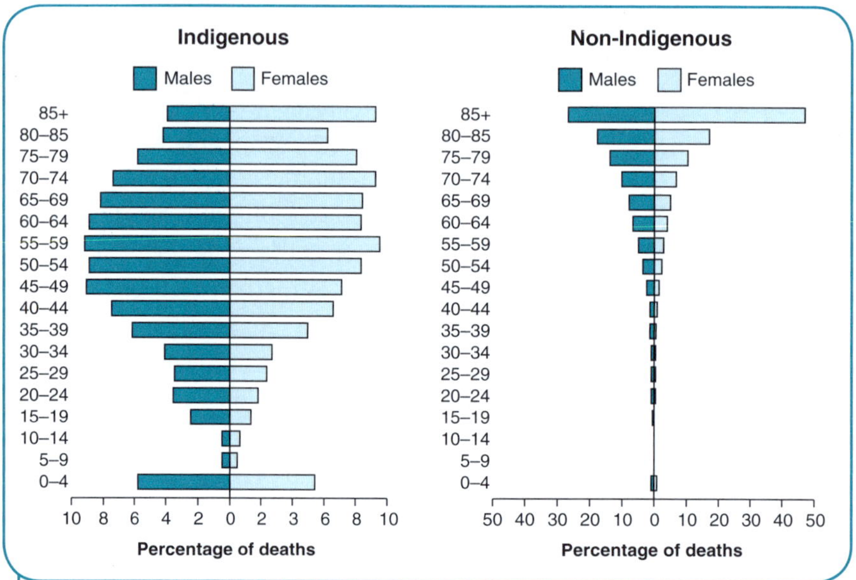

Figure 12.1 A comparison of Indigenous and non-Indigenous death rates by age
Source: AIHW, 2014

To reduce smoking rates, it is important to break down any norms that suggest that smoking is normal. Currently, two-thirds of Indigenous children under the age of 15 share a house with a daily smoker, compared with only a third of non-Indigenous children (ABS, 2011e). It is important to reduce children's exposure to adults and adolescents who smoke and increase the visibility of family and friends who do not. Multiple smoke reduction approaches need to be tried by empowering each community and equipping it with the necessary resources and tools. For remote communities dealing with high smoking rates, schools can play a pivotal role in providing a focal point where people can meet and decide on their own future direction.

Negative stereotypes about Aboriginals and Torres Strait Islanders may also contribute to health inequality. Teachers need to be especially aware of the dangers of stereotyping, as this may affect educational outcomes. Teachers generally expect lower academic achievement by Indigenous than non-Indigenous students (Riley & Ungerleider, 2012). With stereotyping comes discrimination and stigma.

Culture and religion

The cultural context in which you are brought up will guide you in your interactions with others within your culture, influence your respect for laws, guide your approach to religious beliefs, and determine your interactions with those who are from outside your cultural 'reference' group, that is, your in-group members (Helman, 2007). That said, cultural context is not homogenous and thus any cultural guidelines developed in relation to religion or sexual orientation seen as being outside your cultural 'norm' may vary depending on the religion in question. Healthcare professionals need to consider the cultural and religious background of their clients to secure appropriate mental and physical healthcare and outcomes. For example, clients may not be forthcoming with their sexual orientation if it is highly stigmatised within their circles of family and friends. Lacking such information, the healthcare professional may give inadequate advice leading to a less than adequate healthcare outcome and a dissatisfied client.

Sexual orientation

Adolescence is a period of physical and mental growth that comes with several challenges. One of these challenges is physical development during puberty. With puberty comes clearer sexual awareness and a better understanding of one's own sexual orientation. Any orientation outside the societal norm can have serious consequences for the individual. An individual who finds himself or herself outside these norms risks stigma and discrimination from their fellow society members. Social support, including social networks, is very important in enabling adolescents to overcome any sexual orientation challenges. Losing family support can have negative consequences for adolescents, increasing suicidal ideation and attempts, depression, substance use and sexual risk-taking behaviour such as unprotected sex (Ryan et al., 2009). Sexual orientation is sometimes confused with lifestyle: sexual orientation is actually rooted in biology, while lifestyle is a choice (like being a vegetarian). Lack of acceptance can lead to the loss of social connections and support from friends and family, causing social isolation, depression, drug abuse, suicide ideation and suicide attempts.

In Australia, a study of trans men (i.e. those who identified as female at birth but self-identify as males early in life) suggests that the gender identity issue is a predictive factor of suicidal ideation and attempts (Bolger et al., 2014). When mental health in the last 12 months was examined, there was a high rate of depression/anxiety (69%), suicidal ideation (81%) and suicide attempts (35%). Thus mental health seems to be much worse than in the general Australian population (see the mental disorder section of this chapter and ABS, 2011c). Higher rates of suicide ideation and attempts in non-heterosexual than heterosexual adolescents have been consistently found in the US, Canada, New Zealand and Norway (Saewyc, 2011). Substance use is also higher (about three times) for non-heterosexual adolescents; the risk of developing an eating disorder is also higher, and so is the risk of being bullied or harassed (Saewyc, 2011). In a study in Iceland, non-heterosexual adolescents are at a higher risk of suicide ideation or suicide attempts than those who have not experienced any lesbian, gay or bisexual attraction and are not yet sexually active (Arnarsson et al., 2015).

When suicide ideation and attempts are examined across continents, the risks are always higher for non-heterosexual populations (Mathy, 2002). However, the risks are especially high for non-heterosexual populations in Asia, South America and North America. While such issues may be of lesser concern in Europe and Australia, the rate of suicide attempts in Australia is still relatively high (Mathy, 2002).

It is important to emphasise what Saewyc (2011) says in her review when she points out that most non-heterosexual adolescents live a healthy and fulfilling life. They manage to do this despite stigma from society because of the support they receive from family, friends and teachers.

When it comes to research, studies examining non-heterosexual adolescents need to identify risk and protective factors for mental health. Furthermore, very little has been done to evaluate interventions (e.g. employ randomised control trials) to improve mental health despite promising results for programs being run in schools (Saewyc, 2011). Such interventions should target the key support structures that need to be in place to help non-heterosexual adolescents deal with the extra challenges they face. These structures include family, friends, teachers and classmates.

Stigma

It has been suggested that stigma maybe be an underlying cause of health inequality (Hatzenbuehler, Phelan & Link, 2013), thus the more a population is stigmatised the more likely it is to suffer disadvantage in society. But what is stigma? Stigma is a label or a mark that sets an individual or a group aside from other individuals or groups. If you are stigmatised (labelled) then you are likely to suffer negative attitudes, be stereotyped and experience discrimination from other individuals in society. Groups that suffer stigma in Australian society include Indigenous people, non-heterosexuals, the homeless, the poor, asylum seekers, those with mental disorders and other minority groups. Power is generally at play when it comes to stigma and powerful groups will try to stigmatise those who oppose their agenda, thus undermining their ability to express their arguments. Trying to stigmatise opponents is very common in any debate, so labels such as 'activist', 'tree hugger', 'traitor' and 'conspiracy theorist' are all used to undermine the messenger and thus the message (argument) being put forward by the person/groups. As a healthcare worker you need to make sure that you are effective in your work promoting health and wellbeing. People deserve respect and have human rights, but ideas do not deserve respect or rights as they are ideas and not people. This is important to understand, as respect for ideas can become a barrier in your work. For example, domestic violence in Australia is a serious issue and you can never let cultural ideas about male-dominated societies explain this issue away and thus hinder your ability to address this issue in your work. The same goes for ideas in the realm of religion. If your client's abuse is being justified to you through religious-type teachings, you cannot shy away from acting because people deserve dignity and human rights and ideas do not. Australian law is very clear on this matter. Cultural or religious 'laws' do not supersede actual Australian laws (Department of Immigration and Citizenship, 2014).

More seriously for groups such as non-heterosexuals, with stigma comes discrimination and exclusion. With exclusion and discrimination comes social isolation that cuts away your social support, your coping resources and your job opportunities. Any one of these factors is enough to create a stressful situation, but when facing a multitude the situation can become unassailable and potentially lead to drug use or suicide. The research shows this clearly. As mentioned previously, Arnarsson et al. (2015) showed that if you are an adolescent or young adult who is lesbian, gay or bisexual, your chances of suicide ideation or attempts are much higher than if you are an adolescent who has not had any lesbian, gay or bisexual attraction and you are not yet sexually active. Stigma and discrimination directed at adolescents because of their sexual orientation increases the risk of depression, PTSD, suicidality, substance use and risky sexual behaviour (Saewyc, 2011).

Australian asylum seekers are a group that is stigmatised through labels such as 'queue jumpers' and 'illegal asylum seekers'. Such labels are clearly misleading, as there are no queues to jump, and being an asylum seeker is not illegal; both are weak arguments. With such stigmatisation comes prejudice and dehumanisation, two closely related concepts (Greenhalgh & Watt, 2015). Prejudice towards asylum seekers tends to be predicted by low education levels, right-wing authoritarianism and social dominance orientation (Lyall & Thorsteinsson, 2007). Marginalising a group such as asylum seekers reduces the chances of individuals from this group integrating with mainstream Australian society, thus creating a self-fulfilling prophecy about this group's ability to integrate. This group is further disadvantaged through a low SES due to limitations regarding employment (low income and lower-class work) and education (such as opportunities to learn English) (Murray & Skull, 2005).

Discrimination

Discrimination, in this chapter, is used to describe the way in which a group is treated as inferior compared to another group, such as how non-heterosexuals are treated compared to heterosexuals in society (e.g. lack of marriage rights). Discrimination has real impact on those who are being discriminated against. A meta-analysis examining the effects of discrimination on mental health found that it increases your risk of mental illness irrespective of your sex or ethnicity (Pascoe & Smart Richman, 2009). It is your responsibility as a researcher, healthcare professional and not least as a human being to put an end to discrimination. Too often individuals want to twist arguments and claim that if you introduce quotas for any group such as women, the disabled or the Indigenous, you are discriminating in their favour. The answer to this is that you are addressing past and current discrimination and that without quotas you will never address current discriminatory practices. If you don't quantify the participation of different groups, such as the number of women on company boards, you will never address the issue, and the number of women on boards will not change. Some sections of the Australian community are prone to utter 'facts' about Indigenous Australians, suggesting that they don't have higher rates of incarceration or deaths in custody than non-Indigenous Australians if you adjust for SES. However, such assertions are never backed up with reliable statistics and the burden of proof is on the people making such assertions.

Race

Racism is discrimination based on perceptions of race whereby one group of individuals is treated worse than another group. The South African apartheid government was built on racism; look up apartheid (meaning 'being parted'), pitching white against black where black and all non-white South Africans where treated as subhumans with diminished rights. The White Australia Policy was in place from 1901 until 1973, when it was finally fully dismantled. This policy was racism legitimised through law and enabled discrimination against non-white immigrants and even Indigenous Australians. On a more positive note, Indigenous Australians gained the right to vote in Commonwealth elections in 1962 and could vote in all states by 1965. However, voting does not free you from the effects of racism. Racism adversely affects the health of Indigenous Australians (Awofeso, 2011) through entrenched stereotypes that fuel stigma. A national New Zealand survey found that different types of discrimination (e.g. ethnically motivated attack, verbally or physically, and unfair treatment due to ethnicity) negatively affected mental and physical health and increased the risk of being a smoker and developing CVD (Harris et al., 2006). Furthermore, Māori, Pacific and Asian participants were also more likely to experience racism than Europeans. In a national US survey, black women reported greater levels of race discrimination than white women while white women report greater levels of age and gender discrimination than black women (Pavalko, Mossakowski & Hamilton, 2003).

Age

Treating one person differently from another person because of their age is called age discrimination or ageism, and is against the law in Australia (AHRC, 2012). That said, there are exemptions. Denying someone service at a bar or not allowing someone to work at a bar because they are under 18 years of age is not against the law. In an English study, more than a third of participants aged 65 or over said they had experienced age discrimination (Rippon et al., 2014). The findings suggest that you are more likely to experience age discrimination with increased age and higher education levels. Education level may interact with age, causing increased discrimination based on high age and high levels of education making you less employable (e.g. 'old and overqualified'). Other predictors of experiencing age discrimination are lack of employment and low levels of wealth (Rippon et al., 2014). One of the barriers to removing age discrimination is that it seems to be socially acceptable, at least to a certain extent (Finkelstein & Truxillo, 2013). Is it appropriate for workplaces to view new and often younger staff as a burden because they need training and other help to get up to speed in their new job? What about terms like 'being wet behind the ears', 'being green' and 'old guard'?

Barriers to better health

Health inequalities can never be removed if we only ever aim to reduce them. We have to set the goal of removing health inequalities if we want to have a hope of reducing them. A report from the Ministry of Health (2002) in New Zealand warns that health inequalities cannot generally be addressed by the different groups experiencing the inequalities in question. Thus it is not enough for Indigenous Australians or New Zealand Māori to know that there are health inequalities or for them to want to address these inequalities. Inequalities are the results of multiple factors such as class, discrimination, racism and stigma, and these are not changed by one group alone. To address health inequalities, it is necessary to get different groups in society to work together towards a common goal using agreed methods. Collaboration and education need to be the key ingredients here, as well as time limits to implement change. Time limits are needed to put pressure on governments to enact change for the better. Collaboration is needed so that all the groups can be empowered to initiate and maintain changes through education and clear targeted action.

Some might suggest that health inequalities are never going to go away and that they may even be needed as an incentive to encourage people to work harder towards improving their own SES. However, such arguments deliberately ignore the inherent unfairness of health inequalities and the privilege that many have from birth. If we want a society that enables each individual to maximise their potential, we need to remove as many health inequalities as we can. Furthermore, inequalities affect everyone in society; after all, we are all susceptible to the impact of disease (Woodward & Kawachi, 2000).

Informing potential employers can help improve the work participation rates of Australians with a disability, thus benefiting their health and society as a whole. Employers need to be made aware of the potential benefits of hiring employees with a disability and to be informed of the various intervention programs that may be available to help them integrate the disabled worker into the workforce.

Education through informal socialisation, which occurs in schools, sport, recreation and the arts, is needed to foster understanding of different cultures, religions, disability, stigma and sexual orientation. The more people we know who are different from us, the more understanding we are and the more tolerant society will become.

Research

Healthcare professionals trying to untangle the causal chain of events linking the relationship between social factors and health are really up against a web of relationships where causal directions are less than clear. Your race may expose you to racism while your sexual orientation may expose you to discrimination. Discrimination may reduce your chances of getting a job and increase your risk of poverty and homelessness. Poverty will again reduce your risk of getting a job and increase the risk of discrimination against you. Having obese parents will increase your chances of becoming overweight or obese, increasing your chances of being bullied at school and thus negatively affecting your education, in turn reducing your job prospects. Some factors are with us from birth, such as race and sex, while others are determined by our biology, such as our sexual orientation and if we are born as a male or a female. That said, note that hormones and enzymes help determine the development of our sexual organs.

If you are a researcher trying to untangle this complex web of relationships, you should strongly consider running a longitudinal study with enough participants and time points to give you a clear picture of the changes occurring. You also have to consider that when you find differences between groups, such as income differences between an urban Indigenous population and a similar urban non-Indigenous population, you need to try to control for factors such as education. If you find that the children of one group of people (e.g. Indigenous, same-sex couples) have worse or better health outcomes than the comparison group, then again you need to control for other factors such as SES and experience of discrimination.

Maybe if you think about your own life and the lives of your family members and friends, you might like to consider all of the factors that have been discussed in this chapter and think about which factors have affected their lives the most or how their lives might have changed if only one factor had been different.

Mini case study 12.1

According to the ABS (2011a), areas outside major cities have a higher death rate from transport accidents than major cities. Furthermore, for men aged 20 to 24 the death rate in areas outside major cities is 42 per 100 000 while in cities it is 10 per 100 000. Consider that outside major cities roads tend to be in worse condition, speed limits are higher, distances travelled are longer and, in the case of an accident, help may arrive late.

Critical thinking questions

1. As a researcher, plan a research project examining the contributing factors to transport accidents where you compare different geographical regions.
2. As a healthcare professional, consider the different health behaviour change models (e.g. the health belief model) and plan a behaviour change campaign to reduce the transport accident rate outside major city areas.

Mini case study 12.2

Discrimination against people can be based on various factors (e.g. age, race, sexuality, gender and religion) and a combination of these factors.

Critical thinking questions

1. Consider the community you live in and the discrimination you know of in it. As a healthcare practitioner, how would you reduce this discrimination?
2. What groups or organisations could help you reduce discrimination?

Mini case study 12.3

Many Indigenous Australians have to fight discrimination and disadvantaged circumstances on a daily basis.

Critical thinking question

What are these discriminations and circumstances in general in Australia and more specifically in the communities you are familiar with in Australia (e.g. where you live, where you study)?

Summary

- Just as a healthy society values good health, education and openness, an unhealthy society focuses on rewarding wealth (e.g. access to better education, jobs and healthcare) and stigmatises out-groups based on sexual orientation, religious beliefs, poverty, disability and race.
- Factors that contribute to health inequalities are similar from one country to the next, with some factors being more prominent than others by country. As in other countries, these factors affect us here in Australia. However, we are generally moving in the right direction in reducing their impact.
- There are many barriers to health equality, and different groups face different barriers. Education is key in removing barriers, along with the recognition that their total removal can take a generation or two. The education needed is often not through official school curriculums but through socialisation in schools and workplaces where different groups (e.g. religious, race, disability, sexual orientation) get to interact.
- Much of the large survey research comes from government agencies giving an important overview of health inequities and related factors. However, university research is needed in collaboration with government agencies to evaluate the long-term impact of health inequality and potential causal factors. Longitudinal research that can follow thousands of individuals from birth to adulthood and beyond is required to answer more clearly a multitude of health-related questions.

Suggested weblinks

Refer to the companion website at www.cambridge.edu.au/academic/healthpsychology for a list of suggested weblinks.

References

ABS. (2006). *Health literacy, Australia, 2006*. Cat no. 4233.0. Canberra: Australian Bureau of Statistics. Retrieved from: http://abs.gov.au/AUSSTATS/abs@.nsf/Latestproducts/4233.0Main%20Features22006?opendocument&tabname=Summary&prodno=4233.0&issue=2006&num=&view=

—— (2010). *Health and Socioeconomic Disadvantage*. Cat no. 4102.0. Canberra: Australian Bureau of Statistics. Retrieved from: http://www.ausstats.abs.gov.au/Ausstats/subscriber.nsf/0/5703A93771AE2E4ECA2576E70016C8D3/$File/41020_%20healthandseifa.pdf

—— (2011a). *Australian Social Trends March 2011. Health Outside Major Cities*. Cat no. 4102.0. Canberra: Australian Bureau of Statistics. Retrieved from: http://www.ausstats.abs.gov.au/ausstats/subscriber.nsf/LookupAttach/4102.0Publication25.03.114/$File/41020_HealthOMC_Mar2011.pdf

—— (2011b). *Australian Social Trends March 2011. Life Expectancy Trends – Australia.* Cat no. 4102.0. Canberra: Australian Bureau of Statistics. Retrieved from: http://www.ausstats.abs.gov.au/ausstats/subscriber.nsf/LookupAttach/4102.0Publication23.03.112/$File/41020_Lifeexpectancy_Mar2011.pdf

—— (2011c). *Gender Indicators, Australia, Jul 2011.* Cat no. 4125.0. Canberra: Australian Bureau of Statistics. Retrieved from: http://www.abs.gov.au/ausstats/abs@.nsf/Lookup/by%20Subject/4125.0~Jul%202011~Main%20Features~Mental%20health~3150

—— (2011d). *The Health and Welfare of Australia's Aboriginal and Torres Strait Islander Peoples, Oct 2010.* Cat no. 4704.0. Canberra: Australian Bureau of Statistics. Retrieved from: http://www.abs.gov.au/AUSSTATS/abs@.nsf/lookup/4704.0Chapter930Oct+2010

—— (2011e). *The Health and Welfare of Australia's Aboriginal and Torres Strait Islander Peoples, Oct 2010. Mothers' and Children's Health: Children and Passive Smoking.* Cat no. 4704.0. Canberra: Australian Bureau of Statistics. Retrieved from: http://www.abs.gov.au/AUSSTATS/abs@.nsf/lookup/4704.0Chapter650Oct+2010

—— (2012). *Census of Population and Housing: Estimating Homelessness, 2011.* Cat no. 2049.0. Canberra: Australian Bureau of Statistics. Retrieved from: http://www.abs.gov.au/AUSSTATS/abs@.nsf/Latestproducts/2049.0Main%20Features12011?opendocument&tabname=Summary&prodno=2049.0&issue=2011&num=&view=

—— (2013). *Disability, Ageing and Carers, Australia: Summary of Findings, 2012.* Cat no. 4430.0. Canberra: Australian Bureau of Statistics. Retrieved from: http://www.abs.gov.au/ausstats/abs@.nsf/mf/4430.0

AHRC. (2012). *Age Discrimination: Know Your Rights.* Sydney: Australian Human Rights Commission. Retrieved from: https://www.humanrights.gov.au/sites/default/files/content/age/publications/Age%20Discrimination.pdf

—— (2015). *Willing to Work: National Inquiry into Employment Discrimination Against Older Australians and Australians with Disability.* Sydney: Australian Human Rights Commission. Retrieved from: https://www.humanrights.gov.au/sites/default/files/document/publication/discussion-paper-disability.pdf

AIHW. (2004). *Australia's Health 2004.* Canberra: Australian Institute of Health and Welfare. Retrieved from: http://www.aihw.gov.au/WorkArea/DownloadAsset.aspx?id=6442453243

—— (2014). *Australia's health 2014. Indigenous health.* Canberra: Australian Institute of Health and Welfare. Retrieved from http://www.aihw.gov.au/australias-health/2014/indigenous-health/

Arnarsson, A., Sveinbjornsdottir, S., Thorsteinsson, E. B. & Bjarnason, T. (2015). Suicidal risk and sexual orientation in adolescence: a population-based study in Iceland. *Scandinavian Journal of Public Health, 43,* 497–505. doi: http://dx.doi.org/10.1177/1403494815585402

Australian Indigenous HealthInfoNet. (2015). *Overview of Australian Indigenous Health Status, 2014.* Mount Lawley, WA: Author. Retrieved from: http://www.healthinfonet.ecu.edu.au/uploads/docs/overview_of_indigenous_health_2014.pdf

Awofeso, N. (2011). Racism: a major impediment to optimal Indigenous health and health care in Australia. *Australian Indigenous Health Bulletin, 11,* 1–8.

Bolger, A., Jones, T., Dunstan, D. & Lykins, A. (2014). Australian trans men: development, sexuality, and mental health. *Australian Psychologist, 49,* 395–402. doi: http://dx.doi.org/10.1111/ap.12094

Carers Australia. (2012). Statistics. Retrieved from: http://www.carersaustralia.com.au/about-carers/statistics/

Carrillo-Larco, R. M., Bernabé-Ortiz, A., Miranda, J. J. & de Castro, J. R. (2014). Peruvians' sleep duration: analysis of a population-based survey on adolescents and adults. *PeerJ, 2,* e345. doi: http://dx.doi.org/10.7717/peerj.345

Chapman, R., Wardrop, J., Freeman, P., Zappia, T., Watkins, R. & Shields, L. (2012). A descriptive study of the experiences of lesbian, gay and transgender parents accessing health services for their children. *Journal of Clinical Nursing, 21,* 1128–35. doi: http://dx.doi.org/10.1111/j.1365-2702.2011.03939.x

Chapman, R., Watkins, R., Zappia, T., Nicol, P. & Shields, L. (2012). Nursing and medical students' attitude, knowledge and beliefs regarding lesbian, gay, bisexual and transgender parents seeking health care for their children. *Journal of Clinical Nursing, 21,* 938–45. doi: http://dx.doi.org/10.1111/j.1365-2702.2011.03892.x

Crane, M., Byrne, K., Fu, R., Lipmann, B., Mirabelli, F., Rota-Bartelink, A., … Warnes, A. M. (2005). The causes of homelessness in later life: findings from a 3-nation study. *The Journals of Gerontology Series B: Psychological Sciences and Social Sciences, 60,* S152–9. doi: http://dx.doi.org/10.1093/geronb/60.3.S152

Department of Health. (2015). Overview. Retrieved from: http://www.health.gov.au/internet/main/publishing.nsf/Content/health-overview.htm

Department of Immigration and Citizenship. (2014). *Australian Citizenship our Common Bond*. Canberra: Author.

Dunstan, D. A. & Covic, T. (2006). Compensable work disability management: a literature review of biopsychosocial perspectives. *Australian Occupational Therapy Journal*, *53*, 67–77. doi: http://dx.doi.org/10.1111/j.1440-1630.2006.00566.x

—— (2007). Can a rural community-based work-related activity program make a difference for chronic pain-disabled injured workers? *Australian Journal of Rural Health*, *15*, 166–71.

Dunstan, D. A., Mortelmans, K., Tjulin, A. & MacEachen, E. (2015). The role of co-workers in the return to work process. *International Journal of Disability Management*, 4 August. doi: http://dx.doi.org/10.1017/idm.2015.2

Faragher, E. B., Cass, M. & Cooper, C. L. (2005). The relationship between job satisfaction and health: a meta-analysis. *Occupational & Environmental Medicine*, *62*, 105–12. doi: http://dx.doi.org/10.1136/oem.2002.006734

Finkelstein, L. & Truxillo, D. (2013). Age discrimination research is alive and well, even if it doesn't live where you'd expect. *Industrial and Organizational Psychology*, *6*, 100–2. doi: http://dx.doi.org/10.1111/iops.12017

Forrest, L. F., Adams, J., Wareham, H., Rubin, G. & White, M. (2013). Socioeconomic inequalities in lung cancer treatment: systematic review and meta-analysis. *PLoS Medicine*, *10*, e1001376. doi: http://dx.doi.org/10.1371/journal.pmed.1001376

Freeman, B., Chapman, S. & Rimmer, M. (2008). The case for the plain packaging of tobacco products. *Addiction*, *103*, 580–90. doi: http://dx.doi.org/10.1111/j.1360-0443.2008.02145.x

Furnée, C. A., Groot, W. & van Den Brink, H. M. (2008). The health effects of education: a meta-analysis. *The European Journal of Public Health*, *18*, 417–21. doi: http://dx.doi.org/10.1093/eurpub/ckn028

Germain, D., Wakefield, M. A. & Durkin, S. J. (2010). Adolescents' perceptions of cigarette brand image: does plain packaging make a difference? *Journal of Adolescent Health*, *46*, 385–92. doi: http://dx.doi.org/10.1016/j.jadohealth.2009.08.009

Gibbons, R. J., Thorsteinsson, E. B. & Loi, N. M. (2015). Beliefs and attitudes towards mental illness: an examination of the sex differences in mental health literacy in a community sample. *PeerJ*, *3*, e1004. doi: http://dx.doi.org/10.7717/peerj.1004

Greenhalgh, E. M. & Watt, S. E. (2015). Preference for consistency and value dissimilarities in dehumanization and prejudice toward asylum seekers in Australia. *European Journal of Social Psychology*, *45*, 110–19. doi: http://dx.doi.org/10.1002/ejsp.2066

Harris, R., Tobias, M., Jeffreys, M., Waldegrave, K., Karlsen, S. & Nazroo, J. (2006). Racism and health: the relationship between experience of racial discrimination and health in New Zealand. *Social Science & Medicine*, *63*, 1428–41. doi: http://dx.doi.org/10.1016/j.socscimed.2006.04.009

Hatzenbuehler, M. L., Phelan, J. C. & Link, B. G. (2013). Stigma as a fundamental cause of population health inequalities. *American Journal of Public Health*, *103*, 813–21.

Helman, C. G. (2007). *Culture, Health and Illness*. UK: CRC Press.

Kok, G., van den Borne, B. & Mullen, P. D. (1997). Effectiveness of health education and health promotion: meta-analyses of effect studies and determinants of effectiveness. *Patient Education and Counseling*, *30*, 19–27. doi: http://dx.doi.org/10.1016/S0738-3991(96)00953-6

Kondo, N., Sembajwe, G., Kawachi, I., van Dam, R. M., Subramanian, S. & Yamagata, Z. (2009). Income inequality, mortality, and self-rated health: meta-analysis of multilevel studies. *BMJ*, *339*, b4471. doi: http://dx.doi.org/10.1136/bmj.b4471

Krieger, N., Chen, J. T., Coull, B. A. & Selby, J. V. (2005). Lifetime socioeconomic position and twins' health: an analysis of 308 pairs of United States women twins. *PLoS Medicine*, *2*, 645. doi: http://dx.doi.org/10.1371/journal.pmed.0020162

Ljungdahl, S. & Bremberg, S. G. (2015). Might extended education decrease inequalities in health? A meta-analysis. *The European Journal of Public Health*, cku243. doi: http://dx.doi.org/10.1093/eurpub/cku243

Lorant, V., Deliège, D., Eaton, W., Robert, A., Philippot, P. & Ansseau, M. (2003). Socioeconomic inequalities in depression: a meta-analysis. *American Journal of Epidemiology*, *157*, 98–112. doi: http://dx.doi.org/10.1093/aje/kwf182

Lyall, H. C. & Thorsteinsson, E. B. (2007). Attitudes to the Iraq war and mandatory detention of asylum seekers: associations with authoritarianism, social dominance, and mortality salience. *Australian Journal of Psychology*, *59*, 70–7. doi: http://dx.doi.org/10.1080/00049530601148421

MacDonell, G. V., Thorsteinsson, E. B., Bhullar, N. & Hine, D. W. (2014). Psychological functioning of partners of Australian combat veterans: contribution of veterans' PTSD symptoms and partners' caregiving distress. *Australian Psychologist*, *49*, 305–12. doi: http://dx.doi.org/10.1111/ap.12069

Mackenbach, J. P., Looman, C. & Van der Meer, J. (1996). Differences in the misreporting of chronic conditions, by level of education: the effect on inequalities in prevalence rates. *American Journal of Public Health*, *86*, 706–11. doi: http://dx.doi.org/10.2105/AJPH.86.5.706

MacRae, A., Thomson, N., Burns, A. J., Catto, M., Gray, C., Levitan, L., ... Urquhart, B. (2013). *Overview of Australian Indigenous Health Status 2012*. Mount Lawley, WA: Australian Indigenous HealthInfoNet. Retrieved from: http://www.healthinfonet.ecu.edu.au/uploads/docs/overview_of_indigenous_health_2012.pdf

Marmot, M. (2005). Social determinants of health inequalities. *The Lancet*, *365*, 1099–104. doi: http://dx.doi.org/10.1016/S0140-6736(05)71146-6

Mathy, R. M. (2002). Suicidality and sexual orientation in five continents: Asia, Australia, Europe, North America, and South America. *International Journal of Sexuality and Gender Studies*, *7*, 215–25. doi: http://dx.doi.org/10.1023/A:1015853302054

Ministry of Health. (2002). *Reducing Inequalities in Health*. Wellington, NZ: Ministry of Health: Retrieved from https://www.health.govt.nz/system/files/documents/publications/reducineqal.pdf

Murray, S. B. & Skull, S. A. (2005). Hurdles to health: immigrant and refugee health care in Australia. *Australian Health Review*, *29*, 25–9. doi: http://dx.doi.org/10.1071/AH050025

NHMRC. (2011). *A review of the evidence to address targeted questions to inform the revision of the Australian Dietary Guidelines*. Canberra: National Health & Medical Research Council. Retrieved from: http://www.nhmrc.gov.au/_files_nhmrc/file/publications/n55d_australian_dietary_guidelines_evidence_report.pdf

Parslow, R. A. & Jorm, A. F. (2000). Who uses mental health services in Australia? An analysis of data from the National Survey of Mental Health and Wellbeing. *Australian and New Zealand Journal of Psychiatry*, *34*, 997–1008. doi: http://dx.doi.org/10.1080/000486700276

Pascoe, E. A. & Smart Richman, L. (2009). Perceived discrimination and health: a meta-analytic review. *Psychological Bulletin*, *135*, 531. doi: http://dx.doi.org/10.1037/a0016059

Pavalko, E. K., Mossakowski, K. N. & Hamilton, V. J. (2003). Does perceived discrimination affect health? Longitudinal relationships between work discrimination and women's physical and emotional health. *Journal of Health and social Behavior*, 18–33.

Pechey, R., Monsivais, P., Ng, Y.-L. & Marteau, T. M. (2015). Why don't poor men eat fruit? Socioeconomic differences in motivations for fruit consumption. *Appetite*, *84*, 271–9. doi: http://dx.doi.org/10.1016/j.appet.2014.10.022

Regan, J. C. & Partridge, L. (2013). Gender and longevity: why do men die earlier than women? Comparative and experimental evidence. *Best Practice & Research Clinical Endocrinology & Metabolism*, *27*, 467–79. doi: http://dx.doi.org/10.1016/j.beem.2013.05.016

Riley, T. & Ungerleider, C. (2012). Self-fulfilling prophecy: How teachers' attributions, expectations, and stereotypes influence the learning opportunities afforded Aboriginal students. *Canadian Journal of Education/Revue Canadienne de L'Éducation*, *35*, 303–33.

Rippon, I., Kneale, D., de Oliveira, C., Demakakos, P. & Steptoe, A. (2014). Perceived age discrimination in older adults. *Age and Ageing*, *43*, 379–86. doi: http://dx.doi.org/10.1093/ageing/aft146

Rota-Bartelink, A. & Lipmann, B. (2007). Causes of homelessness among older people in Melbourne, Australia. *Australian and New Zealand Journal of Public Health*, *31*, 252–8.

Ryan, C., Huebner, D., Diaz, R. M. & Sanchez, J. (2009). Family rejection as a predictor of negative health outcomes in white and Latino lesbian, gay, and bisexual young adults. *Pediatrics*, *123*, 346–52. doi: http://dx.doi.org/10.1542/peds.2007-3524

Saewyc, E. M. (2011). Research on adolescent sexual orientation: development, health disparities, stigma, and resilience. *Journal of Research on Adolescence*, *21*, 256–272. doi: http://dx.doi.org/10.1111/j.1532-7795.2010.00727.x

Scally, G. (2013). Have we lost the battle to improve health inequalities? *The King's Fund*. Retrieved from: http://www.kingsfund.org.uk/time-to-think-differently/blog/have-we-lost-battle-improve-health-inequalities

Shields, L., Zappia, T., Blackwood, D., Watkins, R., Wardrop, J. & Chapman, R. (2012). Lesbian, gay, bisexual, and transgender parents seeking health care for their children: a systematic review of the literature. *Worldviews on Evidence-Based Nursing*, *9*, 200–9. doi: http://dx.doi.org/10.1111/j.1741-6787.2012.00251.x

Stringhini, S., Batty, G. D., Bovet, P., Shipley, M. J., Marmot, M. G., Kumari, M., ... Kivimäki, M. (2013). Association of lifecourse socioeconomic status with chronic inflammation and type 2 diabetes risk: the Whitehall II prospective cohort study. *PLoS Medicine*, *10*, e1001479. doi: http://dx.doi.org/10.1371/journal.pmed.1001479

Sturm, R. & Gresenz, C. R. (2002). Relations of income inequality and family income to chronic medical conditions and mental health disorders: national survey. *BMJ*, *324*, 20. doi: http://dx.doi.org/10.1136/bmj.324.7328.20

Subramanian, S., Davey Smith, G. & Subramanyam, M. (2006). Indigenous health and socioeconomic status in India. *PLoS Medicine*, *3*, e421. doi: http://dx.doi.org/10.1371/journal.pmed.0030421

Taylor, H. (2015, September 1). No excuses for this Indigenous eye health crisis. *ABC: The Drum*. Retrieved from: http://www.abc.net.au/news/2015-09-01/taylor-no-excuses-for-this-indigenous-eye-health-crisis/6741066

Thorsteinsson, E. B., Loi, N. M. & Moulynox, A. L. (2014). Mental health literacy of depression and postnatal depression: a community sample. *Open Journal of Depression*, *3*, 101–11. doi: http://dx.doi.org/10.4236/ojd.2014.33014

Viña, J., Borrás, C., Gambini, J., Sastre, J. & Pallardó, F. V. (2005). Why females live longer than males? Importance of the upregulation of longevity-associated genes by oestrogenic compounds. *FEBS Letters*, *579*, 2541–5. doi: http://dx.doi.org/10.1016/j.febslet.2005.03.090

Wakefield, M. A., Hayes, L., Durkin, S. & Borland, R. (2013). Introduction effects of the Australian plain packaging policy on adult smokers: a cross-sectional study. *BMJ Open*, *3*, e003175. doi: http://dx.doi.org/10.1136/bmjopen-2013-003175

Wilkinson, R. G. & Pickett, K. E. (2006). Income inequality and population health: a review and explanation of the evidence. *Social Science & Medicine*, *62*, 1768–84. doi: http://dx.doi.org/10.1016/j.socscimed.2005.08.036

Woodward, A. & Kawachi, I. (2000). Why reduce health inequalities? *Journal of Epidemiology and Community Health*, *54*, 923–9. doi: http://dx.doi.org/10.1136/jech.54.12.923

13

Cross-cultural psychology

Learning outcomes

After reading this chapter, you should be able to:

- distinguish between different agents of socialisation
- explain the concept of cultural sensitivity
- interpret the concept of cultural competence
- critically examine the impact of culture on behaviour
- develop an understanding of the concept and implications of cross-cultural psychology for practice.

Introduction

> Homogenization sterilizes. It's the sum of cultures and languages that makes humanity.
>
> (Pierre Bourgault, 1996, p. 13)

This chapter explores the concept of cross-cultural psychology. Initially, we will move from a basic definition of **culture** to a more complex understanding of the term. After gaining insight into the elements of culture as a concept, we will then develop an understanding of the impact of culture. We examine how subjective experiences shape definitions and characteristics of culture. We will explore if culture is a static concept or evolves in response to subtle changes over periods of time.

Why is this topic necessary? Cross-cultural appreciation is a requirement of a health professional's clinical practice, as in today's social, political and economic environments we encounter clients from diverse backgrounds who have concerns that arise from their subjective experience of their world (Christopher et al., 2014). To be able to respond effectively to our client's concerns, it is necessary to achieve a sound level of **cultural competence**, sensitivity and safety, and to facilitate an effective therapeutic relationship and deliver empathetic care while maintaining ethical practices. Cross-cultural appreciation embraces humanity and highlights similarities and differences between cultural groups.

Cross-cultural appreciation also helps reduce bias created by our own ethnocentric behaviours regardless of whether these behaviours are consciously or unconsciously unfolding. There has been an emerging idea in contemporary society that the classical lens of traditional psychology often fails to take into account the impact of culture on an individual's behaviour (Wisniewski & Wu, 2014). The impact of culture on an individual's thoughts and actions cannot be overestimated. The significance is further highlighted by the recent changes in the *Diagnostic and Statistical Manual of Mental Disorders* (DSM-5) (American Psychiatric Association, 2013) with the inclusion of important revisions based on cultural issues and their subsequent therapeutic implications (La Roache, Fuentes & Hinton, 2015). The DSM-5 represents the contemporary classification system for mental health disorders as a guide for practitioners, highlighting common symptomology and facilitating standard diagnosis (La Roache et al., 2015). Notable inclusions in this newest version of DSM are 'cultural concepts of distress' and cultural syndromes (La Roache et al., 2015).

Culture

Before looking at the concept of cross-cultural psychology, it is first necessary to develop a foundation definition for the term. The term 'culture' itself has different meanings depending on the perspective of the person defining it. In 1871 E. B. Taylor, an anthropologist, defined culture as being 'that complex whole which includes knowledge, belief, art, morals, law, customs and any other capabilities and habits acquired by man as a member of society' (1871, p. 42). Broadly speaking, culture relates to the shared characteristics of a group of individuals. Most frequently, to common elements grouped under the broad categories of race, ethnicity, nationality and/or religion. A broad definition of culture can therefore be stated as: 'the total way of life shared by members of a group' (Jones & Creedy, 2012, p. 305).

By using traditional classifications of race, ethnic background, nationality and/or religion, it is thought that we vicariously create a 'them' and 'us' position. In considering culture, we must first look at how the 'us' and 'I' compositions developed. This will require personal reflection, an acknowledgement of our individual core values and beliefs, and an understanding of how and why these emerge. Essentially, before we can consider cross-cultural concepts, we must gain an understanding of 'who' we are through an exploration of self, and reflect on our own cultural affiliations. Attributes of our cultural makeup include: dynamic elements of language; human expression; forms of communication; thoughts about how we perceive, interpret and gain understanding of our world; how we integrate spirituality (as contrasted with religion) into our lives; what our value systems are; our social interaction patterns and so on. These are examples of only a few of the characteristics that we combine in order to position ourselves within a specific cultural framework.

How is an understanding of one's own culture obtained?

The focus of developmental psychology has been contributed to by a myriad of theorists. In this chapter we will consider Piaget's and Erikson's separate models of the stages of childhood and adolescent development and Vygotsky's model of social interaction as a process to develop individual consciousness (i.e. an understanding of the world) (Shiraev & Levy, 2007, p. 121).

Piaget's (1896–1980) theories look at the accommodation and assimilation aspects that a child uses to create organisation in their world. Piaget's view of cognitive development focused on how the environment and genetics impacted on individual achievement, and how these factors are not necessarily similar across all cultures (Keller, 2011); therefore, corresponding developmental processes will also alter between cultures. Piaget's work involved schemas: a unit of intelligent behaviour that records how a person reacts to a stimulus. These schemas are a set of cognitive understandings of an individual's environment. According to Piaget, an individual moves through the processes of adaptations to their world. The first step is assimilation and involves using stored knowledge (schema) to deal with a situation (Jones & Creedy, 2012).

For example, when a child knows how to roll a ball, they have achieved a state of equilibration. When a new challenge is encountered, such as replacing the ball with another toy (e.g. a hula hoop), the task then becomes how to roll a hula hoop (see Figure 13.1.) Disequilibrium (Jones & Creedy, 2012) occurs as at first the child attempts to employ the rolling technique known to work with the ball and then realises that these stored schemas are ineffective with the new apparatus (i.e. the hula hoop). The intelligent child then proceeds to change techniques and experiment to eventually achieve the desired result: rolling the hula hoop. Mastery is achieved and a new schema created. Accommodation of the task has been achieved. In many ways, Piaget sees the **developmental stages** as universal across all children, regardless of cultural factors (Shiraev & Levy, 2007).

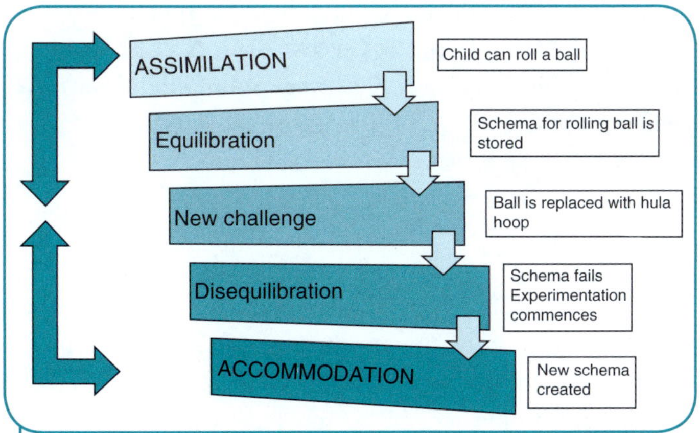

Figure 13.1 The process of assimilation and accommodation

Erikson's (1902–1994) psychosocial theory (Erikson et al., 1959) looked at links between physical and social development and posed a model of sequential social skill development. Erikson's works were greatly influenced by Freud, particularly his 1923 theory of personality structure. Erikson considered that at every stage of the life span, a crisis factor arose because the needs of the individual were in conflict with the needs of society (Côté, 2006). Development in a balanced individual is then achieved by the person being able to work through and find a solution to each crisis.

Vygotsky's work (1896–1934) on sociocultural theory and social development theory is perhaps most widely linked with cultural variants (Keller, 2011). Vygotsky premised that culture is socially constructed and that social learning occurs before development (Gardiner & Kosmitzki, 2002). In contrast to Piaget's work, Vygotsky highlighted the notion that social settings are housed within cultural environments and are key factors in overall development. Vygotsky depicts a downward approach where adults transmit cultural practice to children.

These explanations are a simplistic introduction to the various theorists' works. There are, and will undoubtedly remain, critiques of all models, and those mentioned are no exception. There is no definitive agreement as to the existence or otherwise of a single set of basic processes common to all infants by which they learn about their environments, regardless of culture.

Socialisation

For an individual, acquiring an understanding of their world and shared behaviours and beliefs (i.e. culture) is gained through the process of socialisation. This is defined as the way we learn about our immediate environment, learn what behaviours are acceptable and develop an understanding of moral obligations: that is, what is considered right and wrong in our given situations (Shiraev & Levy, 2007). Socialisation is therefore a social learning theory that establishes norms which are influenced by a bonding process (Rew, 2013).

Socialisation is generally defined as: 'the process of learning the culture of a society or group, its language and customs' (Jones & Creedy, 2012, p. 255). It should be noted that some theories of socialisation propose only two **agents of socialisation** (either primary or secondary), whereas other models consider three: primary, secondary and tertiary. We will now look at each of these agents in greater detail under three distinct phases: primary, secondary and tertiary socialisation environments.

Primary socialisation

Primary socialisation can be defined as the first learning unit (usually the family), where children receive transmission of the unique characteristics of their cultural makeup (e.g. language, beliefs, values, customs and behaviours) (Jones & Creedy, 2012, p. 255).

As the initial phase of learning generally commences within the family unit; the family can be termed an *agent* of primary socialisation. Within this environment, a child will learn about who is a care provider, who will respond to their needs (such as hunger), who is a comforter (i.e. the early associations of who will respond to the need for human contact) as well as who is an attachment versus who is a stranger (Thompson & Lamb, 1983). The child also develops in response to parenting practices, and these clearly vary between cultures. We see some societies embracing a patriarchal system with the male (father) clearly established as the head of the household, tribe or community (Germov, 2014) as is the case with a number of countries such as Saudi Arabia (Al-Rasheed, 2010; Rich, 2015), whereas others favour matriarchal structures such as some communities in New Guinea, including Bougainville (Garasu, 2002). Therefore, parenting styles will have a significant impact on the early socialisation of the child and this is clearly linked to cultural environments (Rew, 2013). Just as all family dynamics differ, cross-cultural and intra-cultural differences also emerge, further emphasising the significance of culture in development (Keller, 2011). Children may model social roles of female and male parents/ carers and this establishes an initial sense of gender roles and responsibilities (Germov, 2014; Grincevičienė & Grincevičius, 2014). As the child develops, they progress to a secondary socialisation environment.

Secondary socialisation

Secondary socialisation can be defined as the learning of behavioural patterns that occurs outside of the family environment, such as within the school system (Nagy & Szekley, 2010). When entering the educational system individuals are exposed to values, beliefs and practices that they may not have encountered within their primary environment. Such experiences may include an introduction to other types of food, different rules for communication such as in a classroom, different types of recreation activities and different terminology for common objects. The impact of peers within secondary school may give rise to considerations of motivation to continue educational engagement, aspire to varying levels of achievement or, conversely, develop a sense of isolation and separateness from the educational system, and influence variations in attendance and possible truancy (Berndt & Murphy, 2002; Studsrod & Bru, 2011; Arnon, Shamai & Ilatov, 2008).

While the role of education in the socialisation process is significant (Grincevičienė & Grincevičius, 2014), as individuals progress through stages of their lifespan, they continue to be exposed to increasingly expanding experiences outside the education system. Examples include interaction with members of the opposite sex, different social languages (including swearing and texting) and different dress styles. The individual makes conscious decisions about their affiliation with these social behaviours (Guliaikhin, Galkin & Vasil'eva, 2013). The adolescent stage of development is often said to have the function of establishing friendships and emotional relationships as a means of belonging and connectedness (Fleming & Towey, 2001; Rew, 2013) along with developing a sense of independence (Jones & Creedy, 2012). To affect a sense of belonging, adolescents will model their behaviours to reflect the group with which they seek to be a member (Guliaikhin et al., 2013). Risk-taking or deviant behaviours often emerge during this stage of the lifespan; however, these are balanced against prosocial factors that also emerge (Rew, 2013; Germov, 2014). At some point, the child attains adulthood and encounters a variety of tertiary socialisation environments.

Tertiary socialisation

Tertiary socialisation can be defined as behaviours that are acquired as a process of engagement with others that occurs outside mandatory formal education, such as in social and free time activities (Nagy & Szekely, 2010).

Tertiary environments continue to expand our exposure to the wider world. With the transition from adolescence into the various stages of adulthood, we experience a number of 'rites of passage'. Examples of the transitions may include dating, consuming alcohol, gaining employment, taking on a religious role, becoming sexually active (Fleming & Towey, 2001), earning money, taking out a loan, purchasing a car, buying a house – these are just some examples. Rew's (2013) research indicated that even in modern society, religious practices and beliefs, along with parenting styles, remain a significant shaping force in determining adolescent behaviours.

The changeover from secondary to tertiary environments is not clearly determined, as adolescents may be working before completing schooling, or they may be members of groups such as sporting teams, religious groups and other units simultaneously. According to Erikson (Jones & Creedy, 2012), it is during this phase – when the adolescent moves into environments beyond education and into other social settings such as recreational sports and nightclubs – that the individual's actual or observed experiences may be attempted or increased; for example, alcohol consumption may also develop during this period (Hoel et al., 2004). While universities are seen as a place of learning, they also have a significant social and leisure time connection. University environments are one of the most common agents of tertiary socialisation in the Western world (Jones & Creedy, 2012). This change of influences also corresponds (within the Western world) with the move to 'adulthood' and reaching the age of 18 years as a legal indication of a capacity to make adult decisions (Nagy & Szekely, 2010). The focus of this stage of adulthood includes selecting a marriage partner, reproduction and gaining work. It is widely accepted that socialisation processes should be considered as lifelong processes that have no strict age limits for the progression from one stage to another (Grincevičienė & Grincevičius, 2014).

The cross-cultural lens

Having examined the term 'culture' and briefly explored how we come to have knowledge of our own culture, we can now move to the concept of cross-cultural psychology.

Cross-cultural approaches require the process of comparison between cultural groups. The cross-cultural lens is a comparative one that highlights both similarities and differences. The actual discipline of cross-cultural psychology is not new, originating as early as the 1960s.

Cross-cultural psychology is defined as 'the systematic study of relationships between the cultural content of human development and the behaviours that become established in the repertoire of individuals growing up in a particular culture' (Berry, Poortinga & Pandey, 1997, p. x). An alternative definition is that of Kagitcibasi and Berry (cited in Keith, 2011, p. 9), who describe it as the 'study of similarities and differences in individual psychological and social functioning in various cultures and ethnic groups'. We can only begin to appreciate the cross-cultural lens (i.e. the comparative lens) once we understand each individual culture in its own context, as well as revealing tendencies that may create a bias; this is achieved through knowing our own culture.

The ethnocentric focus

The explanation so far in this chapter of the agents of socialisation has provided an inherently Western view. In reading the explanations, the majority of readers would have been able to equate the stages to their own situation. This is your individual subjective experience of how you make sense of your own world. This brings us to the next concept, ethnocentrism.

Enthocentricism is defined as 'the belief that one's own culture is the natural, or best, culture' (Jones & Creedy, 2012, p. 251). Ethnocentrism is not a new concept. In earlier times, the term was viewed as an applied prejudice or 'generalized prejudice' (Allport, 1954, p. 66) that often had nothing to do with ethnicity. Cross-cultural psychology is often concerned with how our own ethnocentric behaviours impact on our ability to perceive and understand other cultures.

In delivering interventions, it is necessary for health practitioners to deliver ethical practice. Ethical concepts for consideration are beneficence and non-maleficence. It is here that we begin to gain some insight into the importance of understanding different cultural influences. Even if a method of intervention has been demonstrated to work within a specific demographic area and is found to align with a nominated culture, this does not mean that the intervention is transferable to another location where there are different cultural factors. It is only through gaining knowledge of other cultures that health professionals can maintain ethical practice and adhere to **beneficence**, 'the obligation to do good and to care for people' (Berglund, 2004, p. 12), and **non-maleficence**, 'the paired obligation to do no harm' (Berglund, 2004, p. 13), and reduce ethnocentric or generalised bias (Rew, 2013). Various beliefs and practices need to be understood in order for interventions to be therapeutic. Consider the following case study.

Mini case study 13.1

Hindsight is 20/20.

An example of the necessity of cross-cultural psychology awareness was explored by Christopher et al. (2014) in the aftermath of US-based interventions in response to the 2004 Indian Ocean tsunami. The authors report on culturally

continued ›

Mini case study 13.1 continued ›

mismatched approaches to interventions by foreign aid psychology providers. While 'Western-derived' interventions such as grief counselling and individual mental health evaluations were delivered with the best moral intentions, some practices, such as group interventions and mental health assessments and diagnosis (as general examples) were often at odds with cultural practices that exist in this locality. An illustration of this includes Western practices of encouraging the expression of grief and openly expressing emotions; however, public displays of emotions are not in keeping with the practices of the Hindu and Buddhist cultures that are prevalent in this community (Christopher et al., 2014, p. 646). Additionally, the use of group therapeutic interventions also may not have been in keeping with the caste, religious or gender segregation that also existed (Christopher et al., 2014, p. 646). The result was that anxiety may well have been increased and family dysfunction created rather than a beneficial therapeutic relationship (Christopher et al., 2014, p. 646).

Critical thinking questions

1. Could the term 'ethnocentric' apply to this situation?
2. What situational factors do you think may have led to this condition?
3. Research the concept of non-maleficence. Is this concept related to the case study? Why/why not?
4. What lessons could be learnt from this situation?

Expanding our horizons: gaining insight

How do we achieve these attributes? It is only through reflective practice that we can develop fuller and deeper understanding. Reflective practice or reflexivity is a practice of looking into ourselves as a process of continual learning and developing insight and a critical capacity to evaluate our own behaviours, thoughts and perceptions. To attain knowledge of others, first we must know ourselves; this helps to reduce ethnocentric bias. In acquiring understanding of the concepts of cross-cultural competence, cultural sensitivity and cultural safety are encountered. All of these concepts imply a specialised understanding of the cross-cultural lens. Let's examine these concepts individually.

Cross-cultural competence (CCC) relates to an organisational approach whereby healthcare (for example) is delivered in an effective and efficient manner with significant consideration afforded to the consumers, who have diverse cultural needs (Douglas et al., 2014). This is important, as care provided to consumers is influenced by the organisational culture (Berglund, 2004). CCC can be defined as behaviours, attitudes and motivations that are demonstrated by an individual working in a professional capacity. CCC is often informed by systems within organisations, such as guidelines and policies, and broader social legislation. CCC facilitates an individual's ability to readily understand and develop effective relationships with people from diverse cultures (Flaskerud, 2007, p. 121 cited in Germov, 2014, p. 173; Chen, 2015). Arising from this practice we have seen the emergence of terms such as 'ethno-specific services'. These services predominantly take into account barriers faced by people from culturally and linguistically diverse (CALD) backgrounds. Ethno-specific services are in contrast to mainstream services, where the policy is to provide the same service to all consumers without variation (Germov, 2014).

Cultural sensitivity has been described as an interpersonal skill whereby practitioners can develop empathy, understanding and appreciation of other cultures to facilitate the development of an effective therapeutic relationship (Fleming & Towey, 2001). Developing cultural sensitivity is a professional skill that will enhance individual effectiveness (Fleming & Towey, 2001). Developing cultural sensitivity allows us to acknowledge variances in others' beliefs and practices without classifying them as good, bad, positive or negative. Cultural sensitivity contrasts directly with an ethnocentric lens. Being culturally sensitive enables the practitioner to function effectively within another cultural environment using appropriate interpersonal interactions such as body language, posturing and gesturing.

Cultural safety is a concept with its origins in New Zealand. It gained popularity in the 1980s (Hampton & Toombs, 2013). Cultural safety pertains to a respect for cultural practices by others outside the cultural group and requires that organisations providing services to individuals from diverse cultural persuasions should orientate resources and ways of delivering those services to take into account the cultural nuances (Williams, 2009 cited in Hampton & Toombs, 2013) and seek to maintain cultural integrity (Schnierer, Ellsmore & Schnierer, 2011). Cultural safety practices are intended to reduce barriers that may otherwise oppress or have negative impacts on individuals on the grounds of race/ethnicity (Head, 2013 cited in Hampton & Toombs, 2013). Examples of legislation that can be seen to promote cultural sensitivity include the *Aboriginal Torres Strait Islander Heritage Protection Act 1984* (Cwlth) (Schnierer et al., 2011). Providing a culturally safe environment is linked to the concepts of beneficence and non-maleficence that were introduced earlier.

Is culture a static or dynamic construct?

> Social psychologists have demonstrated that, even when cultural patterns appear to be relatively stable over time, culture is continuously being produced and reproduced in the dynamic interaction between individuals and their social and natural environments.
>
> (Kemmelmeier & Kühnen, 2012)

Durkheim and Parsons (who present a functionalist perspective) considered that while culture was subject to shaping and modification, the rate at which this occurred was generally slow. Marx (who holds a conflict perspective) looked at the dominance of ruling class ideology that was a feature of stratified or class-based societies (Alexander, 1992). Grouping commonalities under broad headings had been a long-held tradition that commonly utilises the domains of race, ethnicity, nationality and religion. An example of this includes Christian and Islamic cultures. It is currently reported that Australia, Malta and the US share predominantly Christian religious practices, whereas the majority of people of Pakistan, Malaysia and the United Arab Emirates follow religious practices that are unique to Islam (NationMaster, 2011). But even within the main classifications, homogeneity does not exist. Within the culture of Christianity, there are smaller subgroups of specific denominations that hold unique beliefs, although Christianity still includes a number of shared characteristics. The same situation can be seen with the followers of Islam: while there are many shared characteristics of a culture, there are also intra-cultural variations; an example of this includes variations between Sunni and Shiah communities.

Based on political and social history, Indigenous culture has often been overlooked or given only slight recognition as a homogenous entity (Sherwood, 2013). It is estimated that approximately 600 variations of Indigenous culture have existed (Schnierer et al., 2011), and their contribution has been drastically underestimated. Where Indigenous culture has been acknowledged, the image of Indigenous Australians has been mainly stereotyped to give a collective identity rather than indicating the vastness of variant practices that exist (Riseman, 2013) and fails to identify 'social and political infrastructures, critical to a sense of community well-being' (Sherwood, 2013, p. 32). Within Indigenous culture, there are a number of variances in characteristics such as language, food, traditional medicine usage, family structures and land boundaries. Australian Indigenous culture is contributed to by an estimated population of slightly under 670 000 people as at June 2011 (MacRae et. al. cited in Sherwood, 2013). Within Australia there are multiple Indigenous communities, each with unique cultural practices, and their culture is transmitted by music, dance, art, architecture and ceremonies (Australian Government, 2015). Identifying characteristics of subgroups within Indigenous Aboriginal culture can include communities that are predominantly sea hunters compared to others that are land hunters. Other examples of characteristics include specialised tools used, and patterns and ways of daily life that have developed alongside these sea and land hunting activities. Cognition and development are also linked to environmental factors, with a number of studies confirming variances in 'hunter and gather compared to pastoralists or farmers' (Keller, 2011, p. 4). Despite the geographical differences, there is a shared concept of 'Country' and links to traditional lands. In the following quote, we can see a cross-cultural focus in relation to Country.

> We cultivated our land, but in a way different from the white man. We endeavoured to live with the land; they seemed to live off it. I was taught to preserve, never to destroy.
>
> (Aborigine Tom Dystra cited in Australian Government, 2015)

Indigenous Australian communities have distinct characteristics; therefore, to consider the group only from a homogenous perspective denies the intracultural subjective experience of each person's specific connection with Country (Fleming & Towey, 2001).

Indigenous communities place significance on Country (note the capitalisation here); that is, the locality of birth and connection with Elders and ancestors. In transmitting cultural practices, there is a strong bond with the land and the places of storytelling (Australian Government, 2015). Locations of cultural significance may be accessible or restricted to outsiders or even to other Indigenous communities (Best & Fredericks, 2014). Knowledge of culture can be transmitted in a variety of forms.

The changing face of cultural transmission

Earlier, we explored the agents of socialisation. In this section we will revisit the concept and note some emerging trends. In 1945, anthropologist Ralph Linton defined a concept called 'non-material culture' as 'the way of life of its members; the collection of ideas and habits which they learn, share and transmit from generation to generation', where the rules for daily living are transmitted from one generation to the next (Linton, 1972). The scripts or narratives that direct and guide individuals in addressing everyday activities have their early basis in folk psychology (Keith, 2011). Transmission of culture through the processes of socialisation often used the medium of song and dance. Folk songs were a way to readily transmit beliefs, practices, morals and values easily from one generation to another regardless of literacy levels. Folk songs are considered a vehicle of transmitting oral and aural history known as folk culture.

Indigenous Australians made use of song, music, art, body decoration and dance as a means of communicating, often across a number of communities that had no shared verbal language (Australian Government, 2015). The practice of *Djaparlagin* is translated as a 'singing corroboree' which uses teaching, demonstrating, talking and mimicking. Using song lines, ceremonies and knowledge of Country, this corroboree is a method of transmitting information from one generation to the next as well as to other groups of interest (Best & Fredericks, 2014). The learning that takes place is translated into *Yatdjuligin*, a term offered by Elder Ivy Molly Booth from the Wakgun Clan of the Gureng Gureng Nation in Queensland Australia that means 'talking in a good way' (Best & Fredericks, 2014, p. 3). A corroboree can then be considered a form of folk culture.

Klimka (2014) indicates that culture often has a traditional basis; however, it is also responsive to other influences, such as media. This catalyst for change can be termed 'mass culture'. Mass culture is defined as ideas, beliefs and values that are transmitted through common exposure to newspapers, television, art and music, and in contemporary society, includes tweets and podcasts (for example). Contemporary communication practices highlight radio, television, print media and even mobile devices and texting practices as shaping cultural practices such as communication and transmission of knowledge (James, 2010). If communication practices unite a community (Ong, 1971), then the emergence of electronic communications can be seen as a reordering and reshaping of the way groups communicate (James, 2010). So in this way we can see a traditional culture that is responsive to elements of social change, impacted by factors such as youth music and fashion.

In relation to processes of socialisation, it is now common for children in Western environments to spend less time interacting within the family unit, even during the period of primary socialisation. This situation has arisen due to the social and economic pressures for both parents to find employment and the increase in single-parent households, necessitating the young child to enter into a care service such as a formal day care organisation or a community- or home-based care provider service. Additionally, the number of children accessing before- and after-school care services has risen over the last several years.

Moving from a primary socialisation unit into a wider environment and establishing relationships outside the family is also occurring earlier within Western societies, where previously this change occurred at the time of adolescence (Arnon, Shamai & Ilatov, 2008). Again, we can see a variation in the meaning and timing of this adolescent period. In Western societies, the transition phase is often accompanied by rebellion and acting-out behaviours (Jones & Creedy, 2012). In some societies the transition occurs earlier; for example, within Australian Indigenous culture, boys are deemed responsible enough to take on adult roles as early as 10 years of age, and this is signified by initiation ceremonies where a boy's body may be painted and often permanent body markings are attained to signify the transition (Indigenous Australia, n.d.). A further example includes the practice of the South American Tukana people, who mark the passage to womanhood with a celebration lasting up to 3 months from the onset of menstruation (Delaney, 1995). Menstruation can commence as early as 9 years of age. Many cultures outside Western environments have practices that involve transmission of cultural knowledge in gender-segregated communities and rites of passage are accompanied by celebrations and rituals that extend over long periods of time, from weeks or months and even up to a year. It can be seen from this that many societies have practices to create cohesive environments either within family, extended family or segregated gender groups. Other indicators of transition can be more visual, such as religious cultural practices; for example, adult males of the Jewish faith (over the age of 13 years) may wear Tallit or a prayer shawl, and commonly, all males wear a hat in the synagogue whereas young, unmarried females may not be required to wear headdress (BBC, 2009).

In comparison, according to Arnon, Shamai and Ilatov (2008), there is a tendency in Western societies for adolescents to spend less time within the family unit and be afforded greater independence and freedom; this can be viewed as creating detachment from the influence of adults and more linkages to peer influences.

Even when a society places a clear indicator for a person to be considered an adult (e.g. the age of 18 years in the US and Australia), an individual may have reached this legal point but not see themselves as a well-equipped adult (Nagy & Szekely, 2010). Arnett (2000 cited in Smith et al., 2015) suggests that this period be termed 'emerging adulthood' and covers the age range of 18 to 29 years. This new phase of adulthood was postulated as being typified by behaviours such as marriage and the establishment of careers – frequently observed as occurring later in industrialised environments – and could be considered to show a delay in attaining the previously held concept of adulthood as stated by Erikson (Smith et al., 2015). Smith et al. further suggest that the delay in marriage was attributed to greater retention within educational environments. In this way, we can see the change in cultural norms and the emergence of a subculture. Subculture can be defined as a subset within any group (Burnard & Gill, 2009). Others argue that the emerging adulthood stage (rather than a specific age or age range) may actually represent a universal concept across cultures. Perhaps we could consider a stage to be universally experienced regardless of culture, and the age range more readily related to specific cultures. More research could be directed to this area to give greater understanding. Again, depending on the viewpoint of the observer there will continue to be much debate on this topic.

The typical Australian situation can be examined in contrast to practices in Pakistan. Pakistan is predominantly an Islamic nation, with approximately 96% of the population being followers of Islam (Hussain, 2005). One significant area of contrast is that generally, Western adolescents are seeking autonomy and individuality whereas adolescents of Pakistan have a culture that is entrenched with values such as obedience and submissiveness (Burnard & Gill, 2009), with the focus on conformity (Imam, 2012).These Pakistani social values are reinforced both within and outside the family unit particularly by the observance of religious practices and the maintainence of social prohibitions such as mixing between genders (Imam, 2012). In this example, the cultural comparison rests on exploration of the freedom afforded the Westernised adolescents and the conformity and tradition instilled in Pakistani adolescents. It is in this comparative analysis that we see the emergence of significant cultural differences. In working with clients from fundamentally diverse backgrounds, there must be an understanding of the cultural constructs in order to develop effective interventions and professional relationships.

Peer relationships are one of the most significant influences on behaviour in the later adolescent period (Steinberg & Monaham, 2007). The influence of peers, which can be termed informal social control, becomes stronger with adolescents as they seek to establish new identities and gain a sense of belonging, and so conform to the expected norms of the aspired-to group. This ties into Erikson's notion of a crisis that arises at each stage of development and requires the individual to solve it (Côté, 2006). In this instance, the crisis is in establishing an identity and asking 'Who am I?' as they move from acceptance of parental views and expectations and juggle these previous beliefs and values against those they observe in the wider environment. The changing influences on adolescents can also be related to social control theory, which focuses on the establishment of a social order and conforming to a given social group (Innes, 2003; Germov, 2014). Depending on the norm – the cultural practices of the group – adolescents may engage in prosocial behaviours such as community enhancement activities including environmental protection and endangered animal advocacy, or they may be drawn into antisocial activities (e.g. graffiti, drug use and promiscuity). The emergence of delinquent behaviour is said to occur when there is a reduced capacity or strength of a social bond (Hirschi, 1969). Social control is, of course, contrasted by self-control. Self-control is an individual's decision-making process in contrast to social control, where moderating or moulding forces are exerted by a particular group (Lowe & Haws, 2014).

Mini case study 13.2

> Imagine there's no heaven.
>
> (John Lennon lyrics)

As an indication of change, let us consider the characteristic of religion within Australia. While remaining a predominantly Christian country, there has been an increase in the number of respondents at census reporting that they have 'no religion'. The 2011 census (ABS, 2013) identified that approximately 1 in 5 Australians have 'no religion'.

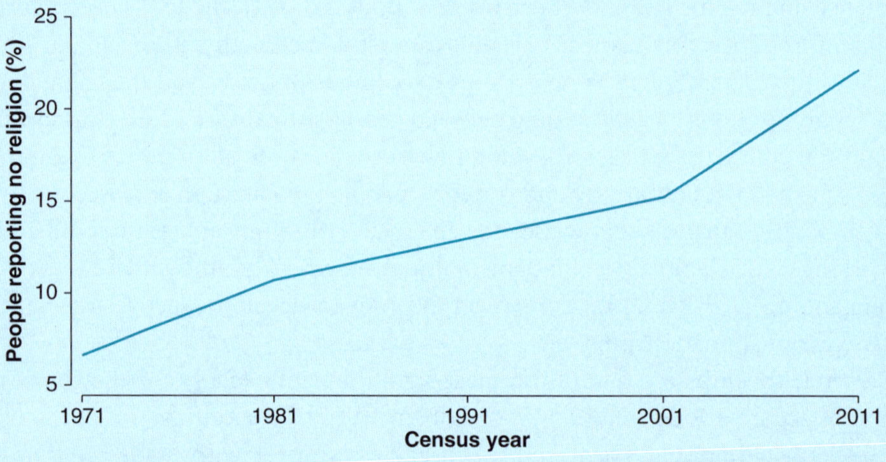

Figure 13.2 Percentage of people reporting no religion, 1971–2011
Source: ABS, 2013

Critical thinking questions

1. What are the cultural elements you note for each situation?
2. How are the situations different?
3. Based on your current knowledge, what changes occurred within these cultures over the past 10 years?
4. Why do you think these changes are occurring?

Impacts of culture on human behaviour

Exploring impacts of culture on human behaviour from a cross-cultural lens is a diverse field. Each writer highlights a collection of different perspectives that are as diverse as the range of definitions for the term cross-culture itself. As we have established, the cross-cultural lens explores both similarities and differences in the behavioural characteristics of individuals within a group. The group itself, as we have determined, is not only related to the constructs of race, nationality, ethnicity and religion but extends to include other areas.

Emics and etics

So far we have considered cross-cultural psychology as a comparative practice between cultures and between groups within cultures. The terms we can now highlight are emics and etics. **Etics** can be defined as the study of unique attributes across cultural groups (a general or reasonably universal characteristic). **Emics** studies characteristics that are unique within a culture or cultural group (Shiraev & Levy, 2007, p. 46; Cheung, van de Vijver & Leong, 2011, p. 593; Gardiner & Kosmitzki, 2002, p. 8). Etics can therefore be seen as an absolutist position whereas emics are a relativist approach to viewing and comparing cultures (Shiraev & Levy, 2007). Cheung, van de Vijver and Leong (2011) researched the impact of emetics and etics using a cross-cultural focus on the interaction between personality and culture. Their comparison groups were Chinese and South African culture. The research included composing personality inventories of the two groups followed by a comparative analysis. The researchers highlighted that even within specific characteristics such as language, cultural implications are significant with variations still evident. For example, in Italy there are permutations of language, described as dialects, which all have their basis in the formal Italian language.

Heuristics

Heuristics is defined as the strategies individuals use to solve problems in everyday life (Jones & Creedy, 2012). In developing a heuristic approach to life's challenges, an individual must rely on skills gained within their cultural environment. Heuristics are 'go-to strategies' or 'rules of thumb' (Nunn, 2012), fundamental strategies we use to address everyday tasks and allow us to make quick appraisals and plan a course of action (Schwikert & Curran, 2014). Schwikert and Curran's (2014) research looks at the notion of familiarity that is contributed to by memory cues. It could then be inferred that culture has an impact on familiarity. These heuristic strategies become part of our routine practices through processes of socialisation and are shaped by our cultural experiences (Nunn, 2012). It should be remembered that moral codes are a product of culture (Norton & Marks-Maran, 2014). Nunn (2012) further examined 'historical shocks' and their impact on cultural replication (i.e. the transmission of beliefs values and norms) from one generation to the next. The issue of trust was a feature for consideration. In making decisions, the notion of whose point of view can be trusted emerges. History is emphasised as a variable that can impact on cultural replication. An example of the implications of trust can be seen in the impact of 'shocks' such as the slave trade, which caused a breakdown in previously known daily activities of those individuals. It reasonably follows that the 'stolen generations' in Australian history will also have significant impact on the transmission of culture and therefore heuristics of Indigenous Australians. These examples clearly impact on cultural norms.

Culture shock

When an individual is positioned within an environment that challenges many of their previously held beliefs, they may experience culture shock (Barnard & Spencer, 2002 cited in Burnard & Gill, 2009). One of the elements of culture shock is the degree to which the current exposures contradict people's understanding of the world as they have previously understood it.

Earlier we spoke of adolescents and their wanting to 'belong' and 'fit in'. For adolescents with families from other cultures, there is often a desire to connect with those from their original culture with whom they can share common experiences. These experiences can be as varied as the use of languages to the implements one uses to eat food (Burnard & Gill, 2009).

Culture shock more often relates to the impact on individuals and groups of catastrophic events. An example is the Nazis' actions in World War II in their attempt to eradicate Jewish people (Burnard & Gill, 2009; Berglund, 2004). Asylum seekers and refugees – those who have been forced to flee their country due to threats on their life (Nicholl & Thompson, 2004) – may also experience culture shock. Another example within the Australian Indigenous experience is the ongoing impact of the stolen generations, where Aboriginal children were forcibly removed from their families to be raised outside their culture and to extinguish links to their identity (Best & Fredericks, 2014). This occurred under government assimilation policies and legislation. The impact still continues, and is one of the most significant issues in Australia's history (Best & Fredericks, 2014; Hampton & Toombs, 2013). One ongoing impact is on language.

> The endangered status of Indigenous Australian languages is illustrated by the decline in the number of Indigenous people who speak an Indigenous language at home. At the 2008 National Aboriginal and Torres Strait Islander Social Survey, 11.5% of Indigenous people aged 15 years and over spoke an Indigenous language at home, compared to 12% in 2002.
>
> (Schnierer et al. 2011, p. 10)

The removal of children from their natural culture has left 'Indigenous peoples' cultures and heritage vulnerable and endangered' (Battiste & Youngblood Henderson, 2000 cited in Schnierer et al. 2011, p. 14), affecting the diverse range of languages, internal governance, spiritually and traditions.

Mini case study 13.3

Read the following accounts of personal stories about stolen generations aired on ABC's regional radio network on Sunday 6 January 2002 (presented by Robyn Williams and produced by Brigitte Seega): http://www.abc.net.au/radionational/programs/ockhamsrazor/the-stolen-generation/3503616#transcript.

Critical thinking questions

1. What were the impacts on the children who were taken from their homes?
2. What are the implications for trust?
3. Does this situation equate to 'culture shock'? Why/why not?
4. What connections can be made between this scenario and non-maleficence and beneficence?

The cross-cultural lens of grief and mourning

Let's look at the emotion of grief. Death and grief are often considered taboo topics in everyday conversation – or at least within a Western context. Many cultures do not openly display emotions, whereas others use rituals to address psychological distress and find comfort. At some time, every individual will experience loss and grief. It cannot be denied that the grieving process is intensely personal. There are a number of models that examine the process of grief from an individual perspective, such as family systems theory which examines family functioning, culture, cognition and developmental perspectives in response to grief behaviours.

The culture of a family includes how the family unit is composed, how the household members communicate, roles and responsibilities, along with power positions within the unit (Rothbaum et al., 2002). It should be noted that family systems theory is a Western approach to understanding as the theory was developed and tested in European and North American cultures (Rothbaum et al., 2002).

In the psychology of grief, we also encounter models such as:

- the Kübler-Ross grief model, which lists five stages of grief
- Therese Rando's model, which details the 'six Rs' of the mourning process
- Stoebe and Strut's dual process model of grief (Jones & Creedy, 2012; Smit 2015).

While these models are exceptionally useful tools for gaining insight into the grief process, could it be that they imply a level of homogeneity and so suggest that there is no variation in grief across cultures (Rosenblatt, 2013)?

From a historical perspective, we can examine the recorded grief practices of Indigenous Australian culture. It has been stated that individuals belonging to the same ethnicity (e.g. Australian Aboriginals) are not homogenous in their practice and often demonstrate significant variances in behaviours, as seen between different communities within the same culture. This remains true in relation to historical burial practices, some of which are still carried out today in traditional communities. An account of Aboriginal cultural practices in traditional Aboriginal communities in northern, southern and central Australia demonstrates significant variances.

In some northern communities, burial practices include a corroboree and may have two distinct phases: primary and secondary (Schnierer et al. 2011). Primary burial involves the deceased body being placed on a platform and exposed to the elements for a number of months until only skeletal remains are evident (Welch, n.d.). Secondary burial then occurs: the bones are collected and sometimes coated in ochre and then disseminated. Some communities bring the bones of their ancestors with them, whereas other communities (e.g. in Arnhem Land) place the remains in logs at sites of significance in their Country (Schnierer et al., 2011; Welch, n.d.).

Grief and mourning practices vary significantly between cultural groups. Religious or spiritual beliefs are a characteristic of many cultures. Such beliefs can offer some assistance for an individual in the way they experience and express their grief. Ata's (2012) research into comparative grief practices of eight cultural groups indicated that cultural practices and religious observances have significant impacts on coping strategies. Having knowledge of a person's cultural background can be a predictor to a certain degree as to the impact the grief experience will have. A person's culture will either permit or prevent the individual from publicly expressing emotions. Ata's (2012) results showed that individuals with greater religious affiliation showed generally lowered anxiety responses to death.

Mini case study 13.4

Susan gave birth to a beautiful baby boy 5 hours ago. Due to complications that arose following her son's birth, he has been placed on life support and airlifted to an intensive care unit at a hospital 500 km from the family home. Only Susan has been able to travel in the air ambulance with her son. Susan's partner is in the military and serving overseas, so she has not been able to speak with him. The remaining family is en route; however, it will take at least 2 hours for them to arrive.

Events unfold and Susan is asked about her preferences for further resuscitation efforts and interventions for her baby, who has subsequently deteriorated. Susan has spoken with doctors about the medical prognosis for her son and available options. On appraising the information, she indicates that she does not wish for any further resuscitation to be undertaken and she requests for the medical equipment to be removed. She asks for a priest to be called urgently so her son can be baptised and given the last rites. Soon after the priest's visit, her son is pronounced dead following a series of further catastrophic events. Susan requests to hold her son. The mother and baby are taken to a private hospital room. She asks to be left alone with her child until her mother and other two children arrive. On their arrival, Susan asks nursing staff for permission to bathe her son as she wants to dress him in the new clothes she had purchased in preparation for bringing home her new addition to the family. Her family helps in the bathing and dressing and each takes a turn at holding the newborn and having their photograph taken with him. Nursing staff assist Susan in taking a snippet of the baby's hair and making hand and foot impressions. The family's request for privacy is respected. After some hours, the nurse and doctor return to speak with Susan about what needs to happen next. Susan is distraught to learn that her son will undergo an autopsy. She is told it is now time to leave her son, who will be taken to the morgue.

Critical thinking questions

1. Reflect on your own culture: your beliefs and practices that relate to grief and mourning. Using a cross-cultural lens, consider the similarities and differences between Susan's behaviours and either your own thoughts and practices OR those of another culture.
2. Thinking about your current understanding of other cultures, list five points you 'know' about another culture's death practices.
3. What processes make you more aware of you own cultural practices in relation to this topic?
4. What are three concepts that you are exploring by personal reflection?

Culture as a shared behaviour across non-traditional groups

So far we have considered the construct of culture as relating to nationality, ethnicity, race and religion. However, if we look back to our definition of culture as 'the total way of life shared by members of a group' (Jones & Creedy, 2012, p. 305), we can see how this can be extended to other groups, or more precisely, subgroups. Subgroups are smaller divisions of a larger cultural cohort; examples we have already considered include some of the smaller assemblies within the larger group of Christianity. We will now consider examples of groups that transcend the construct of disability as a culture; for example, deaf culture. First we need to consider: does this group fit the definition of a culture? Recall that Taylor's definition of culture is 'that complex whole which includes knowledge, belief, art, morals, law, customs and any other capabilities and habits acquired by man as a member of society' (1871, p. 42). Our simplified definition of culture relates to shared characteristics of a group of individuals. Definitions of culture often consider five sociological criteria: language, values, traditions, norms and identity (Padden & Humphries, 1988 cited in Small n.d.). Deaf Australia Inc. (2010) indicates that people belonging to the deaf community do have distinctive characteristics, based primarily on visual orientations. Such characteristics can include unique language (e.g. Auslan in Australia), values (deaf is normal, deaf babies are highly valued), behaviour (including eye contact, physical proximity and touch), greetings and farewells, and use of technology (Deaf Australia Inc., 2010). We can see that these characteristics certainly meet the definition of culture.

New cultural groups?

As we have established, culture is not static but undergoes continual change. So too does the composition of groups that develop their own unique cultural identity. Let's consider the contemporary establishment of gamers as a cultural construct.

Gamers

Gamers can be identified as people who use video technologies, including internet games, for fun and entertainment. Even within this group there are subgroups; for example, casual gamers and hardcore gamers.

Do gamers represent a cultural group? Re-examining our definition of culture – 'the total way of life shared by members of a group' (Jones & Creedy, 2012, p. 305) – it is clear that gamers could indeed be considered a culture. Maxwell (2011 cited in Chmiel, 2012) states that culture is 'a set of transmitted, common knowledge, behaviours and attitudes'. Behaviours, language and other characteristics can be seen as being passed from one generation to the next within the gaming world. Gaming is perhaps the newest version of popular culture. The demographics of this cultural cohort indicate distinct membership characteristics. In Australia, the average age of gamers is 30 years. Male gamers tend towards action-orientated video effects whereas female gamers' preference is for puzzle and family operation games. Interestingly, most gamers are undertaking full-time tertiary study (Brand, Borchard & Holmes, 2008). Demographics aside, gamers use technologies to create new communities, and explore and experiment with varying social orders (Hull et al., 2014; Johnson, 2010).

As internet use has grown, and features and functions have gained widespread acceptance, so have online social connections, either individually or as part of a social group. Gross (2010, cited in Yang 2012) indicates that research has shown computer games and online gaming to be one of the most common recreational activities of children and teenagers. Yang (2012, p. 236) writes that 'the online gaming community provides adolescents not only with the skills for early socialisation but also with an environment for interpersonal and emotional interaction'. In many ways, technology is a mode of cultural transmission and has an effect of changing socialisation practices that over time will undoubtedly be reflected in cultural changes. Yang (2012, p. 236) further asserts that technology, in particular the internet, is more powerful than traditional media in challenging and changing 'the knowledge and values of adolescents'. Logically, then, the impact of computer games on adults is also significant.

Much research has focused on the adverse impacts of gaming, with studies into the shared behaviours of this group revealing that there is often a glamorisation of anti-social behaviours such as violence. Even though such behaviours are simulated and animated, there remains the psychological impact of the acceptance of risk-taking (Fischer et al., 2012; Hull et al., 2014), violent behaviours, aggression and bullying (Yang, 2012), and addiction to gaming (Beranuy, Carbonell & Griffiths, 2013). Internet gaming impacts disorder (IGD) is now mentioned in DSM-5 (American Psychiatric Association, 2013) and relates to characteristics of preoccupation with internet games, withdrawal effects when gaming is discontinued and other factors (King, 2014).

Gaming culture is not all negative. Gaming is also a way of achieving belonging and enabling a degree of social interaction via the online multi-player gaming options. There can be benefits to online gaming, such as providing a way of coping with problems in physical attributes (Beranuy et al., 2013), and it also allows for explorations of other personas and qualities (Hull et al., 2014). Johnson (2010) indicates that depending on the goal or the 'epic win' of the game, benefits may also include developing a collective consciousness, and unified social morality. McGoniligal (2015) asserts that 'when we play a game, we tackle tough challenges with more creativity, more determination and more optimism. We are also more likely to reach out to others for help'. A study conducted by King (2014) indicated the assumption that when used in moderation, internet gaming can be seen as part of a normal and healthy lifestyle. This is a growing area of psychology and behavioural health research.

Cross-cultural psychology and specialised practice

Specialised practice for detention centres and refugee and immigration issues

Of growing interest in contemporary society is the topic of refugees/asylum seekers and immigrants. Australia is home to one of the most culturally diverse populations on the globe, but an increasing disparity in the health outcomes of groups within the general population has been noted (Douglas et al., 2014). Often individuals from minority groups are disempowered, have difficulty communicating their concerns (Jones & Creedy, 2012) and rely on health professionals to advocate for their needs in a way that embraces culturally appropriate care and promotes cultural safety (Douglas et al., 2014).

Refugees/asylum seekers are terms that are often used interchangeably. Technically, asylum seekers are those who have been forced to leave their country of origin and have applied for protection as a refugee in another country (Nicholl & Thompson, 2004). These individuals have fled from their homeland in fear of persecution 'for reasons of race, religion, nationality membership in a particular social group, or political opinion' (Nicholl & Thompson, 2004, p. 532; US Immigration and Nationality Act 1965 cited in Shannon, 2012). Refugees and asylum seekers have made a significant impact, not only in recent times but also from a historical perspective. The numbers of refugees and asylum seekers across the globe continues to grow in response to natural disasters, war, famine, poverty and other factors. It follows then that a number of presentations for healthcare interventions are by members of this cohort (Shannon, 2012). Using a medical approach does not entirely address the needs of these clients, many of whom have experienced trauma, deprivation, lack of access to basic necessities of life and torture: the impacts are seen in presentation of symptoms of post-traumatic stress disorder (PTSD) and other mental health conditions (Nicholl & Thompson, 2004). A biopsychosocial approach provides a more holistic framework for intervention.

Without an understanding of the cultural nuances both between and within (recall the terms emics and etics discussed earlier), there is an increased risk of doing more harm than good, perhaps in interventions that are not tailored to the individual's specific needs. Here we can see how ethnocentric behaviours can emerge. We cannot state that all asylum seekers or refugees have the same subjective experiences, so it is logical to consider that cultural elements should be a significant consideration in developing understanding and formulating safe, effective and empathetic care.

Immigrants are defined as 'those who were born in another country' (Germov, 2014, p. 164). While electing to come to a new country of their own volition, immigrants' cultural practices may be entirely different from those displayed within the society from which they enter, and they experience challenges to their beliefs and practices which extend to health and wellbeing and what are considered 'normal' and 'abnormal' health concerns and actions.

Cultural impacts can be seen in a variety of ways, including the reporting of pain. A study by Kalauokalani et al. (2007) considered pain management variances for cancer patients from varying ethnic backgrounds. The study highlighted that 'minority patients with cancer experience worse control of their pain than do their white counterparts' and 'are at risk for disparities in quality of care' (Kalauokalani et al., 2007, p. 17). To ensure equality of access to care and provide for optimal outcomes, cultural awareness, cultural sensitivity and cultural safety need to be foremost in our considerations.

Summary

- In this chapter we have considered that there may be a biological basis that contributes to our behavioural characteristics.
- Race and ethnicity also define behavioural boundaries.
- Our environment commences in a confined unit – usually the family (primary socialisation) – providing initial exposure to core beliefs and values and imprinting moral codes.
- Secondary socialisation occurs outside the family unit; for example, within the education systems. Here an individual commences initial interaction with 'others' who may either replicate or challenge previous behaviours.
- Tertiary socialisation takes place in the wider environment beyond that of secondary socialisation.

- Psychologists such as Piaget and Erikson have developed theories to explain an individual's physical and cognitive development as well as how individuals gain an understanding of the world around them.
- Challenges at each stage of our lifespan cause us to maintain, moderate or reject our initial belief and value systems and subsequent behaviours.
- As health professionals, we need to have an understanding of our own core beliefs and values before we can develop cross-cultural competence and promote cultural safety.

Suggested weblinks

Refer to the companion website at www.cambridge.edu.au/academic/healthpsychology for a list of suggested weblinks.

References

ABS. (2013). *Australian Social Trends, 2013*. Cat no. 4102.0. Canberra: Australian Bureau of Statistics. Retrieved from: http://www.abs.gov.au/ausstats/abs@.nsf/Lookup/4102.0Main+Features30 Nov+2013

Al-Rasheed, M. (2010). *A History of Saudi Arabia*. New York: Cambridge University Press.

Alexander, J. (ed.) (1992). *Durkheimian Sociology: Cultural Studies*. Oakleigh: Cambridge University Press.

Allport, G. W. (1954). *The Nature of Prejudice*. Garden City, NY: Addison Wesley.

American Psychiatric Association. (2013). *Diagnostic and Statistical Manual of Mental Disorders: DSM-5* (5th edn). Arlington: American Psychiatric Press.

Arnon, S., Shamai, S. & Ilatov, Z. (2008). Socialization agents and activities of young adolescents. *Adolescence (San Diego): An International Quarterly Devoted to the Physiological, Psychological, Psychiatric, Sociological, and Educational Aspects of the Second Decade of Human Life, 43*(170), 373.

Ata, A. (2012). Bereavement anxieties and health amongst the Australian-Italian Catholic community. *Mental Health, Religion & Culture, 15*(6), 555–70. doi: http://dx.doi.org/10.1080/13674676.2011.599370

Australian Government (2015). Indigenous arts, culture and heritage. Retrieved from: http://www.australia.gov.au/about-australia/australian-stories/indigenous-arts-culture-and-heritage

BBC. (2009). Religions: the synagogue. Retrieved from: http://www.bbc.co.uk/religion/religions/judaism/worship/synagogue_1.shtml

Beranuy, M., Carbonell, X. & Griffiths, M. D. (2013). A qualitative analysis of online gaming addicts in treatment. *International Journal of Mental Health and Addiction*, *11*(2), 149–61.

Berglund, C. (2004). *Ethics for Health Care* (2nd edn). Melbourne: Oxford University Press.

Berndt, T. J. & Murphy, L. M. (2002). Influences of friends and friendships: myths, truths, and research recommendations. *Advances in Child Development*, *3*, 275–310.

Berry, J., Poortinga, Y. and Pandey, J. (eds) (1997). *Handbook of cross-cultural psychology, vol. 1, Theory and Method* (2nd edn). Boston: Allyn & Bacon.

Best, O. & Fredericks, B. L. (2014). *Yatdjuligin. [Electronic resource]: Aboriginal and Torres Strait Islander nursing and midwifery care*. Melbourne: Cambridge University Press.

Bourgault, P. (1996). *La Culture. Écrits polémiques*. Lanctôt Éditeur, p. 130, tome 2.

Brand, J. E., Borchard, J. & Holmes, K. (2008). *Interactive Australia 2009*. Sydney: Interactive Entertainment Association of Australia.

Burnard, P. & Gill, P. (2009). *Culture, communication and nursing*. Harlow: Pearson.

Chen, Y. (2015). Examining factors in cross-cultural competence development in Taiwan college students. *Asia-Pacific Education Researcher (Springer Science & Business Media B.V.)*, *24*(2), 329–40. doi: http://dx.doi.org/10.1007/s40299-014-0183-4

Cheung, F. M., van de Vijver, F. R. & Leong, F. L. (2011). Toward a new approach to the study of personality in culture. *American Psychologist*, *66*(7), 593–603. doi: http://dx.doi.org/10.1037/a0022389

Chmiel, M. (2012). Learning about the game: designing science games for a generation of gamers. *Cultural Studies of Science Education*, *7*(4), 807–12. doi: http://dx.doi.org/10.1007/s11422-012-9428-9

Christopher, J. C., Wendt, D. C., Marecek, J. & Goodman, D. M. (2014). Critical cultural awareness: contributions to a globalizing psychology. *American Psychologist*, *69*(7), 645–55. doi: http://dx.doi.org/10.1037/a0036851

Côté, J. E. (2006). Emerging adulthood as an institutionalized moratorium: risks and benefits to identity formation. In: J. J. Arnett & J. L. Tanner (eds), *Emerging Adults in America: Coming of Age in the 21st Century* (pp. 85–116). Washington, DC, US: American Psychological Association. doi: http://dx.doi.org/10.1037/11381-004

Deaf Australia Inc. (2010). Deaf culture. Retrieved from: http://www.deafau.org.au/info/dculture.php

Delaney, C. H. (1995). Rites of passage in adolescence. *Adolescence*, 892–8. Retrieved from: http://cultureandyouth.org/adolescence/research/rites-of-passage-in-adolescence/

Douglas M., Rosenkoetter, M. Pacquiato, D., Callister, L., Hattar-Pollara, M., Lauderdale, J., Milstead, J., Nardi, D. & Purnell, L. (2014). Guidelines for implementing culturally competent nursing care. *Journal of Transcultural Nursing*, *25*(2).

Erikson, E. H., Paul, I. H., Heider, F. & Gardner, R. W. (1959). *Psychological Issues (Vol. 1).* New York: International Universities Press.

Fischer, P., Krueger, J. I., Greitemeyer, T., Asal, K., Aydin, N. & Vingilis, E. (2012). Psychological effects of risk glorification in the media: towards an integrative view. *European Review of Social Psychology*, *23*(1), 224–57. doi: http://dx.doi.org/10.1080/10463283.2012.690969

Fleming, M. & Towey, K. (2001). *Delivering Culturally Effective Health Care to Adolescents*[1]. Chicago: American Medical Association.

Garasu, L. (2002). The role of women in promoting peace and reconciliation, Papua New Guinea-Bougainville. Weaving consensus: the Papua New Guinea-Bougainville peace process. *Acord*, *12*. Retrieved from: http://www.c-r.org/accord-article/role-women-promoting-peace-and-reconciliation

Gardiner, H. W. & Kosmitzki, C. (2002). *Lives Across Cultures: Cross-cultural Human Development.* Boston: Allyn & Bacon.

Germov, J. (2014). *Second Opinion: An Introduction to Health Sociology*. Melbourne: Oxford University Press.

Grincevičienė, V. & Grincevičius, J. (2014). Aspect of life quality in secondary socialization: experience of learners' parents. *Pedagogy Studies/Pedagogika*, *116*(4), 159–69. doi: http://dx.doi.org/10.15823/p.2015.055

Guliaikhin, V. N., Galkin, A. P. & Vasil'eva, E. N. (2013). Young people's and children's social associations as agents of secondary socialization. *Russian Education & Society*, *55*(7), 68–78.

Hampton, R. & Toombs, M. (2013). *Indigenous Australians and Health – The Wombat in the Room*. Melbourne: Oxford University Press.

Hirschi, T. (1969). *Causes of Delinquency*. Berkeley: University of California Press.

Hoel, S., Eriksen, B., Breidablik, H. & Meland, E. (2004). Adolescent alcohol use, psychological health, and social integration. *Scandinavian Journal of Public Health*, *32*(5), 361–7.

Hull, J. G., Brunelle, T. J., Prescott, A. T. & Sargent, J. D. (2014). A longitudinal study of risk-glorifying video games and behavioral deviance. *Journal of Personality and Social Psychology*, *107*(2), 300–25. doi: http://dx.doi.org/10.1037/a0036058

Hussain, R. (2005). The effect of religious, cultural and social identity on population genetic structure among Muslims in Pakistan. *Annals of Human Biology*, *32*(2), 145–53.

Imam, F. (2012). Child rearing and socialisation practices among working and non-working mothers in Pakistan. *Shield: Research Journal of Physical Education & Sports Science*, *7*, 1–7.

Indigenous Australia. (n.d.). Aboriginal initiation ceremonies. Retrieved from: http://www.indigenousaustralia.info/culture/initiation-ceremonies.html

Innes, M. (2003). *Understanding Social Control: Crime and Social Order in Late Modernity – Deviance, Crime and Social Order*. London: McGraw-Hill Education.

James, J. (2010). The folk process through new media. *Indian Folklore Research Journal*, *10*, 65–82.

Johnson, R. B. (2010). Online gaming can make a better world: Jane McGonigal. *Perspectives, University of New Hampshire*, 1–3.

Jones, K. & Creedy, D. (eds) (2012). *Health and Human Behaviour*. Melbourne: Oxford University Press.

Kalauokalani, D., Franks, P., Oliver, J. W., Meyers, F. J. & Kravitz, R. L. (2007). Can patient coaching reduce racial/ethnic disparities in cancer pain control? Secondary analysis of a randomized controlled trial. *Pain Medicine*, *8*(1), 17–24. doi: http://dx.doi.org/10.1111/j.1526-4637.2007.00170.x

Keith, K. (ed.) (2011). *Cross-cultural Psychology: Contemporary Themes and Perspectives*. West Sussex: Wiley & Sons.

Keller, H. (2011). Culture and cognition: developmental perspectives. *Journal of Cognitive Education and Psychology*, *10*(1), 3–8. doi: http://dx.doi.org/10.1891/1945-8959.10.1.3

Kemmelmeier, M. & Kühnen, U. (2012). Culture as process: the dynamics of cultural stability and change. *Social Psychology*, *43*(4), 171–3. doi: http://dx.doi.org/10.1027/1864-9335/a000117

King, D. H. (2014). Internet gaming disorder treatment: a review of definitions of diagnosis and treatment outcome. *Journal of Clinical Psychology*, *70*(10), 942–55.

Klimka, L. (2014). Ethnic culture in processes of socialisation: experience of Lithuania. *Pedagogy Studies/ Pedagogika*, *116*(4), 35–46. doi: http://dx.doi.org/10.1080/13674676.2011.59937010.15823/ p.2014.046

La Roche M., Fuentes M. & Hinton D. (2015). A cultural examination of the DSM-5: research and clinical implications for cultural minorities. *Professional Psychology: Research and Practice*, *46*(3), 183–9.

Linton, R. (1972). *The Tree of Culture*. New York: Knopf.

Lowe, M. L. & Haws, K. L. (2014). (Im)moral support: the social outcomes of parallel self-control decisions. *Journal of Consumer Research*, *41*(2), 489–505. doi: http://dx.doi.org/10.1086/676688

McGoniligal, J. (2015). It's time to think like a gamer. *Psychology Today*, *48*(5), 82–9.

Nagy, A. & Szekely, L. (2010). *Beyond the Family and the School: The Theoretical Foundations of the Tertiary Socialisation Environment and the Youth Profession as an Autonomous Field*. Budapest: Excenter Publishing House.

NationMaster (2011). Religions: countries compared, 18 December 2003 to 28 March 2011. Aggregates compiled by NationMaster. Retrieved from: http://www.nationmaster.com/country-info/stats/Religion/ Religions

Nicholl, C. & Thompson, A. (2004). The psychological treatment of post-traumatic stress disorder (PTSD) in adult refugees: a review of the current state of psychological therapies. *Journal of Mental Health*, *13*(4), 351–62. doi: http://dx.doi.org/10.1080/09638230410001729807

Norton, D. & Marks-Maran, D. (2014). Developing cultural sensitivity and awareness in nursing overseas. *Nursing Standard*, *28*(44), 39–43. doi: http://dx.doi.org/10.7748/ns.28.44.39.e8417

Nunn, N. (2012). Culture and the historical process. *Economic History of Developing Regions*, *27*, S108. doi: http://dx.doi.org/10.1080/20780389.2012.664864

Ong, W. J. (1971). *Rhetoric, Romance and Technology*. Ithaca and London: Cornell University Press.

Rew, L. K. (2013). Predictors of adolescents' health-promoting behaviors guided by primary socialization theory. *Journal for Specialists in Pediatric Nursing*, *18*(4), 277–88.

Rich, A. K. (2015). Riyadh, Saudi Arabia. *Salem Press Encyclopedia*. New York: Salem Press.

Riseman, N. (2013). Racism has a long history we must all understand. *The Drum*. Retrieved from: http:// www.abc.net.au/unleashed/4722082.html

Rosenblatt, P. C. (2013). Family grief in cross-cultural perspective. *Family Science*, *4*(1), 12–19. doi: http:// dx.doi.org/10.1080/19424620.2013.819226

Rothbaum, F., Rosen, K., Ujiie, T. and Uchida, N. (2002). Family systems theory, attachment theory, and culture. *Family Process*, *41*, 328–50. doi: http://dx.doi.org/10.1111/j.1545-5300.2002.41305.x

Schnierer E., Ellsmore S. & Schnierer S. (2011). *State of Indigenous cultural heritage 2011. Report prepared for the Australian Government Department of Sustainability, Environment, Water, Population and Communities on behalf of the State of the Environment 2011 Committee*. Canberra: DSEWPaC.

Schwikert, S. R. & Curran, T. (2014). Familiarity and recollection in heuristic decision making. *Journal of Experimental Psychology: General*, *143*(6), 2341–65. doi: http://dx.doi.org/10.1037/xge0000024

Shannon, P. E. (2012). Refugees' perspectives on barriers to communication about trauma histories in primary care. *Mental Health in Family Medicine*, *9*(1), 47–56.

Sherwood, J. (2013). Colonisation – It's bad for your health: the context of Aboriginal health. *Contemporary Nurse: A Journal for the Australian Nursing Profession*, *46*(1), 28–40. doi: http://dx.doi.org/10.5172/ conu.2013.46.1.28

Shiraev, E & Levy, D. (2007). *Cross-Cultural Psychology – Critical Thinking and Contemporary Applications*. Boston: Pearson.

Small, A. (ed.) (n.d.). Deaf Culture Centre: deaf culture. Retrieved from: http://www.deafculturecentre.ca/public/Default.aspx?I=294&n=Deaf+Culture

Smit, C. (2015). Theories and models of grief: applications to professional practice. *Whitireia Nursing & Health Journal*, *22*, 33–7.

Smith, R. L., Carroll, A. M., Callaghan, K. T., Rowcliffe, M. A., Sullivan, M. A. & Steckler, D. C. (2015). Emerging adulthood: a college student, middle class perk? *Psi Chi Journal of Psychological Research*, *20*(2), 80–5.

Steinberg, L. & Monahan, K. (2007). Age differences in resistance to peer influence. *Developmental Psychology*, *43*, 1530–43.

Studsrod, I. & Bru, E. (2011). Perceptions of peers as socialization agents and adjustment in upper secondary school. *Emotional & Behavioural Difficulties*, *16*(2), 159–72.

Taylor, E. B. (1871). *Primitive Culture*. London: Murray.

Thompson, R. & Lamb, M. (1983). Security of attachment and stranger sociability in infancy. *Developmental Psychology*, *19*, 184–91.

Welch, D. (n.d.). Aboriginal culture. Retrieved from: http://www.aboriginalculture.com.au

Wisniewski, E. J. & Wu, J. (2014). Cross-cultural psychology. *Salem Press Encyclopedia of Health, Research Starters*. New York: Salem Press.

Yang, S. C. (2012). Paths to bullying in online gaming: the effects of gender, preference for playing violent games, hostility, and aggressive behavior on bullying. *Journal of Educational Computing Research*, 47(3), 235–49.

Glossary

AB design	baseline phase (A) followed by an intervention phase (B) in a single systems design study.
Abstinence	voluntarily refraining from a certain behaviour (such as consuming alcohol).
Acute coronary syndrome (ACS)	a condition whereby blood flow to an area of the heart is suddenly reduced or stopped.
Acute myocardial infarction (AMI)	or 'heart attack' occurs when blood flow is abruptly cut off from an area of the heart due to blockage of a coronary artery or its branches, and resulting in cell damage or immediate death.
Adhere	follow advice or recommendations such as recommendations made by a healthcare professional.
Adherence	indicates if people are following the instructions they are given by their healthcare professional.
Adrenalin	(epinephrine) a hormone and transmitter released during the stress response by the adrenal glands. Its effects include increased heart rate, blood pressure and blood glucose levels.
Agents of socialisation	environments of varying complexity and expanse (primary, secondary and tertiary) that contribute experiences which shape our understanding and subsequent behaviours.
Alcohol	drinks that contain ethyl alcohol, which causes intoxication (e.g. beer, wine or spirits).
Angina	chest pain or discomfort, caused by ischaemia.
Antecedents	come before our target behaviour, and may also be thought of as cues, or stimuli.
Anterograde amnesia	an inability to create new memories, while old memories are unaffected.
Anxiety	psychological disorder characterised by feelings of apprehension and fear resulting from the anticipation of a threatening event or situation, that disrupts normal psychological functioning.
Anxiolytic	a drug that reduces anxiety.
Atheroma	an abnormal mass of fatty material that develops on the inner lining of arterial walls.
Atherosclerosis	also known as hardening of the arteries, it is a disease in which a plaque or atheroma forms on the tunica intima of arteries.
Behaviour modification interventions	involving behaviour change based on operant conditioning principles, often by setting up (or changing existing) responses.
Beneficence	an act of benefiting others.
Binary logistic regression	calculating the increase in odds of the dependent variable for every unit increase in a predictor variable, controlling for the effects of the other predictors.
Binge drinking	consuming a large amount of alcohol over a short period of time.

Biomedical model of illness conceptualises health as a direct result of changes to the body, and mental or emotional disturbance as part of a separate process.

Biopsychosocial model acknowledging the biological, psychological and social factors that contribute to health and illness.

Biopsychosocial perspective of pain the idea that pain is the result of a convergence of a multitude of internal and external, biological, psychological, emotional, social and behavioural influences.

Blood pressure the force of blood as it moves through the arterial circulatory system.

Body mass index (BMI) a method typically used to help assess whether someone is underweight, healthy weight, overweight or obese. It is calculated as follows: BMI = kg/m^2 thus a person who weighs 85 kg and is 1.89 cm tall would have a BMI = $85/1.89^2 = 85/3.5721 = 23.8$.

Brain plasticity the incredible ability of the brain to change and adapt following exposure to different experiences.

Bupropion an atypical antidepressant used for smoking cessation, taken orally.

Burden of disease the impact of a disease or an injury on either an individual or at a population level. It can include the economic cost of medical care and other broader costs to society (e.g. those incurred through lost time at work), as well as changes in life expectancy and healthy life expectancy.

Cancer a malignant growth or tumour resulting from an uncontrolled division of cells.

Cannabis a preparation from the cannabis plant, used as a psychotropic drug.

Cardiomyopathy a condition that causes the heart to become enlarged and weakened. Eventually, it will not be able to function properly, resulting in an irregular heartbeat or inability to pump enough blood throughout the body.

Cardiovascular disease (CVD) a range of conditions that affect the heart and blood vessels.

Cardiovascular system (CVS) the heart and blood vessels, which transport blood and hence oxygen and nutrients throughout the body.

Case a person experiencing a disease, health outcome or event.

Case-control studies targeted sampling of individuals with particular health outcomes (conditions) and then retrospective assessment of exposure.

Censoring participants who do not experience the event of interest during the time in which they are followed in a study.

Cerebral infarction ischaemic stroke, the result of an occlusion or rupture of an artery in the brain.

Chemotherapy a form of cancer treatment that uses chemical substances that are toxic to cancer cells (cytotoxic).

Cholesterol a type of fat; low-density lipoprotein (LDL) and high-density lipoprotein (HDL).

Circadian rhythm	near 24-hour rhythm in many aspects of functioning including body temperature, the hormone melatonin, sleepiness and performance.
Classical conditioning	learned associations between two related events.
Cognitive behavioural therapy (CBT)	a form of psychotherapy designed to target maladaptive, unhelpful thoughts and behaviours by replacing them with adaptive, realistic and helpful alternative thoughts and behaviours. This approach is considered the gold standard for mood disorders, such as depression, as well as for chronic pain.
Cohort studies	recruiting a group of participants who do not have the outcome of interest, and following them over time, with repeated measurements, in order to record who develops the outcome during the study and to identify factors that may predict the outcome.
Comorbid	a condition that occurs with another condition; fatigue and depression are comorbid.
Consequences	come after behaviour, and may also be thought of as reinforcing factors.
Coping	the process that individuals use to manage or deal with stress.
Coronary heart disease (CHD)	also known as ischaemic heart disease or coronary arterial disease, it is due to blockages of the coronary arteries.
Cortisol	the primary stress hormone released during the stress response, which causes bodily arousal, such as increased blood pressure and blood glucose.
Cross-cultural competence (CCC)	can be defined as behaviours, attitudes and motivations that are demonstrated by an individual working in a professional capacity. CCC is often informed by systems within organisations such as guidelines, policies and broader social legislation. CCC facilitates an individual's ability to readily understand and develop effective relationships with people from diverse cultures.
Cross-sectional studies	involve sampling at a single time point, and are often used to investigate whether there are differences in the prevalence of a disease or other health outcome in different, pre-existing exposure groups.
Cultural competence	a system that enables organisations to operate across multiple cultures.
Cultural safety	the creation of an environment that acknowledges and incorporates unique cultural identities, practices and behaviours of individuals (including spiritual and physical elements) from diverse backgrounds, to promote trust and understanding.
Cultural sensitivity	personal tools and skills that assist an individual in gaining a deeper understanding of those from different communities.
Culture	an accumulation of beliefs and values that are transmitted from one generation to the next.

Curvilinear trend a pattern in data showing an increase or decrease by an increasing amount for each increasing time unit (e.g. days, weeks).

Depression a state of low mood affecting everyday functioning, ranging in severity and duration. This can affect feelings, thoughts, behaviour and physical wellbeing.

Developmental stages various building blocks of life experiences, including challenges that are encountered throughout the lifespan and that contribute to physical and cognitive maturity.

Diet the type of food and drink that you consume.

Diffusion of innovations a model explaining the spread or uptake of new ideas or practices.

Disability-adjusted life years (DALY) a measure of disease burden calculating the difference between a person's life expectancy and the number of years that they can expect to live free of disability or ill health. One DALY represents one lost year of health.

Discrimination treating someone differently based on one or more qualities (e.g., race, sex, age, sexual orientation).

Distal norms the norms of a less familiar reference group such as broader peer groups or the media.

Duration a measure of how long something occurs.

e-cigarette a device that produces an aerosol containing propylene glycol, flavouring agents and sometimes nicotine in order to simulate traditional cigarettes.

Eating disorder dangerous eating behaviour through which the individual puts his or her health at risk (e.g. anorexia nervosa, bulimia nervosa).

Ecological model a model that puts individual behaviour in the context of social, environmental and societal factors.

Electro-oculogram (EOG) a record of eye activity; waveforms represent electrical activity in muscles surrounding the eye.

Electroencephalogram (EEG) a record of brain activity; waveforms represent electrical activity in the brain.

Electromyogram (EMG) a record of muscle activity; waveforms represent electrical activity in muscles.

Emics unique attributes that exist within a cultural group.

Epidemiology discipline concerned with the frequency of and reasons for disease in different groups of people, as well as the evaluation of prevention strategies and treatment.

Equivalence testing researchers wish to demonstrate that one treatment is equivalent to another.

Ethnocentrism a belief that one's own position, opinions and behaviours are the best and only logical way to function.

Etics	unique attributes that exist across cultural groups.
Exercise	physical activity, usually with the aim of improving health and wellbeing.
Fight-or-flight response	the physiological response, also known as the acute stress response, that occurs one we perceive a situation as threatening or dangerous. It involves bodily and mental arousal and prepares the body for immediate action.
Frequency	a measure of how often something occurs.
Frontal lobes	lobes in the brain located behind the forehead, containing areas that are concerned with risk-taking, attention, planning, problem-solving, motivation and decision-making.
Gate control theory	a revolutionary theory of pain proposed by Melzack and Wall that theorised that descending (inhibitory or excitatory) signals from the brain were the stimulus that opened or closed a gating mechanism in the spinal column, and that this mechanism ultimately controlled the amount of pain signals that could reach the brain.
General adaptation syndrome (GAS)	Hans Selye's general adaptation syndrome describes three main stages that occur in the body from effects of acute to chronic stress.
Generalised estimating equations (GEE)	an extension to regression modelling for longitudinal data that allows specification of continuous or discrete dependent variables and accounts for the within-cluster (serial) correlation in the data.
Genetic testing	testing of DNA from a sample of blood or saliva to identify genetic mutations, or faults, that indicate increased susceptibility to particular diseases or abnormalities.
Glycaemic index (GI)	an indicator of the ability of food to raise blood glucose levels.
Glycaemic load (GL)	an indicator of the effect of food on blood glucose levels; one GL captures the effects 1 gram of glucose would have on blood glucose levels.
Goal-setting principles	these work on successive approximation, and setting up goals that are small and attainable to build towards a larger goal.
Hallucinogen	a drug that causes hallucinations, resulting in experiences of visions, sounds and sensations that may feel real, but are not.
Health	free of illness but also with high levels of wellbeing.
Health literacy	ability to find and understand information about health, both physical and mental.
Health psychologist	a healthcare professional who conducts research into the relationship between behaviour and health or applies such research findings to illness prevention and treatment.
Health psychology	the study of the relationship between behaviour and health.

Heart failure also known as chronic heart failure or congestive heart failure; occurs when the heart becomes too weak to pump blood around the body.

Heavy episodic drinking the consumption of approximately five or more standard drinks on a single occasion.

Heuristics a practical approach to addressing challenges or problems using our core beliefs, values and understanding of our world.

HPA axis a series of connected parts of the nervous and endocrine systems that forms the stress response.

Hypertension abnormally high blood pressure.

Hyponatremia reduced sodium (an electrolyte) levels due to low fluid intake.

Hypnotic a drug that induces sleep.

Incidence the number of new cases over a specific time period in a particular population.

Inequalities where things are not the same; out of balance. Health inequalities mean that different individuals do not have the same chances to achieve good health.

Inhalant a material, such as a solvent, that produces vapour which can be inhaled.

Insomnia sleep disorder characterised by problems initiating or maintaining sleep.

Insulin a hormone that helps regulate blood glucose levels by transporting glucose into skeletal muscles cells or liver cells and is then converted to glycogen, or transports glucose into adipose tissue and converts it to lipid (fat).

Insulin resistance a condition in which skeletal muscle cells no longer respond to the normal action of insulin.

Interval a measure of the period in between occurrences of a target behaviour.

Intervention a treatment to help change behaviour.

Intervention studies focus on comparing health outcomes in two or more groups to determine whether a particular action in one group (e.g. drug administration) is associated with favourable outcomes relative to the other group(s) receiving different or no action.

Ischaemia a restriction in blood supply to an organ or part of the body, especially the heart muscle and brain.

Korsakoff syndrome disorder caused by thiamine deficiency, characterised by anterograde amnesia.

Linear mixed-model regression an extension to regression modelling for longitudinal data that allows specification of fixed and random effects to appropriately account for within and between participant variance.

Linear trend a pattern in data showing an increase or decrease by the same amount for each increasing time unit (e.g. days, weeks).

Longitudinal study	a study that has gathered data from participants at more than one time point with a time lag between time points. It does not generally include experimental studies where participants provide data at more than one time point but with short intervals.
Magnitude	a measure of the size/intensity of a target behaviour.
Meta-analysis	a systematic review of the published literature where the findings are aggregated statistically.
Metabolic syndrome	high waist circumference, high blood triglycerides, low blood HDL cholesterol, hypertension and elevated blood glucose.
Mindfulness	a mental state of heightened awareness that involves being fully and non-judgementally attentive to the present moment.
Model	a representation of relationships between concepts from a theory based on empirical findings.
Morbidity	a disease that may not in and of itself cause death, but that may cause subsequent health issues that may be fatal.
Mortality	another word for death.
Multiple baseline designs	where at least three individuals undertake the intervention, but begin the study with their start times staggered, to help to rule out other potential reasons for behaviour change.
Multiple regression (MR)	calculating the unit increase in a dependent variable for every unit increase in a predictor variable, controlling for the effects of the other predictors.
Naltrexone	a drug that blocks opiate receptors in the brain; used in treatment of heroin or alcohol addiction.
Non-inferiority testing	researchers wish to demonstrate that one treatment is no worse than another.
Non-maleficence	a guiding principle with the aim to 'do no harm', giving consideration to the advantages of an action in comparison to the disadvantages.
Non-randomised intervention studies	involve comparing results in a treatment group to a historical (pre-existing) control group.
Nudge	a term defined by Thaler and Sunstein as a way of influencing choice and associated behaviours in a predictable way.
Number needed to treat (NNT)	a statistical index that gives the number of clients needed to treat for one client to get a benefit. Thus, NNT can range from 1 up. NNT = 1 for drug X means that every person that takes drug X will get the benefit in question associated with drug X. If NNT = 12 then 12 clients need to be treated for one to receive the benefits of the treatment. The benefits of any given treatment or drug that has NNT reported can be in relation to various time intervals. Drug X above may have to be taken for 2 years before you get the benefits while drug Y may have to be taken for 10 years before one out of five sees a benefit.

Nutrition the sustaining elements your diet delivers your body.

Observational studies examination of naturally developing differences in health without investigator interference.

Obstructive sleep apnoea (OSA) sleep disorder characterised by periods of breathing cessation (apnoeas) during sleep, and accompanied by oxygen desaturation and sleep fragmentation.

Occlusion the blockage of blood flow through arteries or veins.

Odds the number of new cases during a time period divided by the number of people who did not become a case during that time period.

Odds ratio the odds of the outcome (e.g. lung cancer) for those in the exposure group (e.g. smokers) divided by the odds for those not exposed (e.g. non-smokers).

Oil type of fat (unsaturated).

Operant conditioning behaviours with positive consequences are likely to recur, whereas those with negative consequences are not.

Operationalisation defining variables clearly, thus enabling them to be measures.

Opioids a group of drugs that relieve pain. In medical parlance, they typically refer to synthetic drugs rather than natural opium extract.

Pain a multifaceted, unpleasant sensory as well as emotional experience, arising in the context of described or observed damaged, or potentially damaged, tissue.

Peripheral vascular disease the reduction of blood supply in arteries leading to the limbs, particularly the legs and feet.

Polyunsaturated fatty acid fat that is commonly found in fish, krill nuts and seaweed.

Population at risk the group of people who would be counted as a case if they were diagnosed with the disease of interest.

Prevalence the number of cases in a population during a particular time period.

Prevention primary prevention programs are focused on stopping a problem/illness from occurring in the first place (e.g. stop adolescents from taking up smoking). Secondary prevention is damage control where you try to minimise the impact of a problem/illness (e.g. help an individual to stop smoking). Tertiary prevention refers to attempts to live with the problem/illness while trying to minimise the impact (e.g. reduce smoking and limit the location of smoking so as not to affect others).

Primary appraisal the first part of the transactional model of stress proposed by Lazarus and Folkman. It involves a preliminary assessment of a situation to determine whether it is harmful or threatening to the individual.

Primary prevention aims to prevent the onset of disease or injury.

Proinflammatory cytokines molecules of protein that increase inflammation.

Proximal norms the norms of a familiar reference group such as close family and friends.

Quasi-experimental study when you compare participants in different groups but the participants have not been randomly allocated to these groups. If you are looking at a study comparing smokers and non-smokers, then you are looking at a quasi-experimental study, as the participants have not been randomly allocated to these two groups; the groups are pre-existing.

Racism believing that one race is somehow superior or inferior to another.

Radiation therapy a form of cancer treatment that uses X-rays or other beams of energy to destroy cancer cells.

Randomised clinical/control trials (RCT) these are intervention studies used to measure the impact of intervention in one or more treatment groups compared to a control group, with measurements taken within groups over time. Participants are randomised to condition: each has an equal chance of ending up in any group.

Rapid eye movement (REM) sometimes referred to as dreaming sleep, REM sleep is characterised by rapid eye movements, flaccid paralysis in the muscles and reports of dreaming if woken.

Rate the number of people affected as a proportion of the population at risk.

Reinforcement consequences of behaviour that strengthen the likelihood of recurrence.

Relative measures types of rate calculations that allow us to describe relationships between exposure to a particular risk and disease outcomes.

Relative risk the risk of the outcome (e.g. lung cancer) for those in the exposure group (e.g. smokers) divided by the risk for those not exposed (e.g. non-smokers).

Response contingencies behaviours that will earn reinforcement.

Risk the number of new cases during a time period divided by the number of people in the population at risk at the start of that time period; also referred to as cumulative incidence.

Ruling class those who hold political power.

Secondary appraisal the second part of the transactional model of stress proposed by Lazarus and Folkman. It involves an assessment of an individual's available coping resources to manage a threatening or dangerous event.

Sedative a drug that is calming or induces sleep.

Serial correlation the inherent relationship between multiple data points collected from the same individual across time.

Shiftwork work schedules that include work hours beyond the traditional 7 am to 6 pm, Monday to Friday work week.

Single systems designs an individual or group of individuals are measured over time to investigate whether an intervention has an effect on a single unit of analysis.

Sleep a state of altered consciousness characterised by disengagement from the environment and often accompanied by closed eyes and recumbent posture.

Slow wave sleep (SWS) otherwise referred to as deep sleep, the deepest, most restorative stage of sleep, characterised by large (delta) waves in the EEG and a high wake threshold.

Social norms patterns of behaviour that are perceived as normal or socially acceptable by a group.

Socioeconomic status (SES) a construct that combines sociological and economic factors to determine an individual's standing in society.

Stable pattern a consistent pattern in data across time units (e.g. days, weeks).

Standardised mortality ratio (SMR) gives a comparison of the death rate in one group of individuals (e.g. anorexia nervosa sufferers) compared with a reference group of 'normal' individuals. If the SMR = 1.00 then the death rate is the same in both groups but if the SMR = 5.86 then that suggests the mortality rate is 485% higher = (5.85 – 1.00) × 100).

Stigma negative labelling of an individual based on the individual's race, age, sex or sexual orientation.

Stimulant a drug that stimulates nervous system activity.

Stimulus control interventions involves the reduction or removal of a stimulus that elicits a conditioned response and prompts undesirable behaviours in order to reduce the frequency of that response, or the introduction or amplifications of stimuli that prompt desirable behaviours.

Stress the physiological and psychological state that occurs from person–environment transactions when an individual perceives a discrepancy between the demands of a situation and their available coping resources.

Stressor an event or situation that can cause stress.

Stroke occurs when the blood supply to part of the brain is disrupted due to vessel rupture, or a blood clot or plaque that has blocked a vessel.

Survival analysis the analysis of time-to-event in datasets where not everyone will experience that event before they are lost to follow up or the study ends.

Survival curve illustrates the cumulative proportion of participants in the study that are 'surviving' or as yet free of the event (*y*-axis) at each time point (*x*-axis).

Sympathetic nervous system (SNS) the part of the peripheral and autonomic nervous systems that triggers the acute stress response.

Systematic review a transparent, replicable process for selecting and appraising research studies in order to answer a clear, focused research question.

Target behaviour the way we refer to a behaviour that we are interested in measuring and/or changing.

Teachable moment a learning opportunity when someone is open to receiving information or motivated to change their behaviour.

Thiamine a B complex vitamin, required for nervous system functioning.

Tobacco dried leaves of a tropical plant that contain nicotine, and may be smoked (in cigarettes or a pipe) or chewed (i.e. chewing tobacco).

Transient ischaemic attack a 'mini-stroke' caused by a loss of blood flow, lasting for a short period of time and causing no residual permanent damage.

Transtheoretical stages of change five stages of change, outlined in Prochaska and DiClemente's model, used to describe one's readiness for behaviour change. The stages are precontemplation (not intending to change), contemplation (thinking about change), preparation (preparing for change), action (implementing change) and maintenance (relapse prevention).

Triglycerides blood lipid energy source based on glycerol and three fatty acids; fats.

Type 2 diabetes (T2D) a chronic condition resulting in higher than normal blood sugar, due to insulin resistance and/or inadequate pancreatic production of insulin.

Varenicline an oral drug used for smoking cessation that blocks the effects of nicotine.

Wellbeing mentally healthy and happy.

Wernicke-Korsakoff Syndrome the combination of Korsakoff syndrome and Wernicke's encephalopathy.

Wernicke's encephalopathy a neurological disorder resulting from thiamine deficiency, associated with changes to balance and gait, confusion and memory loss, frequently associated with chronic, excessive alcohol consumption.

Withdrawal designs an intervention is implemented and then withdrawn (e.g. ABA design).

Years of life lost the difference between age at death and the standard life expectancy at that age.

Index